CORPORATE
WELFARE

CORPORATE
WELFARE

*The Megabankruptcies
of the 80s and 90s*

by Laurence H. Kallen

A Lyle Stuart Book
Published by Carol Publishing Group

A Lyle Stuart Book
Published by Carol Publishing Group

Editorial Offices
600 Madison Avenue
New York, NY 10022

Sales & Distribution Offices
120 Enterprise Avenue
Secaucus, NJ 07094

In Canada: Musson Book Company
A division of General Publishing Co. Limited
Don Mills, Ontario

Manufactured in the United States of America

10   9   8   7   6   5   4   3   2   1

Library of Congress Cataloging-in-Publication Data

Kallen, Laurence H.
    Corporate welfare : the megabankruptcies of the 80s and 90s / by
Laurence H. Kallen.
        p.   cm.
    "A Lyle Stuart book."
    Includes index.
    ISBN 0-8184-0534-1
    1. Bankruptcy—United States.   2. Corporate reorganizations—
United States.   3. Corporations—United States—Corrupt practices.
I. Title.
KF1539.K34   1991   90–21402
346.73′078—dc   CIP
[347.30678]

Contents

This book is dedicated to the memory of
the Honorable Frederick J. Hertz,
friend and mentor, who showed all by example
how to rise above adversity, and who taught me,
amongst other things,
to see the forest for the trees.

Introduction

The 1980s will be remembered for soaring real estate prices, a crashing stock market, megabuyouts—and megabankruptcies. It seemed that every week there were dazzling mergers or a crippled giant filing Chapter 11. While what follows presents the facts of those megabankruptcies, it is much more. It is about how the people who run giant corporations seize opportunities to manipulate the law to tilt the economic playing field very much in their favor, and how federal judges facilitate the achievement of their goals. It is about how in the Eighties the federal bankruptcy system in operation became very little more than a corporate welfare program for those megacorporations that chose to invoke its many benefits. It is about how you and I—the American taxpayers—pay for that massive welfare program.

Sadly, the federal bankruptcy law (there are no state bankruptcy laws) as it applies to corporate reorganizations bears little resemblance in practice to the image of the system held by almost everybody. That state of affairs has existed ever since the federal bankruptcy law was rewritten effective October 1979, but it has gone largely without comment.

ᐟ To most people, bankruptcy is a last-resort safety net for those in deep financial trouble, into which one does not leap unless all other options are foreclosed. Bankruptcy is intended to be the reflection of the American ideal that people should not have to bear the burden of *overwhelming* debt for a lifetime—that *people* deserve a fresh start. Chapter 11 of the United States Bankruptcy Code, which deals with business reorganizations, is supposed to be invoked only under the most dire financial circumstances. In reality, during the past decade many of the largest corporations in this country have treated it merely as a useful corporate tool to be used when convenient to clean up balance sheets, with little actual risk to them. For megacorporations, Chapter 11 has provided both a nearly impenetrable shield against creditors and a powerful sword to strike at adversaries.

How is it that megacorporations came to so dominate the bankruptcy reorganization process? How could the bankruptcy system be manipulated so thoroughly by large companies?

The capturing of the bankruptcy system by megacorporations in the 1980s was based upon a particular confluence of events and circumstances that began to be felt in the 1970s. The decade of the Seventies was marked by worldwide economic turmoil—an unusual combination of extreme inflation *and* unemployment—caused by the hidden costs of the Vietnam "Police Action" and the seizure of control over the world's oil supplies by Arab political leaders that resulted in the greatest transfer of wealth among nations that the world has ever known. Also, the Seventies will become recognized as the decade during which American industry began a serious decline as a result of its own ineptness as well as global economic factors. Fittingly, that decade was capped by a wholesale revision of the bankruptcy law, which had the effect of precipitating the rush to the bankruptcy courts. The Reagan-Volcker recession of the early Eighties then provided a catalyst to the mixture, and an explosion of bankruptcy cases resulted.

Although the economic dislocations of the Seventies and early Eighties caused severe hardship to owners of small companies, this nation's corporate barons quickly learned that they could *profit* handsomely from Chapter 11 with little actual risk to their companies or their cushy jobs. Utilizing their immense size and securing the active help of the judges who were supposed to be supervising them, huge corporations were almost totally successful in overwhelming their creditors and shareholders and bashing their unions. The megacorporations were able to wear down their adversaries by remaining in bankruptcy court for as long as they liked and then exiting bankruptcy at will by paying claims with pennies on the dollar. Through Chapter 11 they cleverly picked the pockets of their suppliers (many of whom were small, struggling companies) and their lenders, callously denied just compensation to people who had been maimed and killed by their products, and boldly canceled collective bargaining agreements that they had agreed to. Under the cover of Chapter 11, employees were fired mercilessly. In short, Chapter 11 allowed megacorporations to run roughshod over everyone in their way.

During the Eighties, Chapter 11 became such a powerful tool of megacorporations that it tipped the balance of financial power in favor of those bold enough to seize it. Chapter 11 permitted megacorporations to perpetuate their financial domination of their industries and provided the wherewithal for their further corporate expansion. It allowed the men who ran them to escape the consequences of their greed and incompetence. If viewed as a government program to provide large amounts of aid to giant corporations, the Bankruptcy Code has been one of the most successful federal programs. If viewed as a program of mercy to help businesses in dire straits, its effect has been retrograde.

The 1990s will impose a new mix of economic pressures. Some major ingredients, such as the mismanagement of American industry and the price of oil, will remain important. Some new problems, such as the collapse of "junk bond" financing and growing environmental liabilities, will create further impetus for financial restructuring of many American megacorporations. It appears that Chapter 11 of the Bankruptcy Code and the judges who administer it will be standing ready to give those megacorporations that choose the bankruptcy option WHATEVER THEY WANT in order to allow them to walk away from their legitimate liabilities.

In order to properly investigate the megacorporate bankruptcies of the Eighties and Nineties, it is necessary first to gain an appreciation of the importance of petroleum to the world's social and economic health and of the massive redistribution of the world's wealth engineered by Arab leaders during the Seventies. Consequently, the story of Chapter 11 must begin at Chapter 1 with a short history of oil politics.

A History Lesson:
Oil and Power

A major determinant of business success or failure, as well as of the standard of living for the world's peoples in the modern, industrial era, is the system of petroleum production and delivery. Oil is indeed the lubricant that permits the wheels of the world to turn, both literally and figuratively.

Oil is the most important commodity, making it the world's highest stakes game, short of war. (As this book goes to press, Saddam Hussein of Iraq has raised those stakes, possibly leading to the point of armed conflict.) The value of the oil trade is greater than that of all other raw materials combined. More than half the tonnage on the high seas at any given time consists of petroleum. Into the 1970s, the quantity of oil consumed by the world doubled every decade, an astounding geometrical progression.

The numbers are staggering. The world consumes about twenty billion barrels of oil a year (about fifteen billion barrels per year are discovered nowadays), 25 percent of it by the United States (with 5 percent of the world's population). The U.S. expenditures for energy are about $450 billion per year, and somewhat over half of that is for petroleum products. Trucks and automobiles in the U.S. burn about 7.5 million gallons of gasoline and 8.5 million gallons of motor fuel a day.

Oil is so important to the industrialized world that its production and distribution have been overseen by governments and cartels for the entire twentieth century. Through the 1960s, the governments of the

United States and England and a very small group of their major oil companies controlled the petroleum industry throughout the entire capitalist world. (Russia controlled it within the Communist countries.) Since the early 1970s, production and distribution have been controlled by a few Arab countries and those same oil companies. Oil is so important that it has been suggested that the petroleum industry from the wellhead through refining and delivery properly should be thought of as one big utility. The utility should be operated for the good of the United States and Western Europe by agencies of those governments, no matter where the oil happens to lie, with or without the consent of the peoples who happen to live above the pools of oil. That, of course, would require military seizure of oil fields in Arab countries. Such a suggestion is not totally bereft of merit.

The story of oil has always been writ large. In past decades, the fountains of riches spewing from oil wells have turned rough speculators with names like Rockefeller, Getty, Hunt, and Keck into the richest people on earth.

Many oil companies are bigger than a good-sized country in sales (GNP) and assets. Exxon and General Motors take turns as the world's largest corporation (based upon annual sales), depending on business fluctuations. Exxon has assets of about $70 billion and annual sales in the neighborhood of $100 billion; it employs over one hundred thousand people. Within the United States, eight oil companies (Exxon, Mobil, Texaco, Chevron, Amoco, Shell, Occidental Petroleum, and ARCO, in descending order of size) are included among the twenty largest corporations. The fifty largest corporations count twenty oil companies in their ranks. Even many "independents," considered pint-sized within the petroleum community, are huge. For example, three independents are prominent in the next rank of America's largest corporations: Phillips (thirty-first), Sun (thirty-third), and the British Petroleum Company (thirty-fifth). Shell is wholly owned by Dutch corporations, and British Petroleum is primarily owned by the British government and the Bank of England.

Company rank is determined without reference to the present market value of proven reserves. If they were included the major oil companies—which also own most gas fields and coal and uranium deposits—would dwarf the megacorporations in other industries. For example, the present market value of Phillips's proven coal reserves is about $1,000 billion, larger than the value of twenty-four General

Motors and E. I. du Pont de Nemours combined!

The actions of these huge corporations, and those of the governments of oil-producing countries, are felt around the world every day in a multitude of ways. The oil geopolitics of the 1970s placed many major industrial corporations in dire straits by the early 1980s. Oil pricing and distribution have a tremendous effect upon the economic well-being of the peoples of the world.

To fully appreciate the scope and power of the oil companies, a brief look at their history and development is in order.

At the end of World War I, with Germany prostrate and the United States lapsing back into isolationism, the more aggressive European powers expanded and solidified their spheres of influence. Among other reasons, they were heeding the view of Winston Churchill that peace is merely a period between wars.

An important part of preparing for the next war was to secure guaranteed sources of petroleum. The newfangled weapons of war—the airplane, the tank, and the oil-powered (instead of coal) warship—demanded it. In addition to dividing the territories that they would oversee under the peace mandate, England and France used both government treaties and corporations to lock in relationships through one-sided trading agreements. Oil matters were handled for England through the Anglo-Persian Oil Company and the Iraq Petroleum Company, nominally private companies; for France through the state-owned Compagnie Française Pétrole; and for the Netherlands through Royal Dutch-Shell.

The method of expansion for those European companies was simple—the companies made offers somewhat akin to the one that led to Manhattan being bought for $24 worth of beads. The companies would approach whatever sheik or other potentate had control over a likely looking area and offer a modest royalty (one-eighth to one-sixth of the profits) for any oil extracted. The local leader thus could establish a source of income that would be munificent by local standards. In return we would give up rights to something under the ground that he could not otherwise locate, extricate, or use—something that was valueless to him.

A new company would be formed made up of the Western oil company and the local government. The company would own all of the oil it found from the moment it was extracted, all of the equipment, and all of the rights to market and distribute the oil. Because the Western partner contributed all of the capital and brought in all of the expertise, of course, the new company so formed would be controlled by that oil company. The local ruler simply could sit back and collect his royalties without worrying his medieval head about details of the business or even how his royalties came to be determined.

Before going any further, some "begats" are necessary to clarify the major players in the development of the world's oil industry and to allow for a unified terminology for the remainder of this book.

First and foremost are the corporate legacies of John D. Rockefeller. As a "trust," Standard Oil was broken up in 1911. The many separate corporate entities that had been parts of the trust became independent operators in theory, and their successes are impressive. Standard Oil of New Jersey was later renamed Humble Oil Company and did business at the pump as Esso; it later gave itself a name that it hoped would bring it better public relations—Exxon. Standard Oil of New York, known as Socony, became Socony-Vacuum after a merger, then Socony-Mobil, then Mobil Oil Corporation. Standard Oil of California, known as SoCal, later changed its name to Chevron. Standard Oil of Indiana became Amoco. John D. would be unhappy to see how his flagship name became a public relations liability to his companies. However, the Rockefellers have continued to enjoy the fruits of John D.'s labors—a government study in 1939 concluded that the Rockefeller family and its foundations effectively controlled Standard of New Jersey, Socony-Mobil, and SoCal.

Other large American oil companies include: Shell, wholly owned by two Dutch companies, Royal Dutch Petroleum Company and Shell Trading Company; Texaco, which originally was named the Texas Company in smaller-minded days; and ARCO, otherwise known as Atlantic Richfield Company. The only major company to retain its original name, Gulf Oil, founded in 1907, was the ninth largest industrial company in the United States when it was acquired by Chevron in 1984. (The Antitrust Division must have been looking the other way.)

For convenience, from here on the oil companies will be referred to by their most modern names.

The eight companies have been referred to as the American "majors," with Exxon being much larger than its nearest competitor in size, Mobil. The eight majors are fully "integrated," with operations at every stage in the extraction, distribution, and marketing process—from the drill in the ground to the nozzle in the tank. In truth these are now "energy companies," with extensive operations and reserves of coal, gas, and uranium. They also have diversified into other industries.

The second rank of American oil companies—huge corporations by the standards of any industry but petroleum—are Occidental Petroleum (owned by Armand Hammer), Phillips, Sun, the British Petroleum Company, Marathon, Cities Service (now controlled by Occidental), Unocal (a result of the merger of Pure and Union), Sonoco (formerly Continental), Signal, and Amerada Hess. Getty Oil was prominent until it was gobbled up by Texaco. These companies are also fully integrated, but are not uniformly strong throughout the various stages of the business. Each of them also is diversified. British Petroleum, doing business as BP America, entered the U.S. market in 1968 by purchasing the East Coast assets of Sinclair and Atlantic Richfield and later absorbed Standard Oil of Ohio (Sohio). It has been growing rapidly in the U.S.

The international oil trade is dominated by a group of companies often referred to as the "Seven Sisters": Exxon, Mobil, Chevron, Texaco, Gulf, Royal Dutch-Shell, and British Petroleum. Unlike seven real sisters, they hardly ever fight. International independents include Compagnie Française Pétrole, Occidental Petroleum, Marathon, Conoco, and Amerada Hess. Russia, controlling its own oil production and that of its colonies, is a player in the West also, the oil business bringing in much-needed hard currency.

The Seven Sisters did not become so profitable and powerful by accident, or even through sound business practices. They became so through sheer hard work—in forming and maintaining one of the world's most effective cartels. A major architect of the scheme was one of the few American businessmen who did not lapse back into isolationism after World War I.

John D. Rockefeller wanted to be part of England's and France's Middle East oil monopolies in order to drill within the territory on the Saudi peninsula that had been "red lined"—that is, circled in red ink on an English-French treaty map. Rockefeller had leverage in that his companies had some market power in England and on the Continent. Also, there was incentive for those European powers to embrace him rather than compete with him. Nevertheless, it took him six years of hard bargaining to be let into the enterprise. On July 31, 1928, Exxon and Mobil were admitted to ownership of the Iraq Petroleum Company, splitting a 23.75 percent share equally. IPC would develop many oil fields in the Middle East in ensuing years, selling its product to its owners at cost.

Shortly after Exxon was admitted to the select group, a code of gentlemanly conduct that would govern further business dealings of BP, Royal Dutch-Shell, and Exxon was established at a meeting at Achnacarry Castle in Scotland. (The president of Exxon said he had been invited to shoot grouse, but that naturally business matters had come up.) The principles allowed the corporations to develop their businesses without conflicting—competing—with each other.

As expanded in agreements of 1930, 1932, and 1934, and by bringing emerging oil companies under its umbrella, the code provided a method of setting production quotas, divvying up the world markets for petroleum, and fixing prices. Among other provisions, companies were encouraged to trade customers to save shipping costs, and they were prohibited from advertising in the marketing territories of member oil companies without consent. Elaborate procedures were adopted for absorbing quota-breaking occurrences (such as the discovery of new oil fields), compensating below-quota companies, and penalizing overachievers. A vast system of collecting and sharing data was instituted, monitored for the group by Price Waterhouse and Company (which is how it became one of the biggest accounting firms in the world).

The cartel's reach extended far beyond the Middle East. For example, in the late 1940s, BP had more oil production than it could market. BP directed the excess to Exxon and Mobil, and in return Exxon and Mobil agreed not to market the oil east of the Suez and Mobil agreed to stay out of the European market. Through interlocking agreements the cartelization of the oil industry was extended to Europe, where consumers were advised that the arrangement would "counteract senseless competition" and end "price chaos." The U.S. antitrust laws prevented direct application of the cartel's rules to operations within the United States, but the offshore elements of it, as well as the gentlemanly attitude of the oil giants to each other, accomplished similar results. (When later investigated, Exxon advised Congress that the enforcement of the cartel's policies had ceased on the eve of World

War II, although no records to that effect could be produced.)

Newcomers threatening to upset the centralized control of the Middle Eastern oil fields were blended into the enterprise. When Chevron struck big pools in Bahrein and in a portion of Saudi Arabia outside the red line, it looked as if competition might break out. However, Chevron easily was co-opted, in no small part because the Rockefeller family effectively controlled it. Chevron was matched with Texaco in a joint venture known as Caltex, which was assigned distribution rights east of Suez and otherwise was tied in with reciprocal contracts. The Arabian-American Oil Company ("Aramco") was formed, with the Saudi Arabian government as a partner, to extract and distribute Saudi Arabian oil, because operating companies that included sovereign governments as partners were not subject to U.S. antitrust laws. When Gulf, then a new company, hit a huge pool of oil under Kuwait, half ownership was assigned to BP and production was tied up under long-term contracts to two buyers: Exxon and Shell.

Soon the entire production of Middle East oil fields was spoken for through intertwined long-term contracts. The arrangement benefited up-and-coming companies by giving them access to the distribution networks of the majors, and the majors thus were able to continue to control production and markets.

Although they could not be set by agreement in the United States, a way was found to establish monopoly-level prices. To support a doubling of oil prices in 1945, the majors reviewed their calculations of their reserves and found them to be shockingly low. Exxon, for one, predicted that it would have no more oil to sell by 1955. Since the government relies on oil company data to determine reserves, it was impossible to verify or reject the oil companies' determinations at the time they were made. By the time a Senate investigation in 1952 found the oil shortage to be a fraud, the majors had been achieving excess profits for seven years, and the antitrust division had given a "pass" to Exxon and Mobil becoming partners in Aramco in order to encourage oil exploration. The oil companies have worked variations on the theme numerous times.

Once the economic power of the oil company majors had been established, only the United States government had enough countervailing power to rein them in. However, World War II had installed them firmly as an important part of the nation's defense and, as such, above the rules that govern ordinary industries. Time and again they have played the national defense card when threatened with antitrust or other laws, and to this day they continue to operate as quasi-government agencies without public oversight. A good example of oil company power involves an antitrust case that ran for sixteen years and ended in a complete victory for the oil companies with the complicity of the United States government itself.

After the Senate investigation of 1952 had branded the oil shortage a fraud, one person who professed to be shocked by the finding was President Harry Truman, who on June 23, 1952, ordered the Justice Department to prosecute the American contingent of the Seven Sisters under the antitrust laws. The basis of the prosecution was to be the Achnacarry Agreement of 1928 and the subsequent agreements enforcing it, and the control of production, marketing, and pricing by the cartel. The Antitrust Division of the Justice Department put some of its best prosecutors on the case, and soon the oil companies were taking a beating in court on pretrial matters.

However, presumably the oil companies began to whisper in the ear of the President's national security advisors, and they into the President's ear, because suddenly Truman "got religion." On January 12, 1953, shortly before leaving office, Truman directed that the criminal case be converted into a civil one. The effect was to make the acquisition of evidence more difficult (no grand jury) and to remove the threat of jail for the oil barons. (Other possible reasons come to mind. In initiating the prosecution was Truman trying to make the Democrats look like big trustbusters, a bluff that would not be carried out when they lost the White House? Or did Truman simply do the dirty work for President-elect Eisenhower in trimming the investigation?)

The Eisenhower administration soon made mincemeat of the civil case. On August 6, 1953, a policy directive of the National Security Council transferred the responsibility for directing the case from the Justice Department to the Department of State. Not only was this feat of legal legerdemain unique in the annals of American law—the State Department directing an antitrust suit?—but it was done in the face of the fact that the defendants were represented by none other than Secretary of State John Foster Dulles's old law firm.

As might be expected, the lawsuit went nowhere, slowly. The National Security Council dealt several crippling blows, quietly decreeing that the government's suit would not challenge joint actions by the

Seven Sisters in production, refining, and distribution, which had been the heart of the case; and would not ask for dissolution or divestiture of the companies, standard antitrust remedies. The government then sat on the case.

By 1960, it became time to dispose of it in the least embarrassing way to the government without actually having to punish the oil companies. A consent decree was entered into by Exxon and Mobil in which they promised generally not to break the antitrust laws in the future. Big deal. And if that was not enough of a travesty of justice, the decrees specifically found that the oil companies' joint operations and agreements were *not* illegal and *would be* permitted. The defendants were expressly permitted to take part in international cartels if such activities were required by the laws of the foreign country in which the activities would take place (such as joining with foreign governments in companies like Aramco), *or where the local custom was such that failure to join in a cartel "would expose the defendant to the risk of loss of the particular business."* In other words, it is legal to act illegally where to act legally *might* result in losing business! In effect, the decree became a government charter for the oil companies to keep on doing what they had been doing.

The oil industry continued to use the case to trample further on the Blind Lady of Justice. An even weaker decree was later entered into by defendant Texaco. Exxon and Gulf, apparently feeling that the charter was not strong enough, had the decree secretly weakened further in an amendment that did not become public until 1969. Mobil and Chevron simply outlasted the government, finally being dropped as defendants when the case was voluntarily dismissed by the government on January 28, 1968. Being a major oil company means never having to say you are sorry.

The lesson of the Great Oil Antitrust Case Fiasco, as well as all other dealings between the Seven Sisters and the United States government, was clear: some corporations *are* above the law. The stage was set for those powerful multinational corporations to aid and abet the Middle East oil producers when they used the Oil Weapon to mug the United States and the rest of the world's countries.

As the importance of the oil companies to the World War II effort became understood, a similar appreciation of the importance of the rather backward oil-producing countries of the Middle East was forming. Discoveries in the 1930s had established the region as the world's oil reservoir. Not only was the Middle East's oil plentiful, it was "sweet" (pure and light) and easy to reach. Strictly speaking, the oil was not pumped out of the ground—natural gas obligingly pushed it up pipes simply stuck in the pool. The actual cost of extraction amounted to only pennies per barrel, far less than for oil found in the United States.

The importance of cultivating friends in the Middle East was not lost on the United States. Besides the fact that access to Middle Eastern oil, especially for its European allies, was desirable, friendship would allow for the continued presence of the major American oil companies and, consequently, for their continued high profits. Finally, fat and happy pro-Western Middle East monarchs would act as strong buffers of any possible southern expansion of Russia. The two greatest successes of that policy were to be achieved with Saudi Arabia and Iran, at least until the Peacock Throne was toppled.

The solicitous attitude of the United States to Saudi Arabia began during World War II. King Ibn Saud, justly famous for his excesses, could not get enough oil to market to support his life-style because of German submarine activity, so he asked Aramco for a $6 million advance. The major oil companies, never ones to spend good money when they can get the United States government to do it instead, asked the U.S. to bankroll the king. On February 18, 1943, President Franklin Roosevelt declared Saudi Arabia to be a "national security ally," entitling it to receive direct payments from the U.S. government.

The care and feeding of the conservative Saudi government in recent decades as a counter to more radical regimes has been a major triumph of American foreign policy in the post-World War II period. During the 1950s, after additional immense pools of oil were discovered along the Saudi Arabia-Kuwait border, the special relationship between the United States and the Saudi government was solidified. In 1951, the U.S. established a major air base at Dhahran, which operated for ten years. Upstart American wildcatters—Getty, Hammer, Hunt, and Keck—were permitted to open fields. When it became inexpedient for the U.S. government to increase its aid, the private American oil companies increased their royalties. American presidents have sold advanced weapons to the Saudis, although a number of sales have been blocked by that special problem that is Israel. It was the Saudi government that successive U.S. administrations used for secret financial support of the Afghan rebels and the Reagan administration operatives turned to for secret funding of the Nicaraguan Contras after Congress cut off funds.

United States policy toward Iran, both public and covert, has had a rockier road. Unlike Saudi Arabia, over which the royal family has maintained firm control, nationalism and revolution have placed Iran at odds with the major European powers and the United States, although it has nevertheless remained a bulwark against southward Russian expansion.

It is not hard to see why the feeling of the Persian people toward the Western industrialized nations is not one of love. The British colonial hand was heavy, blockading all oil shipments from Iran when that country's legislature attempted to nationalize its oil fields in 1951. After the Shah of Iran was deposed in 1953 by a populist government led by Prime Minister Mohammad Mossadegh, the CIA organized a countercoup to return the Peacock Throne to power. When order was restored, British Petroleum assigned 40 percent of its operations in Iran to American oil companies, and the CIA played an increasing role in providing security to the shah and establishing anti-Communist intelligence operations.

The shah proved to be a difficult client. An ambitious modernization program started in 1956 required ever-increasing amounts of oil money. In 1957, that great "friend" of the West became the first Middle East producer of oil to successfully challenge the sole practical control by the oil companies. Iran's petroleum belonged to Iran, he declared, even after it left the ground. The shah formed a competing company to extract the country's black gold. So important to the West was Iran that the shah's actions went unpunished, setting the stage for later, bolder, moves.

Moves that were too bold, however, were punished. When Gamal Abdul Nasser of Egypt attempted to play the oil card by threatening to close the Suez Canal in October 1956, he brought down the wrath of Britain and France on his head—literally, in the form of paratroopers (along with Israeli troops). Increasing Communist-populist activity in the Middle East in the 1950s led to the "Eisenhower Doctrine," which provided that, on request, the United States would help repel armed takeover by any group controlled by international communism. Under that doctrine, U.S. and British troops prevented the overthrow of governments in Lebanon, Jordan, and Iraq by Nasserites. The result was that, in order to protect against threats to the oil lifeline, American self-defense lines had been extended to the Middle East. (That policy would be enforced by the Reagan administration's military intervention into the Persian Gulf to protect shipping lanes during the Iran-Iraq War, as well as the quick U.S. response to Iraq's invasion of Kuwait.)

The lesson that was learned by the governments of the Middle East was that the sleeping giants of the West might be roused by sudden actions that were obvious threats to wrest control of Middle East oil from the hands of the Western powers and their oil companies, but that slow "salami cutting" methods were less likely to draw similar wrath. Therefore, during the 1960s, the Middle East oil producers started to communicate with each other and to organize in small ways.

On September 14, 1960, in response to demands from the major oil companies that the producing countries take a cut in royalties, a formal group, the Organization of Petroleum Exporting Countries—OPEC— was formed by Saudi Arabia, Iran, Iraq, Kuwait, and Venezuela. (Libya and Indonesia joined in 1962, Abu Dhabi in 1967, Algeria in 1969, and Nigeria in 1971.) To the oil companies and the Western industrialized nations, the group was laughable. Everyone knew that the Arabs could not work together, much less counter the power of the West and their oil megacorporations.

In fact, OPEC did little that made news during the Sixties. Its members were busy quietly building the organization and sharing information on oil company contract terms and methods of operation. Through a unilateral reinterpretation of the method of determining royalties in 1962, the OPEC countries managed to increase their income. In 1968, they agreed that each would have the benefit of the most generous contract terms that any one of them achieved—a unilateral declaration of a "most favored nation" clause. Not only that, but they reserved the right to cancel and alter contract clauses if "changed circumstances" were encountered. Meanwhile, during the Sixties, oil had become the most valuable commodity in the world by far. America's new freeways were turning the economy of the country into one based upon the auto and the truck, and the West's usage of Middle East oil had skyrocketed.

The oil companies had learned a few things from the events of the 1950s too. One was that the Suez was too narrow a bottleneck for bringing the Middle East's oil to the European and North American markets. Supertankers were built to skirt the horn of Africa, and new oil fields were developed in western Africa. Those policies were to bear fruit when the Yom Kippur War of 1967 resulted in the Suez Canal being closed until 1975. One element backfired, however. The biggest mistake the American oil companies ever made was to develop the oil fields, during the Sixties, of a sleepy kingdom known as Libya.

By the close of the 1960s, a recipe had been prepared for financial disaster on a scale never encountered before, and the brew was simmering. During that decade, the world's oil consumption had doubled, as it had every decade from 1890. Petroleum had come to constitute more than one-half the tonnage on the high seas. The confused policies of the United States government, as well as the self-interest of the major American oil companies, had resulted in an ever-increasing reliance on Middle East oil. (Foreign imports of oil would *double* during the period of 1969–73.) The power to produce Middle East oil had been centralized in the hands of a few leaders of those countries and the Seven Sisters. OPEC was in place, dominated by Arab countries enraged at the West's past treatment of them. The Suez bottleneck was not the only constraint on distribution—the spigot was also becoming narrow. All that remained was for someone who cared neither for the delicate balance of commerce nor for the partnership of the Middle East with the West to turn up the heat.

In 1969, a twenty-seven-year-old army colonel, a religious zealot, deposed the king of Libya. The officer's name was Muammar al-Qaddafi.

Chapter 2

The Unsettling Seventies

"There is no subtler, surer means
of overturning the existing basis of
society than to debauch its currency."
—John Maynard Keynes

In what has become a hallmark of subsequent presidents, Lyndon Johnson simply left behind his biggest economic problems when he vacated his office—to be solved by, or, more likely, to be blamed on, his successor.

Of course, Johnson's main problem was the undeclared war in Vietnam, which spawned another conundrum: how to pay for it. By the mid-Sixties, two things were becoming apparent. First, in order to accomplish the United States' objectives in Southeast Asia, a massive amount of men and matériel would have to be mobilized. Second, the American public would not knowingly pay the cost of this increasingly unpopular boondoggle. Johnson found an indirect way to pay for much of the cost—by printing money.

In classic economic theory, a ruler must make choices between providing "guns" or "butter." A government must balance spending heavily on military hardware with investing in domestic consumer products. There is only so much production capacity in a country, there are only so many workers, and there is only so much investment capital. Economic theory tells us that when you push suppliers and employees to the limit, they will ask for more money. It also tells us that if additional money is created by the government to pay for those things, it will become cheapened and will fuel demands for even more of it.

Whether Johnson disbelieved economic theory, felt that he was bigger than it, or was just plain desperate is not clear. Perhaps he simply decided to leave the penalties for the violation of economic laws to those who followed him. In any event, his administration stoked the economy, firing up the Arsenal of Democracy while at the same time providing bread and butter. From mid-1965 to mid-1966, military and civilian spending *each* rose by $22 billion. Finally, in 1967 Johnson asked Congress for a 10 percent tax surcharge. However, not only did Congress dawdle until mid-1968, but Arthur Burns's Federal Reserve Board totally negated any effect by easing credit and stimulating the money supply at the same time. By the late 1960s, the American economy was roaring and, incidentally, stimulating the economies of the other countries of the world.

Consequently, the Sixties became a period of great personal prosperity, especially in the United States. With minor aberrations, goods were plentiful and prices stable—the country was a proverbial cornucopia. The War on Poverty benefited greatly from the real war, the percentage of Americans living below the "poverty line" dropping from 22 percent in 1959 to 12 percent in 1970. Because the effective unemployment rate was nil, civil rights gains could be made without pushing out those who already had jobs. As a result, to a great degree the opposition of the American middle class to the war was effectively bought off. They were fat and happy.

The flies in the ointment were the sons and daughters of the middle class, on whom the strategy backfired. They were free to protest, to drop out and turn on, and to go to jail for their causes, without having to fear that they would drop out of the middle class. To them it seemed as if there would always be plenty of money floating around and plenty of jobs to be had for the asking when the time came. Employers had no choice but to hire long-haired, hostile entries into the labor force, who, at best, wore ridiculously wide and loud ties, and, at worst, turned coffee breaks into dope-smoking sessions. The sky was the limit, in more ways than one.

Ultimately it was the youth outside the established work force, aided and abetted by the mass media, who prevailed. The message that they sold was that Americans could continue to enjoy their ever-improving quality of consumer life more effectively without the bother, danger, and moral decay that accompanied the war in Vietnam. When a sufficient number of the mainstream signed onto that message, Lyndon Johnson and Hubert Humphrey became history.

Unfortunately the Vietnam War did not pass from the scene so quickly or quietly. Richard Nixon and Henry Kissinger tried to end the war by expanding it into Cambodia, and the Ohio National Guard brought the war home.

The economic effect of the Vietnam War in the early Seventies was a highly unusual pattern of lackluster business performance in the civilian sector accompanied by excessive wage increases and rising interest rates—what came to be known as "stagflation." The pattern would persist stubbornly throughout the decade. Lyndon Johnson's economic miracle had proven, alas, to be nothing more than a parlor show ending in an exploding cigar. However, LBJ was out of sight and mind, and many business leaders were laying the blame on the unions, which were gaining sizable wage increases for their members.

To Richard Nixon, inflationary pressures were throwing a one-two punch. Not only did inflation drive prices up, but the public, in expecting inflation to continue, factored future inflation into their plans— creating ever higher degrees of inflation. President Nixon felt that extreme measures were called for not only to fight inflation but also to destroy the *expectation* of more inflation in the public's mind. Thus was born what Nixon termed his "New Economic Policy."

On August 15, 1971, Nixon abandoned his fierce lifelong free market capitalism beliefs and announced a course of action almost unheard of outside of wartime: a widespread freeze on wages, prices, and profit margins. What later was to become known as Phase I lasted through November 13, 1971, and then segued immediately into Phase II, which introduced controls for allowing moderate increases in wages and prices. Phase III, which operated from February to June 1973, asked for voluntary restraints. According to *Business Week* magazine, Phase III was "marked by a breathtaking rise in prices at every level of the economic system." Phase III duly was followed by Phase IV, also known as Freeze II.

At each step, the regulations produced diminishing results. They fell prey to the common bugaboo of controls, which is that people learn how to skirt them. Also, it turned out that deficit spending by the

Nixon administration, overstimulation of the economy by chairman Arthur Burns's Federal Reserve System, and the administration's sale of about one-quarter of the U.S. wheat crop to Russia produced strong inflationary pressures that directly contradicted whatever the wage-price regulations had accomplished.

While Nixon was wrestling with stagflation, a far more dangerous situation was developing. It would lead to a threat to the stability of the economy of the United States and the rest of the world that would make the problems of stagflation seem like a holiday from care. Although manipulated by an organization made up of staunch anti-Communists, it would provide perhaps a bigger threat to capitalism than Russia ever had been able to muster in the economic-political arena. OPEC was gathering its power. When it finally flexed its muscles, bankruptcies on a scale never before encountered would result.

After leading the coup that deposed King Idris, Colonel Muammar al-Qaddafi quickly moved to challenge oil company domination of Libya's economy. As the new decade began, Qaddafi boldly told the oil companies with concessions in his country that the price of Libyan oil was too low. He then demanded an immediate increase of forty cents per barrel (a pittance compared with what would follow). To a large extent the demand was merely an attempt to secure a price level that was fair in light of the cartel's pricing mechanisms.

The demand triggered a series of events. The oil companies did not take kindly to Qaddafi's attitude and offered only a token five cents per barrel in response. Qaddafi simply ordered reductions in output for "conservation" purposes. It was not a bluff. Libya had $2 billion in currency reserves, built up in the Sixties, and could withstand a total embargo for four years. That tactic hit Armand Hammer's Occidental Petroleum particularly hard, since Libya was its only source of crude oil outside the United States. Occidental caved in by fall 1970. The other companies followed. That price increase then led to demands by the other Middle East exporting countries for matching price increases—the first time they had ever acted together to hike prices.

With his inflammatory rhetoric and bold action, Qaddafi had ignited the rocket that would send oil prices into the stratosphere. Perhaps that is why, in spite of Qaddafi's political troublemaking in the Middle East over the years, countries like Saudi Arabia have not censured him or taken any action to rid the world of someone whom many would call a "lunatic." They owe him a huge debt of gratitude, for he was the catalyst that turned their leaders from merely rich, irrelevant fops into men rich beyond understanding who could bring the rest of the world's leaders to their knees. As to his place in his country's history, Qaddafi made one of the poorest countries in the world one of the richest, in the space of ten years.

As 1970 ended, the major oil companies knew that they had to act quickly to head off the whipsaw tactics of the Middle Eastern producers. On January 13, 1971, the oil companies secured an opinion letter from the Justice Department to the effect that it had no intention of bringing an antitrust case in the event that they—the oil companies—responded to the situation collectively. Two days later, they proposed to OPEC that joint negotiations be held that would reach one overall pricing structure. Also, an agreement was reached among the major oil companies and a number of independents whereby production losses from any slowdowns imposed by a host country would be made up by other oil companies. This gave Occidental and other independents staying power in facing off against Libya and other OPEC countries where they had concessions. The Libyan threat had quickly brought an end to the decades-old, bitter battles between the Seven Sisters and the unruly independents.

Now it was the turn of oil-producing countries to refuse. Qaddafi and the United States' great friend, the Shah of Iran, saw no reason to stop the game of leapfrogging that was adding cash to the coffers. The oil companies had no choice but to retreat to a position of separate but "connected" negotiations. The OPEC countries then placated the United States government by backing away from threats to close down oil production entirely as a lesson to the West (made mostly by the shah) and also by stating that they would abide by any negotiated agreement.

The results of the talks were the "Teheran Agreement" of February 14, 1971, and the "Tripoli Agreement" of April 2, 1971. They barely made a ripple in the U.S. newspapers, the big news in the United States being the conviction of Lieutenant William Calley. In summary, the oil exporters got about half of their original demands, Libya accomplishing an eighty cents per barrel raise to $2.01 per barrel, and the other Middle Eastern producers getting a phased forty-five cents per barrel raise. The increase would put about $15 billion into OPEC's coffers over the next five years, the life of the agreements. The result was only a three to five cent increase in pump prices, but the die had been cast.

The status quo secured by the five-year agreements lasted five months. In September 1971, the OPEC countries agreed that they would each seek larger ownership interests in the production "partnerships" with the oil companies. The specter of nationalization reared its ugly head.

Once more Libya led the way. Over the course of the next two years, Qaddafi would totally nationalize about one-third of the production within his borders and assume a majority interest in another half, thus increasing his government's take without increasing taxes or royalties. The Seven Sisters shed only crocodile tears, as the nationalization in Libya took away competitive production facilities from the independents. The majors would rather follow Qaddafi than fight Hammer.

The other OPEC leaders became drawn in to a game of one-upmanship—they had to produce gains for their people, too. By spring 1972, the pressure on the moderate Arab countries to follow Qaddafi's lead resulted in demands for increased participation in the oil production companies, the Arab countries taking the position that percentage of ownership issues were not settled in the Teheran Agreement. The Riyadh Agreement of late 1972 laid out the details of the oil companies' transfer of participation to the bulk of the OPEC countries, leading to 51 percent ownership by the host countries.

Also during 1972, OPEC engineered another price increase. When the United States devalued the dollar by 8.6 percent, OPEC deemed that to be, in effect, a price cut. Taking the position that the devaluation was just the sort of "changed circumstance" that triggered renegotiation of the Teheran Agreement, OPEC raised prices to "adjust" for the nick in their revenues.

The oil companies took their lickings quickly and quietly, and the governments of the West did not seem too interested in the proceedings. While this is usually viewed as a horrible mistake, alternate views may have merit. One view is that OPEC had gained sufficient leverage to wrest the control of oil production from the oil companies no matter what was done in opposition. A less charitable view is that the companies simply took a fall—that they had no problem passing leadership to a group that would reverse the competition that independent oil companies had begun to create during the 1960s. Whatever the reason, oil company profits soared. Fourth quarter 1973 profits exceeded the fourth quarter 1972 as follows: Gulf, 153 percent; Chevron, 94.2 percent; Texaco, 70.1 percent; Mobil, 68.2 percent; and Exxon, 59 percent. Exxon's profits for 1973, $2.46 billion after taxes, were the largest ever for an industrial company to that date. It may also have served the purposes of the United States to supply the Shah of Iran with increasing revenues so that he then could buy U.S. arms. A militarily strong Iran would remain independent of pressures from Russia.

It was hardly the time for Western governments to be smug. The industrialized world largely had been converted to oil burning. From 1969 to 1973, while the price per barrel of oil had doubled, so had the world's oil consumption. The huge increase was supplied mostly by Iran (production up by 52 percent) and Saudi Arabia (increase of 129 percent). In 1973, the United States became the world's number one importer of petroleum. Western Europe and the United States had become dependent upon Middle Eastern oil in the extreme, although production from Alaska's North Slope and England's North Sea operations would provide a modicum of continuing supply at controlled prices later in the decade.

The oil companies had little trouble adjusting to the new state of affairs. Taking advantage of the confusion in gasoline prices caused by OPEC's actions, they added substantially to their own margins. (In 1971, the Cost of Living Council, the agency formed to monitor wage-price controls, found that 144 oil companies had violated the price freeze. The Justice Department took no action. Several years later, the Government Accounting Office estimated that oil company overcharges during the early Seventies amounted to $2 billion.) In the name of "national security" five majors—Exxon, Mobil, Chevron, Texaco, and Gulf—were granted exemptions from U.S. antitrust laws and Federal Trade Commission rules to negotiate with OPEC. In return, the companies were "forced" to coordinate international oil shipments. The special exemption, which was to last ten years, was established at a public meeting of the Federal Energy Administration called on six days' notice.

Another spark was ignited in the oil barrel. On October 6, 1973, Egypt and Syria invaded Israel. Egypt's troops would be encircled by an Israeli pincer movement west of Suez within a month. (The canal itself was not a factor. It had been closed since 1967 and would not reopen until 1975.) Shortly after the outbreak of hostilities, OPEC announced a unilateral increase of 70 percent in oil prices—from $3.00 to $5.11 per barrel.

OPEC also flexed new muscles. Starting on October 7, 1973, Arab OPEC countries announced embargoes against the United States. Also, production would be cut generally, to remain constricted until Israel withdrew from territory seized in the 1967 war. However, probably at the urging of Saudi Arabia's oil minister, Sheik Ahmad Zaki Yamani, the Arab producers backed away from the embargo by the end of the year, stating that the goal of teaching the West a lesson had been accomplished. Economic power had been quickly harnessed for political use.

There was no question that OPEC was now catching everyone's attention. Fall 1973 found panic buying lines at gas stations in the United States, and the U.S. government quietly printing ration coupons. In December, with the shah calling for an immediate doubling of the new $5.11 price, an oil auction in Iran drew bids in the astonishing amount of $11.65 per barrel. This, after an April 1973 article in an influential journal had predicted staggering effects on the economy of the world if—and this was not a conservative estimate—oil prices reached $3.50 per barrel *by 1980!*

Having seen bids of the incredible, staggering, unbelievable, ridiculous amount of $11.65 per barrel at the Iranian auction, OPEC simply made that insanity the status quo. It announced that as of January 1, 1974, $11.65 would indeed be the regular price of the industry's marker, Saudi Arabian light crude. Although carrying somewhat different prices due to location and sulphur content of the oil (a negative), other OPEC crudes were adjusted accordingly. Thus OPEC had driven up the price of oil sixfold in slightly more than three years, from $1.80 to $11.65. (OPEC would raise prices another 10 percent in 1975, to make up for the fact that its actions in 1974 had cheapened the dollar.) The cost to produce Middle Eastern oil remained at about twenty cents a barrel.

The incredible price increases produced two major effects. First, the peoples of many oil-importing countries suffered economic hardships unprecedented outside of wartime. Second, the OPEC countries developed a cash flow that swamped them in dollars and threatened to tip the international financial network out of balance. The United States government's policy cynically would use the first effect to profit off the second, which had the result of bankrupting many American individuals, families, and big and small corporations.

Because of the world's commitment to oil as an energy source, the whopping increases produced only a 4 percent decrease in its consumption of oil. As a result, in 1974 oil-importing countries transferred to OPEC countries approximately $100 billion for their liquid gold (compared with about $6 billion in 1970), the Arab contingent receiving about 60 percent of that. That transfer of wealth was certainly the biggest in the history of the world outside of war and possibly bigger than the spoils of any war. Economists calculated that the oil price increases would cost the global economy 2 percent of its economic growth in future years, even with *austerity* on the part of the world's peoples. Whole industries, such as travel, farming (due to fertilizer costs), and utilities, became basket cases. The increase in the oil bill for Americans was greater annually than the cost of the Vietnam War. (Since the oil companies controlled the natural gas and coal industries also, those prices were simply raised commensurate with oil.)

The oil price increase blew the lid off the inflation numbers. While running at about 12 percent a year in the United States during 1974—horrible enough—inflation hit 17 percent in England, 20 percent in Italy (which was narrowly saved from bankruptcy by a $2 billion loan from West Germany), 22 percent in Japan and Mexico, and 28 percent in India. The fabric of democracy was threatened.

Underdeveloped and developing countries became insolvent upon the announcement of the 1974 price increase. Not only did they lack the currency reserves to pay for the oil that was the *sine qua non* of increased standards of living, their elemental economies left less room for oil conservation. India, with foreign exchange reserves of about $630 million, had an oil bill in 1974 of more than $1 billion. The increase in the oil bill of the developing countries for 1974 canceled out all development assistance aid, totaling $11 billion, from the industrialized countries. Oil became another yoke around the necks of people already terribly burdened by large price increases in food and fertilizer.

Meanwhile, the people of many OPEC countries became much richer. The per capita income of the major Persian Gulf OPEC countries increased an average of 115 percent in 1974. Since the $100 billion received during 1974 for oil consisted almost entirely of profit, the OPEC countries amassed $60 billion in additional foreign exchange from that year's trade. That level of profit would lead to additional accumulations of cash in subsequent years, in spite of ever-increasing attempts by OPEC members to spend as much of it as possible. In short order, OPEC countries accumulated $100 billion in monetary reserves, *one-fifth of the reserves in the entire world!*

In practice, the OPEC countries could not possibly spend the major portion of their oil incomes. While the more populous countries of Iran (32 million), Iraq (10 million), Venezuela (11 million), and Algeria (15 million) recycled significant amounts of money by buying goods and services for internal development, and Iran paid $100 million for a one-fourth interest in Krupp Industries, the group of Saudi Arabia, Kuwait, Libya, Abu Dhabi, and Qatar, with 48 percent of OPEC output, together had only 12 million people and limited opportunities for development. (Indonesia and Nigeria had only small shares of OPEC output and used all profits internally). In 1974, OPEC placed only $5 billion in U.S. bank deposits, $5 billion in government securities, and $1 billion in U.S. real estate investments. While it is true that in 1975 Arabs bought a controlling interest in the fourth largest bank in Michigan, Detroit's Bank of the Commonwealth, as well as several smaller ones, that really was done with "petty cash." The world simply was not big enough for OPEC money: four months' oil income to Saudi Arabia totaled enough to buy all of the thirty leading companies on the London Stock Exchange. The U.S. treasury bill market was only $100 million. As a result, a substantial amount of money was siphoned out of the world's economy, making everyone poorer.

Most Arab oil money was placed in English and American banks. However, that was more a curse than a blessing because such short-term funds were very liquid and could not be used as a foundation for long-term loans to other customers. The bankers lived in mortal fear of quick, massive shifts in Arab funds. In fact, when Henry Kissinger hinted of possible military action against OPEC oil fields in the fall of 1974, significant OPEC money was shifted out of U.S. banks and into British banks, causing the dollar to plummet and the pound to rise. He soon changed his tune.

In spite of mediagenic promises, the OPEC countries helped non-Arab Third World governments in only minuscule amounts. For example, most of the $2 billion in grants to underdeveloped countries by OPEC in 1974 went to Egypt, Syria, and Jordan for repair of war damage. Another $3 billion was loaned to countries that were impoverished by the price increases . . . *at market rates!*

The developed Western countries also suffered. Europe and Japan, highly dependent on Middle Eastern oil, were very hard hit. Recessions were triggered in all the industrialized countries, and their per capita income dropped one percent in 1974. Investment capital dried up. European countries embarked on programs of austerity and conservation.

However, the United States was in a position to embark on its own course in response to OPEC, based upon several factors.

First and foremost, while the United States had become a net importer of oil in 1973, it had substantial domestic oil production. (Rosy estimates, though, of the U.S. position proved to be woefully inadequate and resulted in ever-increasing reliance on OPEC oil in the 1970s.) American consumers would be buying oil products at prices that blended the now cheaper domestically produced oil with OPEC oil. Also, after all, good old *American* oil companies were cashing in on the situation, which certainly improved the outlook of a very important sector of the economy. Thus, by early 1975, Henry Kissinger was talking up the concept of getting OPEC to agree *not* to cut prices below $11 per barrel to provide a sufficient "carrot" to American oil companies to explore for more oil. No consideration whatsoever was given to increasing oil purchases from Canada.

It is quite apparent that policy putting primary emphasis on the protection of oil company profits would not also encourage conservation and synthetic fuels. U.S. efforts along those lines—except for improved auto mileage standards, which *do* matter—were fitful and destined for failure. Research into synthetic fuels and solar power has been starved for funds.

Second, the United States was in the best position of any country to recycle OPEC's petrodollars. The Arabs were known to be most conservative investors, and which country offered them the safest, most anti-Communist, place to put their money? Which country offered the largest, most complex economy, thereby providing the widest range of prudent investments? Which country had the biggest stock exchanges, for easy-access investing? Consequently, rather than part company with the leaders of Saudi Arabia and Iran, the U.S. government cozied up to them like the neighborhood coquette batting her eyelashes at the richest boys in town.

This quiet rapprochement went forward in the face of wild public speculation that the major Western powers would take matters into their own hands, in the style of the 1956 British-French seizure of the Suez Canal. Perfectly serious magazines such as *The New Republic* and *Harper's* carried perfectly serious articles laying out the intellectual, moral, and psychological bases for wresting power from OPEC and returning total control of oil to, in effect, the United States. The *Harper's* article went so far as to lay out detailed logistics for a paratroop attack on, and permanent seizure of, Saudi Arabia's oil facilities. For a while, it was assumed that such concepts were not far from actual military preparations. However, in 1975, the Pentagon acknowledged that it was spending $77 million to train Saudi Arabian troops to protect their oil installations, and so obviously the United States government had no stomach for a fight.

To an extent, the policy of accommodation worked as had been hoped. While the Arabs put useless, short-term funds into European banks and Eurodollars, Americans paraded their commercial and farm real estate and corporate opportunities before the sheiks like the auctioneer parades thoroughbreds for sale. (In fact, we sold them those, too!) Significant amounts of money that had sloshed to the Arab end of the world came sloshing back into the United States. If you cannot beat them . . .

However, the results were not very beneficial to the citizens of the United States and in ways hurt more than they helped. There is only so much investment-grade commercial and farm real estate, and so prices increased beyond the means of American investors, to a level that made little sense in terms of traditional requirements of return. Farmers borrowed heavily on the inflated farm real estate values, which led to their problems in the 1980s. The stock market was artificially driven upwards by OPEC money. Because of the extreme financial conservatism of the Arabs, little foreign investment was placed into developing companies and industries. Once Arab money settled into the larger New York and Chicago banks, those institutions lost their fear of large-scale withdrawals. The banks used the increases in Arab deposit balances to go on a lending binge to the oil industry, which directly led to major banking problems—including the insolvency of one of the largest, Continental Illinois Bank and Trust Company of Chicago—in the 1980s.

Of course, the policy of accommodation made the professed federal alternative fuels programs shams. The major oil companies, foreseeing the trend, had already put the American people into a box by quietly becoming "energy companies." They had used their wealth not to explore a significantly greater number of wells, but rather to dominate and control *all* commercial energy resources and most potential sources. The twenty biggest oil companies owned 90 percent of the proven reserves in the U.S., the top eight alone holding two-thirds. Also, just to be sure, between 1964 and 1974 seven major oil companies filed forty-nine of the fifty-two patents for converting coal into synthetic gas and oil. Consequently, to develop those fuels would have required more than the grudging cooperation of the oil barons. The oil companies invested heavily in uranium mines and soon controlled the majority of domestic mining and reserves. (Not surprisingly, the price of uranium began to skyrocket.) When added to large purchases of coal companies in the 1960s, total control over the production of natural gas, and ownership of all gas and oil pipelines, these moves gave the major U.S. oil companies absolute domination and control of domestic energy sources. Make no mistake about it, Americans and their businesses have paid dearly for allowing that to happen because the majors prefer monopoly profits on existing Middle East megapools of petroleum over expensive and uncertain exploration for undiscovered oil fields elsewhere in the world.

Another reason for the waffling attitude of the United States government was the Johnson-Vietnam War phenomenon: no one had the guts to tell the American people that they would have to tighten their belts and conserve and that their standard of living would be headed downward. As a result, U.S. consumption of foreign oil inexorably marched upward during the 1970s. Full effects of the price of oil were blunted by increasing deficits and other smokescreens. As one financial expert observed, "The transfer of wealth to oil-producing countries cannot fail to take its toll on the living standards of the industrialized world, although even here some of the real burden could be shifted to future generations."

The result of the policies of OPEC and the United States government was a weird roller coaster ride for the American economy. Between early 1973 and fall 1974, while the Watergate constitutional crisis raged, more than $300 billion in stock values on the New York Stock Exchange was wiped out. Ordinarily that would signal a serious recession. However, at the same time, the cost of living rose more than 15 percent. The country was suffering its worst inflation in peacetime, about 3 percent of which was directly attributable to the huge oil price increase, and interest rates were the highest in a century. When the auto industry raised prices to cover inflation and resulting higher costs of production, sales dropped 21 percent. American companies cut costs feverishly and thus cut employment. Newly installed as President, Gerald Ford offered solutions: every person should exercise voluntary economic restraint and make a list of ten ways to save energy and fight inflation.

Then the effects of the huge oil price increase really began to kick in. The beginning of 1975 saw the United States in the worst recession since the Great Depression. The unemployment rate went over 9 percent. President Ford told us, "Americans are no longer in full control of their destiny when that destiny depends on foreign oil," but he proceeded to do nothing about it. Instead, viewing the anemic condition of the dollar in June 1975, he remarked that an 8 percent increase in OPEC oil prices would be "justified."

OPEC proceeded to give itself a 10 percent raise, and Kuwait and Venezuela totally nationalized their oil installations. Nigerian oil minister Mofia Akobo said, "It is not up to OPEC to solve the world recession." Odd-even gas days and long lines at stations were triggered. Congress prepared a complex program of taxes, allocation, and rationing, but then lacked the nerve to spring it on the American public. A *Time* magazine survey found that 77 percent of the public felt that things were going badly for the country and that most people had little confidence in Ford or Congress due to their do-nothing attitudes.

The Ford administration then made two big missteps. First, rather than allow the recession to cook the severe inflationary pressures out of the system, hasten energy conservation, and otherwise meld the big oil price increase into the U.S. economy, the administration lost its collective nerve. Instead, Ford and the Federal Reserve quietly stimulated the economy, setting off the roller coaster ride once more. Second, the administration failed to take advantage of the oil-induced recession to put pressure on OPEC, at a time when further decreasing purchases from those countries would have put a severe strain on that alliance. Instead, the U.S. dutifully continued to retain the OPEC countries as its primary foreign suppliers of oil. The stability of Saudi Arabia and Iran continued as a U.S. government policy of the highest priority. (Indeed, the United States was rewarded by Iran with a five-year, $15 billion deal to purchase arms and other goods. The American people's loss was the military's gain.)

As of the last months of 1975, stagflation still held sway in the world. Inflation in the United States continued at a 7.4 percent clip, 28 percent in Great Britain, and 9+ percent in France, Italy, and Japan. Real GNP growth in the United States was negative 2.9 percent.

The Western democracies had given up attempting to organize themselves as oil consumers. The U.S. continued to cultivate Saudi Arabia and Iran. Great Britain, planning on North Sea oil bounty, decided high prices were not so bad after all. France refused to join the International Energy Agency, which had been established to provide energy-consuming countries an organization for unified negotiations with OPEC. Japan was too afraid of OPEC reprisals to fight. Accordingly, contrary to most predictions, it was OPEC that remained strong and united, disparate countries of that group smoothing over their differences for mutual gain; and it was the powerful industrial nations that showed an inability to cooperate.

The close of 1975 brought two interesting, and not unrelated, pieces of economic news. Reeling from high costs of energy and welfare, New York City announced that it was on the brink of bankruptcy. It was saved by a package of short-term loans from the federal government. On the other end of the financial spectrum, the Aramco partners (Exxon, Texaco, Mobil, and Chevron) paid no U.S. taxes on $2.8 billion in profits from Saudi Arabian operations. (Due to a special tax interpretation initiated in 1951, they had paid almost no taxes on their foreign operations during the Sixties and early Seventies.)

Ford's attempt to stimulate the economy did not get him elected in 1976, but it probably made the tally closer. Jimmy Carter had fresh views that were appealing to the public. He campaigned against big arms sales to Iran and Saudi Arabia. He preached solar power and energy conservation. He beat Ford 297 electoral votes to 241, although Ford carried twenty-seven states.

Between the election of Jimmy Carter as President and his taking office, OPEC issued another fiat respecting price increases. Prices were raised 10.3 percent as of January 1, 1977, and increased another 5 percent on July 1. Thus, in January the price of Saudi Arabian benchmark crude stood at $12.81 a barrel. Although the percentage of the increases was not as devastating as the quadrupling of prices three years earlier, because they were based on already substantial prices the effect was another round of economic dislocations and hardships. It was calculated that the increases alone would cut employment by an additional .3 percent and add .2 percent to the inflation rate, both already crippling.

The problem was that the effects were chronic and cumulative. The increases would further add to the worldwide recession and the $170 billion of external debt of the less developed nations, all attributable to the 1974 OPEC price increase. The non-OPEC world had lost $145 billion on GNP in 1974, $215 billion in 1975, $190 billion in 1976, and would lose $220 billion in 1977, directly attributable to the OPEC price increases. In 1977, the OPEC price increases would mean to the United States $75 billion in lost GNP, three million lost jobs, and a loss of $90 billion in disposable income to its citizens. While the latest price increase would add to the $100 billion per year being transferred to the OPEC countries, they were still spending only a small fraction of their income on external goods and services. For example, in 1975 Iran spent $10 billion on imports, Saudi Arabia $7 billion, Libya $4 billion, and Kuwait $2 billion. Thus, in effect, OPEC continued to withdraw vast amounts of wealth from the world's people.

At Mr. Carter's inauguration on January 23, 1977, he walked the parade route. As President, he cut the White House staff by one-third. In a series of televised speeches in April 1977, he preached frugality and promised that his attack on energy costs would be the Moral Equivalent of War. Now this was someone who could shape us up, show us the value of austerity.

However, somewhere between the intention and the execution, the concepts lost their force. The Senate, lobbied heavily by oil and transportation interests and afraid to prescribe strong medicine to the American public, failed to heed Carter's request for wellhead and gasoline taxes. Congress passed the National Energy Act in November 1978, but it contained no conservation measures. While Congress agreed to provide Carter with a Department of Energy, it did not provide the agency with any definitive programs to execute. As a result, 1977 went and 1978 came and went, with no major action being taken. The President's decisive actions were to ask Americans to set thermostats at no more than sixty-five degrees and speedometers at no more than fifty-five. Carter's Moral Equivalent of War began to be referred to by its acronym—MEOW.

OPEC did not help any. Falsely citing civil unrest in Iran as a disruption of oil supplies, it raised prices another 14.5 percent as of January 1, 1978, dealing the world's economy another Arab blow to the gut. And then OPEC complained about the weak dollar. Threats to transfer base pricing of oil to International Monetary Fund special drawing rights set the Carter administration scrambling to prop up the buck. It turned out that OPEC did not abandon dollar pricing of oil, but its *quid pro non* was another 14.5 percent increase in prices in 1979. (Iraq and Venezuela had pushed for 25 percent.)

While oil price increases were a major *major* cause of the American people's troubles, there was a feeling that successive administrations and Congresses should share a large part of the blame for ten years of inflation. *Business Week* surveyed the wreckage of the economy and pessimistically concluded, "Inflation now must seem so deeply imbedded in the foundation of the society as to make the ability to eradicate it seem doubtful. And this is happening because of—not in spite of— the way that the democratic decision making process works in Washington."

Quoth Ronald Reagan: "Our problem isn't a shortage of oil, it's a surplus of government." Exhibit A was federal government spending: from 1961 through 1977, government purchases of goods and services increased by an average of 6 percent per year, and "transfer" payments (welfare, social security, etc.) had average increases of 13 percent per year. Total federal government spending had steadily increased from $196 billion in 1970, with a $2.8 billion deficit, to $496 billion in 1979, with a $48.5 billion deficit.

While there was debate on the proper allocation of blame, one thing was certain: the American economy had become a nightmare from which no one could seem to wake up.

Consider the Consumer Price Index. If the price level for 1967 is taken as 100, except for wartime the levels for the period of 1860 to 1914 were about 22 to 24. After World War I, they did not go below 40. The end of World War II saw it at 58, the end of the Korean War at 80. In other words, slow and relatively steady inflation had brought the index less than 60 points in more than one hundred years. By the end of our large-scale involvement in Vietnam, 1972, it had jumped to 130. By January of 1975, it hit 160, and by the end of 1977, it was pushing 190 heading quickly up through the 200 mark. More than a hundred years of damage had been done in ten.

And the American people suffered every notch on the climb. Although wages and salaries also increased, they did not double during that period as did prices. The average monthly housing expense *tripled.* Those who saved to buy a house found themselves losing ground. Food prices rose 31 percent in 1973–1974 alone and began to climb again in 1978; a head of lettuce, for example, doubling in price in one year. Inflation pushed everyone into higher tax brackets, caused a decline in all income brackets of discretionary income, and squeezed out the luxuries. A luxury that began to disappear was the nonworking wife. Although social security benefits were regularly raised, between 1970 and 1977 actual purchasing power of those benefits declined 25 percent. And inflation did not peter out after raging for a decade. In April 1978, it was clipping along at a 16 percent annual rate, although the rate of all of 1978 would prove to be "only" 10 percent after the Carter administration clamped fiscal and monetary restraints on the economy.

Businesses were whipsawed constantly. Between material shortages, zigzagging government policies, and skyrocketing transportation costs, it became useless to make plans or projections. For example, the Carter administration prodded the economy to foster growth in early 1978, only to slam on the brakes in the fall of the same year, instituting a very complicated set of wage and price guidelines. Longstanding relationships between suppliers and manufacturers, shippers and carriers, and producers and customers were ripped apart. Every day was an uncharted adventure for American business. In many industries, profit margins were eaten up by the inefficiencies generated by these economic conditions.

Not surprisingly, businesses, consumers, and their federal government all tapped into available credit to stay afloat. Because inflation had inflated the values of business equipment and machinery—frequently the market value exceeded the original purchase price—those items could provide the foundation for further borrowing. In 1978, consumer debt rose 15 percent, $136 billion, the biggest annual jump in many years. Mortgage debt jumped from $479 billion in 1975 to $701 billion in 1978. By December 1978, outstanding consumer debt reached a milestone—or was it a millstone?—of $1 trillion. Government deficits, a form of borrowing, had begun to rise at an alarming rate, approaching the unheard of level of $70 billion per year (a figure that would be dwarfed by Reagan administration deficits). In times of expansion, credit expansion is desirable and healthy, but in the economic conditions of the late Seventies, the increases in debt only paid for inflation. Borrowers were grasping at anything to stay afloat.

Another sign of the sickness in the economy was that the huge increases in borrowing were coming at a time when interest rates were at levels previously associated with panic, wars, and gold boomtowns. When the Federal Reserve tried to cool the borrowing craze by tightening credit in 1977, interest rates immediately leaped 2 percent, but the desire for credit did not abate. Posted "prime rates" (interest rates paid by the most sound megacorporate borrowers) marched steadily towards 15 percent, and by 1979 the Federal Reserve rate to banks hit 15 percent. Consequently, the rates that consumers and small businesses paid were pushed upward even further, at times reaching 25 percent—rates previously associated only with the Mafia. Mortgage rates were reaching 15 percent. Lenders were rushing to abandon fixed-rate business, consumer, and mortgage loans in favor of those that had rates that "floated" a certain percentage above the prime rate. (The government deficits were financed by treasury bill sales, but the government was paying the highest interest rates ever recorded, putting it in the same class as the hapless consumer.) The result was a double-barreled blast: high rates fueled more inflation, and the funds required for debt service raised living and business expenses to a level that drained consumers and businesses alike. Simply put, in both business and personal life, it became impossible to turn a profit.

The values inherent in American businesses evaporated, as corporations turned from a weak stock market to expensive borrowing to maintain operations. (Stock offerings had almost ceased since the late 1960s.) In one month in 1978, the stock market plummeted 13 percent, losing $133 billion in corporate values. Returns on assets of American companies, which had averaged 7.7 percent, dictated a reduction in carrying costs. Something had to give and did. Those retailers who lacked sufficient cash reserves or who guessed wrong on the salability of their inventories succumbed to the financial sickness. Auto dealers, many of them decades old, lost their dealerships in droves. Some large retailers bit the dust in 1977, most notably W. T. Grant and United Merchants (Robert Hall stores and its consumer financing subsidiary). Apeco, a photocopy machine manufacturer, badly overextended in a time of business retrenchment, was forced to file bankruptcy.

Of course, this litany of horrors did not apply to the oil companies, who were making fabulous profits. In 1978, the eight major U.S. oil companies earned $8.3 billion. A government study had found that due to tax breaks, incentives, and favorable rulings, the *maximum* effective tax rate on oil companies was 17.2 percent, and many oil companies had "negative" tax rates; as a result, the companies were able to keep nearly all of their cash. For the first quarter of 1979, Exxon had the largest profit of any company ever—$1.925 billion. Texaco's profit was up 97 percent, Shell's 67 percent, Amoco 64 percent, and Gulf 56 percent. And *then* President Carter decontrolled prices in June 1979, letting them float upward to OPEC's level. By 1980, oil company profits accounted for 40 percent of *all* U.S. manufacturing company profits. Of the increase in profits for the period of 1978 to 1980 for U.S. manufacturing corporations, the oil industry accounted for 98 percent! Exxon's $300 million increase in profits during that period almost equaled the profit increases of the entire group of companies listed as 501 through 1,000 on *Fortune's* hierarchy of U.S. manufacturing corporations. In other words, in the late Seventies, the oil industry was about the only profitable business in the United States. It makes sense. After all, the oil industry was the only one that did not suffer from high energy costs!

A major source of profit for the majors was at the gas pump. Having destroyed the independent marketers during the Seventies by choking off their supplies from refineries, the majors did not have to worry about competition from outside "the club." The number of stations was reduced from 220,000 in 1972 to 148,000—for a lot more cars—by 1982. Labor costs were slashed by shortening hours, by selling the public on the idea that they would save a few pennies a gallon by pumping their own gas, and by almost entirely abandoning repair operations (except for Shell). Also, decontrol policies had resulted in unleashing gas station profits, which had been maintained through the 1970s at nine cents per gallon above wholesale prices and taxes, and so by July 1979 profits at the pump were up to 15.4 cents per gallon and rising. Between January and July 1979, prices at the pump increased 55 percent altogether. The oil companies also got incentives amounting to $7 billion over two years for carrying unleaded gasoline. (Hence the reason unleaded costs more than regular gas!) By 1979, the majors had jacked up the price of diesel fuel, which had been deregulated in 1976, to $1.13 a gallon, leading to nationwide protests by truckers.

Prices at the pump were manipulated by a tactic the oil companies by then had perfected. Citing disruptions of production in Iran, the oil companies cried shortage in early 1979. Sure enough, in April 1979, shortages in major cities in California forced them to accept rationing.

Then suddenly the shortages were over. The same happened in Washington, D.C., in June 1979 and in New York in July 1979. The causes were never determined. However, storage facilities on the East Coast were full at the very same time. It was learned that the refineries owned by the majors had slowed output—but why? One thing was for certain: gasoline prices went from seventy cents a gallon in April 1979 to $1 a gallon in May, and up another sixteen cents during that summer.

One thing the oil companies did *not* do was to aid the mythical synthetic fuels development process. It was mythical not only for the unrealistic dreams of energy bounty that it promised, but also because, in fact, the government was doing nothing about it. While Congress gave Carter the Synthetic Fuels Corporation, funded with $19 billion, the agency could not proceed without the active assistance of several major oil companies which owned patents on aspects of the process. Exxon said it *might* become interested if tax incentives were given. They were not. When Ronald Reagan became President, he cut the appropriations in half. In 1982 the United States government offered to fund $10 billion for synthetic fuels development and $3 billion for shale oil research. No companies volunteered. During the period of 1980 to 1982, the Synthetic Fuels Corporation did not fund one project.

Nineteen eighty marked the twentieth anniversary of OPEC. Although the celebration of its two decades in existence was cancelled due to Arab disunity stirred up by the Ayatollah Ruhollah Khomeini, OPEC continued to confound those who still predicted its demise. OPEC oil income had climbed rapidly—$124 billion in 1978, $188 billion in 1979, $272 billion in 1980, and would hit $265 billion in 1981. When the price of oil reached $34 a barrel in 1981, OPEC had succeeded in doubling its revenues from 1978 by selling less at higher prices. The Arab countries were rich beyond imagination.

In spite of all the huffing and puffing, by 1980, the United States had apparently accomplished the true, secret goals of its leaders—to prop up the anti-Communist governments of Saudi Arabia and Iran. As a result the country was horribly, irrevocably dependent on OPEC oil. Although oil usage was on a downward trend from the peak year of 1978, the expenditures for foreign oil continued to burden the American people. In 1973, U.S. foreign oil imports were $7.1 billion; by 1980, that figure had risen to $79 billion. President Reagan appointed a man to be secretary of the Department of Energy whose avowed purpose was to disband it.

The American people continued to suffer from the cost of energy, which had risen by 800 percent during the 1970s *for those who practiced energy conservation.* The poor were cold and isolated due to the cost of transportation. Meanwhile, the suburbs continued their sprawl, based almost exclusively on the private automobile that typically was owned two or three to a family and usually seen on the roads with only one person inside. Twenty oil companies were comfortably ensconced in the top fifty largest U.S. corporations.

The sad part is that it did not have to be this way. Other countries have one hundred-mile-per-hour trains. Japan, whose economy was and is almost entirely dependent on Middle East oil, became an economic tiger during the same decade that the U.S. frittered away its economic might. It is hard to disagree with Senator Adlai Stevenson III when he observed: "Almost every time there has been a choice between what is best for Big Oil and what is best for the nation, Big Oil has won."

Leaving aside the undeniable effects of Big Oil actions, many people might conclude that the hard times, economic and social dislocations, and competitiveness problems of industry that have plagued the United States during the 1970s and 1980s were and are unavoidable consequences of economic forces beyond control. Nothing could be further from the truth.

While economic forces, particularly the seizure of oil power by OPEC, provided severe blows to the world order, America's problems were hugely amplified by the way America's business and government leaders responded. The ineptness and self-aggrandizement of our national administrations and the totally self-interested actions of the barons of American industry and finance did more to harm the American people than any outside forces. They caused the disinvestment in, and the deindustrialization of, the United States. That same federal government allowed megacorporations to use the bankruptcy system to serve those purposes. Together they made the United States what it is today: the biggest debtor in the world, dependent on foreign investment to provide the necessary funds to operate the federal government; the holder of an industrial base that is too shrunken and ravaged of talent to provide the manufactured goods that we need; and the supplier of technologies to countries of the world that use them to eclipse their benefactors.

Proof that it did not have to be this way exists in the industrial giants of today, Japan and Germany. Both countries were more seriously affected by the oil price increases of the 1970s than was the United States. Japan continues to be dependent on the importation of Middle East oil for almost every drop used in that country. Both countries suffered oil-induced severe recessions and high interest rates. However, during the 1970s, they continued to build their industrial bases and strengthen their economies, while the United States became an economic cripple. Take Japan, whose emergence as an industrial tiger is accurately reflected in the same statistics that show the decline of U.S. industries—sales of products within the United States.

As of the beginning of the 1960s, American industry was the colossus. Continuing a trend that extended back to the World War II era, U.S. exports in 1960 were twice those of imports. Those glory years had brought much foreign exchange into the U.S. Europeans were complaining that American companies were "buying Europe." In 1965, the U.S. enjoyed a $5 billion trade surplus.

But American industry was not covering its flanks or planning ahead. For one thing, industrial strategy of the U.S. government was (and still is) centered on military hardware and promoting the interests of the oil companies above all others. Nonmilitary manufacturers began to lag in developing and implementing state-of-the-art equipment. American industry failed to see a need for long-range planning. American workers were gorged on war prosperity and were not inclined to fear for their jobs. They wanted more pay, and they wanted less work. No one in the corporate hierarchy, from the worker on the line through the various levels of management, was concerned about quality.

U.S. manufacturers were finding it more expedient to let someone else do the work. Just like the softened Romans came to hire their armies, American industry found its own mercenaries to man its production front lines. A great number of technologically leading U.S. companies began programs in the 1960s to license their technologies to companies in industrializing countries, such as South Korea and Australia, and to companies in reindustrializing countries in Europe, and to Japan. Japanese companies were particularly eager to acquire technology through licenses from American companies. For example, by 1970

General Electric had licensing agreements with more than sixty Japanese companies, including twenty-four with the Toshiba group. The licenses allowed those companies to manufacture many items that GE formerly had made in the United States, including radar, generators, lamps, and boilers. Goodyear shares its technology with Michelin (French) and Bridgestone (Japanese) and has manufacturing arrangements with Dunlop (British). For convenience and short-term savings, America dealt away its technology. The United States became like the Arab countries before OPEC, trading away a national resource for a pittance.

On the other hand, the Japanese have made big, long-range plans and have then carefully organized themselves to accomplish those goals. Those plans all center around the concept that the prosperity of a nation is related to how well it chooses the strong industries of the *future* and then gives them the resources to capture that nascent market. This is as opposed to U.S. policies, which are activated only to aid failing industries. Many of the Japanese activities are directed by the Ministry of International Trade and Industry (MITI), a sort of government Big Brother to business that we probably would not allow to function in this country.

An example of MITI's abilities is the machine-tool industry, which the United States dominated for decades after World War II. Japanese studies of that industry in the United States (for which they were given numerous guided tours) showed that the way it was organized, with many small producers doing essentially custom work, resulted in undercapitalization, vulnerability to cycles, and inability to quickly apply new technology. The studies also recognized that the next era in the industry would involve sophisticated technology that would produce products by "numbers" programmed into the equipment rather than by measurements constantly undertaken by craftsmen-operators. MITI prepared specific programs for the Japanese machine-tool industry of the future in 1957, 1967, and 1971. Different companies were assigned to different ends of the business. By 1977, Japanese companies still had only a negligible part of the U.S. market; by 1982, they had one-third of the market; and by 1986, they became the world's largest manufacturers of machine tools and totally dominated the computer-aided machine-tool market.

A similar chronology exists in the semiconductor (computer memory chip) industry. After forming a solid base in the technology by "borrowing" most of it from U.S. companies, in 1975 Japanese companies set their sights on beating American companies to the next level of sophistication, the ability to commercially manufacture a chip with capabilities to handle 64,000 bytes of information (64K RAM). Accomplishing that goal in 1980, those companies almost immediately stole away most of the advanced chip sales and decimated the industry in the United States. Companies such as Mostek, with sales of $400 million per year, disappeared or became mere shadows of their former selves, virtually overnight. Over the next year, Japan's output of 64K RAM chips would rocket from 9 million to 66 million on an annualized basis. In late 1980, Japanese companies announced the perfection of a 256K RAM chip, preempting any effective competition for that next stage.

Actually, the vaunted invincibility of U.S. companies in electronics had already been shattered by the Japanese in the manufacture of televisions. Based on licenses granted to the Japanese in the 1950s, in the mid-1960s Japanese companies made a strong run at the black-and-white screen television market. In response, American companies generally conceded the field and moved their remaining production "offshore." By 1972, imports of black-and-white screen televisions were 62 percent of the market; by 1976, 98 percent. In 1962, RCA had licensed its color picture technology to Japanese companies, and the Japanese, always looking for the next "boom items," went to work. While Motorola announced the first prototype solid-state television in 1966, it was Hitachi that produced the first commercial sets in 1969. By 1970, 90 percent of Japanese color TVs were solid state, while U.S. manufacturers were struggling to retool. By 1980, there were only three American television manufacturers, and most of their products were made by employees in Asia. When GE bought RCA in 1986, it sold the GE-RCA television business to a French company, leaving Zenith as the sole American producer.

Foreign manufacture similarly devastated the rest of the U.S. consumer electronics industry. By the mid-1970s, it had entirely vanished.

The rapid development by American companies of television manufacturing in countries outside the United States was not an isolated occurrence. Moving capital and technology "offshore" was the primary response of those companies to foreign competition during the 1970s, even while officers of those companies were making the obligatory promises to get "lean and mean" in their U.S. plants. Major U.S.

banks promoted those moves by shifting their primary lending markets to manufacturing plants in foreign countries. By definition, scarce capital that was diverted outside the United States was unavailable for investment in U.S. facilities. Between the major U.S. industrial corporations and the major U.S. banks, the United States was deindustrialized and disinvested during the 1970s, at a loss to America of countless jobs and substantial wealth.

To a large extent, in making the shift, the corporations and banks were acting just as classic economic theory had predicted. Without letting the American people in on it, by the end of the 1960s the captains of industry and banking had concluded that U.S. manufacturing was becoming uncompetitive and simply acted accordingly. If American workers were overpaid and not docile enough, workers would be found elsewhere who were only too glad to give all for minimal wages. If government policies within the U.S. were contradictory and unpredictable, production would be moved to where long-range planning could be effective. The increasing sophistication and capacity of international shipping would make moving materials between countries as easy as between states. Communications advances would provide almost hands-on supervision of foreign plants from halfway around the world. Since America's stock in equipment and machinery was becoming outdated, it was just as easy to set up the replacements in another land. Also, there was a bonus—U.S. tax and tariff policies actually favored foreign manufacture.

There was also a good deal of nonclassic economic theory at work, as "conglomerates" became the darlings of the day. Corporations concentrated their energies on a great wave of acquisitions, $40 billion spent on shuffling corporate ownership in 1979 alone. As a result, many activities simply involved shuffling ownership of corporations, draining "cash cows" to make diversification acquisitions and then discarding them, achieving increases in profits on paper (but not in reality) through an accounting trick known as "pooling of assets," and other forms of manipulation. Since the real rate of return was less than 10 percent during the 1970s and interest rates were higher, why borrow money to add facilities? Why not confine activities within the United States to mere paper transactions, which will mesmerize stock market investors while the real action takes place elsewhere?

Simply put, it became bad business to invest in facilities in the United States. Depending on the region, between 15 percent and 35 percent of facilities with five hundred or more employees closed during the period of 1967 to 1976. A survey of Fortune 500 companies revealed that during the 1970s, 410 decided to acquire existing facilities rather than build. From 1975 through 1981, the tire industry closed twenty-four American plants, while expanding plant capacity outside the United States. The steel industry similarly slashed U.S. steel manufacturing capacity, even during times of high demand for steel. By 1976, 29 percent of all imports to this country were from foreign plants of American companies. By 1979, 94 percent of Ford's profits were from overseas operations. *The foreign output of U.S. corporations now exceeds the gross national product of every country in the world except the United States and Russia.*

Of course, the jobs went with the capital. General Electric's payroll increased on net 5,000 jobs during the 1970s—through an increase of 30,000 abroad and a decrease of 25,000 within the United States. RCA increased foreign employment 11,000 while cutting 14,000 American jobs. Each plant closing in the steel industry resulted in the loss of thousands of jobs, devastating whole cities in the Northeast. (By 1978, 44 percent of the assets of the steel industry had been deployed to other businesses.) A study disclosed that 35 percent of displaced employees were forced into early retirement. Others had to accept jobs in service industries at greatly decreased wages. With the loss of jobs in major industries came the side effects: bankruptcies of smaller companies in feeder industries and retailers in hard-hit areas; higher government welfare and retraining costs, for which the corporations paid nothing; huge losses of tax income to all levels of government; family dislocations as workers sought mythical "streets of gold" in such places as Houston; and increased mental and physical health problems. It has been estimated that deindustrialization in the 1970s cost the United States 32 to 38 million jobs.

The major American banks knew where the business was heading, and they not only helped, but they made it possible. Aside from bankrolling foreign expansion of U.S. corporations, they directed extensive amounts of funds to foreign corporations. For example, at a time when major banks were refusing to make additional loans to steel facilities in the United States, requiring their closure, they supported foreign steel mills owned by foreign corporations. During the period of 1972 to 1978, the steel company owned by the South African government received $538 million in loans from U.S. banks, 90 percent of that coming from Chase Manhattan and Citicorp. By 1979, that company had become the fifth largest supplier of processed iron and steel to the United States. From 1975 through 1977, Citibank, Chase Manhattan, and Chemical Bank each increased their loans to Japanese steel companies by an average multiple of four, totaling more than $380 million. By 1977, 83 percent of Citicorp's profits came from overseas operations, and the other major New York banks were similarly situated.

American megacorporations also quietly invested a good deal of their funds in foreign corporations. By 1970, General Electric had become the largest shareholder in Toshiba and owned 40 percent of an electronics subsidiary of Toshiba. Westinghouse became a principal shareholder of Mitsubishi. As a result, major U.S. corporations and Japanese companies virtually became partners, a trend that is accelerating to this day. If you cannot beat them. . . . No wonder our government's and industries' attitudes to the Japanese "invasion" have been schizophrenic!

Disinvestment and deindustrialization have led to a situation where United States companies do not have that much domestic production to offer either to U.S. consumers or for export. During the late 1960s, the United States moved to permanent trade deficit, importing more than it exports with respect to almost every geographic area of the world. American corporations have become "hollowed out," for the most part distributing goods made by others. That is why talk of strengthening U.S. exports and righting the massive trade imbalances of the 1980s simply is a cruel hoax.

It is certainly possible to develop a sense of moral outrage at the actions of the major U.S. corporations and banks for their stripping America of its industrial strength. It is clear that their actions were based on careful calculations of profit that totally excluded any human considerations. No weight whatsoever was given to the effects upon the millions of American workers whose lives were harmed. No thought was given to committing resources to improve relations with employees, productivity, or middle management skills. The American worker was abandoned, rather than lifted up, by American megacorporations.

Those policies also can be faulted for being shortsighted. So much technological know-how and skills have been transferred to foreign workers that it has become a practical impossibility to repatriate them. American corporations are so intertwined with foreign corporations that they are no longer free to pursue separate programs. Our major banks have tied up hundreds of billions of dollars in loans to foreign corporations and countries. Any rebuilding of America's economic power must be done in the face of opposition and genuine inability to help on the part of our major corporations and banks. Their interests simply are not identical to the best interests of the United States. This is the true meaning of multinational corporations.

Adding to those facts is another problem: the increasing concentration of American businesses and financial institutions in the United States. Because of the megacorporations' steady march to dominate many industries, fewer individuals direct larger amounts of capital. Fewer competitors remain as checks upon the megacorporations or as innovators.

The government has become ineffective in truly supervising or regulating business activities, if, indeed, it ever was effective. Politics blurs the picture and blunts resolve. The power of the megacorporations to affect government programs in direct and indirect ways is substantial.

In summary, the megacorporations in general and the oil companies in particular do what they want. They will take advantage of every loophole, every weakness in the system. The corporate barons do not hesitate to wield their power with a heavy hand. All decisions are based solely on one overriding principle: to preserve the corporate entity and to improve the "bottom line," whatever the cost to others or the long-range good to society. We, the general public, are only pawns in their game. This principle cynically was applied during the 1980s by seizing upon the loopholes opened up in the bankruptcy laws to unfairly shed massive amounts of debt.

The wild economic gyrations of the 1970s resulted in the flood of corporate bankruptcies in the 1980s. But that would not have happened as it did if there had not been wholesale changes in the bankruptcy law.

Chapter 3

Reform and Revolution in the Bankruptcy Courts

"No man's property is safe so long
as the legislature is in session."
                    —A folk saying

So it was that many of the major policies of the United States government and American megacorporations remained veiled from the Vietnam War era through the 1970s. Even though it may have appeared at times to the American public that the Ship of State was rudderless, those on the bridge had specific goals and intentions. They knew what they were doing, where they were heading.

Apparently, such was not the case with the changing of the bankruptcy laws. No one purposely set out to erect a financial haven for megacorporations . . . or did they? One thing was for sure—the laws concerning financially distressed companies needed some remodeling and updating.

Procedures for dealing with insolvent tradesmen date back to Roman times. In Venice in the Middle Ages, creditors could put a tradesman out of business by destroying his tools. His broken bench ("banca rotta") signified his insolvency. Formal English bankruptcy law goes back to 1542, to the reign of Henry VIII. The English bankruptcy law in effect at the time of the American Revolution lacked many modern features and was essentially punitive. The essence of those early bankruptcy laws was to provide an orderly means for turning over a debtor's assets to his or her various creditors. Debtors' prison awaited.

The Founding Fathers thought that providing for insolvency procedures was such an important matter that the federal government was authorized to promulgate bankruptcy laws by Article I, Section 8, of the Constitution of the United States. The provision did not limit the jurisdiction of those laws to transactions that involved interstate commerce, which was noteworthy. In an era that gave primacy to local laws and customs because of a justifiable fear of the power of central government, it was nevertheless thought beneficial that bankruptcy laws be uniform throughout the country so that neither creditor regimes nor debtor havens would be created. Court decisions quickly confirmed that when a system of federal bankruptcy laws is in place, all state laws on bankruptcy are superseded.

It is clear that the authors of the Constitution were concerned with the insolvency of individuals. Although European commerce included large trading companies, those were aligned with the crowns, and insolvency was not a problem. Rather, insolvency—whether arising from family disasters or business misadventures—was a personal problem, and the most important class of debtors was farmers. If they could awake today, those wise men who laid out our system of government would surely wonder how we have allowed the bankruptcy laws to become the handmaidens of the megacorporations, with those at the helm lacking personal liability.

In 1880, 1841, and 1867, bankruptcy laws were enacted in response to nationwide panics or other financial crises. Until 1841, bankruptcies were only involuntary proceedings. However, the government intrusion into people's lives that bankruptcy allowed was not popular, and since those laws targeted specific types of debtors in specific situations, they were seen as short-lived measures. Accordingly, each of those statutes was quickly repealed once stability was restored. Also, in a young country where risk taking was needed to spur economic development, punishment for economic failure was retrograde, and so, starting in 1921, the states began to abolish debtors' prisons. Out of the inequities generated by those piecemeal responses came the feeling that the federal bankruptcy laws should be more comprehensive and should provide a permanent framework. Rather than doling out special treatment, the bankruptcy laws should strike a general balance between the debtor's need for a fresh start and his obligation to pay his debts if he is at all able to do so.

An analogy may be made to the rules involving the pitcher in baseball. Various factors are constantly being fine-tuned so that there is a fair balance between the pitchers and hitters. Early in the sport, the distance to home plate was altered. As the pitchers got bigger and stronger, the height of the mound was reduced. As they became more accurate, the size of the strike zone was reduced. Otherwise pitchers would have dominated the hitters to the extent that the game would become (even more) boring. So it must be with the bankruptcy laws. The goal is to give relief to a limited group of those in legitimate need, while at the same time not to make bankruptcy so attractive to debtors that they bear little real risk.

The first bankruptcy legislation that was comprehensive and reached an appropriate balance between the debtor and creditor interests was the Bankruptcy Act of 1898. Although it too was the product of a severe financial crisis, it was an uncommon example of a law that was both revolutionary and highly workable. Among its unique features, it allowed a respite from creditors—preventing them from grabbing assets—while allowing a business to reorganize and even offer payments over time. It set a hierarchy of types of claims, to end the "race to the courthouse." For the first time, if a sufficient percentage of creditors approved of a reorganization, the dissidents were legally bound to accept it too. The Chandler Act of 1939 amended the Bankruptcy Act in order to adjust the balance in light of the realities of the Great Depression. New procedural rules in support of the act were promulgated in 1973 to modernize procedures. The Bankruptcy Act of 1898 stands as a monument to the rationalization of debtor-creditor relations.

By the early 1970s, experts in the field began to feel that the Bankruptcy Act was too out of touch with the realities of modern commercial life to serve as an effective mediator between the various financial interests. Business financing had become more sophisticated and complex, and new financial instruments constantly were being created. The consumer credit industry had created a nation of debtors. It was felt that the "whiles" and "whereases" of the credit industry were gaining the upper hand and that, as a *quid pro quo* to being allowed to expand credit, the industry would have to accept more liberal bankruptcy laws. Also, the procedures for business reorganization cases were deemed too likely to lead to liquidation, rather than to provide a fighting chance for decent companies to recover from their mistakes and stay in business.

On July 24, 1970, Congress established the "Commission on Bankruptcy Laws of the United States" to study the problems and make recommendations for changes in the bankruptcy laws. Eight commission members were appointed—two by the President, two by the Senate, two by the House, and two by the Chief Justice of the United States. Named to the commission were Senators Quentin Burdick and Marlow Cook, Representatives Don Edwards and Charles Wiggins, United States District Judges Hubert Will and Edward Weinfeld, Charles Seligson, and Wilson Newman. Harold Marsh, Jr., was selected as chairman. Professor Frank Kennedy of the University of Michigan Law School was named executive director. (Senator Burdick and Representative Edwards later chaired the congressional subcommittees that further developed revisions to the bankruptcy law.)

In 1973, the commission submitted its report to Congress. It was based upon a group of studies and did indeed recommend a comprehensive rewriting of the bankruptcy laws. A bill based on the report was quickly introduced. However, Congress did not act in 1973, being largely preoccupied with the consequences of the Watergate scandal, including the issues of "executive privilege" and the possible impeachment of President Nixon. Had the members of Congress known about the headaches that revision of the bankruptcy laws was to cause, they no doubt would have kept the proposals on a back, back burner!

The first major conflict was created by the National Conference of Bankruptcy Judges, a private organization made up of sitting bankruptcy judges (elevated from "referees" in 1973). Its membership was not pleased with the 1973 bill and had an alternative bill introduced in 1974. The judges felt that their power and prestige should be elevated in the new law.

Issues were delineated, positions staked out, and rhetoric unleashed by more than a hundred witnesses in congressional hearings during 1974, 1975, and 1976. A particularly influential group was the National Bankruptcy Conference, a private association of about sixty bankruptcy "heavy hitters" in private practice and academia. That group developed most of the underlying philosophies of the new law, and nearly all of the group's specific proposals on substantive matters remained virtually unchanged throughout the legislative process and were ultimately incorporated in the final draft of the new law.

In 1977, the versions of the proposed new law began to fly thick and fast. A bill that effectuated a compromise between the commission's proposals and those of the National Conference of Bankruptcy Judges, and superseded those bills, was introduced as House Resolution (H.R.) 8200. That bill was amended several times in committee during the course of more than twenty meetings, reported out of committee, sent back to committee by the House, amended again, and reported out of committee. In the meantime a Senate bill was introduced as 2266. It contained substantial differences from any of the House versions. In February 1978, the House approved a form of H.R. 8200 after adding three amendments and rejecting an attempt to reduce the elevated status proposed for the bankruptcy courts. However, large conflicts loomed with the Senate.

By September 1978, the situation in Congress had become excruciating. The House was forced to vitiate its earlier passage of H.R. 8200 in order to insert a tax provision, and then passed it again. The differences between the House and Senate versions were so serious that a formal conference between the two bodies to iron out a compromise could not be convened. Finally, after hard bargaining during which the House version survived mostly intact with certain creditor-oriented provisions added to satisfy the Senate negotiators, a compromise bill was passed by the House on September 28, 1978, and was passed by the Senate on the same day.

Suddenly, at the "11th hour, 59th minute," in a most extraordinary and ill-becoming move, Chief Justice Warren E. Burger made personal appeals to members of the Senate to delete the portion of the new act that placed bankruptcy judges on an equal level with federal district court judges. He was incensed at the idea that the bankruptcy judiciary would be added to the ranks of the small club of "real" federal district and appellate judges. A host of special interest groups also attempted to get their last licks in concerning their pet issues.

Those appeals were rebuffed, and the Senate passed a form of the bill on October 5, 1978. Technically speaking, the Senate amendment amended the House amendment to the previous Senate amendment, which had been in the nature of a substitute to H.R. 8200. Got it? The House then passed an identical bill through an unusual maneuver that required the unanimous vote of its members to bypass sending the bill to the Rules Committee. For some reason the law was delayed in reaching Jimmy Carter, who finally signed it on November 6, 1978, the last date it could be signed into law.

Thus the "Bankruptcy Reform Act of 1978" became the law of the land as Public Law 95-598, with most provisions to become effective October 1, 1979. The Congressional Bankruptcy Follies were over at last . . . for a while. Like the New Year's baby replaces the old year, the fresh, new code took over from the worn-out Bankruptcy Act. Who knew how the baby would grow?

A major point of contention between the Senate and House in the struggle to create the Reform Act had to do with the status and power of the bankruptcy courts. Those behind the impetus for a new bankruptcy law saw the elevation of the bankruptcy judiciary as a logical and integral part of updating the system and viewed the Tax Court as a model. However, more conservative elements, including the district court judges who were inclined to protect their status, saw no need to create a new class of independent judges. The House tended to back the elevation of the bankruptcy courts, while the Senate leaned toward keeping the bankruptcy judiciary subordinate to the "real" federal judges.

Further complicating matters was an academic issue that made both houses of Congress uneasy. It was the opinion of many constitutional experts that if the proposed act were to give the bankruptcy court wide powers to adjudicate virtually all matters arising out of a bankruptcy case, the judges of that court would have to be full federal court judges as authorized by Article III of the United States Constitution. Those judges would have to have, therefore, the almost-total independence accorded to full federal judges, including lifetime tenure. The Senate never even considered bestowing Article III status on the bankruptcy court, and the House voted it down.

The result of these substantial compromises was the fudging of the bankruptcy court status. The senators and representatives stuck their heads in the sand rather than deal with the serious constitutional issues.

The bankruptcy courts were given broad powers of adjudication over nearly all matters arising out of a bankruptcy case, as opposed to their rather limited "summary" jurisdiction under the Bankruptcy Act of 1898. Unwilling parties who had not subjected themselves to the jurisdiction of the court could be hauled before the bankruptcy judge because the party in bankruptcy wanted that court to adjudicate a dispute. The bankruptcy courts were to become "adjuncts" of the district courts—separate but equal, although without general jurisdiction. On the other hand, they would continue to be courts authorized not directly by Article III of the Constitution, but rather administrative tribunals authorized by Article I and under the control of Congress, staffed by judges serving fourteen-year terms who could be removed by the judicial councils of the federal circuit courts. It was felt that no one would interrupt the practical functioning of the bankruptcy system with arguments about the Founding Fathers' intentions.

Congress was wrong. When a business named Northern Pipeline Construction Company filed a Chapter 11 bankruptcy and then a lawsuit within the bankruptcy against Marathon Pipeline Company based on common-law breach of contract, Marathon challenged the status and jurisdiction of the bankruptcy court. In June 1982, in the case of *Northern Pipeline Construction Co. v. Marathon Pipeline Company,* the United States Supreme Court ruled, in an opinion authored by the same Chief Justice who had lobbied Congress not to elevate the status of the bankruptcy courts, that the jurisdiction granted to the bankruptcy courts could not be exercised by the Article I judges of those courts. The portion of the new law describing the bankruptcy judiciary was declared unconstitutional. The specific findings and philosophy of the decision are almost impossible to delve into, since the case produced a plurality opinion in which four judges joined, a concurring opinion of two judges, and three dissenting votes. The only reliable reading of the case was that the system created by the Bankruptcy Reform Act could not stand. Warren Burger, indeed, had had the last word.

Realizing that simply striking down the system would cause chaos, the Supreme Court in *Marathon* (for reasons which are obscure, if they exist at all, the case is usually referred to as *Marathon* and not *Northern Pipeline*) made the ruling prospective and gave Congress several months to try again. Although Congress did try—very hard—under the circumstances, including lack of guidance from the Supreme Court, it was unable to immediately rectify the situation within the deadline and acquired an extension of the effect of the ruling to December 24, 1982.

When Congress was still unable to refashion the system, the Administrative Office of the United States Courts drafted a model Emergency Jurisdictional Rule that was duly adopted by nearly all federal circuits. It provided that the bankruptcy courts were to be subordinate to the federal district courts; that the district courts were to exercise jurisdiction over all bankruptcy cases, but that matters traditionally central to the administration of bankruptcy cases could be referred to bankruptcy judges for determination, subject to a review by the district court judges; and that as to matters not central to bankruptcy issues but only "related" to the cases (such as the *Marathon* dispute), if the district court chose to refer such a matter to a bankruptcy court, the bankruptcy judge would serve substantially like a special master and could only make recommendations to the district court judge. The rule also removed the power of the bankruptcy judges to conduct jury trials and provided that, in so many words, none of the findings and rulings of bankruptcy judges were entitled to any weight upon review by the district court. (It is no accident that communications from the Administrative Office during this era to and about the bankruptcy judges continued to refer to them as "referees," a demeaning term in that their title had been changed from "referee" to "bankruptcy judge" by a rules change under the prior Bankruptcy Act *in 1973*.)

The Emergency Jurisdictional Rule had its philosophical flaws and downright contradictions, but, after all, who ultimately interpreted it but those "real" federal judges who instituted it? Thus, while a number of bankruptcy judges struck it down (see Merrick chapternote), almost every district court that considered the rule's validity provided a blessing, as did all seven Circuit Courts of Appeal that heard the issue.

The Emergency Jurisdictional Rule was superseded by the relevant provisions of the "Bankruptcy Amendments and Federal Judgeship Act of 1984," which basically codified the rule. The bankruptcy courts remain a subordinate part of the district courts, and all matters that they hear, even on a regular basis, are deemed to have been referred to them by the district courts. The bankruptcy judges can make final decisions in proceedings that are "core" to the bankruptcy process, but act, in effect, as special masters with respect to "noncore" proceedings. In practice, the bankruptcy judges have found nearly all borderline matters to be "core," with little objection from their district court overseers, and district court review of "noncore" recommendations is usually perfunctory, at best. In typical pragmatic bankruptcy fashion, the courts in practice operate just the way the original Reform Act provisions mandated, while giving lip service to the judicial pecking order.

In the power struggle, the bankruptcy judges were put in their place, but what was the result of the Olympian battles upon the practitioner?

Very little. Having established their primacy over bankruptcy judges, the "real" federal judges once more retreated to their chambers while the bankruptcy judges did all the work emanating from the rising tide of bankruptcy filings. With the exception of lawsuits of the type that clearly do not involve any bankruptcy law issues, the bankruptcy judges' control over their dockets is, as a practical matter, nearly complete. Parties that hope to overturn bankruptcy court rulings through *de novo* trials in, or probing reviews by, the district courts that exercise technical jurisdiction over their cases are almost always disappointed. While some megacases have been taken over in whole or substantial part by district court judges, most of the major corporate cases in the country continue to be administered by the bankruptcy courts.

While much of bankruptcy practice returned to normal, the major result of the judicial infighting was that the bankruptcy judges became very uncertain of their authority. The Reform Act had already constrained their abilities to supervise and manage cases, limiting them to adjudicating disputes. The lost battle over their status had saddled them with a long list of limitations on their power. Meanwhile, the new code had unleashed a flood of cases upon them. A significant percentage of bankruptcy judges quit the bench out of despair and sheer exhaustion. When added to the fact that the remaining bankruptcy judges were being called upon to handle large business cases, populated with battalions of aggressive, high-priced lawyers, it is no wonder that the megacorporations were able to get their way before those harried and dispirited judicial officers.

As with judges who claim only to "find" the law that is already in force, the framers of the new Reform Act claimed only to have codified commercial law and practice as it was found to be and to have designed a court that would merely enforce those relationships efficiently. However, in reality judges make the law while finding it, and the bankruptcy codifiers of the 1970s also created new concepts while tinkering with the old.

In many ways, the reconstituting of the bankruptcy laws in 1978 was a true "reform," per *Webster's Ninth New Collegiate Dictionary:* "to amend or improve by change of form or removal of faults or abuses." The bankruptcy laws were updated to remove archaic terms and concepts and to make the laws reflective of current legal and financial realities. The organization and interrelationships of the individual sections were skillfully molded into law's classic "seamless web."

However, much to the surprise of most observers, the reform also led to a revolution, defined in the same dictionary as an "activity or movement . . . to effect fundamental changes in the socioeconomic situation." The balance between creditors and debtors was suddenly sharply tilted in the debtors' favor. Debtors of all kinds, including large corporations, soon learned that the bankruptcy court had become a much more hospitable place for them.

What did everyone think they were fighting about during the reshaping of the bankruptcy laws? What was the unintended revolution in business reorganization practice that resulted?

The main battleground between institutional creditors, such as banks, finance companies, and retail sellers, and those favoring increased debtor relief involved the ease with which consumers might obtain bankruptcy relief and the extent of their "exemptions"—what could be kept by debtors in bankruptcy. After all, were not consumer bankruptcies the "dog" of the bankruptcy practice, and business bankruptcies only a small "tail"? The debates raged endlessly over whether moderated laws would induce large increases in personal bankruptcies, thereby leading to damage to the U.S. credit industry and, ultimately, decreased credit availability to Mr. and Mrs. Middle Class America. It was no small question, since credit had become the engine that drives the American consumer economy.

Without dwelling on specifics, it can be said that the outcome of the battles almost entirely favored increased debtor relief. Now a consumer can easily and cheaply wipe out debts through Chapter 7, or propose a "wage earner's reorganization" through Chapter 13 that turns out to be only slightly more onerous than a Chapter 7 but with the advantage that it can be done over and over again at any time. The federal exemptions are very generous and obviously are intended to open the bankruptcy-court door to the overextended middle class. Mr. and Mrs. America, and the little Americas, can breeze through bankruptcy with nary a glitch in their life-style, keeping their house, cars, and television sets while shedding their debts.

However, the credit industry did manage to secure one loophole that proved to be of great value to creditors. Realizing that Congress was an unsympathetic forum, they managed to have included in the Bankruptcy Reform Act a provision that state legislatures could choose to determine exemptions. It was not an unprecedented concept, since the

Bankruptcy Act of 1898, which had served so well for many years, had relied on state law exemptions.

After securing the loophole, the credit industry shifted its arguments to state legislatures, and almost immediately after passage of the Bankruptcy Reform Act a number of the states "opted out" of the federal exemption statute (although many of those updated their exemption statutes to reflect the Consumer Society).

This was a blow to a major goal of the drafters of the act: the institution of a national standard for exemptions that overrode the quirks and peccadilloes of local laws. (For example, in Florida a residence is totally exempt from the claims of creditors even if it is a multimillion-dollar mansion.) However, the framers of the Reform Act had no one to blame but themselves, as such a reaction clearly indicated that they had exceeded their charter in proposing such liberal exemptions.

In fact, the incidence of consumer bankruptcies did increase dramatically after the passage of the Reform Act, from approximately 200,000 for the one-year period prior to the Reform Act's passage, to more than 400,000 for the first twelve months of the new act, to almost 500,000 for the next twelve-month period. Perhaps the increased filings largely resulted from the economic problems of the era. Perhaps the bankruptcy reform had merely allowed some pent-up demand to be released. Perhaps, as some had predicted, the debtors had been handed the keys to the courthouse and had chased the creditors out. One thing was certain—a much larger segment of the American population found it either necessary or convenient to file for bankruptcy protection, and bankruptcy lost the moral stigma that it once had.

As even the most casual observer knows, the credit industry did not collapse and consumer credit did not disappear. The industry managed to adjust quite nicely and continued to encourage Mr. and Mrs. America to avail themselves of old and new forms of even easier credit through the 1980s.

Congress paid almost no attention to the proposed bankruptcy reforms respecting business reorganizations. While the late 1970s had seen a few large bankruptcies of retailers, and while business filings were on an uptick during the 1970s, there was no real attempt to project the effects of any changes upon the balance of economic interests in the business context. In fact, no one had any real statistical or theoretical basis for making such projections. The historical figures were modest, for example: 163 Chapter X ("public" corporation reorganization) filings in 1974, and 189 in 1975; and 2,171 Chapter XI small company arrangements filed in 1974, and 3,506 in 1975. Clearly, executives felt there was a strong stigma attached to filing bankruptcy. Only those companies in the most dire and unusual circumstances said the "b" word.

As with consumer bankruptcies, the reformers felt that the business reorganization sections were in need of streamlining and updating. The major proposal consisted of eliminating Chapters VIII (railroad reorganization), X, XI, and XII (real estate reorganization) and allowing all business reorganizations to fall under a simplified Chapter 11 scheme. (The new code would have arabic numerals, to distinguish its "chapters" from those under the Bankruptcy Act of 1898.) Unlike Chapter X, Chapter 11 would allow even public corporations to operate their own businesses through their chosen executives during bankruptcy reorganization proceedings without the automatic imposition of a trustee. Unless the creditors proved serious "cause," such as theft by the owners, the ordinary Chapter 11 proceeding would see the management of the debtor company in control of its business, although subject to the general supervision of the court.

That difference was profound. No longer would the operation of a public company in reorganization be turned over to some trustee, whose main qualification usually was that he was the judge's friend. No longer would some outsider have such a unique chance to snoop on those little illegal "tricks of the trade" that so many companies develop. Instead, the same management that got the corporation into trouble could continue in the driver's seat, shielded from creditors, under only the most casual supervision of the bankruptcy court. Many a conservative, antiregulation industrialist would come to realize that not only could he survive with his company in bankruptcy, he could get downright *comfortable* in the protective embrace of Chapter 11.

Another major change in philosophy was the treatment of secured claims. Under Chapter X, secured claims could not be affected; and under Chapter XI, a secured creditor could reclaim its collateral simply by showing the court that the debtor was in default. Thus the banks had very strong positions in bankruptcy court and could "pull the plug" on a company in bankruptcy with ease. Under the new Chapter 11, the debtor would continue to retain possession and use of collateral as long as the total value of the creditor's interest in the collateral was protected. In plain English: in the usual Chapter 11 bankruptcy the company would have continued use of its machinery, equipment, and inventories instead of being forced to turn them over to its banks, and the banks would have to sit and stew just like all the other creditors. It was another change that served to place the Chapter 11 debtor firmly in control.

Another element of the new law that favored the debtor was the time limit by which a business in Chapter 11 had to file a Plan of Reorganization—there was none. Contrary to popular belief, even now there is nothing in the bankruptcy statutes that establishes a time by which a case must end, one way or another. While a judge may require the debtor to move things along if he or she thinks that there is no progress being made, even in small cases that might not occur for more than a year. In the larger cases, it was not too difficult for the management of the Chapter 11 company to convince the judge that the size of the company dictated years in Chapter 11. The megacorporations, almost without exception, would have no trouble holding off creditors for as long as it took to soften them up for the kill.

While creditor groups moaned and groaned about the drift of the changes, no one really knew how the system would operate, and so no one could summon "proof" against the changes. The creditors were thrown a few bones in the final form of the new law, but no one really understood just how much the balance had been shifted. Even the troubled companies did not fully grasp the effects initially. For example, when Chrysler hit bottom just as the new code was becoming law, its effects were too unknown for Chrysler to chance a bankruptcy filing. However, as experience under the code increased, there was a mad dash for the courthouse by companies with unsatisfactory balance sheets.

Added to the big and small changes in the bankruptcy statutes that served to tip the scales of justice in favor of debtors were the natural advantages enjoyed by the megacorporations in bankruptcy. As it is a practical impossibility for the judge or the creditors to truly supervise the operations of a large corporation, they have no choice but to rely on management's judgment calls and its rationalizations in support of them. The companies virtually can do what they want. Also, since the debtor most likely will be paying only a small percentage of its debt to trade creditors upon reorganization, its legal fees are well spent—there is a lot of "bang for the buck." Since the trade creditors know that they probably will receive a pittance on their claims, spending for legal fees and other costs of watching over the Chapter 11 company is a very poor investment and they avoid it. What is the difference if hard work as a creditor simply results in a 9 percent payout instead of a 5 percent payout? To most companies, money spent as a bankruptcy creditor is just money "down a rathole." The business creditors would prove no match for Chapter 11 megacorporations.

At the same time that the balance was shifted so strongly toward the debtor, the Securities and Exchange Commission, that guardian of investors in "public" corporations, almost ceased being a force in bankruptcy court. Unlike the old Chapter X, the new Chapter 11 was not to be a magnet for SEC attention—no longer would the filing of bankruptcy, in itself, be seen as probable cause to impose protective measures on behalf of shareholders. The new bankruptcy code permitted shareholders to organize to protect their interests, just like the creditors. The theory was that the clash of economic interests would lead to a natural mediating of the parties' interests without the heavy hand of government dictating the outcome.

Unfortunately, in practice the system amounted to "survival of the fittest," and it was the debtor megacorporations that would prevail in the new bankruptcy environment.

During the year following passage of the Bankruptcy Reform Act, while the states debated the personal exemption laws and Congress and the federal courts fretted over the jurisdiction and status of the bankruptcy courts, there was an explosion of Chapter 11 cases. Filings were:

Year	Chapter 11s
1980	7,403
1981	11,370 (+53 percent)
1982	22,057 (+93 percent)

Not only were the gross number of filings exploding, but major public corporations began to file cases in numbers not seen since the Great Depression. By the mid-1980s, many, many giants of American business had filed for protection from their creditors under Chapter 11, including: A. H. Robins, AM International, Advent, Air Florida,

Allegheny International, Baldwin-United, Bobbie Brooks, Braniff Airlines, Commonwealth Oil, Continental Airlines, Energy Cooperative, Financial Corporation of America, Frontier Airlines, GHR Energy, Itel, Jartran, Johns-Manville, Lion Capital Group, Lionel, LTV, MacGregor Sporting Goods, McLouth Steel, Morton Shoe, National Sugar Refining, NuCorp, Osborne Computer, Placid Oil (Hunt Brothers), Public Service Company of New Hampshire (Seabrook nuclear plant), Remington Rand, Revco, Rusty Jones, Saxon Industries, Seatrain, Sharon Corporation, Evans Products (Victor Posner-controlled), Storage Technology, Texaco, United Press International, UNR, Western Oil, Wheeling-Pittsburgh Steel, White Motors, Wickes, and Wieboldt Department Stores.

While of course it can be argued that many reasons led to the increase in business Chapter 11 filings, such as the Japanese "invasion" of American markets, high interest rates, and high oil prices, as with consumer bankruptcies it cannot be ignored that American businesses lost their fear of bankruptcy court. In practice, bankruptcy judges were slow to allow secured creditors to sound the death knell of a Chapter 11 company by withdrawing their collateral. Companies found they could control their own bankruptcy cases and shed massive amounts of debt. They learned to use Chapter 11 to humble particularly prickly creditors. Sometimes they were not insolvent when they filed a Chapter 11 case to accomplish some goal.

The net result of the gross numbers of filings and the success of the companies in Chapter 11 was an attitude by business executives that there was no shame to filing a Chapter 11 case, and that the public would not censure them for doing so. The public would be just as likely to consider it a clever move as not. Thus was a basic underpinning of the free enterprise system—the risk of financial loss and the natural elimination of the "losers"—removed for the larger corporations. Capitalism had lost its sanctions because of the rewards offered in the new bankruptcy code.

To fully understand the major insolvencies of the 1980s, a short course in Chapter 11 concepts and procedures is in order, at least insofar as they apply to megacorporate bankruptcies.

Because of the economic problems previously described, and also because of problems in particular industries as well as managerial errors, many large and small companies in the United States during the early 1980s found it necessary to "reorganize"—a generic term, that could refer to restructuring operations, recasting debt, or both. Companies that responded to adversity before their situations deteriorated too far, and who chose not to make their creditors "pay" for their revamping, restructured their operations without the need for any court proceeding. A good example is United States Steel Corporation, which diversified heavily outside the steel business, bought a "cash cow" in Marathon Oil Company, and had enough credit reserves to weather some bad years in the steel business before its modernization programs took hold. The company, now known as USX in recognition of its diversified nature, is quite a different company than it was in the late 1970s.

Although some companies in dire situations manage financial reorganizations outside of bankruptcy, the out-of-court method is very difficult. It lacks the legal strictures of bankruptcy that protect the debtor from its creditors and force all creditors to be bound by a reorganization plan. An out-of-court reorganization virtually requires unanimous approval by the creditors to the debtor's reorganization actions, since there is no legal mechanism for reining in any recalcitrant creditors. Accordingly, there are few examples of major out-of-court reorganizations, except for companies that persuade their banks to recast debt and are able to avoid asking trade creditors to sacrifice.

Chrysler is in a class by itself. As we shall see in the next chapter, it accomplished a massive operational and financial reorganization outside of bankruptcy. To some extent, it is unique because of its size and the fact that it manufactures the most important consumer product in this country. Also, it *made itself unique* by choosing a course of action whereby it became a ward of the federal government, thus making it impossible for the government to allow it to fail. The end result was a radical reorganization very similar to what would have been accomplished in bankruptcy.

Reorganizing through a bankruptcy case means filing a bankruptcy petition under Chapter 11 of the Bankruptcy Reform Act of 1978, now commonly known as the Bankruptcy Code. The sections of Chapter 11 provide the statutory framework for business reorganizations. Companies that file under Chapter 11 are also subject to Chapters 3 and 5 of the Bankruptcy Code, which deal with bankruptcy case administration, but are not subject to the provisions of Chapters 7 (liquidations), 9 (for municipalities), or 13 (wage earner reorganizations). (Why does the Bankruptcy Code have only odd numbered chapters? Tradition—and also to allow for new chapters. In 1988, Chapter 12 was added to the bankruptcy laws to provide new procedures for the reorganization of family farms.) Each chapter also has an underlying set of procedural rules promulgated by the United States Supreme Court.

In most Chapter 11 cases, and all of the megacorporate Chapter 11s, the company is operating at the onset of the bankruptcy and it is essential that it continue to operate while in Chapter 11 in order to preserve its value as an ongoing business. The Bankruptcy Code favors that course of action as the best means of rehabilitating businesses, and so most companies have a fighting chance to hold their place in the market while they attack financial problems. Many companies are able to achieve the goal of having the daily work environment of the production and office employees virtually unaffected by the existence of the bankruptcy case, thus maintaining morale.

Of course, the ultimate goal of the debtor is to use the period in Chapter 11 to correct the problems that caused the filing, recapitalize, and propose payment to the creditors. The proposal is made in the form of a "Plan of Reorganization," which must lay out a coordinated scheme to pay all creditors, consistent with the hierarchy of creditors and other requirements established by the Bankruptcy Code and rules. Once the creditors and the court have approved the plan, the company will emerge from the shadows of bankruptcy into the sunlight of the free market without any hiatus in operations. The balance sheet will be much improved after compromising the creditors' claims through the plan, and the company will be in a good posture to become profitable again.

Any person or entity may file a bankruptcy petition, which is nothing more than a one-page declaration that the party wishes to invoke the protection of the bankruptcy laws. The petition is filed with the clerk of the bankruptcy court in the federal district in which the business entity has its home office, but a large corporation with many substantial places of business can do a bit of "forum shopping." Upon the filing of the voluntary petition, a case number is designated, a court file is opened, and the case is assigned to a bankruptcy judge. The debtor becomes a "Debtor." (The Bankruptcy Code dropped the use of the term "bankrupt" to further weaken the stigma attached to filing bankruptcy. For simplicity's sake, Debtors will be referred to as debtors.) Contrary to popular belief, there is no requirement that a business pass any particular test of insolvency to file a bankruptcy.

At the moment that a Chapter 11 bankruptcy petition is filed, the claims against the debtor are frozen. The debtor cannot pay those debts until it proposes a plan of reorganization to deal with all of them, and the creditors must cease any collection activities. While the secured creditors (e.g., banks, equipment vendors) generally cannot demand return of their collateral at the onset of the case, the debtor must nevertheless reach some accommodation with them that allows the debtor to use the collateral in its Chapter 11 operations—usually monthly payments. The debtor must, in the ordinary course, pay all of its operating obligations that arise after the filing of the petition and are thus considered "costs of administration" of the bankruptcy case.

Between twenty and forty days after the filing of the voluntary petition, a meeting of creditors is held. The meeting is scheduled by the United States trustee and is usually held at the trustee's office. Notice of the meeting is sent to all creditors, and they may attend and ask questions of the debtor relating to the bankruptcy case. In many business cases, the meeting is continued to one or more later dates to provide sufficient time for creditors to formulate questions, investigate the operations of the debtor, and follow up on matters raised at the initial meeting. In a large business case, as a practical matter the creditors' meeting is nothing more than a public relations forum for the debtor. The company is so huge that it is not possible to ask very specific questions or verify management's answers. As with annual shareholders' meetings, the company may take some heat but will shed very little light.

While the creditors' meeting provides a forum for questioning the debtor, it is by no means the creditors' only opportunity to get answers to questions or financial information from the debtor. Generally speaking, any creditor or other party in interest may investigate any aspect of the debtor's past or present operations, finances, and transactions. However, as a practical matter, a single creditor cannot afford to wade through a megacorporation's records.

Even as the filings, meetings, and strategic posturings progress, the company's operations continue, often with little change. Rarely is a trustee appointed to run the business in a Chapter 11 case, and *almost never* in a megacorporate case. It is inherently damaging to drop an outsider into the chief operating officer's place. Since the mandate of the Chapter 11 trustee is to maintain the status quo, such a manager cannot be expected to take any major steps to improve the company's operations. This is why bankruptcy judges will appoint Chapter 11 trustees only if management has engaged in serious fraud or gross mismanagement, issues that are normally absent in megacorporate bankruptcies.

In the vast majority of cases, no one would notice a difference in the everyday humdrum affairs of a company that has filed a Chapter 11 petition. Decisions in the ordinary course of the workday are made by management in the same manner they were before the petition was filed. Although the business is under the theoretical supervision of the bankruptcy court, no court personnel observe operations or watch over the books and records. While the U.S. trustee reviews the operating reports and occasionally takes action if the debtor crosses certain tripwires, the U.S. trustee's supervision of the debtor is normally nonintrusive and passive. The complicated nature of megacorporate life renders meaningful supervision by the judge or U.S. trustee impossible.

Extraordinary actions—outside the "ordinary course of business"—can be taken if prior court approval is acquired. A Chapter 11 company then can borrow additional money and further encumber its property, buy and finance expensive machinery, sign leases for additional space, prosecute lawsuits, and hire top executives or consultants. Such proposals by large corporate debtors are routinely rubber-stamped by judges because management typically has a plausible rationale for its proposed actions, and the court is in no position to second-guess its business judgment. Thus, if the megacorporation is careful not to thumb its nose publicly at the bankruptcy court, it has virtually no restrictions on its actions.

The Bankruptcy Code recognizes that creditors may organize themselves to better protect their interests. Primarily, the code provides for the formation of an Unsecured Creditors' Committee. The United States trustee appoints the members of the committee by soliciting the interest of the larger unsecured creditors. With court approval, the committee may then retain counsel and, in larger cases, accountants and other professional consultants. The fees and costs of such professionals are to be borne by the debtor. This can be a large burden in contentious cases. The members of the committee must bear their own expenses.

The committee is usually comprised of three to eleven members, but larger committees are not uncommon in megacorporate cases. The ideal Unsecured Creditors' Committee, as conceptualized by the drafters of the bankruptcy code, is one that has on it representatives of the major unsecured creditor factions: creditors with small claims, as well as the major creditors; trade creditors and unsecured lenders; and so on. Most creditors do not clamor to be on the committee. The U.S. trustee merely appoints those willing to serve. In many cases with unsecured debt of less than $500,000, and in some larger cases, the unsecured creditors do not show enough interest to form an Unsecured Creditors' Committee at all.

Although permitted by the code, it is unusual to see court-approved committees in addition to the Unsecured Creditors' Committee. However, in very large cases the court may also recognize committees of debenture holders; special claimants, such as state governments or franchisees; or special classes of unsecured creditors, such as product liability plaintiffs, when those claims were a major cause of the bankruptcy.

While committees may be nonexistent or passive in smaller cases, in the larger cases they are highly involved and active. The reason is simple: the Bankruptcy Code provides that the debtor will pay the fees of attorneys, accountants, and other professionals (such as investment bankers and business consultants) hired by committees as long as the court approves their retention. In megacorporate bankruptcies, there is plenty of money sloshing around to pay for these hired guns. It is a price that the debtor pays for the privilege of holding off its creditors. (In the end, it is the creditors who in effect pay those fees, for whatever is paid to the professionals by the debtor is cash that is not available to the creditors in a reorganization.) As a result, in a megacase there is often an unsecured trade creditors' committee, a debenture-holders' committee, and an unsecured lenders' committee, each with its own lawyers, accountants, and investment bankers.

In theory, it is these committees that counterbalance the debtor's power and provide the supervision of the debtor. In theory, they allow the financial interests to protect themselves in the bankruptcy.

In the reality of megacorporate cases, the committees are full of sound and fury, signifying almost nothing. It is simply not possible to stand in the way of the high-powered executives of a megacorporate debtor. The fact that the creditors may also be megacorporations with powerful men in charge is no guarantee that the creditors' committee will meet the debtor's power head on. The executives of the creditor companies are busy running their own businesses and cannot devote sufficient time or allocate sufficient manpower within their own organizations to fully grasp the intricacies of the debtor's operations. It is not worth the cost to fully investigate a debtor company, especially since the creditors are expecting to receive only a fraction of their claims under a reorganization. As a result, most challenges are purely partisan exercises in one-upmanship which do not really provide meaningful alternatives for the judge to act on, even if the court is inclined to buck the debtor's executives. The elegant theory of countervailing power in bankruptcy court is a failure in practice.

The only legitimate goal of a Chapter 11 case is to secure the approval of a plan of reorganization that provides for payment of the company's debt, whether in full or compromised. A number of Bankruptcy Code sections and rules describe the procedures and requirements for proposing a plan, conducting a vote of the creditors, and securing the approval of a plan's provisions by the bankruptcy judge. In a large or complicated case, a plan may not be filed for years.

The Bankruptcy Code does not specify a time within which a plan of reorganization must be filed. The drafters understood that there is a wide disparity in the circumstances of Chapter 11 companies in terms of their size, the amount and the nature of their debts, the complexity of their legal disputes with creditors, the actions that will be required to reorganize operations, and other important elements of reorganization. Even relatively straightforward megacases require megawork in order to move them through the bankruptcy process, and no one expects a quick denouement. It is very rare for a presiding judge to set a deadline by which a large corporation must file a plan. Occasionally a judge may set a deadline after a Chapter 11 megacase has been going on for years, in order to vent his frustration and to attempt to get the case off dead center. Actually enforcing a deadline against a megacorporation by ordering its liquidation or other sanction is strictly a creditor's fantasy.

Although there is no statutory deadline for filing a plan of reorganization, the Bankruptcy Code places a limitation of *creditors'* rights to propose a plan to the court. Commencing on the date of the filing of the Chapter 11 petition, the Chapter 11 company enjoys a statutory

120-day period during which creditors may not propose a plan of reorganization. The purpose of the provision is to give the debtor a breather from the creditors.

In its practical effect the "exclusive period" (as the bankruptcy lawyers call it) is a control mechanism. It removes the creditors' primary means of putting pressure on the Chapter 11 company. As long as it is in place, the creditors cannot achieve payment of their claims whether or not a Chapter 11 company is negotiating in good faith. It follows that in almost every reorganization case the debtor wishes to have the exclusive period extended.

Although the code is silent on whether the exclusive period may be extended—and there is a good argument that Congress intended the honeymoon to last only four months—courts have repeatedly ruled that the presiding judge has the power to extend it. It is common in small business cases for judges to extend the exclusive period sixty days or so. It is common in megacases for judges to extend it *as long as the debtor wishes.* Typically, each time the exclusive period nears termination, the lawyers for the Chapter 11 megacorporation request renewal, painting a picture for the judge of the awful consequences that will befall the company if—horrors!—the creditors are able to affect its future. It is solemnly intoned that the creditors most certainly will act irresponsibly and in ignorance, unlike the debtor's management which will act responsibly and in a wise manner if only it is protected from those crazy people for an additional period of time. The judge, who is scared to death that he might do something that will result in his being reviled in the press or business annals as the one who set the pack onto the wounded giant, pulls out the rubber stamp.

The damage to creditors' rights against a megacorporation in Chapter 11 by serial extensions of the exclusive period is enormous. The filing of the Chapter 11 case stops the creditors' momentum. The maintenance of the exclusive period hands it to the debtor. Aside from the actual wall of protection it builds around the Chapter 11 company, the megacorporation's ability to have the judge come down on its side each time the period is about to end is demeaning to the creditors. (Actually, it gives them a depressingly accurate lesson on their power in a megabankruptcy.) Make no mistake about it, the debtor's ability to hide behind the exclusive period *does* affect negotiations and *does* affect how much the creditors receive in a reorganization.

While neither the Bankruptcy Code nor the Bankruptcy Rules

specify how much a debtor must pay its creditors, they do contain certain requirements concerning the form and content of the plan of reorganization. The plan must:

1. Classify claims and interests (secured, unsecured, etc.);
2. Specify how each class will be treated (debt compromised, payment stretched out, debt paid per its terms, etc.);
3. Describe the means for achieving the payment promised in the plan (from investors, from the sale of the company, from operations, etc.); and
4. Allow creditors receiving stock to have voting rights and a fair share of power within the reorganized corporation.

A plan cannot be confirmed unless the liabilities are divided into appropriate classes. The simplest and most common divisions are: "priority"—mainly tax—creditors; secured creditors; unsecured creditors; and stockholders. A class cannot contain dissimilar types of claims or interests, such as mixing secured and unsecured creditors. Certain priority claims must stand alone, by statute. Also, because each secured claim is usually unique in its terms and treatment of collateral, ordinarily each such claim forms its own class. After the plan describes the nature of the claims contained in each class, it must then state what will be done with each one. Claims within a class must be treated equally.

A group of similar claims can be divided into multiple classes. The debtor may wish to isolate one subgroup that will probably reject the plan or that will require a higher payment than the other subgroup(s). For example, the plan may separately classify bank unsecured creditors and trade unsecured creditors or may place personal injury claimants in their own class. The problem with such fine-tuning of classes is that frequently the class receiving poorer treatment fails to see the legitimacy of the division. It may contest the class distinction, work to sabotage approval of the plan, or both.

The plan also must state how the debtor will acquire the wherewithal to make the payments to the creditors under the plan, and the projection must have some reasonable basis in reality. For example, a plan of a company unprofitable in the recent past that proposes to pay $1 million to creditors out of the next two years' profits may be considered unrealistic, absent some very favorable, demonstrable change in the business's situation. Such a plan may be found to be "not feasible," and therefore not confirmable, by the bankruptcy judge even if the creditors have voted approval. Because of the resources of the megacorporations, the feasibility of their plans is rarely questioned.

The *only* outright plan prohibition in the Bankruptcy Code is that in a Chapter 11 filed by an individual person, his or her "exempt" property cannot be sold, leased, or used without the consent of that debtor. Thus there is a very large category of permissive provisions for a plan of reorganization. The plan may provide for the cancellation of ongoing contracts (including union collective bargaining agreements, as the Continental Airlines pilots learned), the sale of all or part of the debtor's assets (even including the liquidation of the debtor), and the continued supervision by the court of installment payments to creditors. Basically, the content of a plan is limited only by the ingenuity and relative bargaining power of the interested parties.

When the bankruptcy laws were rewritten, the drafters wished to improve the quality of creditor involvement in the reorganization process. If, they reasoned, the key to a democracy is an informed electorate, the bankruptcy law should require disclosure to the creditors of important and relevant facts about the debtor before they are called upon to vote on a plan of reorganization. Thus was born the "disclosure statement."

Before a plan or reorganization can be disseminated to creditors, the plan proponent must produce a disclosure statement and have it approved by the bankruptcy judge in a hearing held with at least twenty-five days' prior notice to creditors. (Here the concept gets slightly schizophrenic. All creditors get written notice of the hearing from the bankruptcy court clerk by mail so that they might express their views if they believe that the disclosure statement is inadequate. However, because the disclosure statement has not yet been approved, it is not sent to the creditors for their review! The result is that the major active parties to the case—the debtor, the creditors' committees, the banks, and the U.S. trustee—who receive copies of the disclosure statement directly from the plan proponent, dominate the hearing.) Once the disclosure statement is approved, the plan and disclosure statement may then be sent together to the body of creditors, who then vote to accept or reject the plan.

The Bankruptcy Code does not list the required contents of a disclosure statement; rather, it provides that it must contain adequate information to enable a reasonable creditor to make an informed judgment about the merits of the plan, in light of the nature of the debtor and the state of its books and records. In order to adequately inform creditors, the disclosure statement should provide some history of the company and place its troubles in context, discuss what it has done to improve its situation, and advise as to what it intends to accomplish in the future. The statement also should describe and analyze the debtor's assets and liabilities. Special circumstances, such as lawsuits, should be disclosed. Of course, creditors should be advised of how the debtor will manage to pay them the amounts promised in the plan. The contents of disclosure statements vary widely.

The plan proponent's statements respecting projections and valuations are supposed to have some factual basis, but verification by an independent source is not required. The debtor will often provide sufficiently dire liquidation values of its assets to remind creditors of how badly they will get burned if they reject the plan and the case is converted to a Chapter 7 liquidation. Values of assets and projections of profits can be quite subjective, sometimes to the point of being downright wishful. In other words, the debtor can usually get away with a good deal of B.S. as long as it does not cross over into obvious, blatant lies. As a result, while sometimes the bankruptcy disclosure process is likened to that mandated by the federal securities laws, in actuality the disclosure statement is not held up to the standards of a prospectus. The disclosure statement is more like an advertisement, attempting to educate and to sell the product while not overstepping the boundaries of "puffing."

Once the bankruptcy judge approves the disclosure statement, it may be sent to creditors, stockholders, and other interested parties along with the plan of reorganization, and a notice of when and where ballots must be filed and the date, time, and place of hearing at which the bankruptcy judge will consider whether to approve the plan. Approval by the creditors simply consists of achieving the requisite votes in favor of the plan, by class. A class of creditors will be deemed to have approved the plan if a majority in number and at least two-thirds in amount of claims of those voting cast their votes for acceptance. The dual requirement gives both large and small creditors a voice in the reorganization. Note that a failure to vote is an abstention, not a "no." Thus those who do not vote have their fate decided by those who do.

The amount of each creditor's claim is determined by the filed claim or, if no claim has been filed, by the amount listed by the debtor. If there is a dispute, the court may be asked to determine provisionally the amount for purposes of the vote. If the debtor seriously wishes to challenge either the amount or the existence of a claim, it will file a formal objection to that claim and have the bankruptcy judge hold a hearing before the plan is considered.

Shareholders and debenture holders whose interests are negatively affected by the plan each form a class and are entitled to vote. Since each unit is equal within the class, approval of either such class requires an affirmative vote of two-thirds of the units for which votes are cast.

It is not uncommon for a plan to totally wipe out a class or classes low on the hierarchy of interests. The grounds are that each such class would receive nothing upon a liquidation (due to the strict rules that each higher class would have to be paid in full first), and so it does not deserve to receive anything upon a reorganization.

The presiding bankruptcy judge must hold a hearing to "confirm" that the plan has received the requisite number of votes for acceptance and that it otherwise conforms to the legal requirements for final approval by the court. Counting the vote is usually very straightforward, although occasionally a vote is challenged as having been procured by fraud, or violating the solicitation rules, or as having arrived too late, or for other such reasons. If every impaired class has voted to accept the plan, the plan has achieved the requisite creditor approval.

About now you are probably thinking that the process is very harsh if the plan proponent can come this far and yet be defeated by the failure of any one class to accept the plan, especially since ordinarily each secured creditor forms its own class. Does one dissenting class constitute an unchallengable veto? What is a plan proponent to do?

The answer is that at the confirmation hearing, the plan proponent requests the bankruptcy judge to "cram down" the plan on each rejecting class. That is, the judge is asked to declare that, pursuant to specific considerations, the dissenting class is being treated fairly and so its rejection of the plan is illegitimate, and it will be deemed to have accepted the plan. (Democracy has its limits, even—or especially—in bankruptcy court. The plan is thus virtually crammed down the throats of the parties in the rejecting class!) Per the Bankruptcy Code, if at least one class of impaired creditors votes to accept the plan, every other class is subject to cramdown.

The cramdown—what a wonderful, descriptive term—may be applied against a class by the judge if he finds that:

1. The class is not being discriminated against "unfairly"—that is, no creditors with similar types of claims have been put in a separate class and given better treatment; and
2. The treatment of the class is "fair and equitable"—a bankruptcy term-of-art that means no class lower in the hierarchy receives anything unless and until the crammed-down class receives 100 percent of its claims.

The method of cramming down a class varies depending on the type of class.

If the debtor wishes to cram down a secured creditor—that is, have the plan confirmed by the judge in spite of the rejection by that class-of-one—the plan must offer to pay that creditor the full value of its secured claim, in one of several ways. The plan may provide that all of that creditor's collateral will be turned over to it; that the collateral will be sold and the secured creditor will receive all the proceeds; or that the debtor will pay for the present value of the collateral either in cash or with payments that include interest. The debtor may even substitute collateral as long as it is equivalent to the original.

What is the advantage to the debtor if it must recognize the full value of the secured creditor's collateral? First of all, it removes veto power from a creditor that has unreasonably voted no. Second, it allows the secured portion of the claim to be limited to the present value of the collateral as valued by the judge, a process most secured creditors fear. (The portion of the claim that exceeds the value of the collateral becomes an unsecured claim.) Third, it shifts the debtor's payment obligation away from the strict terms of the security agreement and allows the debtor, with court approval, to force the secured creditor to accept the debtor's payment schedule. The debtor may even propose a different interest rate. The court then determines if it is an appropriate "market" interest rate, an issue that provokes much dispute.

In extreme cases, the debtor may offer something that looks nothing like the original arrangement, as long as it can persuade the court that the proposal provides for an "equivalent" obligation. For example, the plan may offer an equipment financier payment in bonds secured by accounts receivable. In other words, the deal is rewritten by the debtor and the bankruptcy judge over the creditor's objection (as in "cramdown").

The secured creditor is left a little wiggle room. It may exercise a right provided by the Bankruptcy Code to have its entire claim treated as secured even though the value of the collateral may be less than the amount of the claim. However, should the secured creditor elect to do that, the payments to that creditor need only total the principal amount of the claim, and that creditor is not paid interest or any other compensation for delayed payment.

While the Bankruptcy Code also allows for the cramdown of unsecured creditors, the requirements are so unpalatable to the debtor that it is seldom done. To effectuate a plan over the rejection of a class of unsecured creditors, that class must be paid the total amount of its claims—out of the question, in most cases—or all lower classes of interests must be totally wiped out. Since one of those lower classes consists of the shareholders' interests, an unsecured creditor cramdown is not a very interesting proposition for the people who control the debtor.

The practical result is that plan proponents do not attempt to cram down unsecured creditors. They offer them a few pennies and remind them that if they reject the plan and the company is liquidated, they will almost certainly receive nothing. In fact, rarely do unsecured creditors reject a plan if the debtor knowingly or unknowingly follows a rule of thumb for dealing with unsecured creditors: offer them more than they would receive on liquidation but less than makes them happy!

While most plans leave the equity holders with their ownership interests intact—thus leaving them unimpaired and conclusively in acceptance of the plan—classes of equity holders may also be subject to cramdown. As with unsecured creditors, they must be paid the face value of their interests; if paid less, then every class lower in priority (that is, subordinated equity interests) must be wiped out.

Once the vote has been counted—or ignored, in the case of the cramdown—and the bankruptcy judge has determined that the plan of reorganization has the requisite creditor acceptance, the judge must then confirm that the plan meets certain legal standards before it can have final court approval.

In order to confirm a plan of reorganization, the court must make findings to the effect that:

1. The plan was proposed in good faith;
2. The plan proponents did not use illegal means to gain creditor acceptance;
3. The plan does not contain any provisions prohibited by, or fail to include terms required by, the Bankruptcy Code;
4. The plan provisions must be in the "best interests" of the creditors and equity security holders (read: they will be no worse off under the plan than they would be if the case were converted to Chapter 7 and the debtor liquidated);
5. Each priority claim will be paid either *(a)* in full, *(b)* pursuant to a payment plan specifically authorized by the Bankruptcy Code for certain categories of debts, or *(c)* in lesser amounts only if that creditor consents;
6. The plan proposals are "feasible," that is, the debtor will be able to make the promised payments, and it is not likely that the debtor's performance of the obligations contained in the plan will lead to liquidation or another reorganization of the debtor; and
7. The principal purpose of the plan, if it has been objected to by the government, is not to avoid taxes or the securities laws.

The "good faith" requirement is in the law to allow a bankruptcy judge to deny confirmation on his own initiative, in spite of creditor consent, where it appears that the results of the reorganization will not be consistent with goals of the bankruptcy laws. For example, confirmation may be denied where a fraud is being perpetrated on creditors.

There are two principal reasons why the Bankruptcy Code limits democracy by providing the judge with these veto powers. The first is that, as the "election judge," he or she should not stand by while creditors are defrauded by illegal acts of the plan proponents. The second is that, by requiring court supervision over the plan provisions and procedures, the Bankruptcy Code provides the moral basis for taking economic rights away from dissenters.

Once the plan of reorganization has been confirmed and the company is outside direct court and creditor supervision, it is supposed to follow the mandates of the plan religiously. In practice, the creditors are not too quick to complain to the bankruptcy court if the former debtor is remiss (if they have retained that right), and so the new company has some practical leeway in performing its obligations under the plan. In cases where conforming to the payment schedule contained in the plan is proving impossible, the company may ask the court to reopen the case for the purpose of allowing it to file a modified plan of reorganization and seek approval of the amended proposal. Surprisingly, there is no prohibition against the company filing another Chapter 11. If at first you do not succeed . . .

While many small companies slide down the tubes in Chapter 11, the megacorporations almost all succeed famously. They dominate the committees and bully the judges. They stay ten steps ahead of any feeble attempts at supervision. They use the bankruptcy laws to force plans of reorganization down creditors' throats. And then the executives of those corporations laugh all the way to the bank. Chrysler, the first casualty of the Eighties, would turn out to be one of the last major corporations to fall into dire straits to reorganize outside of bankruptcy.

Chapter 4

Chrysler: The First Casualty

"You can't always get what you want,
but you can usually get what you need."
—The Rolling Stones

Lee A. Iacocca wanted to go head to head with Henry Ford II, his former boss, and whip him. He wanted to take what he felt was his rightful place as King of the Auto Industry, a titan among titans. Offers to head large corporations in a number of different fields had come flooding in after Iacocca was unceremoniously dismissed as president of Ford Motor Company, but Iacocca needed to remain in the auto business if his dreams of glory were to come true. And Chrysler was available.

Iacocca may well have seen himself as Walter P. Chrysler reborn. Walter P. Chrysler, like Iacocca trained as an engineer, became head of an auto division (Buick), but parted company after disputes with the chairman over corporate policies. Already nationally known as an automotive genius capable of demanding a substantial salary, Chrysler took only a minimal one as a gesture of good faith when he was asked to rescue the failing Maxwell Motor Company in 1922. (However, as Iacocca would do half a century later, Chrysler did take compensation in stock options, which would prove very valuable.) Walter P. found and nurtured talented designers and engineers and marketed his cars by appearing in their ads. Meanwhile, he persuaded the company's banks to forgive much of their debt and take stock. Even during hard times,

Chrysler refused to cut funds for reseach and product development. The similarities were spooky. Was Lee Iacocca the Second Coming of Walter P. and, if so, would that be enough to save Chrysler?

Chrysler Corporation was a proud name. One of the Big Three of U.S. auto manufacturers, it was the tenth largest manufacturing corporation in the United States. Since its genesis when Walter Chrysler took over the Maxwell Motor Company (renamed Chrysler Corporation in 1925) and then added the Dodge brothers' factory to his holdings, Chrysler vehicles had earned a reputation as well engineered and well built. In 1924, the company sold 32,000 cars; 192,000 in 1927; and 450,000 in 1929. Chrysler cars ran rings around the Ford Model T when Chrysler introduced the high compression engine in 1926, and Henry Ford was forced to cease production and take a year to retool in order to counter with the Model A. At its peak in the 1940s, Chrysler outsold Ford, capturing about a quarter of the U.S. market. Over the years, Chrysler engineers developed the first air filter, oil filter, modern voltage regulator, electronic ignition, hydraulic brakes, and onboard computers. In 1951, Chrysler introduced power steering. In the early 1960s, Chrysler's Plymouth Valiant and Dodge Dart helped Chevrolet's Corvair and Ford's Falcon drive back the first challenge of foreign compacts arriving from Europe, while the Big Three raked in profits on the sales of their "land cruisers." During the 1960s, chairman Lynn Townsend built a network of manufacturing facilities around the world with the capabilities of matching General Motors and Ford model for model. Chrysler, Ford, and GM continued to grow, buoyed by a booming economy, cheap gas, and $500 billion worth of interstate freeways.

In the midst of national prosperity, Chrysler Corporation suffered from nagging problems. After World War II, with Walter P. watching from the Great Beyond, Chrysler began a long, gradual slide. It was slow to offer new models following the war and ignored the auto industry trend of "selling the sizzle" through newly emerging marketing methods. Although achieving 21 percent of the U.S. market in 1951, sales would drift downward over the decade to where Chrysler would only command 10 percent by 1962. There were some upticks at times, such as when Chrysler led the way to brighter colors, including two- and three-tones, and when it became the first automobile manufacturer to inflict fins on the American public, in 1957. While 1957 was a good year for Chrysler sales, the recession of 1958 hit

Chrysler hard—cutting sales by *a half*—and it did not rebound afterward as strongly as GM and Ford. The company also followed an overly optimistic policy of building many plants and churning out many autos according to its own internal dictates, irrespective of what the market was signaling.

Chrysler directors named Lynn Townsend president of the company in 1961. Although he was trained as an accountant, his interests were in marketing. In conjunction with cost cutting and modernizing (a new IBM computer replaced seven hundred clerks), Townsend introduced and cleverly promoted stylish and well-made models in 1963 and developed the pentstar logo to provide a contemporary image. Townsend's vision of Chrysler was as an international conglomerate. Plants were built or bought in eighteen countries, and Chrysler moved into air conditioning through its Airtemp division, auto leasing, real estate, chemicals, marine products, and space (including rockets for the Mercury program and the booster engines for the Saturn rocket). Townsend was innovative and perhaps ahead of his time in terms of his international view, but he neglected engineering and was satisfied with thin profits even in the good years.

By the late Sixties, Chrysler's product line had slipped out of the groove. Chrysler again fell into the habit of valuing production quotas over all else, even market demand. The capital used to build those foreign plants had been siphoned out of the budgets of the engineering and new product design staffs. Quality suffered, and the company became a "me too" competitor, consistently following GM moves two years after the fact. Chrysler began to suffer with what would become a chronic, nagging problem: as the smallest of the Big Three, it was the least able to bear the costs of retooling and modernizing.

By 1969, Chrysler was dangerously close to being outside the mainstream American market. It was making big, ugly cars, and they were piling up in dealers' lots and at Chrysler holding pens in the Midwest. Chrysler sales dipped 7 percent for the year, while the U.S. auto industry in general enjoyed a 6 percent increase.

The cost of making Chrysler into a "world" auto manufacturer in the Sixties put the company near the brink. The company had almost no bank debt when Townsend took over, but by 1970 when he was replaced, it owed about $800 million (more than GM).

The most pressing job of the new president, John Riccardo, was to cut costs drastically, but the first federal safety regulations in 1970 and emission standards in 1975 tacked additional costs and effort onto Chrysler's burdens. A nationwide credit crunch in 1975 had the indirect effect of almost bankrupting Chrysler. It was saved by the support of its major banks, led by Manufacturers Hanover; however, it emerged from the crisis $200 million more in debt and with a reduced work force.

Unable to allocate sufficient capital to develop a subcompact, Chrysler entered into a relationship with Mitsubishi of Japan to supply it. Though the Chrysler-Mitsubishi cooperative venture would save the American company in the early 1980s, in the early 1970s it was only a minor diversion for Chrysler. Said Townsend: "The subcompacts are just too small. The American people won't climb into them.... [F]ifteen years from today you're still going to see a hell of a lot of big cars." John Riccardo would show the same perspicuity in 1973: "I think the day this company turned around was the day we decided not build [a] subcompact."

The 1974 and 1975 model years sent tremors through the auto industry as the oil-induced recession and rising gasoline prices rekindled the American buyer's interest in smaller, fuel-efficient autos. In 1974, subcompacts made up 17.4 percent of the U.S. market, and the entrants by the Big Three were not doing well. The Chevrolet Vega, Buick Skylark, and Ford Pinto struggled for sales, while Chrysler continued mostly to ignore that market. What small cars the Big Three did offer were stuffed to the roofs with expensive options in a vain attempt to maintain profit margins. Chrysler's behemoths, restyled in 1973, did not sell.

In January 1975, Chrysler achieved a rather dubious "first" for the U.S. auto industry: it introduced rebates in order to get its cars off the lots. Because Chrysler was strapped for capital, it was slow coming out of the severe 1974–75 auto slump, which it did not foresee; and in 1975, it skipped a dividend payment for the first time since the Great Depression. That year Chrysler lost $160 million. It was the company's worst year to that date. John Riccardo, now the chairman of Chrysler, and his president, Gene Cafiero, were forced to slash costs, including investment in tools and research and development. Eighty percent of Chrysler's engineers were laid off or fired.

Chrysler was too enthralled with its success in several growing niche markets to concern itself with portents. Americans were turning in increasing numbers to small trucks and vans as personal vehicles, and

Chrysler was riding high in those markets. By 1975, one-fourth of Chrysler's output in the United States consisted of trucks. Dodge was manufacturing three-fourths of the motor home chassis in the country, supplying most other manufacturers as well as selling models under its name. For a while, buyers did not seem to care about the abysmal gas mileage of those specialty vehicles. As with the introduction of the muscle cars in the early 1970s, Chrysler had countered declining main-line auto sales with gas-guzzling offshoots. After riding the wave for a few years, Chrysler would be sent crashing with it.

By the late Seventies, the turkeys had come home to roost: because Chrysler had decimated its technical staff, the Aspen/Volare was so poorly designed and manufactured that impressive 1976 sales turned into 1977 recalls and massive amounts of warranty repairs. Engines would stall when the gas pedal was applied, brakes failed, and hoods would fly open. Altogether, more than 3.5 million Aspen/Volares were brought back to the dealers for warranty repairs. As late as 1980, Chrysler would still be spending more than $100 million a year to correct Aspen/Volare rusted fenders. Also, for every model year 1975 to 1978, Chrysler was four to eight months late in introducing its models. The company was facing the competition while suffering from self-inflicted wounds—and the competition was getting tougher.

In the second half of the Seventies, the Japanese auto "invasion" began in earnest. In 1976, sales of Japanese-manufactured vehicles in the United States shot up to 1.4 million, and in 1977, they climbed to 1.6 million. When those sales were added to the sales of European autos in the U.S. (mostly by Volkswagen), the imports' share of the U.S. market reached 20 percent. The Big Three were sent scrambling to retool, issuing so many orders that the backlog in the worldwide machine tool industry doubled. (In 1958, Datsun had sold 52 vehicles in the U.S. Toyota had led the way with 274.)

Tooling. Therein lies the key to the success of the Japanese auto invasion. Oh yes, Americans came to appreciate the Japanese manufac-turers for their high quality at reasonable prices, and the efficiency of Japanese manufacturers became legendary, but those were not the major reasons for the huge success of Japanese auto manufacturers. *Very simply, they did not have to retool.* For one thing, the entire Japanese auto industry of eleven producers was forced to build entirely new plants and install all new equipment after World War II. More importantly, as a country that had to import 100 percent of its petroleum and thus discouraged energy inefficiency, Japan *always* has produced small, fuel-efficient autos. When the American consumers needed relief from auto costs, the Japanese had already invested decades of research and development into the products for which those buyers cried out. All the Japanese auto manufacturers had to do was to turn up the assembly lines a few notches, and their products spilled into the United States.

The differential costs of tooling go a long way toward explaining the competitive advantage of the Japanese auto manufacturers over the Big Three. A Department of Transportation study estimated that it would take $60 to $80 billion over eight years, *all of the capital assets of the U.S. auto manufactuers,* for them to comply with just the new mileage requirements. In 1977, Chrysler budgeted $700 million for the year— which it really did not have—for developing smaller cars. The Japanese did not have to concern themselves with expenses like these. Seen in this light, the Japanese advantages in labor costs and employee loyalty were just icing on the cake for them.

Faced with a doubling of cash needs in the midst of sharply declining profitability, Chrysler's search for funds became desperate. Although in mid-1977 Riccardo assured the financial community that the $700 million needed for small car development would come from accounting tricks (accelerated depreciation) and increased efficiency, to no one's surprise Chrysler soon was scrounging for other quick fixes. Over the next several years, Riccardo would preside over the sale of all of Chrysler's business ventures outside production and financing of vehicles and would dismantle Townsend's foreign empire piece by piece.

It was at this time that Lido Anthony Iacocca found himself in the job market, after spending his whole working life at Ford.

Lido virtually was born into the auto business, his father having developed one of the first auto-rental agencies. After graduating with high honors in engineering from Lehigh and taking a master's degree in mechanical engineering at Princeton, he talked himself into a filled training program at Ford. Later, bored with engineering, he went back to Pennsylvania to go into sales. His marketing gifts shone from the hinterlands to Dearborn, Michigan, and he was soon called to join Ford's national sales division. It was during his visits to local dealers in the South that Lido became jus' good ol' "Lee."

Lee was doing it all. He built up Ford truck sales and then became assistant general sales manager. Next, he became general manager of Ford Division in 1960, with responsibility over almost all car and truck sales in the United States and 13,000 employees. He raised the status of market research as a planning tool. He pushed sales to the youth market, conceiving and spearheading the development of the wildly successful Mustang that made its debut in 1964. He scored again with the Lincoln Continental Mark III, overlayed on the basic Thunderbird frame. If it was 1965, he was vice-president, Car and Truck Group, North America Operations; if 1967, executive vice-president for all North American automotive operations, overseeing most of Ford's worldwide business. In December 1970, Lee Iacocca became president of Ford Motor Company.

Iacocca had claimed the peak . . . almost. As with everyone else at Ford Motor, he answered to the man whose last name was on the buildings in the executive compound and on every vehicle going out the factory door, the chairman of the company. And Henry Ford II was a man who had his own ideas about running a car company. Iacocca wanted to develop a smaller car, but Ford said no. Iacocca negotiated a deal with Honda to buy small engines and attached power trains at bargain prices that virtually could be dropped right onto Ford Motor Company "platforms," but Ford countermanded the arrangement. Although recognized as a solid manager and a marketing genius by the rest of the world, Iacocca saw his influence within the company wane as other executives quietly cast their lot with the guy who could not be fired. On July 13, 1978, Lee Iacocca was purged from the Ford Motor Company ranks.

John Riccardo was no fool. He knew a good opportunity when he saw it, and he knew that Lee Iacocca would be good for Chrysler. Personally and through intermediaries, he courted Iacocca even as Lee was wrapping up his affairs at Ford and cleaning out his desk. Although competing with other important companies that placed their chairmanships at Iacocca's feet, Chrysler had something that no one else could offer: the chance for Iacocca to get even with Henry Ford. Shortly after Iacocca became legally free to establish a new relationship, the deal was wrapped up. Iacocca would start as the chief operating officer of Chrysler and would succeed Riccardo as chief executive officer in November 1979 upon Riccardo's retirement. During that first year Iacocca would be Mr. Inside, in total charge of Chrysler's operations, while Riccardo would be Mr. Outside, maintaining Chrysler's relations with its banks and other important constituencies.

Iacocca had known that Chrysler suffered from a capital shortage, but nevertheless, his first several months on the job produced a steady stream of shocks and disappointments. Chrysler's condition was far worse than his worst nightmare. Upon his arrival, Chrysler announced a record loss for the third quarter of 1978, $158.8 million. He found an organizational chart in place that did not provide for proper supervision of subordinates and a corporate culture that discouraged coordination among departments. He found a purchasing department that did not have a system to organize materials flow and did not make regular quality control inspections of incoming parts from suppliers. (Warranty costs were running $350 million a year.) Chrysler also was lacking in perhaps the most important element of auto manufacturing, the strict coordination of all aspects during the thirty-three-month cycle of product development so that all of the thousands of parts in a new model could come together at the same place at the same time. Used to having extensive statistics and financial data for the asking at Ford, Iacocca was dismayed to learn that market research was almost nonexistent, and the company lacked the basic accounting tools to determine the efficiency of the various elements of its operations. (Iacocca has said that his inability to summon sufficient financial data on the company's problems was the greatest jolt he had in his business career.) Iacocca had been handed the crown, but he would have to rehab the castle.

Characteristically, Iacocca moved fast. Three weeks after joining Chrysler, he had a new organizational chart in place. He named a small-car proponent as chief of planning. He improved financial reporting and controls. He fired several vice-presidents. (Eventually thirty-three of thirty-five vice-presidents who had been on board when Iacocca signed on were let go.) He reached out to former subordinates and associates, some still at Ford and some not, to fill key spots. Even at his blistering pace, by the first part of 1979, Iacocca came to realize that revamping Chrysler would take years. He was, as he called it, starting from scratch.

In the meantime, the world in general and the U.S. auto business in particular suffered shock after shock. In January 1979, the shah left Iran, never to return, providing an excuse for OPEC to raise prices drastically. Spring 1979 saw Three Mile Island and severe gas shortages springing up around the country. It was a time of calamity, and consumers were not in a new-car buying mood. When they did buy, they wanted the most gas-efficient autos possible. The Carter administration was calling for a "gas guzzler tax." Small-car sales, sluggish in 1978, became the only car sales in 1979, making it the most violent market swing that the auto industry ever had experienced. Chrysler's recreational vehicle sales hit the wall and crumbled. A grand total of twelve Chrysler RVs were sold in the United States in June 1979. Iacocca commented, "Is this a drop in the market? No, this is a complete disappearance of a market."

The decade of the Seventies was fading into the figurative sunset, a fact for which nearly all Americans could be thankful. It appeared that along with the end of that era another era might also be drawing to a close—that of one of the largest companies in the world, the Chrysler Corporation. The problem for Lee Iacocca and more than 100,000 other employees of Chrysler was that the corporation was making products that relatively few people wanted to buy. The company's sole goal became to survive until the fall of 1980, when the introduction of its redesigned compact car—designated the "K-Car"—would save it. Iacocca had turned the course of the huge company, but would it survive until the changes could evidence themselves at the end of the assembly lines?

General Motors and the Japanese were ready for the new decade, even if Chrysler was not. Because the sale of Japanese-made autos also had been hurt by a general auto slump in 1978, there were plenty of cars sitting on the lots of the importers when the 1979 gas crunch hit. As they were snapped up, sales of Japanese cars hit 24.3 percent of the total U.S. market. General Motors' small-car program, initiated years before, had come to fruition at exactly the right time. In the spring of 1979, GM's light, twenty-four-miles-per-gallon "X-Cars" rolled off the lines to a waiting public. In the first two days after its introduction, every available Chevrolet Citation was sold, and GM had taken orders for 22,000 more. Chrysler, having hedged, saw its big cars rust on the lots while orders for Plymouth Horizons and Dodge Omnis (really the same car but for some trim and the nameplate) were backlogged due to Chrysler's limited small-car production capacity. Also, Chrysler would have only a limited supply of the four-cylinder engines that the public wanted. Years before, it had decided to buy a limited number of four-cylinder engines annually from Volkswagen rather than expend capital on a new plant.

Chrysler losses, and the attendant cash crunch, worsened. The company was forced to lay off 20,000 employees and close several plants permanently. Working capital (current assets less current liabilities), barely adequate at $1.6 billion in 1978, was down to $600 million by mid-1979—perilously close to a technical breach of its banks' lending formulas. Chrysler dug deep into a $560 million standby line of credit, shocking and awakening bankers, who never dreamed that Chrysler ever would need it. Riccardo spent much time on the road calming Chrysler's lenders. *Newsweek* called Chrysler's second quarter 1979 losses of $207 million "staggering" in an article entitled "Can Chrysler Be Saved?" Chrysler's agony had become public and would continue to be so over the next years of its excruciating, slow climb to health.

Riccardo also was knocking on doors at just about every level of government. His first round of talks with federal officials involved his request that Chrysler be exempted from 1980 and 1981 emission standards, which would save Chrysler $500 million in 1979. Riccardo's argument went something like this: since the big, bad federal government had imposed those onerous safety, emission, and mileage standards on innocent auto manufacturers, the federal government had acquired a duty to help the company most injured by them. Riccardo was vague on figures, and seemed to feel that Chrysler should not have to make any sacrifices in return for aid. The arrogance in Riccardo's approach was not lost on official Washington, some public servants having the temerity to suggest that the cost of those items did not come close to explaining Chrysler's losses and, in any event, the mileage standards merely pushed Chrysler towards producing what the public wanted to buy.

Next, Riccardo asked the Treasury Department for an "advance" on anticipated tax credits arising from almost-certain losses on sales and the costs of meeting federal regulations, to be repaid out of future profits. While not unheard of, the pitch for tax credits got nowhere.

While Riccardo's proposals appeared to stall, official Washington was awakening to the fact that one of America's largest corporations, employing more than 100,000 in one of the country's proudest industries, was *very* sick. Chrysler's inventory of unsold vehicles totaled 100,000, worth more than $600 million, and its market share had fallen below 10 percent. Because of its poor financial health, Chrysler had been dropped from the thirty industrials forming the Dow Jones benchmark index. Projections indicated that the company would probably run out of cash before the end of the year. Those same projections showed that Chrysler needed an additional $1.5 billion to survive. As Congress opened debate in the fall of 1979, the main problem was not the form of Riccardo's schemes for relief, but rather that it was abundantly clear that they would be grossly insufficient to keep Chrysler afloat. The company needed more than a life preserver. It needed a heart-lung transplant.

A secondary problem for the government as well as the banks was that Chrysler was asking them to provide lifesaving measures in the dark. Chrysler's bookkeeping system was not sophisticated enough to show exactly how bad things were. Although the federal government, the banks, the union, and Chrysler hired high-priced accountants to attempt to quantify Chrysler's situation, ultimately there was no agreement on figures developed by anybody. The federal guarantees would be based on politics and "a wing and a prayer."

At some point in the fall of 1979, at a time when it appeared that the reaction of the federal government would be inaction, one of Chrysler's arguments began to take hold. The key to rousing the Carter administration turned out to be the specter of more than 100,000 Chrysler employees put out onto the streets *in an election year.* Chrysler was quick to add to the parade of horrors the lost jobs in the feeder industries, the costs of unemployment and other forms of welfare that the various levels of government would be required to expend, the increase in mental health problems of laid-off workers, and on, and on, and on. Suddenly, Treasury Secretary G. William Miller, who had held the perfectly defensible opinion that the government should not make loans that had little chance of being repaid, began to talk out of the other side of his mouth with prompting from the White House. The Carter administration then galvanized support in Congress, support which until that point had been limited largely to members representing Michigan.

Suddenly, no price was too great to pay to save Chrysler. Having previously beaten down Chrysler's aid request to $750 million, Miller did an about-face and suggested that nothing less than $1.5 billion would do the job. Instead of tax credits or other gimmicks, the Carter administration began talking about loan guarantees. The Chrysler management, who had not pushed loans because of the high interest rates then in effect, became believers in federal guarantees.

The central premise of Chrysler's save-the-employees argument was the *a priori* view that there were only two options available: federal aid or the liquidation of Chrysler. On a number of occasions, Iacocca solemnly intoned that the management of Chrysler, in its infinite wisdom, had determined that a Chapter 11 proceeding was an impossibility for the company. Since only Chrysler knew what was possible for Chrysler, the issue was closed—Chapter 11 was absolutely out of the question. In fact, in his public pronouncements, Iacocca consistently— and, one must assume, willfully—ignored the differences between a Chapter 11 reorganization proceeding and a liquidation under Chapter 7 of the Bankruptcy Code. To Iacocca there was only "bankruptcy," and that was liquidation. For example, in his book *Iacocca,* he states:

> What would the largest bankruptcy in American history [Chrysler] have done to the nation? A study by Data Resources estimated that the demise of Chrysler would ultimately cost the taxpayers $16 billion in unemployment, welfare, and other expenses. So much for the bankruptcy option.

Therefore, the options open to the Carter administration were simple: either it would ante up whatever was necessary to save Chrysler, or it would cause legions of unemployed to hit the streets at election time.

Once it had the right lyrics, Chrysler turned up the volume. Recalcitrant members of Congress found their office waiting rooms filled with union members, Chrysler dealers, and suppliers to the auto industry, all carefully orchestrated by Chrysler.

The philosophical and economic arguments in opposition to aid were on solid ground, and Chrysler's request for federal aid was roundly denounced by politicians, economists, business writers, and those business leaders who chose to be quoted, as a raid on the national treasury. Aid to Chrysler would violate two sacred tenets of free enterprise: that the necessary counterbalance to the opportunity for profits was the risk of loss and that losers were not to be rewarded by being propped up. If capitalism was the economic embodiment of the Darwinian philosophy of the "survival of the fittest," Chrysler had provided ample proof that it deserved to perish. In the Senate hearings, James Davidson of the National Taxpayers Union stated:

> The [bailout] will . . . send a signal to all large corporations that

they need not control costs, because in the event that they reach bankruptcy, which is the ultimate consequence, they will be bailed out by the taxpayer.

It was pointed out that because of the size of Chrysler's debt—it was almost 10 percent of the total capital of the fifty largest U.S. banks—propping up Chrysler would lead to a diversion of funds away from many other, more deserving, companies. On considering the proposal of propping up Chrysler, Senator Adlai Stevenson III argued that the United States should not support inefficient producers with public funds, as England had, but should follow Japan's example and encourage the flow of capital to vigorous, growing concerns. The fear was that the federal government, having committed its credit and prestige, would find that it could not extricate itself from the "tar baby."

Practical arguments against aid to Chrysler centered around a number of observations. Despite Chrysler wrapping itself in the flag, it was obvious that the profitable and important battle tank division would continue to exist whether operated by Chrysler or someone else. Also, although it would be moderately embarrassing to Americans to lose a large auto manufacturer, in an era of international competition in the industry the loss of Chrysler's 10 percent market share would not result in an increase in market concentration. Walter Wriston, the chairman of Citicorp, one of the United States' largest banks and a major creditor of Chrysler, doubted that Chrysler had a reasonable chance of repaying its loans and predicted that the banks would refuse to lend any additional sums to Chrysler. The government obviously had failed objectively to determine whether Chrysler might be saved and, if it might, whether the risk was worth the gain.

The arguments against the save-the-employees theme were also cogent. They rested on the reasonable proposition that Chrysler would not simply close up shop and send everyone home but would undergo a massive reorganization, whether in or outside of bankruptcy court. In that scenario, tens of thousands of jobs would be lost anyway, making the jobs lost in the unlikely event of a liquidation only an incremental loss. It was also noted that Chrysler's doomsday figures failed to take into account the absorption of any Chrysler employees into the other automakers or other industries or the switch of Chrysler suppliers into other businesses. The state of the economy and the concentration of Chrysler employees in the Midwest certainly did indicate, however, that there would be substantial heartache if the company ceased to manufacture autos and trucks altogether.

Iacocca's insistence that Chrysler would close its doors before it filed a Chapter 11 was patently absurd. His argument that no one would buy an auto from a company in Chapter 11 was belied by the thousands of manufacturers and retailers who had maintained their businesses while in Chapter 11—after all, what was Chapter 11 for? Companies in Chapter 11 commonly are successful in arguing to their creditors and customers that filing Chapter 11 was necessary to assure that the company would survive. Surveys showed that even people who felt Chrysler would fold continued to buy its cars. In any event, the master salesman would have found a way to turn a bankruptcy to Chrysler's advantage. In addition, the public would have found it easier to ignore the humdrum of a court proceeding than what actually ensued—Chrysler's confessions before Congress, the grandstanding by members of Congress, and highly publicized brinksmanship over federal aid.

In other words, Iacocca's federal-aid-or-bust position was a monumental bluff. It was made for the purpose of acquiring more than a billion dollars in financing through government guarantees that Chrysler could not get otherwise without the sale of profitable assets such as Chrysler Financial Corporation. It was made to prevent Chrysler from having to shrink from a full-line producer. It was made because only the federal government could provide Iacocca with the wherewithal for his greater glory. Iacocca was playing "chicken" with the federal government, and the livelihood of a huge number of people hung in the balance. One cannot help believing that the Chapter 11 petition was tucked away in a drawer, just in case. If the bluff were called, Iacocca still would not lose all.

It was an uneven battle. On one side were legions of paid and unpaid lobbyists, dealers, and employees; a powerful corporation and a powerful union; senators and representatives from the states most affected; and the Carter administration. On the other side were a few congressmen defending Adam Smith, dead nearly two hundred years, and his abstract theories of capitalist economic order. The perceived uncertainties of Chapter 11 loomed large when compared to the misperception of the certainties that would result from government guarantees. Congress was ready to buy a pig in a poke* even though Senator William Proxmire hit the nail smack on the head in confronting Iacocca: "You are asking the government to risk $1.5 billion. If it fails, the taxpayer takes a painful bath. If it succeeds, you will be a famous success and be made very, very wealthy."

Chrysler had one more powerful argument to make to Congress: it was not the first corporation to seek direct federal financial aid during the 1970s in order to stay in business. After the Penn Central Railroad was down to its last $7 million and had been forced to file a reorganization bankruptcy in 1970, Congress had provided $125 million in loan guarantees to grubstake its continued operations. In 1971, Congress had provided—by one vote in the Senate and three in the House—$250 million in loan guarantees for Lockheed Aircraft Corporation. Shortly before Congress was approached by Chrysler hat in hand, it had approved more than $250 million in aid to Jones and Laughlin and Wheeling-Pittsburgh Steel to prop up the American steel industry. The federal government had invested billions in the biggest basket case of them all, New York City. Why should Congress punish Chrysler by deciding to turn off the tap now?

Congress did not know how to defend against Chrysler's plea. Different lessons could be drawn from those forays into corporate finance. No cohesive philosophy had ever been elucidated that would differentiate one corporate request for federal largess from another. Congress clearly was uneasy with its role as Financier to the Financially Irresponsible, but if a policy was emerging from the jumble of situations it was not being verbalized.

There *was* an important lesson to be learned from the Penn Central, Lockheed, steel company, and (indirectly) New York City bailouts, although it has escaped the public's attention to this day. The public does not understand it and the media does not understand it, but Lee Iacocca learned it and many corporate chief executives came to know it. John Riccardo probably knew it, but his high-handed approach to the Carter administration at the onset was a tactical error.

---

* For the uninitiated, a "poke" is a sack, which may be used to carry animals to the farmers' market. It is always wise for the purchaser to remove the animal from the poke to make sure that the animal is of the type, gender, and health claimed by the farmer.

During the 1970s, the principle was established that a corporation can be too big to fail. The really big losers simply had to strike the right chord, wait the proper amount of time for Congress to recover from shock, and sign a few papers, to collect megacorporate welfare. Those in the second rank of megacorporations had more of a problem effectuating the principle . . . until the passage of the Bankruptcy Reform Act. From that point on, another arm of the federal government, the bankruptcy courts, would be available to insure their corporate immortality in the face of the venality, error, or incompetence of their high-priced executives. And so many more companies could be serviced at the same time!

Lee Iacocca was no less arrogant than John Riccardo, but he was blessed with a better public image. Iacocca too tried to frame the issue: "We're not asking for a handout. We're only asking for relief from excessive regulation." No matter that this position ignored the hard numbers to the effect that, not counting gas mileage regulations that actually pushed the auto producers toward higher sales, Chrysler's cost disadvantage as against General Motors due to government regulations was only about $100 per vehicle. Only later in Chrysler's long dance with Congress did Iacocca change his tune, admitting to the errors of (prior) management. Once Iacocca rolled the dice, with Chrysler shareholders' and creditors' money, he was sure they would come up right—so sure that during the many months of presentations to Congress of tense negotiations with many levels of federal officials, he traveled to Washington only twice. Once his federal-aid-or-bust position took hold, he knew that he could spend his time more profitably planning his cars of the future. From his Highland Park headquarters, he notified the Carter administration and Congress that the deadline for aid was Christmas 1979.

Overcoming all obstacles and overwhelming all details, the great bailout bandwagon steamed ahead. The Chrysler Loan Guarantee Act as passed required substantial concessions from many interest groups. The concessions required of the United Auto Workers totaled a whopping $462.5 million. Nonunion employees were assessed $125 million in concessions. Domestic lenders to Chrysler Corporation (160 banks, $1.6 billion in loans) and to Chrysler Financial Corporation (282 banks, $3.2 billion in loans) were required by Congress to make $400 million in new loans and $100 million in concessions on outstanding debt. Foreign banks were expected to contribute $150 million in concessions. Chrysler was required to use its best efforts to cut costs; raise

$300 million in asset sales; negotiate dealer and supplier concessions, totaling $180 million; acquire $250 million from municipal and state governments and the government of Canada; and issue $50 million in additional stock. In other words, Congress had fashioned a comprehensive plan of reorganization very similar to those accomplished every day under Chapter 11 of the Bankruptcy Code.

The passage of the Chrysler Loan Guarantee Act did not save Chrysler. It was only one act in what turned out to be a long-running serial on the order of the Perils of Pauline, with Chrysler frequently hanging from the proverbial cliff by its corporate fingernails.

Chrysler nearly went over the brink shortly after the passage of the bailout, when it ran out of money before the federal loan guarantees could be put in place. A frantic search for fresh cash was instituted after the federal government refused to advance funds and Chrysler's banks turned it down flat. The automaker was saved by loans of $500 million from Household Finance Company and $250 million from none other than General Motors Acceptance Corporation—just like you and me, except on a grander scale! Mitsubishi also extended $400 million in credit to allow Chrysler to purchase its subcompacts.

After Chrysler announced record losses of $1.1 billion for 1979, most of its lenders refused to go along with concessions mandated by the bailout act. Not only was the nature of the required bank concessions vague, but real inequities existed. Also, many bankers had concluded that the company was a goner anyway. As a result of the banks' unwillingness to get with the program, time dragged on and Chrysler teetered on the brink every Friday, when the payroll checks went out, with double jeopardy twice a month when checks to suppliers also went out. On several occasions Chrysler ran out of money, and a sort of rotating triage among suppliers would result, with some having to wait for their checks. In March 1980, the banks informed the Treasury Department that they would not comply with the Loan Guarantee Act.

Chrysler then executed the same maneuver with the banks that it had used on the federal government—it threatened to file a liquidation bankruptcy. It painted horrible pictures for the bankers of claims tied up for five years and impairment of interest claims during the term of the bankruptcy. It vowed to commit a lovers' suicide, taking its profitable finance arm, Chrysler Financial Corporation, with it and threatening to have the bankruptcy court consolidate the CFC and Chrysler cases and the claims against them. If Chrysler were to succeed in that, the banks that held only CFC debt would see their chances of gaining substantial repayment blown out of the water. The major American banks began to understand the concept of "equality of sacrifice" that Chrysler and Congress had been pushing.

Finally, Chrysler was able to build some momentum. Agreements for Chrysler and Chrysler Financial were hammered out with the major American banks in April 1980. Once the major lenders reached agreement with Chrysler, their voices were added to the "equality of sacrifice" chorus. Chrysler then picked off the holdouts one by one, threatening to blame each of those institutions for Chrysler's death if the bailout failed. After all, if every lender had to consent, and the big, bad federal government would not allow Chrysler to make any concessions or side deals, what banker would want to be charged with killing Chrysler? The weapon in each bank's hands became too terrible to use.

The Loan Guarantee Board approved the deal with the banks on May 10, 1980. Congress validated the board's approval shortly thereafter, with only a few senators noting that the specific terms of the entire private aid package as negotiated by Chrysler probably did not comply with the literal terms of the act.

In fact, Chrysler had not come close to fulfilling the requirements set by the Loan Guarantee Act. While the union and nonunion employees had done their fair share as required, all other interests had not. The agreement with the banks did not include any fresh loans. Chrysler had been unable to sell additional stock or as much in assets as the act mandated, or drum up any significant dealer support and concessions. Negotiations for sale of a portion of Chrysler Financial to HFC fell through. An attempt to sell the Chrysler dealers $230 million of convertible debentures, classified as "highly speculative," had been a resounding failure. (Technically, the period during which dealers could buy the debentures had been "extended indefinitely.") In effect, the legislation had been rewritten after the fact by Chrysler and its banks, and passed muster only because the Loan Guarantee Act had given the board the power to accept terms that did not comply with the mandates of the act. Only the American taxpayer and the rank and file had lived up to the bargain. Once more, no impediment—not even an act of Congress—would be allowed to stand in the way of saving a giant corporation. Lee Iacocca, the master salesman, had just made his biggest sale.

Now Chrysler had to get all the lenders to sign on the dotted line.

Achieving consents from each and every lender was an excruciating task. The little banks held out, hoping to be paid off by the big ones. The European banks held out, hoping to be paid off by the American banks. The Canadian banks, and a few small banks in the U.S., simply wanted no part of the deal. (The greater militancy of the Canadian lenders, Canadian government, and Canadian employees of Chrysler caused problems throughout Chrysler's travail.) One by one, each lender was tracked down by a Chrysler emissary and required to state its intentions—sign on to the agreement without demanding any changes or kill Chrysler. Once again the pen was at least as mighty as the sword! The score was kept in a "war room" at Manufacturers Hanover, and the troops sent out on "search and destroy" missions to the recalcitrant banks. By mid-June, eleven U.S. banks and nine foreign banks, holding about 1 percent of the total debt, had not consented to the terms, but the pressure on them by the U.S. government, state governments—Illinois had threatened to withdraw all of its funds from one bank—politicians, Chrysler dealers, union members, and the like, was too hot for them to handle. Their capitulation was none too soon, as Chrysler had been running on empty since the first of June, payments to all suppliers having totally ceased.

The logistics of actually receiving formal consent at a "closing" were daunting. The agreement was reproduced by two printing companies, at a cost of $2 million. The treasurer of Chrysler had to sign 4,000 copies. Even at this stage, Chrysler only narrowly escaped disaster when the entire mountain of paperwork had to be evacuated from the offices of Chrysler's Wall Street lawyers the night before the closing after the building caught fire. (The joke goes that at least one hundred bankers were seen fleeing the scene with cans of gasoline.) While humorous in retrospect, any delay in the closing of the deal might have caused Chrysler to shut down for lack of funds. The moment that the paperwork was completed, on June 24, 1980, Chrysler drew down on $500 million in guaranteed loans, less $13 million pocketed by its investment bankers.

Although Chrysler had succeeded in tapping into the federal treasury, it was not out of jeopardy.

The year of 1980 proved to be a disaster for the American Big Three. Due to the unsettled economy, the American auto market shrank from eleven million units annually to less than nine million, and the foreign manufacturers claimed 30 percent of it. Ford lost $1.5

billion, and even mighty General Motors lost $763 million, its first losing year since 1921. As usual, Chrysler suffered the worst, losing a stupendous $1.7 billion for the year and 1,000 of its 4,800 dealers.

The year also provided evidence that the Master Salesman could err. Chrysler finally introduced its K-car in the fall with much Iacocca hoopla. Unfortunately, there were insufficient inventories in the showroom. Furthermore, those models available were so loaded with expensive options and plush interiors that the increasingly cost-conscious American public once more said "no."

By January 1981, Chrysler was nearly out of working capital again. It was time to do what bankers call "going back to the well." The automaker asked for a $400 million drawdown on its federal line of credit.

As had happened at each stage of the federal aid, the request for the loan installment activated the critics. Whereas opponents of federal aid had only economic theory to cite when Chrysler had first made its pleas, they now had Chrysler's sorry performance in 1980 and its numerous slips to the brink to substantiate their arguments. Chrysler's sales projections had proven to be continually overoptimistic. Although most of the government's exposure had already been incurred, there were those who still suggested that it was not too late to let Chrysler die a natural death.

Even without the urging of the critics, Treasury Secretary Miller was in no mood to grant Chrysler's request. Leaving aside the not-so-minor detail that Chrysler had not achieved asset sales or dealer concessions as required, it was obvious to Miller that simply doling out more loans would not be enough to turn around the troubled automaker. More loans simply meant more money to pay back in the future. Interest rates were at obscene levels. When the new loans were combined with the principal deferrals on prior loans previously agreed to by the banks, Chrysler would continue under a crushing debt load that would come due several years down the road in huge "balloon" payments. Miller was also none too pleased with Chrysler management. Chrysler continually delayed or ignored cost-cutting measures until Treasury put the pressure on. Chrysler was sparing no expense on development of future models—the retooling for the K-car was running $600 million—while seeking the federal dole. On the other hand, to Miller the solution of allowing Chrysler to die, thus triggering the taxpayers' liabilities upon the guarantees, was politically unpalatable. Every interest group, including Chrysler, would have to sacrifice more to keep the concern going—and Miller was the one who would make it happen.

First, Miller went to work on the banks, calling a meeting with the dozen major lenders on January 10, 1981. In it, he proceeded to tell the banks what they were going to do for Chrysler. There would be no negotiations, no stalling. There were hints that the Treasury Department, and maybe the entire federal government, would not be happy with the banks if they did not consent to Miller's proposals for easing the debt load on Chrysler. The terms were: one-half of the loans would be converted to preferred stock, the other half of the debt would be subject to payment by Chrysler at thirty cents on the dollar. In all, the banks would surrender $1.3 billion in debt and receive in return $190 million in cash and stock with a face value of $1.1 billion. When Miller finished, Fed chairman Paul Volcker, a very imposing fellow, entered the meeting to continue beating on their heads. The bankers were sent running to inform their brethren.

Next, Miller demanded more concessions from the United Auto Workers. With help from Volcker at strategic moments, he set out to "persuade" the UAW to accept a wage freeze. (Volcker had his own goals. As chairman of the Fed, he felt that he was striking a blow at inflation.) When the smoke cleared—literally, in the case of Volcker's smelly cigars—the union had granted $622 million in new concessions. Having already agreed in the first round to a precedent-setting concession, that of granting Chrysler a lower wage scale than that of General Motors or Ford, in this round the union leadership grudgingly agreed to two more earthshaking events: wages would be rolled back to their level of January 1, 1981, and they would remain frozen at that level for one-and-a-half years. The average union employee would give up $1.15 per hour, and during the course of the freeze would "donate" about $14,000 to Chrysler's continued existence. (While those terms were dictated by Miller, it should be noted that the union leadership never attempted to seek any form of job security or limits on layoffs and terminations. In the long run, it would be those workers deemed expendable by Chrysler who bore the full brunt of the company's reorganization.) In return for the concessions, Miller had Chrysler set up a profit-sharing program, which must have been a bitter joke for the employees of that highly unprofitable corporation. The vote on the concessions by the union rank-and-file was rancorous, and the package was passed by only a narrow margin.

Miller continued to act upon his vision of what Chrysler needed. Salaried employees were assessed $161 million in concessions. Suppliers were informed that they had granted a 5 percent discount, resulting in a savings to Chrysler of $72 million. The Canadian government was persuaded to grant a $200 million loan guarantee, in return for Chrysler's promise to build a small research facility in Canada. Chrysler was ordered to come up with further cost reductions of $3 billion over time.

Through the force of his will, the treasury secretary truly had reorganized Chrysler's debt. Although the banks received a "sweetener" of an immediate payment of $68 million to overcome their opposition (many bankers thought that the payment was the last they would ever receive from Chrysler), the deal cut Chrysler's bank debt to very manageable proportions. The latest round had resulted in cost savings of $1 billion for Chrysler in 1981, and, because of the reduction in bank debt, $2.2 billion *for every year after that.* Thanks to Miller, Chrysler would now have lower costs than its American competitors. Its break-even point each year would be a mere 1.1 million vehicles, one-half that of 1979.

The application of the time and talent of Miller and his staff to Chrysler's financial problems carried indirect costs. Miller was required to spend about one-third of his valuable time on Chrysler problems over the course of the year that the Iranian hostage crisis raged. Miller was heavily involved with issues concerning international financial obligations to that country and the freezing of Iran's deposits in the U.S. On the last day of the Carter administration, Miller had to halt the final stages of the financial aspects of the Iranian negotiations to sign the permission for Chrysler's $400 million drawdown.

Chrysler was saved—or was it? After fees, Chrysler received $389 million, and it already owed $350 million to its suppliers. It was a much different company than had existed during the 1970s, with only one-third the employees of 1977 and a much leaner cost structure, but it still had to meet the test of the marketplace. Ford's new models were hurting Omni/Horizon sales, and, as usual, the Japanese automakers were having the Big Three for lunch. Rebates, which generated cash but hurt profits, had been the only thing keeping Chrysler going for the prior six months.

In spite of Chrysler's continuing troubles, Lee Iacocca was determined not to go back to the government for the remaining $300 million because of all the negative publicity the loan requests generated. In an interview in *Fortune,* in March 1981, he openly wished for a more convenient form of corporate welfare: "We should have a program to help big business in trouble without them having to go before the bar of the press."

Although Iacocca refused to acknowledge it, that program already was in place in the form of the federal Bankruptcy Code. Nevertheless, the federal government was about to provide Chrysler and other American corporations with bounties beyond belief.

Just when things looked the darkest for Chrysler, there rode out of the West a lone hero who not only would insure Chrysler's survival but would provide grubstakes of hundreds of millions of dollars to the Big Three. Like a true TV hero, he would offer his help gladly, without asking for anything in return. By giving his helping hand indirectly, he would avoid embarrassing the recipients. He would create the illusion that they were helping themselves and would allow them to mask the fact that they were living on the dole.

Ronald Reagan's domestic economic programs provided a financial cornucopia for American megacorporations. Tax rates were chopped. The Economic Recovery Tax Act of 1981 established shortened depreciation schedules, which allowed companies to add to their "paper" expenses each year and thus reduce taxes still further. Companies that were not profitable and therefore could not take advantage of the goodies were allowed to sell their benefits to profitable companies. Over three years, Chrysler alone took in $68.3 million on such transactions, at the taxpayer's expense.

The big score for the Big Three came on April 30, 1981, when the tremendous pressure brought to bear by the Reagan administration induced the Japanese Ministry of International Trade and Industry to state that it would "persuade" the Japanese auto manufacturers to "voluntarily" limit their sales within the United States to 1.68 million units per year for four years, with increases to come only in a 16.5 percent proportion to increases in the total U.S. auto market. Not only was the market share of the Big Three protected, but prices could be increased without fear of normal market forces. Like the aforementioned tax breaks, no sacrifices were required of the Big Three or their banks to "earn" the welfare. There would be no "equality of sacrifice" for Chrysler and its creditors and employees. All would be paid for by the American auto buyer.

The course of the "voluntary restraints" moved predictably. The Japanese automakers offered only token complaints and soon entirely made up for the decrease in the volume of sales in the American market with price increases. Rather than pass on the benefits of cost-cutting measures or try to undersell the Japanese, the Big Three jacked up prices commensurate with the increase in the prices of the Japanese-made cars. On some of the more luxurious models, Big Three prices leaped 50 percent over three years. In 1982, the Big Three together earned $6.3 billion in profits, *thirteen times* their combined 1981 profits and more than 20 percent greater than their previous record year for profits—and that was done in a shrinking U.S. market. By the third year of the restraints, American car buyers were paying more than $5 billion *per year* in the hidden tax, paid directly to the automakers.

Due to the restraints on the Japanese, Chrysler's situation by 1982 had turned around dramatically even though it continued to achieve less than a 10 percent share of the market. Awash in cash, it also raised $432 million within the first few hours of a stock offering and repaid all of the outstanding $1.2 billion in federally guaranteed loans in the summer of 1983, seven years ahead of schedule.

Chrysler executives reaped the benefits of the company's newfound prosperity. Generous raises and bonuses were the order of the day. The company repurchased a corporate jet, which the Treasury Department had forced it to sell in hard times. Stock options for the execs became increasingly valuable, as Chrysler stock price surged. There would be plenty of good work for the staff in the future, since the company was committing itself to spend $1.5 billion in 1983 alone for product research and development. As the chief, Lee Iacocca benefited the most. Although enjoying a modest salary for a CEO of "only" $365,000, by the end of 1983 Iacocca had amassed about $17 million in stock options and was promised options for 450,000 more shares if he would stay at Chrysler. Senator Proxmire had called it correctly: Lido Anthony Iacocca had become a very rich man indeed.

For the immigrants' son from Pennsylvania, there were not only the financial gain in a big salary and a briefcase full of lucrative stock options, but also the glory. Iacocca was named the most respected business executive in the United States in a poll of business leaders. He was named chairman of the high-profile commission to restore the Statue of Liberty. He was the Man Who Saved Chrysler. He was on television and in print *ad nauseam* both as part of Chrysler's ad campaigns and as one of today's Wise Men. He would soon spin his wisdom in two best-selling books. At the end of 1983, he re-upped for three years as chairman of Chrysler. Who could ask for anything more?

Once the good times were back, Lee Iacocca's antigovernment attitude came shining through. In a classic case of "what-have-you-done-for-me-lately?" Iacocca publicly asked the federal government to cancel its stock warrants rather than to exercise them and receive the premium. (Chrysler's stock was trading on the open market at a price in excess of the price that the warrants allowed the government to purchase the stock.) In fact, Iacocca was publicly *outraged* at the unfairness of it all. After all, according to The Great One, the federal government had never had any risk in guaranteeing the notes because Chrysler's assets had been pledged as collateral. Besides, the profit on the warrants amounted to usury on the loans. In effect, the argument was that governments should act only like governments, supplying aid to Big Business on demand, and should not be so immodest as to turn a buck if the venture does not end in a disaster.

Needless to say, the government ignored Iacocca's pleas, perhaps imagining such headlines as "Reagan Administration Gives Away Taxpayers' $300 Million to Big Corporation." Chrysler was more successful in its demands for interest rate concessions on bailout loans from state governments. It is easy to understand why Iacocca has not gone into politics.

Chrysler had finally outdistanced crisis. Thanks to continuing restraints on Japanese autos and a recovering economy, Chrysler earned profits of $700 million in 1983 and $2.4 billion in 1984. (In 1984, Ford earned $3 billion and GM $5 billion.) Beginning in 1983, Chrysler's annual production once more topped one million vehicles. By 1984 the company was bankable, lining up $1.1 billion of (unguaranteed) credit from fifty-eight banks. Chrysler bought a stake in Maserati and gobbled up American Motors. In 1987 and 1988, Chrysler earned more than $1 billion in profits and increased its market share; in 1988, it achieved its first double-million, selling more than a million autos and more than a million trucks.

New challenges now beset the Big Three, but the tactics learned during the lean years of the early 1980s continue to serve them well. The U.S. market continues to shrink. The Big Three are now facing increasing competition from autos made by Japanese companies that are not subject to the continuing import retraints because they are made in the U.S. In 1989, for the first time Japanese companies manufactured more than one million vehicles in the United States. The Big Three saw a sales slump in the first half of 1989. However, in response they cut costs and laid off employees with practiced ease, and so the bottom line nary suffered. For the first half of 1989, Chrysler's profit was $692 million, Ford's $3.04 billion, and General Motors' $3 billion. Under the benign eye of the federal government's antitrust division, all of the American auto companies have continued the trend of increasingly cooperating with foreign automakers. During 1989 alone, Chrysler announced joint ventures with Renault (four-wheel-drive vehicles) and Korea's Hyundai (marketing and development). There is a lot of "blood on the floor," but Chrysler, Ford, and GM have once more become successful in every sense of the word.

In spite of record profits, in mid-1989 the Big Three clamored for *more* government protection from the Japanese, asking for reclassification under the tariff laws of vans and sporty utility vehicles. In making that arcane argument, the Big Three were in effect seeking to impose a 25 percent greater tariff on those vehicles upon entry into the U.S. If the arguments are viewed with favor by the federal government, the results of such a tariff would mean a price increase of between $2,500 and $3,000 for each type of vehicle so reclassified, which will go from each purchaser's pocket directly to the bottom line of the Big Three. Guess which American company will benefit most? Guess who is leading the charge? Ever vigilant for opportunities to wrap himself in the flag, Lee Iacocca expressed his righteous indignation as a purely disinterested citizen in a letter to Treasury Secretary Nicholas Brady: "I am tired of seeing the U.S. government get flimflammed by people who want to . . . cheat the Treasury out of hundreds of millions of dollars." In a private letter to Chrysler dealers, he was more forthcoming, reminding them that a favorable ruling would result in "a $2,000 per truck cost penalty to your [Japanese] competitors."

As 1991 progresses, the Big Three are once more under seige by the Japanese automakers.

Will Chrysler remain profitable? Will Lee Iacocca wring more and varied protections out of the U.S. government? Will Lee Iacocca run for president of this great country? Stay tuned.

What are the lessons to be learned from the Chrysler saga? A series of practical and theoretical answers come to mind.

The Chrysler turnaround was a triumph of state-sponsored capitalism, but not of free-market economics. The same federal government that in the last century opened the West by giving free land to the railroad barons, and at this time is propping up the savings and loan industry, saw to it that Chrysler (and General Motors and Ford) survived and prospered. Chrysler was saved by the credit and the protection of the federal government.

Lee Iacocca is a topflight businessman, but he did not save Chrysler. To say this is not to demean his talents, his efforts, or the decisions he made during the crisis, as he was the field commander during the battle. He was an excellent crisis manager, cost cutter, and product developer at a critical time, when major errors would have meant the demise of the company. Without Iacocca, Chrysler most certainly would not have survived as a major auto manufacturer. Nevertheless, however necessary he was at this juncture in Chrysler's history, his efforts were not sufficient to turn the corporation around. An analogy can be made to Franklin Roosevelt. As President of the United States, Roosevelt probably saved U.S. capitalism through innovative programs that alleviated the harshness of the Great Depression for individuals and reformed the relationship between the federal government and businesses. However, in spite of Herculean efforts by the Roosevelt administration, it was only World War II that got the economy moving again. In spite of the leadership and talent of Lee Iacocca and the dedication of his staff, it was Treasury Secretary Miller who reorganized Chrysler, and it was Ronald Reagan who filled the coffers of the Big Three.

The federal government bore real financial and political risk in guaranteeing Chrysler loans, and the government did become enmeshed in Chrysler's fate. While there were both lofty and self-serving reasons why the Carter administration became committed to saving Chrysler, it is apparent that the government did not have accurate financial data and in the end acted out of short-term political expediency. Thus the federal bailout was vulnerable to the vagaries of the market. Despite Iacocca's protestations after the fact, the federal government would have suffered a loss had Chrysler failed and been liquidated. It is well and good to value an operating plant at $100 million, but how much will it be worth when its owner goes out of business, the industry is in a slump, and the economy is in a recession? It might have taken many years for the federal government to sell off all of Chrysler's assets, most likely at only a fraction of their book value. Of course, the media would have had a heyday had the bailout failed. Treasury Secretary Miller's extensive and time-consuming involvement with Chrysler provided good evidence for the bailout opposition: indeed, once it had reached out its hand, the federal government could not let go of the tar baby.

The cost of saving Chrysler was immense. Since only about one-half of Chrysler's 1977 employees made it through the process, in many ways they paid the most dearly, and for them the bailout was a failure. (Iacocca has admitted that most of these people found other jobs, in and out of the auto industry, a possibility he derided when Chrysler was seeking federal guarantees.) The employees who remained were required to contribute relatively substantial sums to Chrysler's continued existence. Due to federal aid tilting the playing field, many jobs saved or created at Chrysler were at the expense of those at Ford. The United Auto Workers' representation of its members and the gains that it had achieved in the past were compromised by Chrysler's voracious needs for sacrifice. The lenders, usually in the best position of any creditors, were paid only fifteen cents on the dollar two years after the onset of Chrysler's insolvency. They were fortunate to make a profit on their (unwilling) investment in Chrysler's stock. In the end, the American taxpayer and auto buyer paid billions directly and indirectly to prop up Chrysler. The *Wall Street Journal* summed up the "equality of sacrifice" as it played out in practice:

> Under government direction, the company reached into the pockets of its workers for a billion dollars, fired more than half of them anyway, forced lenders to forgive hundreds of millions of dollars in debt, and browbeat suppliers for hundreds of millions more in price concessions.

Several goals were served. Presumably, Carter did indeed "buy" some votes with the bailout. The psyche of the American people was assuaged by the continued existence of an American corporation in a high-profile industry. Chrysler was kept afloat—barely—until the wide-ranging restrictions on Japanese imports could be put into place. Some would say that Chrysler was saved so that Iacocca could achieve what he considered to be his rightful place as a titan among titans. One goal was *not* served. It is quite possible that Americans would have been better off economically had Chrysler died in 1979.

As to the issue of bankruptcy (first posed by Shakespeare as "to b. or not to b.?"), Iacocca was wrong, but it did not much matter. Nothing was done during the bailout that could not have been done by Chrysler under Chapter 11 reorganization proceedings. In Chapter 11, Chrysler could have received the federal loan guarantees, enforced "equality of sacrifice" (with the help of the heavy hand of the federal government), and issued stock and warrants to sweeten the deal. In spite of Iacocca's disingenuous public statements about bankruptcy, especially his failure to separate Chapter 11 reorganization from a liquidation bankruptcy, the company could have continued with its new product development and otherwise kept control over its operations. After the fact, the *Wall Street Journal* observed that "without even admitting it, [Iacocca] has presided over what amounts to one of the biggest bankruptcy reorganizations in American history." It is hard to believe that Chrysler could have suffered any worse publicity in Chapter 11 than it did outside of it, and Iacocca was denied the opportunities to give the classic Chapter 11 pitch to customers and suppliers: *we filed Chapter 11 to show our commitment to saving the company.* Had Chrysler's problems come a few years later, after other large corporations had successfully tested the Chapter 11 waters, Iacocca most likely would have jumped at the chance to file. Chrysler was able to overcome the stigma of bankruptcy, whether declared or not.

In the final analysis, the overriding lesson of Chrysler is that the federal government will not allow a large American corporation to fail, whether it takes direct financial aid, indirect tax breaks, outright protectionism, or the existence of a user-friendly bankruptcy code and federal bankruptcy court standing at the ready.

Chapter 5

The Chairman

Paul Volcker, the former chairman of the Federal Reserve System, likes to tell this story. It seems that a gentleman visited a pet store for the purpose of purchasing a parrot. Three parrots were sitting in cages. Upon inquiry, the storekeeper advised the customer that the birds were, respectively, $100, $200, and $10,000. When the customer asked why the third bird was so valuable, the storekeeper replied, "I do not know the details, but the other birds call him 'Chairman.' "

The Chairman looked across the country from his seat of power and saw that things were not good. After a short lull engineered by the previous leader during his futile reelection campaign, Inflation, the Beast That Could Not Be Killed, once more had broken loose and was raging throughout the land. The populace had lost the will to fight the Inflation Beast. In fact, because all the citizens of the realm expected Inflation to continue its ravages, they had lost their inhibitions and were reveling in the nation's shops even though that meant paying tribute to the Shylocks at levels formerly reserved for debts to the Devil.

The Chairman knew that none of the people's representatives would dare to challenge the dragon, for that would require commitment and risk, and they were weak. The new President was powerful enough to urge sacrifice, but he cared little for the matter; in fact, he had put his faith in voodoo. Who would save the citizens from the scourge of Inflation?

The Chairman knew in his soul that he was the only person who could save the country from the Inflation Beast. He had the will, and he was certain that he knew what was best for the people of the land. And his powers were great because to be Chairman is to have mythical and mystical powers. With a wave of his hand (and the rubber stamp of his council), he could flood the country with riches, or he could cause the wealth available to the people to nearly disappear. Further, as has happened on occasion in history, the appointed advisor had quietly become more powerful on matters within his mastery than was his overlord. Because of his President's disinterest in formulating a strategy to war upon Inflation and the President's willingness to allow the Chairman to solve it as he saw fit, the Chairman prepared to call up all his mighty power for the battle.

The Chairman had not been chosen by the people. There are no elections for that Olympian seat, for its ways have a magic that mere mortals do not comprehend. The Chairman particularly was to be revered, for he had been anointed by a President of one political persuasion and would be reappointed by that President's successor from the opposite end of the spectrum. Truly, he was above politics and above appeasing even his President. The Chairman would see the new administration's reverence for him turn to revilement and the sins of the new administration visited upon his head, and he would receive many missives from the citizenry complaining about his policies, but none had the power to force him to cease his ways. The mantle of the Chairman rested lightly on his shoulders, in spite of his awesome ability to affect the lives of virtually the entire citizenry and their seeming disapproval of his policies.

In facing the Herculean task at hand, the Chairman was not afraid. He was confident of his abilities as an interpreter of the Oracles of the Dismal Science and that he knew what was best for the private barons and the baronets of the minor establishments, as well as the general populace. He was not afraid to see those fall by the wayside who were not strong enough to be led from the ways of Inflation, for the goal was to help the many. Certain of the way, he would hold his head high in the face of the contumely of the people.

This is the story of the Chairman and his battle with the dragon, which raged in every corner of the land and reverberated in every corner of the known world for years.

The United States reeled out of the 1970s and staggered into 1980.

In January 1980, President Carter and his Council of Economic

Advisors painted a cheerless picture of the U.S. economy for Congress. The reports noted the 13 percent "official" inflation rate for 1979 and warned that there was a significant danger of that figure being topped in 1980 amid a likely recession. The administration promoted the increasingly popular notion that the "underlying inflation rate"—the rate of inflation locked into the structure of the economy, which cannot be diminished by ordinary fiscal or monetary policies—had increased inexorably during the 1970s. Accordingly, the President advised, there were no "economic miracles waiting to be performed.... Inflation has been building in our country for a decade and a half, and it will take many years of persistent effort to bring it back down." Also, Jimmy Carter acknowledged a problem that Richard Nixon had recognized in the early Seventies: unless and until the American people became convinced that runaway inflation was being halted, they would make it *worse* by projecting it into their plans and building it into their financial transactions.

Indeed, the first year of the new decade proved to be every bit as punishing as the previous year. Just as Richard Nixon had done, Jimmy Carter would take the American people on an election year roller coaster ride. This time the peaks would be higher and the ride scarier.

By spring 1980, business was slumping badly. During the second quarter, the economy declined at an annualized rate of 9.1 percent, the steepest drop since demobilization at the conclusion of World War II. In midyear, the prime rate touched the 20 percent mark, insuring that no company requiring financing could earn a profit. (Remember that most small and mid-sized businesses pay higher interest to lenders than do their "prime" customers like General Motors and IBM. Many small companies pay 3 to 5 percent over the prime rate.) Carter responded to the Russian invasion of Afghanistan by canceling a $2.6 billion wheat/grain/soybean contract with the USSR, and millions of farmers learned the cost of having a national conscience when farm prices collapsed. Oil prices continued a steep climb, hitting an incredible $40 per barrel by midyear. In 1980, foreign-made autos would attain 27 percent of the American market.

Japan showed no interest in letting the United States get up from the mat. The Japanese automakers captured 21 percent of the U.S. auto market in 1980. The United States' bilateral trade deficit with Japan climbed to $10.4 billion for 1980 and showed no signs of peaking.

Amaya Nashiro, a high MITI official, observed: "The pre-oil-shock era was the age of Pax Americana.... After the oil shock, all this changed." That was not too bold a statement from a representative of a country that was required to import virtually 100 percent of its oil and yet had found ways to grow and prosper in the face of OPEC's actions.

Following in the tradition of Richard Nixon, during Jimmy Carter's election campaign against Ronald Reagan, federal money controls were loosened and the prime rate dipped to 11 percent, which seemed like "free money" under the economic conditions of the day. For a period of several months before the November elections, the economy did not appear to be in crisis, but, of course, that was a temporary illusion. The roller coaster soon would be climbing as if under rocket power.

In November, after the ballot boxes had been emptied, the laws of economics once more applied and the Federal Reserve System was forced to tighten the cord on the federal money bag. By mid-December 1980, the prime rate hit 21.5 percent. OPEC raised its prices by 10 percent to cover the devaluation of the dollar through inflation, thus further adding to inflation as gasoline prices hit $1.30 a gallon at the pump. (By this time there was no question that by having so much cash reserves—Libya alone had $13 billion—the Arab OPEC countries were immune to countervailing pressures.)

Every time the prime rate soared and inflation reared its ugly head, an increasing number of individuals and businesses threw in the towel. In 1980, 303,736 individuals filed Chapter 7 bankruptcy petitions, in which their consumer debts were wiped out. Theoretically those bankruptcy debtors were required to turn over their assets in return for relief from their creditors. However, in practice, generous exemptions created by the code allowed most families to keep their personal assets, including their homes if mortgage payments were maintained; and so the code encouraged people with heavy debt loads to cast them aside in bankruptcy. Chapter 13 filings, by which consumers try to reorganize their debt payments rather than liquidate their assets as in Chapter 7, totaled 106,693. Business failures—liquidations—already up 14 percent in 1979 from the year before, surged an additional 53 percent in 1980. Business Chapter 7 cases, which represent only a fraction of the companies that closed their doors, totaled 46,651 in 1980.

Of course, Big Oil was doing just fine. All buyers pay for oil in U.S. dollars, the international currency, and those dollars earned high interest rates within the United States. During 1980, the dollar would strengthen, making oil more expensive for Europe even when barrel prices did not rise. OPEC received all the nasty publicity for price raises, but the Seven Sisters saw to it that their profit margins expanded, too.

Big Oil suffered an embarrassment of riches when the Securities and Exchange Commission mandated an accounting change for the benefit of investors. In order for the balance sheets of the oil companies to accurately reflect their assets, the SEC began to require them to value their reserves upward to reflect the increased price of oil. As a result, the oil companies' exploration and production profits shot up spectacularly. Exxon's pretax exploration and production profit, valued at $4.6 billion in 1979, became $23.4 billion. Mobil's went from $3 billion to $17 billion; Gulf, $2.4 billion to $12.7 billion; Texaco, $2 billion to $7.6 billion, and so on. While the revaluation did not create additional operating profits, it indicated how understated oil company size had been in the past and highlighted the immense assets that the oil companies hold.

The benefits of the new Bankruptcy Code, so clear to overburdened consumers and their bankruptcy lawyers, were not so obvious to businesses seeking to reorganize. A number of bankruptcy attorneys and financial advisors clung to the conventional wisdom that any sort of bankruptcy filing is the death knell for a company since its customers will abandon it, and its credit will dry up. Among those counseling out-of-court solutions was J. Ronald Trost, a Los Angeles bankruptcy lawyer who persuaded Chrysler's banks that that argument was true. The *Wall Street Journal* surveyed the scene and concluded that "legal experts say vagueness of the new codes [sic] and lack of court precedents are two reasons, but the major deterrent is a fear by companies that some of the protection they had under Chapter 11 has been eroded." The realities of the 1980s marketplace and the mounting experience under the Bankruptcy Code would soon prove how outmoded was the conservative viewpoint. It would turn out that the only thing that big corporations had to fear from bankruptcy was fear itself.

In 1980, the rallying cry for business was the usual: "get Uncle to help us." The bailouts of the 1970s certainly provided precedent. Chrysler's success in achieving $1.5 billion in federal loan guarantees was a shining beacon. If Chrysler could make it onto the federal dole, why not Ford or International Harvester or Remington Rand or Saxon Industries or . . . all of them?

The rationalizations and proposals for tapping into the national treasury began to float out of the business community. The capper was offered by Felix G. Rohatyn, a prominent investment banker and chairman of the Mutual Assistance Corporation, which had been formed to save New York City. Never one to think small, Mr. Rohatyn proposed nothing less than the revival of the Depression-era Reconstruction Finance Corporation. The reborn agency would back loans to businesses, funded by $5 billion from the federal treasury as well as a tax on profitable companies. It in turn would be backed by $10 billion in government loan guarantees. Rohatyn echoed the sentiments of Lee Iacocca perfectly when he defended his grand plan by observing that it would be preferable to "a number of large companies at the same time . . . stumbling around from congressional committee to congressional committee seeking a bailout." In other words, Rohatyn proposed that federal corporate welfare be formally established and then turned over to a semiprivate agency so that the goodies could be disbursed quietly.

The proposals for a more organized form of government largess did not catch on. Because of the dismal state of the economy, the ramifications of formal corporate welfare simply were too overwhelming for Congress to face. For ideological reasons, the incoming Reagan administration could not sponsor the creation of yet another federal agency. (The Reagan administration soon would hand huge subsidies to businesses through tax cuts, changes in depreciation rates, and the restraints upon the Japanese automakers.) In fact, although it was not advertised, Congress had already done its part by enacting the Bankruptcy Reform Act of 1978. The nation's executives would have to follow the clues to discover that new form of corporate welfare.

One clue for the troubled businesses was the slant of the new Bankruptcy Code. In spite of the many open questions about it, well-advised executives were learning of its favorable aspects. The *sine qua non* of business's interest in Chapter 11 was the fact that the Bankruptcy Code had dropped the old act's requirement of a court-appointed trustee in large corporate cases, allowing management to continue to run the company as a "debtor-in-possession." Thus management could feel secure that it would not be replaced—the executives' paychecks would keep on coming while the creditors waited for their due. Further, in Chapter 11, management would gain leverage in dealing with the creditors, since the new code did not allow secured creditors to march into court and repossess their collateral. They would have to wait for the debtor's Plan of Reorganization to resolve their claims, just like the unsecured creditors. The period of 120 days—which could be extended by the presiding judge—during which the Chapter 11 company alone could propose a Plan of Reorganization further shielded the company. It certainly looked like the new ingredients of the Bankruptcy Code provided a recipe for tight control of a Chapter 11 case by a powerful corporate debtor.

Close analysis of the Bankruptcy Code and its history revealed that it had added only one weapon to the secured creditor's arsenal. As a sop to the secured lending industry (banks, finance companies, and insurance companies), no Chapter 11 company with substantial assets pledged for loans could expend *one penny* of its funds without the entry of an order that provided for protection of the lender's collateral and, if the situation warranted it, some continuing periodic payments to the lender for the use of the collateral. According to the strict terms of the Bankruptcy Code, unless such a "cash collateral order" were entered almost contemporaneously with the commencement of the Chapter 11 case, the debtor company would be unable to operate its business and almost certainly it would fail. That provision, giving the opportunity to oppose a debtor's ability to spend money to operate, at first caused a good deal of apprehension on the part of chief executives and their corporate counsel.

Soon it became clear that in practice the judges would not strictly enforce the Draconian measure, which was akin to providing the death penalty for a parking meter violation. In the ordinary Chapter 11 case, they were most reluctant to impose corporate capital punishment—to utterly destroy a company before it had a chance to rehabilitate itself. In a megacorporate Chapter 11, it turned out that the chance of that provision being wielded successfully by a secured creditor was close to zero. The code itself provided an escape hatch: if the debtor and the secured lender could not reach agreement on a cash collateral order, the judge could enter an order that he considered appropriate *even over the objections of the secured creditor.* Accordingly, a bank going for the jugular could find itself on the defensive in front of a judge inclined to help the debtor. It could become the victim of a cash collateral order that actually favored the Chapter 11 company, such as by providing that the debtor need not make any payments on the secured loan during the bankruptcy. Another tactic employed by judges was that, if pressed, they would enter a "temporary" cash collateral order to avoid forfeiture of the company's business and give the debtor company a chance to negotiate a better deal for itself. Others simply looked the other way if a consensual order was not sought immediately upon the filing of the case, thus allowing the business technically to operate outside the law. So much for secured creditor power in Chapter 11 cases.

Corporate Chapter 11 debtors soon learned to turn the requirement of a cash collateral order into an offensive weapon, not against their lenders but rather against the hapless unsecured creditors. The company would allow its bank to improve its position *vis-à-vis* creditors lower on the hierarchy through terms in the cash collateral order that were favorable to the lender. For example, the order might contain a provision irrevocably recognizing the secured creditor's claim in the full amount, thus canceling the requirement that the lender prove all of the technicalities of its claim. Not only did that save the lender time and money, but errors in the lender's perfection of its security interest and questions about how it figured the amount due, both matters that could allow more money to flow through to unsecured creditors, would be buried forever. The order might assign the secured creditor more of the Chapter 11 company's assets as collateral, thereby diminishing the amount of unencumbered assets that would be available to unsecured creditors in the event of liquidation and cooling any ardor on their part for such an outcome.

Why would a Chapter 11 company agree to such a reshuffling of the creditor deck? In return for its concessions to the secured creditor, the Chapter 11 company would gain the goodwill of its most important creditor and acquire a commitment by the lender for secured financing during the bankruptcy—a win-win outcome for them paid for by the unsecured creditors. In the bankruptcy business their agreement is called a "sweetheart" deal because they come into court seeking the cash collateral order practically holding hands.

Once the deal is struck, the Chapter 11 company and its bank then race into court to get the judge's signature on their sweetheart order. If they are fast enough, they can get the order entered by the judge before the other creditors can get organized and oftentimes before they even are notified of the existence of the bankruptcy! One would think that this type of collusion behind the backs of the other creditors would be illegal. However, much to the consternation of unsecured creditors, neither the Bankruptcy Code nor the attendant Bankruptcy Rules prohibited it in the early 1980s, and challenges to orders entered in this fashion usually were to no avail. When the potential for abuse dawned on the judiciary, some judges refused to make those orders final until the other creditors at least had a chance to express their opinions; however, many judges took a justice-is-blind attitude.

Of course, the maneuvering for favorable terms was more important in the small cases, where there actually was a possibility that a bank might close down a company. Many lenders successfully refused to agree to allowing small companies to use cash collateral in Chapter 11, and most flatly refused to provide additional financing necessary to keep the company going during the reorganization cases. However, in the megacases the Chapter 11 companies prevailed in virtually every aspect covered by a cash collateral order, the main negotiations being concentrated on the cost of additional financing during the case. No one wanted the responsibility of putting the last bullet into a big company, no matter how badly it had already shot itself up.

For the executive facing his company's financial problems, filing a Chapter 11 case must have been highly unpalatable at first thought. Some efforts would be made to acquire concessions from creditors, including the company's lenders, in a piecemeal fashion, but each would be suspicious that it had been singled out as "soft." Then word of the company's payment problems would start circulating through its suppliers' sales offices. Soon dealing with the lenders and the suppliers would start becoming a nuisance. With management becoming more and more distracted by creditors, the idea of *turning the tables* on them and *making them pay* for the company's financial restructuring would begin to look like a better idea. In fact, Chapter 11 began to look like a great move for a skilled executive. Once again, the best defense would turn out to be a bold offense. During the depression of the early Eighties, no executives jumped from windows out of shame. They chose instead to march boldly into bankruptcy court, head held high, for a big score.

How had this country come to the point where bankruptcy, even under relatively improved terms, became a serious option for thousands upon thousands of companies? The answer had a great deal to do with the Federal Reserve System and the chairman of its board of governors.

The majority of American businesses certainly needed some form of relief because, just as the inflation/interest-rate roller coaster appeared to be headed spaceward, the Federal Reserve System had slammed on the emergency brakes. The "Fed" did not intend merely to slow the roller coaster. It did not want to gently bring it back downhill. Its goal was nothing less than to throw the train entirely *off the tracks* and onto level ground, and the Fed would not let go of the brakes until that was done. Some would call that a kamikaze mission with the American people strapped onboard. Many, many companies would not survive the crash.

Technically, the Federal Reserve System was administered by a board of seven governors, one of which was appointed as chairman by the President of the United States. Technically, that board operated by majority vote and independently of any other agency or department of the government. However, as a practical and historical matter, the chairman of the board dominated and controlled the Fed's actions, and he in turn was sensitive and responsive to the wishes of the White House. In this manner, the nonpolitical views of the gnomes at the Fed were tempered by the politics of the White House, and vice versa.

When it came time to demonstrate financial restraint to the American people, recent American presidents had not been a positive influence. While the goal of the economy train should be a smooth, safe and boring ride, the chief engineers of the Sixties and Seventies had created a wild ride by turning up the power at the wrong times. To Johnson, Nixon, Ford, and Carter, taking responsibility for slowing the inflation train was more painful than allowing it to run amuck, and each had stepped on the accelerator when the revelers had complained that they were not having fun anymore. The Federal Reserve managers, serving as the firemen-brakemen on the train, had acted under the influence of those presidents and along with them, thereby accentuating the fluctuations in the economy.

At the turn of the decade, there were no obvious clues that the Fed would act differently during the Reagan years than it had during prior administrations. Under the direction of Paul A. Volcker, the chairman of the board of governors appointed by Jimmy Carter in 1979, the Fed had dutifully stoked the economy during Carter's unsuccessful reelection campaign. Subsequent to the balloting, Volcker had started to talk tough about attacking inflation, but that kind of talk had been heard before. All agreed that inflation had been sapping the economic vitality of the United States since the Vietnam Police Action, but no one had actually done anything meaningful about it because of the negative political consequences—most Americans liked belt tightening even less than police actions. So, even if Volcker were serious, would Ronald Reagan, Mr. Nice Guy, ignore the screams of his countrymen caused by Volcker's heavy hand and not rein in his chairman? Could an unelected official such as Volcker blithely ignore the political repercussions of his actions? All would depend upon the particular chemistry of Reagan and Volcker. The attitude of President Reagan towards the economic aspects of running the country would be of prime importance.

Apparently, he had none. Anyone who campaigns on the platform of increasing defense spending, lowering taxes, *and* balancing the budget cannot have too firm a grasp of the laws of economics (although, given the ineffectual economic policies of his immediate predecessors, accomplishing two out of three as president ain't bad!). What Ronald Reagan understood of economic matters could have fit into a thimble, with room left over for a finger. Just as the country paid for the economic fallout of the Johnson-Vietnam years during the entire 1970s, during the decade of the Nineties we will be paying the huge bills coming due from the economic fiascos and excesses of the Reagan era: $500 billion bailouts of the savings-and-loan industry, a trillion dollar borrowing habit, and losses on "junk" bond investments in an as-yet-undetermined amount, to name a few. However, when it came to saving the country from the raging, seemingly uncontrollable, dragon of inflation, Ronald Reagan's ignorance would serve the country well for it would allow Paul Volcker to work his magic.

In stark contrast to Ronald Reagan, Paul Volcker was an acknowledged expert in national and international economics and finance.

Volcker's career could not have prepared him better to direct the nation's monetary policy. His education was impressive: Princeton, Harvard, and the London School of Economics. His practical education began at the New York branch of the Federal Reserve System, where he worked as a research assistant during summer vacation from graduate school. After graduation, he returned there as a money market researcher. He so distinguished himself that Chase Manhattan Bank snatched him away for their own staff of economists. Beginning in 1962, he began living the life of the highly competent technocrat, alternating stints as an international banker with posts at the Treasury Department. In 1979, he was serving as the head of the Federal Reserve Bank of New York when he was called once more to Washington, this time by President Carter, to sit at the pinnacle of the federal banking system.

Once placed in the driver's seat, Volcker was not shy about working the controls. Anxious to break with the Fed's recent ineffectual past, Volcker radically changed its mode of intervention into the money markets almost immediately upon his appointment as chairman. In doing so, he indelibly placed his stamp on the Federal Reserve System, although the full implications of that change were not immediately obvious.

When Volcker was named chairman, the Fed was still using its time-honored form of intervention into the money markets. The Fed affected the interest rates of the country directly, by setting the "federal funds rate" that banks are allowed to charge each other. In the good old days, prior to 1965, when interest rates hovered around 4 percent and barely moved from year to year, there was little chance that the rate decreed by Fed fiat would be challenged by outside "market" pressures. When the Fed nudged the rate one way or the other, the money market was sure to follow. However, Volcker noticed that the traditional methods were not producing the desired effects and apparently had not been for some time. The market seemed unresponsive to the Fed's interest rate manipulations in the fall of 1979. In fact, it seemed to be ignoring the Fed, unimpressed with the agency's power.

Volcker became determined to, as he put it, get the ATTENTION of the market. In effect he decided to put our money where his mouth was—from that point forward, the Fed would follow standard monetary theory that mainline economists believed was correct but that the Fed had not followed in practice. Starting in October 1979, through its daily buying and selling of massive amounts of securities (including U.S. treasury bills), the Fed began to attempt to control the *money supply;* interest rates were set free, to be set by the open market for credit.

Volcker was not just tinkering with the controls. The goal of the Fed's manipulation of the money supply was to beat inflation. It was clear from the basic theory of supply and demand that if the Fed started soaking up money (thus moving it outside the economy), interest rates—the price of money—would rise. Insofar as high interest rates were associated with inflation, the Fed's action would not be a direct cure. Rather, the theory was that high rates would cool the ardor of businesses and consumers for credit, thus causing business activity to decline, thus lowering prices. In effect Volcker's Fed began to suck up a portion of the nation's money supply and to lock it in the Fed's vaults. It would keep its heavy hand on the financial brake, following a "tight money" policy religiously throughout 1981.

Volcker's remedy for the nation's economic ills did not have the full support of its intellectual and political leaders. Economics is the bane of politicians' existence because its elegant theories rarely seem to match real life fully, and Volcker's program suffered accordingly. To Volcker, monetary policy was the muse. To his many critics, it was the will-of-the-wisp.

There was disagreement over whether slamming on the brakes was called for. Inflation ordinarily occurs when an economy is working nearly to capacity and the producers of goods or services are forced to bid against each other for the limited available supplies of materials and workers. Cooling the economy decreases the competition for scarce resources and brings prices down. However, since the later stages of the Vietnam Police Action, the American economy had managed to achieve high interest rates amid a sluggish economy— "stagflation." It was not clear that driving interest rates higher and further damaging business activity was the proper course of action even under classic monetarist theory. Many knowledgeable people argued for an *increase* in the money supply, in order to stimulate the economy and lower interest rates to a level that people could afford and that would allow businesses to make a profit. Under that theory, lower interest rates would moderate inflation by making the cost of doing business and running a home, that is, the cost of credit, lower.

To many, Volcker's course was heartless as well as wrong. Volcker's policies were sure to cause financial hardship, bankruptcies, business liquidations, and ruined lives. What was more important, helping the economy and the people and businesses that comprised it or tilting at the inflation that President Carter had said had become a part of modern life? As the Fed continued to drive interest rates ever higher, the criticisms of Volcker's policies became more shrill. For example, a tart critique of Volcker's views appeared in *Washington Monthly* in an issue with the chairman's face on the cover, eyes closed, bearing the caption "Wake Me When the Recession is Over."

If you believe, as monetarists do, that reducing the growth in the money supply is the only way to stop inflation, then you also tend to believe that this same money supply was itself the only *cause* of inflation. Both ideas are equally daffy.... So that brings us back to the same old bottom-line answer to inflation that, rhetoric aside, always comprised monetarist and Republican positions: start a recession. The shameful thing is that this has become not just the favored way, but the *only* way of assaulting inflation. The arsenal of the Fed was left to blast away all alone. Volcker, so proud of his toughness, so noble looking if you happen to still have a job, somehow made a virtue of shutting down the economy.

To Volcker, the critics were missing a major point. Under his leadership, the Fed had not just signed on to cool inflation a few points. Because the expectation of inflation had become so ingrained in the perceptions and plans of Americans, it was necessary to thoroughly squelch it—*to knock it all the way back down to historical levels*. To Paul Volcker, to fail to do so would mean staying on an ever-rising roller coaster as people built tomorrow's round of price increases into today's calculations of wages and prices, until the system fell apart in a crash that would destroy the fabric of the entire economy. Under the existing conditions of inflation-expectation, to ease up on the brake when the rate of acceleration began to diminish would send a signal that further inflation could be expected, thus kicking in inflation expectations once more.

Viewed in that light, Volcker was on a self-assigned mission of historic significance. He alone would be responsible for straightening the economic framework of the United States, a job that Walter Heller, a widely known economist and the former chief economic advisor to President Kennedy, likened to "sobering up a drunk after a ten-year binge." Of course, Volcker understood the dangers. As he put it in an interview: "You can do all the sensible technical things, but if you can't persuade the marketplace of your long-term intentions and resolve, you've failed. But how do you persuade the marketplace without killing the economy in the process?" Whether Volcker would go down in history as the savior of America or the Don Quixote of inflation remained to be seen, but one thing was for sure: there was going to be a lot of blood on the floor before the mission was over.

As the Fed yanked the country's purse strings tight during 1980 and 1981, with a hiatus in the months before the presidential election, the first major effect of the program was the steep rise in interest rates. By spring 1980, the prime rate had surged over 20 percent. After dropping to 11 percent before the voting, in mid-December 1980 it hit an astounding 21.5 percent, and during 1981, it hovered in the 16 to 20 percent range. It was estimated that almost half of the profits of American corporations were going to pay interest. Business and consumer bankruptcies climbed with the interest rates. In 1980, there were twice as many bankruptcies filed than in the one-year period immediately prior to the installation of the new Bankruptcy Code. (During the Eighties, individuals and companies would continue to file bankruptcies at twice the rate of the Seventies.)

True to predictions, the economy went into a tailspin. Retailers, home builders, and auto dealers faced a double-whammy: not only do they depend upon financing nearly all of their inventories, but their customers were being scared off by their own high interest rates. Sales of American-made autos fell to the lowest level in twenty years, and more than three thousand dealers closed their doors. Like putting a cement life preserver around a struggling swimmer, Volcker's policy was countervailing to the government's bailout of Chrysler, and Lee Iacocca was not shy about commenting. Housing construction dropped to a level not seen since the middle of World War II. Many businesses closed their doors forever. Governmental units could not afford the financing costs of public projects, further wounding the construction industry. Farmers found that food processors were economizing to diminish the effects of high interest rates at just the time that the farmer needed every penny of sales to pay their loan carrying-charges. In 1981 the bankruptcy court clerks logged in 326,276 consumer Chapter 7s; 129,053 consumer Chapters 13s; and 48,655 business Chapter 7s. Chapter 11 filings reached 11,370 in 1980, about five times the yearly average during the 1970s; and in 1981 that figure would double.

As the Volcker policy wreaked havoc on the economy, the screams of the populace were beginning to drown out the debate. Builders were sending Volcker blocks of wood from unsold homes. Members of Congress, besieged by frantic business people and other constituents, made the appropriate angry statements blaming the Fed for the country's economic ills. Senator Jake Garn (Republican, Utah) voiced the concerns of many when he wondered "if the Fed realizes what is going on around the country." Senate Majority Leader Howard Baker (Republican, Tennessee) was more blunt. "It is time for the Fed to give us a little air, to get its foot off the nation's neck and give the economy an opportunity to recover." Representative Henry Gonzalez (Democrat, Texas) called for Volcker's impeachment. Paul Volcker certainly had gotten the country's attention! Nevertheless, when *U.S. News and World Report* asked leaders in thirty fields to name the most influential Americans, Paul Volcker ranked behind only Ronald Reagan.

The Reagan administration distanced itself from Volcker. Treasury Secretary Donald Regan publicly castigated Volcker in testimony before Congress and in the press. President Reagan did not criticize Volcker directly, but he did make his displeasure known by refusing to commit himself to reappointing Volcker as chairman of the Fed when the latter's term ended in 1983. The administration also had a beef with the chairman insofar as it was a borrower. Reagan era deficits of more than $100 billion per year would have to be funded through massive sales of treasury bills, and the Fed was driving up the interest rates that the federal government had to pay. (Actually the Reagan administration should have thanked Volcker for damping the appetite for credit of the business sector, which after all competed with the government for banks' investment funds.)

Although preferring to work behind the scenes, Paul Volcker did not remain silent in the face of criticism from the Reagan administration. He asserted the ultimate defense, one that could not be disproved: that even if the Fed had not followed such a restrictive course, interest rates still would have risen and the economy would have become just as bad. In fact, he engaged in a bit of a counterattack by publicly complaining that the administration was harming the fight against inflation through its fiscal policies. To Volcker, the benefits of the Fed's monetary belt tightening were being offset by the federal government's huge deficits, which not only poured money into the economy but also sent the country a message that it was all right to follow spendthrift ways. The message that Volcker felt that he must send loud and clear was that if the federal government overspent, the Fed simply would put on the brakes that much harder.

Ultimately, the proof of the pudding is in the taste, and Volcker would have had better public relations had the Fed's maneuvering produced unequivocal results. However, control of the money supply of a huge, complex economy is hardly an exact science, and glitches kept popping up. One problem is that there is a lively debate among economists on what forms of near-money are sufficiently liquid enough to be termed "money." For reasons that not even the chairman could explain, some months the money supply apparently took off of its own accord. Large gyrations could not be fully explained. Were people shifting money from savings accounts (not "money") to interest-bearing NOW checking accounts ("money")? Were they finding cash in their mattresses? The Fed lamely blamed unnamed "seasonal" fluctuations. Some economists suggested that the Fed's inability to properly handle the ingredients of Volcker's recipe required that the Fed get out of that kitchen.

But Paul A. Volcker could take the heat. The greater the criticism—inflationary thinking, in Volcker's view—the more he dug in his heels to show the Fed's resolve, proving once again that one person's stubbornness is another person's policy. And *something was happening.* For the last three months of 1981, prices rose at an annualized rate of only 5.3 percent. For January 1982, that figure dropped to 3.2 percent. For the entire year of 1982, the rise in the nation's Consumer Price Index would be 5 percent, high by historical standards but a relief at the time.

The disease of inflation was being whipped, but had the patient lost too much blood to recover? Business failures during the first half of 1982 ran 45 percent ahead of the same period of 1981 and exceeded the total failures for *all* of 1980! The week ending June 15 saw the highest rate of business failures since 1932, while Congress debated whether to back bailouts and home mortgage interest subsidies. The failures continued at the same level during the second half of 1982; business Chapter 7 filings for the year would total 64,467. (Remember, that number does not include businesses that simply shut their doors and handed the keys to their banks without a court-supervised liquidation.) By the year's end, unemployment would stand at a whopping 11 percent. In gross numbers, the wreckage matched the worst period of the Great Depression.

The pervasiveness of the devastation also was impressive. It was no surprise that the small, highly leveraged businesses such as auto dealers and home builders had led the way in 1980. Retailers were a large part of the jump in business failures in 1981. In 1982, wholesalers and manufactures were at the front of the march to oblivion. U.S. copper mines were operating at 55 percent of capacity. The airline industry, in the midst of fare wars, was losing money at the rate of half a billion dollars a quarter. The hiatus in home construction hurt forest products companies, appliance makers, and steel fabricators (who also were hurt by the auto slump). Considering that the average size of the businesses that failed was steadily growing, the scope of the financial debacle that was the Volcker "Recession"—really a depression—was enormous.

U.S. BANKRUPTCY COURT
FILINGS—1980–1983

Year	Chapter 7	Chapter 11	Chapter 13	Total
1980				
Business	46,651	7,403	6,708*	60,762
Consumer	303,736		106,693	410,429
1981				
Business	48,655	11,370	7,956	67,981
Consumer	326,276		129,053	455,329
1982				
Business	64,467	22,057	11,924	98,448
Consumer	306,574		140,082	446,656
1983				
Business	50,519	24,297	9,802	84,618
Consumer	284,571		125,544	410,115
Total	1,431,449	65,127	537,762	2,034,338

* Some small "mom and pop" businesses qualified to use the simplified procedures of Chapter 13, normally considered to be for wage-earner reorganizations, for their business reorganizations.

(For comparison purposes:
Chapter X and Chapter XI
1974   2,334
1975   3,695)

On the other hand, megacorporations were not closing their doors. Although small businesses found themselves in impossible binds, big companies had room to maneuver. They had access to substantial credit, the ability to sell subsidiaries and divisions to raise cash, and the size to absorb the effects of closing units and stores. Employees were expendable. The sheriff would not be out to repossess the furniture in the corporate headquarters. The major companies could roll with the economic conditions. Essentially, the problem of megacorporations was how to ride out the storm in the most profitable, or least unprofitable, way. For many corporate executives, the smart move was to squeeze the creditors and clean up the balance sheet through a Chapter 11.

In 1983, the economy started climbing out of its sickbed. It was still weak, very weak, and would not be truly back on its feet for some time. Consumer bankruptcies and business liquidations decreased slightly from 1982's peak, but Chapter 11s rose another 10 percent. The Fed faced the delicate task of allowing the money supply to expand and interest rates to drop, without getting business *too* excited about it.

Interest rates stubbornly hovered around 11 percent, which was considered too high to fuel a strong recovery, and would go down no further. As soon as industry had sensed that the Fed was loosening the purse strings, its interest in credit had been renewed. Another factor buoying interest rates was Uncle Sam. The United States was in the credit markets in a *big* way, financing what would turn out to be an incredible $200-plus billion deficit for the year. Although as an economist Volcker was horrified at the reckless fiscal policies of the federal government—and he said so publicly—in private perhaps he was a bit pleased that Uncle Sam's needs helped maintain interest rates at a level that would damp any tendencies in the economy to heat up to the point where inflation would be rekindled.

Indeed, it appeared that business had been duly sobered by the Volcker Recession/Depression. There was no mad rush to rebuild inventories from their bare-bones levels. Even with oil prices moderating, profitability was still elusive due to weak demand for just about everything. The fifteen-year-old dragon had been slain, but many of the troops had been killed or severely wounded in the process. The hospitals for the veterans of the fight were the nation's bankruptcy courts. During the early Eighties, they looked like the financial version of *M*A*S*H,* but they were not nearly as funny.

It was 1980. Fate could have picked a better year than 1980 to award Bill Thomas his lifelong dream of becoming an auto dealer.

After toiling many years in the field and showing all the right stuff, working his way up from commission salesman, he had been offered a dealership (a "store" in auto industry parlance) in an affluent, growing suburb of Chicago. The frosting on the cake was that it was no less than a *Cadillac* franchise. He remembered always being in awe of the fat cats who owned Cadillac dealerships. They met the right people in their showrooms and practically minted money. A Cadillac did not have to be *sold* to the customers—they *knew* they wanted the flagship of the General Motors fleet when they walked in the door. And they would not spoil their self-images through hard bargaining. The key to a Cadillac store was also a ticket to the country club and a lifelong annuity.

Thomas had been a successful salesman and manager, but he was not rich. It was all he could do to scrape up the franchise fee from his own savings and borrowings, and so he was stretched thin from the first day he opened the door. Cadillac Division knew that but felt that it was important to reward competence and loyalty.

As had been the competitive practice throughout the country since World War II, Thomas would carry a wide selection on his lot; and like more than 99 percent of the car-store owners in the United States, the cars were financed to the hilt. General Motors Acceptance Corporation, technically a separate company from General Motors Corporation but in practice GM's captive "bank," provided the financing for Thomas to stock his lot and show room. Its collateral was the cars themselves, a practice known as "floor planning." Floor planning is common in American retailing, whether it is Whirlpool Acceptance Corporation financing appliance store owners' inventory of washers and dryers or (was) Borg-Warner Acceptance Corporation lending to automotive stores.

A new, harsh reality of business was coming into focus, but as yet Bill Thomas, other auto dealers, and the rest of American business had not fully been schooled. The American practice of full showrooms and well-stocked back rooms was coming to a crashing end because the carrying charges were beginning to eat up profits. When inflation had held sway in the Seventies, retail prices also kept going up, and so high interest rates could be absorbed. When the Fed doused cold water on the economy in 1980 in its fight against inflation, retailers found themselves paying high interest rates for inventory and loans in a declining, deflationary retail market—but not for long, because they lost money at a very fast rate. Those retailers with strong financial underpinnings, who either had cash reserves or unneeded assets to sell, had a fighting chance for survival. Those who had neither, who were " a mile wide and an inch deep," lost their livelihoods. Those financially in the middle sank after pouring their life's savings into their business in a vain attempt to weather the storm.

Thomas frantically tried to save his fledgling business. He sought help from GMAC in the form of additional financing or a break on his payments, but the lender did not want to set a precedent that would spread to other dealers, almost all of whom were in distress. (GMAC later would soften its policies when the scope of the country's economic troubles became more clear.) No one else would loan Thomas money because his primary asset, his stock of Cadillacs, was fully encumbered by GMAC. Thomas Cadillac had no choice but to file a Chapter 11 bankruptcy in an attempt to prevent GMAC from repossessing the cars.

Chapter 11 provided only a temporary respite. While Chapter XI of the previous Bankruptcy Act did not protect a debtor who was behind in required payments to a secured creditor, under the Bankruptcy Code, GMAC had to allow the dealership some time to attempt to reorganize. However, being protected from the actions of creditors was one thing, and financial reorganization was another. In a few months, Thomas Cadillac was forced to close the doors, and Bill Thomas went to work selling foreign cars. Chapter 11 had not put the dealership out of business, but then again it had not appreciably helped either. Nothing could save Bill Thomas's dream from dissolving into the cold reality of 1980.

Bill Thomas's situation illustrates a sad fact of business bankruptcies, which is that, contrary to popular belief, Chapter 11 is not very helpful to small companies when the country or an industry is in a recession or depression. Lenders do not lend on pie-in-the-sky and quickly abandon small businesses during a downturn. Those companies are unable to show their creditors or the bankruptcy court how they will become profitable. The vast majority of small companies that filed Chapter 11 cases in the early 1980s did not reorganize and were liquidated either through bankruptcy court procedures or by their lenders through foreclosures permitted by bankruptcy judges.

There is a recent trend for the more conservative bankruptcy judges to set arbitrary, short deadlines for the filing of plans and to enforce those deadlines against smaller companies, in spite of the fact that the Bankruptcy Code contains no deadlines for reorganizations whatsoever. The procedure is their way of rebalancing the debtor-creditor relationship in Chapter 11 to a point more to their liking, one that favors the creditors. The practice forces Chapter 11 debtors to come into court to beg for extensions, to justify to the judges their right to be operating under Chapter 11 instead of that being assumed, as the Bankruptcy Code intends. Those judges quickly note what they believe constitutes a lack of reasonable prospects and move to have the company liquidated. The lesson to be gained is that the favorable provisions of Chapter 11 frequently are not sufficient to save small companies in a good economy either.

However, the same is not the case for America's megacorporations—in fact, quite the opposite is true. Some of the largest corporations in the United States learned how the bankruptcy courts could be safe harbors until economic storms blow over. With a little practice they learned that Chapter 11 could be a useful tool for accomplishing all sorts of megacorporate goals, from sprucing up balance sheets in the face of poor operating profits to counterattacking against specific types of enemies of their executive suites. "Bankruptcy for Fun and Profit" and "How I Learned to Stop Worrying and Start Loving Chapter 11" were to be written into the historical record by some of the leading corporate executives of today.

Chapter 6

Big Business Discovers the Bankruptcy Court

The new decade did not begin with a rush of megabankruptcies. The large corporations had a good deal of resources to fall back on, which gave them time to see which way the economic winds would blow. At first, no one could believe that Chairman Volcker would do what he was doing; and when it became evident that he was doing what he said he was doing, no one believed that he would do it for long. It took a while for the level of pain to surpass the megacorporations' threshold. Some got caught counting on inflation well into the downturn and paid for that view later.

Chrysler was creating a wait-and-see attitude in the executive suites of other major corporations. Everyone was waiting to see how the federal government's billion in guarantees would work, whether the Carter administration would help prop up the giant corporation, and whether the whole mess would come down on the administration's collective head. A wonderful precedent for federal aid to megacorporations had been set when Congress allowed the treasury doors to be thrown open for Chrysler, but no one knew how generous Congress felt.

During his program to acquire federal aid, which could have been called "Pay the ransom or I will shoot this dog," Lee Iacocca had given Chapter 11 a bad name. Iacocca just could not keep Chapter 7 liquidation and Chapter 11 reorganization separated. Since he has never been accused of being stupid, one must assume that it was a calculated effort to confuse Congress, which, after all, is not that hard. In any event, Iacocca's constant and consistent prediction that failure of federal aid would result in Chrysler's "bankruptcy"—which he translated into the destruction of the company—had an effect beyond the halls of Congress. A number of prominent bankruptcy specialists echoed the sentiment. With Iacocca proclaiming that bankruptcy must necessarily be the death knell of a company, corporate executives had to be wondering whether "bankruptcy" would be the worst move of their careers. Consequently, most corporate executives waited to see how things would unfold in bankruptcy court before taking the plunge.

As a result of these uncertainties, 1980 would not see a full assault on the creditors of megacorporations through use of the Bankruptcy Code. Only the corporations that had exhausted their ordinary resources and were desperately looking for a rabbit to pull out of their hats gave Chapter 11 a fling.

Lafayette Radio Electronics Corporation was one. The distributor and retailer of consumer electronics was having trouble paying its suppliers and had gone into technical default on some terms of its credit agreement with its lenders. When its banks accelerated the maturity of their loans and demanded immediate repayment, Lafayette virtually had no choice but to run for the cover of Chapter 11 of the Bankruptcy Code, and it kicked off the new decade by filing its petition. Prevented from acting on the defaults, immediately upon the filing of the Chapter 11 case Lafayette's banks agreed to provide interim financing while the company trimmed its unprofitable stores and sought fresh investment capital. Although its lenders continued to press for quick improvement of Lafayette's financial condition, it spent a year and a half edging towards a successful merger with Wards Company, another retailer. Lafayette's ability to get its banks to continue financing and its ability to hold them off during the Chapter 11 case was a lesson not lost on business observers.

Allied Technology also took the plunge. The Dayton, Ohio, company, which made sealants and electronic equipment, had been hurt by problems in the U.S. auto industry. With sales down, it had gone into default with its lenders. When the banks refused to waive the defaults, putting the company in a vulnerable position, it filed for protection from its creditors under Chapter 11 of the Bankruptcy Code.

In April 1980, Penn-Dixie Industries, a cement and steel producer also involved in the construction industry, filed a Chapter 11 petition.

Current management blamed the company's troubles on the former chairman, who had been fired in 1977. Penn-Dixie's immediate cause for filing Chapter 11 was that it had gone into technical default over capital requirements contained in its borrowing agreements with its banks and had failed to make an $825,000 interest payment when due. Because the banks would not make any further loans, the company was desperately short of cash. (Penn-Dixie's and Lafayette's situations were typical of the large, public corporations that choose bankruptcy, in that usually it is vulnerability to their lenders that precipitates their seeking the protection of the bankruptcy courts rather than actions of trade creditors.)

It was a shock to the business public and media when White Motor Company filed its petition on September 4, 1980. Although the giant manufacturer of trucks, farm equipment, and lift trucks had been stumbling through the bad economy, it was a surprise that such a large company would enter Chapter 11. It had $1.2 billion in revenues in 1979, about $900 million in assets, 275 dealers in the United States and Canada, three modern plants, and its own finance company. New management had chopped off 35 percent of the company's salaried personnel and had taken other cost-cutting measures. In 1979, its truck business earned $17.1 million on $809 million in sales, and its farm equipment division earned a $32.2 million profit on $401.7 million in sales.

The downside of the company's huge size was that it had huge debts, including $77 million to twenty-seven lenders and $300 million to suppliers. Its pension program was underfunded by more than $100 million. Because White's truck and farm implement buyers had suffered several major recessions during the Seventies, White had entered the Eighties short of cash and credit. As a result, the company's borrowings were on a short-term line of credit rather than a long-term agreement, and accordingly it was paying a higher interest rate than it would have liked—26 percent per annum, courtesy of Paul Volcker!

In 1980, White Motor Company had begun to lose money by the bucketful as the economy went into the toilet and its farmer and trucker customers went down with it. Of sixty-five thousand trucks ordered in the first half of 1980, forty-four thousand were canceled. During that same period, White lost $46 million, almost exactly the amount of interest that became due on its loans. It did not last that first half of the year outside of bankruptcy protection. The White Motor case was the largest industrial bankruptcy to that date.

The immediate cause for White Motor running for cover was its inability to reach an agreement with its twenty-seven unsecured lenders to "roll over" $77 million in debt. For some time its relations with its bankers had not been friendly, and White and its banks had been testing each other's resolve. Over a period of time, the banks had been taking huge chunks of asset proceeds from White and its subsidiaries, but they were running out of any pieces of fat to grab. In 1980, they offered a gambit, a two-year agreement for a line of credit in return for White granting them a security interest in its assets to back up its promise to pay. White declined the gambit, maintaining its option to acquire fresh loans from other banks who could take a superior position by taking the security interest that White was denying to its existing lenders. Since it was unlikely that the company could service the debt in its present condition, the bankers were hesitant to continue the status quo, which kept them only on a par with White's trade creditors. When two banks in White's hometown of Cleveland, Central National Bank and AmeriTrust, made a quick grab of deposits in accounts at their institutions, scoring on $5 million, White countered with a fast Chapter 11 filing, and, pursuant to bankruptcy rules, they had to give it back.

Viewed in hindsight with the benefit of knowing how Chapter 11 has served megacorporate debtors during the 1980s, it is easy to see that White's bankruptcy filing was preordained.

The first imperative was that White (correctly) refused to provide the banks with security. To grant its lenders security would virtually assure them 100 percent payment if they foreclosed on the collateral, thus encouraging them to foreclose at the earliest opportunity. (White then would have had to file Chapter 11 to halt the foreclosures.) Had White allowed the banks to improve their position in the creditor hierarchy by taking a security interest, the trade creditors would have realized that they were being set up for a fall. Their lawyers would have advised them that the agreement could be voided under bankruptcy's "preference" rules if any three trade creditors holding together at least $5,000 in claims filed an "involuntary" bankruptcy against White within ninety days of the date the lenders improved their position. The natural result would have been an embarrassing involuntary bankruptcy for the company. Also, keeping the banks at the same level as the trade creditors gave White a significantly better position in dealing with the banks.

Another clear advantage of Chapter 11 is the respite from creditor activity that it provides. Ironically, operating under protection of the bankruptcy court gives a debtor *more* stability because it erases the possibility that some big creditor will make the kind of move that White's two banks did. Because it is less likely that something sudden will devastate the debtor's operations, suppliers are *more* likely to continue to deal with the troubled company. They also know that no one else will grab an unfair advantage in payment. Suppliers and lenders hesitant to help a troubled megacompany outside of bankruptcy are *more* likely to do so once a Chapter 11 case is filed, because credit provided during the bankruptcy has a "priority" status under the Bankruptcy Code and will be paid back before prepetition unsecured creditors can get a penny. For White, filing Chapter 11 brought order and stability to its situation.

That order and stability brought by Chapter 11 allows a debtor to concentrate upon necessary changes in its operations. White Motors needed time to undertake and complete the massive restructuring that was called for, and filing Chapter 11 would mean that the company would not have to give concessions to the lenders or give a veto power to them in order to make the changes. Therefore, even if the banks had not made the money grab, White no doubt would have sought the protection of the bankruptcy court while it attended to its financial and operational reorganization. When the deed was done, White's announcement stressed that Chapter 11 "was the most effective way to implement the changes necessary to achieve a strong, vigorous and competitive company."

When the banks grabbed White's deposits, they actually were conceding and forcing the Chapter 11. Although White had allowed its lenders to strip it lean, it was not going to allow them to pick off its remaining assets piecemeal. The banks' exceedingly aggressive, totally self-serving program over the prior year for paying down their loans had gone as far as it could go. They no doubt realized that White was not going to grant them collateral for their remaining outstanding loans. Their action simply insured that White would not "prime" them by giving new lenders security and that it would get on with the Chapter 11 as soon as possible.

The prebankruptcy maneuvering highlights a situation that arises in megacorporate finance, namely the lenders' failure to demand security at the time that the loans are made. Bankers normally consider megacorporations to be such good customers that they willingly lend them money on an unsecured basis, but in a bankruptcy they find themselves at the same level in the creditor hierarchy as the trade and other unsecured creditors. Unlike secured creditors, unsecured claimants are prohibited from continuing to accrue interest against a debtor in Chapter 11. Maintaining its bankers as unsecured creditors, thus stopping their interest clock, is so helpful to a megacorporate debtor that it may become a major cause of a Chapter 11 filing.

Business people around the country anxiously awaited the denouement of the drama. Lee Iacocca had predicted that no one would buy a car from a "bankrupt." Would White Motors' remaining business disappear? Would the industrial customers of Allied and Penn-Dixie become fearful of those Chapter 11 companies' ability to maintain production and go elsewhere? Would bankruptcy court prevent the flexibility that the companies needed to restructure their operations? Would the creditors take over the companies and throw out management?

What happened in the Allied, Penn-Dixie, and White Motors cases through 1980 and into 1981 was . . . nothing much. The creditors took months to get organized. There were meetings, negotiations, and motions in court, to no material effect. White peddled its entire farm equipment division without any complaint from its creditors. There was no flight of customers related to the bankruptcy filings. The attitude of one White truck dealer was typical: "Oh, hell, it's just a reorganization—keep my order in."

Allied would spend one-and-a-half years in Chapter 11, redirecting its business towards certain electronics specialties, before offering its creditors an on-the-cheap plan: $1.2 million in notes and $2.7 face value of stock to cancel $6.1 million in bank debt, and a 20 percent repayment to trade creditors. (They grabbed it.)

White would spend several years in the friendly embrace of the bankruptcy court restructuring its very sick operations before effectuating a formal reorganization plan.

In Penn-Dixie's case, it was clear to observers that Chapter 11 was allowing the company to use its receipts for ongoing operations instead of paying past-due obligations and was permitting management to restructure its operations while protected from creditor actions. Over the next several years while in Chapter 11, Penn-Dixie cleaned up its act. The company canceled an underfunded pension fund and negotiated a settlement of those obligations satisfactory to the federal watchdog Pension Benefit Guarantee Corporation. It sold its six cement plants and a steel-fabricating division. It made plans to modernize its remaining steel-producing facilities by borrowing $38 million when it emerged from bankruptcy. It struck a deal with unsecured creditors of its Penn-Dixie Steel unit to pay them about forty-five cents on the dollar for their claims. Finalizing its settlements with a liberal sprinkling of stock to creditors that greatly diluted the value of outstanding shares—a typical attribute of big corporate bankruptcies—after two years in Chapter 11, it would emerge from bankruptcy court not only enscathed but much stronger.

The experience of Allied, Penn-Dixie, White Motors, and others in Chapter 11 in 1980 was painting a far different picture than Lee Iacocca and other doomsayers had predicted. Chrysler may have achieved custom treatment, but in the Bankruptcy Reform Act of 1978 Congress had created a federal welfare program available to megacorporations without the need for special applications to Congress. It was becoming apparent that there really was little downside to the procedure for them.

Early 1981 saw a number of megacorporate bankruptcies. The new year was greeted by the Chapter 11 petition of Itel Corporation. If it was February, it was Seatrain falling into bankruptcy. March saw Advent, OPM Leasing, and Remington Rand seeking protection from creditors.

Following a meteoric rise, Itel was in danger of burning out. After forming the company in 1967, its two founders, Peter S. Redfield and Gary Friedman, had turned it into a major player in the computer field by selling, reselling, leasing, and servicing them. They then had expanded into navigation and aircraft operation, railroad car manufacturing and leasing, and shipping container leasing. At one point Itel had more than seven thousand employees. Soon Itel owned four container ships, a short-line railroad, and an insurance company.

However brilliant Redfield and Friedman had been in building their businesses, they were not very good at riding herd on their day-to-day operations. Upon reviewing the conglomerate's financial records for 1978, its auditors found "insufficient documentation, employee misconduct, and officer and employee inadvertence." In 1979, Itel's computer-related businesses virtually collapsed, and Redfield and

Friedman were paid about $4 million in termination compensation to take a walk. In October 1980, the concern had reported 1979 losses of $443.3 million, much of it due to charges for discontinued businesses. The company would require rebuilding from the ground up.

Itel was a monster corporation with monstrous debts. Although it had more than a billion dollars in assets, its six thousand creditors were owed about $1.7 billion. Its major liability was to lenders, about half a billion of which was tied to the soaring prime rate. Itel's new chairman, James H. Maloon, spoke plainly about the company's financial condition, saying that Itel was "awash with debt" and that "we aren't close to announcing any settlement with our lenders." It would have been practically impossible for Itel to pare down its debts from the income on its continuing operations since interest expenses on loans were running at $150 million a year. However, fortunately for Itel, only a portion of the bank debt was secured, and so the Chapter 11 filing stopped interest from accruing on a big part of the company's liabilities.

The statutory "First Meeting of Creditors" was pure megabankruptcy theater. Because the bankruptcy court clerk in San Francisco had no facilities large enough to contain the onslaught of creditors, he rented the Gold Room of the tony Fairmont Hotel for the occasion. The chairman of the company commenced his presentation by blaming the bankruptcy on the prior management's mistakes. Angry creditors in the audience were placated by Itel's promise to present a Plan of Reorganization for their review very quickly, perhaps in a month. The corporation's bankruptcy attorney warned creditors that they would be called upon to sacrifice for the company's reorganization, and if they failed to cooperate sufficiently, the bankruptcy could be expected to drag on for years. Having been shown both the carrot and the stick, the creditors were sent home to mull it over.

An unsecured creditors' committee was quickly formed. Its makeup clearly indicated not only Itel's status as a financial megacorporation but also the creditors who counted. Its nine members were representatives from Manufacturers Hanover Bank, Chemical Bank, Citibank, Chase Manhattan Bank, Marine Midland Bank, Bank of America, Girard Bank, and Aetna Life Insurance Company (also a lender).

The committee and its lawyers wasted no time before digging into the company's affairs, trying to figure out the profitability of the conglomerate's operations and the details of its finances. Particularly knotty was Itel's contingent liability in approximately four hundred lawsuits, which had been estimated at $300 million, arising from its ill-fated remarketing of used IBM computers. The committee wanted to be in a position to properly review the reorganization proposal that the company said was imminent. They would wait two years for its arrival.

The bankruptcy case droned on. Itel received extensions of its "exclusive period" to file a Plan of Reorganization. It peddled its remaining inventory of computers and related equipment to National Semiconductor Corporation, receiving $41.8 million in cash and notes. It held an auction sale of many of the sumptuous furnishings and pieces of artwork bought by the free-spending company in its halcyon days. It announced 1980 losses of $75 million on its operations, changed CEOs, and otherwise continued about its businesses. A glitch in its cash flow was caused by its difficulty in collecting upon thousands of shipping container leases with Seatrain, which had filed its own Chapter 11 shortly after Itel.

The bankruptcy-related activities moved in a pattern that would be repeated in megacases across the country: the professionals representing the various interests generated huge fees doing things that amounted to hardly anything at all. There were a dozen law firms representing Itel and the various interests represented in the bankruptcy process. Itel's primary bankruptcy counsel alone logged about $100,000 per month in fees. Itel had retained an investment banker to advise it concerning financial matters, at the rate of $75,000 per month plus expenses. Itel's accountants, put on extra duty because of all the financial information that had to be generated for the creditors, was billing upwards of $400,000 per month. During the initial months of the case, bankruptcy-related expenses were being incurred at the rate of about $2 million a month. Under the bankruptcy law, all of those costs are paid for by the Chapter 11 company, and Itel dutifully cut the checks.

The professionals may have been feeding at the trough, but they were not breaking any laws. They simply were going through the motions of what the megacorporate Chapter 11 process entails. Except for some padding here and there that human nature demands in such situations, the lawyers and accountants in megabankruptcies work hard for their money. The megadebtors are huge and their problems complex, and there are a number of clearly defined interests in each case that have a great deal of money at stake. In fact, it would subject the lawyers and accountants to criticism—and possible liability—if they cut corners to save expenses. The scandal is that—and to this day it is not obvious—*for all of that professional activity and the attendant costs, the creditors' representatives accomplish very little in megabankruptcies.*

Having given the professionals their due is not to say that bankruptcy is the most perfect of all worlds. In spite of the fact that the activities of the parties and the resulting proliferation of fees is expected and even encouraged as a natural concomitant of reorganizations under Chapter 11, in megabankruptcies the flaws in the system do breed excessive costs. The professionals and creditors' representatives cannot help knowing that the megacorporation, although a Chapter 11 megadebtor, has plenty of money with which to pay fees. (Itel had $195 million in the bank at the commencement of the bankruptcy.) Lawyers are not apt to make trouble for themselves and their clients by starting fights with other professionals in the case. The Chapter 11 company, which will be dependent upon the goodwill of the creditors' representatives to recommend approval of its Plan of Reorganization, is not in the mood to object to billings from them. Besides, whatever the costs of maintaining the bankruptcy, they pale next to the savings on interest and other benefits of the bankruptcy to the debtor. In other words, the "juice" money required to keep the Chapter 11 case going is cheap at twice the price to the debtor.

The judge's supervision of fees, as with most other matters in a megacase, is better in theory than in fact. The judge is not going to spend too many of his hours poring over receipts and descriptions of how lawyers have spent their hours. The American judicial system works well only when adversaries dredge up facts to present to a judge in the course of asking him to rule on a dispute, and in the face of what amounts to a conspiracy of silence, no judge is going to effectively supervise fees in a megacase. (The same is not true in smaller Chapter 11 cases, where fees and costs are of a size that can be better grasped, and many judges relish chopping down attorneys of lesser stature.)

The Itel case provided a good example of how the theory of fee supervision does not work in practice. The presiding bankruptcy judge, Lloyd King, quickly overwhelmed by the mountain of fee applications and requests for expense reimbursements, directed Itel to review all such billings and to file objections to those it deemed excessive. Itel's accountants dutifully reviewed the billings, thereby adding another overlay of bankruptcy expenses, but Itel failed to object to any. In an early fee hearing, the judge chastised the parties for their hefty billings, at least in part because they had been publicized in a *Wall Street Journal* article—and then he substantially approved them, as a "vote of confidence" in the professionals and creditors' representatives. (The reasons why he had such confidence in them were not reported.) Judge King simply did not have the time to get bogged down in administrative minutiae involving mere tens of millions of dollars, and, besides, the bankruptcy estate would have to pay the lawyers and accountants for the time they spent preparing for and attending any lengthy fee hearings!

Itel spent a not-uncomfortable two-and-one-half years in Chapter 11 before paying its $1.7 billion in prepetition debt with $327 million in cash; $150 million in notes maturing in 1996; $110 million in notes due in 2002; 975,000 shares of preferred stock; and 1,650,000 shares of common stock. Once again suppliers of a megacorporation had found themselves unwittingly to be its long-term financiers and investors, along for the ride whether they liked it or not. Soon Itel was exercising its conglomerate muscles again, buying Anixter Brothers for $500 million cash in December 1986, an entire container ship fleet in March 1987 for $235 million in cash, 22,000 railcars in February 1988, and 17 percent of the Sante Fe Southern Pacific Railroad in September 1988. Itel's businesses today include heavy marine construction (primarily dredging), rail operations (including leasing), the manufacture of wiring systems, and shipping container leasing. Chapter 11 merely was a rest stop on the path to Itel's greater glory.

Seatrain Lines had been the beneficiary of special United States government programs for much of its existence. In 1951, it went into the ocean cargo business by buying surplus World War II freighters. It specialized in hauling freight under federal programs that were limited to U.S. "bottoms." In the 1960s, its ships hauled military cargo to Vietnam. In the early 1970s, it opened its own shipyard by tapping into a whole collection of federal government subsidies and guaranteed loans. When it closed its shipyard in mid-1979, the Labor Department provided $10.3 million in benefits to its employees, equal to 70 percent of their wages for one year.

For a variety of reasons, shipbuilding was a disastrous venture for

Seatrain, and in the 1970s, it lost money in seven of ten years. As a result, it carried huge government-backed debts into the Eighties. For its fiscal year ending June 30, 1980, it lost an additional $33.9 million. Yet the company continued to operate its shipping business.

How had Seatrain stayed afloat? Trying to retain a merchant fleet, Uncle Sam generously had guaranteed more than $450 million in loans to the company for shipbuilding and tanker operations over a decade, of which more than $300 was still outstanding in 1980. The company had received financial aid from no less than two agencies of the Commerce Department, the Maritime Administration and the Economic Development Administration, as well as the Commerce Department itself. Also, the Maritime Administration had favored Seatrain numerous times with special waivers of rules (over the objections of other companies). When Seatrain played fast and loose with government regulations, fines were, in effect, paid for by Commerce Department loans to the company.

Being so indebted to the Commerce Department had made Seatrain a privileged ward of the federal government. It was beginning to appear that Seatrain could stay afloat forever with its federal sponsors providing a patch whenever it sprung a new leak.

However, Seatrain's precarious position deteriorated suddenly and substantially in 1980. Uncle Sam's alter ego, The Chairman, had so devastated the economy in the last quarter of 1980 that Seatrain dropped a cool $150 million in that quarter alone. In spite of an additional $49.7 million in federal government guarantees in the first quarter of 1981, Seatrain continued to take on water fast. Stephen Russell, Seatrain's president, chief operating officer, and a director, and three other directors of the company abandoned ship in early February 1981. (Mr. Russell joined a company formed to buy a profitable subsidiary of Seatrain.)

In February 1981, three creditors banded together to file an "involuntary" Chapter 11 bankruptcy case against the ailing shipper. If they had any hopes that the bankruptcy court would bring some quick, efficient resolution to Seatrain's financial difficulties, they were quite mistaken. It would be years before Seatrain would accomplish a Plan of Reorganization and leave the safe harbor of Chapter 11.

In Chapter 11, Seatrain had the best of both worlds. It was protected from its lender, Chase Manhattan Bank, to whom it owed $150 million, as well as about four thousand other creditors. Yet, in order to keep the concern going, Chase loaned Seatrain an additional $5 million two days after the bankruptcy was filed. Uncle chipped in with an additional $2 million in April and another $16.2 million in June. Officials of the United States government, the largest creditor, appeared at the First Meeting of Creditors but did not take an active role.

An unusually large unsecured creditors' committee of fifteen was formed, but they would have little to say in the face of Seatrain's mounting losses from operations. Over the next several years, the company would continue to take on water, but with the overt help of the federal Maritime Administration and the covert help of the federal Bankruptcy Code, Seatrain would stay afloat. When in July 1983 it effectuated a Plan of Reorganization, which offered trade creditors and Chase Manhattan Bank stock for their claims while Seatrain continued to carry the debts to the federal government, Seatrain had successfully maneuvered itself through yet another federal government program!

Advent also was in trouble, although on a smaller scale. The company had been a pioneer in the manufacture of modestly priced stereo loudspeakers with excellent sound reproduction characteristics. It also was in the process of pioneering big-screen televisions, which was causing the manufacturer financial problems as research costs mounted. In early 1981, a company announcement summarized its financial situation, which sounded like a perfect recipe for Chapter 11: high interest, overhead, and development costs; and low sales. In March, the company filed a Chapter 11 petition and set about reorganizing its operations.

As it was a smaller concern than many of the other "public" corporations in Chapter 11, Advent's immediate prospects were somewhat dimmer, and its road was somewhat rockier. However, in the forgiving arms of the bankruptcy court, it was allowed to restructure, returning to its roots as a loudspeaker manufacturer and withdrawing from television development, and in mid-1982 it engineered a merger with the International Jensen unit of Esmark.

The bankruptcy of OPM Leasing Services did not fit the mold because it involved white-collar crime on a grand scale.

OPM had helped to create the computer-leasing industry, and had grown large servicing the computer needs of "Fortune 500" corporations. In effect it was in the financing business, leasing computers at rates that were so attractive that its customers would prefer to lease instead of taking out loans to purchase computers. The business came rolling in when OPM offered to take back computers before their seven-year leases were up, because OPM's customers then could be sure that they could keep up with the latest technology simply by canceling their leases and then re-leasing or buying equipment. OPM was taking the risk that it could re-lease the returned computers or sell them used at prices that were a substantial percentage of their prices when OPM had bought them new. It was a bad bet, but it brought in hundreds of millions of dollars in lease rentals when the company was flying high.

OPM's leasing procedures made fraud a very tempting way of doing business. Simply by handing over leases to its lenders as security, OPM could acquire loans based on the future receipts of the leases— instant cash. Since OPM was a "hot" company, the banks were falling over each other to lend it money; and since policing the leases was so tedious, the bankers ceased to attend "closings" when the leases were formally executed by OPM and the customers. (At the time it filed bankruptcy, OPM had twenty-five lenders.) One other factor weighed in. OPM was a private company, jointly owned by its founders, Mordecai Weissman and Myron Goodman, and so it did not have to publish its financial condition in the manner that the Securities and Exchange Commission requires of public corporations.

With the stage set, the play proceeded predictably. With the rapid technological advances in the computer industry, units became cheaper and updating was required more often. As a result, OPM's customers increasingly exercised their rights to return leased computers, and OPM found it increasingly difficult to re-lease or sell those out-of-date used computers. In actuality, the banks' collateral was shrinking in value, but they did not realize it as long as terminated leases were replaced as collateral by new leases. OPM did not have enough new business to cover the terminations, and so the upper levels of OPM's management began creating phony leases and sending them off to the banks. Apparently no one with knowledge of computers looked at the leases for the banks, since an analysis would have disclosed strange, "red flag," leasing patterns by some of OPM's customers.

Of course, there finally was a slip-up in the cover-up, and several banks found out that they had loaned $10 million to OPM based on nonexistent computer leases with Rockwell International. It was widely assumed that many more leases were frauds and that the company would prove to have acquired perhaps $100 million in loans greater than it had computer assets—and that was *before* devaluing OPM's inventory of computers to a realistic fair market value. A lot of bankers had egg on their faces and their jobs on the line, and so lawsuits began to fly thick and fast. (Although Rockwell had nothing whatsoever to do with the phony leases in its name, it was sued for *looking like* it might have leased the computers.) Of course, OPM filed bankruptcy, in March 1981 at the courthouse in Manhattan.

With such a strong scent of fraud in the case—it had not been proved yet—and the company's operations collapsed, a trustee was appointed by the bankruptcy court to salvage what he could. Over the next several years, during which a good portion of OPM's former top executives including Messrs. Weissman and Goodman pleaded guilty to bank fraud, the trustee mopped up the mess. The fraud topped out at $200 million, and later the trustee would pursue OPM's accountants, lawyers, and investment bankers for negligence in failing to discover and report the fraud. According to the trustee, had OPM used proper accounting methods, its financial reports would have disclosed that OPM had lost money every year of its existence. It was not your typical big-company bankruptcy.

At the same time that OPM's bankruptcy filing was making news, Remington Rand slipped quietly into Chapter 11 in Trenton, New Jersey. Quite unlike OPM, Remington's fortunes actually were improving at the time it filed its case. However, although its sales were enjoying a rebound, it was being hounded by creditors' lawsuits and sought the sanctuary of the bankruptcy court while it improved its finances.

The filing of Chapter 11 by the Alton Telegraph newspaper in April 1981 was the first of the "Hey, you can't do that" bankruptcies of the Eighties. Although reasonably profitable, the Illinois newspaper had suffered a $9.2 million libel judgment against it for erroneously naming a local businessman as a criminal in reporters' notes that were turned over to the United States Justice Department. While the case was on appeal, the plaintiff threatened to foreclose on the newspaper's assets, so a Chapter 11 case was filed to halt the collection activities.

In opposing the bankruptcy filing, the plaintiff's lawyers argued that bankruptcy was not meant to provide protection to a party who has lost one lawsuit, fair and square, and who has no other substantial debts. They argued that to allow the Chapter 11 would be to give an unjust advantage to one side in a two-party dispute.

In his ruling the judge considered the basic purposes of bankruptcy. He noted that by its very size the judgment was a threat to the company and observed that the Bankruptcy Code does not discriminate among types of liabilities or require a minimum number of creditors. The court also correctly stated that a philosophy interwoven into the Bankruptcy Code was that bankruptcy was to be an "open" system, generally available for the asking. As a result, there is a strong presumption in favor of allowing a company to remain in Chapter 11, whatever the reason for its choosing to invoke the protections of the bankruptcy court.

The motion to dismiss the bankruptcy was denied. The newspaper held off the plaintiff until a settlement was reached. Little could the judge or the owners of the newspaper know that their precedent would be seized upon in the late 1980s by one of the largest and most profitable corporations in the world, Texaco, after losing a whopper of a lawsuit to Pennzoil.

The year was rounded out by the Chapter 11 filings of two other national companies. Colonial Commercial Corporation, a holding company, had interests in mortgage banking, apparel manufacturing, construction materials, and real estate—industries hard hit by Mr. Volcker's economics lesson to the American people. Colonial would hold off its creditors until 1983, when it would effectuate a reorganization that canceled its debt in return for the issuance of its stock to them. Cooper-Jarrett was one of the first large trucking companies to be forced into Chapter 11 by the state of the economy and deregulation of the industry.

Nineteen eighty-one saw the beginning of the end for dozens of small companies associated with "the oil patch," the oil drilling industry in the United States. Ironically, the easing of the oil crisis during the Reagan era destroyed many companies that had bet their future on *very* high oil prices. When the American refineries (owned by the major oil companies) could get all of the crude that they wished at a relatively good price from OPEC, a good deal of oil under U.S. soil was not worth the cost of drilling. Companies stopped drilling in the United States and stopped buying pipe and other drilling equipment. The small oil companies began defaulting on the bank loans that had been available for the asking a few years before. Banks that had lavished loans upon them began to find the loans uncollectable and the security for the loans (oil in the ground) unsalable.

The effects of the oil industry's setback lasted for several years. Dozens of small oil companies in the United States faded from the scene, furthering the concentration in the oil industry. A number of companies that supplied the oil companies closed their doors. In June 1982, Penn Square Bank, a shopping center bank in Oklahoma City that had made it big by making loans to the oil patch and then packaging and selling them to big-city banks, collapsed. In turn, Continental Illinois Bank and Trust Company of Chicago, which over the prior several years had targeted the oil patch for aggressive lending, stumbled and almost toppled.

The domino effect in the oil industry extended to independent refineries. As part of the Reagan administration's program of deregulation, the federal "entitlements" program was phased out in 1980–81. That program blended oil prices in a way that helped independent refiners of oil compete with the refineries owned by the major oil companies. Without the program, almost all of the buyers of refined oil in the United States bought from the refineries owned by the majors. A good example of the fickle nature of the oil industry and the perilous existence of the independent oil companies is illustrated in the story of Energy Cooperative Incorporated.

When ARCO decided to sell an aging oil refinery in northwest Indiana rather than make renovations in the mid-1970s, there was much interest. During the Seventies, having an oil business of virtually any type was a license to print money.

The ARCO refinery was purchased in 1976 by Energy Cooperative Incorporated, which was made up of some of the largest agricultural cooperatives in the United States, which in turn were owned by thousands of farmers. During the Arab oil embargoes of the 1970s, in order to maximize their profits the big oil companies had cut back on their refinery production of the diesel fuel that farmers used in their tractors, turning the Midwest breadbasket upside down. Thus, purchasing the refinery not only would be a profit-making venture, but it also would prevent the recurrence of a nightmare for those farmers who were members of the cooperatives. ECI put $120 million into refurbishing the facility, and for several years it operated profitably enough to maintain itself, while pricing its products fairly to its owner-customers.

When the entitlements program was phased out, what had been a double-smart move became a double-whammy. Because the refinery could not acquire oil at a competitive price, it could not sell refined products at a competitive price. When it raised its prices to the farmer-members who had pledged to support their own facility, they responded by switching their buying allegiance to the majors' refineries, where they could get product at cheaper prices. A utility canceled a lucrative long-term supply contract. ECI had lost its markets in the space of a few months. The modernized facility, valued at about $400 million, was all dressed up with no place to go. The cooperative owed well over half a billion dollars to creditors.

In May 1981, ECI filed a reorganization proceeding in Chicago. At first there was hope for a turnaround. The presiding bankruptcy judge, Frederick J. Hertz, did nothing to hinder any possible reorganization. Continental Illinois Bank and Trust Company, the lead bank of a consortium owed about $500 million, was allowed to collect the millions of dollars of receivables pending further resolution of the company's situation. (At the court hearing in which Judge Hertz entered that order, which was agreed to by all the parties to the case, one of the lawyers jokingly asked what would happen to the money if Continental Illinois Bank collapsed. There was genuine laughter throughout the room at the thought that there could be any risk whatsoever in keeping money in the largest bank in Chicago. By mid-1982, the bank's circumstances would become no joking matter.)

Attempts to sell the refinery went into high gear. Unfortunately, no one wanted it, at any price. The refinery had become a giant piece of scrap metal. When the asbestos surrounding the pipes began to waft through northwest Indiana, the facility was razed at huge cost to the bankruptcy estate. The bankruptcy degenerated into lawsuits trying to pin blame on someone with a deep pocket. Such was the fate of a bankruptcy of a "little" player in the oil game, far different than the Chapter 11s of the true megacorporations.

Nineteen eighty-two was a banner year in bankruptcy court for megacorporate Chapter 11s.

Bobbie Brooks entered Chapter 11 in January. Its flagship line of sportswear was doing well, but it was burdened with debt resulting from unsuccessful forays into other lines. Its main problem was servicing its debt, and the immediate cause of the bankruptcy was its inability to reach an agreement with its lenders for continued financing. After a year in Chapter 11, it exited with a plan to pay its creditors in full over six years. Apparently the company's prospects had looked so positive that the creditors were able to negotiate an unusually good result for themselves, although there was the risk that the company would not fulfill its projections.

Come February 1982, it was Lionel Corporation going into Chapter 11. To most people, the company, founded in 1901, was a major producer of model trains. In reality it had stepped onto a much faster track in the Sixties and Seventies, playing the conglomerate game furiously. During those two decades, the company bought and sold thirty-one business entities, including a retail toy store chain and a chemical company. In 1967, it acquired American Flyer, but in 1970, it licensed General Mills to make its line of model trains. So, by the time it filed Chapter 11 along with subsidiaries Lionel Leisure Incorporated and Consolidated Toy Company, it had already been out of the model train business for some time except to receive royalties.

Soon after filing bankruptcy, Lionel lined up a $15 million line of credit from Chemical Bank and settled into Chapter 11. Its most valuable asset was an 82 percent interest in Dale Electronics of Columbus, Nebraska, a profitable maker of resistor parts for the electronics industry. Dale was not itself in bankruptcy. Lionel actually needed very little restructuring and did not undertake substantial store closings. The bankruptcy case turned into a running battle with the creditors trying to have an effect upon Lionel's decision about what to do with Dale.

Lionel got rather comfortable in Chapter 11. The company dangled a rather ridiculous ten-year payment plan to unsecured creditors, which was not accepted. In return, the company simply froze them out for a few years, at one point attempting to sell Dale without offering the creditors a reorganization plan. Finally, Lionel's interest in Dale was sold, and the creditors received those proceeds as well as some stock in Lionel. The creditors had waited three-and-a-half years with their noses pressed against the courthouse window.

The spring of 1982 saw bankruptcies around the country springing up like dandelions. Business bankruptcy filings were happening at the rate of five hundred per *week*. The bitter harvest was clogging the machinery of the bankruptcy courts to the point where the judges, even while working long hours, could not keep pace. Creditors found it almost impossible to get the judges' attention for any length of time due to the press of court business. The megacorporations already in Chapter 11 and the fresh megacorporate filings that spring took huge amounts of bankruptcy courts' time and energy, bending the scales of justice nearly to the point of breaking. It was a good time to be a debtor in Chapter 11.

In April and May, the business world was rocked by a tattoo of megacorporate bankruptcy filings. Wickes Companies, with Admiral-Fix-It Sanford Sigoloff at the helm, sailed into the safe harbor of the bankruptcy court in Los Angeles. It was the largest business Chapter 11 filing to that date. AM International filed its Chapter 11 petition in Chicago. Within a week, Saxon Industries, another one of those go-go conglomerates of the Seventies, sought sanctuary from its lenders in the bankruptcy court in Manhattan. Braniff International Corporation, near collapse, asked the bankruptcy court in Dallas to help it reorganize. Connoisseurs of Chapter 11 could appreciate the geographical and industrial diversity of the spring megacorporate filings.

AM International, formerly a stodgy office products producer known as Addressograph Multigraph, had stumbled attempting to become a high-tech manufacturer and then had fallen retrenching. Its research and development costs—funded with borrowed money at high interest rates—had gotten out of hand. Over an eighteen-month span, AMI had lost $300 million.

Who was to blame? Its chairman, Joe B. Freeman, blamed Roy L. Ash, the former AMI chairman (and Litton Industries founder) who had begun the transformation of the company in 1976, for AMI's troubles. Some analysts and executives blamed Richard B. Black, a turnaround specialist who had been chairman for less than a year in the interim between Ash and Freeman, for an inept attempt at restructuring. Everyone involved scorned Black for ordering large write-downs in the value of AMI's assets, which had highlighted the company's troubles and had made it difficult to sell several subsidiaries at a decent price. In turn, Black sued the company, saying that he had been deceived about the extent of the company's problems when he had agreed to take the job. (Black later would be partially vindicated when the SEC brought charges against the company for having inflated the value of its assets in public reports that had deceived investors in the stock market. No individual officers or directors of AMI were charged, and the company got a slap on the wrist from the SEC.) There was enough blame to go around.

The turmoil in the executive suite, including the defections of a number of other officers over the prior several years, had made it impossible for AMI to execute a cohesive plan to achieve profitability in a world of rapid technological change. However, the company had a few things going for it, if only a very few. It was a huge company with substantial cash flow and a number of profitable core products. More importantly, nearly all of its debt to twenty banks was unsecured, allowing it to evade the accrual of loan interest during the Chapter 11 case. Speaking about AMI's filing of Chapter 11 for himself and his colleagues, one banker lamented, "It's a sad, sad day for us."

The bankruptcy of AMI highlighted the ripple effects of bankruptcies around the country upon small and large suppliers of goods and services alike—ripples that were growing to tidal waves as the megacorporate debtors sloughed off their financial problems on those that they did business with. As one creditor holding $170,000 in unpaid bills from AMI noted, Chapter 11 had become "a business fact of life."

For more than a year, suppliers of AMI had been in a quandary. To deny any credit would be to hurt their own sales and anger a big customer and yet to continue to provide the company with services and products would be to risk heavy losses that might throw *them* into bankruptcy. In the end, no matter which course AMI's suppliers had taken, their bottom lines would be damaged by AMI's troubles—dealing with AMI had become a choice likened to "name your poison." For example, one small parts supplier, Pertec Computer, increased its credit line to AMI by two-thirds to $250,000 just a few months before AMI filed for bankruptcy and was caught with a big, uncollectable receivable when AMI went into Chapter 11. On the other hand, a unit of American Hospital Supply Corporation, for which AMI distributed drafting tables, had slashed AMI's credit line and cut its losses; but then it had watched helplessly as its sales tumbled because AMI had lacked inventory to peddle.

The effect of AMI's Chapter 11 filing was described by the *Wall Street Journal:* "All it took was the stroke of a pen on a single sheet of legal boilerplate [the bankruptcy petition] last week and presto: For the time being, struggling AM International Inc. didn't have to pay anybody a dime. . . . But some 8,000 creditors got stuck holding the bag for $465 million in bills. . . ."

Once again the business community waited to see if the invocation of the terrible words "Chapter 11" would scare off customers. Competitors of AMI certainly tried. However, once again all would see that in the upside-down world of Chapter 11, the negatives had become the positives. Since AMI's troubles had been widely reported, it soon became apparent that its operations were no worse off for being under court supervision than they had been before the filing. It became clear that AMI's profitable divisions would not go out of business even if the parent company failed—they simply would be sold intact to some other company. Not paying bank interest and past-due bills created a nice cash kitty for AMI, which went from $15 million at the bankruptcy filing to $45 million six months later. Chairman Freeman observed, "On balance, more uncertainty has been removed than created and by a considerable margin."

In fact, AMI did famously during its Chapter 11 proceeding. It overcame its notoriety with aggressive selling. It strengthened its operations and introduced new products. It acquired Grafcon Corporation. Management went out of its way to soothe shareholders' creditors, and employees, all to good effect. Twenty-eight months after filing its Chapter 11 petition, its Plan of Reorganization was confirmed by the bankruptcy court. It paid $201 million in cash and issued stock constituting 53 percent of its common shares to unsecured creditors. Its secured debt, totaling a mere $2 million, was repaid in full. As with many megacorporate bankruptcies, many suppliers—especially the smaller companies—had suffered to a far greater degree than the Chapter 11 debtor.

Joe B. Freeman, the architect of the turnaround who had been handed the reins of the company only shortly before it went into Chapter 11, was rewarded for his efforts by the AMI board of directors by being fired. The board, apparently piqued that their interests had not been sufficiently attended to by Freeman, said that now that the company had become profitable they would be looking for a top executive with skills in marketing and strategic planning. It seemed that Freeman, an accountant by training, was too much of a number-cruncher and that the board would be happier with a more personable fellow. Another not-inconsistent view, supported by the fate of Sanford Sigoloff at Wickes and other turnaround specialists, is that when the crisis is over the directors do not want the crisis master around reminding them of the necessity for prudence and frugality.

Once out of bankruptcy, the company went on a tear. In June 1986, it bought Harris Graphics Corporation for $246 million in cash and Nicolet Zeta Corporation for $22 million in cash. In 1987, it picked up two more companies, and two more in 1988. In 1988, it had $820 million in sales. Its net current assets (cash, receivables, and inventory) was a handsome $549 million.

When Saxon Industries filed Chapter 11, its balance sheet did not look all that bad either. In its bankruptcy papers, the manufacturer of paper products and seller of photocopy machines listed total assets of $503 million and liabilities of $461 million. Its borrowings, $64.4 million in short-term notes and $157 million in long-term debt, were not out of line.

That is, its debt level would not have been out of line had not interest rates reached levels that the Godfather might have set. Further, although Saxon's twenty bankers were not breaking legs with baseball bats, within recognized bounds they were taking the most hard-nosed stance possible. They had denied Saxon's request for more working capital, and when the company's finances drifted outside of formulas contained in loan agreements, they demanded accelerated repayment of their loans. If all of that was calculated to induce Saxon to provide them with liens on its assets to secure the outstanding loans, they were wrong. Saxon denied their requests and filed a Chapter 11 proceeding.

Perhaps Saxon's lenders had smelled a rat. It seems that Saxon had fallen prey to the same pressures as AMI's prior management, the need to show substantial asset values in order to stay within formulas established by loan agreements and to look good for the stock market in the face of the legal duty to write down the value of obsolete products. As part of the SEC's program to monitor "public" companies to prevent them from overstating their assets during the Volcker Depression, the SEC had snagged Saxon as well as AMI for failing to properly state their assets in financial statements.

During Saxon's bankruptcy, the SEC continued to investigate the company's financial records, and Saxon had independent auditors review its books. The conclusions: through an organized and long-standing program of deceit going back for years involving a number of the company's executives, Saxon had overstated the value of certain assets, including leases of its copiers, to the tune of $115 million, and had listed as assets $95 million of totally nonexistent inventory. Management literally had kept two sets of books. (Was it a mere coincidence that Fox and Company had been the accountants for both Saxon and OPM?)

The effect on the fortunes of Saxon Industries was devastating. Its losses for 1981, previously pegged at a dismal $89 million, became an astounding $299 million. Suddenly, Saxon had a negative net worth of $174 million. Stanley Lurie, Saxon's longtime chairman, president, and chief executive officer (an accountant by training—who else could have kept track of the phony bookkeeping?), was removed from the company and charged in a complaint by the SEC. He later received a five-year prison sentence. Well into the Chapter 11 case of Saxon, the creditors finally understood why the company needed the protection of the bankruptcy court.

In a way Saxon's task became the same as Lurie's had been: to make something from nothing, or at least from little. The company brought in William J. Scharffenberger, who had guided Penn-Dixie through Chapter 11, as chief executive officer. The company concentrated its efforts in the areas of paper distribution and envelopes. In the second half of 1984 Saxon was sold to Alco Standard Corporation, which paid $116.8 million in cash and $26.5 million in stock to fund a reorganization plan.

The remainder of 1982 saw a steady stream of large corporations taking advantage of the Chapter 11 process.

The shakeout in the oil and gas industry sent Nucorp Energy scurrying for cover. Nucorp had ridden the boom in oil and gas drilling, going from $38 million in sales in 1979 to $416 million in 1981, and then had ridden the industry down. The company had failed to foresee the crash in domestic oil and gas production and had invested heavily not only in exploration in the U.S. but also in hundreds of millions of dollars of drilling pipe that had no immediate use. In its bankruptcy papers, the corporation listed $777.1 million in assets as against a mere $683.6 million in debts. However, much of the value of its assets consisted of oil and gas in the ground and fifty acres of steel pipe inventory that would not be producing income in the near future. Nucorp's investors had ridden the roller coaster with the company—its stock went from $21 a share in August 1981 to $1 at the time of the bankruptcy.

While Nucorp's problems stemmed from its depressed industry, its own mistakes had added to its woes. In addition to not anticipating the market swing and failing to react quickly when it was happening, weak central management had allowed units to overbuy. Instead of reducing high-interest debt with profits during the boom in the oil business in the late 1970s, Nucorp had borrowed money voraciously in breakneck expansion. Despite being in an industry where a shift in the winds from Arabia can instantly destroy corporate charters, Nucorp found its errors smoothed over by Chapter 11, which allowed for a reorganization. In 1984, the corporation would pay $177 million to its creditors, resulting in large losses to them, but Nucorp would live on.

The settlement was a nasty blow to Continental Illinois Bank and Trust Company of Chicago, which had loaned Nucorp $173 million— near the bank's lending limit to one customer. Then again, the bank had been staggering under heavy blows to its financial stability for some time. Its aggressive loan program to the oil industry during the late 1970s, during which it actively sought out borrowers to throw money at, had come back to bite it in the 1980s. It lost about a billion dollars from loans accepted through Penn Square Bank alone. Continental also was a major lender to AM International, Wickes Companies, and Braniff International. Like Nucorp, Continental's own policies and mistakes had magnified the effects of the downturn. The availability of Chapter 11 to Contintental's debtors further added to Continental's problems, almost bringing it down. It was saved only by being taken over by the Federal Deposit Insurance Corporation, which in many ways could not afford to allow Continental to collapse.

The 1982 bankruptcies kept on coming. Records are made to be broken, and the championship caliber shown first by White Motor, then by Itel, and then by Wickes was eclipsed on August 16, 1982, when Johns-Manville, newly renamed Manville Corporation, filed that special, powerful piece of paper with the clerk of the Bankruptcy Court in Manhattan. Manville weighed in with more than $2 billion in assets.

With the Manville filing, something was amiss in bankruptcyland. Manville's liabilities on its books were considerably less than its assets. The company was making money hand over fist. Granted that Chapter 11 was proving to be a paper tiger, but why was one of the largest, most profitable, companies in the United States volunteering for special duty? Would Manville not only break a size record but set a new standard for the reach of the Bankruptcy Code?

Ironically, Manville had filed Chapter 11 because in one important way it was *not* like the other companies in bankruptcy that had been caught by the economic downturn. Indeed, like the well-managed company that it was, Manville carefully was planning ahead for its *future insolvency*! It would become one of the foremost "Hey, you can't do that" bankruptcies of the 1980s.

Manville's major problem was not its banks nor its suppliers. Its major problem was thousands of people around the country who were sick and dying because of breathing in its primary product, asbestos, over a period of time. They were factory workers who had helped to manufacture asbestos products. They were construction workers who had installed asbestos insulation in ships and buildings. They also were the surviving family members of those breadwinners whose lives had been shortened by asbestosis or various forms of asbestos-related cancers. There was every reason to believe that health claims against Manville would be made for decades to come and would include those made by people with accidental exposure to asbestos, such as those who lived or worked in structures containing asbestos installation.

Manville had filed Chapter 11 for the express purpose of compromising those health claims. No company ever before had filed a bankruptcy to "reorganize" a large group of personal injury cases. Further, Manville was demanding that its Chapter 11 reorganization bind people who would be getting sick from its asbestos products *in the future* and would not even know enough to make claims in the bankruptcy. If Manville were to succeed, Chapter 11 would rise to new heights as a corporate tool, but more on that later.

KDT Industries, a large discount department store chain (and Continental Illinois Bank customer), filed Chapter 11 in 1982 in order to, in bankruptcy parlance, "reject" a number of its store leases, as authorized under the Bankruptcy Code. "Rejection" of a lease pursuant to Chapter 11 is nothing more than a breach of the lease by the tenant. Under ordinary circumstances, a tenant vacating premises still has to pay what remains on the lease. If there is a year to go, the landlord is entitled to the full twelve months payment. Not so in Chapter 11. The Bankruptcy Code limits the period of time on a canceled lease for which the landlord can make a claim. Also, even though the breach of the lease takes place during the bankruptcy, by the express terms of the Bankruptcy Code the landlord is not considered to have a "priority" claim arising during the case but rather is relegated to prepetition unsecured creditor status—which, of course, means that the claim will be paid in highly discounted dollars. For a company like KDT chafing under a number of unwise leases entered into during times of optimistic overexpansion, the lure of Chapter 11 can be irresistible. KDT quickly moved to close one-third of its stores, laying off thousands of employees.

KDT used its stay in Chapter 11 to cancel a good many of its leases and to improve the terms of some leases by threatening cancellation. Money saved then was applied to the purchase of inventory for the remaining stores. When the company completed its restructuring, it presented its Plan of Reorganization to its creditors, which consisted of paying them stock for their claims. Since every company has only so much equity, the only effect of issuing stock without receiving any payment for it is that the existing shareholders suffer dilution of the value of their holdings. Thus, with a wave of the Chapter 11 magic wand, KDT wiped out all of its debt existing on the date of the bankruptcy, wiped out all liabilities to landlords for cancellation of leases, and made its shareholders pay for the whole thing. The exercise cost the company nothing whatsoever. Now *that* is a reorganization!

Revere Copper and Brass, whose roots can be traced to a copper-rolling mill founded by metalsmith and famous horseback rider Paul Revere, also sought protection from its creditors. The company had been plagued by unwise long-term power and raw-materials contracts. Chapter 11 allowed it to "reject" those agreements similarly to KDT's lease cancellations, as well as to halt environmental claims against it. After emerging from Chapter 11, it was taken over in a leveraged buyout in 1986. As of 1988, it had $601 million in sales.

The economic downturn also had caught a pretender to the megacorporate throne before he could build his empire. In October 1982, DeLorean Motor Company filed its Chapter 11 petition in Detroit. The corporation owed about $80 million, but had few hard assets that might be sold for cash. (The manufacturing facility in Belfast, Ireland, built with much aid from the English government, was liquidated separately under British law.) One supplier's attorney observed, "I'm just not sure if there's much there besides office furniture."

The year fittingly closed with the bankruptcy of a company that liked Chapter 11 so much that it filed for it a second time. HRT Industries, a discount retailer and apparel manufactuer, had filed a reorganization proceeding in 1974 when it was known as Hartfield-Zodys. This time around, the large chain, whose stock was traded on the New York Stock Exchange (as with nearly all the corporations being discussed in this book), had been hurt by its customers' financial problems owing to the Volcker Depression and by high interest rates. A peculiar problem of the retailer was the devaluation of the Mexican peso. Stores near the Tex-Mex border and in Los Angeles had been hit extra hard.

Executives of HRT handled the bankruptcy with practiced ease. Advertisements reminded customers that Chapter 11 did not mean liquidation. Employees exuded semiknowledgable confidence. Suppliers were persuaded to keep shipping, and the stores remained adequately stocked.

The company slipped into Chapter 11 so smoothly that cynics among its thousands of suppliers thought they saw much method in the madness. They noted that, even though HRT's profitability was suffering, the company recently had reported record sales. Although Edward D. Solomon, the chairman of HRT who had put the company into both bankruptcies, stated that the newest case had been filed only after much "soul-searching" due to "very recent" cash flow problems, creditors felt that Chapter 11 had been invoked merely to help the company over a temporary snag. (The company did close some stores and let go more than 10 percent of its employees.) Also, the bankruptcy was timed perfectly to come after HRT had received most of its shipments of Christmas merchandise but before the company had paid for it. The creditors were not jolly about playing Santa to HRT.

One of the more accomplished bankruptcy-liquidation vultures, Schottenstein Stores Corporation, of Columbus, Ohio, was drawn to the scent of the wounded company. Together with the McCrory unit of Rapid American Corporation, Schottenstein funded a Plan of Reorganization that gave creditors fifty-five cents on the dollar and 35 percent of HRT's stock. McCrory and Schottenstein together ended up with 55 percent of HRT's stock. HRT's shareholders at the time of the filing of the bankruptcy were left holding only 10 percent of the reconstituted company's shares. By the time HRT's Plan of Reorganization was approved in February 1984, it had managed to hide in Chapter 11 for two Christmases. (Shortly thereafter, McCrory bought out Schottenstein, which went on to scavenge many more retailers during the Eighties.)

Nineteen eighty-three was a busy year in the halls of bankruptcy . . . and in the courtrooms, too!

GHR Companies was an oil, gas, and chemical conglomerate owned and operated by John R. Stanley. Stanley was (and still is) quite a colorful character who has cut a swath through the courts of America, including the nation's bankruptcy courts. In the bankruptcy reorganization case(s) of GHR Energy Corporation, one of the subsidiaries of GHR Companies, Stanley would establish a world-class level of audacity and manipulation of the bankruptcy process.

John Stanley may have been raised in Massachusetts, but he was a Texan at heart. Stanley started in the energy business as a gas station attendant in Worcester and then moved on to own a string of service stations. By thirty-three, he was a millionaire. Pursuing a dream of establishing an energy empire, he then began accumulating gas and oil fields in Texas and Louisiana. The gas jockey from Massachusetts was riding high in the oil patch, for there was much money to be made in oil and gas in the first half of the 1970s. However, a shift in ammonia prices created a financial crisis for Stanley's ammonia plant; and in 1975 that operating entity, then known as Good Hope Incorporated, filed a bankruptcy reorganization case under Chapter XI of the Bankruptcy Act. Stanley would continue to build his empire in spite of little inconveniences such as operating under bankruptcy court supervision.

Although immensely wealthy, Stanley found the bankruptcy court to his liking. He bullied creditors, litigating fiercely within the bankruptcy court against those who attempted to stand up to his tactics. The court procedures that would restrict his actions simply were ignored. During the *five* years that Good Hope was in bankruptcy, Stanley continued to engineer its growth. Finally, the company emerged from bankruptcy by promising to pay creditors in full over four years, largely with money borrowed from its new bank—you guessed it—Continental Illinois. Once out of bankruptcy, Good Hope was renamed GHR Energy Corporation, and its home office was moved to Louisiana.

Stanley learned a valuable lesson managing Good Hope in bankruptcy: the creditors were paper tigers. He learned that if the company in reorganization fought them tooth and nail, they could be rendered impotent. He realized that he risked only slaps on his wrist by judges for fighting unfairly, which would come only very much after he had accomplished his goals. John Stanley had perfected the contentious court reorganization, where creditors are worn down and tired out by the aggressiveness and litigiousness of the Chapter 11 company before being offered crumbs from the debtor's table. Chapter 11 easily had become the sword as well as the shield.

There was a corollary to the rule that Stanley had perceived. It is easier to make money if one does not pay one's bills.

With $3.3 billion in annual income by the early 1980s, Stanley's GHR Companies ranked as the third largest privately held industrial company in the United States; but GHR Energy Corporation, the operating arm of the empire, was once more in deep trouble. At a time when the devastating shakeout in independent oil refineries that had claimed Energy Cooperative was raging, Stanley had poured $900 million (largely in borrowed money) into what he hoped would be a state-of-the-art refinery in what became Good Hope, Louisiana. However, the economics of the oil industry would not cooperate with Stanley's grand plan. Operations at the refinery were halted shortly before GHR Energy filed a Chapter 11 proceeding in January 1983.

When compared with the Seven Sisters oil companies, GHR Energy was only a small oil and gas concern. Nevertheless, with $1.1 billion dollars in debt owed to more than a thousand creditors, it was one of the largest bankruptcy cases ever filed. The case was filed in Stanley's home court of Worcester, Massachusetts, a courthouse unfamiliar with the arcane world of oil and gas except for Mr. Stanley's company.

Uncharacteristically, in a weak moment, Mr. Stanley had let his lenders get a jump on him. During 1982, when GHR Energy was foundering outside the safe harbor of bankruptcy, Stanley had allowed the consortium of banks to improve their position by taking control—taking a lien, in effect—of $375 million worth of oil and gas fields. That move gave them a leg up on the trade creditors for a good portion of their loans and provided them with some leverage against Stanley. (Stanley referred to the tactics the banks used to gain security as "a reign of terror.")

Although having the lien was better for the banks than being wholly unsecured, it did not end the banks' woes. It would be some time before the collateral in the earth could be turned into cash, and Stanley proved to be a master at negating the banks' power in court. By the way, Continental Illinois Bank and Trust Company of Chicago was a prominent lender, to the tune of $82.5 million.

Mr. Stanley was upbeat after the filing of the Chapter 11 case. He predicted a quick sale of some assets, possibly even the flagship refinery, to either undisclosed companies or undisclosed countries. He valued his gas reserves at $1 billion and claimed that he would soon be squeezing $250 million a year in revenues from them. He boasted,

"When I'm finished, we'll be known as the Chrysler of the energy business." The analogy was not exact—he would have to do without direct federal largess. However, he would have the benefit of the federal megabankruptcy welfare system. It would have been more accurate had Stanley pictured himself as the Marathon Man of the bankruptcy court, for his company's second court reorganization would last almost as long as the first.

The banks had had enough of John Stanley's cheery vision. Memories of GHR Energy's last reorganization were still fresh—partly because the company was still making payments on that plan! They quickly put together a proposal to oust Stanley, attempting to induce the trade creditors to go along by promising them a payout of $200 million over fifteen years, which seemed a ridiculously long period at that time but would prove close to the mark. They persuaded Stanley to allow outside directors to sit on his board. They had the case moved to Houston, to a courthouse filled to overflowing with oil and gas bankruptcies. If they thought that any of those moves would unseat John Stanley, hasten the end of the Chapter 11 case, or even slow Stanley down, they were greatly mistaken.

GHR Energy settled into Chapter 11. Five more of Stanley's twenty-six units joined GHR Energy there, bringing the total debt of the bankruptcy contingent of Stanley's companies up to $1.4 billion. Proceeding with his dream for the Good Hope refinery, Stanley proposed to spend $24 million to improve refinery capabilities of the shuttered facility. (The refinery was well named!) The operations of the gas fields were expanded through innovative drilling deals and other arrangements that minimized GHR's cash outlays. The Chapter 11 company did so well that Stanley even gave himself a raise. His wife, a daughter, a son, and two sons-in-law remained on the payroll. For his own reasons, Stanley decided to change the name of GHR Energy to TransAmerican Natural Gas Company.

Some of John Stanley's maneuvers were questionable under the bankruptcy laws, and the creditors were forever attempting to keep up with his latest move. It was difficult to tell which receipts of Stanley's companies outside of bankruptcy belonged to them and which should have gone into the companies in Chapter 11. Stanley used $500,000 of TransAmerican's money to set up a company nominally owned by his wife—and therefore outside of bankruptcy court supervision—to service TransAmerican's wells at a price higher than an independent company would have charged. Eventually, at the urging of creditors, the judge forced Stanley to bring those operations within the bankruptcy. In all, the John R. Stanley family did not suffer during the bankruptcy, and in fact it prospered mightily. Even the *Wall Street Journal* commented that "seldom have the burdens of a Chapter 11 case fallen so heavily on the creditors—and so lightly on the debtor. . . . [B]y not paying its bills promptly, TransAmerican has sucked the life out of so many small oil-field companies that it is known in South Texas as 'Transylvania,' after Dracula's stamping ground."

True to form, Stanley took his time exiting from bankruptcy. By October 1986, he had wrung $200 million in debt concessions from his weary creditors and had offered to pay the remaining debt over ten years. (They had the choice of taking the long-term payout or 30 percent in a quickie settlement.) Never in a hurry actually to pay creditors, Stanley kept the negotiations up in the air into the spring of 1987. By that time, at least five hundred creditors had dried up and blown away like Texas tumbleweeds and would not have to be paid anything at all. At that point, a frustrated creditor, Coastal Corporation, attempted to propose its own plan; but TransAmerican fought back, accusing Coastal in a mud-slinging public relations campaign of plotting to interfere with its reorganization effort (!) and filing a $2 billion damage suit against the creditor.

It was then that Stanley concluded that he had ridden Chapter 11 as far as that horse could go. He made peace with Coastal and wrapped up the reorganization in August 1987. GHR Energy/TransAmerican had been in its last Chapter 11 case for four years and eight months and in reorganization proceedings for a total of nine years out of the previous twelve. Considering the delay in payment that the creditors endured as well as the terms of the reorganization plan, they had received very little for more than a billion dollars "invested" in Stanley's dreams. If there is a Bankruptcy Hall of Fame, John R. Stanley most certainly is in it.

Even as new megacorporations were ducking into Chapter 11, others were exiting. The American economy of 1983 was not great, but it was better than it had been for several years, and many of the early Chapter 11s of the Eighties were ready to cast aside the protections of the bankruptcy court. Besides, they had accomplished all they wished in bankruptcy.

In March 1983, Itel's Plan of Reorganization was approved by its creditors and the presiding judge. Its unsecured trade and bank creditors received $341 million in cash (the company had accumulated $417 million in cash while in Chapter 11) plus notes and stock. The company claimed that the total package resulted in about a 66 percent payout to unsecured creditors, but because Itel's projections under its plan had been rosier than early 1983 reality had turned out to be, the value of the notes and stock was less than the creditors had hoped. In the end, about $800 million of the legitimate claims for loans, goods, and services by thousands of companies had disappeared into the maw of the bankruptcy court, canceled under the authority of the Bankruptcy Code. The creditors also bore the risks inherent in holding the long-term notes that were a big part of their payout under the plan. The shareholders of Itel saw their holdings diluted to 7 percent by the issuance of the stock to creditors.

Even though the plan was approved, it was recognized that disputes over some major claims remained undetermined. They had to be settled or litigated to a conclusion before the reorganization plan could be finalized and payouts begun. It would not be until September 19, 1983, that Itel was cleared to exit from bankruptcy and execute its Plan of Reorganization. Itel had been in Chapter 11 for thirty-two months.

Itel still faced a struggle. Its railroad and shipping container businesses were in sick industries. Its days as a computer leader were long gone. Its major asset—and it *was* a major asset—was $370 million in "net operating loss" (n.o.l.) tax benefits that could be used to shelter future profits or, more likely, to shelter the future profits of profitable companies that Itel might acquire. The investment banking house of Kohlberg, Kravis, Roberts and Company already was sniffing around for leveraged buyout possibilities. Because of the n.o.l., the American taxpayers would pay a good portion of maintaining Itel's existence.

Having cleaned up its balance sheet, Itel was able to make it through tough times in the leasing industry though it continued losing money. It was not until the first quarter of 1985 that the company made its first profit—a small one at that—since prior to bankruptcy.

Itel's improving fortunes attracted a takeover enterpreneur by the name of Sam Zell, who became chairman. Zell then used Itel as a springboard for an unwanted takeover of Great Lakes International, Itel paying $129.7 million. In 1987, Itel bought Flexi-Van Leasing for

$222.1 million and Evans Transportation for $225 million. In 1989, it had revenues of $750 million.

White Motors continued retrenching furiously in Chapter 11. During a fifteen-month period ending March 1981, White had lost $146 million on operations and $165 million on discontinued businesses. In August 1981, White had sold its pride, its heavy-duty truck manufacturing operations, to Sweden's AB Volvo, for a mere $70.4 million in cash and notes. In mid-1982, White sold its finance subsidiary for $33 million in notes, leaving the company a mere shadow of its former self. By 1983, White's new direction was set. It would continue on as a small automotive-parts producer, and, since it had sold its name to Volvo, it would henceforth do business as Northeast Ohio Axle. White did carry one highly valuable asset into its future operations, a huge net operating loss tax benefit that would shield profits from Uncle Sam for a long time to come.

The treatment of creditors in White's Plan of Reorganization is instructive on what lenders who fail to take security can lose. In the White plan, the lenders were treated separately, constituted as their own class of creditors denominated as "senior debt claims," and they were paid 53 percent of their claims. Under the plan the trade creditors were paid forty-nine cents on the dollar. In other words, the lenders received very little monetary recognition for their almost honorary position as "senior debt." Had they held security they could have neared full repayment of the principal amount of their loans.

In 1983, Baldwin-United Corporation got tangled in its own financial web and threatened to take a lot of innocent customers down with it.

Based in Cincinnati, the financial services company had built a huge business selling "single premium deferred annuities" to older middle-class people through a number of insurance company subsidiaries. The program offered individuals a fixed income for life starting at a retirement age, in return for one large initial premium which could be on the order of $100,000 or more. In the interim, income on the premium—promised by Baldwin to be very substantial, in the neighborhood of 14 percent a year—would accumulate for the benefit of the policyholder but was not subject to income tax until actually paid out. The annuity program was innovative, attracting $3.2 billion in policy premiums, but it also was controversial. It depended upon the funds administered by the company earning handsome returns. Also, similar to bank deposits or standard life insurance—or a Ponzi scheme—it worked only if not too many policies were turned in at once and the company kept on selling a sufficient number of new ones.

Since the annuities were a form of insurance, the Baldwin subsidiaries that offered them were regulated by state insurance departments. However, the agencies found it difficult to follow Baldwin's tangle of financial arrangements. For example, some capital requirements of Baldwin units were met by holding stock in other units. When any state agency required a Baldwin unit to write down the value of its portfolio and acquire additional capital, often that was accomplished by shifting securities of another Baldwin company into the portfolio. Baldwin also canceled dividends to outside investors so that it could concentrate its funds on paying dividends to its own affiliates, thereby boosting the value of their stock. In other words, Baldwin's finances began to go around in circles.

The circles began to look like they were swirls down a drain by mid-1983. In the first quarter of 1983 alone, Baldwin had to write off almost $600 million, due to state insurance departments insisting that portfolios be devalued. News of Baldwin's troubles with states' insurance regulations caused a number of customers to redeem their annuities even though they suffered 5 percent penalties. Redemptions in turn set off more capital problems, which in turn stimulated more redemptions. Redemptions began to exceed sales of new policies. Lenders were asked to enter into "standstill" agreements whereby they would not enforce defaults by Baldwin. In July, regulators in Arkansas and Indiana halted redemptions of funds in those states. While that action stopped the hemorrhaging of those funds, it worried yet more policyholders around the country—not to mention Baldwin's banks, who scrambled to take security. Victor H. Palmieri, a turnaround specialist who had been the president and chief executive officer of Baldwin only since May, began to talk about one of Baldwin's noninsurance subsidiaries, MGIC Investment Corporation, becoming the new profit center of the company.

In September 1983, Baldwin-United Corporation filed for protection from its creditors under Chapter 11 of the Bankruptcy Code at about the same time that several of them filed an "involuntary" Chapter 11 petition against it. Baldwin listed its assets at $9.38 billion, which, even allowing for overvaluation of many assets, made it a whopping big bankruptcy. The company had about a billion dollars in short-term debt alone. MGIC was not included in the bankruptcy, and the company put it up for sale. Baldwin also announced that it would sell its namesake business and its flagship in simpler times, Baldwin Piano and Organ Company, to raise operating cash.

The bankruptcy filing hit all of the interested parties hard. Everyone blamed everyone else for pushing Baldwin into Chapter 11 and moaned and groaned about the fees and other expenses that would be incurred in the bankruptcy. There were fears that Baldwin's financial organization was so complicated that the judge would not be able to figure it out. On the other hand, none of the creditor groups offered immediate compromise or additional cash.

The first issue in the bankruptcy was how many creditor committees should be appointed. To appoint committees of the fifty or so classes of creditors Baldwin had created with its financing techniques would have been to bury the case in the committee's lawyers' and accountants' fees. To limit the number of creditors' committees would be to render them deadlocked because there would be so many diverse interests. The judge limited the creditors to one committee, the only other being a common shareholders' committee. Immediately upon the naming of representatives of the various creditor groups to the unsecured creditors' committee, intense backbiting and jockeying for position within the bankruptcy ensued. A fight erupted over how to use $2 million—really petty cash, in the context of the case—in profits that Baldwin was receiving from banks in which it had an interest.

The numbers in the Baldwin case were awe inspiring. In 1984, the company announced that it had lost $1.4 billion the previous year and that its net worth was a negative $1 billion. It sold MGIC for considerably less than the $1.2 billion it had paid for it. The litigation over the annuity business threatened to overwhelm the restructuring of the company, the lawyers and accountants racking up millions in fees.

Through the haze of battle, a reorganization plan emerged. Throughout most of 1985 and 1986 it developed as litigated matters were finalized. About $170 million were paid to the states of Indiana and Arkansas to free Baldwin's annuities from purgatory. Unsecured creditors received $70 million in cash and notes for another $105 million. (Some more money may have become available through several pieces of litigation that dragged on past the confirmation of the reorganization plan.) Creditors were awarded 87 percent of the stock in the company.

The company that emerged from Chapter 11 in November 1986 was a mere shadow of its former self. Its main businesses were trading stamps, employee motivation programs, travel agencies, and, yes, some insurance. The bulk of its income would come from subsidiaries Top Value Stamps and S&H Trading Stamps. It even changed its name, to Phicorp, and moved its main office from Cincinnati to Philadelphia. Victor Palmieri, who had managed the company through the reorganization, remained as chairman. There was no resemblance between the prebankruptcy Baldwin-United and Phicorp—but Chapter 11 had permitted and encouraged the transformation, for whatever it was worth.

Another notable bankruptcy in the fall of 1983 was that of a pretender to the megacorporate ranks. In May 1981, a Silicon Valley jouranlist, Adam Osborne, had revolutionized the computer industry by introducing a portable computer and "bundled" software for it at the West Coast Computer Fair in San Francisco. For two short years, the world had beat a path to Osborne's door, but in 1983, his house of cards toppled.

As the first computer to combine a disk drive, screen, and keyboard into one portable unit, the Osborne I was the grandfather of today's laptops and, at $1,795, a heck of a bargain to boot. It filled an immense demand for a computer that could be carried easily to business meetings, accountants' audits in the field, etc. Its software was innovative and easy to master. It was such a pleasure to use that Osborne Computer Corporation did not have customers, it had fans, many of whom organized Osborne I computer clubs around the country just for the fun of it. (Many of those customers, still swearing on the usefulness of their Osborne I's, gobbled up the company's inventory later when the company was liquidated.)

Osborne Computer Corporation took off like a rocket. In 1981, Osborne sold forty thousand units. At the start of 1982, the company's income was $1 million a month. By the end of 1982, it was taking in $10 million a month. It attracted $32 million in investment capital from people dreaming of becoming filthy rich by helping to start the next IBM. However, competitors such as Kaypro and Compaq quickly had entered the field with good products, and future development would have to be carefully managed.

Adam Osborne was a good thinker and a very good promoter, but he had no idea how to manage the rapid growth of the corporation or stay on top of the company's finances. When the company's books were audited in 1983 preparatory to a large stock offering that would finance its future growth, all involved received a rude shock. Ever-increasing sales of computers and software had masked the fact that the company was losing money on each sale! At about the same time, word leaked out that the company would soon be introducing the Osborne II. Dealers cut their orders for the original model, but development problems stalled introduction of the new model. The company had fallen between the stools precisely at a time when it needed strong cash flow.

Actually, the company needed more than good sales; it needed a miracle. Anticipating its stock offering, Osborne had borrowed heavily on a short-term basis to finance research and development and, it turned out, losses on sales. However, the audit had raised so many questions about Osborne's operations that it was impossible for the company either to raise additional money from investors or to borrow further funds from banks. Like Wile E. Coyote in the Sunday morning cartoons, Osborne Computer Corporation had gone over the cliff and had been hanging in midair for some time, but it did not fall until it looked down.

There was talk of selling the rights to the computer to other companies and talk of bringing in new management, while the computer market whizzed right by the prostrate company.

In mid-1984, with Adam Osborne gone from the company, a Silicon Valley veteran by the name of Ronald J. Brown and his attorney made a proposition to the creditors' committee to jump-start the company. Brown, who had little money of his own, essentially wanted to use the Osborne name as a vehicle to raise investment capital in order to sell portable computers made in Europe. With nothing to lose, the creditors accepted a plan providing some cash, mostly on the "if-come," and 20 percent of the stock in the recapitalized entity.

Brown and his sharp lawyer had spotted a loophole. Under a provision new to the bankruptcy law in the Reform Act of 1978, companies issuing stock as part of a reorganization no longer have to comply with securities laws. The statutory formalities required under the securities laws, including the requirement of a prospectus, are overriden by the Bankruptcy Code. The thinking of the drafters of the code was that the requirement of a Disclosure Statement in the bankruptcy law insured that those being issued the stock would have sufficient information to guide them. Under Brown's proposal, stock not only was given to creditors but it also was sold to the public, under the cover of the bankruptcy law. Its legality was not challenged.

Osborne emerged from Chapter 11 in January 1985. Brown indeed got Osborne going again, offering products manufactured by others, but the magic had gone out of the Osborne name. In an industry that is so fast moving that people can get conservative about their buying habits—the main question being "Is it IBM compatible?"—the company was never able to shake the ignominy of its collapse. A little over a year later, the company was declared in default of its payment plan and was liquidated.

Osborne's fall put a chill on investment in what had been the go-go computer industry. It provided a strong note of caution that still guides investors in computer hardware today.

Nineteen eighty-four marked the Chapter 11 filing of another computer industry high-flyer, Storage Technology Corporation. Unlike Osborne Computer, it had achieved megacorporate status before it hit turbulence, and accordingly its fate was far different.

Storage Technology was in the news a lot during the early 1980s, and the news was all good. Whether the company was issuing $100 million in debentures or issuing press releases describing how much demand there was for its product line, it gave every indication of a growing company. (It helped that rival IBM was having trouble developing its own disk device.) Its 1980 sales were $603.5 million, almost exactly double those of 1978, and, unlike Osborne's, they were profitable sales. With the corporation flush with cash, its chairman Jesse Aweida pursued his dream of producing total computer systems. Just before the end of 1981, it announced the purchase of Magnuson Computer Systems with nothing more than 1.8 million of its own shares. It confidently announced another product-to-be, an optical disk data storage device that would handle much more information than existing devices.

Storage Tech rolled right into 1982. As of the beginning of the year, it had a $485 million backlog of orders. It snagged an $80 million contract with the Army to supply tape, disk, and printer products. During 1982, the company racked up about a billion dollars in sales.

In the midst of all its success, Storage Tech had a bugaboo that it could not shake. It seemed that everyone in the computer industry, as well as every stockbroker specializing in analyzing that industry, was assuming that sometime soon Big Blue—IBM—would get its act together and swat Storage Tech down like a fly. They were right. When IBM did finally come out with a disk drive, it had leapfrogged Storage Tech's technology with a superior product, and Storage Tech was left playing catch-up ball. In 1983, IBM shipped fifty-five thousand disk drives, compared with fifty-four hundred units for *all* other manufacturers.

Storage Technology limped into 1984 and went downhill from there. In January, it canceled its attempt to build a mainframe computer, which had cost it $75 million to that date. With money in short supply, other research projects that were the future of the company also were in danger. In the third quarter, it lost $60 million, which was not a devastating amount for a megacorporation; however, that was the company's fifth straight quarterly loss, and the company announced that it might have to write down the value of its assets. On October 31, the company filed a Chapter 11 petition in Denver. Its fourth quarter 1984 loss, reflecting write-downs as well as declining sales, was $419.2 million.

Was this the end of Storage Technology? The market having spoken, should not the company fold up its tent? Not necessarily, because Storage Tech had an ace up its sleeve. Of $694.5 million in liabilities, only $15.7 million was secured debt—and the company had Chapter 11 to fall back on.

While in Chapter 11, Storage Technology concentrated on stabilizing its cash position. It quickly laid off about four thousand workers and trimmed other operating costs as much as possible. Over the objections of the trade creditors, it took out an $80 million loan for working capital. Restructuring accomplished by fall 1985 stood to save the company about $50 million a year. Finally, reluctantly, management announced the cancellation of the company's efforts to build an optical disk drive, once considered critical to the company's future but now a research and development cash sponge that already had soaked up $100 million.

As happens in Chapter 11s, the year passed quickly. As 1986 was ushered in, Storage Tech's restructuring had started to take hold, and it had become marginally profitable. Discussions proceeded in earnest concerning a Plan of Reorganization. The shape of a reorganization came into focus and—what do you know?—another year became history while the parties negotiated and drafted.

It was not until June 1987 that the Plan of Reorganization for

Storage Technology and its subsidiaries was confirmed. About $800 million in liabilities were canceled by the payment of $321.5 million in cash, the issuance of ten-year notes at 13.5 percent interest in the face amount of $285 million, and the issuance of 192 million shares of stock. The company took with it out of bankruptcy roughly $740 million in assets, subject only to $345 million in (long-term) debt. It also took with it $380 million in tax-loss carryforwards that would be used to shield future income from federal income taxation. Shareholders' equity stood at about $200 million. There is nothing like Chapter 11 to clean up a balance sheet!

Chapter 7

Wickes Meets
Ming the Merciless

It was early 1982. To call the recent performance of the business group known as Wickes Companies "countercyclical" would have been charitable. A more honest observer might have said that it was doing everything wrong. It was a very sick conglomerate in a very sick economy.

"Conglomerate" had been the buzzword for corporate executives during the 1970s. The theory was that an executive who was competent enough to run a company in a profitable manner could run *any* company profitably, since success merely was a matter of analyzing balance sheets and maintaining the proper financial ratios. The concept was and is hogwash, of course. Computers provide data, but not wisdom. Creating a profitable company is not a science (and, in fact, science is not as cut-and-dried as most people think). Circumstances can screw up the best-laid plans, as Bobbie Burns once said. Nevertheless, one small section of the Internal Revenue Code made the theory a balance-sheet winner.

Under the IRS rules then in effect, merged companies were considered to have "pooled" their assets. As one might expect, the rule allowed the assets listed on the companies' balance sheets to be added together to form one consolidated total. As one might *not* expect, past profits could be added together to create a revisionist history of the ongoing business. As a result, poor performance could be turned into ever-increasing balance-sheet profits through serial mergers. During the 1970s, corporations drove trucks through that loophole, creating excellent profits on paper without having to take the trouble of actually getting their products out the door efficiently.

Unfortunately, as with accelerated depreciation or junk bonds or any other forms of purely paper manipulation, economic reality must set in eventually. Accountants could make the conglomerates profitable on paper, but they could not run the companies profitably. The whiz kids in the executive suites made tyros' mistakes when assigned to unfamiliar industries. As any blue collar down on the assembly line could have told them, making tires is not like selling machinery which is not like operating a finance company. Wickes was learning that lesson the hard way. Also, it was borrowing large chunks of money to buy companies at a time when interest rates were becoming deadly. Wickes was blindly following an expansionist conglomerate plan in a contracting economy.

Originally called the Wickes Corporation, it had made its mark after World War II by developing America's first lumber supermarkets. During the Seventies, under the leadership of E. L. McNeely, Wickes had become one of the largest national retailers in two fields, building supplies and furniture, through its Wickes Lumber, Builder's Emporium, and Wickes Furniture chains. That spectacular internal growth of Wickes was but part of McNeely's grand plan, which was one of the most ambitious in recent corporate history. Following the conglomerate muse, McNeely started a consumer finance company and engineered the acquisition of MacGregor Golf Company; and then he looked around for more companies to gobble up.

McNeely spotted what he called "a once-in-a-lifetime opportunity." He would add to his conglomerate by buying . . . a conglomerate. Gamble-Skogmo and its subsidiaries, based in Minneapolis, Minnesota, were available. Under the G-S umbrella were the Red Owl Supermarkets; Snyder's Drug Stores; Alden's, a well-established catalog house; J. M. McDonald Department Stores; Howard Brothers Discount Stores; Howard Brothers of Phenix City, Alabama; Woman's World Shops; Southland Wholesale Distributors, a marketer of grain and beans; Airstar, a financial services subsidiary; and 21 percent of retailer Garfinckel, Brooks Brothers, Miller and Rhoads. In one massive purchase, Wickes would gain retail operations throughout the United States and Canada. Wickes would become a grocer and a druggist. It would operate department, variety, and fabric stores. It would be the fifth largest mail-order company in the country. In all, the acquisition would double Wickes's size. Now that was an acquisition that Emil McNeely could get behind!

The deal did not even take much cash. Wickes was able to scoop up G-S in 1980 for $125 million plus 2.8 million of its own shares. However, as part of the deal, Wickes assumed $563 million of G-S debt, a deferred, but very real, part of the purchase price that would prove to be a stone around McNeely's neck.

As McNeely's vision unfolded, reality intruded upon his dream. He had been unconcerned about the fact that the G-S acquisition had served to double Wickes's debt, but 1981 would not be a good year for carrying that heavy load. Wickes's cost of debt service went from $38 million for the company's fiscal year prior to the acquisition to $200 million (!) for 1981. Sales plummeted during 1981 as the Volcker Depression KO'd consumer spending in its fight against inflation. When the construction industry went into hibernation in the face of 20-plus percent financing costs and 15 percent home mortgages, Wickes's core lumber and furniture businesses suffered greatly.

Another problem for McNeely was that reality was putting the lie to a basic assumption of conglomerate theory. It turned out—not surprisingly, really—that all businesses were *not* alike, that running a company meant more than shuffling accounting statements and trading corporate charters. Wickes had not looked deeply enough into G-S's many businesses to see that some of them were stagnant and others poorly managed. When knowledgeable G-S managers were axed and replaced with Wickes's executives who were unfamiliar with those businesses, they suffered further decline. In 1984, *Fortune* magazine would label the Wickes-Gamble-Skogmo merger among the worst of the prior decade.

Embarrassingly enough, the economic downturn revealed that Wickes itself was not the paradigm of good management. It had turned out that while McNeely was conquering an empire, he had forgotten to watch the store. Wickes had continued to rely on construction contractors, perhaps the hardest hit segment of the economy, as its prime lumber customers while other lumber companies had done a better job of moving into suburban areas and catering to do-it-yourselfers. McNeely's policy of moving managers around from business to business—in conglomerate theory they are all interchangeable parts—prevented them from picking up trends. Another major blunder had been McNeely's failure to foresee the country's economic trend and to conform his quest for power to the conditions that prevailed.

Management's errors had left the conglomerate, renamed Wickes Companies after the absorption of Gamble-Skogmo, wide open to the one-two-punch of high debt and declining retail sales, and it was sent reeling. For the 1981 fiscal year (actually ending January 31, 1982), the conglomerate lost $80 million, which would have devastated most retailers. However, Wickes was a heavyweight, with more than $4 *billion* in sales, and the company was able to stagger through the year.

E. L. McNeely reacted to the crisis belatedly, and he seemed to be unable to develop a unified plan for responding to the serious threats. McNeely moved to spin off some of the conglomerate's businesses, but his pride would not let him offer bargain-basement prices just to raise cash, and they languished on the market. He also entered into negotiations to sell several of the conglomerate's "cash cows," which would bring in operating capital but also would limit future opportunities for profit.

In February 1982, McNeely was able to dodge a bullet when he patched together an agreement with a number of banks to roll over $580 million in short-term debt that was coming due. The banks' price for rolling over the debt was the scheduling of a $70-million-debt payment for April 30, but almost before the ink was dry on the debt agreement, Wickes was forced to begin negotiations for a moratorium on that payment. Wickes had been given a reprieve, but it was obvious that the lenders would not be so easy to deal with the next time the loans came up for renewal unless the company could show some progress.

Wickes's board of directors, which had been very docile during McNeely's twelve-year tenure, decided that firing McNeely and his top executives would be "progress." To the board, the man who had dominated the company and engineered its spectacular growth was not the one to manage crisis and consolidation in a declining economy. The directors most closely associated with McNeely, five out of eleven, resigned. McNeely's top executives were sent packing. Management had paid for its sins, but the ritual cleansing of the executive suite did not in itself solve the mess that the company was in. Banishing a leader for leading them astray was one thing, but finding the right person to lead them to safety was another. Choosing McNeely's successor was a corporate life-or-death decision, and yet the board's options were very limited by the circumstances.

It was imperative that the giant company immediately find a chief executive to attack its monumental problems quickly and expertly. The new top man would have to know how to operate in the executive suite of a national conglomerate—there would be no time for on-the-job training in corporate procedures. He would have to be an expert in crisis management rather than strategic planning. However, the board had a problem. Executives who had risen through the corporate ranks during the 1970s had been trained on the gospel of growth and acquisition. In order for their personal merit badges to remain untarnished, they had steered clear of becoming responsible for any corporate basket-case. What accomplished businessman was an expert in poorly performing companies? What sort of high-powered executive thrived on chaos and cutbacks? What dynamic leader enjoyed, in effect, picking up a shovel and cleaning up after the parade?

Sanford C. Sigoloff was available.

When Wickes was looking for help, there were almost no business executives who specialized in joining troubled corporations and attempting to return them to profitability. Because the touchstone of American industry is growth, growth, and more growth, the corporate world was loath to admit its failures. During the 1970s, large corporations did not admit to their internal problems. Now that business failures and bankruptcy have become ingrained in the American way of life, there are more self-proclaimed experts in fixing troubled companies. However, because the nature of command in such a crisis situation is so different than traditional business training teaches, there will never be very many "turnaround artists."

The personal characteristics required of a good turnaround artist also limit the field, for they are most unusual in a corporate executive. He must thrive on living a leader's nightmare: being the captain of a sinking ship, over and over. He must know how to exercise his authority and expertise through the smoke and confusion of crisis. He must be able to make instantaneous life-or-death decisions. How can the vessel hold off its enemies and fight on, though dead in the water? What can be jettisoned to lighten the load, and what must be retained on board for later battles? Who among the crew can be saved without endangering the whole enterprise? In the midst of solving all of those predicaments, the holes in the hull must be located and plugged, using only the materials already on board.

It is a grueling job. Impending disaster does not allow for planning committees, elaborate financial projections, vacations, quiet weekends, or even civilized lunch hours. The executive suite is a crisis center, receiving emergency notices and issuing rapid-fire orders with too little information at hand, for months on end. There are no little problems because in the company's weakened condition, any one of them could spell disaster. There is never enough money to fill all the needs and never enough time to do the job right. Decision making tends to be one long exercise in triage. There are few humans who actually seek ecstasy in the midst of that agony.

Among the few true turnaround artists existing in 1982 was Sanford "Sandy" Sigoloff, who had distinguished himself by turning around two mid-sized companies during the 1970s. Although he was temporarily parked at Kaufman and Broad, a national home builder and insurance concern, as vice-chairman and chief operating officer, he was looking for the next adventure. "I'm the kind of guy who loves a very, very tough challenge," he would say when piped on the board of Wickes. There was no doubt that he had shown some promise, but was he tough enough to turn one of the largest conglomerates in the country from its course before it hit the shoals?

Sigoloff's early career was so successful that it actually served to argue against his attempts to build his image as a turnaround artist. In college in California, Sigoloff studied physics and chemistry and upon graduation he became a nuclear scientist. In 1960, he was lured into private industry to develop products on the leading edge of technology. A few years later, the company he was working for was bought by another obscure one and Sigoloff, having been awarded with a nice piece of the new company's stock, became a vice-president in charge of technical development. That company was Xerox, and for the next six years he took part in exciting advances of xerography, printing, and facsimile transmission. Sandy Sigoloff was rich and happy.

In 1969, Sandy Sigoloff showed a restless and independent streak. When Xerox moved its offices to Rochester, New York, he refused to go. He quit the company, saying that he liked southern California's sun. When a banker friend asked Sigoloff to take a look at the Republic Corporation, a conglomerate that had grown like Topsy but had fallen into Chapter 11, the idea of remixing a company instead of chemicals appealed to him. Within three months, he was president of the company, with responsibility for the conglomerate's hundred businesses in dozens of lines, including specialty steel, aviation, film processing, and graphics. Scientist Sandy had not been promoted merely to captain, he had been named *admiral* of a sinking *armada*! Was he tough enough to plug all the holes in the midst of the storm?

Sigoloff indeed was tough enough! To turn the company around, he closed down more than forty of its businesses, sold unprofitable units, and reorganized its core industries. Sigoloff exhibited the ability, even the *desire*, to take whatever steps were necessary to save a company, even if those actions led to many people being out of jobs. His energy, his long hours on the job, his insatiable appetite for conflict and crisis, and his ability to make the hard decisions shone through the wreckage. Although smaller for Sigoloff's ministrations, the leaner, meaner Republic became profitable, and the creditors were paid in full.

It was an important learning experience for Sigoloff. One thing he learned in dealing with Republic's creditors during the four-year process was how little bankers and business people knew about working with troubled companies and how ignorant they were about Chapter 11. He was already one step ahead of them.

The experience did not catapult Sigoloff into the ranks of turnaround artists, but the aftermath did. Sigoloff envisioned settling into Republic's executive suite, but the qualities that had served him so well during the company's battle for existence did not work well in peace-time, and when the board of directors reined in his shoot-from-the-hip managerial ways, he quit the company. Although he had fared very well financially, he was unhappy to have been ushered out the back door after he had done the board's dirty work.

Sigoloff may have realized at that time that the turnaround expert, like the hired gun, is the ultimate outsider. If he did, perhaps he understood his growing fascination with the job. It was the loner in Sigoloff that drew him to the work.

Young Sandy had had no social life. His father, a doctor, had enlisted in the army during World War II and had been assigned to a series of military posts in the Deep South. If it was not bad enough being a northern army brat below the Mason-Dixon Line, his life was made distinctly worse by being Jewish. According to Sigoloff, in all his teenage years in the South, he never was invited into the home of a classmate.

Of course, Sigoloff carried his past into his present. As a turnaround expert, he would find that typically he would come into town, drop himself onto the top of a corporate culture that he was not part of, practice his dark profession, and then leave. His autocratic philosophy of management was a logical outcome. Sigoloff explains, "I believe in the single-man theory.... [H]e makes the last decision. If sixteen guys out of seventeen vote yes and he votes no, it's no."

A corollary is that the human element does not count for much. To Sigoloff, good employees give their all, day and night; do what they are told; and never, never cross the boss. If someone fails to meet any one of Sigoloff's criteria, Sigoloff has no problem removing that person from his life. There do not appear to be any other human factors in his equations for producing a profitable company. Perhaps that attitude comes with the territory, but it also cost Sigoloff one of his trusted aides, who was banished for using a corporate plane without clearing it with him first.

In 1974, a year after his departure from Republic, Sigoloff was called in by Daylin Incorporated, a Los Angeles-based discount retailer and producer of health-care products with $600 million in annual sales but no profits. Sigoloff put the company into Chapter 11—it was one of the largest to that date—and began to weed out the losers. During the course of the bankruptcy, Sigoloff chopped off 120 unprofitable stores, firing eight thousand employees in the process. He did such a good job of turning around Daylin that it attracted a hostile takeover by W. R. Grace and Company in 1979. Although Sigoloff had been compensated handsomely, he did not possess the financial resources to prevent the advances of the unwelcome suitor. Having put the company back on its feet, Sigoloff was back on the street.

It was during his tenure at Daylin that Sigoloff acquired a nickname which he continues to carry with pride today: "Ming the Merciless," after the coolly efficient nemesis of Flash Gordon. It is obvious that the life-or-death power that Sigoloff has over employees of troubled companies is one of the attractions of the job. He and the close associates who travel with him have various code words and euphemisms to make light of deciding to fire someone, such as "Let's invite him to get a suntan." It is with relish that Ming observes, "There are times when you put the cape on, and you might have six executions simultaneously, some of them in public." For one magazine article, a smiling, slightly-built Sandy Sigoloff posed with a five-foot-long sword.

Sigoloff was susceptible to the siren call of the Wickes directors. Although he had been a solid vice-chairman at Kaufman and Broad, he had become bored with the humdrum of ordinary corporate life. He did not like being someone's lieutenant, even to Eli Broad, a friend from his Xerox days. Further, Wickes had assented to Sigoloff's three demands: he would be chairman of the board of directors, president, and chief executive officer, an unusual concentration of power in a megacorporation; the *directors* would serve at his pleasure, an unheard of power; and he could bring his own cadre of executives with him. If he joined Wickes, he clearly would be in command.

Once more Sanford Sigoloff threw himself into the breach. Within two weeks of being contacted by Wickes, Sigoloff was on the job (with the blessing of Broad). "I'm a war-horse," he explained. "I couldn't resist it. How many times in a lifetime do you get an opportunity to put your stamp on a business of this magnitude?"

Indeed, there was great magnitude. Sigoloff suddenly had nearly absolute control over twenty-three retail chains, five wholesalers, four manufacturers, three leasing companies, two finance companies, and an insurance company (but no partridge in a pear tree). He received a $400,000 signing bonus and was promised $300,000 a year in salary plus benefits and the opportunity for bonuses. The Wickes directors had missed a good bet—he probably would have done it for free.

It is hard to conceive of being handed the wheel at a mega-corporation with hundreds of facilities and tens of thousands of employees. It is even harder to grasp if that company is "troubled," a euphemism that understates the chaos existing when a business is almost out of money: suppliers are refusing to ship absolutely necessary inventory; the better executives (the ones who can get jobs elsewhere) have bailed out; the accounting system needs a complete revamping in order to provide absolutely necessary information about where the company is hemorrhaging; the lenders want an immediate presentation of the company's financial condition and management's plans for paying them; equipment is breaking down because money for maintenance has been needed elsewhere; landlords are pressing for additional security deposits; competitors are frightening the customers; and on, and on, and on. There is no strategic planning—everything is triage. A mistake, a slighted creditor, a hiatus in inventory deliveries, or any one of a thousand things that could cause problems for other companies could mean the *demise* of the company in such an unstable condition.

Indeed, Wickes was one troubled company. In a little over a year, it had lost more than $400 million dollars, an astounding capital drain. Its stores had become shabby. Inventory was spotty, and so were the floors of the stores due to leaky roofs. Parking lots were in dire need of deferred maintenance—a delivery truck had to be towed out of one Wickes pothole. Inadequate financial reporting and controls did not permit proper supervision of the far-flung operations. The payroll of forty-five thousand employees was too large for the conditions that prevailed. It was $2 billion in debt. Sigoloff had arrived not a moment too soon. Had he arrived too late?

Sanford Sigoloff quickly re-formed his team. His chief lieutenants, who together with him were nicknamed the Sigoloff Seven, ceased their other endeavors and reported in. In all, Sigoloff's management group and other trusted confidants who would be imposed on top of the Wickes corporate hierarchy would total sixty-five. Duty having called, they canceled their social engagements for the next several years, kissed their wives good-bye, and started logging backbreaking, nerve-racking, head-splitting workdays. Not only would Sigoloff and his crew be well compensated, they would have no time to spend their earnings foolishly!

The Sigoloff management team hit the ground running. On the Sunday before Sigoloff was to start at Wickes, his staff already had been formed into ten crisis teams to try to get a handle on the company. On his first day on the job, four of his teams were flying to Wickes outposts to show the flag. Sigoloff would say of his team, "I'm fortunate that I'm able to draw on a cadre of seasoned people who have loyalty and are willing to work eighteen-hour days." Sanford Sigoloff was in his element.

The employees of the Wickes Companies greeted the arrival of the Sigoloff Seven with a great deal of apprehension. They were well aware of how difficult it would be to match the frenzy of the crisis junkies newly installed in the executive suite. Sigoloff's reputation as a demanding taskmaster had preceded him, and he was not above reinforcing his image as a do-or-die leader with a little gallows humor. Sigoloff summoned managers from the hinterlands to company headquarters to answer hard questions about operations. Each manager was handed a letter opener with the Wickes logo as a memento of the grilling, along with directions from the boss on how to use it: the stiletto was to open the manager's bonus envelope if he succeeded on the job or, in the event of failure, plunged into himself, to escape Sigoloff's wrath. Ming the Merciless had landed.

When Sigoloff piped the crew to battle stations for an indefinite period, the desertions began. The order extending the workweek to six days for all executives led to a number of resignations, including those of the entire financial department. Many middle management types defected due to the demands put on them by the Sigoloff Seven. Some of the leave-taking was not so voluntary—Sigoloff quickly initiated the company's "diet," as he put it, by ordering a 10 percent reduction in the work force.

Wickes's lenders, a consortium of forty-four banks and insurance companies, were pleased with the change in management. The bloom had been off McNeely's rose for some time with them, and they were buoyed by Sigoloff's reputation for saving companies. In public, they expressed hope and confidence. However, behind the bravura, there must have lurked a cold fear over what Ming intended to do about their outstanding loans. After all, Wickes was choking on $580 million in short-term debt and $618 million in long-term debt, and something would have to be done about it if Wickes were to turn around. Private negotiations commenced.

Although Wickes had been beleaguered by its creditors, the arrival of Sanford Sigoloff led to a 180-degree change. It may have seemed to a casual observer that the Sigoloff Seven was outmanned and outgunned, but their experience in debtor-creditor warfare tipped the scales in their favor. While the Wickes creditors specialized in lending money or selling goods, the new Wickes executives specialized in fighting off creditors and whittling down their claims. A banker later commented on Sigoloff's tactical abilities:

> The case started with Sigoloff and his troops in full control and continued like that . . . to the end. For a long time we didn't know what the hell was going on. They hired the best professional talent available, kept control of the data and the timing, and very deliberately set creditor against creditor.

Since the creditors had no Flash Gordon on their side, Ming could have taken them on with one sword tied behind his back.

Sigoloff also knew that, if he wished, he could improve his position by invoking Chapter 11. The debtor-oriented provisions of the Bankruptcy Code stood as a safe harbor for Wickes if necessary. Further, at a time when corporate utilization of bankruptcy reorganization was in its infancy, Sigoloff was already an expert in maneuvering in those waters.

Not only was the Bankruptcy Code generally helpful to Wickes, but buried in its arcane language was a weapon that could prove conclusive in the battle.

Under the Bankruptcy Code, all creditors are not equal. There is a strict hierarchy that must be followed when making payments to creditors. At the top of the heap, ahead of the Internal Revenue Service, ahead of employee wage claims, ahead of bills incurred during the bankruptcy case, stands the secured creditor (usually a bank). Generally speaking, the bankruptcy law does not disturb the bargain struck between the debtor and that creditor prior to the bankruptcy in which credit was extended in return for the borrower providing some or all of its assets as collateral (also referred to as security). Because the secured creditor holds a lien—a mortgage, if the collateral is real estate—on *specific assets* of the debtor, it does not merely have a general claim for payment. In the event of nonpayment, it may choose to seize the collateral, sell it, and apply the proceeds against the outstanding balance, by following established rules. Although since 1979 the debtor's bankruptcy prevents the secured creditor from acting on its special status (under the previous Bankruptcy Act the filing of bankruptcy did not stop the secured creditor from foreclosing on its collateral if the debtor was behind in payments), the law does not destroy its interest in the specific property of the debtor that constitutes its collateral.

It is the nature of American business that, in most cases, a corporate debtor will have bank loans that roughly equal the liquidation value of its assets. It is the nature of American banking practices that a loan to a business be secured by a "first" lien—a security interest that is not subordinate to any other creditor's secured claim—on assets. The most common practice is that the lender takes a "blanket" lien on all of the company's assets to be sure that it is fully secured. Because lenders to companies almost invariably hold substantial security that they can look to, in a Chapter 11, their claims cannot be compromised as greatly as those of unsecured creditors. They are in a relatively good position to protect their rights.

When it comes to me and you and small to mid-sized companies, the banks have an ironclad rule: secured lending only, with security taken on as much business collateral as possible, and, if possible, on the owner's personal assets and firstborn child. There is a large underground market for foreclosed children. (Just kidding.) However, for megacorporations and wheeler-dealers to whom the bankers want to toady up, money is for the asking and rules are for the breaking.

A big company with a good track record can get loans for the asking based on reputation only. Bankers are dazzled by their brush with corporate barons. Also, they are too lazy to really dig into a big company's financial situation and too unskilled to really understand a business's operations. When a company looks like a winner, bankers throw money at it. It does not matter that the business may be a money hog—the more it borrows, the more the bankers like it. The largest companies in America will always pay their debts, right? Also, because bankers actually cannot tell which companies will be successful in the future, they are herd animals. They do not want to be left out of what seems like easy money, and so they fall over each other to lend to borrowers who are "hot." As a result, just as night follows day, unsecured lending constantly comes back to haunt the bankers. Nevertheless, they repeat it over and over with favored borrowers. (That is precisely how banks and savings-and-loan institutions got into so much trouble investing in "junk" bonds. Why bother trying to figure out which loan applicants are winners when it is so much simpler to hand the money over to Drexel Burnham Lambert for bonds carrying a handsome interest rate, while pocketing an outrageous transaction fee to boot?)

E. L. McNeely had been a master at playing on the bankers' greed and limitations. When he went shopping for expansion fuel or funds to cover losing operations, he never offered security. If a banker had the temerity to ask for collateral for millions of dollars in loans, McNeely would say, in effect, "We are Wickes. We do not give security. Hurry up and jump on the bandwagon, or you will be left behind." The vaults would be thrown open. As a result, *the forty-four lenders of well over a billion dollars to Wickes had neglected to take security*! As incredible as it may seem, the banks had made huge loans to Wickes over an extended period of time based solely on the good name of the company.

The short-term lenders had wised up a a bit when Wickes hit the

skids in 1981. When the short-term lending agreement had been renegotiated in February 1982, they had closed up some loopholes and
improved their position. However, they had a window of vulnerability.

The Bankruptcy Code provides that improvements in a creditor's
position within ninety days prior to the filing of the debtor's bankruptcy can be *voided in bankruptcy*. The purpose of the provision is to,
in a rather crude manner, maintain a fair parity among creditors by
rolling back favoritism towards any particular creditor on the eve of
bnkruptcy. An unintended result of the provision is that it allows a
debtor an out. It can placate an important creditor in an effort to stay
afloat, but if its situation continues to deteriorate, it can file a Chapter
11 proceeding and toss out the prebankruptcy agreement.

While Sandy Sigoloff was negotiating for some relief from the
banks, Ming the Merciless was ready to wield the sword on the short-
term lending agreement if necessary. Wickes began siphoning money
out of its accounts with lender banks, so that they could not grab it and
apply it to their loans. Day after day, funds drifted into accounts at a
bank that had not made loans to Wickes until Wickes had a $135 mil-
lion fund free from its lenders' grasp—a "war chest" in bankruptcy
lingo.

Although the war-horse originally had anticipated the battle happily,
during April 1982, he was finding the early going to be tough trench
warfare, with gains measured in inches. Sigoloff completed the sale of
MacGregor Golf Company, which brought in $17 million. On the
other hand, suppliers were demanding COD for needed inventory, and
the lenders were unwilling to provide fresh funds to help Wickes's
dismal cash position. The $70 million payment on the short-term lend-
ing agreement scheduled for April 30 loomed ahead.

Sanford Sigoloff faced a painful dilemma commonly present in troubled companies. Sale of the more profitable businesses would provide
the largest transfusion of much-needed working capital, but selling off
too many profitable operations would leave the company with a very
mediocre future. Of course, no one wants to pay a good buck for the
dogs, which must be made profitable, practically given away, or
closed, as soon as possible. Sigoloff's men desperately were trying to
get a handle on Wickes's far-flung operations to find out which were
profitable, which were expendable, and which were outright losers, but
such a detailed inspection of a megacorporation like Wickes could not

be done instantaneously. An error in the mix of sold, closed, rehabilitated, and untouched businesses could have seriously mortgaged the giant company, but time was of the essence. McNeely had hurt Wickes by delaying his decision on which units to sell, and further delay by Sigoloff could compound the problem.

Sigoloff showed his boldness. He backed off the sale of the agricultural division as well as the sale of a two-thirds interest in the Red Owl Supermarket and Snyder Drugstore chains, both of which McNeely had negotiated. Sigoloff mysteriously explained "Maybe I know something about those areas." (Maybe Mr. Sigoloff had been spending some time down on the farm?) The supermarket/drugstore package alone would have brought in a quick $55 million.

Ordinarily, it would have been prudent for the new skipper to review the course that the previous captain had set, but under the circumstances, it was an open question as to whether Sigoloff's initial decisions had bought Wickes more trouble. The buyer for the supermarkets and drugstores claimed breach of contract—although that was a clue that McNeely possibly had "given away the store"—and had filed a lawsuit that tied up those divisions' assets, including their funds. So, while Wickes retained title to those divisions, it lacked access to their cash flow and had given up the cash that their sale would have brought in. Was Sigoloff really looking beyond the present troubles, saving the better divisions for Wickes's future, or had he decided that there was a Chapter 11 move in the future, which would help Wickes's cash problems?

Sigoloff also had to shepherd Wickes's limited working capital. In order to conserve cash (and build a war chest), Wickes began to stretch out payments to suppliers. It soon stretched them out so far that it looked suspiciously like the company was not paying its bills at all. The credit fuel-gauge was reading near "empty." The Wickes showrooms were beginning to look bare.

As the end of April 1982 approached, Wickes and the lenders were negotiating furiously. Was there really any chance for a deal? Given Sigoloff's past and Wickes's present, an objective observer would have to bet that Chapter 11 would soon be in the picture. It was no coincidence that one of Sigoloff's lieutenants was Jeffrey Chanin, formerly an attorney with a Los Angeles firm that specialized in bankruptcy law. Sigoloff has admitted privately that he made "truly impossible requests" upon the banks. In other words, it would have taken such extreme concessions by the lenders to provide Wickes with the benefits that it could take for itself in Chapter 11 that as a practical matter no banker could voluntarily do it. While Sandy Sigoloff was negotiating, Admiral Ming was readying the ultimate financial weapon—Chapter 11. It would alter the balance of power conclusively.

On Friday, April 23, Wickes Companies' computers indicated that the funds in the accounts at the friendly bank had reached a peak. The war chest had reached its maximum level.

On Saturday, April 24, the Wickes Companies filed Chapter 11 petitions in Los Angeles. Los Angeles was chosen by Wickes as the venue for the case because, although corporate headquarters were in San Diego, Sigoloff as well as Southern California's big-time bankruptcy lawyers were based in Los Angeles. In receiving special dispensation to file the case on the weekend, Wickes had followed a procedure that became *de rigueur* for megacorporate Chapter 11 filings, which was to do the dirty deed after the stock market, the financial media, the creditors, and the creditors' bankruptcy lawyers had closed for the Sabbaths. It prevented total chaos for those trading in the company's stock and gave the Chapter 11 company just that much of a lead out of the blocks.

Sandy Sigoloff followed the filing with a public announcement stating that balky suppliers had forced Wickes to file the Chapter 11. Br'er Rabbit had been thrown into the briar patch.

By filing Chapter 11 petitions, the Wickes Companies improved their circumstances instantly. Simply not having to pay all of the bills outstanding on the date of bankruptcy—at least not until a Plan of Reorganization was approved—increased Wickes's effective working capital substantially. Funds now could be rerouted to pay for future purchases instead of past due bills. Because the banks were unsecured, *they could not force the company to make any payments during the bankruptcy on $1.2 billion of debt!* Also, while Wickes's loans would have continued accruing interest during the bankruptcy had the banks been secured, because they were unsecured *Wickes's interest clock stopped during the Chapter 11 proceeding.* That one bankruptcy provision alone would save Wickes more than $100 million a year. The provision in the short-term loan agreement requiring Wickes to make a $70 million payment on April 30 became unenforceable, even though Wickes only recently had solemnly promised to do so. (Wickes's inability to service its debt load materially affected the profits of banks across North America, from Security Pacific National Bank [the lead bank of the consortium] to the Bank of Nova Scotia.)

It may sound as though Wickes had no secured creditors, but that is not quite true. One vendor, Whirlpool Corporation, acting through its finance arm, Whirlpool Acceptance Corporation, had succeeded in obtaining a security interest in the appliances that it had sold to Wickes for its furniture stores. Its claim was relatively modest, only about $10 million, but it apparently was the only creditor that managed to prove to the court a position that entitled it to full payment. (Without wishing to appear immodest, Whirlpool was represented by none other than Laurence H. Kallen.)

The biggest fear of a company on the eve of Chapter 11 is that the suppliers will cease selling necessary inventory upon the declaration of bankruptcy. However, as has been shown time and again, suppliers do not punish their naughty debtor. Often much goodwill has been built up over the years, and suppliers will help out a struggling company just because they genuinely want to help out. Even absent goodwill, most trade creditors do not get "mad" at a deadbeat company, continuing instead to take the usual business factors into consideration when determining whether to sell to a Chapter 11 debtor. Also, they hope that reorganization will bring them a substantially larger percentage of repayment on their outstanding accounts than liquidation (a hope that invariably turns out to be a fantasy). Further, if the debtor makes it out of Chapter 11, they have retained a grateful customer who will provide profits in the future. Few vendors are so mad at the debtor that they will not even sell for cash and most will even sell on credit. As Chapter 11s became almost a way of life for American business during the 1980s, suppliers became positively blasé about dealing with them.

Chapter 11 companies do not even fare badly in gettting credit from their vendors, because once again the realities of bankruptcy produce results that the average person would not predict. Because debt incurred during a bankruptcy receives priority of payment in either a reorganization or a liquidation, ironically, suppliers are better protected selling to a Chapter 11 ward of the court than to a company outside of bankruptcy. (It is another one of those unintended results of the bankruptcy law that increases the attractiveness of filing a Chapter 11.) Because of the strange dynamics of Chapter 11, suppliers who had stopped credit sales to Wickes began to offer credit again, and so

Wickes was better able to acquire inventory as a debtor-in-possession. Like a modern version of a biblical miracle, bankruptcy had calmed the financial waters for Wickes.

In filing its bankruptcy petition, Wickes entered the Guinness Book of Records for losers—in sales it was the largest company to file Chapter 11 in the entire history of the American bankruptcy laws to that date. (In terms of assets, it was number two behind the Penn Central Railroad bankruptcy of the Seventies.) Emil McNeely indeed had made his mark on American business history. Although Wickes would lose its title a scant four months later, when the Manville Corporation would run for cover from tens of thousands of injury lawsuits, its numbers remain impressive. The companies operated 1,200 retail outlets, The bottom lines of the balance sheets of the Wickes's Companies showed about $1.5 billion in assets and a whopping $2 billion in debt. Although it had $4 billion in annual sales, it lost more than $100 million in the fiscal year that ended just prior to its bankruptcy filing. Wickes Companies had in excess of 250,000 creditors; the required list filed with the clerk of the court was thousands of pages long. The related companies had managed to acquire about $400 million in trade debt—a substantial unintended investment in Wickes by suppliers that was sure to be a loss. Sigoloff's stinginess in paying trade creditors before the bankruptcy had resulted in a cash kitty of $180 million.

Trade creditors and lenders were not the only ones directly concerned with Wickes's financial health, or the lack thereof. Hundreds of millions of dollars had been put into Wickes Companies by investors large and small. The public's involvement consisted of no less than three types of stock in the companies and nine bond issues, all carried on the New York Stock Exchange. On May 9, when all trading in Wickes's issues was halted due to the Wickes Companies' bankruptcies, common stock traded under $4 a share. Not too long before that it had traded at more than $17; however, it was Wickes's poor condition that had depressed the stock, not the bankruptcies in themselves.

The cases of the Wickes Companies were assigned to Bankruptcy Judge William Lasarow, and they immediately began clogging up his courtroom. Not only were there motions respecting the thousand-and-one administrative matters, but also there was the initial jockeying for position that a megacase entails. Even though it was clear that pursuant to the scheme of the Bankruptcy Code no trustee would be appointed, because of the public importance of the Wickes cases, Judge Lasarow made an unusual announcement advising that he would *not* be appointing a trustee unless unexpected circumstances would later present themselves. Wickes would be handled with kid gloves to insure that nothing was done by the bankruptcy court to harm its sales or its image with consumers. The courtroom matters would be meaningless lawyers' exercises, largely irrelevant to the course of the cases.

In every bankruptcy, a meeting of creditors is called about a month after the petition is filed. The purpose is to subject the bankruptcy debtor to the scrutiny of the creditors. The debtor is fair game for almost any question related in any conceivable way to the debtor's past, present, or future finances. Theoretically, the debtor has filed financial information on court-mandated forms with the clerk, so that creditors can become informed prior to the meeting. "Theoretically" is the key word here, because most corporations receive extensions on the grounds that they need more time to gather the required information. Not incidentally, the extension usually carries past the first meeting of creditors, so that they are usually flying blind during the questioning. When the debtor is a megacorporation, no creditor can become familiar enough with the debtor's finances to undertake a meaningful interrogation. As a result, the first meeting of creditors becomes a public relations exercise for the debtor's management. The meeting of Wickes's creditors followed true to form.

In preparation for the meeting of the creditors of Wickes Companies, the clerk of the Bankruptcy Court for the Central District of California thoughtfully reserved the largest venue in Los Angeles short of having the meeting in a stadium, namely the Los Angeles Convention Center. Creditor representatives obligingly halted at checkpoints at the entrance to register and to receive name tags. Inside, the atmosphere was like that of a seminar. At the table on the stage were several Wickes executives as well as the representative of the clerk of the Bankruptcy Court, who would ask them some basic questions about the companies' finances.

The questioning of the Wickes representatives by the clerk might have had some meaning in a "mom and pop" bankruptcy, but they constituted a pure formality in the case of Wickes, since detailed, and thus useful, answers would have taken a team of accountants and lawyers weeks. Instead, the audience received vague generalities. For example, in response to a question about how much money Wickes had lost during the prior fiscal year, Wickes executives reported that the companies' financial statements for the fiscal year ending January 31, 1982, had not been finalized in time to present to the meeting. (How convenient for Wickes!) As a result, all that they could say was that it was likely that the Wickes Companies would report losses of something more than the $80 million that had been publicly projected by prior management. Within a few weeks, Wickes would admit to losses *over three times* the projection.

At the conclusion of the initial questioning, Sanford Sigoloff took center stage. As he began discussing Wickes's circumstances, it was obvious that Sigoloff's alter ego, Smooth Sandy, was in attendance—Ming the Merciless was nowhere to be seen. The meeting of creditors quickly turned into a Sigoloff lecture, complete with charts, graphs, and a slide projector.

The centerpiece of Sigoloff's presentation was a chart with a lopsided "v" curve, steep on the left-hand side but rising ever so gradually to the right. Wickes's present financial circumstances, Sigoloff explained to the creditors, placed it precisely at the lowest point of the "v." Wickes's fortunes had taken a sharp drop, but the company had hit bottom and it would be climbing slowly out of the trough over the next several years. Any foolish actions by creditors or other intermeddlers would lead Wickes's health line to plunge off the bottom of the chart. The patient was very sick, but Dr. Sandy could cure it if given enough time and forbearance by those in the audience. Until the patient's climb out of the hospital bed was assured, there was no point in talking about the payment of the patient's bills. The lecture ended with the Chapter 11 ritual warning that creditors would get a mere pittance at best if the patient died, but if the patient got well, everyone would be made fat and happy from the patient's munificence.

The floor was opened to questions. Most were of the "softball" variety and were easily—almost *eagerly*—handled without error by one Wickes exec or another. Attempts at harder questions dissolved in confusion. What sort of meaningful, incisive question could a creditor ask that could be answered without a two-day review of the companies' financial records and without being turned into a self-serving response by the Wickes executives? The painfully obvious answer to those who had traveled thousands of miles to achieve enlightenment was "none."

Contrary to elegant bankruptcy theory, the meeting had not meaningfully informed the creditor group about the Chapter 11 debtors' circumstances. (That problem was repeated in megabankruptcies across the country during the 1980s.) It had not been an interrogation, it had been a lecture. As the hall fell into silence, the projector was turned off, and the pointer put away, it seemed to me (who had been diligently taking notes in the twentieth row of the amphitheater seating) that there was a danger that Dr. Sigoloff might declare a surprise quiz and order the creditors to take out a pen and paper and number from one to a hundred! Most certainly, if the subject were Wickes's finances, none of us would have passed.

In the days after the creditors' meeting, Wickes announced more bad news. Effective immediately, it would be closing down forty-four department stores and the divisional headquarters operated by its J. M. McDonald unit. Separately (as they say in the *Wall Street Journal*), Wickes announced that, indeed, it had lost more than $80 million during its most recent fiscal year—more like $258.3 million! In the twelve weeks immediately preceding its Chapter 11 filing, which was subsequent to the closing of the prior fiscal year, Wickes Companies had lost an *additional* $156.4 million, totally wiping out the shareholders' equity on the books. (The losses included not only deficits on operations but also reserves for anticipated store closings.) Perhaps Dr. Sandy had avoided these matters at the creditors' meeting to avoid heart attacks in the audience. The creditors could only hope that Wickes had not fallen through the bottom of the "v."

Those surprise announcements were but the first of many. As the case proceeded, the creditors and shareholders would find that they could not keep track of Wickes despite following all of the rituals of bankruptcy that were supposed to lead to their enlightenment and empowerment. The confusing, useless creditors' meeting in the convention center would typify the megabankruptcy process for them. They would learn that in spite of having gone through all the motions, they were not really in the game.

The creditors and shareholders were duly organized into committees. Because Wickes was such a huge conglomerate, in all there were four official committees, each with its own lawyers, accountants, and investment bankers. At any given time, meetings of the committees, their subcommittees, or their retained professionals might be taking place in offices all around Los Angeles. An important meeting with Wickes representatives might draw hundreds of representatives of the creditors and shareholders. Each committee kept busy communicating with

Wickes, each other, and the court, although little of substance ever came of it.

Much ado was made by the representatives of the creditors and shareholders about supervising the debtor-in-possession, as contemplated in the bankruptcy scheme. However, the size and complexity of Wickes's operations as well as the ease with which the Sigoloff Seven could hide its intentions and "bury the bodies" insured that the outsiders would always be three steps behind the real action. Also, as with all megabankruptcies, the presiding judge was deathly afraid of being blamed for any harm that might befall the conglomerate, and so he would do nothing but rubber-stamp management's requests. An example occurred when Sigoloff proposed to expand Howard Brothers by buying another chain for $11 million. When the creditors objected, suggesting that the money be used to pay down their debts, Sigoloff's reaction could be paraphrased by the rhetorical question "Who is running this company, me or you?" The judge knew the right answer and quickly supplied his rubber stamp to the action.

Bankruptcy law dictates that the debtor cooperate in committees' investigations into its finances, but once again philosophy collapsed in the face of megadebtor maneuvering. Early in the case, the committees made demands for definitive financial information, but Wickes said that its internal reporting systems could not produce it, leaving the creditors in the dark. At one point after the committees complained about the lack of financial information, Wickes dumped so much raw data on them that they were unable to make use of it. In private, Sigoloff referred to that tactic as "taking them deeper into the swamp." The results were predictable—the creditor and shareholder representatives lapsed into befuddlement. In negotiations during early 1983 concerning the outlines of a possible reorganization, the creditors, lacking hard numbers on which to base their positions, could not agree on a unified position. Having once failed to discover Wickes's $135 million war chest, some creditors were sure that Sigoloff again was hiding money from them, this time for later empire building; but they could not find it in the mass of unsorted financial information. Although Sigoloff claimed to be frustrated by the creditors' inability to get their act together, he tipped his hand when he let it be known out of the other side of his mouth that his proposal was only the first step in negotiations.

With the Chapter 11s in place and the creditors put on the defensive,

Sigoloff did not have to waste much of his valuable time negotiating with creditors. In spite of all the cross talk, they virtually had no choice but to sit tight and wait for the master scientist to create a new, improved competitor from the pieces of the monster. The lights burned late in the lab.

Over the three months immediately following the filing of bankruptcy, Wickes cut its losses to a third of those for the prior quarter, but that improvement had nothing to do with the hard work of the Sigoloff Seven; rather, the marked change in Wickes's finances was courtesy of the United States Bankruptcy Code. During that period, the bankruptcy saved Wickes approximately *$50 million* in interest charges on its outstanding loans. With the improvement in Wickes's finances that Chapter 11 wrought, suppliers were falling back into line.

The costs of the bankruptcy were inconsequential to the giant conglomerate. Although Wickes had large extraordinary expenses of $7.5 million (primarily legal and accounting fees) related to the first three months of its Chapter 11 case and would continue logging those expenses at the rate of millions of dollars a month during the bankruptcy, that "protection" money more than covered itself in interest savings alone. Sales were down somewhat but it was hard to tell how much of the drop-off, if any, was due to the Chapter 11 and how much was due to the Volcker Depression, which greatly hurt Wickes's core businesses. Whatever the cost of the bankruptcy, it had bought Wickes valuable time and had actually helped the companies to acquire inventory.

Over the summer, the creditors began getting restless. They were learning how much the bankruptcy law favors the debtor-in-possession, and they gained ample reasons to believe that the court was very solicitous of Wickes. The only real leverage that the creditors could have wielded would have been to threaten to propose a Plan of Reorganization of their own. However, Wickes was within the statutory 120-day period subsequent to filing bankruptcy during which it alone could propose a Plan of Reorganization; and since the creditors lacked that remedy, there was no need for Wickes to negotiate seriously with them. For the time being, they were along for the ride whether they liked it or not.

One group of creditors thought that they saw a crack in Wickes's defenses through which only they might be able to squeeze. Over the summer of 1983, representatives of the Gamble-Skogmo creditors had narrowed the scope of their inquiry to the G-S operating entities, and a coherent picture began to come into focus. It confirmed their suspicions that it was McNeely's companies that had been poorly run and had dragged down G-S, not the other way around. They calculated that if G-S were severed from the Wickes units, G-S's businesses would be sufficient to repay G-S's creditors *in full* over time. To those creditors, the figures showed that, contrary to the conventional wisdom being proffered by Wickes's management, if the G-S acquisition had been too big for Wickes to swallow that was not G-S's fault. Like Jonah in the whale, G-S and its creditors would be a lot better off if Wickes would spit them out. In August 1983, the G-S creditors petitioned the judge to cut loose the G-S cases and allow them to propose a Plan of Reorganization of their own. It was a serious threat to Sigoloff's vision of *his* Wickes. Other admirals were trying to steal half of his fleet!

The question of whether to sever one or more of a group of related companies in Chapter 11—called "consolidated" cases—for separate treatment was, and continues to be, one of the great gray areas of bankruptcy law. That decision can greatly affect the creditors' rights, yet there are no good guidelines to limit the judge's power to choose as he pleases. It all depends upon how he wishes to handle them.

It is clear that bankruptcy judges have the power to handle related corporations as a group, either by "administrative" consolidation or "substantive" consolidation. If cases are administratively consolidated, one judge will hear matters that arise in any one of them, but they remain separate bankruptcy cases. They each may proceed at their own pace, and each must file a separate Plan of Reorganization that meets bankruptcy law standards without reference to how creditors are treated in the other related cases. If cases are consolidated substantively, for bankruptcy purposes the entities cease to be separate. Their assets and liabilities are lumped together, as are their creditors' claims; and they will be reorganized, if at all, through one Plan of Reorganization.

All the parties to related bankruptcy filings are vitally interested in which type of consolidation the judge chooses. Because subsidiaries of megacorporations can themselves be giant corporations, in the typical megacorporate bankruptcy, there will be creditors who did not rely on the creditworthiness of the umbrella organization but rather dealt with one of the corporate entities only. Under nonbankruptcy law, it is clear that any contraact between two corporations does not bind other related companies, and, in fact, "parent" corporations commonly stand upon that basic rule of law in refusing to pay claims that are against a subsidiary. However, when the parent company decides to file a Chapter 11 proceeding, it usually wants to treat its separate units as one so that the stronger ones can keep the others going. In that way it will be the management of the debtor who decides which units to keep and which to close; otherwise a group of the creditors will "cherry-pick" the better companies and leave the other businesses to sink on their own. Also, management and the shareholders want to knock creditors' claims against the stronger units down to the lowest common denominator of the group, so those will get paid less upon reorganization.

As one can see, the judge's ruling respecting consolidation is of the utmost importance; however, the Bankruptcy Code gives no guidelines whatsoever, and so the judges do what they want to do. What creditors in megacases throughout the United States found out during the Eighties was that the judges wanted to do whatever the Chapter 11 companies wanted them to do. Wickes wanted to keep the half of the enterprise that had been Gamble-Skogmo. So, in spite of the fact that the creditors of Gamble-Skogmo had a perfectly reasonable argument for severance of those cases, the judge refused to do so.

With creditors clamoring to file their own plan, Wickes was in danger of losing its lock on the bankruptcy process when its statutory "exclusive period" ended in August 1982. To counter that threat, Wickes petitioned the court to enter an order under its own authority extending the period for six months. The judge entered such an order . . . and kept entering such orders each time the exclusive period was about to terminate.

The Wickes creditors had learned another hard lesson, one which creditors of megacorporations across the country also were learning: creditors would not be allowed to interfere with megacorporations' control of their Chapter 11 cases by proposing their own Plans of Reorganization. It was a course of conduct by American bankruptcy judges that would further tilt the Bankruptcy Code in megadebtors' favor, leaving creditors with almost no bargaining power. In the Wickes case, in a pique after haggling with creditors over to which of two entities a *mere* $10 million in assets belonged, Sigoloff decided that he would stop wasting his time trying to negotiate a consensual plan and that he simply would propose a plan that was to his liking.

No one could stop him.

The Wickes shareholders and debentureholders tried another tack. They filed a lawsuit against the men who were the directors of Wickes during McNeely's tenure as well as those who were the past and present officers, for securities-law violations under Section 10(b)(5) of the Securities and Exchange Act. That provision allows investors in publicly held corporations to collect damages personally against any corporate executive who takes part in misleading the public about the company's financial condition. Of course, the "automatic stay" in the Bankruptcy Code unequivocally prevented the shareholders from suing the corporate bankruptcy debtors, but nothing in the code prevents suit against individuals who may have incurred personal liability through their own actions. In fact, a general provision of the code states that only bankruptcy debtors shall have the benefits of the code's protection from creditors.

Wickes responded to the end run by asking the judge to enter an injunction against the suits. Since the company lawyers could point to no part of the code that prohibited such a suit against people who had not filed bankruptcy, it asked the judge to enter an *ad hoc* injunction based upon his general powers as a judge. Sure enough, the judge sided with Wickes and enjoined the suit, on the grounds that it might distract Wickes's executives from concentrating on the bankruptcy and that it might somehow prejudice the corporations even though they were not parties to the suit. That episode provided *another* object lesson on the power of the corporate debtor.

While the lawyers engaged in essentially meaningless battles—because Wickes always got what it wanted—Ming the Merciless was cutting a swath through the conglomerate's operations, liquidating some units and selling others. The three leasing companies and a machine tool company were sold. A total of three hundred poorly located stores, including fifty-five lumber yards and twelve furniture stores, closed their doors forever, and their employees were terminated. The efforts in cost cutting paid off. After six months in Chapter 11, Wickes's cash position was up to $520 (!) million, most of which was earmarked not for creditors but rather for business improvements, including expanding the more successful retail operations. It mattered not whether the creditors opposed Ming's choice of units to ax, the prices he negotiated for those he sold, or his spending plans—realistically, the creditors had no way of forcing changes in his business plans or redirecting more of the funds to them. The titanic struggle over Alden's Catalogue Company was a classic example of the megacorporation's ability to render archaic the concept of Chapter 11 court and creditor supervision.

Alden's was the fifth largest catalogue house in the United States, with $300 million in annual sales. It was as close to an institution as an American company can be, having been in business for ninety-three years and serving millions of customers across the country. Alden's 2,600 employees in a blue-collar suburb of Chicago were so loyal and so tenured—the average length of employment was seventeen years— that it was more like a family than a company. Unfortunately, in 1982, they were still keeping track of orders by hand entries into big books. Also, the quality of the mailing list was deteriorating. Alden's had been treated as a "cash cow" and mismanaged for a number of years prior to Sigoloff's arrival on the scene, and the bottom line was showing the damage.

Sanford Sigoloff claims that he tried hard to keep Alden's going. He claims that he considered trying to save it, and then he tried to sell it. He says that he agonized over closing it down. However, by mid-December 1982, after a disappointing Yuletide selling season, just before Christmas Day, Sigoloff ordered Alden's to be liquidated, and he turned its employees out on the street. As he did so, he expressed his regrets. "This isn't closing a business, it's annihilating a family," said Sigoloff, in an appropriately sad manner.

The sufficiency of Sigoloff's attempts to save the Alden's family is open to debate. Sigoloff no doubt was correct when he said that McNeely had let Alden's decline; that McNeely's officers had made many marketing mistakes; and that Wickes's problems had starved Alden's for credit to buy inventory. However, Sigoloff's conclusion, that it was too risky to keep Alden's in operation, does not necessarily follow. Sigoloff made it clear that he begrudged the amount of time the Sigoloff Seven had to spend on Alden's troubles. Could it be that he simply decided "off with its head!"?

Sigoloff's means of dealing with Alden's was not above attack. Investment bankers were given very little time to try to peddle the large company before it was closed. Critics felt that Ming's shoot-from-the-hip style had not done justice to Alden's substantial assets and that Sigoloff had been overly discouraged by the poor sales of one mailing. Some business experts said that the risk and cost of rehabilitating Alden's had been overestimated, and that Wickes mistakenly had let go a business with substantial customer loyalty that would have bounced back when the Volcker Depression subsided. A number of Alden's former employees said that they would like to get their hands on Ming the Merciless just once, and apparently a few tried. The creditors had almost nothing to say about the matter.

Besides fielding daily crises during his first year at the helm, Sanford Sigoloff had been reshaping the many-tentacled conglomerate. In addition to closing Alden's, he had sold Wickes's agriculture division, an auto-leasing unit, an equipment-leasing unit, the fabric stores, and the Maxwell furniture division. Put up for sale were Toy World, Rasco, J. M. McDonald, Farmaster, and Wickes Engineered Materials. In all, Ming would preside over the sale or liquidation of fifteen business units of the conglomerate, cutting the Wickes work force by more than seventeen thousand human units. Red Owl stores had been remodeled and merchandise upgraded, other retail lines had been spruced up, and twenty Woman's World stores added. Sigoloff's fifteen Wickes Furniture stores were producing the same sales level that twenty-seven of McNeely's Wickes Furniture stores had produced the prior year. Sigoloff could announce that he felt comfortable with the core group of businesses that he had selected to be Wickes's future.

Sigoloff was now free to turn his attention to a Plan of Reorganization, or, more precisely, to turn his attention to chiseling the creditors' claims. Like the bankruptcy court pro that he was, Sigoloff was following a basic rule of Chapter 11 debtorhood: management should make its repayment proposals to the creditors as soon as the CEO is sure that he sees the light at the end of the tunnel, but before it is obvious to outsiders that the company has made the turnaround. The creditors cannot see the future of the company the way that management can because they lack inside information. They only know that they have been along for the ride in a dark, dark tunnel for a long, long time. All they want is off the train, and they most likely have arrived at the point where they will pay for the privilege of jumping.

The time was ripe to make a proposal to the Wickes creditors. The loss for the full year under Sigoloff was about equal to the last year under McNeely's stewardship, a breathtaking $250 million, and *that* was accomplished on only two-thirds of the receipts! (Costs associated with the bankruptcy were $25 million.) However, there was a trend. After suffering horrendous losses during the first half of 1982, Wickes had accomplished an infinitesimal profit for the third quarter. Then for the fourth quarter of Wickes's fiscal year, it had showed only a small loss. The creditors could follow the results each quarter, but it was hard for them to tell how the pieces had made up the puzzle. For example, a large portion of the losses on the books was due to charges on the balance sheets for closed stores. It was hard for the creditors to tell how many of the problems had been put behind the company. Sigoloff felt that Wickes had bottomed out. Would the creditors take the bait and get hooked on Wickes's proposal?

Sigoloff had dangled the framework of a plan in front of the creditors in February 1983, and after letting it sink in for a while he continued to press it. After deciding in the fall of 1983 to stop truly negotiating with the creditors on the terms of a reorganization, he started telling some of the major banks that, in effect, the train was moving out of the station and they had better jump on board. Sigoloff avoided the lawyers and other intermediaries by delivering his message directly to bank presidents at one-on-one dinners.

Wickes's proposal involved some cash but more notes, debentures, and stock. The stock payment to creditors would substantially dilute the value, such as it was, of the stock held by Wickes shareholders. Behind closed doors, Sigoloff also offered creditors the Chapter 11 debtor's classic enticement: stick with me and you will get lots of profitable business after the company is out of bankruptcy. The beauty of the line is that it can be spoken with great earnestness and commitment, but it costs nothing and it is not enforceable.

It had been the G-S creditors who had wanted G-S cut loose from the weaker debtor corporations, but it was the creditors of a Wickes unit to whom Ming offered special dispensation. At the end of September 1983, Wickes Companies announced that creditors of its Wickes Credit Corporation would be paid in full through a Plan of Reorganization that covered WCC only. The banks that had outstanding loans to the credit arm of Wickes were so happy to have it separated from the morass that, in return for a face-saving token payment from WCC of $10 million—over time, no less—the lenders would reinstate WCC's line of credit, which was a shade under $100 million. Also, they promised to help WCC line up $50 million more in standby credit. The benefit to the banks: the interest clock could start ticking again. The benefit to Wickes: increased sales, by resuming in-house financing to Wickes's customers.

Finalization of the plan terms dragged on into 1984. Sigoloff was getting a little nervous—not that Wickes would fail, but rather that the creditors would catch on to the turnaround before Wickes's Plan of Reorganization could be effectuated. "We're in a danger zone," Sigoloff said to a confidant. "If we wait much longer, the creditors will see that total liquidation would bring them one hundred cents on the dollar." He sweetened Wickes's proposal a bit.

In February 1984, Wickes announced that it had an agreement in principle with the various creditors' committees on the shape of a Plan of Reorganization. The package that Wickes offered was to pay the creditors $289 million in cash, $524 million in face value of notes, and common stock that would add up to 82 percent of the stock in the company when issued. As living proof that "some animals are more equal than others," the lenders would receive higher percentages of their claims than trade creditors. Sigoloff did not want to embarrass them too badly since he knew that soon he would be knocking on their doors asking for more money for his postbankruptcy exploits.

Some last minute concessions satisfied hold-out groups at little cash cost to Wickes and insured that they would not want to derail the plan. Wickes agreed to pay creditors holding $45 million in claims against the Howard Brothers unit $9 million in cash, $36 million in nine-year notes, and a small amount of stock. The shareholders were thrown a bone when Wickes added warrants for them to buy 3 percent more stock to its proposal. During spring 1984, everyone fell into line.

In its final form, Wickes's Plan of Reorganization fell far short of paying the creditors in full. The cash and the "present value" of the notes constituted about 60 percent payment of the creditors' claims against Wickes and Gamble-Skogmo. Alden's creditors received only $16 million of the total package, constituting less than 40 percent of their claims, even though Alden's had more $200 million in accounts receivable when it was closed. By issuing a mix of notes, some for a term of twenty years, Wickes had made its creditors into long-term lenders. Wickes was well positioned to rocket out of bankruptcy, but all the creditors knew was that they would have the excruciating situation behind them.

It would take seven months for the giant company to complete the formalities of gaining approval for the Plan of Reorganization and nearly a year until all court procedures had been completed. Formalities they were, for once the creditors' committees had provided their stamps of approval, the chances of some rump group of creditors organizing an effective challenge to the settlement package were nil. Any challenge would have been prohibitively expensive—under bankruptcy rules, Wickes had paid the fees of the official committees, as well as their costs in contacting creditors to recommend approval, but dissidents would have to finance their own communications with hundreds of thousands of creditors. Also, a fact of life in megacases is that the judges do not let anyone roll a log in front of the bandwagon.

During the interim, the company maintained an even keel. Wickes announced a tiny profit for the fiscal year ending February 1984, on sales that were up 9 percent from the previous year. The lackluster profits were all right with Sigoloff. He did not want the creditors to know of the progress that Wickes was making every day. On the other hand, he was impatient to wheel and deal. Over the summer, he wheedled a $140 million line of credit from some of the lenders to have at the ready when Wickes emerged from Chapter 11.

On September 21, 1984, the Plan of Reorganization was approved by the court. Wickes had dragged its creditors through the briar patch. It could now run free on open ground.

There is an epilogue to the story.

Wickes emerged slimmed and trimmed from Chapter 11, with everyone sobered by the effort that had been needed to save the company from McNeely's purchase of Gamble-Skogmo. Well, not quite everyone. Sigoloff was trying his best *not* to ride off into the sunset this time by turning his attentions to what normal megacorporate executives do: gobble up other companies.

Not only did Sigoloff find an acquisition, it was a whopper—the consumer and industrial products group of Gulf + Western Industries, with sales of $2.85 billion a year. Gulf + Western was in the process of "deconglomeratization," and those units were available for a mere $1 billion in cash. Wall Street observers had doubted that any one buyer would take its entire hodgepodge of businesses that had been put up for sale, but they had not considered Sigoloff's voracious appetite for corporation shuffling. The merger that Sigoloff proposed would about double Wickes in size, bringing such businesses into the fold as Catalina and Cole of California apparel, Supp-Hose and Burlington hosiery, Simmons mattresses and Selig furniture, and automotive parts distributed through one thousand four hundred Big A stores, as well as other apparel and manufacturing concerns. The price Wickes was offering to pay was $200 million over the value of the companies' assets, providing Gulf + Western with a handsome premium.

Wickes did not have sufficient cash and credit in place to swallow the G + W spin-offs. To complete the merger, Wickes would have to raise $500 million (which was approximately twelve times Wickes's earnings for the previous fiscal year). To do that, Sigoloff was planning to harness the financing wizardry of a young stockbroker located in Los Angeles, Michael Milken, who had described to Sigoloff how the issuance of high-yield bonds could attract capital to finance acquisitions of companies. After the merger, Wickes's obligations for principal, interest, and preferred dividends—that is, its financing expenses— would total $260 million a year. Its operating income was $290 million a year. G + W would be a big meal to swallow.

Had the ghost of Emil McNeely entered into Sanford Sigoloff's body? Would this acquisition be Wickes's Nightmare on Wall Street, Part II? To Sigoloff, "The parallel is a poor one." It was an "unusual opportunity," said Sigoloff, unintentionally coming very close to echoing McNeely's characterization of the acquisition of Gamble-Skogmo as a "once-in-a-lifetime opportunity." Very much like McNeely, Sigoloff was betting the store on the merger. At least he knew how to live with Chapter 11, if it came to that!

While the acquisition had inherent risks for Wickes, it was the chance that Sanford Sigoloff had been looking for. Sigoloff may have been playing "bet the company" by proposing to load Wickes with debt to swallow the G + W divisions, but he was determined not again to be tossed out of an executive suite that he had rebuilt. The action presumably would impress Wall Street critics that Sigoloff could run 'em as well as fix 'em. Not incidentally, the debt load and the plethora of subsidiaries would make Wickes so unattractive to corporate raiders that Sigoloff would maintain his bailiwick. Perhaps the self-proclaimed war-horse had temporarily had his fill of life on the front lines. His remarks to the press indicated that, after tackling a job that turned out to be even more complex and draining than he had expected, he was not yet ready to face the next sick company.

However, he was ready to face some that were well. With the G + W divisions in the Wickes fold by June 1985, he dashed after more megacorporate mergers. In quick succession, he launched three multibillion-dollar hostile takeovers, for National Gypsum Company,

Owens-Corning Fiberglas Corporation, and Lear Sigler. He was thwarted in the takeover attempts, but like any credible corporate raider at the time, he came away with large profits when bought off. Sigoloff successfully purchased a large textiles concern, Collins and Aikman, for $1.16 billion and added five retail chains from W. R. Grace (the company that had snatched Daylin from him).

In 1988, Sigoloff made an offer for another company—his own. With the help once again of Michael Milken's junk bond genius, a Sigoloff-led group proposed a leveraged buyout of Wickes Companies for $478.2 million. The financing of the buyout would push Wickes's debt well over $2 billion. The public would have been only too happy to sell its stock to Sigoloff, since his takeover binge had not endeared him to Wall Street and at the time Wickes operations were oscillating around a break-even point. Also, Sigoloff was proposing to offer $12 a share for stock that had hit a high of $7 in 1986 and a low of $2 after October 1987's Black Monday (a range that was not substantially different than that during the bankruptcy). If accomplished, the outsider could no longer be cashiered. He would own the fleet.

Just as it looked like the deal would go through, it was torpedoed by one of Sigoloff's own prior acquisitions. Dr. Sigoloff had failed to diagnose serious illness in Collins and Aikman when he brought it into the Wickes camp. After the division announced a $40 million loss for the third quarter of 1988, breaking Wickes's delicate financial equilibrium, Drexel Burnham Lambert backed out of the financing.

Sigoloff's actions had put the company "into play," as the takeover artists say, and it drew the interest of sharks in the corporate waters. Shortly after Sigoloff announced the withdrawal of his buyout offer, a leveraged buyout led by an investment banking house (not Drexel) took Wickes private, and Sigoloff was forced to resign his command. Although he made a good deal of money from the buyout by cashing in his investment in Wickes, once more against his wishes he had been mothballed when the war was over. No doubt he cried all the way to the bank.

In 1989, Sigoloff was called out of retirement to attempt to resuscitate the American branch of the L. J. Hooker Corporation, which included B. Altman's and Bonwit Teller. But that is another story.

Among the combatants, who were the winners, and who were the losers?

There are a number on each side of the ledger. The trade creditors were fortunate that the banks had been remiss in taking liens as security for their loans; they received at least four times what they otherwise would have been paid. For the same reason, the banks had done themselves out of hundreds of millions of dollars in lost interest receipts. The terms of the plan hurt the stockholders of the Wickes Companies the most. Because the other creditor groups received stock as part payment for their debts, the common (what a term!) shareholders saw their stock values, already hammered from mid-teen highs during Wickes's go-go year to about $4 a share, mostly dissipated.

If one looks at the whole forest instead of merely noting which trees got nicked, it is reasonable to say that all the creditors lost out—that the reorganization process was nothing but smoke and mirrors. In other words, the Chapter 11s of Wickes Companies may have benefited no one other than Sanford Sigoloff and his friends.

Liquidation would not have been the financial disaster that it is usually painted to be. Liquidation of a conglomerate does not mean that all of the assets are sold piece by piece in some gigantic auction. The only difference between what Sigoloff did in wheeling and dealing Wickes's units and what a liquidation would have entailed was that the units retained by Sigoloff for Wickes's future would have been sold, no doubt at a good price.

Sigoloff's public and private statements also tell us that the creditors got taken. In a required Disclosure Statement to creditors at the time of the vote upon the Plan of Reorganization, Wickes purported to show that the creditors would receive $400 to $500 million more through the Plan of Reorganization that they would if Wickes were liquidated. Bankruptcy professionals know that the Chapter 11 debtor's assessment of liquidation values is highly self-serving because the debtor wants to persuade the creditors to accept the reorganization proposal instead of demanding liquidation and notoriously unreliable because there is no analysis done by an objective expert. Assuming that the disclosure statement was as helpful to Wickes as the Wickes authors could make it, at best there was only a relatively small additional dividend from reorganization over and above what liquidation would have brought. Sigoloff's private sentiments, most certainly a more accurate assessment, indicated that there was no differential at all given what he had offered the creditors to settle their claims. Even *if* there were some additional values recognized through keeping the conglomerate intact, a liquidation would have produced all cash while more than $500 million of the package offered to creditors as part of the reorganization was in notes, some bearing a twenty-year maturity. In return for their original risk of lending or selling to Wickes, the creditors received . . . more risk.

Other factors also work in favor of liquidation. Had the liquidation of Wickes been commenced on Day One of the bankruptcy, its creditors would have received payment of their claims years earlier than they did through the reorganization. Due to the high costs of the Chapter 11 and the substantial compensation that the Sigoloff executives took for themselves, it would have been far cheaper to have hired Ming as a liquidator—and Sigoloff would not have had a chance to go on his acquisition hunts with other people's money after the bankruptcy was over.

Why did that large group of sophisticated lenders and business people allow themselves to get the short end of the stick? Why did they not demand a larger repayment of their claims or vote to break up the conglomerate? Were they stupid? Did they have bad advice? Did Sanford Sigoloff bamboozle them? The answer is that they had no choice—Chapter 11 had disarmed them.

By its very existence, Chapter 11 eliminated the creditors' option to liquidate Wickes before or during bankruptcy. Had they begun to enforce their claims at any time prior to April 24, 1982, Wickes could have stopped them in their tracks before they got very far by filing the bankruptcy proceeding at that time. Once Wickes had invoked the protections of Chapter 11, realistically there was no way that the creditors could have achieved a quick court ruling stripping Sigoloff of his prerogatives and requiring the immediate sale of the conglomerate's assets. Once the case had gone on for more than two years and a Plan of Reorganization had been proposed, the only way that liquidation could have carried the day would have been if the creditors could have proved to the judge's satisfaction that the liquidation value of the companies was greater than the repayment offered in the Plan of Reorganization. That valuation hearing would have been a lengthy, tremendously expensive process that no doubt would have produced inconclusive results, which would have allowed the judge to exercise his inherent bias in favor of the megacorporate debtor.

Of course, the creditors could have exercised their right to vote down Wickes's plan, but that would not have been too smart. It would have left an angry Sanford Sigoloff still in total control of Wickes Companies and their Chapter 11s. He easily could have kept the creditors on ice for another year or two, with the interest clock shut off and them having to beg for every snippet of useful financial information in order to try to figure out what Sigoloff was up to. It is no wonder that the creditors tucked their tails between their legs and slunk out of bankruptcy court.

The winners of the titanic struggle were the Wickes executives. Although the creditors choked on the numbers, Ming rammed through an $18 million (in cash) bonus package for his executives. That was on top of very substantial salaries that they had received during the bankruptcy with the blessing of the creditors and the court. After all, the spoils of war are fair game for the victorious mercenaries—that is why they sign on for the campaign. To Sigoloff, it was merely recognition of the great job he and his boys had done.

Of course, Sanford Sigoloff was the big winner. Although the judge had the power to void Sigoloff's prebankruptcy employment contract with Wickes, it was considered sacred during the Chapter 11, and under it Sigoloff earned about $1 million a year. (No one wanted to get Ming mad.) His share of the bonus pie was about $3.5 million. Certainly Sigoloff's star shone brightly before, during, and after the Wickes Companies' bankruptcy. He was able to maintain his image exactly as he liked it. He was able to have his fun as he defined it, tinkering with one of the largest conglomerates in the world—and thousands of peoples' lives—with almost no constraints other than his own sense of right and wrong.

Was Sanford Sigoloff worth all that? Had Admiral Sigoloff really made the ships seaworthy, or was it the rising tide of the economy at the end of the Volcker Depression that had lifted the fleet? Sigoloff as much as acknowledged the ambiguity in his performance when he said, "You can say we were good or you can say we were lucky. Take your pick." The question was, who cared?

Was the public's interest served?

Wickes can be cited as a "classic" Chapter 11. In the case of Wickes, the bankruptcy process had operated in the way that the drafters of the law had intended and consistent with the public's expectations of the system. In spite of its huge size, it was clearly in dire financial straits—a deserving candidate for the protection from creditors that the Bankruptcy Code offers. While in the protective confines of the court, the conglomerate was reorganized financially, operationally and structurally; and then, having been given a new lease on life, it was able to emerge from the confines of court supervision.

A view from the creditors' side of the ledger might not be so favorable. By filing one piece of paper—the Chapter 11 petition—Wickes avoided *hundreds of millions* of dollars in interest for loans that it had sought and received. Creditors were made to wait for payment for years, stripped of enforcement rights, until management was ready to throw them some money (and even more promissory notes). The process as it served a megacorporation was not a dialogue or a financial democracy; rather it was a dictatorship of the debtor. Instead of being forced to bargain with creditors in the marketplace, Wickes was able to put them aside for years. The bargaining power of the parties was reshuffled by the arcane rules of a chamber that was outside the mainstream of commerce and superimposed over their freedom of contract.

In the final analysis, the reorganization was substantially, though indirectly, funded by taxpayer dollars. The $400 to $500 million premium gained for the creditors according to Wickes's disclosure statement equaled the net operating loss carryforward on Wickes's books. Under our tax laws, that entry entitled Wickes to shelter all future profits from corporate income taxation until they reached that amount. Had Wickes folded, the tax benefits would have died with it, but since Wickes survived the Chapter 11 process that $500 million in tax-loss benefits survived with it. That n.o.l. possibly was the reorganized Wickes's most valuable asset—courtesy of Uncle.

For Wickes the new Chapter 11 provisions had achieved the wishes of Lee Iacocca and Felix Rohatyn for a form of government largess that did not entail begging for bucks from Congress in the glare of public exposure. Through the bankruptcy and tax laws, Wickes's losses had actually been spread to the American public—corporate welfare.

Was it not worth it, in order to save Wickes Companies' jobs? In corporate reorganizations, it is the employees who are the most expendable. The surviving Wickes Companies employed slightly more than half of their former number of employees. Had Wickes been liquidated, no doubt its strongest units would have been sold as ongoing businesses, saving most of the surviving jobs anyway. With respect to divisions that would have been closed, Wickes's competitors would have moved into niches formerly served by Wickes, hiring employees in the process.

In the end, it cannot be proven that Chapter 11 helps anyone other than those who take advantage of its shelter. The whole bankruptcy reorganization system has been founded on shaky, unexamined premises. When it is invoked in desperation by small companies, it affects the shape of the national economy but a small bit, and the bankruptcy reorganization program can be chalked up to mercy for "the little people." However, now that the Bankruptcy Code has been seized upon as a financial tool of megacorporations, with numerous cases affecting billions of dollars of other people's money, its unexamined premises have become an embarrassment. As a huge, hidden welfare program for megacorporations and their executives, it is a scandal.

Chapter 8

Boffo Battle: Big Business in Bankruptcy Busts Brotherhoods

> "The prophecies of what the courts will do
> in fact, and nothing more pretentious, are
> what I mean by the law."
> —Judge Oliver Wendell Holmes, Jr.

The Bankruptcy Reform Act of 1978, which was codified into the Bankruptcy Code now in effect, held many mysteries for bankruptcy experts as well as the uninitiated.

Everyone was dealing with an entirely new regulation scheme. In the early years of its existence, courtroom argument often was characterized by the lawyers and the judge frantically thumbing through the seven hundred-plus pages of the code and related statutes and rules in order to find the key that would unlock the conundrums seemingly created by the new law. The drafting of the code was excellent, and it was almost perfectly internally consistent, but *still* ambiguities and inconsistencies popped up regularly. It took ten years of practice under it to settle most of the uncertainties that it had raised.

When statutory language proves to be ambiguous, there are legal principles for coming to a conclusion on its meaning. The judge first should look to other provisions of the statute to see if some interpretation can be adopted under which all the related parts of the law can be read to form one cohesive whole, with no dissonant parts that must be ignored. If that does not solve the problem, the statutory language must be investigated in the light of its usages in other contexts and prior rulings in other cases. Of course, there are limitations in following the "common law."

Sometimes when other means of statutory construction fail, it is necessary to undertake that most dangerous of investigations, a determination of the "legislative intent" of the august body that had passed the statute. The pursuit is admirable, for the courts are charged with the responsibility of enforcing the laws as enacted by the country's elected representatives. Unfortunately, the result is often a fiction because there is no real agreement on the "mind" of the legislature concerning the particular problem at hand.

A very large question in battles that have been fought up and down the federal court system has had to do with the extent of the ability of Chapter 11 debtors to "reject"—cancel—or "assume"—force the other party to continue with—contracts that were entered into prior to the filing of the bankruptcy. Sometimes issues revolve around whether the subject of the dispute is a contract at all, sometimes whether it has been fully canceled prior to the filing of the bankruptcy and thus no longer is in existence. In nearly every kind of situation, however, if the court concludes that the debtor is a party to an existing contract, the debtor is allowed to reject it and to continue operations free from its terms. The cases turn on factual matters, not issues of major philosophical import, except when the contract in question is a collective bargaining agreement with an entity that represents employees.

Lawyers are quick studies, and almost immediately after the Bankruptcy Code became law, it was noticed by some bankruptcy attorneys that there was no statutory exclusion naming any situations when a debtor could not reject a contract. Could it be that a debtor's ability to reject a contract that it was not happy with was a *sine qua non* of Chapter 11? Could that be true even when that pique bumped up against a strong federal policy, such as the support of unions and the protection of union activities from unfair tactics of employers? What good would be the rights to organize and to negotiate a contract over working conditions when the employer could cancel it simply by filing Chapter 11? The ultimate resolution of the disputes would turn upon that tricky inquiry: what did Congress mean when it passed the Bankruptcy Reform Act without including any exceptions or limitations on rejecting collective-bargaining contracts? Did it really mean that union contracts were like any other? Did it have any intent at all on the subject? What standard, if any, should the courts supply on their own initiative?

The issues had been around for a while because the Bankruptcy Act had allowed the rejection of contracts. However, it was not an important issue under the act because companies would not think of damaging their reputations by filing a bankruptcy just to deal with union problems. The few cases split on how seriously the union contract had to affect the company in order for it to cancel it. It took the economics and philosophies of the Reagan era to define the boundary. During the 1980s, labor warfare increasingly would spill into the bankruptcy courts, with judges being asked to decide whether union contracts were just like any other contracts that could be broken by the company using its business judgment under the authority of the bankruptcy laws, or whether there was something special about them.

The first case under the Bankruptcy Code to catch the attention of bankruptcy lawyers around the country did not involve a mega-corporation, but a small New Jersey builders' supplier named Bildisco. The Bildisco dispute involved eighteen unionized employees, whose number, due to the company's business problems, would be reduced to three by the time the final decision on appeal would be entered. The savings projected from the rejection of the company's collective-bargaining contract with its teamsters was a grand total of $100,000 per year—hardly a monumental sum but an amount, according to the company, that would allow it to compete effectively with nonunion shops. Other companies had broken their union contracts in Chapter 11 prior to Bildisco, most notably Revere Copper and Brass, but it was the Bildisco case that marched upward irrevocably through the appeals process and would provide the legal precedent upon which the other cases around the country would turn.

Bildisco won round one, the judge presiding over the reorganization of the company ruling that it could reject the union contract. Teamsters Local 408 not only appealed the decision to higher courts, it made an end run around the bankruptcy by filing unfair labor practice charges before the National Labor Relations Board, which still was oriented towards labor. When the company declined to appear before the NLRB, citing the "automatic stay" of the Chapter 11, the board awarded the union a victory. Apparently, Bildisco's union had won round one also! The dispute was turning into an unseemly power struggle between arms of the federal government.

In July 1982, the Third Circuit Court of Appeals ruled on the Bildisco appeal. The court's opinion opened with a technicality, namely that for many purposes the "debtor-in-possession" existing in the bankruptcy is considered to be a different entity than the one that existed just before the filing of the case. For example, the books of account of the troubled company are frozen as of the date of filing, and new ledgers are opened on the first day of the bankruptcy. To the appellate court, the fact that the debtor is a new entity gives it a certain amount of distance from its actions taken before bankruptcy. As you can guess, that concept has rather limited utility given the many ways that Chapter 11 companies are viewed as continuations of their prior selves.

The opinion then analyzed the Chapter 11 situation and concluded that the most important value to be served was the successful reorganization of the company. After all, if a company cannot reorganize, the unionized employees will have no jobs anyway, and so the better choice is to allow rejection. Given the ambiguity of circumstances at the onset of most Chapter 11 cases, the court felt that it would not be feasible to make a determination of just how burdensome union obligations are. Therefore, the court ruled that it would be the company's decision as to the necessary action to be taken that will prevail, as long as it appears to have made a "reasoned determination." If it does so, the court ruled, its action cannot be an unfair labor practice, and a union cannot file charges with the NLRB. Round two went to Bildisco.

The screams of organized labor echoed across the country and through the halls of Congress. What had happened to labor's special status with the federal government? What had happened to Section 8(a)(5) of the National Labor Relations Act, which required an employer to bargain to impasse before implementing a change in the terms and conditions of employment? Where was a Democratic president when you needed him?

While tiny Bildisco and its three teamsters fought their way to the United States Supreme Court, some heavyweights joined in the battle. Braniff Airlines filed a Chapter 11, citing labor headaches among its financial problems. Then Wilson Foods and Continental Airlines signed onto the battle, each company saying that its union contracts were *the* problem. The ante had been upped for organized labor to stay in the game.

The deregulation of the airline industry first energized it and then decimated it. Hundreds of undercapitalized, fly-by-night airlines started business and disappeared shortly thereafter, along with many well-known air carriers. There were a number of causes for the turmoil, all set in motion by the fare wars that erupted when the deregulation of the industry was accomplished in 1978.

For the first time, pressures were put upon airlines to operate efficiently. Costs that simply had been passed on to the public as part of regulated fares had to be tamed under the era of deregulation. Wages of skilled employees that had been allowed, and even encouraged, to rise to excessive levels under the benign eye of the regulators could not be supported in the air of free competition. (Those same cost-cutting pressures also led airlines to skimp on maintenance and delay modernization, but that is another story.) The skies had turned unfriendly for traditional airline operations, and any carrier not fast enough to adjust quickly to changing conditions was a goner.

The cut-rate competition that erupted favored the new carriers. Using employees willing to work at modest wages in order to break into the industry or because they had been laid off by the established carriers, the new airlines had a decided price advantage to offer customers in order to build up business. The threat to the established air carriers varied with their size. The large established carriers had their own advantages. They had sideline service businesses, such as reservation systems, that other airlines paid to use. Most importantly, they had staying power—they could absorb losses by increasing their debt until the smaller airlines were driven out of business. The companies that fared the worst under deregulation were the mid-sized, established airlines such as Braniff, Continental, Eastern, and others like them, that were trapped into wage structures that their operations no longer could support.

The employees of the established airlines recognized the problem and provided wage and benefit concessions to the carriers piecemeal during the early 1980s. The major question was: how much is enough? The mid-sized airlines felt that they had to dig very deeply into their employees' pockets in order to survive. The struggles of the Eighties between those airlines and their unions would center around whether the companies were demanding excessive concessions as an easy way to cut costs or whether the unions' refusals to give in further at any point threatened the existence of the airlines. Would that decision on where that line was be solely in the hands of the companies, or would it be the result of negotiated compromise? Would rulings on that issue emanate from the NLRB or from the bankruptcy courts? The economics of the country in the early 1980s would decide the forum of the debate.

If deregulation was a dream come true, it happened during a period of economic nightmare in the United States. The carriers felt they had to expand service to stay viable, yet fares were low and costs, including jet fuel, were high. The Volcker Depression had led not only to decreased demand for tickets, but also high interest rates on money borrowed for expansion. Under those circumstances, the appellate decision in the Bildisco case certainly raised an interesting possibility for the second-tier air carriers. Due to the nature of the beast, savings in skilled labor costs would have a huge positive impact on an airline. However, the customary wisdom in the industry was that an airline filing a Chapter 11 was committing suicide. No major air carrier ever had filed bankruptcy.

By spring 1982, Braniff International had come to the end of its ability to do business. It had gambled on deregulation by adding high risk routes and borrowing heavily to finance expansion, including the purchase of forty-one planes for $925 million. American Airlines had moved its home base to Dallas, which had been Braniff's bailiwick, and the head-to-head competition and price cutting had bled Braniff dry. Because of the unremitting fare wars, it no longer could hold on until its new routes became profitable. Late in the day on May 12, 1982, the airline called all of its planes back to Dallas-Fort Worth Regional Airport, canceled all further flights, and told most of its nine thousand five hundred employees not to report for work. The next day it filed a Chapter 11 bankruptcy petition.

Not only was Braniff *in extremis*, but many aspects of its situation militated against revival. Vern Countryman, a Harvard law professor and a leading expert on bankruptcy, commented on one, the cessation of Braniff's operations: "That's absolutely crazy. When you file for reorganization, the last thing that you want to do is cease operations altogether. I can't remember another case where someone's shut down, laid off employees and then filed for bankruptcy."

Braniff's competitors quickly filled the gaps in domestic service. They petitioned the Federal Aviation Administration for Braniff's takeoff and landing slots and flooded the Civil Aeronautics Board with applications for Braniff's foreign routes. At every airport where Braniff had done business, its competitors were lined up to grab its gate allocations. Since it had ceased operations, it would have almost no cash flow to build upon, creating a difficult situation in which to persuade lenders and other creditors to accept reorganization. Because of the economic conditions in the industry, no one wanted to pay any meaningful price for any of Braniff's aircraft. Because of its poor planning, it would have no "war chest" to draw on during the bankruptcy case.

The opinions of experts were unanimous—the only thing that remained was the burial. The lead line in the *Wall Street Journal*'s news story sounded the knell: "Braniff International's decision to cease operations and seek protection under bankruptcy law almost certainly means the death of the airline." One of its bankers stated that "filing for Chapter 11 is an exercise in futility." Was it possible that Chapter 11 could work a miracle cure on a broke, shut-down company dependent upon consumer confidence to resume operations? Braniff would provide the ultimate test to the can-do framework of the bankruptcy reorganization statute.

The portents in the early stages of the bankruptcy case were not good. The Dallas-Fort Worth airport asked the court to be allowed to evict Braniff from its headquarters and terminal facilities. Since the FAA's regulation of takeoff and landing rights is for safety reasons and not for the collection of debts, its actions were not stayed by Braniff's bankruptcy, and it held a lottery to reassign Braniff's slots.

In spite of all the disastrous aspects to Braniff's situation, in the through-the-looking-glass world of bankruptcy the negatives began to become pluses. Not operating meant that losses would be stemmed. The actual sale value of Braniff's operating assets, mostly airplanes and related equipment, was so poor in the short run that no one was in a hurry to start the auction. Since the airline could be picked up at a relatively good price, it had started to draw suitors who had their own reasons for wanting to enter into the airline business or use Braniff to expand existing operations. The creditors smelled corporate death and destruction. Others smelled a good deal in the offing.

The bargain hunters would have time to do a deal. While a smaller company in Braniff's situation would have been liquidated without any further ado, Braniff was accorded the knee-jerk reaction that a megacorporation receives in bankruptcy court. It was not until January 1983 that Braniff, still with nonexistent operations, floated a reorganization concept. The two-page memorandum proposed to drastically cut creditors' claims. In return, Braniff would turn over sixty-two of its aircraft to its bankers and retain ground and service operations. Braniff had already reached a tentative agreement with another airline, PSA, which would transfer certain of Braniff's planes and facilities in sixteen cities to PSA on a lease-or-purchase basis. The PSA deal would hinge upon Braniff's ability to abrogate its collective-bargaining contract with its machinists' union, in order to bring its operating costs down. It was a plan developed in desperation. Nevertheless, Braniff was still alive.

The reorganization concept, including the PSA deal, met with a storm of opposition. The unsecured creditors saw the deal as producing almost nothing for them. Competing airlines, including American, who held the status of Braniff creditors or assignees of Braniff's routes, opposed the deal for their own reasons. The company's lenders, who favored the proposal, had not agreed on divvying up the assets scheduled to be turned over. The FAA challenged Braniff's rights to turn over its slots to PSA. After several months of negotiations failed to bring widespread agreement with the creditors or a better contract with Braniff's machinists' union, PSA withdrew its offer.

Even at this low point, in January 1983, Bankruptcy Judge John Flowers granted Braniff's motions to reject its union contracts with its machinists and flight attendants, citing the Bildisco case as precedent. In his ruling, the judge acknowledged that he was canceling the contracts to pave the way for a reorganization and invited PSA to reconsider.

Indeed, PSA was wooed back by the judge's decision, and Braniff renewed its motion for approval of its proposed arrangement with PSA. The hearing, which included objections by Braniff's competitor-creditors and the FAA, drew the attendance of approximately one hundred lawyers, which in number was about half of Braniff's then existing employees! The judge, having already stated the necessity of the PSA deal to revive Braniff, had no trouble overruling objections to the proposal. However, on appeal the approval was reversed, the appellate court ruling that such an important restructuring of Braniff could only be done through the affirmative vote by creditors upon a formal Plan of Reorganization. Thus the judge was barred from bypassing the creditors to give Braniff a boost, and Braniff had to develop a reorganization plan.

The interregnum had allowed another White Knight to come to

Braniff's rescue. Integration of airline and other travel-related services had become all the rage in the travel industry, and Hyatt Corporation saw Braniff as an opportunity to add an airline component to its hotel empire. The thinking was that travelers could be induced to use both components as part of packages, and so each business could help the other. (Other companies in the travel industry also were conglomeratizing. For example, United Airlines bought Hertz. As usual with conglomerates, within a few years the synergy of the travel conglomerate proved to be an illusion.)

After substantial Hyatt and creditor group haggling, by July 1983 a plan had been pieced together to breathe life back into the moribund company. Hyatt agreed to infuse up to $75 million in capital and loans into Braniff, which would allow thirty of its aircraft to operate. Under the plan, the secured creditors would fare the best, receiving about 84 percent of their claims in cash and stock. Unsecured creditors would receive eight cents on the dollar in cash and stock. The shareholders of Braniff would do just as well papering a room with their certificates—they were offered one share in the "new" Braniff for every 125 of their existing shares, a value of about fifteen cents per share. The new Braniff would be owned 80 percent by Hyatt, 10 percent by Braniff's prepetition unsecured creditors, 6 percent by the secured creditors, 2.3 percent by other creditors, and 1.7 percent by the existing Braniff shareholders. The revived company would have about two thousand employees. It was not very much but it would "save" Braniff, whatever that meant.

A Plan of Reorganization was mailed to Braniff's eighty thousand creditors. As is customary, the package to creditors included letters urging a favorable vote from the creditors' committees that supported the plan as well as from the company's management. The creditors voted approval of the plan, and Judge Flowers confirmed it over one committee's objections to the balloting procedures. The last hurdle was cleared when the federal Pension Benefit Guaranty Corporation agreed to compromise its claim for $48 million in pension benefits that Braniff had failed to pay, in return for $1 million.

The Braniff reorganization was cleared for takeoff in the sixteenth month of its bankruptcy. About a billion dollars in debt had been wiped out. Because management had been so foolish as to wait until the company was prostrate before seeking the warm embrace of bankruptcy court, it had lost control of the reorganization and was duly banished by Hyatt. Hyatt had obtained an airline for relatively little money, much of it in loans that could be pulled back by Hyatt. Along with Braniff's hard assets and remaining airport rights, Hyatt acquired an asset that easily exceeded its financial exposure—$300 million in tax credits, which could be used to offset any profitable operations that Hyatt could funnel through the Braniff entity. Between those tax loss carryforwards and the compromise with the PBGC, the American taxpayer once more had contributed mightily to the continued existence of a megacorporation, with rather dubious advantages, if any, accruing to the public. In 1988, Hyatt would sell Braniff to another investor group.

At the time it filed its Chapter 11 petition, Braniff was in so much trouble that its union contracts were not the main issue in the reorganization. The judge's action in canceling the bargaining agreements was just another sweetener, albeit a very important one, in attracting the scavengers. However, the era was dawning of the Union-Busting Chapter 11, in which the primary goal by far of corporate reorganization would be the extinguishment of collective-bargaining agreements fairly negotiated and voluntarily entered into.

Soon after Judge Flowers voided Braniff's union contracts with its machinists and cabin attendants, Wilson Foods Corporation threw down the gauntlet to unionism. Wilson was not just any food processor—with sales well over $2 billion a year, it was the largest pork processor and fifth-largest meat-packer in the United States. Wilson was not bankrupt by traditional concepts, and its Chapter 11 filing with no warning stunned many. However, its management insisted that its agreement with the United Food and Commercial Workers Union was causing it to become unprofitable; and that the Manville Corporation bankruptcy, filed in August 1982, provided precedent for filing bankruptcy while solvent. Accordingly, although the company had plenty of cash and credit and had no plans for closing any of its twelve plants or laying off workers, it immediately rejected its collective-bargaining agreements pursuant to the bankruptcy law and cut wages 40 to 50 percent for most of its nine thousand employees. A typical meatcutter earning $22,000 a year suddenly found his annual pay fixed at $13,500, not really a living wage for someone supporting a family.

Wilson became the latest of the "Hey, you can't do that" Chapter 11s, and it drew the usual experts' disapprobations. Lawrence King, a law professor at New York University Law School and a leading expert on the Bankruptcy Code, clucked that Wilson's Chapter 11 "smacks to me of improper use of the bankruptcy laws." Professor Frank Kennedy of the University of Michigan Law School, another bankruptcy expert, decried the action, accusing Wilson of "taking the law into its own hands." Harvard law professor Vern Countryman, filling out the triumvirate of the most prestigious academic experts on the Bankruptcy Code, stated flatly, "It's improper to file for Chapter 11 when your only purpose is to reject a collective-bargaining agreement." *Business Week* followed the customary wisdom when it said "Chapter 11 is supposed to be a safe harbor reserved for use by those who need it."

As usual with respect to megacorporate bankruptcies, the academics and other observers were overlooking one of the primary unwritten rules of the bankruptcy courts: there is no such thing as an illegitimate use of Chapter 11 when it involves a megacorporate debtor. It was not that professors King, Kennedy, and Countryman, and others, did not know their legal theory; it just was that during the 1980s, established legal principles became mere hurdles to be circumvented by courts anxious to do the megacorporations' bidding.

Wilson had prepared the best it could for Chapter 11. It had an extensive public relations campaign, which was ready to go on the date of filing. It had planned a program of personal contacts with its most important creditors to assure them of its viability. However, by necessity, no creditors were given prior notice of the Chapter 11 filing. Although Wilson had given some signals about its profit problems to its lenders, it had left even them in the dark about the extreme action that it would be taking. Consequently, one open issue was the extent of cooperation by Wilson's banks, led by none other than Continental Illinois Bank and Trust Company.

Continental Illinois wanted out. Already suffering big problems with its oil loans, the tottering bank could not afford to be identified with another company in Chapter 11, even a solvent one. Because Wilson was in such sound financial condition, it quickly negotiated an $80 million line of credit with Citicorp.

Of course, when a company tears up its union contract, it incurs the threat of a strike (although often the union members refrain from striking because they are afraid it will cause the company to fold). The advantage to the company is that its cancellation of the union contract, if found to be legal by the bankruptcy court (which it generally is), cannot be found to be an unfair labor practice by the National Labor Relations Board. Wilson's union was so confused by the company's move that it took a wait-and-see attitude.

Wilson got an extra bonus from its Chapter 11. Occidental Petroleum Corporation, which already owned a meat-packing company (IBP), pursued an unwanted takeover of Wilson but was thwarted by the bankruptcy. Occidental requested that it be allowed to present its Plan of Reorganization for Wilson to Wilson's creditors, but the presiding judge denied Occidental the opportunity, limiting the right to file a plan to Wilson. Consequently, the only plan that the creditors saw, which was approved, was that presented by Wilson.

Wilson exited its Chapter 11 proceeding about a year after it had entered. Its creditors were paid their debts over a two-year period. The company had spent some time and effort in the Chapter 11 attempting to further chisel its creditors, but its balance sheet was too strong. Nevertheless, it had accomplished its goal, a radical reordering of its wage structure. Wilson's top management was so pleased with its success that it voted itself 36 percent raises.

Unlike Braniff, Continental Airlines did not wait until it was down to its last penny to attack its unions. While true that Continental, the eighth largest airline in the U.S., had lost $60.8 million in 1982, the company was nowhere near the end of the line, and it had recently achieved $100 million in concessions from its employees. When it filed its Chapter 11 proceeding on September 24, 1983, it had a $58.2 million cash war chest and $230.2 million in receivables.

There was no mistaking Continental's reorganization program. Upon filing Chapter 11, it unilaterally canceled its collective-bargaining agreements, fired all of its twelve thousand employees, and then rehired about a third of them at about half of their prebankruptcy wages or less (senior flight attendants were cut from $35,700 to $15,000), with orders to work longer hours for the pay. The company said it took the actions because in its judgment its labor contracts were burdensome, and rejection would increase its reorganization chances—the emerging standard for bankruptcy rejection under the Bildisco and Braniff cases.

Of course, the attitude of Continental Airlines was really the attitude of one Francisco A. Lorenzo. Lorenzo was cut from a different mold than the polished and faceless corporate barons who guided their companies through Chapter 11 without drawing undue attention to their methods and goals. In 1982, Frank Lorenzo had used the freedom of deregulation, his small Texas Air Corporation, and his own brand of *chutzpah*, to swallow the much larger Continental Airlines. After he gained control of Continental, he single-mindedly began to reshape the company and did not bother to disguise his moves. Frank Lorenzo would fight all the fights that had to be won to get to the top of the heap in the airline industry.

To Frank Lorenzo, at the center of the storm, it was very simple to see how to fly through it—Continental needed to be a low-cost carrier to compete with the industry's giants, and the high wages of Continental's skilled, unionized employees stood in its way. Since Lorenzo (through Texas Air) had paid $134 million for the company, it was his to do with as he wished. If cleansing the company through bankruptcy would do the trick, it was going to be done.

Lorenzo's actions were based on two assumptions: there were plenty of people with dreams of becoming pilots and flight attendants, even at wages lower than offered at the major airlines; and any bad image of Continental and loss of support by travel agencies generated by its labor problems and bankruptcy could be countered by cheap fares. He was right, across the board. In the end, in spite of picketing, full-page ads, and every public relations ploy that organized labor could conceive of, Continental's most important constituency, the American public, was all too happy to pay lower fares to ride what would become the cattle cars of the air.

The bankruptcy filing did increase the intensity of Continental's internecine warfare with its unionized employees. Members of the Air Line Pilots Association as well as the Union of Flight Attendants struck the carrier just one week after the bankruptcy was filed. Continental kept its planes in the air with those employees who chose not to fight Lorenzo's vision of the new era and with new hires. Continental even claimed that the strike was illegal because the provisions of the labor laws setting preconditions for strikes had not been complied with by the unions! The company slapped a libel suit on striking mechanics for implying that it was using unskilled workers in servicing its aircraft. The once proud bird of the skies had chosen to get down and dirty with its own.

Whether Continental was abusing the law or acting legitimately depended on which side of the fence one was on. There was a good deal of unease even in business circles at the apparent success of Bildisco, Braniff, and Continental in radically altering labor-management patterns that had been built up over the course of many years. Even *Business Week*, hardly a dupe of the unions, expressed the view in an editorial that the bankruptcy courts ought to "send issues such as labor problems back to the bargaining table." Amid the tsk tsks was an opposing view printed on the editorial page of the *Wall Street Journal*:

> This skewing of the market forces by the labor laws, and the non-consensual nature of collective-bargaining agreements generally, make them a particularly appropriate subject of the rejection mechanism. The ability of a bankrupt employer to reject an onerous collective-bargaining agreement aids the reorganization effort and thus represents a small step toward redressing the economic imbalance created by the labor laws.

Among the commentators to the media concerning Continental's bankruptcy filing was the ubiquitous Professor Vern Countryman. Immediately after the announcement of the bankruptcy, Countryman stated for the media record that "if their sole purpose of going into Chapter 11 bankruptcy is to get rid of their collective-bargaining contracts, then it's a misuse of the chapter, and the courts won't allow them to do it." He soon was retained by Continental's unions to challenge the validity of the Chapter 11 proceeding.

Frank Lorenzo had supplied the professor and his clients with some good ammunition. While others would have muddied the waters over the causes of Continental's Chapter 11 filing, if for no other reason than to improve the company's legal position, Lorenzo had been quite direct. When asked why Continental filed Chapter 11, Lorenzo had replied, "It wasn't a problem of (insufficient) cash or too great a debt load. Our sole problem was labor." The gauntlet had been thrown down, the challenge issued clearly. It would be responded to by one of the foremost academic experts on the bankruptcy law. Would the courts punish the brash Mr. Lorenzo for polluting the sacred bankruptcy text?

The filing by Continental spurred union lobbyists to step up their efforts to persuade Congress to legislate against the use of Chapter 11 to abrogate collective-bargaining contracts. Union arguments in opposition to the tactic focused on the view that companies would not have to bargain with them anymore if they could act unilaterally through bankruptcy. At the time, Congress was wrestling with the fallout from the Supreme Court's *Marathon* decision, and the union movement was hoping to have its legislation piggybacked onto any corrective bankruptcy action. In the end, Congress was too tied up with the problem of bankruptcy court jurisdiction and too beset with countervailing lobbying by businesses to prevent unions from being dragged through the bankruptcy courts. Corporations' ability to challenge union power through the bankruptcy process would prove to be yet another successful means of setting unions back on their heels during the decade of the Eighties.

Ultimately, organized labor failed in its attempts to paint Lorenzo as the devil incarnate because it was he who struck a popular note for the times, not the unions. In the midst of the Reagan years, it was all right to be a tough capitalist. All was fair if one's heart was free of a desire for government regulation. The marketplace would correct all. Lorenzo proudly cast himself as the quintessential capitalist in an interview: "Deregulation is working the way it has to work. One shouldn't look too hard at the short-term disruptions that may have to occur. Continental is right out on the leading edge of this wave of deregulation, and we're saying, 'Look, we're going to solve our problems ourselves.' We're not running to Congress trying to get the laws changed." Lorenzo did not have to run to Congress—he had the federal government's Bankruptcy Code on his side.

If Frank Lorenzo was carrying the banner, there were many who were ready to follow. The most visible effect of Continental's Chapter 11 involved a company that did not file bankruptcy at all, Eastern Airlines. Two days after Continental filed its bankruptcy proceeding, Frank Borman, the chairman of Eastern, told the airline's 37,500 employees that if they did not agree to cut wages by at least 20 percent on top of concessions already agreed to, Eastern soon would follow Braniff's and Continental's lead in canceling its labor pacts through Chapter 11. Over a period of the next several years, Borman would use that threat to extract serial concessions from Eastern's employees. (Nevertheless, the worst nightmare of Eastern's employees would come true in 1986, when Eastern was taken over by Texas Air.)

Although Continental obviously had bought itself a good deal of trouble by filing for bankruptcy, soon the great advantages of being in Chapter 11 began to kick in. Freed from its collective-bargaining agreements, the company began banking the millions of dollars that were saved by the reduction of wages and the size of its labor force. More millions were saved by the stoppage of the interest clock that had been running upon much of the company's debt. By December, which was only Continental's third full month in bankruptcy, the company announced its first monthly operating profit in some time. Once again, the early tension of a megacorporate Chapter 11, the dire predictions of imminent collapse, the threats of the appointment of a trustee to replace management, all proved to be mere fantasy. Once again, the true nature of the bankruptcy courts' service on bahalf of megacorporations came to the fore.

Bankruptcy Judge R. F. Wheless, Jr., did his part. At Continental's request, he prohibited the company's suppliers from refusing to sell to it, a most unusual abrogation of the basic legal right of any business to refuse to sell to any customer unless the refusal constitutes an antitrust violation. When Continental balked at disclosing financial information to creditors as required by bankruptcy law, the good judge obligingly told the company that it did not have to. This is how the *Wall Street Journal* reported the proceedings:

> How much cash Continental has is a mystery to most creditors and the public. The federal bankruptcy court judge hearing Continental's bankruptcy proceedings entered a sweeping secrecy order that prohibits disclosure of Continental's cash position, cash projections and profit-and-loss projections. Continental officials declined to answer most questions relating to the company's current or projected financial condition.

Perhaps no one had informed Mr. Lorenzo that he actually would be expected to give Continental's creditors some hint of the company's financial circumstances as a price to pay for asking the court's protection from paying them their just debts! In any event, the broad secrecy order was weakened substantially on appeal.

Lorenzo also successfully covered his flank. To counter union lobbying in Congress, in April 1984, Lorenzo testified before a joint hearing of the Senate's Judiciary and Labor Committees. Not only did he offer a defense of the use of Chapter 11 to shed unwanted union contracts, he put in a special caution concerning Continental. Lorenzo warned that if Congress passed corrective legislation that had the effect of voiding Continental's cancellation of its union contracts, Continental would not have the resources to make its employees whole retroactively. If forced to do so, Continental would have no choice but to fold. In other words, the blood of Continental's corporate body and the pain of its employees' layoffs would be on the hands of Congress. Frank Lorenzo had placed Continental in a position that Congress could not bear to affect—a twist on Lee Iacocca's approach.

Meanwhile, the unions were making no headway against union busting in court. In response to motions by Continental's unions asking that the bankruptcy case be dismissed, in January 1984, Judge Wheless ruled that it was acceptable for Continental to file a Chapter 11 case because it was *threatened with insolvency.* Judge Wheless still was considering the legality of Continental's cancellation of its union contracts when the United States Supreme Court made his job easier, the high court ruling in January 1984 in the Bildisco case that it was relatively easy for a Chapter 11 company to reject its union contracts.

Justice William Rehnquist, the most conservative Supreme Court judge at the time, wrote the high court's opinion in the Bildisco case. Once Justice Rehnquist had set out the general principles that the Supreme Court found existed in bankruptcy law, there was no doubting the direction that the decision would take. To the judge, the dispute must be viewed against the backdrop of the "policy" of Chapter 11 to "permit successful rehabilitation of debtors," and the fact that rejection of contracts is "vital" to the purposes of Chapter 11.

The first part of the decision involved the issue of whether a Chapter 11 company could unilaterally declare a union collective-bargaining agreement void. By a bare 5 to 4 majority, the court ruled that the authority to cancel labor agreements reposes in the Chapter 11 company and that it need not first request authority from the bankruptcy judge to do so. That ruling insured that bankruptcy cancellation of union agreements would be a *fait accompli*, with employees suffering and unions relegated to litigating the matter for many months after the fact while the company's restructuring proceeded, perhaps irrevocably.

The second portion of the decision, setting the standard that a Chapter 11 company must meet in order to have its rejection of a union contract ratified by a court, was by unanimous vote of the Supreme Court. The court ignored concepts previously developed by lower courts, rejecting the standard of unfettered "business judgment" as too favorable to businesses and the standard of "necessary for reorganization" as too onerous for them. Instead, avoiding an inflexible standard and refusing to base its ruling on technicalities, the court chose a rather nebulous middle ground, ruling that in order to reject a labor pact in bankruptcy, a company must show that the agreement is burdensome, that it had made reasonable efforts to get the union to modify it, and that, on balance, the facts favor rejection. To the court, that balance should be struck with due regard for the interests of the debtor and the creditors as well as of labor, none of the interests being inherently paramount.

An unheralded portion of the Supreme Court's opinion also provided a big boost to business. In addressing the issue of what happens if and when a court determines that a company has acted wrongfully in canceling a union contract in bankruptcy, Judge Rehnquist insured that the result would be nothing but a slap on the wrist. In such a situation, the court ruled, claims for damages would be treated as prepetition claims which could be compromised in a Plan of Reorganization. The wrongful rejection would not be deemed to be an unfair labor practice, the labor laws taking a subordinate place in that matter to the purposes of bankruptcy reorganization. Since the matter would be taken care of in the bankruptcy, the National Labor Relations Board would not have jurisdiction to punish the company. The natural result of that ruling would be to encourage companies to cancel their union agreements whenever a situation was ambiguous or whenever cancellation would be the least bit colorable.

The Supreme Court's opinion also was notable for what it did not say. Virtually no mention was made of the special status of organized labor, the court merely advising that judges should be "somewhat stricter" in reviewing the rejection of labor agreements than other types of contracts. No hint whatsoever was given that it might be illegal to file a Chapter 11 case for the sole purpose of rejecting a collective-bargaining agreement. Given the opinion's treatment of unions as barely different from any other party who had entered into a contract with a company that then files for bankruptcy, the clear message was that the court would not disapprove of such a motive for filing Chapter 11.

Corporate lawyers were jubilant, and union attorneys failed to see any good in the Supreme Court's Bildisco opinion. Although the Bildisco case involved the National Labor Relations Act and railroads and airlines technically came under the Railway Labor Act, neither side saw any significant chance that the two similar laws would be viewed differently on this issue by the courts. Because rulings in the future would depend upon a balancing of facts rather than a hard-and-fast legal rule, and because factual findings by trial-level judges are generally almost impossible to upset on appeal, it could be predicted that compliant bankruptcy judges would provide corporations with an easy path to attack unions. Although companies would have to meet a minimal standard to abrogate union contracts, the Supreme Court had spoken fairly clearly about the deference to be accorded to companies in reorganization. The message was: stay out of their way!

No one was surprised when Judge Wheless ratified Continental's rejection of its labor contract with the pilots' union. In making his ruling in June 1984—nine months after Continental began operating without union approval—Judge Wheless stated that the collective-bargaining agreements were "burdensome to [Continental's bankruptcy] estate. Reasonable efforts to negotiate a voluntary modification have been made and are not likely to produce a prompt and satisfactory solution, and the parties' inability to reach agreement threatens to impede the success of the debtor's reorganization." The judge also stated that the balance of equities favored Continental and its creditors over the pilots. The judge's findings were carefully consistent with the standard set by the Supreme Court in the Bildisco case.

Subsequent to the Supreme Court's Bildisco decision, organized labor was successful in getting Congress to address the issue. When Congress finally enacted amendments to the Bankruptcy Reform Act to deal with the problem of bankruptcy court jurisdiction that had bedeviled it since the Supreme Court's *Marathon* decision, it included an amendment that modified the court's Bildisco rulings to at least keep unions in the game. Effective July 10, 1984—and not made retroactive to affect Continental—a Chapter 11 company has to apply to the presiding bankruptcy judge in order to reject a union contract (as it must for rejection of all other kinds of contracts), and it has to show that it already has followed certain steps in making a good-faith proposal to the union that would allow a reorganization. If the union has rejected the offer without good cause, and if the rejection of the bargaining agreement is necessary for the reorganization of the debtor, the court will allow the debtor to reject the pact. By picking bits and pieces from other court cases as well as the Supreme Court's Bildisco decision, Congress had managed to supply a reasonable standard without unduly offending either business or labor. It had finally been forced to state its "intent" respecting the issue.

The major problem with Congress's carefully drafted compromise language is that it is largely irrelevant in megacorporate cases. Companies' compliance with the standards and procedures set out in the statute is supervised by the United States Trustee in each federal district. The U.S. Trustee is part of the Justice Department, the same department that intervened in the Bildisco case at the Supreme Court level in order to argue for the most relaxed standards in the rejection of labor agreements. The U.S. Trustees are not hard on companies that wish to cancel their union contracts. Further, the factual findings respecting labor contract rejections are made by judges who are dedicated to successful reorganizations of megacorporations. An added factor is that during the last decade of Republican control of the White House, the men and women filling those judgment seats increasingly have been conservative Republicans unlikely to see matters the unions' way. Who said life is fair?

Continental did not have to worry about how judges would interpret the new statutory standards. Its collective-bargaining agreements had been canceled prior to the passage of the corrective legislation. During 1985, its unions called off their ineffectual strikes, officially raising the white flag.

Having securely established its new persona as a discount airline staffed by nonunion personnel, Continental was ready to move out of the friendly confines of bankruptcy court. Before it did so, like other megacorporations in Chapter 11, it spent a good deal of time dangling a plan in front of creditors that would keep an unwarranted amount of cash in its pocket. However, Continental got serious when court procedures began to get in the way of its substantial expansion plans. Also, it became difficult to cry poor in the face of its own projections showing a quintupling of its operating profits over the next four years. At some point, even the best executives lose the ability to talk out of both sides of their mouths at once!

In September 1985, Continental's creditor groups agreed to a Plan of Reorganization. The proposal provided for full payment of its debts; however, Continental reserved for itself the right to pay most of it over time, some of it over ten years, with interest. That provision provided Continental with one last bankruptcy benefit—an involuntary loan from its creditors of more than $700 million. Continental's shareholders were not given the usual bankruptcy shaft because most of Continental's stock was owned by Frank Lorenzo's Texas Air unit.

After completing the reorganization formalities, in June 1986, Continental emerged from Chapter 11. Its creditors had waited almost three years on the sidelines for the first payment on their debts owed at the time of the filing, and most of them would wait for many more years before they would be fully paid. Continental's management proudly called it one of the most successful reorganizations ever undertaken. By September 1986, Bankruptcy Judge T. Glover Roberts, who had taken over the Continental case from Judge Wheless and had issued a number of rulings highly favorable to the company in its labor disputes, was comfortably ensconced as a partner in Continental's Houston law firm.

As Continental emerged from bankruptcy, Frank Lorenzo started his program to impress the financial market with Continental's and his strengths, in order to make the next steps in his careful plans become reality. Continental's management reviewed its own financial records and announced, by golly, that its most recent projections were far better than those that had been presented to the creditors during the bankruptcy. Not only did those figures predict substantial profits over the next five years, those profits would be double good—they would be sheltered from taxation by more than $200 million in federal income tax credits. Having earned his stars as a crisis manager (and with the bankruptcy laws in reserve), Frank Lorenzo would be able to attract all of the financing that he needed for his flights of fancy.

In what had become a rather commonplace occurrence for Chapter 11 megacorporations, Continental shot from the box lean and mean. While Continental rebuilt its routes and established itself as a major discount airline, Lorenzo also managed the operations of Texas Air and two other airlines. In a crowning achievement that established him as the premier operator in the airline industry, in 1986 Lorenzo (through Texas Air) purchased Eastern Airlines *and* Frontier Airlines *and* People's Express. Frank Lorenzo came to control about 25 percent of the domestic airline industry—and the bankruptcy law was his most important partner.

After tiny Bildisco had led the way, giants Braniff, Wilson Foods, and Continental Airlines took major steps in making the bankruptcy courts safe for megacorporations. Instead of being thrown out of court ignominiously, they had extended the power of the bankruptcy courts to aid in the reorganization of corporations at the expense of others. Although Congress could claim credit for righting the imbalance created by the Bildisco decision, it would not be Congress that would be presiding over megacorporate bankruptcies. It would be a simple matter for Mr. Corporate Executive earnestly to explain to a friendly bankruptcy judge that, yes, his company had bargained oh so reasonably with that unreasonable union, and, yes, it would be necessary for the company's reorganization to ...

But it was not to be Bildisco, Wilson or Continental that would take the provisions of the bankruptcy code to its furthest extent to date. That honor was to fall to Johns-Manville.

Chapter 9

Manville: The Giant at Bay

Monster, dread our damages.
We're the jury,
dread our fury.
—Gilbert and Sullivan
Trial By Jury

Everything was coming together for John Rossi in 1978. At thirty-three, he was about to be made a partner in his New York City law firm. His wife Nancy was six months pregnant with their first child. He was living a charmed life.

Then something went wrong. Rossi had no energy. He was losing weight but suddenly had a protruding stomach. The doctors ran tests; the results were a death sentence. There was an inoperable tumor in his abdomen. Despite chemotherapy, John Rossi died on December 17, 1978, one month before the birth of his son.

When an autopsy was performed, asbestos fibers were found in the body. It seems that when Rossi was twenty years old, he had counted asbestos sheets before unloading them from a truck. He had done this for two weeks.

After her husband's death, Nancy Rossi, looking at their wedding pictures, was to wonder, "Was that asbestos sitting there in his body the day of our wedding, just waiting to start its rampage?" The answer was yes.

What is the value of a life? What measures should be undertaken by a company to protect the health and safety of its employees, those who may use its products, and the general public?

How should a corporation be punished for policies which show a disregard for people? Should it in effect pay a fine to parties injured by its products, in the nature of "punitive" damages? If so, what legal limits on the punishment should be set? When, if ever, should corporate officers and directors bear personal liability for corporate actions? When, if ever, are injured people better served by a system other than that already available through the standard court procedures? When should the criminal justice system be invoked to censure business activities?

When answers to those questions emerge from the crucible of our political and judicial systems, to what extent should the dictates and goals of the bankruptcy system be allowed to change them? Should bankruptcy be permitted to cheapen the value of life? Are there times when the bankruptcy system should not be permitted to override the level of liability established by other courts? When, if ever, is bankruptcy in the best interests of creditors? Should injured claimants take precedence in bankruptcy court over commercial creditors? Can potential future claimants have their rights taken away before they can learn that they have them?

These thorny social and legal issues—and many more—arose in the odyssey of Johns-Manville Corporation from pillar of the "Fortune 500" to reviled defendant to rehabilitated corporate citizen.

One job of the civil courts within the United States is to compensate people injured by the wrongful actions or failures to act of others. These wrongful actions or failures to act are known as "torts." An action or failure to act is wrongful if it does not meet standards of care established by statutes and case decisions. A tort may cause physical injuries or even death, but in the end, the pain, suffering, inconvenience, and incapacitiation of the injured person are reduced to one common denominator: money damages.

A manufacturer is not liable for all injuries caused by its wrongful actions or failures to act. The law limits a miscreant's liability to those who the manufacturer should have foreseen would legitimately use or come into contact with its product. Who is a "foreseeable" claimant in the law's eyes is not determined by common sense or even actual experience. He or she simply is any injured person the law deems to be within the ambit of compensable victims. Generally speaking, under early tort law, an injured person is a "foreseeable" claimant against a manufacturer only if he or she purchased that manufacturer's product directly from it. To a large extent, the story of tort law in the twentieth century has been the inexorable enlargement of the group of users of products and bystanders affected by products deemed to be foreseeable under the law. The major issues in the injury lawsuits brought against Johns-Manville involved the extent of its "foreseeable" liability as well as whether its actions lived up to its duties of care.

Although judges set the general legal standards of foreseeability and due care, in practice, it is juries who apply the facts to the law and who decide the ultimate issue of liability in nearly all personal injury cases in this country. That is because the constitutional right to a jury trial almost always is exercised by experienced plaintiffs' attorneys instead of a "bench" trial. The judge can set the ground rules for the conduct of a trial and charge the people in the jury box to follow only dry statistics and rules of law, but when the common folk retire to the jury room, they are relatively free to apply their "people's justice."

Most attempts to impeach a jury's decision on the grounds that the jurors were swayed by emotion or were otherwise not objective are doomed to failure—judges *do not want to know* what went on in the jury room! For example, in a seminal case decided against the major asbestos manufacturers, in responding to the companies' arguments that special questions answered by the jury were inconsistent with its general verdict, the appellate court stated:

> It has long been the rule that consistency in general verdicts is not required. Whether the jury's verdict was the result of carelessness or compromise . . . is immaterial. Juries may indulge in precisely such motives or vagaries.

While juries are not particularly proplaintiff in determining liability—contrary to the disinformation campaigns of the insurance industry, on the average civil plaintiffs win only approximately 50 percent of cases that go to trial—juries most assuredly recognize the human factors when considering the amount of damages to be awarded to a successful plaintiff. A crass and inhumane defendant can expect to pay for lapses in decency. And, yes, big impersonal corporations may feel the ire of the juries in the dollar amount of verdicts against them. Some may call those exactions a tax on big corporations as recompense for the ways they tax the citizens' sense of control over their own lives.

A more express recognition of the jury's right to enforce a sense of outrage is its ability to assess "punitive" damages, which are designed not to compensate the plaintiff for loss but rather to punish the defendant for shockingly deficient conduct. (A judge may award punitive damages when he or she sits without a jury but is far less likely to do so.) At the point that punitive damages are assessed, the system has crossed over from a civil to a quasi-criminal mode. To the plaintiffs' attorneys, punitive damages are the primary means of forcing big corporations to change abusive policies where the companies are able to absorb ordinary compensatory damages awards as mere costs of doing business. To companies that frequently find themselves in court as defendants, punitive damages are evidence of a system run amuck, where there are no recognized standards for setting the amount of the award and the plaintiff receives a windfall over and above true damages and financial loss. There are also *sub rosa* issues: plaintiffs' attorneys get their percentage of the punitive damage awards too, as part of their fee, which provides additional fuel for their "outrage"; and punitive damage awards are not covered by corporations' liability insurance policies and must be paid directly out of the companies' coffers. For better or worse, the availability of contingency-fee legal representation and punitive damages in civil suits allows the "little people" on the jury to send a message to corporate America, and the mega-corporations do indeed say "ouch." (Yes, the plaintiff does receive a windfall. Some states have passed legislation that cuts the state government in on a substantial percentage of punitive damages entered in state courts. No sense allowing all that money to escape the politicians' hands!)

There are limits upon the jury's ability to award punitive damages, although they are ill-defined. Generally the judge presiding over a trial serves a "gatekeeper" function, allowing the jury to consider imposing punitive damages if substantial evidence of shocking conduct on the part of the defendant has been presented at trial but prohibiting the jury from doing so when, in the judge's opinion, that threshold level has not been reached by the plaintiff's case. As one might suspect, in jurisdictions where the judiciary is more conservative, the threshold level is higher; and some judges virtually will not permit punitive damages to be considered in personal injury cases. Even after a jury has been allowed to impose punitive damages, the award may be reduced or eliminated by the presiding judge or on appeal if it is felt that *too much of a message* has been sent.

Aside from the windfall problem, many judges are concerned that companies that are sued many times over chronic problems—such as the asbestos manufacturers—may become overpunished through suffering successive punitive damage hits. Of course, those defendants are quick to complain to the judges presiding over trials of the unfairness of having to face their own reprehensible actions over and over across the country. Some judges will bar the consideration of punitive damages for that reason. Thus far, defendants in multiple cases involving their defective or hazardous products have been unsuccessful in persuading most trial judges or any appellate courts to put a definitive limitation on any one company's exposure to punitive damages.

Not only do litigants and their attorneys fight on the micro level in individual lawsuits, they also fight on the macro level, for the hearts and minds of the American public and their elected and appointed representatives.

On one side are attorneys who specialize in representing people who are injured in accidents or by manufactured products. To that increasingly sophisticated group, the individual tort lawsuit, with its constitutional right to a jury trial, is the only effective means of discovering the skeletons in big corporations' closets and achieving adequate compensation for those injured wrongfully. In other words, not surprisingly, they believe that the rights of injured individuals against big companies depend upon an aggressive, entrepreneurial plaintiffs' bar. The necessary concomitant to individuals' rights to sue for injury is the "contingency fee" arrangement, whereby the party's attorney agrees to take a percentage of any settlement or award in the client's favor, commonly somewhere between 25 and 35 percent. The substantial percentage stems from a recognition that for those cases lost at trial, the attorney may take away nothing for hundreds or thousands of hours of work. While an hourly fee arrangement may produce a more reasonable fee in many cases, few injured individuals can afford to make that type of commitment. Consequently, plaintiffs' attorneys will fight to the death to protect the place of the contingent fee and jury trial in American jurisprudence in order to secure the rights of injured people and, not incidentally, the chance to earn big bucks on multimillion-dollar cases.

"Institutional defendants"—those insurance companies and manufacturers that find themselves in court frequently defending against such suits—like the tort/court system just fine when it serves to pit impecunious plaintiffs against big corporations and produces logjams that delay the days of reckoning for years. However, when a group of litigants begins to improve the odds by accumulating embarrassing evidence against defendants from case to case, when hordes of injured people begin to learn that they might have causes of action against particular companies or industries, or when juries begin to show their feelings for certain defendants' lack of concern for employees or the general public by imposing punitive damages, then suddenly to those companies the jury-trial system becomes "inefficient." Those defendants begin to express concern that plaintiffs are not receiving adequate compensation because of plaintiff attorneys' contingent fees and that the court system is becoming overloaded. That concern becomes manifested in calls to replace the existing tort system with an administrative procedure that would compensate large groups of claimants "efficiently," not incidentally limiting their awards to some table of damages and, of course, prohibiting punitive damages.

That pattern—growing plaintiff's power generating counterattacks by large corporations—is being played out at this time. The assault upon the megacorporations by those injured by hazardous and defective products, dangerous chemicals in the workplace, toxic waste, and pollution is now building in America. The story of Johns-Manville Corporation is illustrative of the past, present, and future of these large forces at work, and the bankruptcy denouement that often is the culmination of the struggle.

Asbestos is a strange and wonderful substance. It is nothing more than any of several minerals that nature has formed into soft, thread-like fibers. Because its spongy composition traps air like wool, it is an excellent insulator. Because it is made up of strands of fibers, it can be formed into mats and even woven into textiles. Because it is rock, it will not burn or easily conduct electricity. A method has been devised for spraying it onto surfaces as a coating. Its fibers are flexible, strong, and not affected by most chemicals. As a result of those admirable characteristics, asbestos has thousands of uses. Asbestos textiles are used for firefighter's clothing and fireproof curtains in theaters. Asbestos wrapped or sprayed around electrical wiring, pipes, ducts, and in walls prevents heat loss and keeps rooms cool, whether on land or in ships. It has been used widely for ceiling tiles in schools. It is a crucial material for brake linings. Mixed with other materials it adds heat-resistant and insulating qualities to caulking, cement pipes, floor tiles, wallboard, and plastics. In all of its various forms, it was heavily used in houses and public buildings through the 1970s. Who knows how many fire deaths asbestos has averted?

Now for the bad news: asbestos is extremely hazardous to human health. Those miracle fibers, when inhaled, tend to stick in the lining of the lungs and stomach. When taken into the lungs even in small amounts over a moderate amount of time, asbestos tends to cause certain diseases: asbestosis, a type of fibrosis which blocks the lungs with fibrous tissue; bronchial cancer (aided by cigarette smoking); and mesothelioma, a cancer of the chest or abdominal lining. Since all of those diseases are degenerative, and since no cure is known for them, they are invariably fatal. Asbestosis often produces right-side heart failure. With increasing dosages, time of exposure, or both, the chance of incurring one or more of those diseases also increases. The families and friends of asbestos workers are also at risk to those diseases through contact with clothing that carries asbestos "dust." However, the period between cause and effect is extensive, and it may take up to forty years for asbestos-related diseases to manifest themselves. Of course, the incubation period and the severity of the resulting disease are a function of the degree of exposure to asbestos as well as such other factors as the general health of the individual, other environmental insults, and whether the individual is a smoker. (A sure recipe for early death from a lung disease is to be an asbestos worker who smokes.) Accordingly, a major issue in asbestos litigation has been how much the asbestos manufacturers knew about the health hazards of inhaling asbestos—and when.

Other products dangerous to human health have been loosed upon our society, but none has been so widespread. The combination of the usefulness of asbestos, the severity of the resulting diseases, and the slow-acting nature of the hazard has proven to be a deadly mix. The stuff is virtually everywhere—in buildings, ships, houses, and cars. No careful records pinpoint the locations of asbestos insulation, since until recently it carried no warning labels and builders were casual about its use. As a result, about 21 million people have been exposed to it regularly on the job, including a majority of construction workers and about 1.4 million teachers. The Environmental Protection Agency has estimated that asbestos insulation is in about 700,000 buildings and 31,000 schools. California alone has about 200,000 homes with asbestos-lined air ducts. An East Coast study estimated that about 30 percent of homes have asbestos insulation. As to those exposed to asbestos on the job, it has been predicted that eight thousand to ten thousand deaths per year will result through the end of this century. One study found that one quarter of a million people may die from asbestos-induced diseases over the next several decades. No one really knows—or, apparently, wants to even think about—the number of deaths in the general population aside from asbestos workers that will be caused by the mineral fiber. The cost of removing asbestos from our environment will be a burden on our generation and the next.

For much of the period discussed in this chapter, less than twenty companies doing business in the United States "manufactured" asbestos—that is, mined the fibrous minerals and prepared them for the various types of insulation duties. Johns-Manville Corporation was one of the first American companies to enter the business and maintained its postion as the largest producer and industry leader throughout the Age of Asbestos. PPG Industries, formerly known as Pittsburgh Plate Glass, bought into the industry when it acquired Corning, which had previously gobbled up the asbestos operations of Owens-Illinois. Raybestos-Manhattan is a big producer of asbestos brake linings. Some companies—Forty-Eight Insulations, Keene Corporation, Fiberboard Paper Products Corporation, Amatex, Eagle-Picher, and Union Asbestos and Rubber Company (UNARCO)—are not well known but nevertheless have been big producers of asbestos. Until litigation became a major cost of the business, the manufacture of asbestos was solidly profitable. For example, Johns-Manville's profit margin on asbestos operations hovered around 27 percent, about three times that of its other products. (In 1981, Johns-Manville Corporation changed its name to Manville Corporation and relegated the Johns-Manville name to its asbestos division. Raybestos-Manhattan has become Raymark. For convenience, those companies will be referred to as Manville and Raymark, respectively.)

The history of asbestos-related litigation in the United States is a story of the slow but steady accumulation of power by injured claimants to the detriment of the manufacturers.* It features the Little People against the Big Corporations, with the litigants' chosen champions displaying great ingenuity and dedication in the thrust-and-parry of shifting tactics and grand strategies. It is a long-running story, covering most of the twentieth century and having a large cast of characters.

In its summary form, the progression of events must seem obvious, even preordained; however, in reality, it was not so simple and easy for the plaintiffs and their attorneys. Rather, the story unfolded like a good mystery, with clues to unsolved issues appearing only after dogged investigative work, often then providing hints of other pieces of evidence whose existence had not been suspected. Unlike the classic mystery novels, the detectives were not police or even glamorous private eyes, but rather tenacious members of the plaintiffs' bar who spent many thousands of hours and dollars tracking down the evidence. It was only after decades that sufficient pieces of the puzzle were in place to allow a climax to the story, when the attorneys for injured claimants could point the finger at whodunit for juries around the country. The executives of the asbestos industry have never admitted guilt or fault of any kind, insisting to this day that no corpus delicti or smoking gun has ever been found. In the running battles over half a century, a great many people afflicted with the scourge of asbestos-related diseases went uncompensated, beaten by the system, and died losers in court or awaiting trial.

Asbestos began to be recognized as a cause of disease in the early 1900s. In England, autopsies established asbestosis as a cause of death. In the United States, a number of insurance companies noted the abbreviated life-spans of asbestos workers and some refused to issue life insurance policies to them. When some asbestos workers began filing lawsuits against the manufacturers for asbestos-related diseases, the cases were quietly settled for small amounts. When a rash of lawsuits by rockworkers for silicosis—a lung disease similar to asbestosis, found most frequently in workers in granite and sandstone—

---

* A detailed history of asbestos-related litigation in the United States was done by Paul Brodeur, a reporter for *New Yorker* magazine, whose extensive investigation of the asbestos industry laid bare the dismal safety record of the asbestos manufacturers first in "Annals of Law—The Asbestos Industry on Trial," which appeared in the *New Yorker* on June 10, 17, and 24, and July 1, 1985, and was later published as *Outrageous Misconduct: The Asbestos Industry on Trial* (Pantheon Books, New York, 1985).

broke out in the 1930s, the states' workers' compensation laws were expanded to cover lung diseases of the types caused by asbestos and silica. As a result, while Parliament reacted to a study of asbestos workers in England by passing a law in 1931 that required better ventilation and dust control in asbestos factories, companies in the United States continued their sloppy practices, and the victims of the manufacturing process were shunted through state workers' compensation systems. Due to the relatively low compensation allowed under the state systems, the fees that companies had to pay to support them were so reasonable that injured employees simply became another (minor) cost of doing business.

By the 1930s, asbestos manufacturers in the United States were well aware of studies by English doctors and American insurance companies that established asbestos as a health hazard. Industry executives girded for an increase in workers' claims while at the same time attempting to head it off through public denials of that danger. Workers who claimed lung injuries from asbestos were scorned as laggards by the industry's executives. As late as 1961, the medical director of Manville would advise industry executives that "irresponsible reporting [in medical journals should] be eliminated to avoid the high cost of compensation and product liability litigation." By the time litigation really did heat up, in the late 1960s, the industry had "forgotten" about its past knowledge of the hazards of asbestos and neglected to produce important, incriminating evidence in thousands of cases for more than a decade—many, perhaps, lost by injured claimants for just that reason.

This double-think view of the hazards of asbestos led, predictably enough, to a two-faced policy regarding protections against inhalation. Government inspectors were allowed to review health records of employees for statistical purposes, but the companies required that all information be kept confidential. (Until the Occupational Safety and Health Act [OSHA] was passed, government health agencies had no authority to enter factories other than under terms dictated by the companies.) Slowly and quietly, the asbestos manufacturers used that information to raise their standards of cleanliness for asbestos dust, and the dirtier facilities were closed entirely and gutted, sometimes under pressure from governmental safety agencies; but no hint of the dangers was allowed to escape the executive suites. No warnings were placed upon packages. No safety instructions were provided to contractors or their employees who installed asbestos products in shops and buildings. The industry had "externalized" the hazard to people to whom the asbestos executives did not feel any duty to warn or protect. Through the early 1960s, the two-pronged strategy produced excellent results, with employees of the asbestos manufacturers being forced to run the workers' compensation gauntlet of short statutes of limitations and heavy burdens of proof, and insulation workers employed by independent contractors seemingly cut off from suing the manufacturers of products that they handled (and inhaled) regularly.

In 1964, the cat got out of the bag. A report was presented at the Conference on the Biological Effects of Asbestos by a team of researchers, led by Dr. Irving Selikoff of Mount Sinai Hospital of New York, based upon an extensive historical and X-ray investigation of asbestos insulators. Because the researchers were not beholden to the manufacturers in any way, the report frankly laid out the undeniable fact of disease and death visited upon those construction workers as a result of their contacts with asbestos. The report was so thorough and objective that it supplied claimants' attorneys with virtually determinative evidence of the dangers of asbestos to workers outside manufacturing plants. The report was so public and so uncontrovertible that the asbestos manufacturers would have no choice in later lawsuits but to admit knowledge from the date of the report of the dangers outside the factory gates . . . but *only* from the date of the report.

The fact that the asbestos manufacturers were required to defend against lawsuits at all is a classic example of how changes occur in our "common law" system, where an argument made on behalf of a nobody by an unknown can stir the conscience of a court which is then followed by other courts. It sealed the fate of Manville. And it all started with a small-town Texas lawyer named Ward Stephenson.

The year was 1961.

Ward Stephenson was a partner in a small law firm in Orange, Texas, on the border with Louisiana, specializing in representing workers in industrial accident claims. An asbestos insulator by the name of Claude Tomplait had asked Stephenson to make a workers' compensation claim on his behalf for asbestosis, which had just been diagnosed. Stephenson had not handled an industrial disease case before, but in his law practice he had become familiar with the administrative claim format dictated by the workers' compensation laws. In early 1962, Stephenson filed a claim on behalf of Tomplait with the Texas

Industrial Accident Board asking that the employer at the time of the diagnosis, or its insurance carrier, be required to pay Tomplait $14,035, the maximum allowed for total disability at that time by the state's workers' compensation laws.

Stephenson soon learned the difference between an industrial *accident* case and an industrial *disease* case. Injury claims arising from industrial accidents usually produce a rather simple cause-and-effect situation; but the facts of Tomplait's claim immediately became muddled. The insurance company's doctor pronounced Tomplait to be suffering from emphysema, self-inflicted through smoking. Tomplait's own doctor erroneously included silicosis in his diagnosis, which could not have been acquired on the job as an asbestos insulator. As a result, the claim was denied by the board in late 1962, and, although Stephenson filed an appeal for Tomplait, Stephenson was not encouraged by the prospects. Accordingly, when a settlement was offered for $7,500 in 1966 as the case dragged on, he advised Tomplait, whose condition was steadily worsening, to take it.

Ward Stephenson was not pleased to advise his client to settle the case. Although he fulfilled his duty to follow the practical and realistic course in his client's best interests, he felt that more could and should be done for Tomplait and others like him. Stephenson decided to take a novel course by seeking a court ruling that would authorize Tomplait to bypass the workers' compensation system and allow a direct suit against manufacturers of the asbestos with which Tomplait had worked. In other words, Stephenson was going to take on, *en masse*, a group of the largest corporations in the world. In undertaking it, he committed a great deal of his time and effort over the next several years of his life, for which he never could be fully compensated, on the chance that he could set American law heading in a direction that would be more fair to America's workers. Indeed, it would prove to be his life's work from that point on, as the historic victory which he would win on appeal would be handed down just days after his death.

On behalf of Tomplait, Stephenson filed a complaint that advanced the theory that the manufacturers had a duty of care to asbestos installers—that is, it was "foreseeable" that they would become injured by asbestos products—but that they had acted negligently in failing to place warnings on their products. Before trial five of the six defendants settled, for a total of $75,000 (by state law that was diminished by the $7,500 that Tomplait had received in the settlement of his workers' compensation claim), but Fiberboard Paper Products Corporation refused to settle and forced the case to trial in 1969. Stephenson would challenge the conscience of the court with a simple question: why should the asbestos manufacturers escape the deadly consequences of their own products?

The law may proceed by grand theories, but trials are won with hard evidence of specific facts. Tomplait's trial showed the difficulties inherent in penetrating corporations' defenses. Lacking direct knowledge of what the defendant manufacturers knew respecting the risk of asbestos-related diseases to insulation workers, Stephenson could only establish that some studies had been done and some papers had been written during the proceeding forty years, mostly in England. Fiberboard produced polished and experienced executives and company medical personnel who swore that nothing about the dangers of asbestos had been known. Tomplait was tripped up in cross-examination, unable to remember exactly when he used Fiberboard's brand of asbestos. In May 1969, the jury returned a verdict against Tomplait.

As a professional, Ward Stephenson could be satisfied that he had gone the extra mile for his client, and in fact he did quite well for Tomplait financially through the settlements. But as someone who continually represented blue collar workers, Stephenson was not satisfied. He had acquired a number of asbestos installers with similar claims, and he knew that he had to present a credible threat of winning at trial if he was to help them. He decided to add a twist to his theory of manufacturer liability.

Stephenson began to characterize asbestos as inherently dangerous, analogizing it to a defective product. Companies that make dangerous or defective products can be found liable to those who foreseeably might use the product and become injured, if an adequate warning of the dangers had not been given. If Stephenson's arguments were adopted by the courts, the manufacturers could be held liable even if they exercised all possible care in the preparation and sale of the asbestos—*plaintiffs would not have to prove that the manufacturers were negligent in order to prevail.* Also, a manufacturer could not defend against a claim on the grounds that the plaintiff acted with "contributory negligence" for his own safety, such as by smoking or not wearing a mask when applying asbestos. Such a defense can overcome a claim for negligence if proven, but is not permitted as a defense to a "strict liability" claim such as Stephenson would be advancing. Selikoff's 1964 report provided a factual basis for Stephenson's theory, and a respected commentary on the law, the Restatement of the Law of Torts, provided additional credentials for the view.

Although Stephenson filed suits for a number of claimants, his breakthrough case involved an asbestos insulator who first came into the law office in the summer of 1969. Clarence Borel had a similar work history to Claude Tomplait, working for many years at various oil refineries and shipyards in southeast Texas for a number of installation contractors. He was weak and short of breath, and his doctors had advised him that his chronic pneumonia was caused by advanced asbestosis. Stephenson quickly filed suit for Borel against the major asbestos manufacturers, alleging not only negligence but strict liability, but by the time the case went to trial in 1971, Borel had been dead a year of mesothelioma and it was his probate estate that was the plaintiff.

At the trial the defendants' witnesses painted the manufacturers as good citizens who were concerned for the health of those using their products, but who could not have known of the dangers to installers until 1964. On cross-examination, Stephenson scored points by securing admissions that company executives knew that asbestos was generally dangerous, but that the companies had failed to test construction workers or otherwise attempt to investigate the effects of asbestos on workers outside the manufacturers' plants. Stephenson could not prove their actual knowledge of danger to construction workers because it had all been withheld by the defendants. The defendants' attorneys countered Stephenson's theories of liability with the argument that the producers had no duty to investigate the dangers to nonemployees, just as an aspirin manufacturer need not follow the product home to make sure that it is not abused. To the asbestos producers, injury to construction workers was not "foreseeable." The jury retired to consider the evidence.

The jury's verdict proved the wisdom of Stephenson's line of attack. Although the jury found most of the manufacturers guilty of negligence, it also found Borel guilty of contributory negligence for failing to wear an available respirator. Borel's claim for negligence thus was negated, and round one went to the manufacturers. Round two, and the knockout, went to Borel when the jury found the defendants to be "strictly liable" for Borel's death. Stephenson's brainstorm had carried the day, but would it hold up on appeal?

In front of the United States Court of Appeals for the Fifth Circuit, the defendants attempted to impress the judges with the enormity of the possible effects of adopting Stephenson's arguments. How could the court be the first to declare an entire industry liable for occupational diseases that took decades to develop? Why should the court open the floodgates that protected important corporations to the onslaught of claims by large numbers of laborers? Should not the many benefits of asbestos in saving lives from fires outweigh the few who became ill from the product? In short, the asbestos industry argued that Ward Stephenson was a very unreasonable man, espousing a dangerous and unreasonable position.

Viewed from a certain angle, Ward Stephenson indeed was an unreasonable man. A small-town, small-firm lawyer, he chose to fight hugely profitable corporations and the best legal talent money could buy. He asked the courts to bypass a system of compensation for workers that had been developed before his birth, in a manner that was sure to instigate a flood of litigation. He ignored one of the basic lessons of nitty-gritty law practice, to find out what the prevailing case decisions and customs are and to work within them. Whom did Stephenson represent, but a bunch of broken-down laborers, whose lives were worth very little in the scheme of things? Who in their right mind would fight major legal battles for them, tilting at the windmills of the legal system? It is not known whether Stephenson had read any works by George Bernard Shaw, but he certainly would have related to one of Shaw's observations: "A reasonable man adjusts himself to his environment. An unreasonable man tries to adjust his environment to himself. Therefore, all progress depends upon the unreasonable man."

Against all odds, unreasonable Ward Stephenson persuaded the appellate court that protecting asbestos workers, and by implication other people who come into contact with dangerous products, was the decent thing to do. Injuries to workers not directly in the employ of manufacturers of asbestos were deemed to be "foreseeable." Asbestos was "unreasonably dangerous" because the manufacturers had not made clear warnings of the dangers that they knew or should have known of. Because warnings had not been given, the producers would be held "strictly liable" for any injuries that the product caused. Manufacturers would be held to the standard of knowledge of the experts in the field—they would not be permitted to fail to inform themselves of the latest research. Accordingly, they had the duty to thoroughly test the effects of their products upon likely users. The judgment of the jury in favor of Clarence Borel and against the major asbestos manufacturers was affirmed.

Ward Stephenson would have felt deep satisfaction at the Fifth Circuit's *Borel* opinion, but he never saw it. He died of natural causes four days before the ruling was handed down, although apparently a friendly soul on the appellate court's staff, knowing of his condition, telephoned him with the news shortly before his death. No doubt he would have been a leader in the battles that would rage across the country between asbestos workers and asbestos manufacturers.

The first shot had been fired in the revolution, but, as with most things involving the legal system, the response was in slow motion. News of the dangers to asbestos workers spread across the country by word of mouth and through union literature (many installers belonged to the International Association of Heat and Frost Insulators and Asbestos Workers), and ill workers began drifting into lawyers' offices. Manville selected a case in another federal circuit to appeal, hoping to receive a favorable ruling that would start leading courts away from following *Borel*. (Since each federal circuit is coequal with the others, the appellate court in each circuit is not required to follow a decision of another circuit, although opinions of other circuits are carefully reviewed. At times, circuits may have widely varying rulings on an issue, and the Supreme Court then may end the confusion by providing its last word on the subject, which all federal courts are requrired to follow.) At the district (trial) court level, Judge Miles Lord, who would gain more fame later as a a judge hard on polluters and devastating to A. H. Robins, had followed the restatement viewpoint and had charged the jury to consider strict liability. In the fall of 1975, the Eighth Circuit Court of Appeals stunned Manville by decreeing that the *Borel* ruling on strict liability would be followed in that circuit also. As with many, many cases that would be brought against the asbestos manufacturers, the plaintiff had died before his victory on appeal.

In spite of the lost appeals, at the trial court level through 1977 the manufacturers were giving as good as they got. For every jury that felt that the manufacturers had failed in their duties to asbestos workers, there was a jury that accepted the manufacturers' defenses that they had not known of the dangers of asbestos. The manufacturers forced each plaintiff to laboriously prove facts about asbestos and the manufacturers' operations that had already been proven in prior trials, and not every plaintiff's lawyer was as skilled as Ward Stephenson had been. In fact, by mid-1978, the scorecard on major cases going to trial stood at 8 to 8.

As the number of asbestos-related claimants increased, from tens to hundreds to thousands, the leading plaintiffs' attorneys began to pool their knowledge and energies. In 1976 a number of leading asbestos claimants attorneys formed the Asbestos Litigation Group, an informal cooperative, and many others joined. Information gained and arguments honed, bit by laborious bit, were shared; and the identities of friendly witnesses spread across the country by word of mouth. It was becoming cost-effective for attorneys with hundreds of clients claiming asbestos-related injuries to undertake costly and time-consuming searches for the skeletons in the producers' closets—and virtual closets they were, often consisting of musty storehouses containing decomposing boxes of crumbling papers decades old. Claimants' attorneys began to find out a lot of things that the asbestos manufacturers did not want juries to know!

By the late 1970s, plaintiffs' attorneys had accumulated a good deal of hard evidence concerning the cynicism in the corporate boardrooms of asbestos producers towards asbestos injuries. Animal studies from the 1930s and 1940s commissioned by asbestos manufacturers and showing asbestos to be a very harmful substance were unearthed. (In one study, *all* the test animals that breathed in asbestos fibers developed asbestos-related diseases.) Internal studies were found that disclosed asbestos's dangers in the 1940s and 1950s. Evidence of management tactics to hide the dangers from employees—including willfully failing to advise them if their X-rays disclosed early signs of asbestos-related disease—was pieced together. As juries became more fully advised of the extent of the complicity of corporate executives in the injury and death of innocent people, the defenses of the asbestos manufacturers developed more holes than could be plugged.

The target of choice for the plaintiffs' attorneys was Manville. It was the largest manufacturer by far, which meant that more people came into contact with its products—and *remembered* coming into contact with its products—than those of other companies. It also was the industry leader in almost every way, including the suppression of harmful evidence about asbestos. By the late Seventies the pack began to bite at the heels of the strongest fighter in the herd.

By 1980, Manville's primary insurance coverage of $16 million became exhausted. Seeing almost certain losses to the limits of their coverage, its secondary, "excess coverage" insurers refused to concede that their policies had become triggered; and Manville was left to defend itself and pay all judgments against it while it sued them. (Suits by asbestos producers against insurance companies denying coverage would slog through the courts around the country for the entire decade of the Eighties.) It faced thousands of asbestos-related injury claims, spread across almost every judicial district in the country and generating ever-increasing judgment awards and, therefore, settlement demands. The giant was at bay.

In the midst of its deteriorating litigation posture, Manville started playing hard(er) ball. The move reflected the thinking of chairman John McKinney, who could not be persuaded that any health claims were legitimate or that any plaintiffs' attorneys had anything but the basest motives. Manville virtually ceased settlement discussions, began to stonewall legitimate requests for documents in pretrial processes, and at trial presented only the most obstreperous posture. Its lawyers were instructed to admit nothing and to challenge the authenticity of documents already accepted into evidence in many prior trials. Although the tactic served to increase the company's legal fees, no doubt to the delight of its hundreds of retained counsel across the country, the result desired by Manville was achieved: the cases became bogged down and court calendars became backlogged. For example, by 1980, the federal court district for eastern Texas alone had three thousand pending asbestos-related cases. In August 1980, McKinney scoffed at the thousands of lawsuits against his company, stating to a Senate subcommittee that there was no surer proof of the frivolousness of the complaints than the fact that the company had not suffered one punitive damage award. He soon was to eat his words.

It did not take long before the strategy began to backfire, as Manville began taking big hits in the cases that went to trial. Fewer settlements meant more exposure to juries' sensibilities. Not only were juries becoming more generous to injured workers, they were becoming enraged at what they heard in court, and they began awarding punitive damages. (Most importantly, the presiding judges in the trials, having heard the same evidence, began *allowing them* to consider awarding "punitives.")

Each judgment was another hole in the fortifications carefully erected over the years by Manville, and it was not too long before the holes sent them crashing. In Los Angeles in 1980, a jury returned a $1.2 million verdict against Manville and Raymark in a test case for more than a thousand suits in that district. In quick succession, a Philadelphia jury hit Manville and other defendants with $450,000 in punitives, and a Cleveland jury punished Manville with $500,000 in punitives, both in addition to compensatory damages. A July 1981 judgment of $1.8 million against Manville by a Jacksonville, Florida, jury (including $750,000 in punitive damages) was affirmed by an appeals court that cited Manville's "wanton disregard" for the users of its products and its "reckless disregard for human life." If it was the fall of 1981, it was $300,000 in punitive damages from a New Jersey jury. If it was the first half of 1982, it was $1 million in compensatory damages (for one claimant) and $1 million in punitive damages in Texas; $280,000 compensatory and $220,000 punitives in Tennessee; $100,000 compensatory and $1 million punitives in Pennsylvania; $391,000 compensatory and $125,000 punitives in Mississippi; and $800,000 compensatory and $1.5 million punitives, also in Tennessee. The average punitive damage award against Manville for 1981 and 1982 was $616,000. By 1982, the asbestos companies had paid out about $600 million to settle more than twenty-three thousand claims— their insurance companies funding about two-thirds of those—and industry and insurance officials were predicting *billions* more in claims, perhaps *tens of billions*.

Manville's situation was steadily eroding. Manville had tried to sue the federal government in federal court for running an unsafe shipyard, but struck out at all court levels. Suits in the United States Court of Claims against the federal government for demanding asbestos in wartime ships languished in the backlog and later would prove futile. The courtroom scenes in the injury cases were getting ugly; managing the thousands of lawsuits was taking more and more of management time and energy; and the court costs, attorneys' fees, and judgments were getting expensive, even for a megacorporation.

It was time to make an end run around the court/tort system. It was time for the higher-ups at Manville to telephone some friends in Congress asking them to dust off some legislation that had been in the hopper for more than a year. One friend was United States

Representative Millicent Fenwick, a Republican from a district that included Manville, New Jersey, the home of one of Manville's larger plants. Another friend—a strange bedfellow indeed—was United States Senator Gary Hart, a Democrat, of Colorado, who had introduced asbestos litigation in 1980. Hart's interest may be put more into perspective after considering two facts: Manville had recently moved its corporate headquarters to Colorado; and Hart was in need of beefing up his business relations within his state for reelection purposes.

Although the two bills were not identical, they had common attributes. Both were termed the "Asbestos Health Hazards Compensation Act," both were approved of by the asbestos industry and were most certainly drafted with industry help, and both served the asbestos manufacturers' goal of removing the claims from the court/tort system. Fenwick's bill would compensate victims from a federally administered fund, with all claims accruing before January 1, 1980, *to be paid out of the federal treasury*! Later claims would be paid out of a fund formed with contributions by the asbestos and tobacco industries and the federal government. In effect, the federal government would swallow whole the asbestos manufacturers' arguments that Uncle Sam's World War II effort was the predominant cause of asbestos disease in the United States. A worker who could prove total disability would receive $500 to $1,000 per month, depending on dependents, under Fenwick's bill. Hart's asbestos compensation system would be run by the states along the lines of their general workers' compensation systems, possibly with federal guidelines on a schedule of minimum payments for different degrees of injury. Both bills would prohibit injured individuals from suing in court and, therefore, would cut off access to juries and punitive damages by those dying of asbestos-related diseases.

The insurance and asbestos industries tried a number of different strategies to "educate" the public and Congress on the "unfair" court/tort system. As late as 1982, the party line of the industry in dealing with Congress was that it could not have known of insulators' susceptibility to asbestos-induced disease until the 1964 Selikoff report. (By that time that assertion had been debunked totally in thousands of court cases, but there were no plaintiffs' attorneys cross-examining Manville witnesses in the halls of Congress.) Commercial Union, an insurance company that possibly had more than a billion dollars of liability as one of the prime insurers to the asbestos industry, issued and widely circulated a polemic in May 1981, entitled "Asbestos: A Social Problem." Solemnly it decried the court/tort system as too slow for injured plaintiffs and too costly due to plaintiffs' lawyers' fees. (When have you ever heard an insurance company complain of that!) Noting the astronomical numbers of asbestos claims expected, the paper proceeded to present a parade of horrors ending with the collapse of the entire insurance industry and the resulting worthlessness of every person's homeowner, health, and auto insurance policies. Since asbestos claims were a "social problem" that affected everyone in the country, why then the only logical solution was for the federal government to take care of it!

Even Congress, those folks who brought us numerous bailouts and other forms of corporate welfare, was not going to buy this one—as usual, for both lofty and base reasons. There was enough informed opposition to warn Congress that it might not be wearing the White Hat in passing any such legislation. Also, in a prototype situation involving coal miners with black lung disease, the cost to taxpayers of a federal benefits program had become an embarrassment; and the Reagan administration most assuredly was not in the mood for taking on an additional obligation to workers. The dark side of Congress's studious attempt to ignore the pleas of the industry is the consistent failure of the federal government to consider any responsibility—or liability—for mass toxic torts that it has committed in the name of national defense. Hiding behind the shield of "sovereign immunity," which is an ancient doctrine that the king cannot be sued (that is, "the king can do no wrong") unless specifically agreed, and legislation that expressly makes the government immune for acts of the military, the federal government has refused to take part in any litigation to compensate soldiers and civilians for diseases caused by atomic testing in Nevada and "Agent Orange" in Vietnam. For all those reasons, no branch of the government of the United States seriously considered tapping into the treasury to help the huge numbers of people who have had the misfortune of intentionally or unintentionally coming into regular contact with asbestos. Accordingly, when the bills were reintroduced in 1981 by Hart and Fenwick, they never emerged from committee.

By the early 1980s, the rain of lawsuits was beginning to erode Manville's corporate foundation. Because the flagship name "Johns-Manville" had become identified in the public's mind as a "bad" company, the conglomerate was forced to change its name to "Manville Corporation" and work hard to promote itself as a "good" company specializing in forest and building products. Nevertheless, the potential liability of the conglomerate for asbestos health claims was so large that Manville's accountants "qualified" its balance sheet for 1981, hurting the company's stock price. The management of Manville was coming under pressure to estimate the company's future liabilities, a move that surely would hurt it further.

The combination of circumstances propelled Manville on a tricky path fraught with danger. It would have to make a plausible determination of its product liability exposure that would allow it to fulfill its securities-law responsibilities and return to a balance sheet that was in a standard form for a "public" corporation. However, even the Manville executives and board of directors were being forced to recognize that the legal picture was too bleak to simply continue following the current path; and that when that liability was quantified, the company might be deemed insolvent. If the risk analysis produced too large a number, the company might appear so hopelessly insolvent that it simply would be liquidated for the benefit of its creditors. No, the number must be large enough to support a bankruptcy reorganization proceeding, but not so large that it would provoke liquidation.

It is no exaggeration to say that when Manville started down the path of maximizing sales by failing to warn its employees and other asbestos workers of dangers—when its top executives decided to be unconcerned about people's lives rather than to show them how to use its product safely—it chose to eventually reach the sorry end to the trail at which the officers and directors of Manville found themselves in 1981. The company's policies were figuratively and literally bankrupt. Although the management team of John McKinney, who became chief executive officer of Manville in 1977, must bear responsibility for its arrogant and cold decision to give no quarter in litigation for as long as possible, to a large extent those responsible for Manville's predicament had fed full from the corporate trough and enjoyed status as captains of industry . . . and were long gone from their earthly battles. The Manville case illustrates a recurring theme of industrial America: today's generation is paying for the waste and pollution of earlier generations. Not only is that true of those who have been maimed and struck down by asbestos, but also the executive managers of those companies who must devote a good portion of their talents to managing environmental burdens placed on their companies by their predecessors.

In July 1981, Epidemiology Resources, which had been retained by Manville to quantify its product liability exposure, returned its report. Because of its wide margin of error, the report was considered incomplete, and the company was asked to refine its methods. Additional experts were consulted. After a year of combined efforts (and, some have charged, a massaging of the statistics by Manville staff), a scenario was produced that envisioned 139,000 asbestos-related diseases in the United States between 1980 and 2009 that would generate about 48,000 new lawsuits against Manville. Applying an average cost of $40,000 to dispose of a claim, Manville's future liability was pegged at about $1.9 billion. There is great debate about the accuracy of those figures, because each step in the process required assumptions that cannot be proven conclusively, and neither Manville nor its creditors can be said to be without motives. (There is some support for figures double those used by Epidemiology Resources.) However, two things are clear: when shown the results of the study on August 4, 1982, the board of directors of Manville believed the figures contained in it to be a credible basis on which to proceed; and, as such, Manville could not tough out the product liability claims. It would have to file a Chapter 11 proceeding to deal with its tormentors. Amazingly enough, the megacorporation had been run to the ground by legions of the dead and dying.

Chapter 10

Stalemate

By mid-1982, Manville was defending against more than sixteen thousand product liability claims for asbestos-related diseases to workers; it had to process about five hundred new lawsuits every month; and it was being hit frequently by large judgments and punitive damages—but when Manville filed for protection under Chapter 11 of the federal bankruptcy laws on August 26, 1982, *then* all hell broke loose!

Because the preparations for the bankruptcy were accomplished in total secrecy, Manville was able to fire the first shots in the public relations war. Manville was portrayed as the victim of unforeseen circumstances and the calumny of others. John McKinney stated that Manville's businesses were "in good shape" and that the company would not have had to file for protection from its creditors had not both the federal government and the company's insurance carriers shirked their clear duties to share the liabilities from asbestos-related diseases caused by Manville's products. McKinney went so far as to say that if either the government or the insurance carriers would own up to their responsibilities, "It is certainly possible that we can emerge from Chapter 11 with everyone getting what is coming to them." To insure that the media record properly enshrined its point of view, concurrently with the filing of the bankruptcy case Manville placed a full-page ad in major newspapers, pointing fingers everywhere else but into its boardroom. Attempts by the health claimants' attorneys to respond through the media were fragmented and could not match Manville's preplanned publicity blitz.

Apparently Manville was pleased with its ability to speak directly to the American public, because within six months of the bankruptcy filing, the corporation ran a series of upbeat ads to the effect that it had embarked upon a course that would make it a leaner, meaner competitor and a stronger company. One effect was to infuriate and frustrate injury claimants and their lawyers, who lacked a public relations department and an ad agency.

The media were appropriately flabbergasted at the filing. The *Wall Street Journal* called it "highly unusual" and "unexpected" and termed Manville "financially strong." To *Business Week*, it was "unorthodox" and a "surprise." *Newsweek* puzzled that "it was one of the biggest industrial bankruptcies in American corporate history, but the company insisted that its business was in good shape," and predicted that the case would break new legal ground each step of the way. Numerous articles and commentators marveled that a company with $2 billion in assets and a net worth on the balance sheet of $1.1 billion, that had earned $60 million on $2.2 billion in sales in 1981, could find itself in bankruptcy. Of course, the full story had not yet found its way into the mass media. Still, the antiestablishment journal, *The Nation*, smelled a rat, calling Manville's attempt to deal with its asbestos liability through the bankruptcy filing "one of the neatest pieces of corporate sleight of hand ever perpetuated on the American public."

Insofar as the filing of bankruptcy was intended to create sympathy in Congress for financial aid, Manville had badly miscalculated. Rather than bending to help the fallen giant, Congress chose to remain on its lofty pedestal. Because of the Supreme Court's *Marathon* decision, Congress already had more bankruptcy court headaches than it could handle, and its leaders were none too pleased that Manville had handed them another hot potato. Was Congress supposed to devote huge amounts of time to deciphering the constitutional ramifications of the Supreme Court's Delphic ruling, cobble together another compromise among the many factions, and come up with a concept of bankruptcy court jurisdiction that would pass constitutional muster, only to have the media trumpet that it had reconstituted the bankruptcy court to serve the likes of Manville? Senator Robert Dole of Kansas was most certainly speaking the thoughts of many of his colleagues when he stated, "America's bankruptcy system can ill afford the additional strains placed upon it by those who would use its protection for shelter against personal or corporate attacks where other remedies ... would seem more appropriate," and promised to have the Senate Judiciary Committee investigate the filing. Rather than moving ahead with the bailout bills that had already been put into the hopper by Millicent Fenwick and Gary Hart, Congress would spend some time investigating whether Manville's filing was an abuse of the system but would end up doing nothing whatsoever about the filing of bankruptcy by Manville or any other megacorporation.

Manville's inability to secure a bailout provided further proof of the method behind Lee Iacocca's madness in threatening to close down Chrysler rather than file a Chapter 11 proceeding. Once Manville filed bankruptcy, Congress could wash its collective hands of the problem. Why should Congress go before the bar of public opinion in a high profile manner and dispense public funds, when all of the thorny issues could be thrashed out by lawyers filing legal briefs in some courtroom? In any event, Congress had provided the means to help Manville and others like it, and that aid was called the Bankruptcy Code.

The filing of bankruptcy by Manville Corporation and twenty of its subsidiaries caught commercial creditors, many of whom had a long relationship with the company, flat-footed. Although the purpose of the Chapter 11 expressly was to bring the industrial-disease cases under control, the commercial claims were just as surely caught up in the bankruptcy net. Especially bitter about being dragged through the bankruptcy were the trade creditors of Olinkraft, the forest products division, who had relationships dating from the time that Olinkraft was strong and independent before Manville bought it in 1979.

Also caught by surprise were the other asbestos manufacturers. Because Manville was the largest asbestos producer by far and the acknowledged industry leader, the bankruptcy filing was a psychological blow that called into question the ability of any of them to survive outside of bankruptcy court. Also, it removed from thousands of cases the party that had taken on the primary duties of defense and had provided the "deepest pocket" for payment of judgments and settlements.

Sadly, the bankruptcy filing amounted to a triple-whammy for Manville's employees. Not only did it signal layoffs, and not only was it a threat to the viability of pending claims for asbestos-related diseases, but the company's pension fund was the largest holder of the company's plummeting stock.

The primary claimants' lawyers seemed to have been genuinely surprised at the bankruptcy filing and were most certainly dismayed that the quarry had found refuge. Having spent years developing their evidence and skills in order to put Manville on the run, they now found that the company would turn and fight again in an arena that they knew nothing about, armed with new weapons. The stay against actions threatened not only the financial welfare of sick and dying workers, but also the livelihood of hundreds of attorneys across the country who had built law practices on litigating against Manville. Now that was serious!

Although Manville had stolen the march on the claimants, it turned out that their attorneys already had the mechanism in place to organize for the battles to come. By the time of the bankruptcy filing, the Asbestos Litigation Group, formed by a handful of claimants' attorneys not too many years before, had grown to about 150 lawyers, including all of the most prominent asbestos litigators. The group received approval from the bankruptcy judge to form an official Committee of Asbestos-Related Litigants and/or Creditors, later redenominated as the Asbestos Health Claimants Committee, and packed that committee with the movers and shakers from the group roster. Those committee members, veterans of many cases against Manville, saw the bankruptcy as another test of their manhood in the seemingly never-ending struggle against the evil asbestos empire. The committee chose Stanley Levy, of the New York City law firm of Kreindler and Kreindler, as its chairman. Levy specialized in trying asbestos injury cases with large numbers of plaintiffs.

Technically, a corporation should file a bankruptcy case in the federal district in which it has its primary offices, but as a practical matter, a megacorporation has a number of locations which might qualify, and so they can engage in what lawyers call "forum shopping." Although Manville had moved its headquarters from New York to Colorado ten years earlier, it chose the federal court sitting in Manhattan as the venue for its Chapter 11. Aside from the convenience for its Wall Street lawyers—no small matter—there was further method to Manville's choice. The federal court sitting in Manhattan is recognized as the preeminent commercial bench in the country, and its bankruptcy division has substantial experience in handling large business bankruptcies. The difference between the sophistication of that court and the federal court sitting in Denver is immense.

In fact, Manville did reap great benefits from its forum shopping in that its case was assigned to the honorable Burton R. Lifland, a bankruptcy judge of only a few years experience on the bench who was nevertheless smart, tough, able . . . and in the process of building a reputation as strongly favoring Chapter 11 megacorporations over their creditors. Judge Lifland would prove to be perfectly capable of dominating the high-priced lawyers for the creditors and shareholders and dragging them, kicking and screaming, through a reorganization process that, from the very beginning, he willed *would* be successful.

The Asbestos Health Claimants Committee decided to ask the judge to dismiss Manville's bankruptcy on the grounds that the company was solvent and that in filing its bankruptcy petition it had acted in "bad faith." In making that argument, the committee would be taking the position that the bankruptcy court should discount Manville's study of the statistical likelihood of future disease claims, and, therefore, the company had a healthy balance sheet with a positive net worth. That argument would be the first bite at the apple respecting the treatment of injury claims. If the committee did not succeed and Manville remained in bankruptcy, later the committee could renew the issue by arguing that future claims should not be covered in any reorganization plan, thus negating any value of the bankruptcy proceeding for Manville.

The Asbestos Health Claimants Committee filed its motion to dismiss the bankruptcy on November 8, 1982. Similar motions also were filed by commercial creditors and a group of asbestos producers and insurers to the industry that were codefendants with Manville in the thousands of lawsuits across the country. The philosophical issue was whether the bankruptcy court should take cognizance of those who would manifest an asbestos-related disease after the bankruptcy case and any reorganization plan had been completed. The technical issue was whether those people had "claims" to be recognized in the bankruptcy case. There was plenty of room to argue either way, as the term "claim" was not defined in the Bankruptcy Code in sufficient detail to cover the delayed-action claimant.

In the brief in support of the motion, the committee made a highly legalistic argument, asking the judge to ignore the virtual certainty of thousands of future claimants by finding that they did not yet possess "claims." The other three movants made similar technical arguments as to when a "claim" springs into existence under the Bankruptcy Code, much as medieval clerics debated the number of angels that could fit on the head of a pin.

In focusing on the legalities, the movants hoped to counter an instinctive point of view to the effect that it was more fair to the mass tort claimants to include future claims into a bankruptcy so that everyone could get something. Many familiar with the asbestos cases considered it less fair that early claimants receive adequate compensation and later plaintiffs risk that the company will have been forced out of business by the earlier claims. While certainly a debatable issue, Judge Lifland would show that he strongly adhered to this view; and the plaintiffs' lawyers continually would face the charge that, by attempting to block the bankruptcy of Manville, they cared only about earning their fees as quickly as possible in the pending cases.

If the movants won the battle of the "claim" definition, they were still not all the way home. While the result would be to knock future claims off the balance sheet and return Manville to a positive net worth, that alone would not result in Manville being barred from Chapter 11. The movants would have to then take the next step, to persuade the judge that because Manville had manageable liabilities, it had engaged in "bad faith" in filing the bankruptcy case. It would be "bad faith" that would result in the expulsion of this Adam from the garden since solvency is not a sin in bankruptcy court.

It was necessary for the movants to make the argument of "bad faith" because, strangely enough, there is no requirement that an individual or corporation be "insolvent" in any of the several definitions of the word in order to file either a Chapter 7 liquidation or Chapter 11 reorganization case. In broadening the scope of the bankruptcy law in 1978, Congress had chosen to eliminate that barrier to a company or individual voluntarily seeking the protections of the bankruptcy court. If accepted by the court, the movants' "bad faith" argument would return an insolvency requirement to the bankruptcy law indirectly.

A weakness in the argument was that "bad faith" already was a bankruptcy term of art for situations that did not exist in the Manville case. As ordinarily used in the bankruptcy context, bad faith exists when the debtor seeks the automatic stay against creditor actions *solely* as a delaying tactic, and there is virtually no chance that the debtor can actually reorganize through the proceeding; or when the debtor has sought refuge in bankruptcy to evade the consequences of a dispute with a *single* opponent. The classic example is the real estate partnership that has been defending a mortgage foreclosure proceeding for a year. Unable to find refinancing, it files for reorganization the day the foreclosure judgment is entered against it. In that and similar situations, the bankruptcy court will exercise its *inherent* right to refuse to be part of a sham. (Note that it is a doctrine of self-protection developed by the courts themselves. There is no statutory requirement of "good faith" in the Bankruptcy Code.) Thus those that sought to remove Manville from bankruptcy were asking the court to give the term new meaning—an uphill battle.

In order to induce Judge Lifland to toss Manville out of the garden, the Asbestos Health Claimants Committee charged the corporation with a litany of sins, which, when added together, amounted to the venal sin of attempting to manage its liabilities to health claimants through an overall settlement. The essence of the committee's position was stated by Stanley Levy in an affidavit in support of the motion to dismiss (here cleansed of its invective):

> Instead of doing its best to meet its obligations as an ongoing business, Manville dedicated itself . . . to going into bankruptcy in order to . . . defeat the rights of a single class of creditors. . . . It did not "reluctantly" accept bankruptcy of "necessity," as an "economic imperative." It rushed forward to embrace it. . . . [Manville's plan is] so illusory and prejudicial that it confirms Manville's true plan was not to save a failing company . . . but to proceed through bankruptcy to impair and defeat the rights of the asbestos victims. . . .

Had the experts and academics who drafted the Bankruptcy Code been present at a reading of the Levy affidavit, most likely they would have responded in unison with a rousing "So what?" The statement merely paraphrased the purposes of the law. To "embrace" bankruptcy is not a perversion, it is an acceptable act under the Bankruptcy Code. Impairing the rights of totally innocent creditors is the integral mechanism of bankruptcy reorganization. As to the view that the health claimants somehow were unique creditors, since 1934 it had been clear that tort (personal injury) claims could be compromised in a reorganization. *Of course* Manville was attempting to rid itself of a large number of debts. What else was bankruptcy for? Manville may have been in bad faith in the colloquial sense, but not as far as the bankruptcy law was concerned.

Nevertheless the Asbestos Health Claimants Committee was driven by missionary zeal to prove that Manville was the devil incarnate. Its attack went well beyond the bankruptcy "bad faith" argument. It included indictments of the safety and health policies of Manville for the past fifty years, its recent corporate restructuring, and its study conducted by Epidemiology Resources. The committee would spend huge amounts of time, energy, attention, legal fees, and out-of-pocket expenses over the course of a year, attempting to develop evidence that the study, and thus the bankruptcy, were frauds. That included hiring its own epidemiologists, conducting fifty-five days of depositions, and sifting through mountains of documents.

In attempting the theological proof of Manville's wickedness, the health claimants (really, their attorneys) had fallen into a common bankruptcy trap. They had convinced themselves that if they showed the judge that Manville had been a "bad" corporation, he would cast it from the court in an act of moral righteousness. Accordingly they had directed their efforts toward that end rather than more potentially fruitful avenues. However, every bankruptcy judge had seen it all before: creditors pitiably complaining to the court about being unfairly unpaid; a debtor that did not live up to standards; and supplicants asking him to ignore the bankruptcy laws because they *really deserve* to be paid. Those heartfelt pleas would have no more effect this time. Bankruptcy judges see so many "bad" debtors each year that they are not inclined to find any one more bad than the others. Further, when it comes to megacorporations, the job is the same with the "good," the "bad," and the "ugly"—get it reorganized at any cost.

Although the attack upon Manville's bankruptcy was quixotic, the conclusion of the Epidemiology Resources report on future liabilities to health claimants—the *raison d'être* of the filing—actually was vulnerable to attack because the statistical analysis in the report could not stand up to a rigorous review. Basic data concerning the relevant lung diseases was "soft." A number of underlying factual assumptions used in calculations were arbitrary or unproven—for example, the assumption that there would be no further incidence of asbestos-related diseases after 1984. The methodology contained junctures where a leap of logic or faith was required. (At one point the report referred to its methodology as "quick and dirty.") Because of those deficiencies, the calculations could not be reliable. Making the conclusions further suspect, the questionable decisions made during the course of the study had the effect of reducing Manville's future liabilities, thereby diminishing the amount of money Manville would have to commit to fund any reorganization plan that included them.

Having threaded through a statistical minefield of elusive facts, unproven assumptions, and hidden bias, all of which were multiplied through levels of calculations, the Epidemiology Resources report ended with a "bottom line" that really was more like a smudge. Although Manville religiously cited the report as stating that it would face approximately 48,000 suits over thirty years, what the conclusion of the report really said was: "[A] reasonably central projection of the number of lawsuits seen from 1982 on is likely to be about 45,000, with a reasonably firm lower bound of 30,000 *and a very indefinite upper bound on the order of 120,000.*" [Emphasis added.] A reading of the report brings to mind a basic precept of computer science on the accuracy of number-crunching: garbage in, garbage out.

The most important test of the Epidemiology Resources report would be what Judge Lifland would think of it. Would he be skeptical about it because of Manville's sponsorship? Would he apply a rigorous analysis to it? Would he aggressively seek the truth about the number of future claimants? It turned out that the questions hung in the air for a year, while the health claimants' committee reviewed mountains of documents and took scores of depositions in an effort to prove that Manville was "bad."

When Judge Lifland did make rulings during that first year of the Chapter 11 case, it had been to help Manville.

Judge Lifland repeatedly extended the period during which Manville had the exclusive right to file a Plan of Reorganization, thereby depriving the creditors of the leverage of threatening to file their own plan. (Although the Bankruptcy Code provides for only one 120-day "exclusive period," during the entire four and one-half years of the case, it would remain firmly in place.) Like a Greek god on Olympus affecting the combat of mere mortals on the plain, the judge had chosen to aid Manville by denying the creditors the power to force the case to proceed to the reorganization stage. As the bankruptcy case dragged on, with John McKinney hanging as tough as he had during the personal injury cases, it became apparent that Manville's hardball stance was bolstered by the knowledge that the creditors could not force the action.

Soon after the filing of the Chapter 11 case, Judge Lifland extended the benefits of the bankruptcy to those associated with Manville. Creditors were enjoined from filing suits against past or present officers or directors of Manville personally for fraud. Creditors were similarly enjoined from suing Manville's insurers directly. The creditors thus would be required to focus their attentions entirely on the Chapter 11 case and thus would remain firmly under Judge Lifland's control.

Judge Lifland's exercise of his prerogatives on Manville's behalf is an object lesson on the power of bankruptcy judges. Although a number of his orders were highly unusual and flirted with the outer penumbra of legitimate bankruptcy court power, they were upheld on appeal almost casually. Not only were the appellate judges unwilling to interject themselves into a complex reorganization case, but they too understood the true nature of a megacorporate Chapter 11: give the company whatever it wants.

Well into 1983, the parties continued to shout at each other from their mountaintops. Manville steadfastly refused to offer any substantial amounts to the health claimants and insisted that any claims procedure be along the lines of workers' compensation. The health claimants' attorneys would not hear of any claims procedure that did not provide for the right to jury trial and punitive damages and refused to allow the rights of future claimants to be taken away by the bankruptcy case.

Some of the creditors' actions got pretty far out. Two asbestos manufacturers, tired of paying judgments in which Manville should have shared liability, asked the United States Supreme Court to declare that because Congress had not passed legislation in response to the *Marathon* decision, the bankruptcy courts were entirely nonexistent, and Manville had no place to hide. The court did not give them a hearing. The jailhouse lawyers in Attica Prison filed a class action lawsuit against the asbestos producers for unspecified diseases due to asbestos in the prison walls.

The Attica action was quite a joke . . . or was it? Shortly after, the Los Angeles School District filed a claim against Manville (and lawsuits against those asbestos producers that were not in bankruptcy) for unspecified damages resulting from asbestos in school walls and heating/ventailating systems. So many similar "property damage" claims were filed that the judge allowed the formation of an unofficial Committee of Property Damage Claimants, which named subcommittees for schools and hospitals; state governments; and "big city" claimants. (An unofficial committee has standing to be heard by the bankruptcy judge, but the Chapter 11 debtor does not have to pay its legal fees.)

The property damage claims represented a huge threat to Manville *and* the commercial, trade and health creditors who had been taking part in the bankruptcy. If Manville were deemed to be responsible for the cost of ripping out asbestos and reconstructing buildings afterwards, or of tearing down buildings and replacing them, the sum total of the company's obligations to property damage claimants could equal or exceed its liabilities to existing and future health claimants and arguably make the reorganization of Manville impossible. However, the state of the medical knowledge about the health hazards of simply being inside buildings lined with asbestos was—and still is—in its infancy. Therefore, the property damage claimants were not particularly shrill or aggressive in the bankruptcy case, allowing all the major players and the judge to look the other way throughout the entire bankruptcy even as they tiptoed around that time bomb.

The battles spilled over into congressional hearings. Manville was called upon to defend its bankruptcy filing. The organization of asbestos plaintiffs' lawyers contested the legitimacy of Manville's tactics and its projections of future claims and asked Congress to force Manville to pay all claims as made. The major asbestos manufacturers, speaking through the innocuous-sounding Committee for Equitable Compensation, petitioned Congress to force claimants to use a system modeled after workers' compensation and to create a superfund-type pool to pay claims. Congress declined to choose sides.

Negotiations were protracted throughout 1983 and resolved nothing. The Manville executives had not expected the bankruptcy process to be so cumbersome, at the initiation predicting that the case would be over within a year. The plaintiffs' attorneys had proven more tenacious than the corporate barons had ever imagined, and a whole host of nettlesome legal issues remained unresolved. On the other hand, the Asbestos Health Victims Committee had been unable to get Manville to significantly compromise, and the clock was ticking loudly for the dying claimants and their families. Bank and trade creditors, caught in a businessman's nightmare, oscillated in support of the factions and often found themselves serving as involuntary mediators. Through it all the judge kept on extending Manville's exclusive period for filing a plan—October 1983 saw the ninth such extension—leaving the creditors without a dramatic way of shifting the balance of power.

By late October 1983, the situation had become excruciating for the creditors' and claimants' attorneys. Health claimants' lawyers complained that Manville only appeared to negotiate near the end of each "exclusive period;" when Judge Lifland would grant another extension, Manville would then lapse into an uncommunicative state. John Jerome, a lead counsel for the commercial and trade creditors, fumed at the "antediluvian, atavistic, and moronic" attitude of Manville's management. (Those Wall Street types sure can call high-class names!) Codefendants complained of being ignored in negotiations while having to in effect carry Manville's burdens in injury suits. Even the Securities and Exchange Commission chimed in, saying that the continuing extensions of the "exclusive period" violated the spirit and intent of the Bankruptcy Code.

The patience of District Judge David N. Edelstein, nominally one of Judge Lifland's overseers under the jurisdictional morass that had arisen due to the Supreme Court's decision in the *Marathon* case, began to wear thin. The district court's supervision of Lifland's steady hand had been more honored in the breach than in the observance, but Judge Edelstein began to threaten to "remove" the case from Lifland unless progress could be shown. Edelstein even went so far as to suggest that any Manville Plan of Reorganization should include a twenty-year sinking fund to pay health claimants, funded with all of Manville's future profits.

None of this appeared to ruffle the Manville management. Having been protected from paying its prepetition bills, loans, judgments, and settlements and having suspended dividends, Manville's retained earnings had increased by $200 million during the Chapter 11. Cash rich, Manville could do its own financing internally, and so it was not dependent upon what the credit markets thought of it. On most days it was business as usual in the executive suite, and that was not too bad at all. Chapter 11 has its benefits.

Although Manville was feeling no pain from the proceedings, the strategists at Manville came to realize that the logjam would have to be broken, or at least *appear* to loosen. The judiciary was getting restless. Judge Lifland wanted progress and had ordered around-the-clock negotiations. Nevertheless, in typical Manville fashion, "progress" would be narrowly defined and carefully managed. Manville's sole concession in the negotiations was to increase its offer to health claimants to a fixed sum (a "limited pot") of $400 million, about half of what the Asbestos Health Claimants Committee was demanding. (Manville chairman John McKinney wanted Manville to withdraw any lump sum offer entirely.) In reporting later to the judge, the parties agreed that the marathon talks had produced "frank " discussions, but that was all they could agree on! Judge Lifland complained, "I am dealing with generals and colonels instead of statesmen." The lawyers dutifully marched off to more meetings.

While the parties negotiated throughout the first weeks of November 1983, the Asbestos Health Claimants Committee filed thirty pounds of documents with Judge Lifland in support of its contention that Manville could have paid all creditors, including those who would suffer from asbestos-related diseases in the future, without filing bankruptcy.

With negotiations having become reduced to trench warfare, on November 21, 1983, Manville filed its reorganization plan, which weighed in at three hundred pages. The company had sweetened its schedule of awards for various types and stages of disease from an average of $13,500 for each health claimant to a $15,000 average, still less than half of what the Asbestos Health Victims Committee was willing to settle for. The schedule would award $50,000 for mesothelioma, which is almost always fatal within two years of diagnosis; from $1,500 to $45,000 for other cancers; and from $1,500 to $40,000 for asbestosis and other forms of impairment. A computer would absorb the relevant information about a claimant and spit out the amount of the award.

Manville's funding mechanism under the proposed Plan of Reorganization achieved the best of both worlds for the company, allowing it to take credit for moving off its "limited pot" offer while not actually allowing a serious attack on its present or future treasury. Awards would be paid from Manville's "free cash flow"—defined as *future profits in excess of those needed to fund Manville's operations*. Those excess profits would be split evenly between two groups, health claimants and the rest of the creditors, until the commercial/trade creditors were fully paid, estimated by Manville to be eight years. Thereafter, any excess profits would be directed to the health claimants under the plan. The manner of determining "free cash flow" was necessarily vague, since the determination of the number each year would have to take into consideration a myriad of factors.

Manville had handed the health claimants a pig in a poke and had asked them to buy it without looking at it too closely. Not only was the level of funding an indeterminate amount under the best of circumstances, but the Manville management could shrink it each year at will by declaring that additional expenses were necessary for increases in salaries and bonuses, the purchase of new equipment, expansion, or just generally staying competitive. It would be impossible effectively to monitor the company's day-to-day activities that would lead to the bottom-line figure. Certainly there was a risk to the health claimants that that might not be enough to fully pay awards. Due to the nature of the proposal, it could not be determined how big the risk was, but given the history of the litigation, the health claimants could make a good guess!

Manville sought to establish a claims procedure through its plan that would be independent of the tort/court system which not incidentally would hold down the size of individual awards. The part of the award equation for each claimant that involved the degree of impairment would be determined by a medical panel chosen and paid for by the company, with a right of appeal to a special appeals board, subject to review by the bankruptcy judge. There would be no right to a jury trial of the tort claims.

Manville added a zinger to its plan, a pet position of John McKinney. Terming the legal fees earned by plaintiffs' lawyers "completely unreasonable [and] exorbitant... [b]ecause the amount of legal work performed by counsel is so small in comparison to the potential monetary awards," the company requested the bankruptcy judge to void the contingent fee contracts entered into by all of the plaintiffs' counsel. The court was requested to review all services by each plaintiff's lawyer and award a "reasonable fee." The reaction of the claimants' attorneys to that proposal was not hard to predict, especially of those attorneys who had chased Manville from court to court, trial to trial, negotiation to negotiation, for many, many years.

It should have come as no surprise that the creditors disapproved of the proposals, because they were not new. Essentially the same terms had been rejected months before by the creditors. Manville's insistence on prohibiting access to a jury trial had been a main cause of the breakdown of negotiations. Thus the formal presentation of the plan to the bankruptcy court simply was one more illusion of progress that Manville conjured for the judge.

The filing of the formal Plan of Reorganization was more than merely the publication of old news, it was the publicizing of proposals that were hugely offensive to the health claimants and their attorneys. To them the plan offered an awards schedule that ignored the present

litigation picture, which would be applied through a valuation procedure that was operated by Manville's minions and that Manville
could avoid actually paying! The reaction of the claimants' attorneys
to the fee review proposed by Manville will not be reprinted here.
Perhaps the Manville management sensed that the Asbestos Health
Claimants Committee did not approve of the plan when its lead counsel
called it "unconfirmable, illegal, and unconstitutional."

The plan was a nonstarter. Because of the lack of consensus, Manville did not call for a vote of the creditors. In fact, the plan would be
prosecuted no further by Manville during the entire case. Although on
the surface, the failure of the plan seemed to be a setback for Manville, the truth was more subtle and totally to the opposite effect. In
reality Manville was in a "no lose" situation, and Manville management had every reason to be pleased with the situation.

Just by *being*, the plan had tilted the playing field Manville's way.
The filing of the plan satisfied Judges Lifland and Edelstein for the
time being and helped Manville's public relations. Because Judge
Lifland had continued to bar the creditors from filing a plan on this
evidence of "progress," by default the one-sided proposals contained in
it set the terms of debate and negotiation. It was "progress" in
Manville's definition of the word, the corporation achieving all of those
benefits without actually having to compromise its positions
significantly.

In addition, given the extreme nature of the proposals, the goal of
the Manville executives could not have been truly to achieve a reorganization at that time with that plan. They knew well the reception
that it would get. In reality the plan was merely a tactic in the grand
strategy of wearing down the creditors and their lawyers. Since approval of the plan was not the immediate objective, there could be no
disappointment at not having achieved it. Had the creditors by some
chance agreed to the plan, Manville would have made out like a ban-
dit.

Having been outmaneuvered by Manville, the creditors counterat-
tacked with a flurry of motions. The Asbestos Health Claimants Committee asked for the appointment of a bankruptcy trustee to operate
Manville. (Denied.) Smarting from the challenge to their fees, the
plaintiffs' attorneys requested the judge to cancel Manville's directors'
fees and to reduce the pay of the officers by one-third. (Denied.)

In addition to the new motions, the "atom bomb" motions—the four separate motions to dismiss the bankruptcy, filed long before by the Asbestos Health Claimants Committee, a group of codefendants, and two trade creditors—were rearmed. The motions were reactivated, the issues were briefed, and on January 5, 1984, Judge Lifland heard oral argument.

While the other three movants made technical arguments concerning "bad faith" in its usage as a bankruptcy term of art, the Asbestos Health Claimants Committee went straight for the jugular, attempting to persuade the judge that Manville was not morally worthy of being a Chapter 11 debtor. Using charts during the presentation before the judge, the committee argued that a sequence of events showed the bad faith of Manville. Manville's management was accused of manipulating the study of future liabilities; then fraudulently claiming that accounting rules had required it to recognize potential future liabilities in its annual report, which would have provoked its lenders into calling their loans had not the company filed bankruptcy first; then "dup[ing]" its own board of directors into approving the filing of the bankruptcy petition; and then attempting to reorganize to insulate itself from its just liabilities, all when it had enough cash flow to pay its debts in full. To the claimants' attorneys, the charted actions were adequate proof that Manville had committed the perversion of "embracing" bankruptcy, thus committing "bad faith."

As is common with important matters, the judge did not rule upon the motions to dismiss at the conclusion of the hearing. However, he issued his decision a relatively short time later considering the complexity and centrality of the issues and the mountain of documents submitted by the litigants. On January 23, 1984, the parties received the judge's determination in the form of a written "opinion," which is a ruling that not only contains the bare yea or nay but also includes express findings of fact, conclusions of law, citations to the legal authorities upon which the judge relied, and a reasoned statement of the judge's thinking. The movants, especially the members of the Asbestos Health Claimants Committee, would be bitterly disappointed by the contents of that opinion.

Although the denial of the motions was, as characterized by the lead counsel for the Asbestos Health Claimants Committee, "no surprise," the tone of the judge's written opinion was a shocker. In black and white, for the whole world to see, Bankruptcy Judge Burton R. Lifland did not just deny the motions, he savaged the movants' arguments and heaped scorn on their tactics. Further, he made it abundantly clear that Manville *would be* reorganized through the Chapter 11 proceeding, come hell or high water.

Judge Lifland commenced his opinion by stating the causes of the bankruptcy in terms that had been promoted by Manville. He accepted that "the sole factor necessitating [Manville's] filing is the mammoth problem of asbestos health suits brought against it because of its substantial use [sic] for many years of products containing asbestos which injured those who came into contact with this lethal substance." The bankruptcy filing was necessitated by "the crushing economic burden to be suffered by Manville over the next 20–30 years." No mention was made of any contribution by Manville's management to the rise of "the problem."

The judge obviously had not concerned himself with the details of the disputes. He did not bother to analyze the calculations comparing likely claims to Manville's likely earnings to see if a Chapter 11 was necessary. In effect deemed irrelevant was the copious amount of evidence brought to light over a decade of litigation respecting the culpability of Manville, which had led juries repeatedly to punish the company. Also ignored were the depositions taken and the documents laboriously collected during the course of the bankruptcy to the same effect that had been submitted to the court by the health claimants' attorneys. That evidence was referred to derisively by the judge in the opinion as, variously, "a multitude of volumes," "multitudinous submissions," and "tomes of material." Lifland would not expend his time and intellect upon ancient history or financial projections.

The period of history in which Judge Lifland *was* interested began at the filing of the bankruptcy and enveloped a mere sixteen months. In his legal opinion, he laid a charge at the movants' feet: why had they not prosecuted the motions to dismiss the bankruptcy earlier? If Manville had blemished the integrity of the court by using it in bad faith, why had they not immediately stepped forward to protect it?

> If there was merit in the motion [of the Asbestos Health Claimants Committee] to dismiss on the ground of lack of good faith, it could have been fervently pressed a year ago instead of tolerating this alleged misuse of the courts. This same assertion of untimeliness can be made regarding the other co-defendant proponents of dismissal of the petition because they too may be

pressing these motions as a last resort as a result of frustrations at the bargaining table. This court must therefore bear in mind the strategical motivations underlying the pursuit of these motions at this time as well as recognize the progress toward a successful, perhaps consensual, reorganization that has already taken place. It is against this backdrop of progress and achievement accomplished by the key constituencies toward a resolution on perhaps a sweeping basis of the asbestos problem that the . . . motions are now placed before me for determination.

The judge had viewed the circumstances through his own particular filter. The perceived motives of the creditors had come through loud and clear, while their legal arguments and factual presentations had not. Manville's unsupported plan was seen as evidence of "progress and achievement," and Manville thus would be encouraged to press ahead, even if everyone else had to be dragged along behind.

Although Judge Lifland questioned the motives of the creditors, he had no trouble with Manville's. The judge only needed to know that "Manville is a real company [that is, not formed for the purpose of filing bankruptcy—one test of bad faith] with a substantial amount of real debt and real creditors clamoring to enforce this real debt." The "real debt" theme was repeated several times in the opinion, a clear dig at the health claimants' attorneys who were hounding Manville unmercifully, demanding huge sums for their clients, yet asking the court to ignore the likelihood that, if allowed, they would be hounding Manville unmercifully in the future on behalf of new clients. Employing a common judicial tactic, the judge buried the attacks upon the objectivity of the statistical research that Manville had commissioned and upon which it based its bankruptcy filing, by neglecting to comment upon them at all. The opinion merely noted that the Epidemiology Resources report was a "lengthy, careful and detailed analysis." To Judge Lifland, Manville had done much "soul searching" before it had filed the petition commencing the bankruptcy case. So much for the health claimants' primary argument of moral "bad faith."

After making those findings, Judge Lifland had no trouble locating sufficient legal authority in the expansive philosophy of the Bankruptcy Code to support Manville's Chapter 11 status. To the judge, a principal goal of the Bankruptcy Code is "open access" to the bankruptcy process for the rich and the poor, the solvent and the insolvent. A business should not have to wait until its financial situation has deteriorated so much that it cannot be rehabilitated. Because a goal of the bankruptcy law is to save jobs, any substantial company that has any significant chance to reorganize must be given that chance. Since Manville is a substantial company whose goal is to reorganize, it cannot be in "bad faith."

Through his opinion Judge Lifland not only had denied the motions to dismiss the bankruptcy, he had provided a blueprint of its future course. Just in case he had been too subtle for anyone, he closed the opinion by stating, "It is *undeniable* that these proceedings *will* result in a delivery system for Manville tort claimants, whether in the present questionably efficient tort system, a newly-created claims-estimation facility, or another form." [Emphasis added.]

Manville had successfully walked the line. Through its self-serving study, it had convinced the court that it faced substantial future liability for asbestos-related diseases, even though the exact amount was in question and medical science could not determine exactly which people would be affected by asbestos. The estimate of liability was not so small that compromising creditors' rights would be inappropriate nor so large that a reorganization proceeding was hopeless—as long as everyone ignored the immense potential liability for property claims.

As if a single roundhouse of a ruling were not enough for one day, the Honorable Burton R. Lifland let fly with the remainder of a one-two combination. Having decided that the case would continue, the judge would now begin to build one of the major foundation blocks for a successful restructuring of Manville.

By order and opinion dated the same day as the ruling on the motions to dismiss, Judge Lifland granted a pending motion for the appointment of a "legal representative" for those people who did not know yet that they would have claims against Manville for asbestos-induced disease. According to the judge, "It is abundantly clear that the Manville reorganization will have to be accountable to future asbestos claimants whose compelling interest must be safeguarded in order to leave a residue of assets sufficient to accommodate a meaningful resolution of the asbestos related health problem." In other words, future claims would have to be wrapped up in the bankruptcy so that Manville could continue in business free of them.

Actually the judge did not go the whole ten yards because he did not decide whether future claimants had "claims" that would be recognized in the bankruptcy. Rather, he only issued a provisional ruling to the effect that they were "parties in interest," a term used in the Bankruptcy Code to indicate individuals or entities who technically may or may not be creditors but in any event have a substantial stake in the outcome of the bankruptcy. (For example, the Securities and Exchange Commission is a statutory party in interest in cases involving "public" companies.) Parties in interest have standing to receive all court papers, make motions, and appear before the judge in order to advise the judge of their wishes. Since obviously future claimants could not appear in person or hire legal counsel, the judge would appoint someone to play their part. A ruling on the recognition of their claims in the bankruptcy would come later, but in terming them "a central focus" of the proceedings, Lifland was leaving no doubt as to what that ruling would be.

Judges, like emperors, do not appreciate it when their carefully created fictions are pointed out. A self-styled future claimant, an asbestos worker with early signs of an asbestos-related disease, who appeared in court at the hearing asking to be named as the representative of the future claimants, was given scant attention by Judge Lifland. The "legal representative" would be of the judge's own creating. At a later date, the judge denied a semifacetious motion that he disqualify himself from presiding over the Manville case because he was a potential future claimant, putatively having been exposed to asbestos in the office building where he had practiced law. The judge chose not to see the truth in the jest: that it was not possible to tell who future claimants were or how they might view their interests in the bankruptcy. Indeed, for all that is known, all the judges in the courthouse and all the attorneys in the case may be future claimants, but that thought would be too monumental to capture Judge Lifland's attention.

Judge Lifland was not interested in conundrums, paradoxes, philosophical inquiries, or even careful legal reasoning. The "can-do" attitude of the bankruptcy court was shining through. Step by practical step, Manville would be reorganized. The judge was not concerned with anything more.

Had Burton R. Lifland been a philosopher or a legal scholar, he would have been more troubled with the concept of a "Legal Representative" in the Manville case. Whether that person truly was an average future claimant, with a background and legal rights very similar to the core of the group, or like a trustee or attorney, how could that person learn about the characteristics, desires, and best interests of the group at large? How could he or she get instructions from them? Or, if the representative simply were to use his or her best judgment, how could the judge or anyone else tell if indeed that was in the best interests of the group? How could notices be given to future claimants? How can one tell if a respondent to a notice is a future claimant? Given that many courts had ruled that a claim for personal injury upon which a lawsuit is to be based does not arise until the injury is manifested (so that plaintiffs do not lose their rights to the statute of limitations before they know that they have those rights) under what consistent theory could the court rule that for the purpose of bankruptcy the claim for asbestos injury arose upon exposure even though at that time the person could not legally or practically file suit?

There were no good answers to those questions. In fact, there could be no rational answers at all to them. The judge's "Legal Representative" is an example of what law scholars term a "legal fiction," which is defined in *Webster's Third New International Dictionary* as "an assumption of a possible thing as a fact irrespective of the question of its truth; specifically, an allegation or supposition in law of a state of facts assumed to exist which the practice of the courts allows to be made . . . and refuses to allow the adverse party to disprove." Use of a legal fiction by a court allows a change in the law to be masked because its real purpose is not apparent. The judge had created a brand new, controversial position but had cloaked it with an innocuous title.

Apart from the pretzel logic of the situation, it had appeared that Lifland would have to overcome a serious obstacle, namely a contrary decision by a federal district judge in another case. However, it turned out that the delay until January 1984 in deciding the issue, which was not, strictly speaking, Lifland's doing, had solved the problem for him.

Shortly before Manville had filed bankruptcy in 1982, UNR Industries, a much smaller asbestos producer, had filed a Chapter 11 case in Chicago. In March 1983, Judge William Hart, a district court judge, had ruled that future asbestos health claims could not be treated in the UNR bankruptcy. Had Lifland been called on to rule upon the motions to dismiss the Manville case at that time, he would have been hard pressed to decline to follow Hart's ruling.

The problem for Judge Lifland was that Judge Hart's ruling was based solidly on traditional precepts of law. In his written legal opinion and order, Judge Hart observed that it is legal gospel that with respect to personal injury cases, each one presents unique facts and liability issues. For example, even if a product were clearly dangerous, issues in a case would include whether in fact it injured the plaintiff, whether the plaintiff misused it, whether the label adequately warned the plaintiff, how damages would be determined, and so on. If cases did not have common facts, how could one "legal representative" act for all? To Judge Hart, "It would be impossible for one legal representative to represent adequately the claims of tens of thousands of future claimants."

Judge Hart's opinion then reviewed the concept of due process in civil (as opposed to criminal) litigation. The requirement of due process is solidly embedded in this country's jurisprudence—it is one of the things that makes us different from so many societies around the globe. It is basic, unassailable law ("black letter law" in legal jargon) that due process in a legal proceeding requires that reasonable notice be provided to those whose rights may be affected. It was obvious that notice was impossible when people reading it would have no idea as to whether they should respond. The judge characterized the attempts of UNR's lawyers to argue around the insurmountable problem:

> They argue, in effect, that the Congressional intention to provide the possibility of a "fresh start" to entities suffering under grave financial disabilities includes the intention to subordinate to the "fresh start" concern the statutory and constitutional rights of those who do not yet know that they will in the future suffer from a dread disease.

To Judge Hart, the conclusion was inescapable: a bankruptcy case could not deal with injury claims that would become manifest after the likely conclusion of the bankruptcy. He acknowledged in his opinion that his ruling may result in the liquidation of UNR Industries, but he could not avoid the reality that courts have limited power. He closed his opinion by suggesting that a solution to the legal bind just be found in Congress, if at all.

Fortunately for UNR, Manville, and future generations of Chapter 11 megatortfeasors, Judge Hart's ruling was vacated by the Seventh Circuit Court of Appeals in mid-January 1984. The specific decision of the appellate court was no decision—the matter was deemed premature for consideration by either the district or the appellate courts, and so the appeal was dismissed without a ruling being made. UNR's case would be allowed to proceed through the many stages of a complex Chapter 11 reorganization before the issue would be presented again for ruling. By that time, UNR would no longer be in the lead, as Manville already would have a reorganization plan approved and the issues under consideration on appeal. The asbestos bankruptcy debtors had narrowly dodged a bullet.

Important for Judge Lifland's purposes, the Seventh Circuit had added some words of wisdom as an aside in its order dismissing the appeal. The court had noted that, under the realities of asbestos-related litigation, there would be no reason for a Plan of Reorganization to go forward if it did not take care of future health claims. The order then mused that the Bankruptcy Code "just might" have enough built-in flexibility to include future injury claims in a reorganization plan, which could be tested when a future claimant filed a claim. (No mention was made of how that might occur.)

Judge Hart must have been thoroughly confused. A humorous boast of trial level judges is "Sometimes 'in error' on appeal, but never wrong," and as a matter of textbook law, Judge Hart indeed was not wrong. His description of UNR's argument, quoted above, was right on target. His analysis of the legal precedent was correct. The judge's "error" was to place considerations of law above the reorganization of corporations. In the real world, those companies are more important than the mere mortals whose interests must be subordinate to the laws.

For a nondecision, the order had substantial repercussions. Quickly taking the cue from the Seventh Circuit, the UNR bankruptcy judge in Chicago directed a court-appointed official to develop information on the number of prospective claims in order to advise the court if they could be dealt with in the bankruptcy case. Judge Lifland took the comments in the Seventh Circuit's order to have great import, as, in effect, an advisory opinion of a higher court, and acted accordingly.

The Seventh Circuit had given Lifland just enough room to maneuver through his written opinion. As suggested by that court's order, he would not make a final ruling on the status of future claims but would bring future claimants into Manville's bankruptcy through a "legal representative." Also, he borrowed a maneuver from the Seventh Circuit. Although professing not to rule on the final status of those parties, in a lengthy footnote in his opinion, he analyzed the theory by which such claims might be included in a plan.

Judge Lifland also adopted the Seventh Circuit's posture that the uniqueness of the situation demanded a unique solution. In his opinion, he observed that traditional means of legal analysis and traditional procedures (which stood in the way of his theory as to the status of the future claims) might prove inadequate in the Manville case. Judge Lifland then commented, "It is the unprecedented, extraordinary nature of these proceedings that mandates a declaration the [future health claimants] are parties in interest." Was there any doubt over how he would rule respecting the status of future claims in the bankruptcy when the time would come to decide whether they held cognizable "claims"?

The judge concluded the blockbuster of an opinion by setting a hearing to hear the parties' advice regarding the form that a "legal representative" would take and the nature of that person's duties. No doubt the judge knew perfectly well what he would do at the conclusion of that hearing, but it is always wise to maintain the illusion of considering the parties' arguments. It tends to make rulings reversal-proof.

Suddenly, a new concept appeared on the scene that reshaped the dialogue.

John Jamieson, a member of the Unsecured Creditors' Committee, proposed that a trust be created to administer any approved Plan of Reorganization. The trust would operate through independent trustees, who would administer the claims process. Claimants would be required to go through the process, but dissatisfied claimants could then file a lawsuit and pursue their remedies in court. Manville would contribute a specified amount of cash and all available insurance coverage. Jamieson also proposed that the *trust would own a majority of Manville's stock, which could be sold on the open market to supplement the fund.*

Manville had no choice but to negotiate over the terms of Jamieson's proposal, so strong was the ground swell, and some progress was made. The company conceded that the trust could own its stock, but it bargained hard over the exact percentage. Manville conceded that in the first step of the claims process, the negotiations could be between the health claimant and a representative of the trust, rather than Manville. At least $100 million would be contributed to the trust initially, with annual infusions of perhaps $10 million.

Then the Jamieson proposal caught Manville-itis. There were lots of negotiations, and the general shape of the deal could be perceived, but actual agreement on the many parts of the proposal eluded the participants. As spring turned into summer, the dialogue stopped entirely. Manville's defense had bent but had not broken.

The Asbestos Health Claimants Committee then showed its displeasure by wildly litigating within the bankruptcy. It went ahead with its appeal of Judge Lifland's failure to dismiss the bankruptcy; it appealed the appointment of a "legal representative"; it filed a lawsuit in the district court demanding a right to jury trial for the determination of the health claims; and it filed and then withdrew a demand that the court appoint a trustee to manage Manville's affairs. However, the flurry of activity failed to overcome the inertia of the case. No ruling was forthcoming that would break the logjam created by Manville. None of the district court judges hearing the appeals was the least bit interested in sticking a hand into the hornets' nest.

Typical of the topsy-turvy world of bankruptcy, the one favorable ruling that the health claimants committee was able to secure helped them not one bit. A district court judge ruled that, yes, the jurisdictional mess caused by the Supreme Court's *Marathon* decision required that full district court judges and not subordinate bankruptcy court judges conduct trials on the thousands of health claims filed in the bankruptcy case; but, no thank you, the district judges would not hear them just now. According to the ruling, the issues for a trial would not be ripe until it was determined whether a plan would be approved which provided for an agreed hearing process outside of court. Thus the health claimants had succeeded in prying the determination of health claims away from Judge Lifland but had not succeeded in getting any other judge to actually hear the claims.

The ruling conceding that it was the responsibility of full district court judges to hold hearings on personal injury claims in bankruptcies, which was technically correct, held immense implications. The ruling had the effect of dumping some twenty-five thousand pending health claims in the bankruptcies of Manville and several smaller asbestos bankruptcies into the laps of district court judges—a sort of a karma-wheel result given the considerable role that they had exercised in limiting the power and position of the bankruptcy judges. In fact, the implications were so immense that the real-life result has been to put tremendous pressure on the district court judges to rubber-stamp *any* Plan of Reorganization approved by a bankruptcy judge that contains *any* format for hearing injury claims that does not require them to preside. So, rather than truly help themselves, the ruling secured by the health claimants only made it doubly certain that any reorganization of Manville would not be overturned on appeal.

While the action was in the district court, the issue of who would become the "legal representative" of future claimants remained up in the air. Once more the judge rebuffed a volunteer, this time the AFL-CIO, thousands of whose members would have claims. If a union could not represent thousands of its members, and the judge had already rejected a likely future claimant as a representative, then who could represent the group? While the lawyers jousted, people continued to take sick.

In desperation, a peripheral group of attorneys for health claimants filed a class action asking for a declaration that, because of the *Marathon* muddle, the automatic stay (injunction) against proceeding with lawsuits against Manville was ineffective. It was not so much a constitutional argument as a plea for mercy, as Manville's codefendants already had failed with a similar argument. The lead attorney stated simply, "It has been over two years since Manville filed its Chapter 11 petition. Some of our clients are dying." Needless to say, the suit got nowhere. Plaintiffs' atttorneys began to take video depositions of their dying clients so that they could "testify" against Manville when their estates were accorded a hearing sometime, somewhere.

While the stalemate continued in the Manville bankruptcy case, other asbestos producers were buried in fierce litigation across the country. Plaintiffs' attorneys continued to find damning evidence against them, and they were suffering judgments in ever-increasing amounts and were therefore required to pay handsome settlements. Hospitals and governmental entities were filing blizzards of lawsuits against them that totaled in the billions of dollars for property damage relating to asbestos in their buildings. Lawsuits between the asbestos companies and their insurers over coverage continued unabated. Courts in some districts were so overburdened with asbestos cases that other types of civil suits could not be heard. The only reason that the number of claims was not higher was that the United States Environmental Protection Agency had banned asbestos for most uses in schools in 1973 and for all uses in 1978.

Rather than remain the center of activity, the Manville case had become practically inert. The chemistry of the personalities in the case had produced much heat but little light. Judge Lifland began to understand that his solicitousness of Manville had been abused; but he did not appear to favor the demands to which the plaintiffs' attorneys had clung. Accordingly, the judge readied the introduction to the case of what he hoped would be a catalyst for the creation of a Plan of Reorganization that would attract and bind all of the factions. The judge would appoint his choice of a "legal representative" for the future health claimants.

Chapter 11

In Silverman We Trust

Bankruptcy Judge Lifland knew what the Manville Chapter 11 case needed to get it moving—and what it did not need. Having breathed life into the fictional character to be known as the "Legal Representative," the judge set about shaping him . . . in his image.

He did not want to appoint a delegate from the class of future claimants. He did not have in mind someone who was a composite of the workers who would fall to the slow death that asbestos wrought, perhaps a strapping forty-year-old who had installed asbestos insulation for twenty years or an immigrant who had supported her family sewing asbestos textiles. Such a person might truly carry the standard for the group, and to the judge, the last thing that the case needed was another faction vigorously and vociferously demanding the best deal for it alone.

Judge Lifland was thinking more of someone who would command the attention of the combatants and lead them towards a consensual reorganization of Manville. Although that person formally would be charged with estimating future claims and assuring their payment, in reality his job was to be a mediator/special master/judge's proxy to find the best path to save Manville, act as an intermediary, fashion a Plan of Reorganization, persuade all parties to go along with his proposal, and, if necessary, cram the plan down their throats.

To Judge Lifland, the perfect person to do the job was Burton R. Lifland. However, since the judge could not climb off the bench to actively manage Manville's reorganization, the Legal Representative would have to be his alter ego, someone who would understand, without the need for detailed instructions, what Judge Lifland would do if he could. It would be the bankruptcy court version of the TV series *Mission: Impossible*. That Legal Representative later would describe the judge's place in the successful reorganization of Manville:

> [I] should emphasize what has been said before in these proceedings [citation] but simply cannot be said enough times or with enough vigor. The guidance, direction and determination to achieve what is now an unparalleled result flowed from this Court [Judge Lifland]. In taking the steps that have led to a successful reorganization, the Legal Representative and Counsel, as well as the other parties to this reorganization, were attempting to fulfill the mandate clearly and repeatedly set by the Court. . . . [T]he simple fact of the matter is that the one person without whom, under any set of circumstances, this reorganization could never have happened and who consistently and effectively compelled everyone to attain the results which are now so celebrated, was this Court.

What credentials should the Legal Representative bring to the case? The key was that the fractious crowd constantly before Judge Lifland in court was not made up of injured laborers, nest-egg shareholders, small-town suppliers, and regional banks *but rather of their New York lawyers*. The *"legal representative"* must be just that—a counselor-at-law. Of course, he had to be from a well-known New York law firm and be tough enough to push around the other big boys.

Leon Silverman was that man.

On August 14, 1984, Judge Lifland named Leon S. Silverman, a senior partner and cochairman in the New York law firm of Fried, Frank, Harris, Shriver and Jacobson, as the Legal Representative of persons who, without fault of their own, would not realize that they had a claim against Manville for causing a disease until after the period for making claims in the Manville bankruptcy had expired. Mr. Silverman had excellent educational credentials, having been graduated from Yale Law School and the London School of Economics. After school he had been an assistant United States Attorney for the Southern District of New York and an Associate Deputy United States Attorney General, signs that he was politically well connected. Evidence of that was his appointment as special investigator in the probe of former

Secretary of Labor Raymond Donovan. His office was filled with plaques in recognition of service with various lawyers' groups. He was not a bankruptcy lawyer. He was a member and a past president of the American College of Trial Lawyers, an elite group made up of attorneys who commonly defend large corporations in lawsuits.

The judge granted Mr. Silverman the status of an official committee, coequal with the other official committees before the court. Of course, everyone knew that, as the judge's man, Silverman was "more equal" than the others. Technically, he would be represented by his law firm; fees and expenses would be paid by Manville. Since the Lone Committeeman had no cohorts and no specific clients, he surely would be an efficient operation!

Almost immediately, the appointment was challenged. A boilermaker who had handled asbestos extensively asserted his status as a future claimant and indicated that he did not want a "representative." His attorney was, almost needless to say, a member of the Asbestos Litigation Committee. The objection was withdrawn when Judge Lifland threatened to find that the attorney had a conflict of interest and would be barred from representing present claimants. Of course, the Asbestos Health Claimants Committee also opposed the appointment for legal (lack of due process in taking away rights) and tactical (run Manville to the ground) reasons. It filed an objection, arguing that the appointment showed an intent by Judge Lifland to include future claimants into the reorganization.

However, time and the tide were favoring Manville on the future claimants issue. The concept, so foreign to the entire history of Western jurisprudence, was gaining credence through repetition and lack of other alternatives to keep the asbestos companies going. Companies facing mass tort claims had sought refuge in the bankruptcy system, and it would be up to the courts to save them from themselves. Before the appeal would play out in the Manville case, the bankruptcy judge presiding over the UNR case would appoint a representative of future claimants, and the Third Circuit Court of Appeals would reverse the lower court's refusal to appoint a representative in another smaller case.

Silverman immediately met with the major interest groups. He found them to be dug into hardened positions. There was virtually no communication among them. Not only did they mistrust each other, they also mistrusted Silverman, each creditor group thinking that Silverman was in the pocket of Manville. At the same time, Manville was distrustful of Silverman's power in the case. Meetings consisted largely of attempts to co-opt Silverman.

Never lacking for confidence, Leon Silverman quickly came to his own conclusions about the path the megacase would travel. His clear mandate from the judge was to reorganize Manville as it existed, and so he never seriously considered selling off Manville's divisions to raise money. To Silverman, the opposing sides more or less canceled each other out, leaving him free to work his own alchemy. Manville *would* be reorganized *his way*, no matter how many square pegs had to be crammed into round holes.

One factor was of prime importance to Leon Silverman in developing his own plan for the participants. It was an article of faith to Silverman that the uncertainty generated by the health claims was hurting Manville in the eyes of Wall Street, a constituency that Silverman thought was highly important. To Silverman, a megacorporation without the ability to go to the capital markets was a pitiful, helpless giant, and he would not allow that fate to haunt Manville. Accordingly, to Silverman a major goal of Manville's reorganization would be to see that company emerge from bankruptcy with sufficient cash and the likelihood of substantial, unencumbered future profits to maintain its good standing in the megacorporate club.

With the establishment of that goal, the logistics of a plan were obvious—at least to Silverman. Silverman simply would make his own determination of how much spare cash the company was likely to have in the foreseeable future (including as much in insurance proceeds as could be squeezed out of Manville's insurers) and then tell Manville it would have to pay it and tell the creditors that is what they would be getting. Finalizing a plan would consist of making the suppliers and lenders reasonably happy, perhaps with a liberal sprinkling of Manville stock, performing some miracle to make the property claims go away, and leaving the rest of the pot of money for health claims.

There was a certain efficiency in Silverman's approach. Since his plan was not based on an estimate of the likely future liability of Manville to health claimants, he was free to ignore epidemiological predictions of the incidence of future illnesses caused by Manville's asbestos, as well as the estimates of the number of claims that would arise from them, which he felt were imprecise. In fact, he was free to ignore *all* of the issues surrounding the health claimants over which everyone else was fighting. He made no attempt whatsoever to communicate with asbestos workers, and, after one abortive meeting with the AFL-CIO, he ignored the workers' unions, too. Silverman's bottom-line view also meant that he was totally disinterested in assigning any blame to Manville or in pursuing the officers and directors responsible for Manville's health policies, since neither activity would add any substantial percentage to the pot for claimants.

Silverman's basic philosophy dictated that he not actually be the champion of the rights of future claimants, and in that regard he walked a fine line that may not be visible to many others. For example, although his standing in the case was based solely on his designation as the Legal Representative of the future claimants, he steadfastly maintained that he was not their "guardian ad litem" (a legal term of art that signifies that a person is the legal guardian for another in a particular piece of litigation, with the power to act for, and bind, that person). That he would waste no time or energy championing the cause of the future claimants was made quite clear when he stated in negotiations and in court that he would try to achieve fair compensation for *all creditors*, and although he would try to include future claimants, *he would take no position on the legality of that view*! The calculated ambiguity of Silverman's position is illustrated by his own description of his job in his fee application addressed to Judge Lifland:

The specific mandate of the Legal Representative and [his] Counsel was to represent "future claimants." This was an untested and controversial role. However, in describing the services rendered, we will not be describing services rendered strictly on behalf of even this broad constituency. Nor did the Legal Representative and Counsel—as in the normal reorganization—merely react or respond to the proposals of the Debtors or others. In fact, the Legal Representative and Counsel acted with respect to every aspect of this reorganization. Rather than speak for the narrow interest of a single constituency, in every important matter the Legal Representative and Counsel devised the solution or took a lead role in arriving at the resolutions and points that found their way into the Plan of Reorganization.

In other words, the outcome of the case was dictated by a litigant who had no financial or legal interest in it whatsoever and who did not represent anybody except insofar as he was the judge's man. Since he did not speak for future claimants, and they could not speak for themselves, they remain in limbo to this day.

Recognizing Manville's hardball attitude, and wishing to overcome the distrust of the creditor groups, Silverman first communicated with the creditors. During the spring and early summer of 1985, a plan evolved in the office of the Legal Representative without the participation of Manville. The wishes of potential future health claimants, the putative constituents of the Legal Representative, also were deemed irrelevant to the plan process.

As the bankruptcy case drifted through 1985, Manville seemed mired in the proceeding—or was the right word "entrenched"? True, Manville had filed to purge its balance sheet of health claims through a quick reorganization but found that even provisional resolution of some issues was linked to resolution of other issues that defied settlement. However, for Manville during this period it was "business as usual," minus the asbestos division, which finally was folded. McKinney's salary had gone up 56 percent during the bankruptcy. Big raises and bonuses for Manville's execs were the rule. If bankruptcy court is purgatory, it was the creditors who were suffering in it.

By summer 1985, Leon Silverman was ready to engage Manville in discussions, and the company professed to be ready to deal. However, when Silverman met with Manville's negotiators, the sides just talked past each other, Manville making what Silverman considered to be inadequate offers and Silverman lecturing Manville about what he was going to require the giant company to do. (The creditors had not been invited.)

As the third anniversary of the case neared, the team of Lifland and Silverman made its move. The judge announced darkly that he expected to see *real* progress by that date. Silverman drafted a plan that reflected his view of fairness and presented it to the factions. When Manville balked at its terms, Silverman refused to be drawn into negotiations. Instead, he fired off the ultimate threat to the Manville management: if the company did not come along quietly when he proposed his plan, he would support the appointment of a bankruptcy trustee to manage the affairs of the company in place of its executives. Further, certain expansion plans that Manville was proposing would be opposed. It would *not* be business as usual for Manville in the future. Was there any doubt how Judge Lifland would rule in the event that

Leon Silverman took those positions in court?

(The creation of the Plan of Reorganization that would eventually carry the day is another illustration of Silverman's obsessive desire to control everything but be responsible for nothing. From August 1985 on, there was no question that the reorganization scheme that would dominate the remainder of the case—and in fact that finally was adopted—was Silverman's. It was Silverman's requests, not Manville's, that maintained Manville's "exclusive period" in order to effectively immobilize the creditors and shareholders. It was Silverman, along with Manville, who prevented the shareholders from changing the company's officers and directors. Yet, when Silverman's Plan of Reorganization eventually was formally proposed, Manville was the sole official sponsor—Silverman's name was nowhere to be seen.)

Silverman's threat got the attention of the Manville executives! They could delay payment to thousands of dying people, they could spend endless amounts of time in negotiations, they could see the company become one of the most disliked companies in America (per a *Fortune* magazine poll), and they could allow the value of the company's 28 million shares of stock to be dissipated, but they could not endure the possibility that they would lose their positions and power. By the end of July 1985, the board of directors had approved the principal elements of the Plan of Reorganization developed by Leon Silverman.

For all of Manville's protestations, Silverman's plan was quite favorable to the company.

An essential element of the plan was that the whole world would be enjoined from ever making another claim for asbestos-induced disease against Manville Corporation or any of its subsidiaries—what the lawyers called making the company "bulletproof." After all, that was a primary purpose of Manville's filing the Chapter 11. It also was consistent with Silverman's primary goal of making Manville creditworthy.

Silverman's proposal favored Manville's view of a claims procedure. All present and future health claimants would be required to file claims against a trust that would be created for that purpose. The trust would establish a claims facility that would operate independently of any influence from Manville. Claimants would have no right to jury trials. (Silverman could never gain the support of the Asbestos Health Claimants Committee on that provision, and he eventually sided with them—over the fierce objections of Manville—in allowing health claimants access to court procedures at the conclusion of the administrative process if they were not satisfied. As we shall see, that right became essentially meaningless, a fact that Silverman may have anticipated.)

In Silverman's plan, although claimants could attempt to prove punitive damages, all such claims were limited to a puny $5 million fund provided by Manville at the commencement of the process. With the inclusion of that provision, Manville achieved its other major goal of the bankruptcy: to shield itself from the wrath of the juries. To Silverman, eliminating punitive damages was a small matter, since moral culpability was not an issue that interested him. Also, as a lawyer commonly on the defense side, he adamantly was against the entire concept of permitting serial punitive damages against mass tort defendants.

As to the funding of the trust, Manville finally had been forced to sweeten its "limited pot" offer. In addition to initial funding at a level that Manville had agreed to for some time, Manville would make additional contributions if needed to bolster the fund. Specifically, Manville initially would contribute $200 million and would add $75 million in the fourth through twenty-fifth years of the trust. Also, the trust could acquire up to an additional 20 percent of Manville's profits after the fifth year, in the event that the funding proved inadequate.

The financial aspects of the plan stirred great debate among the health claimants' lawyers. Some concurred with Silverman's position to the effect that his plan would scoop up all of Manville's loose cash that could reasonably be deemed available to pay creditors. Others felt that too much deference had been accorded to continuing the mega-corporate life-style to which Manville had been accustomed and argued for a greater portion of the income stream to be diverted to the health claimants. In that dissenting view, the $75 million per year was nothing more than a modest fee for the privilege of staying in business that would be a minor cost for the giant corporation. The dissenters pointed to the company's internal business plan, which projected extremely strong sales in the near to mid-term future.

Under Silverman's proposal, the trust's assets would be enhanced substantially by all of Manville's insurance coverage, as it eventually would be determined through litigation or settlement, estimated to be $650 million. Although that was a big number, agreement on that asset never was a problem since really it belonged only to health claimants under any circumstances. Manville could afford to be magnanimous with it, since it did not cost Manville a penny to provide it to the trust.

Manville's shareholders were the big losers under Silverman's Plan of Reorganization. The trust would hold as an asset 50 percent of the common stock of the company, which could be sold to raise cash; and preferred shares, which could be converted to an additional 30 percent of the common stock. (There were some restrictions on the trust's voting and transfer rights, the most important being that the shares could not be used to oust management for the first four years of the plan. No dummies, that management!)

Several major assumptions of the plan were questionable. It could not be said with any certainty that the insurance proceeds would total such a large amount. Further, the success of the plan was predicated on paying only $50 *million* for nine thousand five hundred property damage claims on file (but not approved) as of June 1985 totaling $69 *billion*. If that could be accomplished, squeezing the property claimants would rank as the greatest benefit of the bankruptcy for Manville. Manville quickly took the first step in the long march by initiating a challenge to a sampling of governmental claims on the grounds that they could not prove the extent of use of Manville products. However, the school districts were contesting the matters vigorously and would not so easily see their claims wished out of existence.

Large issues had not been agreed upon. There was no provision for the "codefendant claims" that were ripening constantly for sums that other asbestos manufacturers had to pay to health claimants in lawsuits for which the companies might have a right of "contribution" from Manville. Silverman's plan baldly assumed that the trade and banking creditors would waive interest that had accrued upon sums that Manville had been withholding because of the bankruptcy injunction; however, that had been a sore subject with them, and they had conceded nothing.

As any good student of the Manville saga could have predicted, the Silverman plan got bogged down. Every interest group objected to some provisions and balked at being counted as being in the fold. The health claimants' attorneys were divided, some ready to take for themselves and their clients whatever they could get, and others incensed that only a small percentage of Manville's future earnings would be devoted to its past sins. In any event, negotiations on terms, provisions, phrases, percentages, definitions, time periods, exceptions, warranties, representations, rights, and duties, large and small, went around in circles. One creditor's attorney called the plan a "dead issue," but, as with Mark Twain, such reports of its demise were premature. (The Plan of Reorganization formally filed by Manville in November 1983 was not dead either. It just was a sleeping dog, never having been brought to a vote.)

Judge Lifland did not sanction Manville nor did he appoint a trustee, because it appeared to him that "progress" had been made. To Lifland, the negotiations were in a "delicate" stage, and he could "almost see the light of day." Perhaps he was wearing rose-colored glasses. It would be several more years before the Manville bankruptcy would play itself out.

Meanwhile, people suffered through every breath, lost their lungs, and died, unable to achieve any compensation from Manville. That deprivation caused enormous hardship across the country because of Manville's pivotal place in the industry. As the biggest producer, Manville had the most employees exposed to asbestos. As the major national distributor, it caused injuries in almost every locale. Even though many health claimants had come into contact with asbestos from multiple manufacturers and had lawsuits against other asbestos producers in addition to their claims against Manville, the other companies refused to pay in settlements what they considered to be Manville's share of liability, which could be substantial. Leon Silverman briefly considered asking that some interim payments be made to health claimants during the bankruptcy, but the logistics seemed too daunting to him.

During the late summer and fall of 1985, Leon Silverman and a cadre of lawyers from his office slogged through a round robin of negotiations. The parties were beginning to peek out from their entrenched positions and to consider making concessions to the mild-mannered man who was nonjudgmental and eminently practical, caring not who was right or what the legalities were but rather only how a consensual plan of reorganization could be fashioned. Not only was Mr. Silverman a natural mediator and conciliator, but he also carried an air of inevitability which permeated the discussions. After all, he did carry the judge's imprimatur. He was a man on a mission, and he gave every appearance of knowing how to get it done.

The positions of the Manville management and the creditors began to drift together. Although John McKinney remained adamant in his view that the whole shootin' match was caused by the greediness and unreasonableness of the plaintiffs' attorneys, Manville's other officers and directors began to concede that the company was going to have to pay big money in order to emerge from Chapter 11 and get on with its corporate life. The company firmed up its commitment by agreeing to provide a $1.65 billion bond as security for its promised yearly payments of $75 million. Silverman's settlement numbers were so large that his plan began to receive favorable reviews from many on the Asbestos Health Claimants Committee. The committee pressed for a substantial majority of Manville stock to be provided to the trust, and neither Silverman nor the Manville negotiating team seemed inclined to quibble about it. The bank and trade creditors and the preferred shareholders had a bit of leverage that they were exercising, and it would take stock sweeteners to bring them into line later, but they were not a major problem.

Not everyone was happy with the drift. The representatives of the holders of common shares on the Equity Holders' Committee viewed the situation with alarm, as each succeeding compromise was sweetened with a portion of common stock. The common shareholders watched as the 50 percent of the common stock to be given to the trust ballooned to two-thirds, and then to 80 percent, a devastating dilution of the shareholders' position if approved. The commercial creditors continued to nibble at the remaining common shareholders' holdings in negotiations; and when the preferred shareholders began to talk about dipping into that pool as the price for their consent to a plan, the Equity Holders' Committee broke up in recriminations. It was obvious that Manville's management had lost the will to represent the interests of the common shareholders.

The common shareholders decided to exercise one of the basic rights of our capitalistic system: they called a shareholders' meeting. Although the bankruptcy laws are silent on the subject, the management of Manville had suspended all shareholder meetings during the course of the Chapter 11 case, thus denying the shareholders of the corporation the exercise of economic democracy for more than three years. To the shareholders, they had every right to name directors who would represent their wishes as the owners of the company. That right was inalienable, was it not? It could not be snatched away even in the Through-the-Looking-Glass world of bankruptcy, could it? A lawsuit was filed in Delaware, the state from which Manville had received its corporate charter. The complaint asked that the corporation be ordered to hold a shareholders' meeting for the purpose of electing directors.

The Manville management reacted as if barbarians had surrounded the palace. A motion immediately was filed before Bankruptcy Judge Lifland asking that the shareholders be enjoined from proceeding witth their lawsuit. In the motion the attorneys for the corporation ascribed evil motives to the shareholders. The shareholders were using an *illegitimate method* to influence the company and thus to *force* themselves into the discussions from which they had been excluded. Their interest was *narrow* and not in the best interests of everyone. Insofar as shareholders had bought into the company after the commencement of the bankruptcy, they were mere *speculators*, not entitled to the time of day from the other parties to the case. The case had seen real *progress*. The negotiations were in the *most delicate state*. If the shareholders were allowed to hold such a meeting, *chaos would result*, the plan negotiations would suffer a blow from which they could not recover, and Manville would be *liquidated*. The creditors and Silverman, not relishing the prospect of another interest group becoming militant, eagerly subscribed to the parade of horrors and weighed in on Manville's side. The negotiating patterns of the major interests having been established over the course of several years, no one wanted to upset the relationships by admitting interlopers.

Of course, the position of the Manville management, as forwarded by the corporation's attorneys, was entirely self-serving. Management had not called a shareholders' meeting during the bankruptcy because management had feared that the shareholders might take umbrage at the mess that it had gotten the company into. The officials of Manville had feared all along that they might get the boot, and the status of the negotiations only increased that possibility. The management would fight against a shareholders' meeting for precisely the same reason that the shareholders wanted it: the shareholders would end up with management that they wanted.

In a way, Leon Silverman's opposition to a shareholders' meeting also was self-serving. He had worked himself into control of the case, and he was not about to let it get out of his hands. Needless to say, he had the support of Judge Lifland.

As with the issues surrounding the rights of future creditors, once more the immovable objects that are the foundations of American jurisprudence met the irresistible force that is a megacorporate bankruptcy.

Once more the needs of Manville's reorganization clashed with settled nonbankruptcy law, to the effect that the officers and directors of a corporation are beholden to the shareholders first and foremost. The 1978 changes in the bankruptcy law had left a loophole, and Manville went charging through. The conflict must be seen in a historical context.

From the Great Depression and until the creation of the Bankruptcy Code, different chapters of the Bankruptcy Act governed companies in which the owners were the directors, officers, and managers, and those "public" corporations whose stock largely was owned by passive investors. It was assumed that the interests of the "mom and pop" businesses and their owners coincided, and so as a rule no trustee was named in the ordinary Chapter XI case. However, as a result of a crusading Securities and Exchange Commission commissioner, William O. Douglas, who later would have much more to say about the direction of American law, public corporations organizing under Chapter X would see trustees appointed in every case. The express purpose of replacing management's control of the corporation was to protect shareholders from the abuses by corporate insiders and bankers that were rampant at the time. The trustee supervised operations; investigated the previous management for fraud and mismanagement, and reported his findings to the court, shareholders, and creditors; and also formulated a Plan of Reorganization. Chapter X was not too popular with the captains of industry.

Those differentiations between owner-managed and public corporations disappeared in the legislative maneuverings that resulted in the Bankruptcy Code. The SEC had proposed that trustees be appointed in cases involving $1 million or more in debt and three hundred or more shareholders, and the Senate draft of the bill contained such a provision. However, the House's view, that it was more important to stimulate reorganizations by maintaining the "debtor in possession" unless fraud or gross mismanagement was first proved, prevailed, and bankruptcy became a much kinder and gentler place for large corporations. In the 1980s, under Reagan administration policies, the SEC would withdraw from even monitoring megabankruptcies.

The conflict in bankruptcy between the shareholders and the management of a company arises because the Bankruptcy Code forces management to have divided loyalties. Outside of bankruptcy, management's duty to act in the best interests of the corporations is coextensive with its duty to act in the shareholders' best interests.

However, a Chapter 11 company acting as a "debtor in possession" acquires a bankruptcy duty to act for the best interests of the creditors in addition to its corporate law duty to represent the shareholders' interests. In a Chapter 11 case of a "public" company where reorganization may be accomplished by the issuance of a good deal of stock to creditors in partial or full payment of their claims, in effect management sells the corporation's shareholders down the river. That was the case in Manville.

Rather than fight the shareholders' suit in the Delaware state court, Manville dashed into Judge Lifland's court seeking an injunction against the suit. Consequently, the locus of the dispute was shifted into a courtroom highly favorable to Manville. By that move, the deck was stacked against the shareholders.

Judge Lifland had a problem. In two other bankruptcy cases, shareholders had been successful in forcing corporate meetings. In the Lionel bankruptcy, the judge had allowed the matter to be decided in state court under state corporate law considerations, and that court had ordered the corporation to call such a meeting. In the Saxon case, the state court judge also had ordered a formal shareholders' meeting, observing that the right of shareholder governance was "clear" and "virtually absolute." In both cases, increased shareholder leverage did not scuttle reorganizations. The shareholders simply got a little bigger piece of the pie and then aided the passage of a Plan of Reorganization. Judge Lifland would have to make an end run around the corporate law in order to keep his man in total control of the Manville reorganization.

In his opinion granting Manville an injunction against shareholder action, Judge Lifland crafted his loophole. To the judge, while under corporate law the shareholders' right to elect directors was very strong, that right could be overridden by bankruptcy considerations. If a Chapter 11 case shows great progress towards a potentially successful Plan of Reorganization, and it is likely that new directors elected by the shareholders will reverse the process, they will be enjoined. To Judge Lifland, it was improper for shareholders to use their right to elect directors as leverage in plan negotiations. In other words, shareholders in bankruptcy, being the lowest interest on the bankruptcy totem pole, had no right to a management that would reflect their views.

Judge Lifland had gone way out on a limb to keep Leon Silverman in control, and the Second Circuit Court of Appeals would not follow him. Following more traditional concepts, the appellate court ruled that shareholder rights ceased only if there was a "clear abuse" of them. Having recognized that standard, the court was rather hard pressed to come up with examples of illegal abuse. Merely utilizing a shareholders' meeting to acquire additional bargaining power in a bankruptcy was *not* clear abuse. Using an election of directors to secure a board that would follow shareholder wishes was *not* clear abuse. If shareholder action resulted in delaying the promulgation of a Plan of Reorganization, that was *not* clear abuse. To the appellate court, only substantial evidence that shareholder action would cause "irreparable harm" to a reorganization of a company—virtually resulting in corporate suicide—would allow for a ruling of "clear abuse." The appellate court sent the case back to Judge Lifland to conduct a hearing to determine if the facts warranted such a finding.

Judge Lifland was not a fumbler. He knew how to take that ball and run with it. He duly held a lengthy hearing, during which Manville executives provided some rather nebulous and self-serving testimony, for example that of Executive Vice-President and Director G. Earl Parker (who is an attorney by training):

> I think also further exacerbating the situation would be the necessary delay and confusion and expense and prolonging this proceeding even beyond the four years that we have engaged here. I think all of those things would have a disastrous and probably fatal effect on the reorganization.

That hardly seems like the sort of testimony that could establish "clear abuse" as defined by the appellate court, but Judge Lifland thought it powerful enough to cite it in his written opinion. Leon Silverman argued that horrible things would happen to the wonderful progress of the case if the shareholders rose up and smote the Manville management. After due deliberation, Judge Lifland agreed, simply fitting his first ruling on the issue to the standards enunciated by the Second Circuit. His opinion was replete with references to the sin of shareholder democracy that was threatened, summing it up with appropriate bombast:

> Thus, in light of all the evidence before it, the court can only

conclude that it has always been and remains the *in terrorem* intent of the [shareholders' group] to call a shareholders meeting, *with a full awareness of the devastating consequences to the fabric of the reorganization,* in order to elect a new Board of Directors *who will withdraw or substantially modify the plan of reorganization.* [Italics in original.]

Further venal sins included the possibilities that shareholder action might destroy the "fragile consensus" of the other parties; might result in the company ending its "exclusive period" so that the shareholders could propose their own plan (horrors!); or might result in a motion for liquidation. According to the judge, another fatal flaw of shareholder action was that it would bring down the wrath of Leon Silverman, who threatened to ask for a trustee if the shareholders changed management.

Through Judge Lifland's opinion, in effect it became illegal to criticize Leon Silverman's plan for Manville. Further, the appeals/hearings process had taken well more than a year, and the case had passed by the shareholders' action. Lifland's ruling was issued in October 1986, but the Silverman plan had been formally filed earlier in the year. The shareholders never caught up to the action after Lifland's ruling.

Whether the shareholders' attempted end run had an effect on Manville's management is hard to say, but in July 1986, Manville announced that John McKinney would be retiring as chairman and chief executive officer. George C. Dillon, an "outside" director and formerly the chairman of Butler Manufacturing Company, a $500-million-a-year prefab building company, would step up to the chairman's position. Dillon was an experienced hand and could be expected to provide solid leadership during the firm's emergence from Chapter 11. The new chief executive would be W. Thomas Stephens, the chief financial officer since 1984, when he came to Manville in the Olinkraft acquisition. Stephens represented a breath of fresh air in the smoky negotiating rooms, displaying more flexibility and a stronger desire to get out of bankruptcy than had McKinney. Coming from the forest products division, he was not associated with the asbestos operations. Also, he projected a youthful, squeaky-clean image that Manville sorely needed. For one thing, he was named one of *Fortune* magazine's "25 Most Fascinating Business People" for 1988. (Judging from the number of times he was featured in business magazines after he was elevated, Manville's public relations department must have been working overtime.)

The changing of the guard had proceeded in typical Manville bankruptcy fashion as developed and perfected by the Silverman-Lifland tag team. Having had a big part in the disenfranchising of the Manville common stockholders, Silverman then exercised a heavy hand in the choosing of the successors to McKinney and in forcing out of the company another high officer because Silverman felt that he was associated too closely with the "old" Manville. When Manville objected in court to outside influence in its selection of corporate officers, Judge Lifland gave the company forty-eight hours to, basically, knuckle under. Stanley Levy of New York City, a nationally prominent plaintiffs' lawyer in the field of toxic torts and the chairman of the Asbestos Health Claimants Committee, was named as a director of the company, to help make sure that the "new" Manville would be a "good" Manville. With no legal right in choosing officers of the company, Silverman had managed to exercise a virtual veto power in the process. Once again, Silverman had wielded immense power without being cloaked in *de jure* authority or accepting accountability.

Leon Silverman was not a one-issue leader. During the period when the shareholders were litigating up and down the court system for the right to have a corporate meeting, Silverman was tackling the problem of the property damage claims.

Silverman had been advised by the "old" Manville executives that the idea that building owners had claims for the cost of removing asbestos was wholly fatuous, but he felt that the executives were sticking their heads in the sand. Although building owners had not been successful in the first few state court cases, the analysis by Silverman's law firm was that property damage plaintiffs would win a substantial percentage of future cases once they got the hang of it. That prediction later was to prove correct, but at the time, the parties were flying blind as to a reasonable estimate of Manville's liability to property damage claimants. A further problem was that *no* ordinary settlement of property damage claims was possible due to the numbers involved. Since claims had risen to about $80 billion, even a 20 percent settlement—ordinarily a good deal for a defendant in a highly contested case—was too much for the company to pay over any reasonable period of time.

Then a funny thing happened: a group of claimants actually acted in a statesmanlike manner. The property damage claimants, consisting of

hundreds of state and city governments, hospitals, and schools, agreed
to settle their claims for $125 million—.1 percent of the face amount of
their claims—to be administered by an independent trust and claims
facility. The reasons why they did it essentially boiled down to the fact
that they did not want to take (too much) money out of the hands of
the citizens within their districts who had injury claims against Manville. The importance of the settlement to the property damage
claimants was that it established a certain recognition of the validity of
their claims, which, it was hoped, would start the ball rolling in state
court actions. Perhaps for that reason, Manville's G. Earl Parker
termed the settlement "wholly inappropriate" and "excessive." Being a
megacorporation means never having to say "thank you."

Leon Silverman did not particularly care what the Manville officers
thought of the settlement. He liked it a lot, and what he thought
counted. Silverman gleefully recounts how Manville was advised of the
settlement ten minutes before it was to be presented in court,
Silverman's manner becoming that of dictation, not negotiation. When
Manville balked, Judge Lifland began musing about what would happen if a trustee were appointed to replace Manville's management. The
settlement was quickly approved.

Irrespective of Manville's carping, the settlement of the property
damage claims may rank as one of the most important benefits of the
Chapter 11 to the company. If the resolution of the claims did nothing
more than eliminate litigation costs in every state in the land over what
surely is going to amount to Asbestos Litigation—Part II for the asbestos producers, its value is great. *The property damage settlement has
given Manville a benefit far greater than the asbestos producers outside of bankruptcy are likely to achieve.*

During 1986, the segments of a plan were thrashed out. Silverman
proposed that Manville pay to a health claimants' trust $150 million in
cash and receivables; a $50 million note payable in the fourth year
after the approval of the plan; $5 million as a cap on all punitive dam-
age claims; $75 million per year starting in the fifth year after
effectuation of the plan, secured by a $1.65 billion bond; 20 percent of
Manville's annual profits in the event that additional cash was needed
to pay claims; and 7.2 million shares of preferred convertible stock, if
necessary to pay claims. The biggest portion of initial funding, an
estimated $615 million that later would turn out to be more than $700
million, would come not from Manville but from likely settlements

regarding insurance coverage. Lenders and suppliers would be paid about one-half of their claims upon confirmation of the Plan of Reorganization, and the rest over four years. Their claims for interest in the amount of $200 million were paid with eleven million shares of stock, warrants to purchase another seven million shares of additional stock, and seventeen-year bonds paying a total of $170 million in installments. Preferred shareholders received a promise of dividends and ten million shares of common stock. Property damage claimants would get $125 million.

As a result of the rather free issuance of Manville common stock to creditors to meet their final settlement demands, the common stock that had been outstanding at the time the bankruptcy was filed was diluted 98 percent. The shareholders were not consulted on the final form of the plan or on the extent of their sacrifice for the good of the company.

While a majority of the health claimants' committee felt that they had gone about as far as they could go in the context of the case, a minority opposed the plan. They felt that the plan was too vague about how health claims would be handled by the trust. Also, many felt that Manville had grossly underestimated the number and amount of claims that would be filed through the end of the century, and that therefore the trust would go broke quite quickly. A very active member, Aaron H. Simon of Los Angeles, resigned from the committee in disgust at the relatively small amount of its assets Manville would be contributing.

Simon wrote to committee members, detailing his calculations. To Simon, the entire settlement package had a "present value" of $1.4 billion, of which almost half came from Manville's insurance companies. Through the kindness of Uncle Sam, the settlement would generate a $100 million tax refund and $750 million to $900 million of loss carryforwards that could shelter future profits from taxation. Manville's obligation of future contributions to the trust would be deductible as business expenses in the year made. By Simon's calculations, Manville's actual cost amounted to $250 million, with the first dollar of that coming due no earlier than the fifth year after confirmation of the plan. To Simon, the definition of "profits" that had been agreed upon grossly understated Manville's actual operating profits, and so the promised 20 percent really worked out to 5 percent. By Mr. Simon's analysis, it was a heck of a good settlement for Manville.

A study commissioned by the Asbestos Victims of America

determined that the creditors would do better if Manville were liquidated, producing $1.3 billion in "present value." The report was
roundly ignored by the major players in the case.

The creditor interests approved the plan. Clearly, neither the health
claimants' committee nor the existing claimants themselves played
"Simon says" or read the AVA study, because more than 90 percent of
the health claimants voted to approve the plan. (The health claimants'
committee was permitted to "piggyback" its recommendation to the
health claimants that they vote "yes" into the packet of voting papers
sent out under the authority of the clerk of the Bankruptcy Court.
Almost no one saw or heard of the details of Simon's calculations.) All
other voting classes approved the plan except for the group of common
shareholders. Judge Lifland utilized powers granted by the Bankruptcy
Code to find that the stockholders were treated fairly under the circumstances of the company's assets and liabilities, and so their disapproval could be disregarded.

The Bankruptcy Code required Judge Lifland to review the Plan of
Reorganization, make sure all bankruptcy rules were followed, and
determine that the projections made to justify future payments were
correct. Needless to say, the good judge had no problem with the plan.
After all, he was its spiritual creator. Some of the required findings
necessitated a legerdemain of the type at which Lifland had become an
expert. He found Manville to be insolvent and therefore a legitimate
candidate for reorganization, in spite of the fact that no one knew
exactly how much the claims against the company totaled. Because the
health trust would hold a substantial portion of Manville's stock, the
judge found it unnecessary to determine the number and amount of
health claims in order to see if the trust really would have enough
money to pay them all.

Manville's Plan of Reorganization was confirmed on December 22,
1986, and the judge entered concomitant orders barring any suits or
punitive damage claims arising from the use of asbestos from ever
being brought against the Manville Corporation, its related entities, its
present or past officers and directors, or its insurance companies. All
further asbestos health claims were required to be filed with the facility
handling the trusts created through the reorganization.

The "new" Manville emerged from bankruptcy ready to concentrate
on its businesses of forest products, including paper, cartons, and ply-
wood, businesses that had rebounded nicely while Manville was under

court protection; fiberglass products, including home insulation; and some specialty products, such as lighting fixtures and industrial filters. Shortly after the reorganization plan was given final approval, Manville announced that sales for 1986 had been $1.9 billion, providing $91 million in operating profits from ongoing units, up 20 percent from the year before. The lean and mean Manville could easily dominate its industries.

By the deadline in May 1987, six appeals of the controversial aspects of the confirmation of the Plan of Reorganization were on file. Because reversal could have affected the organization or operation of the health claimants' trust, the plan could not be effectuated until the appeals could be completed. The official committee representing the health claimants filed briefs in the appeals supporting the plan and Judge Lifland's related rulings.

Ironically, the reorganization of Manville did not answer many of the nagging issues concerning asbestos health claimants. Leon Silverman's contribution to the matter was to insure that the facility that handled the claims would be independent of Manville's influence and thus would be perceived positively by the health claimants' lawyers. The independent trust that was to administer the claims procedure was given neither guidance nor restraints on its manner of operation, the types of claims that it should recognize, the level of proof that it should require, or the amounts of damages that it should pay for the various types of injuries. Although Silverman insisted that the health claimants be barred from seeking punitive damages outside of the symbolic $5 million fund provided through the reorganization, on the other hand his plan allowed claimants to seek court relief for ordinary damages if they were not happy after going through the administrative claims procedure. Thus, in the final form, the plan did not limit health claimants' remedies to the trust's administrative procedure.

In what is both an outgrowth and a symbol of Silverman's methods, *the bankruptcy never determined the issue of "future claims."* Silverman assiduously avoided doing anything that technically could be called binding the future claimants, even though the effect was the same, and Judge Lifland just as industriously kept any likely "future claimant" or realistic representative, like the asbestos workers' union, from gaining any standing in the case. The judge's confirmation of the Plan of Reorganization was based upon the fiction that the trust would have sufficient funds to pay all asbestos health claims that had or would arise against Manville—however many those were—and so the need to separate the health claims into classes of existing and future claims was obviated. All of the sticky issues of constitutional rights to notice and to be heard involving future claimants were ignored, Silverman's philosophy being that such matters were mere technicalities that were irrelevant because he, in his own wisdom, had acquired for claimants all that could be acquired. Since no one could have done better than Mr. Silverman—according to Mr. Silverman, the human embodiment of economics' Invisible Hand—there was no need to inform potential claimants of the elements of the reorganization plan, trust, or claims facility. Leon Silverman had made a complicated matter simple.

Perhaps more than one hundred thousand people would find out after the confirmation of Manville's reorganization plan that Manville had made them sick. They then would find out that their rights under the personal injury laws had been altered not by Congress or state legislature, but essentially by a very few men who had not been elected by anybody. They would come to find out that Big Business had reached out to strike them down, and Big Bankruptcy had fashioned their rights of recovery, and no one had ever asked them about it.

Of course, the Second Circuit Court of Appeals could have restructured the process. After all, it is the job of an appellate court to be mindful of the larger legal issues and values that sometimes are lost or wrongly compromised in the tumult of lower court battles. However, lawyers know that it also is the (unofficial) job of appellate courts not to get caught themselves by tar babies, and the Manville case was one big, sticky problem after another. Besides, the Chapter 11 case had already proceeded five years by the time argument was heard on the appeals, and any reversal and remand to correct illegalities would have delayed the case even more. Yes, the Second Circuit could have reversed Lifland's rulings. The appellate court judges also could have enjoyed sticking their hands into hornets' nests. They did not do either.

Approval of the Manville reorganization required the Second Circuit to execute the same moves that Leon Silverman and Burton Lifland had choreographed, and it turned out that the appellate panel picked up the dance without missing a step. First, at the urging of the ubiquitous Leon Silverman, it dismissed the appeal of an undeniable future asbestos health claimant on the grounds that only Mr. Silverman represented future claimants. Then it adopted Mr. Silverman's position that *there was nothing for future claimants to appeal because at the time the trust commenced it would have funds to pay claims*. The court recognized that future claimants may challenge the injunction against suing Manville directly at some time in the future if and when the trust ran out of money, although in the same breath it raised the troubling possibility that at that time those claimants might then be barred from advocating any position contrary to that taken by their "Legal Representative" in the Manville bankruptcy. All other actions by Bankruptcy Judge Lifland, including the validity of his finding that the trust funds would be sufficient to effectuate the plan, were affirmed as "not clearly erroneous," the minimal standard for supporting the lower court judge.

In November 1988, Manville's Plan of Reorganization was consummated. The attorneys and accountants involved were paid handsomely. Leon Silverman charged $2.3 million for his work in the bankruptcy case and Judge Lifland awarded him another $2.3 million as a bonus.

Manville was looking every bit the megacorporation. John McKinney had retired from Manville with a $1.3 million (cash) send-off, leaving Tom Stephens to shepherd the company's booming businesses and its $274 million cash kitty above and beyond its cash flow requirements. A number of Manville's banks quickly put together a $220 million line of credit. The company began to exercise its muscle in the forest products industry.

The trust for health claimants kicked off its operations in 1988. Following its mandate to treat claims on a first-in, first-out basis, the trust staff began wading through claims that had been pending at the time the bankruptcy was filed, six years earlier. (Some of those had been backlogged in court for several years prior to that.) It mailed its first settlement checks by Christmas of that year. By October 1989, the trust reported that it was almost out of money. Talk about "a day late and a dollar short!"

The operations of the trust were affected by several pressures. Given the long delay that the claimants had suffered, an effort was made to expedite their claims. Thus although the trust was in operation only part of 1988, it had cranked out twelve thousand settlements before the end of the year. Also, it was felt that the trust had to bend over backwards to be fair in the initial cases, so that claimants' lawyers would perceive the trust as impartial and feel comfortable settling their cases with it. As a result of those factors, initial settlements averaged

$38,000 apiece, instead of the $25,000 each that Manville had predicted. Although the trust held twenty-four million shares of Manville stock as backup, pursuant to restrictions in the reorganization plan, it could not sell them yet to raise additional funds.

The picture for the trust painted at the end of 1989 was not pretty. The trust had about 100,000 cases pending and expected to see a total of 200,000 claims altogether. The huge backlog meant that claims would be on file for many years before being attended to. To preserve assets, claimants already were being asked to accept only 40 percent of their settlements in cash and to accept a payment plan for the rest. At one meeting during 1989, a trust official predicted that someone who filed a claim at that time might not be paid for twenty-five years. The following year the trust confirmed that there would be about a twenty-year delay. That much delay would mean that claimants would exercise their rights to file suit, causing the trust to spend a portion of its funds on court expenses, exposing it to costly judgments (per the injunction, Manville could not be sued), and otherwise negating the reasons for its existence other than to shield Manville from liability. Of course, if the bleak picture were even partially accurate, damages would be paid on claims long after the claimants had died and long after the families had to pay the medical bills and the burial costs.

Although the picture at the end of 1989 was bleak for the trust, the same could not be said of Manville. It announced record earnings for the year.

In the spring of 1990, two judges, Jack Weinstein, a federal district court judge, and Helen Freedman, a New York state court judge, who had joined forces to attempt to handle a group of asbestos court cases, strongly criticized Manville's insulation from liability. Struggling under the load of hundreds of cases arising from a shipyard in Brooklyn, now closed, the judges came to realize that the assets of the non-Manville defendants were inadequate to fund any settlement or judgment. They became frustrated that Manville, the only asbestos producer large enough to contribute significantly to the resolution of the cases, could not be made a party, and that the assets of the Manville trust also were inadequate.

In June 1990, Judges Weinstein and Freedman called for Manville to become a party to the group of cases or to contribute to the payment of any judgments or settlements. The judges ordered Manville and the trust to return to bankruptcy court to find additional funds for the benefit of health claimants. Judge Lifland responded quickly, appointing a high-powered New York attorney to investigate what he called the trust's poor performance. That investigator was none other than Leon Silverman. No investigation of Manville's ability to pay more money was initiated. The trust was ordered to cease making payments while its operations were being reviewed.

Ironically, in the very week that the two judges called for Manville to pick up its share, a medical study was made public that found alarmingly high levels of cancer and lung damage in the wives and children of asbestos workers and in construction workers who do not work directly with asbestos. If the trust is to recognize their claims—and there is nothing in its mandate which suggests that it will do otherwise—a further burden will be placed upon the already inadequate trust funds. Of course, that burden will be felt only by the health claimants, the innocent bystanders to the asbestos industry in America.

In the face of what looks to most people like a debacle, the architect of the program, Leon Silverman, is sanguine. He freely admits that he had anticipated that the trust would run out of money, although he had thought that it would take a few years longer. (No formal projections ever were done.) His position is that he never claimed to have solved the health claimants' problems—that he just got as much money for them as he could. He feels that the funding of $75 million per year plus a percentage of Manville's profits will suffice to pay claimants, although they will have to wait to receive their money. He suggests that perhaps someone will challenge the injunction against Manville sometime in the future and be successful in upsetting the company's "bulletproof" status. He does not indicate what position he will take, as their "Legal Representative," when that litigation commences.

What did the reorganization of Manville accomplish?

With a big boost from Burton Lifland and Leon Silverman, Manville accomplished a great deal. Although its tour of duty in bankruptcy court was longer than it had expected, it managed to shed all health and property claims against it through the payment of, and the promise to pay, sums apparently well within its financial means. No action whatsoever was taken to determine the personal culpabiltiy of any officers of the company for the injury and deaths of thousands of people, it being considered by Leon Silverman too minor and distracting a matter with which to be concerned. Manville achieved a moral victory by greatly limiting the health claimants' punitive damages against the trust. Exempt from all asbestos suits, it is once more a strong and healthy megacorporation, well situated for future profitability. That profitability, as well as that of other companies it may gobble up, will be shielded from income taxation by hundreds of millions of dollars in tax benefits.

What did the health claimants gain from Manville's reorganization? It is hard to say. They did gain a less combative opponent in the trust. The total amount that Manville will contribute to the payment of health claims is more or less established. However, as to the eighteen thousand people with claims against Manville on the day the bankruptcy was filed, having given up six years of time that the bankruptcy took, they then were told that they would have to go through an administrative process and *then* file suit *again* to fully enforce their legal rights. For those who will be making claims in the future, if the amount set aside for health claimants over the years is enough to pay all of their legitimate claims in a timely manner, then they have gained through the provision of an orderly process. If the trust fund proves inadequate and Manville prospers, an injustice will have been done. The situation at this time seems to favor the latter result.

Even with all of the open questions, the Silverman plan has established a powerful precedent. UNR reorganized in Chicago in 1989 after seven years in Chapter 11, under a plan similar in most aspects to the Silverman plan even though there is a big difference between the two companies. UNR is much smaller than Manville, and so its contribution to its trust consisted solely of its own stock. For that act, UNR was able to bind $11 billion in claims to its plan. The stock, worth about $150 million *if* the trust could sell it all, obviously cannot come close to fulfilling a mandate to pay all health claims; and so the underlying rationales for taking away people's legal rights do not exist. (UNR now makes steel tubing, commercial racks, and related products.) Another asbestos company, Pacor Incorporated, which sought bankruptcy protection in July 1986, accomplished a reorganization in late 1989 using the Silverman format. Pacor contributed a scant $10 million to its trust and will contribute at least $50,000 a year out of its profits for the next twenty years, to settle billions in claims. Thus far, only a few other asbestos producers have chosen to escape the unremitting personal injury battles and the growing attacks by property damage claimants by seeking the safe harbor of Chapter 11. What are they waiting for?

There are many things about the Manville Chapter 11 case that are troubling, but the one factor that stands out is the judge's extreme commitment to the goal of reorganizing the megacorporate Chapter 11 debtor. Under that circumstance, anything or anybody that threatens to get in the way is treated as the enemy by the court. The Chapter 11 company knows that it cannot lose. When a judge becomes a litigant, whether through bribery (of which there is no evidence whatsoever in Manville) or through an unwavering desire to help one side, by definition there can be no justice, regardless of the result accomplished. One cannot have a fair chance when his opponent is sitting on the bench to which he must argue.

What is wrong with Judge Lifland appointing a "Legal Representative" of his own creation—or, as is more common, an "examiner" of a Chapter 11 debtor's operations and finances as authorized by the Bankruptcy Code, or a "master" as authorized by civil litigation rules? The answer depends upon how much power that person has. If he or she merely serves the function of independent investigation or acts as an intermediary among parties, justice is aided. The format also helps a judge stay judicial, available to rule on disputes but not drawn into the development of evidence that may be part of litigation. If that person becomes "The Judge's Man (or Lady)," whose function is to do for the judge what the court wishes to do but cannot do directly, the process becomes illegitimate. After all, the appointee has neither a financial interest in the matter nor a right to represent any party who has such an interest. The appointee becomes nothing more than what is known in law as an "officious intermeddler" into other people's rights and affairs.

The Manville bankruptcy case extended the potential for sanctioned abuse built into the system to new limits. The case was driven by Judge Lifland and Leon Silverman acting in tandem. There was no chance whatsoever that an alternate view of the course of the case could prevail. (The higher courts did their parts by turning away from any actual inspection of, or introspection about, what was going on in Judge Lifland's courtroom, in order to avoid harming Manville's reorganization.) The interloper was provided with false papers as "*the* Legal Representative" of the group of future claimants and then raised to the level of a demigod. Silverman followed nothing more than the mandate from the judge to reorganize Manville and his own ego in deciding what was right and what was wrong, secure in the feeling that his superior intelligence, experience, and practicality would produce the best/right result. Maybe he was right and maybe he was wrong, but in this country we are not supposed to let people do such things.

Lest there be any doubt as to the place of Leon Silverman in the Manville case and his own estimation of the result, consider Mr. Silverman's own words, contained in his fee application presented to Judge Lifland:

> The Legal Representative and [his] Counsel were prime participants in every aspect of the analysis, negotiation and drafting which led to the Plan and related documents and disclosure statement. . . . Many of the ultimate documents were originally drafted by [the Legal Representative's] Counsel. The Legal Representative and Counsel sat at the head of the negotiating and drafting table with respect to every document and participated in every negotiation which included singly or collectively every other constituency that was part of the ultimate consensus. . . . The ultimate Plan of Reorganization has recently been referred to as "a work of art, a stunningly magnificent document."

Chapter 12

Robins Becomes a Prisoner of Its Own Device

"Many people denounce crime
in the street, but few examine
crime in the skyscraper."
—Miles W. Lord,
U.S. District Court Judge

A lot of money can be made selling drugs of one kind or another. Street sellers of illegal hard drugs are called pushers, because of the methods they use to addict others to their wares and thus assure themselves of steady demand. Drug companies are never called pushers, even when they pass the boundaries of safety and necessity in order to persuade the public to use their products. Selling drugs can make someone wealthy and widely known, whether in the ghetto or the genteel South.

The Robins family roots in the drug business go deep. In 1866, at a time when many worthless patent medicines were sold by unscrupulous people who moved from town to town to avoid their former customers, Albert Hartley Robins became a registered pharmacist and settled into an apothecary shop in Richmond, Virginia. In 1896, his son Claiborne joined the operations. A second business—A. H. Robins Company— was spun off from the retail business and specialized in selling drugs to physicians. Claiborne died quite young, but his wife Martha continued the wholesale business for twenty-one years until their son E. Claiborne received his degree in pharmacy. It was 1933—in the depths of the Great Depression—and the business had not been particularly successful up to that time. However, a base of customers existed, and E. Claiborne's hard work started the sales growing, to $100,000 in 1942 and $1 million in 1948.

As the drug industry grew in the United States, the Robins family prospered with it. E. Claiborne developed a number of drugs and often took to the road to personally introduce them to doctors. His policy was to develop drugs to deal with common problems arising from everyday living, particularly in the fields of gastrointestinal and digestive upsets, coughs, colds, and arthritis. Using aggressive traveling salesmen and choosing products for their sales potential, A. H. Robins Company charged ahead through the 1950s, hitting $50 million in annual sales in 1963. During the 1960s, Robins expanded beyond its base of medicines by buying several other product lines, and it chose wisely. Many of Robins's products did very well, and several became household words: Chap Stick, Robitussin cough syrups, and Sergeant's products for pets. To E. Claiborne Robins, free enterprise was the touchstone and federal regulation an anathema. Hard work had made the Richmond Robinses very rich—about $150 million net worth—and philanthropy would show their humbleness in the face of it.

Although its drug products were showing no signs of flagging, the company was constantly on the lookout for new products. To fail to develop and change in the drug industry is to fall behind. In particular, Robins wanted to get into the rapidly growing market for intrauterine devices for contraception, which had doubled in the four years since 1966. It was not prepared to undertake the arduous and expensive task of developing a proprietary IUD, but it would be receptive to an opportunity to buy into a product that had already been developed. E. Claiborne Robins, Sr., was getting near retirement, but he wanted to bring A. H. Robins Company into that field as a crowning achievement to an impressive career. The new IUD would be a money machine already in place when Claiborne, Jr., fresh out of business school, reached the top of the corporate ladder.

The fact that foreign matter in the uterus prevents pregnancy has been known for thousands of years; however, the problem has been to eliminate the unwanted side effects. Certain materials, copper for example, interact chemically with the body to prevent pregnancy, but that same reaction can introduce toxic chemicals into the body. Also, in nature's scheme, the uterus is to be an antiseptic chamber, especially during pregnancy. Anything that introduces contamination directly, by carrying bacteria on its surface, or indirectly, by providing a pathway for bacteria to enter the uterus, becomes a serious "fifth column" threat to the body's defenses. Infections can result, including pelvic inflammatory disease (PID), which racks the body with pain and can cause serious damage, including infertility.

Even the best contraceptive device or chemical does not thwart nature with complete infallibility. Unlike chemical contraceptives, if the IUD fails to prevent pregnancy, it remains as a foreign substance in the same grotto as the developing fetus. It may later induce a spontaneous abortion by which the body attempts to expel the contaminants (a "septic abortion"), which is life threatening. If an IUD pregnancy goes to term, the baby may be born with one or more congenital defects.

Thus even if a modern intrauterine device for contraception is manufactured to be chemically inert, it can still cause serious physical problems. The insertion of an IUD must be done with great care and skill in order to make sure that it will not cause discomfort or pain or be expelled. A poorly designed IUD can cause perforation of the uterus and may then migrate to the bowels where a blockage is created. Because all modern IUDs have a string that protrudes from the uterus into the vagina, in order to provide evidence that the IUD has not been expelled and to make removal easier, there is a danger of infection if the material allows bacteria to use it as a wick up through the cervical canal.

Assuming valid reasons for avoiding the danger, parental responsibilities, and financial hardship of unwanted pregnancy, and leaving aside religious issues, the benefits of intrauterine contraceptive devices to the peoples of the world are substantial in spite of the potential problems. It avoids the need for daily self-medication of contraceptive pills, an important plus especially in countries where it is likely such a regimen will not be followed. Ideally, the device should be safer than the introduction of chemicals into the body by the "Pill." Properly produced and inserted, the IUD should have a failure rate comparable to that of the Pill, that is, on the order of a few percent.

By the 1960s, the IUD began to look like the contraceptive product of the future. Although silver IUDs developed in the 1930s caused problems and the IUD had gone out of favor, in the late 1950s the Japanese developed a chemically inert IUD made of—what else?!—plastic, which seemed to offer promise. Several variations were developed in the United States, the most well known of which was the Lippes Loop. In 1962, the media introduced the American people to the threat of the world "Population Bomb," created by the explosion of births and the decrease in infant mortality in Third World countries. In the United States, the initial skirmishes of the Sexual Revolution were being fought. Reports began to filter out about the negative effects of high dosages of the early versions of the Pill. When the early field experience with the modern IUD devices was satisfactory, the race was on to tap into the giant worldwide market.

There were a number of peculiarities about the medical testing of the new IUDs. The exact mechanism by which an IUD prevents conception is unknown, and so achieving satisfactory results is a matter of trial-and-error. Testing it upon animals will not produce results which can be applied reliably to a woman. Therefore, there is a need to, in effect, experiment upon women by placing this foreign object into their bodies to see what happens; yet because the IUD is a "device" and not a "drug," it was outside the jurisdiction of the Food and Drug Administration. Being outside FDA purview meant a company bringing a new IUD onto the market would not have to prove that the device was safe or that it was effective. (To a large extent due to Robins, the jurisdiction of the FDA would be extended to medical devices in 1976.)

The development of a type of IUD by Dr. Hugh J. Davis illustrates the peculiarities and pitfalls of the process.

In 1964, Dr. Davis was an associate professor of obstetrics and gynecology at Johns Hopkins University School of Medicine, although he was not certified by the American College of Obstetrics and Gynecology. Davis literally had an inventive mind: he had already developed several new medical devices and viewed deficiencies of medicine's tools as challenges for innovation. He was highly motivated to develop a new IUD because he wanted to make his fortune as an inventor, and the common feeling in the medical community was that the patent holder of a successful IUD would become very wealthy very quickly. He was well situated, with time to do research and access to Johns Hopkins University's clinic for the poor of Baltimore.

Over the course of the next several years, Davis created IUDs in various forms, which he tested on the clinic's patients. He patented a form of an IUD and sold it to a drug company; however, the design did not achieve satisfactory results, and it was never marketed. In 1967, he helped a create a new design, a shield holding a curled wire.

Or did he? There are a number of murky aspects concerning the early development of the shield, and Dr. Davis has attempted to dissociate himself from it. Hugh Davis has insisted that the shield was the invention of Irwin Lerner, an electrical engineer who was a friend of his, and offers as proof that the patent was taken out in Lerner's name. Strong circumstantial evidence suggests otherwise. It seems unlikely that the engineer developed the contraceptive device without the doctor's active participation. Further, Davis had a 35 percent interest in the corporation formed to hold the patent, with rights to become the majority owner in the event of Lerner's death. Leaving Davis's name off the patent also would avoid any claims to the patent by either the drug company to which he had transferred his prior IUD patent or Johns Hopkins University. (Later those institutions would be quite happy that they had not made any such claims.)

Even so simple a matter as the naming of the product is clouded in denial. It was named the Dalkon Shield, seemingly in honor of Davis and his friends and business partners Irwin Lerner and Robert Cohn, an attorney. However, that has been denied by the principals. The shareholders of the Dalkon Corporation, formed to market the shield, were Davis, Lerner, and Cohn.

Perhaps the mystery had something to do with the early marketing of the Dalkon Shield. Just as the development process was being completed, the dangers of the Pill were coming to the forefront of the public's consciousness. Davis introduced himself into the public debate under the guise of being an objective researcher in the field, and while playing on the public's fears about the safety of contraceptive pills, he touted the Dalkon Shield as a much preferable alternative. In 1970, Dr. Davis was handed two opportunities that would serve to herald the Dalkon Shield.

In January 1970, Dr. Davis testified before a committee of Congress investigating the safety of the Pill. He roundly condemned nearly everything and everybody associated with it, saying, "I think it can be said fairly that the widespread use of oral contraceptives [that] has developed in the United States in the past ten years, has given rise to health hazards on a scale previously unknown to medicine."

The testimony is eerie in retrospect, given Davis's hand in a product that would create a whole new scale of disaster, dwarfing the problems with oral contraceptives. Davis went on to score the drug companies for selling oral contraceptives before, he alleged, they had been fully tested. He then launched into the virtues of IUDs, claiming (erroneously) that some could provide 99 percent protection from pregnancy. Without mentioning the Dalkon Shield, he spoke of an IUD that had been used at the Johns Hopkins clinic quite effectively. He also spoke of a recent advancement, the development of smaller IUDs for women who had smaller uteruses because they had never borne children. The Dalkon Corporation was the only manufacturer of this "nullip" IUD.

Hugh Davis's marketing strategy almost came unglued at the conclusion of his remarks. One of the counsel to the committee asked Davis about reports that he had recently patented an IUD. In an instant, Davis deftly dragged a red herring across the trail, directing the discussion to his *prior* patent and honestly informing the committee that the drug company now owned one half and that he had assigned all the rights in his half to Johns Hopkins. No mention was made by Davis of the Dalkon Shield or the fact that he would receive compensation as an officer of Dalkon Corporation. However, the committee's attorney persisted, asking, "Then you have no particular commercial interest in any of the intrauterine devices?" Davis replied, "That is correct."

The hearings were just the sort of thing on which the media feeds. On its front page, *The New York Times* repeated Davis's charge that oral contraceptives were still "experimental." Magazines picked up the story, with *Time* running a picture of Dr. Davis along with its two-page article. Davis was asked to give a number of interviews and became a source for the media on contraceptive matters. Thanks to Davis, the public saw nothing but a steady stream of puffery about the Dalkon Shield.

The second opportunity to get the bandwagon moving followed quickly on the heels of Dr. Davis' appearance before Congress. In February 1970, the *American Journal of Obstetrics and Gynecology* published an article by Dr. Davis that reported his twelve-month study in summary form. The journal was a highly regarded bible of that specialty (notwithstanding that it had no policy of rigorous review of the claims made in its articles), and the article allowed Davis directly to address doctors across the country who specialized in OB-GYN. Davis extolled the Dalkon Shield as a new generation of IUD that had a pregnancy rate of only 1.1 percent, that is, less than half of that for oral contraceptives. Nowhere in the article did Davis mention his affiliation with the Dalkon Shield.

That statistic—a 1.1 percent failure rate—shined like a beacon to those seeking a safe and effective means of contraception. As with other IUDs, the Dalkon Shield would avoid the dangers of adding hormones to women's bodies. In addition, the Dalkon Shield apparently had achieved a level of protection from pregnancy that had eluded the other IUDs on the market, thus promising greater efficacy than the Pill. The 1.1 percent figure would propel the Dalkon Shield to millions in sales over the course of several years. However, it was untrue.

The problem was that Dr. Davis's study did not really provide reliable proof of the efficacy of the Dalkon Shield. Although the period of his study was one year, the average amount of time that a subject wore the shield was five and a half months, far too short a period to determine its contraceptive abilities. Davis's article was submitted about a week after the study ended, suggesting not only predetermination but perhaps intent to exclude from the statistics women who were pregnant at the close of the study but who would not learn of it until later. (When those figures were inserted into Davis's figures, the pregnancy rate was increased to more than 3 percent, a percentage that rendered the Dalkon Shield an unexceptional alternative method of contraception at best.) The high drop-out rate of the clinic's patients, with no follow-up on those women, further blurred the figures. To cap it off, Davis had recommended to his study subjects that they also use a contraceptive foam during the time that they were likely to be ovulating—a fact that Davis neglected to mention when tossing about the 1.1 percent pregnancy-rate statistic that was the crowning achievement of his study.

Davis and Lerner soon muddied the picture even further by continuing to tinker with the Dalkon Shield after the conclusion of Davis's study. In fact, just about every element of the shield was altered. The plastic mix was changed to make the shield more flexible, and the shield was made thinner, in order to aid in removal. Powdered copper was added to aid in the molding process and to provide added strength. Copper sulfate also was added to the plastic mix, in the hope that it would render the Dalkon Shield more visible to X-rays.

Unfortunately, one thing that Davis and Lerner did not change was the configuration of the string, or "tail," that was attached to every

Dalkon Shield. It was basic IUD technology that the string be a monofilament, that is, a solid piece. Also, it could not be made of nylon, which tended to deteriorate inside the body. The Dalkon Shield's string would have to be strong, solid, and carefully produced and attached. It was none of those things.

A nonstandard IUD tail was necessitated by the shape of the Dalkon Shield. The same configuration of barbs that reduced the chances of accidental expulsion made the shield extremely difficult to voluntarily remove. Lerner and Davis hoped to solve the problem by turning to a suture material called Supramid manufactured in Germany. It had good tensile strength being used primarily in the repair of horses' leg tendons. It achieved that strength by combining hundreds of strands inside an outer sheath of nylon.

The choice of Supramid for the tail is one of those puzzling aspects of the Dalkon Shield saga. Davis knew full well that the multifilament presented a risk of wicking, but he did little to verify its safety. Lerner did a simple visual test, in which he determined that a knot would prevent colored water from climbing up a Supramid string dangled in it. From that, he was satisfied that the string would not "wick" bacteria into the uterus. There were no flexibility tests to see if the string would crack, no statistically valid laboratory tests of wicking, and no field inspections of the condition of strings attached to shields in women. In fact, neither Davis, Lerner, nor A. H. Robins Company later would *ever* engage the string in any other tests. They would rue that fact, as would hundreds of thousands of women.

The Dalkon Shield, haphazardly designed, improved through mere tinkering, and inadequately tested, was ready to be marketed as "superior," "advanced," and "scientifically engineered."

As Dr. Davis earlier had done with his first form of IUD, his Dalkon Corporation desired to sell or license the Dalkon Shield patent to a major drug company with the marketing expertise, sales network, and capital to assure wide distribution. Although Dalkon Corporation would lose the opportunity to reap the full profits from the sales of the shield in the future (it had sold twenty-six thousand even with no marketing staff), the royalties alone from a larger company's efforts could make Dr. Davis and his partners rich with very little further effort. During early 1970, the company engaged in negotiations with the Upjohn Company.

While Dalkon Corporation was searching for a suitor, it retained a small-town doctor, Thad Earl, to act as medical director, in exchange for 7.5 percent of the stock in Dalkon Corporation. Earl had sought out Davis and Lerner after reading about Davis's claims about the Dalkon Shield's efficacy. What Earl lacked in sophistication and formal credentials, he made up for in enthusiasm. Earl's job was to travel to trade shows and otherwise make doctors aware of the Dalkon Shield, and also to search for a buyer for the Dalkon Shield patent. In reality, Earl was more of a salesman than a true medical director.

In May 1970, the fates brought together the Dalkon Shield and A. H. Robins Company. Thad Earl was manning the Dalkon Shield booth at a medical convention when a salesman for Robins, impressed with the claims for the product, asked him if the rights to it were for sale. When Earl answered in the affirmative, a demonstration was scheduled at his office for Dr. Fred Clark, Robins's medical director, and a doctor who was a consultant to Robins, during which they watched Earl make a few insertions. After that, Earl made a presentation to Robins officials, employing a silent "home movie" of an insertion in his office and advising them that he had no problems whatsoever with the Dalkon Shield in his practice. The top brass at Robins, anxious to enter the IUD field, was hooked. From that point negotiations moved with lightning speed.

The technical people at A. H. Robins Company had some caveats. Dr. Clark had noted the pregnancies listed in Davis's research papers that had been reported only after the close of the twelve-month study. To Clark, the additional experience with the Dalkon Shield translated into a pregnancy rate above 3 percent. Dr. Jack Freund, a vice-president of Robins, noted that the term of the study was too short to come to reliable conclusions. Oscar Klioze, director of pharmaceutical research and analytical services, noted that the Dalkon Corporation had never tested the plastic of the shield to see if it would deteriorate inside the body. Robert Nickless, a project management coordinator, passed on a cautionary warning from Irwin Lerner about the possibility that the multifilament tail might wick. Roy Smith, the Robins salesman who had approached Dr. Earl at the medical convention, had doubts about selling a shield in such a different configuration to that used in Dr. Davis's study. Smith also questioned the inclusion of the copper sulfate, which was not inert inside the body, in the shield's plastic mix without prior testing. The worries of these men were contained in memos to the top Robins officers, who in later lawsuits would be required to explain why the company had so thoroughly ignored them. (The most common explanation: "I never saw it.")

By June 12, 1970, less than a month after Davis's initial contact with the Robins representative, the deal was done: for $750,000 and 10 percent royalties to Dalkon Corporation's shareholders, Robins had the patent rights. Davis, Lerner, and Earl also received consultants' contracts. Dalkon Shields would be manufactured at Robins's Chap Stick plant in Lynchburg, Virginia, for twenty-five cents apiece and would be sold for $4.35. Robins quickly geared up for production.

The speed at which the Dalkon Shield was brought to market by its developers, and at which A. H. Robins bought the rights to it, was astounding considering the nature of the product. The principals were intent on entering the growing, lucrative contraceptive market as soon as possible. As an added incentive, quick introduction of the product would steal the march on threatened federal legislation that would extend FDA jurisdiction to medical devices, which would have the effect of requiring FDA approval for new products such as the Dalkon Shield. Within six months of announcing the purchase of the rights to the Dalkon Shield, Robins's aggressive sales force of more than five hundred was informing doctors of its virtues.

Many questions remained open about the safety and efficacy of the Dalkon Shield even as it was brought to market at the close of 1970. However, there is no evidence that there was any curiosity whatsoever about the scientific basis for Davis's claims at the highest levels of A. H. Robins Company management. Those men simply did not care about such things. Robins did not have an OB-GYN on its staff and did not seek the aid of one. Middle-level executives who questioned the safety or efficacy of the shield were ignored. The last thing that the corporation wanted was to delay matters while further studies were done. The primary considerations were *will it sell* and *how fast can it be produced?* Robins had failed to snap up the Lippes Loop when it had been offered, and the Robins family was determined not to make the same mistake again. Instead, they made different, far more serious, mistakes.

The officers of Robins also were indifferent to the manufacturing process of the Dalkon Shield beyond the question of how to make it as cheaply as possible. That attitude turned the concept of quality control on its head. Production commenced at Robins's Chap Stick plant in Lynchburg before any quality-control procedures were in place, and, in fact, before Wayne Crowder, Chap Stick's quality-control supervisor, was informed! The assembly procedure magnified the Supramid string's potential for wicking and virtually guaranteed that the tail of the Dalkon Shield would cause bacterial infection. The tails were *hand tied* to the shield and *hand knotted* at the end—a process more akin to making fishing lures and flies than medical devices—which mashed and cracked a significant percentage of the somewhat brittle Supramid strings. When Crowder rejected several thousand strings because the protective outer sheath had been damaged in assembly, he was over-ruled by Robins's management, and the production department was directed by the top echelon of executives *not* to reject for shipment shields with mashed tails. Thus a significant percentage of Dalkon Shields were damaged and dangerous at the moment they left the factory.

In a perverse way, the Robins officials were right when they concluded that damaged strings did not matter. Cutting the string to size created openings at both ends. The knot at the lower end of the string, and to some extent the knot that tied the string to the shield, were the only barriers to bacteria introduced into the vagina climbing through the inside of the string into the uterus. If that defense mechanism were insufficient to stop bacteria, even an undamaged string would cause infection inside the uterus. If the Supramid wicked when knotted, it need not be damaged to become a pathway for disease. Wayne Crowder could not get that potential hazard out of his mind, even though the assembly process for the Dalkon Shield had been established and the packaged product was heading out the door.

Although Lerner had previously done an informal test that had not produced wicking, Crowder conducted his own experiment on the wicking potential of the Supramid string. He found that when left standing in a glass of water for several days, the string would allow water to move through and past the knot barrier and up to the top end. Apparently Irwin Lerner had not allowed sufficient time for wicking in his experiment. If the Supramid string would wick water, it had the potential of providing a pathway for bacteria also.

Crowder attempted to inform the company of the problem. He expressed his concern to his immediate superior, Julian Ross. Ross berated Crowder for investigating something that was not supposed to be his concern. When Crowder persisted, saying that he could not let the issue pass in good conscience, Ross reminded him that his conscience did not pay his salary and that if he valued his job, he would do only what he was told. When Crowder could not interest the president of Chap Stick, Daniel French, in the hazard, he wrote a memo directed to Robins's officers detailing his wicking experiment and suggesting that the ends of the string be heat-sealed. When Ross found out about the memo, he again threatened Crowder with his job. It is not known which officials of Robins saw the memo.

Unbeknownst to Crowder, his warning to Daniel French did have some effect. It began to gnaw at his mind, too. In August 1981, French picked up the telephone and called Dr. Fred Clark, Robins's medical director, to express his fears about the wicking problem. Rather than give deference to the Chap Stick president, Clark apparently told French to mind his own business, which, as it applied to the Dalkon Shield, was to keep the shield coming off the assembly line as cheaply as possible. The dressing down was so complete that French felt compelled to cover himself using a form of classic corporate revisionist history, the follow-up memo. He wrote to Clark: "As I indicated in our telephone conversation, it is not the intention of the Chap Stick Company to attempt any unauthorized improvements in the Dalkon Shield. My interest in the Dalkon Shield is to produce it at the lowest possible price and, therefore, increase Robins's gross profit level."

As French was preparing that bit of fealty, he no doubt felt very sorry that he had stuck his neck out so far for Crowder, a man now in fear for his job. One by one, and in a number of ways, the underlings in the Robins organization were getting the message: time is of the essence, do not stand in the way, get with the program, or get gone. A. H. Robins was going to run with the Dalkon Shield as fast and as far as it could, philosophical, ethical, and engineering matters be damned.

Consequently, the Supramid strings were double trouble. Under the best of circumstances, they would wick bacteria into the uterus. If and when they were damaged by Robins's assembly process, they would be even more hazardous to the wearer. To be dangerous, the Dalkon Shield would not have to be inserted improperly nor would the string have to break or deteriorate in the body, although those things would happen, also. Robins was selling disease and death to the unsuspecting multitudes, in a plastic bag.

Having spent the minimal amount of initiative, time, and money in investigating what one judge later would refer to as a "time bomb" within women, Robins proceeded to throw its energies and expense budget into selling it. Robins marketed the hell out of the Dalkon Shield, and Robins knew how to market! In selling the Dalkon Shield, A. H. Robins Company would build an image of a product of tomorrow come today.

Using the statistics generated by Davis's study, the Dalkon Shield was touted as the new, improved generation of IUDs that offered protection from pregnancy superior to *any* other contraceptive. A comparison with other IUDs was printed, in which the Dalkon Shield, unencumbered by statistics developed by independent testing, was shown to have lower pregnancy rates than other brands. Robins disseminated eighty thousand copies of Davis's journal article as well as 200,000 copies of an article by him in *Good Housekeeping*. In September 1971, Davis published a book entitled *Intrauterine Devices for Contraception*, in which he—surprise!—extolled the virtues of the Dalkon Shield and repeated the 1.1 percent pregnancy rate statistic that he must have known was false. In none of the publications was Davis's relationship to the Dalkon Shield disclosed.

At first, Robins's truth was the only truth. In all, Robins flooded the market with five million pieces of promotional literature, and most recipients were unable to determine or uninterested in the validity of the studies upon which Robins based its claims. The company turned down a number of requests to fund independent studies due to "a limited research budget." The results of additional research done by Dr. Davis to counter the growing number of complaints were never made public.

Robins directed advertising to the ultimate consumer, the woman who was looking for a long-term contraceptive. Such an aggressive marketing technique had never been done before with a contraceptive, the customary thinking being that information on such a product should be directed to the doctors who would counsel their patients and dispense it. In addition to direct advertising, a number of public relations devices were used to plant in the mass media seemingly unbiased reports that served to promote the shield. When the other IUD makers refused to adopt Robins's marketing slant, a situation was created where those women asking their doctors for an IUD often would mention the Dalkon Shield specifically.

Robins did not neglect the medical profession. In another bold marketing decision that defied custom, the company directed promotional literature not only to OB-GYNs but also to general practitioners, including osteopaths. Part of Robins's sales pitch was that insertion of the shield was exceptionally easy, a boast that would prove to be ludicrous given the extreme pain that would accompany many insertions. Because of that marketing strategy, a wide range of medical practitioners were encouraged to make insertions of the Dalkon Shield into their patients. (When the complaints started coming in, for some time Robins blamed ham-handed doctors. Only much later would the company suggest a painkiller be used during insertion and a general anesthetic for removal.)

There was no doubt about it, the A. H. Robins Company was stocked with marketing geniuses. In 1971, only 12 percent of OB-GYN specialists dispensed the Dalkon Shield, but by 1972, that figure had jumped to 33 percent. Robins was selling shields as fast as the assembly line could put them out. With some truth, a Robins flyer could crow: "Before 1970, IUDs were seldom considered as a contraceptive method of first choice. The Dalkon Shield is changing that." All that was required was a willingness to play fast and loose with the truth and to tell doctors and their patients what they wanted to hear, that the Dalkon Shield was painless, almost infallible . . . and, believe it or not, that it gave great sex! One brochure directed to women extolled: "A recent survey of women using the Dalkon Shield noted a marked improvement in sexual relations. Some of them found it much easier to reach an orgasm than with the other methods of contraception. This is another reason why wearing a Dalkon Shield can be a rewarding experience in your married life." Robins later would advise that the "survey" was an informal poll of clinic patients by Dr. Hugh Davis. (There is no truth to the rumor that the A. H. Robins Company promised that the Dalkon Shield would remove the drudgery of housework.)

Great efforts were made by the A. H. Robins Company to avoid regulation of the Dalkon Shield while encouraging the widest possible usage by women, the "copper story" being an outstanding example. The metal had been added to the plastic mix without any prior testing, in order to give the Dalkon Shield a drug-induced boost as a contraceptive, but the addition also introduced a potentially hazardous dose of a heavy metal into the body. Robins was aware that the FDA had taken jurisdiction over G. D. Searle and Company's "Copper 7" IUD because Searle had claimed additional effectiveness due to a copper additive, and Robins did not wish to get caught in the regulatory net. At a meeting of executives project management coordinator Robert

Nickless advised: "I don't believe we need to go into the many reasons why the copper story can be damaging to us.... I strongly urge we take protective action on this matter." Robins's general sales manager Robert Burke directed all sales personnel, "In view of recent developments regarding the regulatory status of copper-containing intrauterine devices, it is essential that you avoid any suggestion or implication that the copper additives contribute to or enhance the contraceptive effectiveness of the Shield." Accordingly, neither doctors nor consumers were advised of the additive. Rumors of the Dalkon Shield's copper additive were denied to doctors. Having taken defensive measures, Robins was able to avoid the agency's regulatory grasp simply by denying to it that the Dalkon Shield had any drug effect. Although A. H. Robins Company was looking over its collective shoulder at the specter of the FDA, Dr. Hugh Davis, ever the supersalesman in doctor's clothing, had touted the value of the Dalkon Shield's copper additive to the women of America. In his piece in *Good Housekeeping*, he advised readers that the copper would make the shield "virtually 100% effective in preventing pregnancies."

Under Robins's ownership, the Dalkon Shield became a fierce competitor to the established brands. Six months after Robins's official commencement of sales on January 1, 1971, doctors were inserting shields at the rate of sixty-six thousand per month. Propelled by the advertising and publicity blitzkrieg, the shield soon captured one-half of the burgeoning market. By January 1972, more than 800,000 women were wearing it.

Along with the success of Dalkon Shield sales, almost immediately came the complaints. Doctors could not understand why they could not achieve the 1.1 percent pregnancy rate that Dr. Davis had promised. They were having trouble with insertions and finding normal removals to be almost impossible, and women were passing out from the pain that resulted. Bleeding was common from what doctors were referring to increasingly as Robins's "harpoon" or "fishhook." Reports of pelvic inflammation began to circulate in the medical community, and a number of doctors wrote to Robins about such experiences. In response Robins blamed poor insertion and removal techniques, oddly shaped uteruses of their patients, and unclean sex practices. In brochures Robins still claimed "outstanding medical safety" and a pregnancy rate equal to contraceptive pills and admitted only to mild, temporary cramps as a possibility upon insertion. Women were advised that "the insertion procedure is generally tolerated by even the most sensitive person."

When sales flagged in 1972 as doctors learned of wearers' problems with the shield, Robins brought out more marketing artillery. The centerpiece was an eight-page brochure that Robins termed a "progress report," which was placed in major medical journals beginning in November 1972. The Dalkon Shield was presented—falsely—as a new generation of IUD that was scientifically engineered to fit the uterus. The important element of the report was the reference to four studies that seemed to prove Robins's claims for the Dalkon Shield. In effect, Robins was saying to doctors that no matter how bad their own experiences had been with the Dalkon Shield, they could rest assured that statistically the shield was the best choice of contraceptive.

The studies were not accurate and independent, but most doctors reading the glossy ad would not know that. One study was the original by Dr. Davis, with the false 1.1 percent figure. The second was done by none other than Thad Earl. Of course, Davis's and Earl's affiliations with the Dalkon Shield were not disclosed. The third study was done at two California Planned Parenthood clinics, providing an impressive imprimatur to Robins's report. Actually the figures in Robins's report, leading to a bottom line of a quite nice 1.9 percent failure rate, were only preliminary figures provided by the group during the study. Robins failed to print the final figures for the study, containing a 4.3 percent pregnancy rate and an astounding 24.4 percent removal rate for bleeding or other medical reasons, in spite of the fact that the final figures had long been available and an article using them had been printed in the May 1972 issue of the *Family Planning Digest*. The fourth study had been done for Robins by an independent doctor, but earlier in 1972, Lester Preston, Robins's own biostatistician, had circulated a memo analyzing that doctor's work and termed it so flawed that it was useless. (In 1983, Robins would destroy all remaining copies of that study, expressly acknowledging that it was factually erroneous.)

The problem was that no amount of hype could hold back the truth of the performance of the Dalkon Shield. Although Robins steadfastly refused to sponsor any research, beginning in the summer of 1973, results from independent studies began to appear. A British group reported a 4.7 percent pregnancy rate; a Boston hospital reported a 10.1 percent pregnancy rate; and a San Francisco study found a 5.1 percent pregnancy rate and a 26.4 percent rate of removals for bleeding or pain. Research initiated by Robins in response, the results of which were never disclosed to doctors or Robins's sales force, at first determined a 4.1 percent pregnancy rate and a 15.8 percent removal rate, but when unreliable data were removed by Robins in a review, the pregnancy rate jumped to 7.2 percent. (However, in a March 1973 communication to doctors, Robins used incomplete data from its unfinished studies to claim a 2 percent pregnancy rate.)

The string was proving to be a huge problem for the Dalkon Shield wearers, and it was not hard to see why. Due to the nature of the material and Robins's manufacturing process, an independent study of *new* Dalkon Shields found that 9 percent had defective strings. Tests of used strings revealed that infectious bacteria invariably had penetrated the surface and that the amount of bacteria increased like clockwork over time. On strings that had been in place six months, obvious breaks in the protective outer shell were found on 42 percent; of those in place for twenty-four months, 67 percent were so damaged. Once the bacteria reached the uterus, infection was a good possibility.

A turning point for Robins came in the spring of 1973. Up until then Robins's views had dominated the debate concerning the safety and efficacy of the Dalkon Shield. The company had papered doctors' offices with its brochures; had controlled the slant of the print media through ads, Davis's book and articles, and public relations activities; and had reached women directly through advertising. Doctors making piecemeal complaints or warnings did not have the statistics or the confidence to effectively challenge Robins's bland denials. However, tales of some of those negative experiences had reached the halls of Congress. Dr. Davis had effectively used a congressional hearing in 1970 to put the fear of oral contraceptives into the public's collective mindset; in 1973, another congressional hearing would do the same to IUDs in general and the Dalkon Shield in particular.

On May 30, 1973, hearings of the Intergovernmental Relations Subcommittee opened to investigate the safety of medical devices and to explore whether they should be regulated. The panel would look at pacemakers, artificial heart valves, and other such mechanical contrivances, but it would lead off the hearings with testimony about IUDs. It was the sort of action by Congress that Robins had feared and a primary cause of Robins's rush to market with the Dalkon Shield. Although the subcommittee hearings would prove to be insufficient to prod Congress to give jurisdiction over medical devices to the Food

and Drug Administration, the reputation of the Dalkon Shield and the
A. H. Robins Company would be severely tarnished. (It would not be
until 1976 that Congress would move to regulate medical devices, in
the face of the Dalkon Shield tragedy as it by then had unfolded.)

The prime witness on the subject of IUDs was Dr. Russel Thomsen,
a major in the Army Medical Corps. He carried no special credentials
other than the fact that he had complained to FDA Commissioner
Charles Edwards about the Dalkon Shield. He became the first to
explain to the public that, with respect to Robins, then reigning
sovereign over IUD sales, "the emperor has no clothes."

Dr. Thomsen had done his homework. He analyzed Robins promotional literature and Davis's writings in detail. He showed the panel
how the claims for the Dalkon Shield were false and how the purported
statistical basis for them was not respectable. For example, he pointed
out for the first time publicly that Davis's own study figures led to an
average insertion time of only five and one half months—a figure that
could easily be determined by Davis's own raw numbers, but which no
one to that date had done. He pointed out that buried in the footnotes
was the fact that Davis had recommended that a contraceptive foam be
used for the first three months. To Thomsen, the level of deception in
Robins's advertisement containing the comparisons with other IUDs
was nothing short of "amazing." Thomsen was none too pleased about
the statistics of IUDs in general, but the other manufacturers had not
made the patently false claims for their products that Robins had; and
so, Robins was skewered from stem to stern.

Thomsen had more to say. He described his experiences with IUDs
as a practicing physician. He told the panel about the high failure rates
of IUDs, often ending in spontaneous miscarriages. He told of
women's pain, and the heavy bleeding that IUDs often initiated. He
told of IUDs perforating tissue and migrating to other parts of the
body; and of twenty thousand otherwise unnecessary X-rays given each
year, some to pregnant women, for no other purpose than to try to
locate an errant IUD.

The testimony before the subcommittee was so devastating, and so
widely reported in the media, that Robins was forced to respond in
kind. The company asked to appear before the panel as soon as possible and was granted a hearing on June 13, 1973.

Robins sent a deputation to Congress, apparently chosen to provide a
spectrum of support for the Dalkon Shield. It consisted of Dr. Jack

Freund, a vice-president and head of the medical department; Kenneth Moore, the project director for the Dalkon Shield; Ellen Preston, Robins's liaison with doctors; Donald Ostergard, a practicing physician who had been prominently featured in Robins's "progress report" as the leader of a study that had produced favorable results with the Dalkon Shield; and H. Bradley Wells, an independent biostatistician. If the congressmen noted that the owners and primary operators of the company, the Claibornes, were absent, nothing was said.

There were elements of the group that would have made for great press had they been pointed out to the panel. Ostergard was the doctor whose study had been dismissed in the memo to Robins's officers by Robins's house biostatistician, Lester Preston (Ellen's husband), as statistically flawed. Since presumably Robins now considered Lester Preston to be unreliable, it was necessary for the company to bring in Wells.

The testimony by the Robins witnesses consisted of the practiced assurances that the company had been giving to doctors. To Freund and his group, the Dalkon Shield was a quality product that was being worn around the world with great success. On behalf of the A. H. Robins Company, Freund "categorically" denied charges of fraudulent advertising, without going into specifics. The witnesses stated that Robins had defensible reasons for choosing its statistical base. Although the Robins witnesses faced some pointed questions, after the hearing Freund would conclude that the gamble had worked out pretty well.

Up to a certain point, Freund's analysis was correct. Robins had put up a defense, rather than defaulting to the negative testimony initiated in the subcommittee's hearing. The Robins witnesses had avoided admissions that would have devastated Robins's sales program. However, the benefits ended there because the testimony was really nothing more than damage control. Robins had no hard evidence to persuade Congress and the American public that the Dalkon shield was a superior product. The public's confidence had been shaken. Doctors could feel more sure that their bad experiences with the Dalkon Shield were not isolated occurrences, nor were the problems their own fault or some fault of their patients. Women had learned that their safety depended upon them turning away from IUDs and especially the Dalkon Shield. Injured women, and their attorneys, could feel that suing Robins was the right thing to do.

During the developing crisis, the top executives at Robins retained a calculated air of indifference and ignorance. A request by a staff researcher to do a simple $90 study of wicking was denied. The company generally expressed disinterest in receiving feedback from doctors around the country. There was no change in corporate policy even after Kenneth Moore, the Robins project coordinator, recommended in a written memo dated February 7, 1973: "Considering that we have been marketing the device for going on three years, it is about time that data are collected on the effect of the uterine environment."

The negative communications failed to remain in the corporate consciousness, and many also failed to remain in the company's records. Negative information that was received was treated as a series of isolated, unrelated incidents that were not worthy of true concern. Complaints were commonly met with countercharges from Robins that questioned the doctors' techniques and their patients' hygiene, a strategy that was carried over to litigation with a vengeance. The company followed a policy of isolating negative documents at the lower executive levels, so that senior management would not be bothered and later could claim ignorance. When the number of liability suits grew to worrisome proportions, the policy changed to one under which Robins's attorneys kept all communications and other documents not consistent with the party line. If asked, *every* Robins employee could state truthfully that he or she did not even know of the documents' existence. (Under court rules, documents in the possession of a party's attorneys are considered to be in the possession of the party; however, for the employee of the corporate party answering in a deposition, it truly is a case of "what you do not know cannot hurt you.") Written complaints frequently were "lost" when it came time to respond to FDA inquiries or requests for documents by opposing lawyers.

Maintaining ignorance of the Dalkon Shield's failings required the officers of Robins to develop a sort of amnesia. When questioned in depositions after the company had halted sales of the Dalkon Shield, chairman E. Claiborne Robins, Sr., and president and chief executive officer E. Claiborne Robins, Jr., would display less knowledge of the Dalkon Shield than the janitor might have had. They would not recall seeing numerous memos from subordinates, on which they were listed as having received copies, warning of dangers of the "tail" or suggesting the need for testing of the product. They would not recall discussions about the Dalkon Shield at board meetings, in spite of the fact that corporate minutes definitively placed them there. The chairman would have no idea how many women had been injured by the Dalkon Shield. The president would state that he was not familiar with *any* problem emanating from the Dalkon Shield. The following took place between a plaintiff's attorney and E. Claiborne Robins, Jr., during his deposition in 1983:

Q: Excluding conversations with your attorney [which are "privileged" and need not be disclosed], do you have any recollection of any discussion with any company member, employee, board member, or consultant about the Dalkon Shield . . . at any time?

A: I do. . . . Only one. . . . It was a letter relating to the Dalkon Shield.

Q: Was that one of [Robins's] "Dear Doctor" letters?

A: Correct.

Q: Now as I understand it, Mr. Robins, outside of this one conversation concerning the Dalkon Shield . . . you don't have any recollection of any other conversations with anyone within the company at any time . . . , is that correct?

A: Correct.

Dr. Davis caught the amnesia too. In an early deposition, he "forgot" that he had received at least $300,000 in royalties from Robins's sales of the Dalkon Shield.

If the Robins family could see no evil, there was no evil. The company could continue shipping out a product destined for placement inside women's bodies, and management could make damage control a regular corporate activity, apparently all in good corporate conscience. Indeed, in the press release that would be issued upon the discontinuance of sales of the Dalkon Shield (one step ahead of the FDA), Robins would baldly assert that the shield "when properly used, is a safe and effective IUD." Now that took *chutzpah*!

Of course, there was some method in the forgetfulness and bland denials of Robins's officers. The profit margin on the Dalkon Shield was excellent—40 percent in the United States and 70 percent abroad—and top management was loath to do anything that would slow the flow of cash. As the numbers of septic abortions, unwanted pregnancies, birth defects, and pelvic infections induced by the Dalkon

Shield steadily climbed, so did the lawsuits, and the word in the Robins executive suite was that loose lips could end the cruise. It got to the point where the company could not admit a problem involving the Dalkon Shield, improve the product, or provide better instructions or warnings because management feared that the move might be taken as an admission of guilt in some lawsuit. The Dalkon Shield became the tail that wagged the dog.

Robins fought every lawsuit. Plaintiffs' attorneys were made to fight for every piece of paper that they received as well as the many that the company failed to produce. It took plaintiffs' attorneys numerous court appearances, numerous conferences with Robins's lawyers, numerous court orders, and a seeming lifetime to get a few documents out of the company files. Robins's counsel around the country were directed to be aggressive in dealing with the female plaintiffs—a good offense would be the best defense. The strategy involved pretrial depositions, where Robins's lawyers attempted to poke into every facet of claimants' sexual history, inquiring about sexual practices and intimate health habits and asking for the names and addresses of all sex partners for the prior several years. The tactic of intimidation was mildly successful in that a number of suits were dropped out of sheer embarrassment by women who could not steel themselves to face the relentless questioning by Robins's attorneys. (Robins rarely, if ever, actually used such "evidence" at trial if the plaintiff stayed the course.) In addition to placing the blame on the women, Robins commonly attempted to point the finger at the competence of their physicians. While it was a moderately effective litigation tactic, it damaged Robins's goodwill with doctors, that had been built up over a century.

In the spring of 1974, Robins was still fighting hard to win the public relations battle, but its position was eroding. Robins staged a conference at its Richmond headquarters, at which IUD experts other than those under Robins's control were permitted to take part. The Robins participants were able to blunt criticism of the Dalkon Shield, and the conference adjourned without making conclusive findings—a victory for Robins. Learning that an article was going to be published in the June issue of an influential professional journal linking the Dalkon Shield with "sepsis," a serious and sometimes fatal blood poisoning caused by pelvic inflammatory disease, Robins in May staged a pre-emptive strike by sending a letter to physicians recommending that quick tests be given to Dalkon Shield wearers suspected of being pregnant and that the shield be removed if a pregnancy had occurred. Whether due to the letter or the continuing bad publicity, or both, Robins sale figures got progressively worse as more doctors and clinics dropped the Dalkon Shield from their inventories.

In the meantime, the FDA was closing in. In April 1974, the agency refused to approve a communication from Robins to doctors that advised of precautions but failed to state *why* those procedures should be followed. In May, three officials of the medical devices division of the FDA asked Robins to voluntarily suspend sales pending further study of the safety of the Dalkon Shield, but the company refused. However, by June, the FDA's medical advisors were recommending agency action to stop sales, and Robins hurried to "voluntarily suspend" sales rather than to be the subject of an FDA order. The merit of the suspension was confirmed in hearings held by the FDA in August 1974, which took evidence on two hundred twenty septic abortions, including eleven fatalities, caused by the Dalkon Shield.

Throughout the merry chase, Robins was able to keep a secret behind its closed doors: no one had focused on the structure of the Dalkon Shield's tail as a primary cause of problems with the shield. It was not until after Robins's staged conference that someone unconnected with that company thoroughly investigated a shield. Dr. Howard Tatum, the inventor of the Copper-7 IUD and an invited participant at the conference, discovered that the Dalkon Shield's tail was not a monofilament and conducted experiments that disclosed Supramid's tendency to act as a wick. However, Tatum did not disseminate his findings. Robins managed to avoid divulging the wicking problem to the FDA for the entire decade of the 1970s, a disclosure that if made most certainly would have led to a recall order. Robins may have stopped selling the shield, but thousands of women still had the device in their bodies.

Robins was facing dilemmas similar to those presented to Manville in the five decades following 1930 and indeed presented to many companies every day. At what level do the unintended negative effects of a product upon health or safety call for further study, warnings, changes in the product, special handling, or the discontinuance of sales? Should a company take action to revise or recall a product although not yet found liable for its hazard and not yet ordered to do so by a governmental agency? In other words, at what point do the interests of consumers and the general public outweigh the interests of corporate shareholders and executives in maintaining sales and profits? Knotty questions also are raised about the reasonable limit to manufacturers' purview. When does a manufacturer "know" of problems that its product is visiting upon those outside the company's control? What duty does a company have to seek out such information?

Of course, there are no easy answers to these troublesome questions, since they involve conflicts among values that our society promotes. The dividing lines are often painstakingly drawn in numerous courtrooms over many years. Manville and the other asbestos producers were found wanting by juries in personal injury cases in a process that took decades. As to A. H. Robins Company, apparently juries did not have the same difficulties establishing the line over which the company had strayed, because Robins's downfall would not take nearly that long. As those injured by Manville and Robins would find out, an added problem is that the fine lines of accountability and legal liability painstakingly established by the tort system are then blurred by the operation of the bankruptcy system.

In spite of the growing pressure from the FDA in 1974, Robins stayed one step ahead of the agency. By attacking its attackers at the FDA hearing in August, Robins was able to create some uncertainty over the Dalkon Shield's track record. Then, while dickering with the FDA over Robins's own proposals for modifying the configuration of the shield and the material of the tail, Robins suddenly announced the "voluntary" permanent cessation of production and sales of the Dalkon Shield.

In making the announcement, Fletcher B. Owen, Jr., the director of medical services for the A. H. Robins Company, stated that the cause of the action was the unfair bad publicity that had been generated, which had the effect of hurting sales. According to Owen, the termination of production was "based upon economic considerations rather than any real concern regarding the safety and/or the efficacy of the Dalkon Shield." Although Robins's failure to acknowledge real problems with the Dalkon Shield was typically cold-blooded, in fact, sales had slipped so badly that it was becoming clear that the Dalkon Shield would no longer be profitable. Now *that* was something the Robins officials could understand!

Because Robins had acted on its own initiative, the FDA never would hold additional hearings focused on the Dalkon Shield. The FDA never would issue any formal order that Robins cease and desist from manufacturing the Dalkon Shield; and, in spite of considerable pressure, it never would require Robins to recall the Dalkon Shield from doctors and wearers. With the Dalkon Shield off the market, the FDA simply moved on to other matters, in spite of the Robins "time bombs" existing within many women. Robins would trumpet the FDA's failure to act in trials across the country. (With an eye toward the legal repercussions, Robins would not recommend until 1981 that wearers of the shield have it removed.) It would not be until 1983, in a petition filed by the Women's Health Network, that the FDA was informed of the wicking problem. In terming Robins's failure to disclose the problem to the FDA "objectionable," FDA Commissioner Lillian Yin observed that Robins "knew about the problem with wicking from day one and didn't tell us. . . . In 1974, they acted so innocent."

In spite of Robins's twin tactics of aggressive defense and bland denials from the witness stand, in February 1975, Robins lost the very first case to go to verdict. The plaintiff's injuries were not severe, and the Wichita jury awarded her only $75,000 in compensatory damages. However, Robins was shocked by the jury's wrath in awarding $250,000 in punitive damages. The plaintiff's lawyer was Bradley Post, a personal injury specialist who had been convinced to direct the case at Robins rather than his client's doctor by the fact that Dalkon Shield referrals, involving a number of different doctors, suddenly had started flowing into his office. The key to Post's presentation in court was the 1970 memo of Fred Clark that had pointed out the deficiencies in Davis's study even before the Dalkon Shield had been purchased by Robins. Robins had unintentionally produced the memo for Post in a pile of papers. That note proved to the jury that Robins knew all along that the claimed 1.1 percent pregnancy rate was invalid.

Robins had been stung. Characteristically, top management blamed the process rather than the product. Roger Tuttle, Robins's in-house counsel who had been handling Dalkon Shield litigation, became the designated scapegoat. Blaming the loss on his incompetence, Robins removed him from litigation duties and later eased him out of the company. In his defense, Tuttle has blamed the loss on the memo (in other words, the truth) and has blamed disclosure of the memo upon a management that refused to take litigation seriously and failed to adequately cooperate with its litigator. Robins would come to rue its treatment of Tuttle.

The truth would not be dismissed as easily as Tuttle was. The fact was that the Dalkon Shield was not more effective than other means of contraception, and it was considerably more dangerous than the other IUDs on the market. The Centers for Disease Control, an agency sponsored by the federal government, determined that Dalkon Shield wearers were twice as likely as the wearers of other IUDs to be hospitalized with complications. An independent study covering 1976 to 1978 found that Dalkon Shield wearers had five to ten times more chance of suffering from pelvic inflammatory disease than the wearers of other IUDs. Robins's insurer, Aetna Casualty and Surety Company, did secret tests on the Dalkon Shield in order to prove its safety and efficacy, but in the end it settled cases rather than disclose the findings.

Personal injury lawsuits against Robins arising from the Dalkon Shield increased steadily. By mid-1974, there were forty-seven. By 1977, more than three hundred lawsuits had been filed alleging Dalkon Shield injuries. By 1980, there would be more than nine hundred, and by 1984, fourteen thousand. The reason was as simple as the operation of a wick. Because of Robins's refusal to recall Dalkon Shields, the tails continued to deteriorate and infections continued to be caused. Although missing crucial documents, plaintiffs' attorneys built credible cases that shocked the juries into entering verdicts against Robins, which totaled $130 million by the end of 1982. Yet Robins's management, developing a siege mentality, grimly fought on, never wavering from the position that somehow the Dalkon Shield was getting a bum rap and that the A. H. Robins Company was being unfairly persecuted.

In February 1978, Aetna pulled the plug on Robins. It declined to renew Robins's liability insurance policies. As with the asbestos insurers, Aetna unilaterally declared the "manifestation" theory of coverage and refused to defend against or pay upon injuries that manifested themselves after the termination of the policies, even though they had been incurred during the period that Aetna had insured Robins. Robins was unable to secure another insurer and was forced to "go naked." Robins then sued Aetna for a court declaration that Aetna was liable as Robins's insurer for all Dalkon Shield claims by women, since Aetna's policies had been in force during the entire period that Robins had sold shields. The two companies were at each other's throats, and the litigation would drag on for many years. In 1984, they would settle the dispute prior to trial, Aetna agreeing to contribute $70 million towards paying claims in addition to the $130 million it had already paid out.

As 1983 drew to a close, there was no untoward concern in the A. H. Robins executive suite over the Dalkon Shield litigation. Only a few dozen cases had actually gone to trial, and Robins had won about half. The company's actual costs of defense and punitive damage awards (which are not covered by liability insurance policies) totaled a modest $40 million, the remainder having been borne by Aetna. It looked like the company would negotiate a settlement with Aetna that would provide the wherewithal for the court fights. Unlike Robins's antagonists, life went on pretty much as before for the management at the company.

The company's litigation tactics had been working reasonably well around the country. As is commonly the situation with injury litigation, judges had not concerned themselves overly with pretrial matters; and so Robins generally was able to get away with its cavalier attitude towards "discovery" and its intimidation of the female plaintiffs. After stonewalling diligently for years, as trial approached Robins's attorneys suddenly would decide that further work needed to be done on the case and that trial postponements would have to be requested. While fighting fiercely, Robins was not above settling if its tactics had softened up the plaintiff or her attorney to the point where the price was very "right."

Robins also had learned to cut off evidence that—and attorneys who—might prove troublesome in later cases. For example, when faced with a devastating test of wicking done by Stanford University for a California case, Robins offered a settlement to the plaintiff that was too good to refuse, only on the stipulation that the results of the test be destroyed and the scientists who conducted the test agree never to testify in a Dalkon Shield case. Lawyers who had built up an expertise in Dalkon Shield litigation were required to forswear future representation of claimants in return for good settlements for their present clients.

Although the executives of Robins could not know it at the time, 1984 would be much worse for the company and its officers. The downturn began innocently enough in December 1983, when twenty-one cases in the federal district encompassing Minneapolis were assigned to United States District Judge Miles W. Lord.

The Honorable Miles W. Lord, now retired from the bench, was not your run-of-the-mill jurist. One journalist accurately defined his approach as "the last breath of frontier populist justice."

His was The American Story brought to life. Born in the hardscrabble region of northern Minnesota in 1919, a Golden Gloves boxer in his youth, he supported his wife and child through a series of part-time jobs, sometimes three at a time, while attending the University of Minnesota Law School. The one blemish on his career after his graduation from law school occurred when he failed as an insurance adjuster because the company thought that he was too generous with claimants. He then combined a law practice in Minneapolis with politics within Minnesota's unique Democratic Farm Labor Party. He was a protégé first of Orville Freeman, who later would become governor of Minnesota and then secretary of agriculture in the Kennedy administration, and then of Hubert Humphrey, with whom he had a lifelong friendship. In 1954, he was elected as state attorney general, earning a reputation as a tough law-enforcement officer. (Although a popular favorite, in 1958 Lord declined to run for the United States Senate in a race that ended in the election of Eugene McCarthy.) In 1961, he was appointed United States attorney for the federal district encompassing Minnesota. When he was appointed a federal judge for that district in 1966, Humphrey predicted that "he'll be a people's judge." He was not wrong.

Most judges stay above the fray and allow the adversarial process, like the gladiatorial process, to produce a winner no matter how unevenly the combatants are matched. Judge Lord has always been concerned that the process produce *justice*, which requires inquiry into the substance of cases before him. He has always understood that the federal bench can be a bully pulpit for an activist judge, and he has not been shy about using it when he feels the time is right. Consequently he can be a bother to carefully mapped-out strategies, and he can be fearsome to those who he has concluded wear the "black hats."

There are those who decry his style. The judge's detractors complain that he should not intervene in the head butting that is the adversarial process and should simply allow the side with the hardest head to prevail. Many say that the judge takes his surname too literally and is too insistent on placing his view of justice upon the parties before him. To those people, he should stick to "the law" in the narrowest sense of the word.

The judge does not totally deny the charges. In an interview for a magazine article, he summarized his philosophy: "I think that my job as a judge is to see that justice is done. The whole object is to get at the truth. If you just don't read the lawbooks, you get lots done."

One of Judge Lord's pet peeves is irresponsibility in the executive suite. In 1974, at a time when serious environmental laws were only in their early stages, he shut down one of the biggest employers in the state, Reserve Mining Company, for dragging its heels at proposing a plan to stop polluting Lake Superior with its tailings. In a speech given to a church group several years prior to receiving the Dalkon Shield case assignments, Judge Lord observed:

The law has recognized [through criminal conspiracy laws] that more than one person acting together multiplies the danger to society, except in the instance of the corporate structure where many people can be gathered together and the law only looks at . . . the corporation acting as one person. . . .

If the corporate officers direct their corporation into violating the law to make a profit, and they are caught, they pay a fine. That is looked upon as a nuisance, a nonrecurring obligation it says in the books, and an unfortunate incursion by outsiders. The corporate official, the individual who is caught with his fingers in the pie and making antitrust arrangements, polluting, or making unsafe goods, or other arrangements which are contrary to the law, suffers almost no disgrace either in the eyes of his corporate officials and employees or the public at large; but rather his conduct is looked upon as being the norm, but for the fact that some nosy government investigator looked in and blew the whistle on him. These people are not punished, demoted, or fired. If they are, it is in such a way that they suffer no economic consequences therefrom. . . .

THOU SHALT NOT STEAL applies to every corporate official who sells shoddy, dangerous, or unusable merchandise in the name of profit.

THOU SHALT NOT KILL applies to the corporations and agencies of those who are killing and maiming through industrial pollution. . . .

Yes, we are our brother's keeper.

Judge Lord would not take kindly to the pollution of women's bodies by the executives of the A. H. Robins Company.

The timing of the case assignment to Judge Lord could have been better for Robins. That month the judge had wrapped up a case that angered and frustrated him, a case that was not unrelated to Robins's litigation philosophically.

The U.S. Justice Department had asked Lord to approve a plea bargain agreement in a criminal case involving overcharges to the United States by Sperry Corporation on an MX missile contract. Sperry had agreed to pay $650,000 plus interest as damages, and a $30,000 fine; it would also forego $300,000 of its attorneys' fees otherwise chargeable to the government. Most judges would have rubber-stamped the request and signed the order with a "job well done" attitude, and in fact the prosecutors were congratulating themselves over the settlement; but Judge Lord wanted to know the facts. To his dismay, he found out that the Defense Department had documented $3.5 million in overcharges. Further, the damages Sperry would pay would be tax deductible. (Fines are not.) No penalty whatsoever had been sought against any individuals. So, this was the "message" that the Reagan administration was sending to defense cheats!

Judge Lord was furious. He attempted to learn if officers of the company should be punished. He tried to determine if the case should proceed on the original charges. However, he received no help from the government, and he reluctantly approved the plea agreement. With that experience in corporate iresponsibility—and, perhaps, governmental irresponsibility—ringing in his head, he turned to his Dalkon Shield case assignments.

Judge Lord had received the assignments because some ambulance chasing, 1980s style, in his district had resulted in hundreds of Dalkon Shield cases being filed there. Two Minneapolis lawyers had taken advantage of a recent U.S. Supreme Court decision allowing attorneys to solicit clients. They had circulated brochures on the Dalkon Shield advising women that they may have the legal right to sue the A. H. Robins Company. The program had generated a significant number of claims from around the country, which were filed in the federal district court in Minneapolis.

Whether such soliciting by lawyers is an affront to the legal system or a needed counterbalance to giant corporations depends upon whose ox is being gored. The aforementioned Supreme Court ruling has had the effect of promoting competition in the professions by allowing professionals such as attorneys, accountants, doctors, and dentists to tell the public what they can do for them; but it has also contributed to a decline in ethics, since many professionals now see themselves as little more than businessmen or businesswomen. For better or for worse, the relaxed rules have allowed law firms to accumulate cases arising from a single product or incident. To plaintiffs' lawyers, the right to solicit cases and to charge a contingency fee counterbalances corporate power to injure people. To manufacturers, the practices generate groundless claims and require the expenditure of funds for unnecessary court costs.

The iron laws of economics are a cause of client solicitation by personal injury plaintiffs' attorneys. Hardball defense of product liability suits by large corporations (and of malpractice suits by insurance companies) is common. Plaintiffs and their attorneys are made to pay for their effrontery, in more ways than one. A full-blown trial against such a stubborn adversary can tie up several lawyers in a firm for months. For example, it cost a law firm about $800,000 in expenses and about $3 million in attorneys' time (if billed on an hourly rate) to try the first *two* Dalkon Shield cases in the Minneapolis federal court. Without the ability to accumulate cases, plaintiffs and their attorneys are forced to accept insufficient settlements for claims that they cannot afford to try. Lawyers with a drawer full of similar claims are more able to try cases and to apply the lessons learned to other cases, and the defendants know it.

The mass tort defendant can apply a countervailing tactic, by insisting on trying nearly every case. On the average in the United States less than 5 percent of the civil cases asking for money damages go to trial, and so it is not hard for one recalcitrant mass tort defendant to jam up the system. A. H. Robins increasingly was following the lead of the asbestos manufacturers in forcing trial and then requiring the plaintiffs' attorneys to fight to put into evidence the same things about the product that had been admitted into evidence in previous trials. Not only does the tactic delay justice for plaintiffs, but it drives the cost of trials sky-high, even for law firms that have multiple claimants. A Dalkon Shield case tried by a fellow judge in Lord's district had consumed four months and almost nine thousand pages of transcript and involved the testimony of thirty-seven witnesses and the introduction into evidence of almost six hundred documents. Each trial of a Dalkon Shield case could be expected to generate similar statistics, a fact that worried the plaintiffs' attorneys as well as the Minneapolis district court judges.

Although an unusual number of Dalkon Shield cases had been filed in the federal district of Minnesota, strictly speaking that alone had not made the backlog worse than elsewhere. Robins had struck back at the attorneys who had solicited the cases by attempting to have them disbarred, and the hundreds of cases being handled by them languished while they battled Robins for their licenses. (Robins would be unsuccessful.) Eventually, the two attorneys were forced to give up their Dalkon Shield cases to another law firm.

In order to get the cases moving again, the judges in the Minneapolis district court spread them among themselves, and that was what brought twenty-one Dalkon Shield cases to the Honorable Miles W. Lord, chief justice of the district. The tenacity that would be shown by Lord and the law firm that took over the cases (ironically named Robins, Zelle, Larson and Kaplan) would make Robins sorry that they had challenged the other attorneys.

Judge Lord saw the problems inherent in successive trials, but his options were limited. He knew that class actions of thousands of personal injury claims respecting one product are complicated and generally are not allowed, and that if he declared one Robins would sidetrack the cases with class action issues and appeals. Characteristically, Miles Lord innovated.

Judge Lord proposed to the attorneys involved in the twenty-one cases before him that they agree to a "consolidation" of the cases on the underlying issue of Robins's product liability. Technically the cases would remain separate and independent, but the evidence presented once would apply to each. The group of plaintiffs' attorneys quickly assented (not all the cases were those of the Zelle firm). While consolidated trials presented a possibility of losing all of them at one time, they were confident that Robins would lose once the jury heard the facts. At the hearing concerning scheduling the cases, counsel for Robins could not disclose the company's strategy of delay to the judge, and so when Lord refused a suggestion that he send the cases of women from outside Minnesota to other jurisdictions (to start again at the bottom of some trial calendar), Robins's lawyers had no choice but to assent to the judge's plan.

The group of plaintiffs' lawyers chose the Zelle firm as lead counsel. Not only had that firm successfully tried two Dalkon Shield cases in the district, but it also had an admirable record as plaintiffs' counsel in other product liability cases, including mass tort cases. Further, it was a large firm with the people-power for the showdown.

Judge Lord was not through with his streamlining of procedures. He advised the attorneys that at the start of the consolidated trials he would deem as already entered into evidence all documents and testimony relating to product liability matters that had been accepted into evidence in one of the previous trials in the district. When the company's lawyers attempted to delay the trial date by demanding depositions of all the plaintiffs, the judge set them concurrent with the starting of the trials so that they would not have to pay for two trips to Minneapolis to testify in a deposition and again at trial. A Robins request to delay the trials for the depositions of the plaintiffs' doctors was rejected, since issues involving the possible negligence of the doctors would not come up until part two of the trials when the facts of the individual cases were to be considered. The judge also asked that the plaintiffs' attorneys shorten the time that they had been taking to prove their cases. Having reduced the massive trials to a very manageable package, the judge set an early January 1984 trial date.

The judge had another requirement. He specifically ordered the lawyers for the company to refrain from asking women those "dirty questions" in depositions. In his view it was a blatant attempt at intimidation. Further, according to the judge, Robins's sales had benefited from the climate of sexual freedom, and so he would not hear any evidence that tried to blame Dalkon Shield problems on sexual practices.

The judge's approach set a fire under Robins, but not the kind that the judge had hoped. His instructions generated *seven* motions by Robins contesting them, including a motion to disquality him and a motion to stay all proceedings until that motion could be heard. Almost nonstop hearings were generated by Robins's recalcitrant attitude during the pretrial "discovery" process. Time and again Robins would argue issues to death and then fail to abide by the judge's order when a ruling was entered, which then required further court action. In the first three months of Lord's supervision of the Dalkon Shield cases, more than sixty pleadings were filed by the parties, and the judge held seventeen hearings and conferences and issued dozens of written and oral orders, almost all involving Robins's objections to requests for information and failure to produce documents or witnesses.

Two weeks prior to the trial date that had been set by Judge Lord, Robins was still angling for complication and delay. Of the seventy-two depositions that Robins's lawyers said they needed to take, in the intervening time since Lord's first scheduling hearing they had taken exactly one. They informed the judge that they had no power to make E. Claiborne Robins, Sr., appear for the trials, because, although he was the *chairman* of the A. H. Robins Company and a paid *consultant* to the company, he was not an *employee* subject to company orders. Besides, said Robins's lawyers, he and Fred Clark were too sick to travel to Minneapolis for the trials. In fact, volunteered an attorney, the company may decide not to bring any Robins people to the trials. When Lord authorized the plaintiffs' attorneys to take depositions of Robins executives in Richmond in lieu of their appearances at trial, Robins's counsel was so obstreperous that the depositions threatened to take forever. The trial date was pushed back.

The plaintiffs' lawyers were struggling with three related elements of Robins's litigation strategy. The first was to render the lines of responsibility within the company so diffuse that they would be invisible to the outsider's eye. About this, another judge who had been handling a large group of Dalkon Shield cases since 1975, Frank Theis of the U.S. District Court in Wichita, noted in frustration: "The project manager for Dalkon Shield explains that a particular question should have gone to the medical department, the medical department representative explains that the question was really the bailiwick of the quality control department, and the quality control department representative explains that the project manager was the one with authority to make a decision on that question. . . . [I]t is not at all unusual for the hard questions posed in Dalkon Shield cases to be unanswerable by anyone from Robins." A variation on the theme was practiced by Robins's attorneys. Most aspects of the case, including document production, were handled by Robins's Richmond law firm. However, many times it was one of a number of Minneapolis attorneys who had been retained by Robins as local counsel who actually went to court. Consequently, Robins counsel appearing before Lord often knew only what they had been told by other attorneys outside the judge's courtroom. Neither they nor the judge knew whether what they were saying indeed was the truth. At one point, Lord tried to get each Robins attorney who had worked on a document or pleading to sign it, so that he would know who was responsible for it.

The second and third elements worked in tandem and reinforced the first. As already described, the Robins officers and staff developed corporate amnesia whenever an outsider raised the subject of the Dalkon

Shield. Virtually, no one at Robins could remember talking to anyone, or reading anything, about any remotely controversial matter concerning the shield . . . ever! Finally, *the first two strategies worked only if the ordinary and usual papers that were part of operations at such a large company—copies of correspondence, intraoffice memos, statistics, files, and notes—were kept away from the eyes of plaintiffs' attorneys.* Robins and its attorneys had done an awesome (an overworked word, but applicable here) job of that during twelve years of litigation.

When Robins's defense strategy was erected in Judge Lord's courtroom, the struggle became redefined: it became Robins's impenetrable stonewall against Miles Lord's resolve, the immovable object versus the irresistible force. The plaintiffs' attorneys became almost bystanders in the drama. In the end, Judge Lord would not just crack the structure, he would knock a hole in it big enough to drive trucks full of documents out of the A. H. Robins Company's vaults and cause the whole fortification to crumble.

The wedge was handed to the judge through a phone call. On January 23, 1984, one of the plaintiffs' attorneys called Judge Lord from Richmond, complaining about the inability to get E. Claiborne Robins, Sr., to remember the first thing about the Dalkon Shield. In response to a question, Mr. Robins had allowed that his recollection *might* be refreshed if he were to review the minutes of the company's board of director's meetings. However, the lawyers for the company had refused to produce the records, claiming that the material was "privileged" because the company's attorneys were present at the meetings. Lord ordered the minute books brought to Minneapolis for his review, so that he might rule on the question of privilege.

What the judge saw made him furious. The corporate minutes clearly showed that E. Claiborne Robins, Sr., when he was at the helm, and E. Claiborne Robins, Jr., from the time he became an officer of the company, were active, informed, hands-on executives. Of course, it had always been beyond belief that they, the leaders of a multinational megacorporation, were the detached ignoramuses that they had claimed to be in depositions, but the minute books provided the first hard proof. The corporate minutes had the effect of Richard Nixon's tapes, without the erasures. The contents of the minute books were far from being "privileged" and told a story highly unlike that being spun by Robins officials in depositions.

After seeing the minute books, Miles Lord realized that the

adversarial process was being abused, and so no amount of effort by plaintiffs' counsel could produce the facts. Judge Lord reasoned that there *had to be* many other records of Robins's operations and decision-making processes that had not yet been produced by Robins. Accordingly, he was dubious when Robins's attorneys assured him that all documents that were not "totally irrelevant" or "privileged" as communications with counsel had been produced for inspection by plaintiffs' attorneys either in the cases grouped before Judge Theis in Wichita or the Minneapolis proceedings. The value of those representations of Robins's lawyers was brought into question further by the fact that shortly before Judge Lord commenced supervision of the consolidated Dalkon Shield cases, Judge Theis had reopened "discovery" that had long been closed in the cases he had been supervising upon learning that Robins had withheld some evidence during the pretrial process.

Most judges would have done nothing about the fact that Robins was waging what Judge Lord would call a "war of attrition." However, because of the judge's activist nature, he was drawn into the battles and, not uncharacteristically, he took unusual and bold action to see justice done. He was forced to extend the trial date again due to Robins's (in)actions, but he would use the interim period to good effect.

Judge Lord became involved personally in the "discovery" process. He worked long hours supervising and writing opinions and orders. Once, he traveled to Robins's home office in Richmond to sit in on and supervise depositions, a level of attention to civil suits that is virtually unheard of. On February 8, 1984, he issued a carefully worded order requiring Robins to produce for inspection documents in ten categories. Since Robins apparently was claiming "privilege" for roomfuls of documents, he appointed two lawyers unconnected to the cases as "special masters"—agents of the court—to oversee Robins's compliance with "discovery" requests and orders. The special masters would review documents that Robins claimed did not have to be given to plaintiffs' attorneys and would determine whether in fact they came within any of the recognized exceptions to production.

Robins quickly filed an appeal to the Eighth Circuit Court of Appeals, asking that the order be struck and that Judge Lord be ordered off the cases. Just as quickly, the appeal was denied. Robins then filed an appeal to the Eighth Circuit asking for more time to comply with the order for document production, which was denied. During oral argument in front of the appellate panel concerning Robins's request to delay the document production, Robins's attorney made an astounding argument on behalf of a company that had represented to many judges around the country over a period of many years that it had produced all relevant, nonprivileged papers. The company and its attorneys needed more time to properly preview the requested documents, he contended, because *the file drawers containing the documents requested, if laid end to end, would be more than a mile long*.

Although the court of appeals had given the discovery disputes almost instantaneous hearings, the appeals did work some delay. Through February 24, when the Eighth Circuit denied the motion to delay discovery, Robins still had not produced one document to the judge's special masters. Judge Lord was forced to reschedule the trial for the end of March. Lord's special masters began work in earnest. Robins knew that they were on the trail of the tail.

Robins fought a rearguard action to protect the secrecy of its files. It engaged in picayune arguments over definitions of documents, the means of production of documents, and the scope of inquiry allowed to the special masters. It buried the special masters under paper by claiming "privilege" on truckloads of documents. In the meantime, Robins was settling Judge Lord's cases as fast as possible—money no object. (The plaintiffs in the last two cases to settle received *more* than they had asked for.)

In spite of Robins's need to settle all of Lord's cases, it fought hard to avoid agreeing to several collateral conditions for complete settlement of the cases being pressed by the plaintiffs' attorneys. One condition simply was the actual payment of several prior judgments. Robins did not want to pay the judgments because, according to Robins's attorneys, that might be deemed an admission of guilt in other cases . . . an unusual excuse and a fanciful reading of the law. The major sticking point in the negotiations involved the documents for which the plaintiffs' attorneys had fought so long. The special masters had located perhaps 100,000 (!) documents that, judging from the labeling of Robins files, should have been produced long ago for inspection by plaintiffs' attorneys, but there had not been time to review them. The plaintiffs' attorneys considered it to be very important to get an agreement respecting the availability in other cases of the as-yet-unseen drawers of documents, but, not surprisingly, Robins wanted no such limitations. In the balance lay the future of thousands of other Dalkon Shield cases around the country.

Because agreement could not be reached concerning retention of Robins's Dalkon Shield documents, once more the plaintiffs' attorneys were forced to go to court to protect their discovery gains. When plaintiffs' attorneys asked Judge Lord to enter an order against Robins destroying any documents respecting the Dalkon Shield, a Robins attorney claimed to be insulted. The order was unnecessary, he said. "We do not destroy documents. We feel that the entry of such an order . . . is an insult to the integrity of [Robins's] lawyers." (If any objective observer could still believe that such an order was unnecessary, events several months later would put that view to rest. Robert Tuttle, the Robins house counsel who had suffered ignominy in the Robins executive suite after he had lost the first Dalkon Shield trial, unburdened his soul in a deposition. He provided details of how Robins employees, upon orders from top management, threw incriminating documents into Robins's furnace in 1975. He even brought a peace offering to the deposition—a packet of documents that Robins's management thought had been destroyed. Robins denied the charges, terming Tuttle a "disgruntled former employee." To most, Tuttle appeared more like a man who had just been relieved of a big burden.)

With the "nondestruct" order in place and the special masters diving into its business records, Robins *really* wanted to settle the last two cases before the Honorable Miles W. Lord. It agreed to a series of terms that would keep its records available for inspection by plaintiffs' attorneys in other cases and that would result in quick, substantial cash payments to a number of plaintiffs. The company claimed that the settlements were made because Judge Lord had poisoned the minds of prospective jurors. Later, thorough reviews of the cache of papers at the offices of Robins and their attorneys would produce a mother lode of information for plaintiffs' lawyers, including a full appreciation of the place of the Dalkon Shield's tail in the tragedy. Among the thousands of documents that would be found relevant to Dalkon Shield injury litigation and improperly withheld during twelve years of lawsuits, there were more "smoking guns" than there were in Dodge City in its heyday.

Judge Lord's bold action had placed prying eyes within Robins's fortifications, and the information discovered would cause the company's defenses to crumble. Once the documents had found the light of day, they would be used in Dalkon Shield litigation across the country. Any testimony by Robins witnesses that was out of sync with the records simply served to discredit them, and they lost their effectiveness at trials. By the end of 1984, Robins would suffer more than $17 million in punitive damage awards. Adverse judgments and settlements paid in 1984 alone would exceed $40 million. However, at the time the Robins management thought that they had limited the reach and effect of Miles W. Lord by quietly agreeing to settle the cases before him. They were sorely mistaken.

Although settlements in civil cases are commonly accomplished by filing a simple motion with the judge and receiving back a perfunctory order dismissing the case, things would not be so simple with the Dalkon Shield cases. For two reasons, Judge Lord had a final hearing with officers of the A. H. Robins Company present in court. First, the judge wished to address the men directly, having dealt with them indirectly through the company's lawyers on so many important matters. Second, the plaintiffs' attorneys had demanded the presence of Robins's officers at the hearing so that the record would be clear that they knew about, understood, and agreed to the terms respecting the future availability of the company's documents.

Technically, it was not necessary that the judge actually approve the settlements' terms since the parties always have the right to dismiss a personal injury case by their private agreement. The judge would not—and most likely could not—deny the plaintiffs their hard-won settlement proceeds, but he was galled that Robins might benefit from the morally ambiguous nature of a settlement. The judge wanted to do some good beyond that which he had done for his twenty-one plaintiffs, to say something that would have an effect on other business cases in general and Dalkon Shield cases in particular. He hoped to persuade the controlling shareholders and officers of the A. H. Robins Company of the error of their ways. His judge's bench would become a bully pulpit. Neither the company nor its executives would be permitted to slink from the courtroom of the Honorable Miles W. Lord. They could be happy that the hearing date was February 29 and that they would be spared anniversaries of the hearing date three out of every four following years.

When the bailiff called the courtroom to order, before the judge stood A. H. Robins president E. Claiborne Robins, Jr., senior vice-president for research and development Carl Lunsford, and vice-president and general counsel William Forrest. The attorney for E. Claiborne Robins, Sr., had advised the court that the senior Claiborne was "too ill" to appear, and the judge had not pressed the matter.

Judge Lord opened the hearing by asking the attorneys for the various plaintiffs to review the document containing the proposed settlement terms to be sure they agreed with them on behalf of their respective clients. The judge then had his clerk hand the three Robins officials transcriptions of the judge's 1981 speech on corporate responsibility. During the short recess that the judge called to allow the Robins officers an unhurried reading of that text, his special masters telephoned from Richmond to advise him that they thought at least 100,000 Robins documents had been wrongfully withheld from Dalkon Shield cases.

Next the judge asked the Robins officers to read silently the text of remarks that he had laboriously prepared for the hearing and had handed to them. "Please don't rush through the document," he requested. "It is a very important, profound document which I have been working on for weeks, and I hope it burns its mark into your souls." After allowing them a period of time, Judge Lord began to question Carl Lunsford in a manner that made it clear that questions for the other two would follow. The judge plainly was attempting to get the Robins representatives to admit the wrongs that they and their company had done relating to the Dalkon Shield. Lunsford declined to answer, on advice of counsel. At that point, in the courtroom only the Robins contingent had copies of the text and could know what it said. It had not been read into the record nor had the judge filed it with the clerk.

Once again, the bad attitude of the Robins officials would lead them into trouble. Frustrated at the lack of dialogue, the lack of any indication of remorse or apology, and his inability to test if the men had actually read his statement, Judge Lord ordered the clerk to file it (thus making it a public record) and proceeded to read it out loud. The world would soon learn what was on the judge's mind.

This is what the judge read, in part:

> It is not enough to say, "I did not know," "It was not me," "Look elsewhere." Time and time again, each of you has used this kind of argument in refusing to acknowledge your

responsibility and in pretending to the world that the chief officers and the directors of your gigantic multinational corporation have no responsibility for the company's acts and omissions. . . .

Gentlemen, the results of these activities and attitudes on your part have been catastrophic. Today as you sit here attempting once more to extricate yourselves from the legal fact that more than nine thousand women have made claims that they gave up part of their womanhood so that your company might prosper. . . .

If one poor young man were, by some act of his—without authority or consent—to inflict such damage on one woman, he would be jailed for a good portion of the rest of his life. And yet your company, without warning to women, invaded their bodies by the millions and caused them injuries by the thousands. . . .

[W]e simply do not know how many women are still wearing these devices, and your company is not willing to find out. The only conceivable reasons you have not recalled this product are that it would hurt your balance sheet and alert women who already have been harmed that you may be liable for their injuries. You have taken the bottom line as your guiding beacon, and the low road as your route. This is corporate irresponsibility at its meanest. . . .

I see little in the history of this case that would deter others from partaking of like acts. The policy of delay and obfuscation practiced by your lawyers in courts thoughout this country has made it possible for you and your insurance company, Aetna Casualty and Surety Company, to delay the payment of these claims for such a long period that the interest you earn in the interim covers the cost of these cases. What other corporate officials could possibly learn a lesson from this? The only lesson could be that it pays to delay compensating victims and to intimidate, harass and shame the injured parties.

Judge Lord then referred to Robins's attempts to get Congress to limit plaintiffs' rights to punitive damages, balancing the comments against Robins profits for the prior year of $58 million. He then described Robins's litigation strategies of harassment, stonewalling, and delay, causing not only injustice for injured women but also the waste of an inordinate amount of precious judicial and other court resources across the entire country.

After the conclusion of his prepared text, the judge was forced to face his limitations in the cases. Because they had been in the nature of tort claims for damages, under the law the judge could not provide any other remedy, such as requiring A. H. Robins Company to recall all the devices that were being worn by millions of women around the world or to present the evidence in its files to the FDA. He closed with a plea that the Robins officials cleanse their souls by confession. Immediately upon the close of his remarks, one of the Robins attorneys leaped to his feet to object to them. Throughout the judge's presentation, the Robins representatives had maintained an air of studied indifference.

The judge quickly wrapped up the hearing. Upon receiving assurances from the plaintiffs' attorneys that the settlement agreement was acceptable to them as drafted, he scrawled "so ordered" upon the settlement terms that had been set before him at the start of the hearing and signed his name below.

There can be no doubt that, after standing mute during Judge Lord's rebuke, the Robins officials had a few things to say when they returned to the executive suite! Instead of Robins avoiding the glare of trial with quiet settlements, Judge Lord had seen to it that the spotlight of publicity had shined brightly on the company's misdeeds. Miles Lord's actions, words, and moral indignation made him a hero to more than one of the women victimized by the Dalkon Shield.

Robins once again was put in the position of posturing as a form of damage control. At the company's annual meeting, E. Claiborne Robins, Jr., defended the safety record of the company and stated that the judge's comments were wrong because no evidence had been presented to him. (However, Lord had stated on a number of occasions, including the final hearing, that he had read transcripts of depositions.) In addition, Robins attacked the judge for becoming an advocate for the plaintiffs' bar, which was interested in nothing more than "how to pick our corporate pocket." In a deposition in June 1984, Carl Lunsford continued to deny any personal responsibility and stated the judge's remarks had not caused him to discuss deficiencies of the Dalkon Shield with anyone. Apparently the judge's comments had generated little of the desired response within the Robins executive suite.

An appeal was filed, asking that the court record of the judge's remarks be expunged and that even his "so ordered" be wiped out. Robins also filed a judicial misconduct complaint, alleging that Judge

Lord was biased and had make remarks that would affect other cases. The disciplinary complaint would be heard by the same court that would hear the appeal of the order, the Eighth Circuit Court of Appeals. The company did not ask to upset the settlements.

On the surface, the end of the clash between the populist judge and the multinational corporation ended in a draw. The Eighth Circuit Court of Appeals ruled that the judge's comments were in error because the A. H. Robins Company and the three officers of the corporation had a right to a prior hearing on the judge's charges before such statements could be made. The record was ordered expunged. Robins even won the right to a clean copy of the settlement agreement, unsullied by Judge Lord's offending "so ordered" notation. On the other hand, the circuit panel dismissed the judicial misconduct complaint against the judge, simply noting that the decision on appeal had taken care of the matter sufficiently. In a follow-up statement, the panel put the matter into perspective:

> A trial judge should not fear that because of comments he or she makes from the bench, which in good faith the judge feels are related to the proceedings before the court, he or she ultimately may be subject to a disciplinary sanction by the Judicial Council. Disenchanted litigants or other citizens should not be able to influence a federal judge about a judicial decision through the threat of disciplinary sanction.

As to things that matter, indeed the judge accomplished his view of justice. Plaintiffs' attorneys would mine the mother lode of documents that Judge Lord's special masters had uncovered and would find many nuggets of information damaging to Robins. Because of that information transfer, Robins would be forced into more costly settlements rather than go to trial and would lose more trials that it did undertake. For example, after Judge Lord made his comments for the record, Robins paid $38 million to settle 198 other cases pending in Minnesota, a per-claim average more than $150,000 greater than earlier settlements. Shortly after Judge Lord's rebuke, Robins started a program of recalling shields, 2.2 million of which had been sold in the United States. The Robins family may have tweaked Miles Lord's nose, but Judge Lord's comments would live on in the "public record" of the media if not in the formal hearing transcript and would directly benefit thousands of women. (However, the battle is never over until the last bankruptcy card is played.)

The Eighth Circuit had found Judge Lord to be "in error" in making his comments, but was he *wrong*? In June 1984, the Colorado Supreme Court upheld a $6.2 million punitive damage award against Robins as a legitimate response of an outraged jury to the facts of the case. In January 1985, the Eleventh Circuit Court of Appeals ruled that sufficient evidence existed to the effect that a regular Robins expert witness, Dr. Louis Keith, had committed perjury in describing his favorable tests of the Dalkon Shield. In February, Judge Lord's two special masters filed a report that advised of the existence of sufficient evidence to find that Robins had fraudulently misrepresented the safety and efficacy of the Dalkon Shield—in part because Dr. Hugh Davis could not be viewed as a credible expert or scientist—and that the company had wrongfully destroyed many documents relating to the Dalkon Shield. In court the company was taking it on the chin with regularity. In May, a jury awarded an injury plaintiff $1.1 million in compensatory damages and a record punitive damage award of $7.5 million— one hundred times greater than the first punitive damage award in 1975—as compensation for her losing, as Judge Lord had put it, her "womanhood" to the A. H. Robins Company.

Robins attempted to soften the blows. It continued to lobby Congress to limit punitive damages to the first case in which they are awarded. Its executives began to complain about the contingency fee system utilized by the plaintiffs' attorneys. It filed its own action in the courtroom of its hometown federal judge, Robert R. Merhige, Jr., asking that he consolidate all pending cases. Surely one pillar of the Richmond community would help another! Judge Merhige disappointed the Robins family by denying the request.

At the end of 1984, Robins took an internal audit of the scope of the Dalkon Shield problem. The financial statement for the year was a study in contrasts. Sales were up strongly, by 12 percent to $631 million, and profits on operations were up 21 percent to $128 million; but earnings were anemic due to Dalkon Shield legal expenses, judgments, and settlements. The average settlement cost had risen to about $40,000 compared with an average of $8,000 in 1976, and three thousand five hundred cases were still pending. A study of the likely progress of the injury litigation estimated that eighty-seven thousand women in the United States would be injured by the shield, which would result in twenty thousand new claims against Robins.

As a result of the number-crunching, in April 1985 Robins set aside a $615 million accounting reserve (unfunded) against future claims. When applied to the financial statement, it resulted in a loss for 1984 of $416 million, which was greater than Robins's net worth. (Neither the study nor the resulting accounting reserve took account of women in foreign countries.) Whether intentionally or not, the A. H. Robins Company had laid the groundwork for the filing of a Chapter 11, although the company denied that it was considering filing a bankruptcy proceeding. Senior vice-president G. E. R. Stiles stated, "We are not in danger of [bankruptcy]. We are operating today just as we did yesterday. It is business as usual."

Chapter 13

A Toxic Tortfeasor Dives for the Bankruptcy Bunker

The problem for Robins was that "business as usual" meant defending against some four thousand injury lawsuits, which were increasing at the rate of about three hundred per month, and paying for the removal costs of thousands of Dalkon Shields. As Robins had feared, it had stimulated both types of claims by its campaign to recall shields after Judge Lord's rebuke. (The costs of publicizing the recall alone had set Robins back more than $4 million.) The bad news of a litigation strategy in retreat kept arriving, such as the ruling by the Ninth Circuit Court of Appeals that claimants may not be barred by state "statutes of limitations" (which limit the time period for filing a suit, usually to a period of a few years after discovery of an injury) because of Robins's concealment of the Dalkon Shield problems. Almost at the same time, the Eleventh Circuit reversed a hard-won Robins trial victory because of the perjury of its medical witness, Dr. Louis Keith.

By July 1985, Robins was running out of wiggle room. The company had suffered more than $300 million in judgments and settlements, plus more than $24 million in punitive damages. Dalkon Shield liabilities and court costs had grown to about $15 million per month. Although the majority of the injury claims and court expenses had been paid by Aetna in the past, under the settlement agreement with the insurer, Robins was now on its own; and the $70 million that Robins had received in the settlement was dissipated. In fact, Robins's out-of-pocket expenses had passed the $200 million mark and were rising fast. On July 23, Robins's last hope for managing the injury litigation had been dashed when Judge Merhige denied its request to bring all Dalkon Shield punitive damage claims into one class action in his courtroom, citing the historic inapplicability of class actions to personal injury claims. Robins would have to conjure up some other way of having its legal problems heard in its home court.

Robins found the way. On August 21, 1985, it filed a Chapter 11 case in the Eastern District of Virginia, Richmond Division. Although run-of-the-mill bankruptcy cases were assigned as a matter of course to a local bankruptcy judge, the A. H. Robins Company would not be treated similarly. Its case immediately was withdrawn from Bankruptcy Judge Blackwell N. Shelley and reassigned to . . . the Honorable Robert R. Merhige, Jr.

The first order of business for Judge Merhige was to defend his stewardship of the bankruptcy case. Because of the national brouhaha over the jurisdiction of the bankruptcy judges, technically it was correct for the district court to directly supervise a case. As to the assignment to Merhige specifically, the judge angrily denied allegations that he would be biased in favor of the A. H. Robins Company. The judge stated that he was not a personal friend of E. Claiborne Robins, Sr., who was a neighbor of his, although he thought the Robins patriarch to be "a fine man." Judge Merhige *had* met with Robins shortly before the filing of the bankruptcy, although according to the judge, it was only done to get some information for an upcoming meeting of judges handling Dalkon Shield injury suits. That gratuitous compliment and meeting would be insufficient to enable a group of plaintiffs' lawyers to persuade the court of appeals to order Judge Merhige off the case. Robins had managed to segue from the stern gaze of Judge Lord to the friendly confines of Judge Merhige's courtroom. The difference would be *very* noticeable. Judge Merhige would be *very* helpful to Robins.

Financial schedules were filed with the court that showed a textbook example of a well-run company but for the Dalkon Shield fiasco. The company listed $373 million in assets and, not counting the reserve for future liabilities, $215 million in debts. For the first six months of 1985, Robins had earned an operating profit of $64 million on $331 million in sales. However, the listing of approximately five thousand pending claims and the accounting entry for the reserve, standing at that time at $550 million, darkened the financial picture considerably.

Robins and Judge Merhige moved quickly once the bankruptcy was filed. Almost immediately—and months before a trade creditors' committee or a health claimants' committee could be organized—Robins asked for an extremely short "bar date" (a date beyond which making a claim against the company would no longer be acknowledged) for all health claims. Although the request was well within the law, more commonly time limits for claims are not set until the bankruptcy case has received some notoriety among its creditors and the case has matured to the point where it is likely that the Chapter 11 company will be filing a Plan of Reorganization. The judge established April 30, 1986, as the last date on which any health claimant could file a claim against the A. H. Robins Company. The judge also allowed Robins to hire Kidder, Peabody and Company as its investment banker; ordered all injury lawsuits across the country to be transferred to him in order to be administered by him within the bankruptcy; and enjoined the world from suing Robins's directors or officers, Aetna Casualty and Surety Company, or Aetna's directors or officers, in any court in the land respecting Dalkon Shield matters. All of this happened before any creditors' committees could get organized.

Judge Merhige had retilted the playing field. Unlike Judge Lord, Judge Merhige would hear no motions from Robins to reconsider each order, no same-day appeals to the higher courts, no obvious attempts to challenge his authority to act. Those activities would not be necessary. All of Robins's pugnaciousness could be directed back at its injury claimants and their attorneys. There were immediate benefits. The injunction stopped some nasty suits against the two Claibornes, and the judge's orders (in addition to the automatic "exclusive period" during which only Robins could file a Plan of Reorganization) left the company firmly in command of the bankruptcy case.

Much to the surprise of the Robins executives, Chapter 11 also provided figurative and literal bonuses. The first benefaction was that the Chapter 11 had barely dented Robins's sales, so popular were its name brands. In October, the company made $9.1 million in profits on sales of $30.5 million, up 5 percent from the same month of the year before. The second gift was courtesy of the automatic stay against all payments by Robins to creditors existing on the date of the bankruptcy filing, which allowed Robins's cash kitty to increase by $13 million. Robins officials celebrated by voting substantial cash bonuses for themselves. Meanwhile, because of the bankruptcy, no payments at all were being made to injured women.

Robins's plan for notifying potential claimants of the bankruptcy and the need to file a bankruptcy claim was controversial. The company proposed to spend more than $2 million on print ads (including those in the *National Enquirer*) and TV spots. However, there were areas of the country where the only announcements would come in the form of national magazines, and it seemed certain that some women would miss the announcements. The extremely short date to respond magnified the deficiencies in the plan. Outside the United States, the program was limited to news releases and direct communications with doctors and health ministries. The foreign program was plainly inadequate, since Robins had sold well over a million IUDs for use outside the United States, but the *sub rosa* agreement among the interest groups active in the bankruptcy was that large numbers of foreign claims would not be stimulated.

The claims procedure that was adopted was complicated. To avoid having her claim barred forever, a woman first would have to file a "notice of claim" with the federal clerk's office in Richmond by April 30, 1986, *and* a more detailed final claim on a form provided by the clerk no later than June 30 (July 30 for foreign claims). The dual filing requirement was chosen in spite of the fact that the Bankruptcy Code and related Bankruptcy Rules require only one simple, one-page form to become a creditor of record in a bankruptcy.

Filing the two acceptable forms merely registered a claim. Robins retained the right to object to any or all of them later and to require that they be proven under some procedure that had not yet been established. Thus claims would be cut off very quickly, but it could be years before they were actually investigated in conjunction with a Plan of Reorganization. Because of the likely large number of claims, it most certainly would take at least several *more* years for that process to play itself out.

By acting quickly, Robins had seized control of the claims procedure, something that Manville had not been able to do, and shaped it to its liking. (Do you suppose that Robins had learned from Manville's mistakes?) The notification program was limited, the claims schedule was tight, and hurdles had been placed in the procedure. Many women would find that they had lost their remedies through ignorance or mistake. Five thousand claims that were filed would be disqualified by the court. No one knows how many legitimate claims were not made at all.

The attorneys for the injury claimants were no match for Robins's concerted actions and the judge's quick rulings. They did not come into the case with an already-existing organization and acknowledged leaders, the way the asbestos plaintiffs' attorneys had done. Also, the case had moved rapidly ahead before the thirty-eight-member claimants' committee could become effective. Robins's train, with Judge Merhige at the switches, had left the station while the claimants' representatives were still searching for the boarding gate. In fact, the claimants' committee *never* would become an effective force in the bankruptcy. At the beginning of the case, the committee was badly split philosophically over what attitude should be taken toward Robins. Judge Merhige then would see to it that the committee was rendered impotent for the duration.

Soon after the claimants' committee was established, a number of militant plaintiffs' attorneys on the committee asserted themselves. That group wanted to challenge the legitimacy of the bankruptcy and to prosecute a lawsuit against Aetna as an active coconspirator in Robins's fraud, making the insurer equally liable with Robins for injuries. Those attorneys also wanted to dig for more damning evidence against Robins, in spite of the fact that, from the bench, Judge Merhige had advised them that they should leave any investigation of criminal wrongdoing to the government (which was not doing an investigation). They soon wanted to dump the committee's counsel, Murray Drabkin, and Drabkin's law firm, the Washington, D. C., office of Cadwalader, Wickersham, and Taft, a Wall Street firm, because they felt that Drabkin was proving too soft on Robins and was not counseling the committee to use its "full legal remedies"—in other words, he was not advocating all-out warfare.

There was a movement afoot to replace Drabkin with Robert Rosenberg, who had been forced to resign as the counsel for the asbestos-related claimants in the Manville case when he switched law firms. (He was "conflicted out" because his new firm had done work for Manville in the past.)

Another contingent on the committee saw the bankruptcy as a fact of life. They saw legal challenges to the bankruptcy and the judge's orders as tilting at windmills, as demonstrated in the Manville bankruptcy. They wished to concentrate energies on working with Robins on a Plan of Reorganization and a claims hearing procedure.

Although the differences of opinion were causing problems within the committee, apparently the arguments against Drabkin were persuasive because the members voted thirty to one to replace him. According to Bradley Post and Mary Beth Ramey, two attorneys on the committee, when the judge heard about the vote he was furious. The judge quickly moved to disband the committee.

In March 1986, Judge Merhige ordered the dissolution of the claimants' committee and ordered the United States trustee to replace it with a committee made up of no more than seven members. The judge described the committee as paralyzed by internal conflicts and the fight over naming a committee counsel.

The order by the judge was quite unusual, to say the least. One of the basic philosophies underlying the Bankruptcy Code is that the committee is a microcosm of economic democracy and that all sides should be represented. The different viewpoints, interests, and personalities are to be worked out through negotiations—thus will be produced the best overall solution under the circumstances of the case. As a concomitant to that concept, bankruptcy law and practice assume that a creditors' committee will be a fractious group made up of representatives of diverse interests; and judges routinely deny requests to remove unpopular members, whether under the guise of "streamlining" a committee or making it "more efficient" by removing dissidents. Further, for such a large, contentious case as the Robins bankruptcy, a claimants' committee of seven members would be unusually small.

Upon receiving the judge's order, ten (now-former) members of the claimants' committee asked the judge to recuse himself for bias.

In two weeks, the judge responded in a blistering fifty-nine-page opinion. Given the speed of the decision and the length of the opinion, it is doubtful that the judge spent much time agonizing over what to do! Having considered the motion to have himself disqualified, and having found himself free from bias, he denied what he called the "ill taken" motion to recuse him from the Robins bankruptcy. Taking a cue from Judge Lifland's ability at times to find movement in the Manville case when there was none—or perhaps he had his own view of headway—Judge Merhige stated that "the court will not allow these movants to further delay the progress of the case." He then stated that he would assign the matter to another federal judge solely on the issue of whether the movants should face sanctions for making the motion. (One of the ironies of American jurisprudence is that parties have no other recourse when they think a judge is biased than to make those allegations to that very same judge. Most lawyers would rather swallow poison than make a recusal motion, for obvious reasons. The slow professional death if the judge refuses to disqualify himself is much more painful!)

At the same time, the judge buttoned up a few loose ends. He retained Murray Drabkin as "special counsel," in spite of the fact that prior to being disbanded, the claimants' committee had voted so overwhelmingly to replace him. Judge Merhige also appointed Francis McGovern, a law professor at the University of Alabama and an expert in negotiations over complex issues, to be the judge's special advisor.

A new claimants' committee was duly appointed by the U.S. Trustee for the Richmond district. It consisted of Dr. Nancy Worth Davis, a professor at the George Washington University School of Law, the chairperson; Dr. Helen R. H. Clemo, a member of the Department of Physiology and Biophysics at the Medical College of Virginia; Judith J. Rentschler, an attorney in private practice in San Francisco; Ann E. Samani, an attorney recently with the bankruptcy court in Lexington, Kentucky; and Gorman H. King, an attorney from Fargo, North Dakota. Rentschler and King had been on the original committee and had favored cooperation with Robins. Davis, Clemo, and Samani supposedly were claimants, although the extent of their injuries was not disclosed and militant plaintiffs' attorneys claimed that they could find no records of them ever having filed suit against Robins. It was evident that the reconstituted committee of only five members was really a blue-ribbon panel rather than a group committed to fighting for the injury claimants. Noticeably absent were the attorneys formerly on the committee who directly represented thousands of Dalkon Shield claimants. To no one's surprise, Murray Drabkin was retained as counsel for the committee.

The removal of dozens of plaintiffs' attorneys from the claimants' committee could not help but have a profound effect upon the case. Not only were they cut off from shaping the actions of the body that would be considered to represent the interests of injury claimants, but they would be cut off from meaningfully taking part in the case at all. That is because the only parties entitled by the Bankruptcy Code to be on the "service list" to receive, by mail or hand delivery, copies of all notices, motions, and briefs filed by parties and orders entered by the judge, are the debtor, the U.S. Trustee, and the attorneys for the committees recognized by the judge. Becoming *personae non grata*, the former members of the committee were placed in a legal purgatory.

The filing of a claim by a woman injured by a Dalkon Shield would be of little help in bringing her or her attorney into the information loop. Although individual attorneys may request the court to add them to the service list, and in smaller cases that motion is granted as a matter of course, in large cases the judges routinely deny such motions because otherwise the cost of "service" would get out of hand. Creditors themselves receive notices from the court clerk only, and only on very few occasions which are specified by the Bankruptcy Code, most notably *after* the Chapter 11 debtor has filed a Plan of Reorganization or asks the judge to approve the sale of an appreciable amount of assets. In a case such as Robins's, with a large number of claimants, the cost and logistics of sending the creditors notices would be such that only the very most important notices would be sent to them, the judge having the right to waive notification. (Why does the judge have that right? Because it is assumed that the creditors' committees truly represent the interests of the larger group, and so notice to the committee produces the same result as notice to all the creditors—a dubious proposition in some cases.)

The "outsiders" get left behind. Those not on one of the committees are left in the dark about matters large and small until long after they have occurred and so find themselves to be strangers to the case. The viewpoint of the committees becomes nearly determinative, and others who attempt to address the court on important issues are viewed as officious intermeddlers and are given short shrift. Thus, ironically, in the larger cases the degree of involvement by creditors is diminished.

Bradley Post and Mary Beth Ramey, who had been booted off the committee in spite of representing numerous injury claimants, were reduced to begging the judge to enter a special order adding them to the service list so that they could find out what was going on. In that motion, Post and Ramey blasted the new committee. Not only were Davis, Clemo, and Samani pretenders to the role of injured claimant, but King, supposedly a representative of the plaintiffs' bar, had never tried a Dalkon Shield case. To Post and Ramey, "No one with the backing of the majority of Dalkon Shield victims or their lawyers is representing the interests of the Dalkon Shield victims in this bankruptcy." Soon after, a group of former committee members filed a motion that the new claimants' committee be dissolved because it was not representative of the claimants' group as a whole. Both motions would be heard by none other than the Honorable Robert R. Merhige, Jr.

It was harder to discern the implications of something else that happened at about the same time: Robins fired its bankruptcy counsel, the San Francisco firm of Murphy, Weir, and Butler. Although not a large firm, it was (and is) a nationally known bankruptcy and creditors' rights "boutique." It was doubtful that it had been doing an inept job—the firm was too good. Robins vaguely indicated that the firm had not been moving the case forward fast enough. The nature of the strained relations between Robins and the law firm would not become apparent until some months later.

Just when Robins and Judge Merhige thought that they had everything under control, everyone's attention was drawn to a loose cannon on deck, an assistant United States attorney by the name of S. David Schiller.

The Justice Department is the "law firm" for most federal agencies, including the Internal Revenue Service, in many litigation matters. Accordingly, the United States attorney's office in each federal court district across the country represents the IRS in the many bankruptcy cases in the district in which it has filed a claim. Because most federal tax claims have statutory priority, if a company wishes to have a successful reorganization, it must render to Caesar.... The ordinary reason for mere mortals to jockey for position in the bankruptcy, to see who will get more and who will get less, is not applicable to the IRS; it *will* get its "fair" share. Accordingly, almost without exception the U.S. attorney's office will simply monitor a case to see when it should collect the check.

The Internal Revenue Service had filed a claim of $61 million against Robins for back taxes (which Robins denied was owed). Schiller had been assigned to monitor the case, which in itself was not unusual. What was unusual was the fact that Schiller did not stick the file into his cabinet, with a reminder to give the company's lawyers a call in a year. By poking around in Robins's financial statements, Mr. Schiller discovered that Robins was cheating—not the IRS, but the general creditors and the court itself. He blew the whistle, much to the judge's discomfort.

S. David Schiller filed a motion over the imprimatur of the Justice Department that asked Judge Merhige to find the A. H. Robins Company in contempt and to appoint a trustee to manage its affairs.

According to Schiller, Robins's records disclosed that it had paid out more than $6 million to prebankruptcy creditors, an action, if true, that clearly was in violation of the Bankruptcy Code. It is unarguable—"black letter law"—that a company cannot file bankruptcy, subject its creditors to the automatic stay, and then pay favored creditors. According to Schiller's allegations, the company had not just favored outsiders; its payments included more than $1 million in deferred compensation to its senior executives. Apparently the Robins family did not consider themselves to be bound by the rules of bankruptcy.

Schiller filed a brief with the judge in support of his motion, in which he did not pull any punches. To Schiller, "a raid on the estate's assets by corporate insiders cannot be tolerated." Testimony by Robins executives that they *knew* the payments were illegal "highlights the callous indifference [Robins] has accorded the Court's Orders" and shows Robins's "utter arrogance." Noting that the company had recently announced increases in executive compensation and bonuses, the brief charged that the "compensation decisions [are] grossly insensitive to the thousands of claimants awaiting payments for needed medical care."

Schiller reminded the court of Robins's other transgressions while in bankruptcy. According to Schiller, Robins had attempted to funnel illegal payments through a subsidiary to its banker, Central Fidelity Bank. This maneuver was thwarted when the claimants' attorneys found out. According to claimants' attorneys, the Robins family controlled the bank, and so not only had there been an attempt to make unauthorized payments to a creditor, but there had been an element of self-dealing by Robins. Schiller then described how the A. H. Robins Company had tried to sell a subsidiary's plant without seeking court approval on notice to creditors, another violation of bankruptcy law that was blocked when the U.S. Trustee informed the court. (When the claimants' committee had requested information on the transaction, the company had failed to respond.)

To Schiller, Robins "is out of control and only the appointment of a trustee can set it back on course." He argued that although the Bankruptcy Code disfavors a trustee in a Chapter 11 case, the judge could find ample causes to replace management. For one, the company "arrogantly and systematically flouted a clear, unambiguous order of this court." Further, "the record demonstrates the instances of fraudulent conduct, dishonest dealings, incompetence and gross mismanagement constituting cause for appointment of a trustee." Schiller also asked the judge to bar the company from indemnifying the officers and directors of the company if they were found to be personally liable for Dalkon Shield injuries because of their own part in the fraud (a common corporate practice that Judge Lord had decried in his speech to the church council).

For a while it looked like the Justice Department was going to pick up the fight of the militant claimants' lawyers and expose Robins for what they thought it was. If the judge were forced by the disclosure of Robins's wrongdoings to have a trustee appointed, the balance of power would shift mightily.

Then, for whatever reason, Schiller compromised his position and allowed himself to be removed as a factor in the case. Prior to beginning depositions on the illegal payments, Schiller agreed to withdraw his motion if Robins would allow the appointment of an independent director, who would, presumably, serve as a watchdog against further skulduggery. The judge threw Schiller a curveball by refusing to approve the deal. Although the compromise had been compromised, Schiller seemed to lose all steam and more or less disappeared from sight in bankruptcy court.

The flurry of accusations did clarify one issue. Robins claimed that their former chief bankruptcy counsel, Penn Ayers Butler of Murphy, Weir, and Butler, had failed to fully advise the corporation of its limitations in bankruptcy and had orally approved the payments. Butler angrily denied the charges, and it did not appear that anyone involved in the case, including the judge, seriously believed that the experienced and highly qualified law firm had dropped the ball so miserably. The most likely scenario was that the law firm and the corporation had parted ways because the law firm would *not* go along with Robins's program.

The matter of unauthorized payments did not die entirely, even without Schiller's stridency. The final evidence disclosed unauthorized payments of $7.3 million, including $1.7 million to Robins executives.

Robins had violated a basic, if unspoken, agreement in such situations: if a party is to enjoy the benefits of a favored litigant before a judge, it should not do anything to make the judge look bad. Judge Merhige had been sticking his neck out for Robins, and would continue to do so, and yet in their greed the Robins executives had thought nothing of insulting the court. Perhaps they thought that they could do no wrong in that courtroom. Perhaps they were right.

Indeed, Judge Merhige continued to tilt the playing field in Robins's favor. He rejected all objections to the makeup of the claimants' committee. He struck down a challenge to the short claims period, finding notice to be adequate in the United States and ruling that foreign claimants have no constitutional right to adequate notice anyway. He had bolstered Robins's corporate fortress when he had quashed the outside director agreement, and he did it again when he denied the motion to prohibit the A. H. Robins Company from indemnifying individual directors and officers who might be found to be personally liable to health claimants. Thus the company was spared prying eyes, and the Robins family was insulated from any financial repercussions.

More subtle aid to the A. H. Robins Company by Judge Merhige came in the form of the judge's continual professed state of frustration with what he averred was the slow pace of progress in the case. He frequently applied pressure on the parties to produce a Plan of Reorganization. In actuality the bankruptcy was proceeding quite briskly, especially for that of such a large corporation. Perhaps, as a full federal judge with little experience in supervising bankruptcy cases, Judge Merhige was mistaken about the speed at which resolution of the thorny issues should arrive. However, the judge certainly must have seen that the Robins bankruptcy was proceeding more quickly than many simpler pieces of ordinary litigation on his calendar. While applying the pressure, the judge continued to extend the "exclusive period" by court order, so that health claimants and other creditors remained barred from proposing a Plan of Reorganization and seeking acceptance of any such plan from the creditor body. Thus the judge's pressure would be felt the most by the claimants' lawyers, who were left no alternative—other than capitulation—by the "exclusive period" except to be naysayers in order to eventually force Robins to propose a better plan.

Even though the judge had ordered a hearing on the illegal payments, the betting was that Robins would not incur serious sanctions. Robins had been careful to retain as its new bankruptcy counsel the Wall Street law firm of Skadden, Arps, Meagher and Flom, better known as a heavyweight in the corporate takeover field but also having an excellent bankruptcy department. The Skadden firm provided some Wall Street respectability, and so presumably the judge could be comforted that it would not stand for any further schemes by Robins. (Not

that Butler's firm had done so.) Having been caught with their hands in
the corporate cookie jar, the Robins execs had given back the compensation that they had illegally paid to themselves; thus making available
the basketball player's plea to the referee, "No harm, no foul." At the
hearing, the Skadden firm had thrown Robins upon the mercy of the
judge rather than attempt to deny the facts.

The judge was merciful. Although he virtually was forced by the
bald facts to find Robins in contempt of court, he managed to avoid
actually penalizing anyone. There was no finding of criminal contempt
at all. The corporation was found in civil contempt, but there was no
finding on any individual responsibility. (Although the company had
more or less conceded that it had done wrong, as many outsiders had
already learned it had been impossible to pierce Robins's defenses to
pinpoint who actually had responsibility for the offending actions.) The
only remedy that the judge imposed was that an "examiner" would be
appointed to review Robins's finances to make sure that they were in
order. (The examiner later would aid Robins by facilitating the
development of a Plan of Reorganization, something that the judge
surely had in mind when he ordered that "penalty.") As to real punishment, the judge solemnly intoned, "Now is not the time for the court
to impose sanctions." He did not say when that time might arrive.

Longtime bankruptcy practitioners could only shake their heads.
Because the Chapter 11 "debtor in possession" system operates on the
assumption that the Chapter 11 company can be trusted to follow the
rules without on-site supervision, misdirecting funds in violation of
clear bankruptcy rules is a direct challenge to the fair operation of the
reorganization laws. Accordingly, those actions are the quickest way
for management to find itself replaced by a court-appointed trustee.
Further, the payments are criminal violations if intent to bypass the
bankruptcy law is proved. It is hard to find another case in which more
than $1 million in wrongful payments to the owners and executives of
a Chapter 11 company was discovered, and the presiding judge did not
refer the matter to the United States attorney for a criminal investigation. (Perhaps it would have been assigned to S. David Schiller!)

After the embarrassing sideshow, Robins got back into the driver's
seat. In early July 1986, Robins circulated a draft of a proposed Plan
of Reorganization, but it was so penurious that even the reconstituted
claimants' committee opposed it. The committee was not permitted to

present its own plan proposals to the court.

The late summer of 1986 saw additional rulings that were favorable to Robins. Judge Merhige allowed Robins to go on what lawyers call a "fishing expedition" when he granted its request to ask a sampling of claimants about their sexual practices. He ruled that those claimants who got sick during the Robins bankruptcy case would be treated as if they had manifested injury prior to the filing, so that their claims could be limited through a Plan of Reorganization as prepetition debts. (If their claims were deemed to have arisen after the bankruptcy petition was filed, they would have to be paid in full.) He not only rejected the challenge to the makeup of the Dalkon Shield Claimants' Committee, he suggested that he may impose sanctions on those attorneys who had brought the motion. He forced plaintiffs' attorneys to drop a class action suit against Aetna.

Another embarrassing situation for the judge was narrowly averted. The Robins directors, apparently oblivious of the fact that large bonuses would be offensive under the circumstances, voted management $2 million in executive bonuses for 1986. It required a compromise worked out by the judge's advisor to quiet the bad publicity. Under the compromise, although the Robins execs gave up their 1986 bonuses, they were permitted to keep their substantial bonuses for 1985.

The judge started applying financial pressure on the creditors by using his power of the purse string. In a Chapter 11 case, the bankruptcy debtor must pay all professional fees of the official committees, as well as its own. Because those fees are out of the ordinary course of business, the judge must approve them before they can be paid out of the funds of the bankruptcy estate. Naturally that function provides the presiding judge with a powerful means of rewarding "cooperative" attorneys and punishing those who have fallen into disfavor. Expressing his impatience with the progress towards a Plan of Reorganization, in January 1987, Judge Merhige cut the percentage of fees that would be paid to the attorneys for Robins and the committees on interim fee applications to 60 percent.

That bite hurt the claimants' attorneys the worst. Robins bankruptcy attorneys, Skadden, Arps, Meagher and Flom, could live without the fees temporarily, in order to help out the client's strategy. The Skadden firm was *especially* able to ride out the storm because the corporate world was going through the Reagan-era takeover binge, and ever since Joel Flom had virtually invented the unwanted takeover, the law firm had been awash in huge fees. (It was not unusual for a Fortune 500 megacorporation to pay Skadden, Arps a fat retainer for doing nothing, just so the law firm could not represent anyone who might want to take over the company!) The trade creditors' attorneys were not terribly active, since their clients were really just spectators to Robins's battles with its customers. Mainly, it would be the attorneys for the Dalkon Shield Claimants' Committee who would feel the financial pressure of the reduced interim fee payments. The judge's use of fee awards as a pressure tactic would also lead the claimants' attorneys to think twice about the judge's reactions before a motion was made or opposition raised to something that Robins wished to do.

Robins, however, was feeling no financial pain. Customers of Robins's other products obviously did not care about the Chapter 11, because sales had continued to rise nicely during the bankruptcy proceeding. Sales for 1986 were $789 million, a healthy 12 percent over 1985 (which had been a good year). Profits were $81 million, dented slightly by bankruptcy-related costs. In fact, with bankruptcy court protection, the company had become something of a cash cow that was not being milked, with cash reserves up to $193 million by the end of 1986. Of course, due to the automatic stay, no health claimant had received a dime since the filing of the bankruptcy petition.

There was more than a little method in Robins's hiring of the Skadden law firm. Robins's high profile had drawn the attention of other medical companies seeking acquisitions. No doubt that is why Robins, its shareholders' committee, and the claimants' committee each had retained investment bankers early in the case. Skadden would be one-stop shopping for Robins's legal needs, and as an added bonus, no acquisition-minded megacorporation would have Joel Flom as its attorney.

American Home Products, a company with a product line much like that of the A. H. Robins Company but with more than six times the sales, expressed its interest in gobbling up the Chapter 11 company. Robins's over-the-counter products would blend nicely with AHP's, which included the likes of Anacin, Dristan, Advil, and Preparation H (as well as Chef Boy-Ar-Dee and Woolite). AHP was a handsome suitor, with $845 million in profits in 1987, $700 million in the bank, and almost no debt. It quickly offered $20 per share for Robins, plus a $1.5

billion trust fund for the Dalkon Shield claimants. Then it just as quickly withdrew the offer, to study some angles to which it had not given sufficient attention. Nevertheless, the interest of AHP showed that on the open market Robins was worth a substantial sum which could be used to deal with the health claims.

That is, Robins would be salable if the total amount of the health claims was not too outrageous. All involved in the Robins bankruptcy turned their attention to the health claims, and what they saw was not encouraging. More than 300,000 "notices of claim" (the first step) had been received—an astounding number, which must have cast a pall over Robins's executive suite when it was disclosed. On the other hand, about 152,000 of those women had failed to return the longer follow-up form that legally would place the claim on the court's claims docket. Another five thousand filed claims were disqualified as inadequately prepared. Robins's fate was boosted further by the paltry returns from outside the United States and the fact that future claims were barred from ever being recognized. Because of the ambiguity of the results, it was not possible to get a good fix on Robins's ultimate liability to Dalkon Shield users.

As the claims period drew to a close, the controversy over its adequacy once more raged. The two-part claims process had generated differing predictions about its fairness and effectiveness when it was instituted, and the statistics of actual filings similarly generated opposing viewpoints. To Robins and Judge Merhige, the substantial returns "proved" that notice had been effective. To plaintiffs' attorneys, the substantial returns "proved" that so many more people were injured than Robins had let on, that the process should be revised to make sure all injured women were brought into it. The small amount of claims from foreign countries, which had generated sales for the Dalkon Shield roughly equal in size to the U.S. market, "proved" that the international notification process had been a disgraceful cop-out.

Of course, the facts of the claims made did not "prove" any argument. Guess which view prevailed? Guess which black-robed person had the only vote that counted when it came to deciding whether the process had been sufficient?

The case was becoming focused upon reorganization issues. Aside from the attention being paid to the level of health claims, a number of buy-out proposals were being considered. Rorer Group, a conglomerate about the size of Robins that carried brand names such as Maalox and Ascriptin, began to kick the tires. Like American Home Products, Rorer Group had made an offer and then withdrew it; like AHP, Rorer appeared to be working upon a more complete and sophisticated offer.

Robins proposed a plan that would pay $1.65 billion into a trust fund for health claimants, to be raised by the sale of "junk" bonds. However, a number of procedural rules proposed by Robins concerning the claims process appeared to stack the deck in the company's favor, and the claimants' attorneys vowed to fight them. Of course, the shareholders thought that Robins was giving *too much* to the claimants.

The plaintiffs' attorneys were not sure that they liked the "limited pot" proposals, irrespective of the amount of the trust fund. If the trust funds were fixed at the time of the confirmation of the Plan of Reorganization, the risk that the fund would prove insufficient would fall on the health claimants. The plaintiffs' attorneys were loath to see the Robins family benefit from a shortfall. However, they might go for it if the fund were substantial and the fixed contribution provision were necessary to sell A. H. Robins to some other megacorporation.

During the summer of 1987, the Robins family negotiated fiercely to secure the best deal for itself. As the 40 percent shareholders of the A. H. Robins Company, they were most interested in the price per share that a purchaser would pay. There also were the matters of protecting the senior and junior Claibornes from judgments against them individually and providing continuing income to them. In July, Robins signed a letter of intent with Rorer Group for the sale of the company.

The proposal to the creditors hardly amounted to a model bankruptcy Plan of Reorganization. The shareholders of the Chapter 11 company would receive Rorer stock valued no less than $30 per share ($735 million in total), a handsome value for the shares considering that in the bankruptcy hierarchy of payment the shareholders rank dead last. Commercial and trade creditors of the A. H. Robins Company would be paid in full, with interest, while Dalkon Shield claimants would be limited to a trust funded by the sale of junk bonds. Several banks would receive $24 million in fees "up front" for floating the junk, which was nonrefundable even if the issue did not sell. Further, if the issue flopped and the trust were underfunded, Dalkon Shield claimants would still have no recourse against Robins's assets.

The Dalkon Shield claimants and their attorneys were not amused by the proposed plan. It was viewed as the flawed Robins's plan of several months earlier but with $200 million more going to Robins shareholders—of which the Robins family would receive its 40 percent. The proposal was especially cruel in juxtaposition to a ruling just the prior month by a unanimous Kansas Supreme Court that confirmed that Robins had known that the Dalkon Shield was not as safe or effective as the company had touted and that the company had concealed and destroyed documents during litigation.

The judge's maintenance of the "exclusive period" on behalf of Robins, which protected the company from competing plans, continued to aid it immeasurably during this period as it proposed plan after unacceptable plan. At one point Judge Merhige even fined a law firm $7,500 for making a financing proposal that the judge deemed to be the elements of a plan proposal. An interesting aspect of the situation was that the maintenance of the "exclusive period" not only barred claimants and other creditors from proposing an alternative Plan of Reorganization, *that bankruptcy ruling also prevented other companies from attempting an unwanted takeover of Robins, a protection that similar companies outside of bankruptcy do not enjoy.*

Judge Merhige had been doing a yeoman's service on behalf of Robins, but finally he was becoming impatient with the company. All of his important rulings in favor of Robins had been rubber-stamped on appeal without too much trouble, providing Robins with a "dream" bankruptcy. Those orders had helped maintain the company in a position of power even while in bankruptcy, but they also had allowed the company to get comfortable in the embrace of Chapter 11. In spite of the avid interest of at least two megacorporations, negotiations had bogged down. It was becoming plain that the Robins family was utilizing the court's protections to attempt a big score on the sale of the company, and that the Robins family might embarrass the judge again by its greediness. Judge Merhige started prodding Robins. At one hearing he went so far as to wonder for the first time on the court record why the company had never admitted that it had made a product that had turned out badly.

Upon feeling pressure from the judge, in late August 1987, the A. H. Robins Company filed a formal Plan of Reorganization. It provided for two trusts: the first a "limited pot" fund for Dalkon Shield claimants, the second for indemnification of the company's officers and directors as well as doctors and hospitals that also may have been sued along with Robins for Dalkon Shield injuries. It posited junk bond financing, but many details were vague or absent.

Judge Merhige was ready to sign on the dotted line. He indicated his personal requirement: a *reasonable estimate* that the plan's funding would be adequate to pay the Dalkon Shield claims in full. The *actual* trials or other means of determining the validity and amount of each claim would come later, after the vote on the plan had been completed. That comported with a requirement in the Bankruptcy Code that all disputed claims be estimated by the presiding judge at the time a Plan of Reorganization is considered. Thus the need to hold trials or other forms of lengthy hearings to determine disputed claims need not delay the confirmation of a Plan of Reorganization. It was also consistent with the observation of the Fourth Circuit Court of Appeals in an earlier Robins bankruptcy appeal that individual trials of the Dalkon Shield claims "would likely consume all the assets of [Robins]." However, there is a danger inherent in the procedure. If the plan provides for a "limited pot" and it turns out that the judge's estimate of the total amount of disputed claims was too low, each claimant in that class of creditors will receive less than projected. Under the judge's procedure, the Dalkon Shield claimants would be at risk.

Additional terms were disclosed several weeks later. Rorer sweetened the proposal by offering to put up $500 million as the initial funding for the Dalkon Shield trust. (Robins had been offering only $75 million.) It was also disclosed that the A. H. Robins Company would become a subsidiary of Rorer Group, to be managed by essentially the same group of officers as had been operating Robins. Even though Robins would be a wholly owned subsidiary of Rorer, it would have its own board of directors—a structure almost unheard of in the corporate world. The chairman of the subsidiary's board of directors would be none other than E. Claiborne Robins, Jr.

It appeared that the Robins family had achieved the best of everything. The Dalkon Shield problem would be cut off and isolated, relegated to the junk pile of Robins's history. The company would be sold at a tidy profit, yet the Robins family would continue as the stewards of the A. H. Robins Company brands. There was every reason to believe that the combined companies, having formed a pharmaceutical giant, would be well positioned to make substantial profits, and E. Claiborne Robins, Jr., would be well positioned to rise to the top office of the conglomerate even if it had not already been promised to him privately. Because the shareholders of Robins would receive Rorer stock instead of cash, they would share in Rorer's future. The shares of the A. H. Robins Company owned or controlled by the Robins family would be translated into about 15 percent of the outstanding shares of Rorer stock, a substantial and powerful block. Within the friendly confines of the bankruptcy court, the Robins family had negotiated one hell of a merger deal.

As always, the losers in the deal were the parties not represented at the bargaining table. The Dalkon Shield claimants would be relegated to making their claims against the trust, a separate and independent entity. In so far as Robins/Rorer succeeded in the future, the profits as well as the increase in stock value would be out of reach of the injured women. They would bear the risk that the trust fund would prove inadequate.

In spite of what appeared to be a "sweetheart deal" for Robins, as summer 1987 drifted into fall, Robins had not yet produced a signed contract, and Judge Merhige wanted to know why. In October, Judge Merhige summoned not only E. Claiborne Robins, Jr., but also seventy-six-year-old E. Claiborne Robins, Sr., to appear in open court and to account for the delay. It was explained to the judge that Rorer wanted to put restrictions on the Robins family's ability to vote and sell its block of stock—discretion being the better part of valor for the Rorer top executives—and the Robins family was holding out for diminution or elimination of the proposed restrictions. In so many words, the Claibornes were telling the judge that the plan, and therefore payment to injured women, was being held up while the Robins family jockeyed for position in, and possibly future control of, the conglomerate to be formed by the merger.

Although the Claibornes could be thankful that it was not Judge Lord that they were standing before, the judge's reaction was icy. He observed that the Robins family appeared to have acquired a conflict between their duties to the A. H. Robins Company and to themselves as shareholders, and, if he should find that to be true, he would probably have to remove the Robins family representatives from the company's board of directors. He also observed that the types of restrictions that Rorer wanted were common in such deals, and the Robinses should have expected such limitations to be placed upon their new shares of stock. In other words, the Robins family was unreasonably delaying progress in the case. In other words, the Claibornes were in trouble. To underscore his mood, the judge ruled upon an unrelated motion by fining E. Claiborne Robins, Jr., as the president of the A. H. Robins Company, $10,000 *personally* for failure to act expeditiously to collect all of the improper payments that the company had made to creditors before it was caught.

Apparently, Judge Merhige got the attention of the Claibornes. Twenty-four hours later, the agreement between the A. H. Robins Company and Rorer Group was signed, sealed, and delivered. The Rorer offer would provide $150 million to trade and financial creditors, $735 million worth of Rorer stock to the A. H. Robins Company shareholders, and $1.75 billion over time in a trust for Dalkon Shield claimants. The next task for Robins was to provide sufficiently credible evidence to the judge that the Dalkon Shield claims were equal to the proposed contribution to the trust fund.

Once more, everyone's attention was turned to the Dalkon Shield claims. However, it was not a simple matter of toting up the amounts of the 195,000 claims filed with the clerk of the court (taking up some 1.7 linear miles of a special facility). The magic number that everyone was looking for was not the gross amount of claims filed, but rather the likely gross amount of claims *as they would be allowed by a court*. Accordingly, corrections would have to be made for faulty, late, duplicate, and inflated claims; and, since it was impossible to review each claim and analyze its likelihood of success, an estimate in gross of those corrections would have to suffice. Accordingly, all eyes turned to a survey of the Dalkon Shield claims done by the judge's advisor, law professor Francis McGovern.

Unfortunately, the import of the professor's statistical exercise differed with the beholder, and so the study did not end the controversy over the proper size of a fund. One problem was that the methodology of the study was not above legitimate attack. For example, 42 percent of the women who received the professor's sampling form did not respond, making the study subjects a highly self-selective group who may or may not have been representative of the whole. Further, as with beauty, any opinion formed about strength of the various types of claimants' cases (perforated uterus, pelvic inflammatory disease, and so on), after supposedly giving due regard for different fact patterns and availability of evidence, struck many as highly subjective. (One plaintiffs' attorney had called any such endeavor "guesswork dressed up as statistics.") Nevertheless, in spite of all of the arguments to the contrary, the McGovern sampling was all that anybody had to work with, and in the end it formed the starting point for all debate.

The wide range of conclusions drawn from the McGovern report was ludicrous. To the Robins executives, the study showed that Dalkon Shield claims would total a paltry $698 million, an estimate that quickly was amended up to $1.2 billion. (With Rorer putting up the money, there was no sense trying to sell a number that was so low that it might lead the judge to dismiss the bankruptcy.) The shareholders' committee, which had an interest in paying as little as possible and preserving as much of the assets of the company as possible, estimated Dalkon Shield claims at $1 billion. The trade and commercial creditors came in at $1.6 billion. Aetna, facing possible liability for whatever Robins failed to pay (not as an insurer but as a coconspirator of Robins), estimated health claims at $2 to 2.5 billion. The Dalkon Shield Claimants' Committee read the same McGovern figures as everyone else and came up with a whopping $7.1 billion value for the claims. Obviously these were not objective opinions!

Because of the inability of the various interest groups to reach agreement respecting the Dalkon Shield claims, Judge Merhige was required to hold a valuation hearing. It would be a historic hearing, being the first time that a bankruptcy court had estimated mass tort claims, as well as a pivotal point in the bankruptcy. It also would be one of those exercises in public life that discloses just how haphazard decision processes can be, even with regards to large and important matters.

The hearing was carefully orchestrated to avoid chaos. Although more than two hundred signed up to speak, the judge declined to hear injured individuals and those not sponsored by the attorneys that had been appearing regularly before him. Nevertheless, the hearing took six days, under the watchful eye of a gallery that included reporters and hundreds of women wearing black-and-white Dalkon Shield patches. Outside, more women protested against Robins and for payment of Dalkon Shield injuries.

Karen Hicks was one of those women. Hicks had had a Dalkon Shield inserted in 1971 after her female gynecologist called it the "Cadillac of contraception." For the next seven years, Hicks, who had been healthy and active before, was constantly sick. It was always something, from bronchitis to bladder infections, and she had a disturbingly heavy flow during her periods. But all the doctors she went to could not discover the root of the problem. After awhile Hicks was dismissed as a neurotic, something she came to believe was true.

In 1978, her new gynecologist found that the IUD had drifted and lodged in Hicks's cervix. The doctor took it out.

Karen Hicks's medical problems were still not over, although her marriage was. She was so devoid of energy that she allowed her ex-husband to have custody of their daughter—who had been born before the Dalkon Shield insertion. Hicks tried to get her life back on track in Bethlehem, Pennsylvania, where she worked at Lehigh University as an administrator. Gradually the years went by, and she felt she had enough stamina to cope with the vagaries of life—as long as there were not too many of them. Then in 1984, at the age of thirty-six, she decided to remarry. Her fiancé was forty, and they both wanted to start a family while there was still time.

Three days after the wedding, Karen Hicks blacked out from pain, from what was later diagnosed as pelvic inflammatory disease. Seven days after the wedding, Hicks had a complete hysterectomy; her entire reproductive system including the cervix was removed. "I was castrated," she was to say later. It was only then, after the emergency surgery, that the first doctor of all the many she had consulted over the years suggested that perhaps the Dalkon Shield had been the source of her pain and misery.

At first Hicks was demoralized and too depressed to take any action. Then she filed suit against the A. H. Robins Company. She felt a good portion of her adult life had been stolen from her, and she was damn well going to get restitution. Her case was in the discovery stage when the bankruptcy was filed. Karen Hicks felt castrated for a second time. Her rage was such that she would not be a passive victim, a number in the bankruptcy files. She did not want her fate to be decided by a "bunch of suits" in the Richmond courthouse.

Hicks organized the Dalkon Shield Information Network after claimants were told not to bother the court with their questions. With fifteen hundred paid members, she has estimated that her volunteer group has talked with some fifty thousand victims. She spent endless hours on the road to Richmond—once getting herself thrown out of Judge Merhige's courtroom—and she organized protests such as the one at the valuation hearing. "We wanted the lawyers to see our faces. We didn't want to be invisible."

At the hearing, the primary witnesses were experts produced by the parties, each of whom interpolated the McGovern report to reach a "bottom line" of the gross amount of estimated Dalkon Shield claims . . . consistent with the position of the party that hired the expert, of course.

If anything was proved during the hearing, it was the adage that it is possible to prove almost anything with statistics. Robins's expert witness opined that less than 30,000 of the 195,000 claims were of the type for which Robins had paid substantial damages in litigation. He read the 42 percent nonresponse rate to McGovern's survey to indicate that 42 percent of injured women would not pursue claims. He also assumed that many who pursued claims would be thwarted by problems of proving that the Dalkon Shield caused their injuries and by statutes of limitations. His analysis buttressed Robins's estimate of $1.2 million, grudgingly increased to $1.6 million at the hearing to allow for the weakness of the assumption that only 58 percent of the claimants would stay the course. At the other end of the spectrum, the expert for the claimants concluded that Robins would end up paying an average of $37,112 for 173,000 Dalkon shield claims that had been manifested prior to the bankruptcy, $717 million for claims that had arisen during the bankruptcy, $571 million for women not showing signs of injury yet, and $5.6 billion for claims that would arise after the bankruptcy had been finalized.

In the clash of titans, the appointed representative for future claimants was barely heard. Stanley Joynes was involved in the activities but was a peripheral player. Unlike Manville, which had to deal with diseases of long gestation periods, Robins insisted that nearly all of the repercussions of the ill-fated Dalkon Shield had been visited on its users. As a result, Joynes's position, that future claimants' rights could not be taken away from them by the bankruptcy as a matter of due process, was a problem relegated to the back burner. Joynes did not make more noise because he felt, rightly or wrongly, that a claims facility set up through a reorganization plan would provide a remedy for those women.

Judge Merhige was a reluctant Solomon. Because of the inherent vagueness of the topic and the ferocious self-interest of the parties, he had been given very little realistic evidence upon which to make a decision. Any finding that was not without the consent of all the major intrests would surely be appealed, which would delay the final funding. Subsequent to the hearing, the judge called in the primary lawyers in the case and told them to reach agreement on the valuation of the claims. He also told them that no fee applications would be approved until they did. (About $20 million in professional fees had been paid out by Robins and about $10 million was owed. The hiatus in interim fee allowances may have hurt the lawyers, but it was an added bonus for Robins.)

If the judge had expected a miracle to be worked upon the parties tussling over claims valuation, he was destined to be disappointed. After a period of frustration, Judge Merhige was forced to issue his ruling. His estimate of the total of valid, enforceable Dalkon Shield claims as would be determined over the next several years by some claims procedure (as yet to be determined) was—ta da!—exactly $2.475 billion. Presumably, it was a sum that would up the ante for Robins to buy its way out of bankruptcy and complete a desirable merger, yet not be so large that it would blow the deal. Robins and Rorer said that they would try to meet the figure.

The delay had allowed other drug companies a second chance. American Home Products, which really had not gone away, continued to follow the proceedings and talk with the parties. Sanofi, an international drug company 60 percent owned by petroleum giant Elf Aquitaine, expressed its interest. When Sanofi agreed to pay $600 million to Robins shareholders for only 58 percent of its stock and allow Robins to run as an independent subsidiary, the Robins family jumped into its corner. Rorer cried "breach of contract." However, neither Rorer nor Sanofi yet had put in place the financing to reach the estimated value of the claims set by the judge. It looked like the best that they could offer would be funding for the trust over a period of years.

The delay allowed the largest company of the group, American Home Products, to finish putting together the offer that would send the other companies away. AHP, being much larger than Sanofi and Rorer, was better able to raise the kind of cash that would persuade everyone that, whether or not they loved the deal, at least the trust would not end up with less money than promised. AHP simply offered to produce $2.375 billion on the day the Plan of Reorganization was approved, or $2.475 billion one year from that date.

After some tussling over dollars, duties, delineations and details, the Fourth Amended Plan of Reorganization of the A. H. Robins Company was presented to the court. It contemplated payment in full of all valid claims of all types, although not necessarily instantaneously. Trust No. 1 initially would be funded with $2.255 billion in cash from American Home Products and Robins, $75 million from Aetna, and $5 million from the Robins family. In addition, Aetna would provide an insurance policy for $250 million that would come into play if the trust fund proved inadequate. It would pay out on Dalkon Shield claims as determined by a claims procedure that was not yet fully formulated. A second trust, Trust No. 2, would be funded by $45 million from Robins and $5 million from the Robins family, and would hold a $100 million excess claims insurance policy to be issued by Aetna. That trust would attend to claims not covered by Trust No. 1, such as claims for indemnity by doctors and hospitals. Aetna and the Robins family had not sweetened the pot out of the goodness of their hearts. In return, the bankruptcy injunction barring suits against the A. H. Robins Company once it had reorganized would be extended to cover them—a highly unusual and controversial use of the bankruptcy powers.

All of the major interests represented in the bankruptcy agreed upon the AHP plan. The major claimants' attorneys felt that the practical limit had been reached. The lenders and trade creditors had achieved full payment of their claims. The shareholders of the Chapter 11 company received $29 per share, a total of $700 million. The Robins family would receive $280 million (!) in stock for its holdings, making the $10 million contributed to the trusts in order to gain immunity from suit a small price to pay, indeed. AHP obviously felt that adding Robins's products to the fold was well worth the price. Stanley Joynes felt that he had covered the future claimants by filing a claim in the bankruptcy on their behalf, and he was satisfied that the trust funding was fair.

If there was a loser in the deal it may have been Aetna. Considering that it had settled its liability through litigation with Robins prior to Robins's bankruptcy filing, it was paying dearly in the final form of the plan. Aetna's sole benefit appeared to be inclusion under the bankruptcy umbrella by way of Judge Merhige's order that enjoined anyone receiving injury benefits from either of the trusts from ever suing Aetna. On the other hand, it could be argued that Aetna had made a perfectly accurate assessment of its potential liability from suits claiming that it had a further duty to pay Robins's claims or that it was a coconspirator in Robins's fraud. In that view, Aetna had become a loser not through poor negotiating during the bankruptcy, but rather when it had blithely continued to insure Robins without requiring that the Dalkon Shield be stringently tested before it was marketed.

Many of the Dalkon Shield injury claimants felt that they had not been well served by the Dalkon Shield Claimants' Committee during the negotiations and that they would not be well served by the Plan of Reorganization. Because of the makeup of the committee, its positions were inherently suspect to the bulk of claimants and their attorneys. They were not impressed that the Dalkon Shield Claimants' Committee had taken part in the process that had increased the funding of the claimants' trust. Many health claimants were unhappy that the committee had not succeeded in shifting the risk of inadequate funding to the giant Robins/Rorer company-to-be and were worried that the money would run out before the claims did. Accordingly, they gave little weight to the committee's recommendation that claimants vote for the plan.

The Dalkon Shield committee was not the only element of the case viewed with suspicion by many. Other aspects of the bankruptcy as they appeared from the outside looking in did not help the attitudes of many Dalkon Shield claimants.

A major irritant was the ability of the Robins family to skate through the proceedings. Not only did its members avoid significant legal liability while profiting handsomely as shareholders of the Chapter 11 company, but they had suffered no moral opprobrium whatsoever in the bankruptcy. The ancient adage of commerce, "payment cures all," had been the basic philosophy of the judge and the lawyers; and the consensual plan would effectively deny the Dalkon Shield claimants their day in court to point the finger at the men who had changed their lives for the worse. Except for Roger Tuttle, the former in-house attorney for Robins who had salved his conscience, *no top executive of the A. H. Robins Company had ever said he was sorry or even admitted that the Dalkon Shield was a defective product*, and none of the central players in the bankruptcy proceedings seemed the least bit interested in pursuing the subject.

To many Dalkon Shield claimants, the bankruptcy lawyers appeared to be a very chummy group. Now that the negotiations had reached fruition and each side had begun the psychological process of rationalizing the outcome and becoming a believer in the package, there was a great release of tension within the case. The familiarity built up across the negotiating table over a period of years, often breeding contempt during hard bargaining, now turned to camaraderie. A feeling of "job well done" began to wash over the lawyers. As always, the lawyers would walk away from the case handsomely compensated; however, the health claimants would only be *beginning* a claims process that would take more years to complete even *if* they could carry the burden of proving their damages. The leader of one group of Dalkon Shield victims expressed a view of the bankruptcy process that appeared to be widespread. "This is not a system of justice, this is a business plan. You should have seen the lawyers for the claimants' committee patting lawyers from Robins on the back. I want human beings accountable for criminal wrongdoing."

Of course, there was no chance that the Robins executives would have to face up to their deeds in criminal court. Having been ignored as inappropriate in bankruptcy court by those most familiar with the whole story, the subject was unlikely to be taken up elsewhere. One journalist understood the full meaning of the situation: "[U]nless a U.S. Court of Appeals rules against that financial settlement in the coming weeks, the paltry payoff will stand—and the U.S. Bankruptcy Code will be one step closer to becoming the shelter of choice for corporate criminals." No doubt many claimants recalled Judge Miles Lord's observation concerning crime in the executive suite.

The track record of the Reagan administration on business crimes also must have given comfort to the Robins management. The Justice Department had ignored the request of the FDA that felony charges be brought against Eli Lilly for failing to report forty-nine deaths and nine hundred injuries outside the United States arising from its arthritis drug Oraflex and against SmithKline Beckman for a similar indiscretion involving thirty-six deaths and more than five hundred injuries from its high blood pressure drug Selacryn. The department merely had brought misdemeanor charges against the corporations and had settled for miniscule fines ($25,000 from Lilly). The Justice Department would not be heard from further in the Robins case, except to collect its tax claim.

During the spring and summer of 1988, the Dalkon Shield once again was in the news. Injured women and their lawyers would have to decide whether to vote for the plan.

In order to win approval of Dalkon Shield claimants, the Plan of Reorganization would have to win two-thirds approval of that class of creditors. The normal bankruptcy requirement is that a plan achieve approval of one-half of the *number* of claims voting and two-thirds of the *amount* of those claims. Thus the larger, presumably more important, claims will have a weighted vote. Notwithstanding whatever magic Judge Merhige had used to divine the total of the claims as they would be allowed, the logistics absolutely precluded determining, or even estimating, approximately 195,000 individual claims in order to assign each one an amount for voting purposes. The result was that each claim not already voided for some procedural reason would be assigned one vote. At the close of two decades of the sexual revolution, the motto would be "One woman, one vote."

Because of the cost, it was not possible for any group of Dalkon Shield claimants to communicate in person or through direct mailings with the class as a whole concerning the vote. However, the official Dalkon Shield Claimants' Committee was permitted to piggyback its recommendation to approve the plan onto materials sent to health claimants under the auspices of the court clerk. As a result, women who filed claims received in one "official" package not only the proposed reorganization plan and other papers necessary to conduct a mail-in vote, but also the voting recommendation of the claimants' committee. In effect, the precinct captain had been allowed into the polling booth. (Allowing a committee to communicate with its members by piggybacking onto the court's mailing is a way a judge can encourage approval of a Plan of Reorganization, and it is not unusual. It is another element of the power that the creditors' committees can swing.)

Dissenters had come forward from the ranks. A coalition led by the International Dalkon Shield Victims Education Association claimed that the settlement amounted only to thirty-five cents on the dollar. The case against Robins's plan was made mainly through the mass media. Not only was it a subject that the media could grab onto, it was not feasible for any groups to do a mailing to hundreds of thousands of Dalkon Shield claimants. The outcries were full of sound and fury, but in the end signified nothing.

On July 26, 1988, a month short of three years after A. H. Robins had filed its Chapter 11 petition, the buy-out proposal of American Home Products and the attendant Plan of Reorganization were easily approved in their final form, the Sixth Amended and Restated Plan of Reorganization. In the end, 94 percent of the Dalkon Shield claimants who voted did so in favor of the plan. Judge Merhige made the necessary legal findings, not the least of which was that the estimate of 100 percent payment to the health claimants allowed the shareholders to receive compensation for their shares.

In later hearings, Judge Merhige efficiently dispatched other issues in a manner that fulfilled preconditions to the final closing of the merger and AHP's participation in funding the Plan of Reorganization. To no one's surprise, the judge disallowed all punitive damage claims. Judge Merhige ruled that because punitive damages were not capable of being estimated, it was within his equity powers to aid the reorganization of Robins by denying the right to claim them. An additional reason was that it was inappropriate in bankruptcy to be concerned with punishment or deterrence, the twin goals of punitive damages. He also established a national class action, in his courtroom of course, for anyone so foolish as to pass up the Robins trust in order to sue Aetna as a coconspirator or doctors for malpractice. In doing so, he ignored substantial legal authority to the effect that class actions are not suitable for numerous personal injury claims, including his own prior ruling denying class action status to Robins, a ruling that had precipitated the Chapter 11.

Judge Merhige's heavy hand would not be lifted easily. The judge announced that as an extension of his supervision of the bankruptcy case, he would personally supervise the operations of the trusts, an unexpected move that caused a good deal of apprehension on the part of the plaintiffs' attorneys. When the trust machinery was being assembled, he insisted that his man, Michael M. Sheppard, clerk of the Bankruptcy Court in Richmond, be hired to the $150,000-per-year post of managing director. He rejected the counsel for the Dalkon Shield trust, refusing the trust's request to retain the law firm that had represented the Dalkon Shield Claimants' Committee. When the trustees' organizational efforts were proceeding too slowly for him, he removed three of them.

Robins had saved a surprise until the Plan of Reorganization had been approved. The company objected to the proof of claim that had been filed by Stanley Joynes as the court-appointed representative of the future claimants. Apparently Robins did not believe its own advice to Judge Merhige that there would be a mere $9 million in claims arising after the approval of the reorganization plan. Perhaps they feared that the number would be closer to Joynes's estimate, $289 million, which could tip the Dalkon Shield trust fund into the red in the future.

The very next month after Judge Merhige approved the reorganization plan of the A. H. Robins Company, an IUD was back in the news. A jury in St. Paul returned a verdict for $8.75 million against G. D.

Searle for injuries received by a wearer of Searle's Copper-7 IUD. The jury found that the device had been insufficiently tested, and it appeared that a number of plaintiffs' attorneys were gearing up to expand the number of cases against Searle. With Robins in mind, investors started a run on the stock of Searle's parent, Monsanto, sending its stock tumbling 13 percent in two days.

Although there was no turning back, almost immediately after the creation of the Dalkon Shield trust, many claimants must have wondered whether they had made a mistake. Having waited in limbo for years, now they were being stampeded.

Whether intentionally done or not, the initial funding of the trust had put a fear of not settling quickly into many claimants' heads. The trust had been funded with $100 million in seed money during appeals of the judge's approval of the Plan of Reorganization and the grant of immunity from suit to Aetna, and a natural reaction of claimants surely must have been that the limited fund could disappear entirely in the event of an adverse ruling. Claimants' attorneys charged that women who called the trust's hotline were told that the trust would soon run out of money.

Further, the trust had started off its activities with an aggressive program to induce—and, some said, advise and mislead—claimants to settle *cheaply*. A claims schedule was established that offered an almost automatic payment of $725 for minor injuries or for injuries for which there was little proof. The settlement process with respect to other smaller claims was geared, avowedly, towards persuading claimants to use a schedule and not to use lawyers. Then, just before Christmas, presumably when claimants' needs for cash were at their greatest, the trust mailed out its no-muss-no-fuss settlement package. Claimants' attorneys felt that the trust's form settlement offer was in a tone that made recipients feel that they had to hurry up and accept it or the money might go away. While the trustees denied that intent, the letter explaining the trust's offer stated that the trust "will stop making payments under this option as soon as the reorganization plan is given final approval by the appellate courts." The letter further advised that if any part of the plan were to be struck down on appeal, settlement payments would cease.

The procedures appeared daunting to those Dalkon Shield claimants who were considering refusing the quickie settlement offer. In order to undertake negotiations for a higher settlement, a claimant would have to retain an attorney—an act, due to the acknowledged antilawyer stance of the trust, that a claimant legitimately might fear would lead the trust's negotiators to "punish" her and result in a diminished chance of collecting anything in the foreseeable future. Also, as a prerequisite to agreeing to a substantial settlement, the trust demanded proof akin to that customarily required in pretrial procedures. If negotiations failed, the claimant would have to file a lawsuit (against the trust *only*), follow the usual court procedures, wait on backlogged court calendars (in many districts caused primarily by asbestos cases), and prove the same evidence at trial, as she would have had to do prior to Robins's bankruptcy . . . except three years had been lost.

The result of the procedures chosen through the bankruptcy and the attitude taken by the trust administrators was to create extreme psychological pressures on the Dalkon Shield claimants against restarting adversarial processes that had been set in neutral for years and would have to be pursued for years more. The quick, low-ball offers left women in a quandary over whether to spend money on medical documentation and lawyers in order to meet the trust's burden of proof for higher payments (such as proving that the injury would be "long lasting") or whether simply to request the modest check, end the uncertainty, and be done with it.

Many women decided to be done with it. More than 70,000 claimants out of approximately 195,000 accepted the trust's first offer of $725 rather quickly, almost double the estimate that the judge had used to set the trust's funding. The morality of that depended upon one's viewpoint. To the trustees, more money was left available for those claiming serious injuries. To many Dalkon Shield claimants' leaders, it was a travesty of justice. In any event, the trust's work would continue on, and by seizing the initiative at the onset of the process, the trustees certainly made their future job easier.

The fact of so many women meekly settling their claims could not have been lost on the panel hearing the appeals objecting to the Plan of Reorganization. Add to that the strong general tendency not to disturb the rulings of a presiding judge—especially a district court judge wearing his bankruptcy court robe—with respect to bankruptcy matters, the deference accorded to megacorporations in Chapter 11, the almost total unwillingness to disturb *any* Plan of Reorganization that saves a company and moves a Chapter 11 proceeding off the court calendar, and the lack of enthusiasm of an appellate court to take a fresh look into such a complex matter when affirmance will make the whole problem go away, and you have a lot of good reasons why the dissenters' odds on appeal were miniscule.

The appellate court did not upset the oddsmakers. In June 1989, the Fourth Circuit Court of Appeals issued a series of opinions that upheld every facet of the reorganization scheme, up to and including Judge Merhige's heavy-handed supervision of the Dalkon Shield trust. Rubber-stamping the plan of reorganization was easy. Rationalizing the injunction against suing Aetna or the companies' officers or directors required some legal gymnastics. The legal analysis contained in the one hundred seventy-five pages of the decisions can be reduced to one proposition: if it is necessary to allow the reorganization to become effectuated, than it is O.K.

The affirmance of the plan of reorganization, including the judge's estimate of Dalkon Shield claims, took only slightly more than nineteen pages of text. The first clue was when the opinion termed Robins's bankruptcy plan "the carefully designed reorganization." It noted the substantial vote in favor of the plan and the similarity of the case to that of Manville. It found Judge Merhige's estimate of the Dalkon Shield claims not to be "clearly erroneous," the standard for reversal.

As to a central element of the reorganization, providing Aetna and officers and directors with immunity from suit from any Dalkon Shield claimant who sought compensation through the Robins trust, affirmance required hurtling a number of legal obstacles. One problem for the court was the clear language of a section of the Bankruptcy Code, which provides that "discharge of a debt of the debtor does not affect the liability of any other entity on, or the property of any other entity for, such debt," and a number of prior court decisions which found that the language barred extending protection of the bankruptcy injunction to those not in bankruptcy. The court simply ruled that the statute does not apply all the time, such as under the circumstances of the Robins case "where the entire reorganization hinges on [it.]" The court quoted the Manville appellate court when it approved Manville's plan: "Particularly since the insurance settlement/injunction arrangement was essential in this case to a workable reorganization, it falls within the bankruptcy court's equitable powers which traditionally have been invoked to the end that . . . substance will not give way to form, that technical considerations will not prevent substantial justice." Case closed.

Another task for the appellate court provided an even higher hurdle. The court's opinion approving the establishment of a class action for those who chose to sue Aetna as a coconspirator rather than claim through the Robins trust was a monster of one hundred seven pages. The court was required to undertake a series of gymnastic moves in order to ignore substantial legal authority denying class actions in mass tort situations. To the court, due process is a "flexible concept," a viewpoint that then allowed the court to turn the prior case authority on its head and to decide that a class action was *preferable* in the Robins/Aetna situation.

Since the court had decided in its wisdom what was best for the Dalkon Shield claimants, those who had appealed Judge Merhige's ruling were interlopers of a sort, not acting in the best interests of the larger group. Speaking about the appealing Dalkon Shield victims, the opinion delivered the unkindest cut of all: "Class certification cannot be defeated simply because a few claimants—actually, their attorneys—" feel that they could do better for themselves by going it alone. It was the syndicated Mr. Dooley who observed that judges read the election returns, and most certainly these judges had read the creditors' vote in favor of approving the Robins Plan of Reorganization.

The appellate ruling not only approved the establishment of a class action suit, it denied the right of any plaintiff to choose any other form of suit or forum—a highly unusual use of the class action format. It was the belief of the appellate judges that the trust would provide compensation for the injuries. Further, after some gratuitous analysis of the claims that the Dalkon dissidents wished to make against Aetna, the appellate court opinion concluded that they were not very good and had little chance of success. Thus it followed to the court that because the Robins program was so good not only did the situation warrant a class action certification, it warranted a class that no one can "opt out" of, a very rare form of class action. Of course, affirming the lower court's rulings by mandating the class aided in the overall reorganization as well as the settlement of the Robins claims against Aetna, killing two big, bothersome birds with one stone. Accordingly, no one who bypassed the Robins trust to sue Aetna, officials of Aetna or Robins, or doctors would be permitted to sue in any court of the land except the one court where the class action had been established— presided over by none other than the Honorable Robert R. Merhige,

Jr.

There is no absolute right of appeal to the United States Supreme Court for a commercial case, and the "writ of certiorari" requesting a hearing filed by dissenting Dalkon Shield claimants was denied by that court. The road had reached an end for those who felt that the Plan of Reorganization and the attendant rulings by Judge Merhige had been unfair and wrong.

The tone of the Fourth Circuit's rulings and the effect of the Supreme Court's failure to rule were clear. When reviewing bankruptcy reorganization plans of megacorporations, details were for defeatists. Legal precedent in bankruptcy and other areas of law would be viewed through a prism that would distort it so that a picture could be painted to match the strokes that made up the sections of the plan. The rational arguments of dissenters would not be allowed to outweigh the wishes of the megacorporations and, in Robins's case, the vote of the creditors. Companies that had injured so many people, making adequate compensation difficult, could turn to bankruptcy to settle the gross liability, set it aside, and, if possible, sell the company at a handsome profit to the shareholders. When done as part of a megacorporate reorganization, corporate officials and other companies who have not suffered the obligations of bankruptcy can nevertheless piggyback onto the case to acquire its benefits. The bankruptcy courts—and their overseers, the higher courts—will be happy to serve as, to use the motto of *Forbes* magazine, the megacorporations' "capitalist tool." (Congress, too. Thanks to special legislation, Robins/AHP and other companies creating a pool to pay for mass injuries can deduct all funding as a business expense in the year that the money is set aside; they need not wait years until the funds are actually paid out to claimants. It is the taxpayers' unwitting contribution to the welfare of mass toxic tortfeasors.)

The Robins bankruptcy case also stands for another proposition: it is perhaps the ultimate example of how a presiding judge can aid a corporate reorganization.

One of the unique aspects of bankruptcy is how much supervision by the court is required over a long period. Ample opportunities are presented for the presiding judge to set the tone of the case, reward cooperative attorneys and punish those who do not go along with the program, and throw the court's considerable weight behind the debtor's reorganization. No other form of adversarial litigation—and, make no mistake about it, bankruptcy is one form of that—requires so much hands-on supervision by a judge. No other type of case demands so many rulings by a judge on matters great and small that can affect the outcome, for which the protections of a jury are unavailable. (Although ordinary pieces of litigation can take years, nearly all of the activity of those cases proceeds without the judge's intervention or, usually, knowledge.) In no other type of proceeding can the ultimate outcome hinge on estimates of liability untested by actual trials subject to the law's strict rules of evidence. In no other kind of court proceedings do judges have such a regular, and in effect sanctioned, interest in aiding one of the parties. No other type of rulings by the presiding judge is granted the deference, and usually the disinterest, of the higher courts—and that goes double when the presiding judicial officer is a full district court judge.

By calling on the protections afforded by the Bankruptcy Code, the A. H. Robins Company not only stacked the deck in its favor legally, but it chose its own dealer. By filing a piece of paper, the one-page Chapter 11 petition, Robins brought litigation from courtrooms all over the country—Robins had kept the cases isolated when it was a help—into the courtroom of the friendliest possible judge in the friendliest possible city. When it comes to what lawyers call "forum shopping," the A. H. Robins Company had found the best bargain of all. As of this writing, it is too early to tell the fate of the claims being made to the Dalkon Shield trusts.

Chapter 14

The Late Eighties:
The Song Remains the Same

"Can we ever have too much
of a good thing?"
—Miguel de Cervantes,
Don Quixote

During the late 1980s, economics in general, and bankruptcies in particular, ceased to be hot topics. The inflation dragon had been killed. Although oil prices fluctuated frequently, threatening to leap several times in 1989, OPEC disunity kept prices hovering around $20 a barrel—a level once thought bizarre but by then treated as ordinary. Because no one specter (with the exception of Japan) affected the majority of Americans, President Reagan, with the magic that only he could employ, assured us that everything was all right. So what is there to write about?

It is a myth that the economy went back to what had been normal before the late Seventies. Whole industries, such as steel, were unprofitable. By the close of the Eighties, the Japanese automakers had backed all the others to the wall. In spite of the talk of increasing the competitiveness of American business, substantial energies of the top corporate executives were diverted from mundane things like production efficiency and capital investment by the development of "junk" bonds and merger and takeover mania. What did look the same as the Sixties and the early Seventies was the megacorporate fascination with conglomeratizing. Because banks found it easier to invest in junk bonds and foreign governments than to try to figure out whether their customers were creditworthy, funds for start-ups and small businesses were hard to come by. For the American middle class, the late Eighties meant hidden inflation in housing, health, and transportation costs and an increasing reliance on credit cards and home equity loans to make ends meet.

The number of bankruptcies filed by Americans continued to rise throughout the late Eighties. To see approximately 200,000 personal bankruptcies in 1979 was to view an ominous signal. To have 300,000 in 1981 was saddening. To count 430,000 in 1987 was to become jaded. When Americans set a new record by filing 600,000 personal bankruptcies—predicted for 1990—it hardly will be newsworthy. As long as no one coherent threat can be detected, we can go on thinking that the personal finances of the American public are peachy-keen.

Business bankruptcies did not keep increasing during the late Eighties, but they did not recede either. About 40,000 business Chapter 7 liquidation cases were filed each year. Although there was some fluctuation, an average of 20,000 Chapter 11s per year were recorded.

The cessation of the extreme economic conditions of the late 1970s and early 1980s took some of the financial pressure off the mega-corporations, but there still was plenty of overexpansion and other forms of corporate blunders to keep the bankruptcy courts busy. The steel industry provided several major bankruptcies. A number of mega-corporate bankruptcies commenced in the early Eighties, most notably Manville's and Robins's, lumbered through most of the late Eighties. Both Sanford Sigoloff and Frank Lorenzo did an encore, and the Texaco and Hunt brothers fiascos provided more colorful characters to the bankruptcy scene. In general, whatever the form of corporate folly, the forgiving arms of the bankruptcy courts were there to catch the corporate barons before they fell; and whatever the scheme to make others pay more than their fair share, the bankruptcy laws could be harnessed to provide a helping hand.

The American steel industry has milked protectionism for all it is worth. Protected from competition for many years by high tariffs, it has fallen behind foreign manufacturers. As protective tariffs were eliminated, in the late Eighties a number of steel producers sought another barrier to hide behind—the protection from creditors offered by Chapter 11 of the Bankruptcy Code. As of mid-1990, two major U.S.

steel companies continued to operate while insulated from competition by the bankruptcy laws, further delaying their days of reckoning.

In April 1985, Wheeling-Pittsburgh Steel took the plunge. In a desperate attempt to modernize during the early Eighties, Wheeling had borrowed heavily at the same time that it was suffering operating losses. By 1985, it was one of the more modern U.S. steel producers, but it had run out of credit. Facing $219 million in upcoming debt payments and unable to wring concessions from its lenders and unions that it considered sufficient, the seventh largest steelmaker ($1 billion in assets) resorted to Chapter 11. It was a sign of the times that the initial reaction of the business media focused on the competitive advantage the company would have when it completed its court case, rather than any possibility that it would be liquidated because of the bankruptcy.

The Wheeling-Pittsburgh Steel case introduced a new element into the megacorporate Chapter 11: the underfunded pension plan as a major aspect of the case. At the time of the bankruptcy filing, the pension fund that covered about ten thousand pensioners was woefully underfunded, and a $60 million contribution was coming due. In crisis talks held when the company was trying to avoid bankruptcy, the company was willing to give its lenders additional security on $300 million of unencumbered assets in return for agreeing to defer scheduled payments, but the United Steelworkers union would not acquiesce to the restructuring. The union feared the concessions would be insufficient to really turn the company around and that no assets would be left free to pay union contributions. Instead, the union demanded that *it* receive the security instead, to guarantee the company's obligation to its members. The bankruptcy was precipitated by that impasse. Immediately upon the filing of the Chapter 11 case, the company announced that it would move to terminate its pension plan and renegotiate its labor agreement with the union.

At the time, the bankruptcy filing by Wheeling Steel was thought to be a setback for its aggressive chairman, Dennis J. Carney. The word was that Carney had struggled quite hard to avoid the embarrassment of Chapter 11. The company claimed to be quite concerned about possible customer defections. However, most of them turned out to be wise enough in the ways of Chapter 11 to know that the bankruptcy filing had *increased* the chances that Wheeling Steel would be around to deliver the orders placed with it. The 5 percent discount Wheeling offered not only enticed those wavering on the edge of seeking another supplier, it even helped to bring in some new business. In bankruptcy Wheeling set about busily reorganizing operations and canceling onerous contracts while protected from creditor actions, and in mid-1986 turned its first quarterly profit in two years. The Chapter 11 would help Wheeling survive a period of sagging steel demand and stiff foreign competition until its modern facilities could have an effect.

Of course, wage relief was part of the package that allowed Wheeling to stage its comeback. Although Wheeling was not as successful beating down the steelworkers' union as the airlines had been with their unions, it benefited greatly from the leverage it gained in bankruptcy.

While Bankruptcy Judge Warren W. Bentz had no trouble granting the company's motion to reject its labor contract, and the federal district court affirmed the ruling on appeal, a panel of the Third Circuit Court of Appeals reversed the rulings. The appellate court added a new twist to the theme. The court ruled that it was unfair for the company to cut wages so deeply without granting employees their request that wages improve in the future as the fortunes of the company improved—a so-called "snapback" clause. The company's rejection of its labor accord was disallowed, and the parties were told to try again.

In practical terms, the ruling was not a serious defeat for Wheeling Steel or, in terms of precedent, for other employers. All it said was that employees cannot be handed what is too obviously the short end of the stick in industries where factors other than labor costs are important, too. In any event, the rejection of the pact had already benefited Wheeling. The appeals court decision did not come until more than a year after Wheeling had filed bankruptcy, and the company had already used the leverage supplied by the bankruptcy law's rejection provision to negotiate a more favorable contract with the union. The union had pursued the appeal in order to seek a favorable ruling on the law. Because the parties had already renegotiated their relationship, the appellate court's ruling did not result in any change in their new agreement.

It took Wheeling Steel three years in Chapter 11 to wear down the Pension Benefit Guaranty Corporation. The PBGC, another one of those "off balance sheet" agencies created by Congress, has the job of reimbursing employees whose terminated pension plans lack sufficient assets to fulfill their obligations. In having its pension fund terminated at the onset of its bankruptcy, Wheeling Steel had dumped a shade under $500 million in pension liabilities onto the PBGC, and the agency, reeling under a $2 billion deficit, had tried to make the company fund a large share of it. In April 1988, a settlement was reached. Wheeling would contribute a modest $85 million towards the mess it had created, the PBGC picking up the rest of the liabilities to Wheeling's pensioners.

The PBGC put its best face forward when the settlement became public. Its announcement of the accord emphasized that it was sending "a clear message that it's going to be very expensive for companies to back out of their pension promises." In reality, the 17 percent settlement transmitted exactly the opposite meaning to the likely recipients of that message. Another form of unacknowledged megacorporate welfare had been developed.

Although the settlement with the PBGC appeared to clear the last hurdle standing in the way of the reorganization of Wheeling-Pittsburgh Steel Corporation, the company still was in no hurry to step from behind the protection of the bankruptcy court. As the reorganization proceedings neared the five-year mark, a shareholders' group led by an investment banking house threatened to propose its own plan, but the company was successful in co-opting it. A new crisis then emerged—the failure of the company to reach an updated accord with the United Steelworkers, the same problem that had precipitated the bankruptcy many years earlier. However, this time a new contract was reached.

Between April 1985 and mid-1990, Wheeling has negotiated at least two collective-bargaining agreements with the United Steelworkers, closed several inefficient plants, restructured its operations, and seen three chairmen pass through its executive suite, but the company still had not emerged from Chapter 11. Apparently, for Wheeling the world of competition is just too cold and cruel to face without the help of some form of federal welfare, and the bankruptcy system ranks among the best.

LTV Corporation followed Wheeling Steel into bankruptcy in July 1987. Like Wheeling's, LTV's Chapter 11 was still unfinished midway through 1990.

In April 1982, at the peak of the rain of bankruptcy filings, the *Wall Street Journal* did a feature piece on LTV. The article compared Nucorp Energy, which had not yet filed Chapter 11 but was obviously too much in debt, and LTV, which had pared its short-term debt down to nothing in a heroic manner over the space of a few years. The section on LTV was entitled "The Survivor." LTV continued as a solidly financed company into the late Eighties. In 1984, it created a stronger steel division by merging its Jones and Laughlin unit with Republic Steel Corporation. When it filed Chapter 11 in order to ditch its pension liabilities and chisel its union, it had about a billion dollars in the bank.

LTV filed Chapter 11 on July 17, 1986. With LTV, the number two steel producer in the U.S., joining number seven Wheeling-Pittsburgh Steel Corporation in Chapter 11, fully 20 percent of America's steel production came under bankruptcy court supervision.

The bankruptcy filing of LTV caught the financial world and the steel industry by surprise. Although LTV was not operating profitably, it appeared to have sufficient assets to withstand the need to file bankruptcy. Since LTV's immediate financial situation did not appear that dire, competitors who had not chosen the bankruptcy route fretted at the edge LTV would be handed through the bankruptcy laws. How times had changed!

LTV was (and still is) a huge corporation. At the time it filed its Chapter 11 petition, it listed its assets at $6 billion and its debts at $4.2 billion. In addition to its steel operations, it was a big player in the aerospace and energy businesses. Its income from steel was a little less than $6 billion a year, and the profitable aerospace business generated more than $2 billion a year in sales. It employed fifty-six thousand and had some thirty-six thousand creditors. In all, sixty-six bankruptcy petitions were filed for the conglomerate's related corporations, and the required financial disclosures ran to ten thousand pages. The paper work and telephone calls generated by the case sent the bankruptcy clerk's office to overload, and the conglomerate soon got its own outpost of the clerk's office with its own file managers and telephone number. LTV was (and still is) the largest industrial concern to seek protection of the bankruptcy law.

Although LTV's home office is in Dallas, the Chapter 11 case was filed in Manhattan. Since most of the interests would be represented by Wall Street firms and other New York bankruptcy heavyweights, there was not much point in having them log expensive, billable hours traveling interstate to court. Executive travel time between Dallas and New York was cheaper and wasted less important time. There also may have been an element of forum shopping. The big, important case was handed to the judge most experienced in megacases, the Honorable Burton R. Lifland.

A primary cause of the bankruptcy filing was LTV's liability to its present and former employees. The company owed $920 million in accrued obligations for benefits, compensation, withholding, and social security taxes, and current payments to retirees, *in addition to* what was estimated at the time of filing as more than $1.5 billion in pension obligations that were totally unfunded. If the company had not filed for bankruptcy, it would have had to pay $375 million to pension funds in 1986, in addition to more than $500 million in other debt payments. LTV had already spent that money, and stubbornly soft markets for LTV's steel products gave little hope that the company would have substantial amounts of cash to meet its payment schedules.

Because the conglomerate's pension obligations were so overwhelming, when company executives stated that major terminations of the conglomerate's pension plans would not be undertaken after bankruptcy was initiated, no one really believed them. The company insisted that it would only cancel one "small" pension fund with fifteen thousand beneficiaries, not the larger pension plan that had an estimated $1.5 billion in unfunded liabilities. Of course, to no one's surprise it soon canceled its plans covering 59,400 retirees. After all, what is the point of filing a Chapter 11 if you do not try to evade as many of your just debts as possible? The fact is that jettisoning company obligations to many thousands of loyal employees, if possible, is what passes for "good business."

LTV's effect on the national system of private pensions was substantial. Since LTV's pension obligations, which turned out to be *$2.3 billion*, were unfunded, the entire load was dumped on the Pension Benefit Guaranty Corporation, doubling the PBGC's obligations. Congress immediately was forced to triple federal employer insurance premiums in order to prevent collapse of that agency—another dose of corporate welfare given without the public knowing. The retirees from LTV (and from corporations that it had acquired) began receiving their benefits from the PBGC, but since the benefits were limited to 38 percent of the plans' obligations, many retirees suffered. The PBGC was left with a claim against the bankruptcy estate of LTV, which made it the largest unsecured creditor of the company by far.

The bankruptcy filing by LTV caused one of the early blips on the junk bond chart. A number of LTV's debt issues qualified as junk bonds, with ratings below the dividing line of BBB, and at least $1 billion of those were held by the public. However, rather than pull back from the mania of junk bond financing that was going on at the time, buyers were encouraged to continue funding junk bond offerings by higher interest rates that then were offered as inducement. Therefore, the net effect of the LTV bankruptcy was to make junk bond issues riskier because they promised investors larger returns.

LTV quickly began to use Chapter 11 to its full extent. The company canceled several long-term raw material contracts that had proven improvident, freeing it to buy at the lowest cost available, and pared off the parts of its steel operations that had poor potential for profit. It negotiated concessions from the United Steelworkers—it did not have to actually reject the bargaining agreement, it only had to point to Wheeling Steel's precedent. Bankruptcy has allowed the company to cut its steelmaking costs by at least 20 percent.

So far LTV has escaped paying a penny towards the pension liabilities it dumped on the PBGC. However, the issue of how much, if anything, LTV will have to pay is being litigated. Judge Lifland helped LTV fend off a counterattack by the PBGC when he denied the agency's request to force LTV to take back its pension liabilities because the company had included a new pension plan in its renegotiated contract with the United Steelworkers. Lifland's ruling was upheld on appeal in May 1989. (More on that in a later chapter.)

Being in Chapter 11 suits LTV just fine. Every day the company stays in bankruptcy, it avoids having to pay interest on hundreds of millions of dollars in loans. Besides denying the PBGC motion, Judge Lifland has allowed LTV to have the best of both worlds by entering an unusual series of orders, first permitting LTV's profitable aerospace unit to operate autonomously as if it were not in Chapter 11, then denying the motion of LTV's lenders to split off that unit for a reorganization separate from the beleaguered steel operations. All the while the good judge dutifully extends the protections of the "exclusive period."

Because of the fine treatment LTV has received in the bankruptcy court, the conglomerate, which had not been profitable for several years, became so beginning in the quarter during which it filed for Chapter 11. However, one of these days LTV will have to exit from bankruptcy court protection and face competitive pressures without the crutch of federal welfare. On second thought, maybe it will not!

During the late 1980s, the bankruptcy courts continued to see their fair share of colorful and widely known characters, mainly because the oil patch continued in deep recession and the bottom fell out of Texas real estate. (Those same features contributed mightily to the "bankruptcy" of the nation's savings-and-loan system. Everything in Texas is bigger than life!) Those who lost their fortunes in the crash of Texas real estate and who were forced to file bankruptcy included Clint Murchison, only shortly before considered one of the richest men in the world, former Treasury Secretary John Connally, and heart surgeon Denton Cooley.

The bankruptcy court in Dallas presided over the dissipation of another one of the largest personal fortunes in the world, that amassed by H. L. Hunt and left to his sons Nelson Bunker, William Herbert, and Lamar, and to several family trusts controlled by them. The debacle also touched the family businesses, most notably Placid Oil Company, Penrod Drilling Company, and Hunt International Resources Company (oil, gas, sugar, and real estate). (A sister, famous for her careful ways, was not severely harmed by her brothers' incredible level of mismanagement.) It took a rare combination of piggish greed, hamhanded tactics, and extreme naïveté for the Hunt brothers to lose all of their share of their daddy's fortune, but they managed to do it. It all started when the boys decided that they could be so very much richer if they cornered the silver market.

Controlling a commodity has been a dream of a number of financial megalomaniacs in the history of capitalism. Not only does it bring monopoly-level profits, but it makes the holder famous—bigger-than-life, a King of Capitalism. However, reality almost always has stepped in to thwart the fantasy, the nearest example of success in cornering a market in modern financial history being the failed attempt of one of the great robber-barons of the 1800s, Jay Gould. In 1869, Gould was within a hair of cornering the gold market, and it took President Grant's order opening the Treasury Department's vaults to halt him.

The Hunt brothers too learned that their wealth could not buy them everything that was for sale. As with Gould, the federal government played a part in preventing the Hunts' monopolization of the precious metal, although it was unintentional in the Hunts' case. In spite of being thwarted, Gould made out quite handsomely from his investment; the Hunts, on the other hand, lost a substantial fortune in their brush with fame.

The Great Silver Run started in August 1979, when the price of silver began to show surprising strength on the open market. In the silver "pit" at the Chicago Board of Trade, there was always a buyer, even if the price was "limit up." From a level of around $10 an ounce, by January 1980 the price of an ounce of silver hit $50. Like the herd animals they are, investors around the United States began to speculate on further rises in the silver market; and as is common when rampant speculation grips a bull market, they attempted to leverage profits by borrowing to fund their silver investments.

Rumors began to circulate that the Hunt brothers, historically big investors in silver, had been increasing their holdings substantially. In fact, by early 1980, the Hunt brothers and their related entities had amassed 120 million ounces of silver, more than one-third of the world's annual production, and had acquired rights to 50 million ounces more.

The Hunts' plan began to unravel when Paul Volcker's anti-inflation efforts drove up interest rates. Investors shied away from borrowing to finance their investments, and the price of silver could not be supported at the lofty level to which it had been driven. When the slide in silver prices became pronounced, the silver that the Hunts had used for collateral in order to purchase more silver was valued at steadily lower prices. This led their banks to demand more collateral and their brokers to make "margin calls" asking for more funds to cover the Hunts' positions.

Once that happened, the Hunts were caught in a downward spiral, having to pledge more and more of their assets. Within a short period of time, nearly all of their assets, from Placid Oil to the racehorses to the works of art to the boys'—and their wives'—personal effects, were pledged to banks for $1.1 billion in credit. Slowly but surely the banks began to liquidate collateral to pay the Hunt brothers' debts, with the Hunts fighting them every step of the way. The Hunts had bet that a billion dollars could corner the silver market, and they had come up short. Bunker observed, "A billion dollars is not what it used to be."

As the financial disaster continued to eat away at the Hunt brothers' resources, eventually their affairs spilled over into bankruptcy court. In March 1985, debentureholders threw Hunt International Resources into an involuntary bankruptcy. Over the next several years, the Hunts' trusts (including Lamar's, which owned the Kansas City Chiefs professional football team) and corporate entities filed Chapter 11s in a piecemeal fashion to stave off foreclosures and other credit crises. Their bankers attributed the sporadic filings as serial attempts to muddy bankruptcy court supervision of the holdings and to mask the Hunts' unreorganizable insolvency. The Internal Revenue Service further muddied the situation by claiming $1 billion in back taxes related to the debacle. When the Hunt brothers suffered a $312 million judgment against them personally for damages caused to a Peruvian company by their failed run at the silver market, Bunker and Herbert were forced to file individual Chapter 11s, with Lamar settling his share.

Over the next several years, the Hunts held off creditors and countersued their bankers, all the while keeping their fingers crossed for the gusher that never came in. Although their claims against their bankers for pulling the plug were not litigated to a conclusion, they did manage to gain agreements from them to allow reorganization of Placid Oil and the family trusts. They bet their remaining interest in Penrod on their ability to raise further capital, but when that failed, they lost it in March 1990. Bunker and Herbert were not able to shake the large judgment against them, and their assets were eventually stripped from them (although the IRS got most of the proceeds).

To the Hunt brothers, it was not enough to be wealthy—they had to make the big play that would make them famous in history as the master businessmen. Instead they became infamous, victims of their hubris. They had bet the farm on one roll of the dice and came up losers, and they will be remembered in history for that.

John McKinley of Texaco earned his dubious place in history, as well.

The United States government has many programs to encourage oil exploration. Nevertheless, during the early 1980s, the major oil companies constructed their own *de facto* program for finding oil, consisting of finding an oil company with proven reserves on its books and buying it. It was so much easier than actually exploring the wilds, and, because oil reserves are generally undervalued on companies' books, buying oil known to be in the ground was a good deal for the purchaser. As one of the largest oil companies in the world, Texaco was a major player in this game.

Texaco was not in quite the same position as the other majors because it had developed somewhat differently. While they had concentrated on finding oil in the ground and had added distribution networks to get it to market, Texaco had concentrated its efforts on refining and distribution. The reason stemmed from the fact that the founder of "Texas Co.," "Buckskin Joe" Cullinen, had a knack both for missing out on the big Texas geysers and for organizing ways to get other companies' oil to market. For those reasons, Buckskin Joe's financial backers, businessmen from the Northeast, were reluctant to back oil exploration and instead directed the energies of what became known as Texaco into the more sure money of refining and distribution. (That control by Yankee money is why Texaco's home office has been and is in White Plains, New York—a fact that would hurt Texaco immensely in its fight with Pennzoil.)

Texaco's distinctive history had its pluses and minuses. It is the only oil company to have substantial filling station operations in all fifty states at the same time. On the other hand, although Texaco had some presence as a driller in Louisiana and the Middle East, in the Seventies and early Eighties, the company was frequently short of oil stock to run through its system and had to pay high prices for the oil it could buy. When the word went out that Getty Oil Company was for sale, it would not be too strong to say that Texaco was desperate to buy it.

Getty Oil Company also had a colorful character in its past, J. Paul Getty. J. P.'s father, George, actually started the oil business, but from the time J. P. took it over in 1934 (pushing his mother aside to do it), it grew magnificently. One of the more clever wildcatters and oil company builders, J. P. Getty amassed one of the largest fortunes in the world by developing oil fields in Texas and the Middle East. He had five sons by five wives and was quite famous for being a curmudgeon to them as well as to the world in general.

By the time J. P. died at eighty-three in 1976, three of his sons were old enough to already have had experience in the family business and to continue the dynasty. Ronald had run the European operations. Paul had supervised Getty Italiana. Gordon had worked both in Saudi Arabia and in the United States for arms of the company. (George, the oldest son of J. P. and the most capable businessman of the offspring, had died unexpectedly in 1976 at age forty-eight. J. P. III has had a tragic history. When he was kidnaped and his ear cut off in 1973, his father agreed to pay the ransom only if it were considered a loan to be repaid. At age twenty-four, J. P. III had a stroke that left him blind and paralyzed.)

Alas, J. P.'s boys lacked the feistiness of their father. Ronald did not like oil and went into the movie business instead. Paul "dropped out" in the Sixties. Gordon was, and is, an accomplished composer and musician, a patron of the arts, and an indifferent businessman. Gordon has been described variously as a naïve dilettante in business matters and as a competent manager of the Getty family interests, depending on the side the speaker is on. Perhaps there is an inherent contradiction between being cultured and being a megacorporate baron, but in any event the truth about Gordon probably lies in between the poles. Gordon appears to be a decent man who got caught between two cutthroats when he decided to sell Getty Oil, and therein lies the tale.

In 1983, Gordon Getty was the sole trustee of the family trust that owned 40.2 percent of Getty Oil; the rest was owned 48 percent by the public and 11.8 percent by the J. Paul Getty Museum. The chief executive officer of Getty Oil was Sidney Peterson, a financial man who had risen through the ranks at the company by presiding over its diversification. Gordon Getty and Peterson were vying for dominance over the company's affairs.

The museum, run by trustees, attempted to stay neutral in the power struggle. However, when Peterson tried to dilute the family trust's percentage of ownership while Gordon Getty was out of town, the museum's lawyer, Martin Lipton, halted the power play and negotiated a cease-fire. When Peterson instigated a suit to have Gordon removed as trustee of the family trust, the museum trustees and Lipton were angered and helped Gordon take control of Getty Oil. The museum trustees and Lipton eventually would have a lot to do with the sale of the company.

The scrapping caught the attention of Pennzoil Company, a mid-sized oil company with "only" $2 billion a year in revenues. It bought 590,000 shares of Getty Oil on the open market, and on December 28, 1983, it initiated a tender offer for 20 percent of Getty Oil stock at $100 a share. The $1.6 billion offer was 25 percent above the market price of the stock. Gordon Getty's reaction was that J. Hugh Liedtke, the chairman and CEO of Pennzoil who had been a family acquaintance, could help him take Getty Oil private. Gordon wanted complete control. So Getty initiated contact with Liedtke. Hugh Liedtke thought that an alliance with Gordon would be a useful stage in *his* taking over

Getty Oil.

On January 1, 1984, Hugh Liedtke and Gordon Getty agreed to cooperate in taking Getty Oil private at $110 a share, with the Getty family trust to own 57 percent and Pennzoil to own 43 percent. The public and Getty Museum shareholders would gain through a sweetened offer, and the two purchasers still would have a good deal. Martin Lipton drafted a short Memorandum of Agreement to memorialize the price terms and a few other aspects on which Getty and Liedtke had agreed. The memorandum was signed on January 2 by Liedtke for Pennzoil, Gordon Getty for the Getty trust, and Harold Williams, the president of the museum. The outline of the deal still had to be ratified by the entities' respective boards. Gordon also signed a letter drafted by Liedtke stating that Gordon would support Pennzoil's part of the deal when it was presented to the Getty Oil board of directors and would vote to remove any directors that opposed the proposal, subject to Gordon's fiduciary duties.

None too pleased at Gordon Getty's extracurricular activities, the other members of the board of directors of Getty Oil rejected the proposal by a 9 to 6 vote, although they agreed to accept the offer if it were sweetened. Liedtke balked at increasing Pennzoil's offer, and an attempt was made to fashion a sweetened offer that the Getty board and Pennzoil would agree to. In the evening of January 3, the Getty Oil board voted 15 to 1 to accept Pennzoil's offer if it would include a $5 per share "kicker" to shareholders that would come into effect when Getty Oil-Pennzoil sold an insurance subsidiary. Before the board adjourned, it was informed that Liedtke had agreed to the sweetened terms. That night, Gordon Getty and Hugh Liedtke celebrated their deal. On January 4, a press release was issued by Getty Oil, Pennzoil and the museum describing the status as an "agreement in principle" that was "subject to the execution of a definitive merger agreement." That press release later would play a big part in litigation over the sale of Getty Oil.

When Liedtke had at first refused to increase Pennzoil's bid, Getty Oil was thus "put into play," as the investment banking vultures call it. While the parties fashioned the deal that the Getty Oil board agreed to on January 3, two different investment banking houses, trolling for bidders, contacted Texaco. Was Texaco interested in acquiring a company that was ranked ninth among U.S. oil companies in reserves and crude oil production and sixteenth in refining capacity?

Does the sun rise in the east?

Texaco was very interested. Texaco, a former client of the museum's attorney Martin Lipton, advised Lipton not to have the museum execute any agreement until Texaco had a chance to bid. John McKinley, Texaco's CEO, telephoned Peterson, who advised him that Getty Oil still could entertain offers other than Pennzoil's. In the evening of January 5, McKinley met with Lipton and Getty. Apparently, in that meeting Lipton told Getty that he would advise the museum trustees to sell their shares to Texaco for $125, rather than to Pennzoil. Since Lipton had thrown the museum's weight to Texaco, Gordon was faced with the prospect of becoming a minority holder of Getty Oil when Texaco bought the public's shares too. Consequently, he agreed to cause the family trust's shares to be sold to Texaco also.

The deal moved quickly. Lipton worked all night to draft the necessary documents, and by 5:30 A.M. on January 6, the museum had signed over its shares in Getty Oil to Texaco. Because the museum trustees were worried about getting caught in the switches, Texaco agreed to indemnify them against any liability to Pennzoil that might be found. The Getty Oil board soon withdrew its acceptance of the Pennzoil offer and approved the Texaco proposal.

Litigation over the matter moved quickly also. On January 6, Getty Oil (with Texaco's approval) filed a lawsuit seeking a ruling that the sale of stock to Texaco was legal. On January 10, Pennzoil filed a suit in Delaware (as with many megacorporations, Delaware is Getty Oil's technical place of incorporation) asking the chancery court judge to enforce its agreement with Getty Oil. It was then that Texaco made its first—or second, if you believe that it should not have muscled in on Pennzoil's deal—major tactical error. It delayed in filing an appearance in the Delaware case, and so Pennzoil was allowed to dismiss its own complaint, without any repercussions, for the asking. Then Pennzoil quickly filed a revised complaint in Harris County (Houston), Texas, asking for $7 billion in actual damages and $7 billion in punitive damages. Pennzoil demanded a jury trial in the Texas case, a right that was not available in Delaware's chancery court. Pennzoil would be fighting in its home court against that Yankee company from White Plains, New York—whose main operating office actually was close to Pennzoil's in Houston.

It was then that Pennzoil made a move that was so brilliant that it could just as well have been disastrous: Pennzoil hired a personal injury lawyer to try its case. Its trial counsel, Joseph D. Jamail, was one of the better personal injury attorneys in Houston, but a p.i. attorney nevertheless. Jamail had acquired million-dollar judgments for his "leg-offs," but could he obtain billions in a corporate fight? Why would one of the richest companies in America hire what some might call an "ambulance chaser" to litigate a major corporate dispute? Because Jamail was a good ol' boy, a master at talking to juries, and Texaco's fate would be decided by a Houston jury of common folk, not a panel of corporate lawyers—that's why. Of course, Jamail was backed by the finest legal talent of one of Houston's major corporate law firms, but it would be Mr. Jamail who would be sweet-talking to the jury on Pennzoil's behalf when the case would come to a close.

It did not hurt that Joe Jamail's law firm had given a $10,000 contribution to the reelection campaign of presiding Judge Anthony J. P. Ferris. When Texaco moved to disqualify the judge, always a dangerous move, the judge angrily declared that he could not help it if state law allowed lawyers to contribute to judges' campaigns, and, besides, he could not be bribed for a mere $10,000. Motion denied.

Texaco chose an experienced corporate litigator, Richard B. Miller, who had a reputation for "playing hardball." The two would be at each other's throats for the entire trial.

For a case that involved so much money, the issues were very simple. The main issue was: did Pennzoil have a binding contract with Getty Oil? If so, should Texaco have known it; and, if so, should it pay punitive damages? If there was a breach of contract, it would not be hard for the jury to figure the amount of actual damages. Pennzoil had come up with a way of figuring damages at about $7.53 billion, based upon the value of Getty Oil's reserves that had been denied to Pennzoil, and Texaco was so disdainful of Pennzoil's case that it did not bother to contest the figures greatly. However, because of the aggressiveness of the combatants and the amount of money involved, the simple case—which could have been tried in three days if it had concerned $25,000—took nineteen weeks. At every point, the attorneys jockeyed for the extra edge, the most gratuitous insult, the sneakiest way of poisoning the jurors' minds.

Each occurrence and document involving the contest for Getty Oil was placed before the jury *ad nauseam*, and each side gave its spin to the action. When the Getty Oil board had agreed to the sweetened price, did that make the four-page Memorandum of Agreement, which

Getty Oil had not formally signed, an operative agreement, or was that just one step along the way? Did the press release evidence a "done deal" or indicate that more work had to be done on details before there could be a complete contract? When Gordon Getty and Hugh Liedtke shook hands on the deal, was not that enough? Is not a man's word his bond? Was it dishonorable for Texaco to put the squeeze on Gordon Getty, and, if so, should that action make Texaco liable for billions? Did the fact that Texaco gave indemnities to the museum, the Getty family trust, and Getty Oil evidence the fact that Texaco knew it was doing wrong, or were they simply an ordinary by-product of a mega-corporate merger?

The judge was rather lax in his rules of evidence. Much testimony for both sides was provided by lawyer-witnesses who were allowed to give wide-ranging opinions as well as to describe factual matters. Liedtke was allowed to give his opinion that Texaco had destroyed some notes, without any factual basis whatsoever. Each side attacked the methods and the intentions of the other, both in the Getty situation and in other deals.

After building the molehill of facts into a mountain of evidence, each side rested its case. In closing arguments, Miller stressed the complexities of any merger and that Getty Oil and Gordon Getty had done the right thing by keeping open the bidding to get the best price for Getty Oil's shareholders (as involuntary as that might have been). Jamail advised the jury that Texaco's assets were $48 billion and that every billion in damages would add only forty-three cents per barrel of reserves acquired by Texaco. Pennzoil's counsel told the jury that an oral contract could be binding and that it could rule on "the ethics" of the situation. Then the jury—a letter carrier, an equipment salesman, and other blue collars and clerks—repaired to the jury room to decide the fate of the multibillion-dollar deal and the two giant corporations. Only in America. . . .

The jurors did not like Texaco. According to one account, they found chairman McKinley cold and another officer aloof and combative. They felt that Hugh Liedtke and Gordon Getty had shaken hands on the deal and that Texaco had muscled in, putting the squeeze on Gordon Getty; so they found that Texaco had knowingly caused Getty Oil to breach its contract. Since Texaco had failed to adequately address the issue of the amount of damages (probably not wanting to encourage the jury to compromise by finding for Pennzoil with moderated damages), the jury had no trouble awarding Pennzoil the full $7.32 billion (!) in compensatory damages for which it had asked. The jury was all over the lot on punitive damages, until it adopted one juror's suggestion that it award $1 billion for each of the three indemnities that Texaco had handed out. On November 19, 1985, the jury finalized a judgment for $10.53 billion in favor of Pennzoil. The big numbers had not fazed the jurors one bit.

Texaco and its shareholders were horrified, and the business community was scandalized. John McKinley had bet the store on one roll of the dice. The fate of a business deal involving the highest orders of business and legal acumen had been decided by people who had never negotiated more than a house purchase. The jurors had made it clear after the trial that it was very simple: people should not go back on their word. That simple concept, insufficient in contract law (as every first-year law student learns) and absent from the mores of Big Business, threatened to turn business methods across the country upside down.

The post-trial maneuvering was every bit as dramatic as the buildup. In order to block Pennzoil from seizing its assets while it appealed, Texaco had to post a bond. To post a bond equal to the judgment would have violated Texaco's covenants with its lenders, and so Texaco, desperately trying to gain a home court advantage, got a friendly federal court judge in White Plains to reduce its appeal bond to a mere $1 billion. The appeals marched up the court system—Texaco's appeal of the judgment working its way up to the Texas Supreme Court, and Pennzoil's appeal of the bond ruling heading through the Second Circuit Court of Appeals to the United States Supreme Court.

April 1987 was April Fool's month for Texaco. Texaco's bankers started asking for security to cover ordinary banking transactions. The Texas Court of Appeals upheld the jury verdict, although it cut punitive damages to $1 billion. The United States Supreme Court overturned the lower federal courts' rulings on Texaco's bond, saying that under the circumstances, the federal courts had no right to countermand the state court's bond rules. Texaco offered to pay $100 million, nonrefundable, in return only for Pennzoil's promise not to foreclose on any of its assets during its appeal to the state supreme court. Hugh Liedtke refused it. Texaco offered Pennzoil $2 billion to go away entirely. Liedtke refused it. Facing possible seizure of its assets by Pennzoil and unable to post such a huge bond, giant Texaco filed a Chapter 11 petition—in White Plains, of course. Its bankruptcy counsel was Harvey Miller, of the New York firm of Weil, Gotschal and Manges.

It was a strange bankruptcy case. It had all of the accoutrements of a megacorporate Chapter 11, including the official committees, but the entire case rested on making one creditor happy. Texaco had no problems with its lenders, suppliers, or shareholders, who after all were naturally aligned with Texaco against Pennzoil. The architect of the debacle, John McKinley, was gone. The new president and chief executive officer, James W. Kinnear, had to begin his tenure as the head of a Chapter 11 company, bargaining desperately with the disparate interests represented in bankruptcy court.

Of course, there were cries of "foul" after Texaco filed its Chapter 11 petition. Pennzoil threatened to do every nasty thing under the sun that could be done to a bankruptcy debtor, including having the bankruptcy dismissed, replacing Texaco's management, and investigating and limiting Texaco's operations. Pennzoil also claimed that it would have its status as an unsecured creditor raised to secured. Business commentators discoursed on how Chapter 11 would hurt Texaco.

Although the level of vituperation and commentary was at a higher volume than most Chapter 11 cases, actually it was nothing more than the usual background to a megacorporate bankruptcy. Did anyone really believe that Bankruptcy Judge Howard Schwartzberg would close down or harm in any way one of the top ten corporations in the United States just because one jury had said Texaco had been too pushy?

In the press and in court, Texaco gave as good as it got from Pennzoil. Texaco representatives castigated Liedtke's intransigence, calling him unreasonable and wrong, and charged him with trying to destroy a mighty company. Pennzoil had put Texaco's back to the wall, but that had given it a new tactical advantage. As long as Texaco was in bankruptcy, Pennzoil could do nothing to collect its debt, interest on the liability would cease running, and Texaco's operations could continue without change. It soon became clear that Texaco fully appreciated the newfound Chapter 11 strength. Shortly after the bankruptcy filing, Kinnear announced, "I'll tell you damn straight: my number today is less than it was yesterday."

As a leading megacorporation, Texaco received some favorable reviews of its part in the long-running morality play. The *Wall Street Journal* termed the jury's finding of a Pennzoil-Getty Oil contract to be a "Ten Gallon Outrage" and a "national embarrassment." The editorial told the Texas Supreme Court in no uncertain terms to get on the job, warning, "Now that Texaco has the protection of a federal bankruptcy court, Texas itself is even more on trial than before. The only way Texas can begin to repair its reputation is for its supreme court to reverse the trial judgment." The federal Securities and Exchange Commission filed a brief in Texaco's appeal to the Texas Supreme Court that asserted that the Pennzoil-Getty Oil agreement violated federal securities laws, although that was not the express issue in the appeal.

It is an open question as to whether the support from those outsiders hurt Texans' pride, but it sure did not help Texaco any. In November 1987, the Texas Supreme Court affirmed the judgment as amended by the intermediate court. The ruling was not totally unexpected, since it had been assumed widely that the Texas Supreme Court, at that time under considerable fire for being susceptible to political pressures, would favor Pennzoil. What was surprising was that the court entered its decision on the $10 billion judgment without bothering to provide Texaco a hearing! Judge Roy Bean would have been proud. Although the ruling established the law of the case and fixed the amount of Pennzoil's claim against Texaco, Pennzoil was restrained from acting upon the judgment by the Chapter 11.

Since the only remaining appeal for Texaco was a low-percentage chance that the United States Supreme Court would hear the matter, the focus of attention turned to the hard bargaining going on in bankruptcy court. Both sides had been hedging on the final verdict, negotiating over the amount of a nonrefundable initial payment by Texaco and a cap on any judgment if Pennzoil prevailed. However, Texaco's best offer was $370 million and a cap of $2.6 billion, and Pennzoil's bottom line was $1.5 billion with a $5 billion cap. After the Texas ruling, talks focused on a flat sum, but both sides were hanging tough. The logjam was broken when the equity-holders' committee, acting as an intermediary, talked both sides into a settlement. In the end, the primary pressure on Texaco to settle came not from the exigencies of Chapter 11, but rather from the fact that "corporate raider" Carl Icahn had bought a 12.3 percent stake in Texaco's stock and was pressing for the company to get on with its corporate life.

The final settlement with Pennzoil was a big pill for Texaco to swallow—$3 billion in one lump sum, at least ten times greater than any damages ever upheld by a court. The payment to Pennzoil and the catch-up payment of other creditors' claims against Texaco knocked 20 percent off the company's net worth.

Viewed from a different angle, the settlement was not such a bad deal for Texaco although it was a windfall for Pennzoil. No doubt Texaco had earned about as much in interest on its war chest as it had to pay to its trade creditors at the conclusion of the bankruptcy. Texaco had saved about a billion in canceled stock dividends and other savings by filing the Chapter 11 case. The remaining $2 billion differential was probably made up by the relatively good price that Texaco paid for Getty Oil. Also, Texaco walked away with the prize—Getty Oil—that it had so desperately needed to maintain its preeminence. Pennzoil, a company with $2 billion in revenues, had acquired a large war chest for future acquisitions. After separate copies of the settlement agreement were signed in the companies' respective offices, Kinnear and Liedtke wished each other good luck.

Kinnear would need it. The settlement agreement required shareholder approval, and Carl Icahn (whose ownership share in Texaco by then was up to 14.5 percent) was not happy. Although Icahn's personal shuttle-diplomacy had helped create a monetary settlement well within Icahn's parameters, he was incensed at the extra goodies that Texaco had tucked into the agreement. If and when the shareholders approved the settlement with Pennzoil, they also would be ratifying the small print that canceled all claims by Texaco shareholders against Texaco management for their actions in the fiasco, including the nineteen shareholders' suits already pending. The settlement agreement also provided that Texaco would maintain its antitakeover provisions.

Instead of luck, the Texaco management had Judge Schwartzberg. In January 1988, the judge denied Icahn's request to be allowed to present a competing Plan of Reorganization for a vote. The judge stated that he did not think that the shareholders' rights against Texaco management were worth anything. With the creditors' and shareholders' choices limited to approving the settlement agreement engineered by Texaco's management or voting for continued warfare, of course the Plan of Reorganization was approved. Judge Schwartzberg had no trouble confirming the plan on March 23, 1988, over the objections of some shareholders to the releases from liability of Texaco's management. Texaco was free at last. (After Texaco strengthened its antitakeover provision, in June 1989 Icahn sold his stake in Texaco for a cool $2 billion.)

Texaco was vindicated indirectly in September 1989 when the Second Circuit Court of Appeals, deciding an unrelated case, ruled that an agreement to purchase a company is preliminary and unenforceable when important terms are still open to negotiation and a final contract document is contemplated. That ruling only confirmed what every corporate lawyer knows—there is many a slip betwixt the principals' handshake over a merger concept and the final agreement on the myriad of terms that constitutes a done deal. Some still defend the Texas Supreme Court decision by saying that technically the Second Circuit decision concerned only New York law, not law west of the Pecos.

Another high profile bankruptcy of the late Eighties was the Chapter 11 proceeding of Eastern Airlines. In the early Eighties, Frank Borman had used the specter of Frank Lorenzo to win substantial concessions from Eastern's unions. The next thing they knew, that dreaded cost cutter had bought Eastern.

In early 1987, Frank Lorenzo combined the operations of Continental Airlines with two of his acquisitions, Frontier and People's Express, and another of his units, New York Air. The result was an airline doubled in size but in operational chaos, and Lorenzo felt required to remove Continental's president, Martin R. Shugrue, and take over the job himself. From that time Lorenzo was required to spend quite a bit of his time establishing the "new" Continental while still keeping costs to the bone. Eastern suffered from too little of Lorenzo's attention, and according to the Federal Aviation Administration, too little maintenance.

Was Frank Lorenzo the problem or the solution? Lorenzo was widely viewed as a good dealmaker, but also as impulsive, untrusting, and a poor manager. He had created the second largest (behind American) air carrier, but could he turn his collection of losers into winners? He could make an airline, but could he run an airline?

Under Lorenzo's hand, Continental indeed came around; however, Eastern fell off the chart. By early 1989, Continental had become one of the most profitable airlines in the United States. Its sister airline went from making a slight profit in 1985 to losing more than $100 million in 1986, almost $200 million in 1987, and almost $400 million in 1988. On March 4, 1989, in response to Eastern's insistence that they take pay cuts, Eastern's pilots, machinists, and flight attendants walked out, idling the vast majority of the company's thirty thousand employees and greatly restricting its operations. Lorenzo had prepared by creating a $400 million war chest to outlast the unions, but Eastern was in danger of losing business permanently.

It then became clear why Lorenzo had not folded Eastern into Continental. He had foreseen that Eastern's problems would be endemic, and he had wanted to maintain his option to put Eastern into bankruptcy even as Continental took off on its own. On March 9, 1989, he did so. Eastern became the fifth largest bankruptcy in U.S. history.

The Eastern bankruptcy was not Continental-Part II. Eastern's machinists union had historically been a maverick local. Eastern's problems ran a lot deeper than its wage scale. The company was unable to come even close to being profitable. It had suffered from excessive debt since the late 1970s. Perhaps a problem was the travelers of the late Eighties, who asked for more service from airlines. Perhaps travelers had tired of Lorenzo's shoddy operations. Perhaps, as some speculated, the airline industry was headed irrevocably toward further consolidation, and companies like Eastern would be broken up and their parts sold to the dominant air carriers. That remains to be seen.

Another wild card in Eastern's bankruptcy concerns its presiding judge. The case was filed in Manhattan, and Eastern drew the ubiquitous Burton R. Lifland. Eastern could be confident that the judge would not take any harsh measures to close it down. On the other hand, as the case has progressed, it has become clear that, as with the Manville case, the judge is intent on putting his personal stamp on the Chapter 11 megacorporation. Unlike the Manville case, however, the judge did not waste years sitting on the sidelines.

Immediately upon the commencement of the Chapter 11 case, the parties handed Judge Lifland a perfect excuse for appointing a representative who would begin to shape the proceeding. Eastern had sold some assets to its parent, Texas Air, shortly before the filing of bankruptcy, and Eastern requested that the judge appoint someone to review the sale and, presumably, advise the court and the unions that it was fair. Since the Bankruptcy Code provides for the appointment of an "examiner" when a court wishes to investigate the books and records of a Chapter 11 debtor to make sure that the laws have been followed in its prepetition actions, Eastern asked that such a person be appointed. The unions, believing that Lorenzo was following a plan of gutting the airline by transferring its best parts to other Lorenzo units, asked for the removal of management and the appointment of a trustee.

In response to the motions, within weeks of Eastern's Chapter 11 filing, the judge appointed an examiner. However, in typical Lifland fashion the examiner was cloaked with broader powers than the title implied. In addition to investigating Eastern's transactions with its parent, the examiner was given the cachet of labor mediator, with the duty to address "impediments to a reorganization," and—in an unspecified manner—the "public interest." Lifland was outspoken about his goals, referring to his appointment of the examiner as "a way of banging heads together" and stating that he wanted the strike ended and planes flying as soon as possible. The judge delayed ruling on the unions' request for the appointment of a trustee pending the examiner's report, thus reserving for himself another opportunity to appoint a surrogate. He did not desire to take the drastic step of appointing a trustee for a megacorporate debtor unless he absolutely had to.

Even as the examiner, attorney David Shapiro of Washington, D.C., began work, Lorenzo plunged ahead with divestiture plans. He wrapped up a deal he had been working on for several months, the sale of Eastern's East Coast Shuttle to Donald Trump for $365 million. He then entertained bids from the Pritzker family of Chicago (the owners of Hyatt Hotels and Braniff Airlines) and a group headed by Peter V. Ueberroth (the former baseball commissioner and media darling), agreeing to sell Eastern minus the shuttle to Ueberroth. Of course, the deals would have to be approved by the bankruptcy court, but it seemed that Lorenzo would wash his hands of attempting to make Eastern Airlines profitable.

Eastern's three unions were ready to rid themselves of Mr. Lorenzo. In April 1989, they agreed to wage concessions in the event that the Ueberroth group acquired the airline—concessions that they had denied to Lorenzo. However, they wanted their last pound of flesh from Lorenzo, insisting that a trustee be appointed immediately to baby-sit for the company until its sale to Ueberroth could be finalized.

The deal collapsed over that issue. Eastern's unions insisted that they would not go back to work for Lorenzo, even on an interim basis. Lorenzo, fearing the always-present possibility that the preliminary agreement might fall through before it could be closed, refused to turn the company's operations over to a trustee. "We were waving the white flag and [the unions] tried to take the flagpole and beat us to death with it," said Lorenzo. Ueberroth, perhaps gaining a vision of what life with Eastern's unions would be like, quickly backed away from the deal. Eastern was taken off the auction block, and actions to replace striking workers were accelerated.

The company quickly floated a reorganization plan—a dose of strong medicine. Eastern proposed to sell $1.8 billion in assets and slash its service by 40 percent. The company would sell its Philadelphia hub and expand its one in Atlanta. Employees would be cut down to seventeen thousand. According to Eastern, the moves would produce $744 million in net cash by the end of 1989, which could be used to begin payments on the $2.8 billion in debt. Remaining reductions of debt would come from projected profitable operations of the reorganized air carrier.

The response was hardly unanimous. The creditors were wary. Union representatives alleged that the plan was but the first big step of even deeper cuts that would chop the airline to bits. Examiner Shapiro, cognizant of Judge Lifland's desire that Eastern be sold in one piece, told the judge that there were still parties interested in buying the airline. Even though Eastern obviously lacked consensus for its plan and did not immediately ask that it be brought to a vote, it turned down an offer by the Pritzkers in May, saying that the air carrier was not for sale.

Also in May, the sale of the shuttle to Trump was completed. Besides bringing Eastern much-needed cash, approval of the move by Judge Lifland was a signal that he was allowing Lorenzo to take a shot at a reorganization. Perhaps the judge was changing course because the suitors whom the unions were dredging up—including an options trader, a diamond merchant, and a union pension fund—did not really present the viable alternatives to Lorenzo that the judge had in mind. After Judge Lifland's approval of the shuttle sale, Lorenzo and Eastern's president, Phil Bakes, began to tout Eastern's reorganization plan to whomever would listen.

Eastern's unions continued to back Anybody But Lorenzo as the company's restructuring went forward. The options trader, offering no small amount of money for the company, was deemed unsuitable by the creditors' committee. The machinists' union was still standing tall. According to one member, "They can confirm his plan till the cows come home, it doesn't mean we'll give up if they confirm it around us." After the pilots' union turned down a penurious offer, in June

1989, Eastern moved to reject its collective-bargaining agreement. That left Eastern standing tall, but actually hurting from an inability to bring enough new pilots on line to fulfill scheduled flights.

The strike indeed had an effect on Eastern. Its revenues from operations were only a small fraction of prestrike levels, and management had to work hard both to drum up business and then to assemble enough workers to complete flight assignments. One of Eastern's tactics unintentionally resulted in a bit of black humor. After the company offered to give frequent flyer miles to funeral directors who shipped bodies on the carrier, wags suggested that the airline change its motto to "They're dying to fly Eastern." Eastern's plight was eased some when the pilots' strike began to crack and a few began drifting back to work. With help from Continental, Eastern scheduled 53 percent more flights in September.

The bad news for Eastern was that it was having trouble selling the amount of assets that its restructuring plan had posited. The company could not unload its Miami maintenance center. The sale of its lucrative South American routes to American, seemingly well along the way in the spring, floundered on American's demand that Continental (its arch enemy since the days of Continental's Chapter 11 filing) drop a lawsuit over American's reservation system. With no other airlines having a good fit with the South American routes, it began to look as if Eastern would have to revitalize them itself. That would take money that Eastern did not have and would put the company even further behind schedule in raising cash. Frank Lorenzo even met with Donald Trump to see if he could interest him in buying a piece of Continental.

By November, Eastern's inability to move off dead center was getting embarrassing to everybody. Experts were consulted, but no easy fix was found. Eastern was forced to delay the presentation of a revised reorganization plan because the correct numbers kept getting farther out of reach. The frosting was put on the cake when a labor arbitrator decided a dispute with the pilots' union that predated the bankruptcy, ruling that Eastern owed those pilots something in excess of $60 million. Eastern was forced to go back to American with a discounted offer to sell the South American routes. Thanksgiving brought Eastern a blessing—its pilots' and flight attendants' unions voted to end their strike—but the company could only respond with more job eliminations and pay cuts. Meanwhile, Eastern's sister airline Continental was completing an order for $4.5 billion in new planes.

After several delays, Eastern unveiled its latest reorganization concept to creditors at the end of January 1990. It had finally succeeded in reaching a deal to sell its South American routes to American, after American had skinned Eastern for a discount of several hundred million dollars on the original price and had gotten Texas Air to drop its antitrust lawsuit against American's reservations network. The new plan retreated from Eastern's longstanding promise to pay creditors in full. Unsecured creditors were offered 10 percent in cash, 70 percent over ten years without interest, and the other 20 percent in what amounted to rights to 40 percent of Eastern's common stock. The creditors were not happy.

Spring 1990 only brought more slippage for Eastern. A loss of $852.3 million in 1989 was reported. Between new hires and returning strikers, the company finally had a full complement of employees, but its business continued to fall off. Due to Eastern's abysmal service record, travel agencies were afraid to book their clients on the carrier. Further reductions in expenses were planned. An agreement with pilots to cut wages, some up to 25 percent, was effectuated, but a week later the company announced that it might have to ask for more. The net result was that Eastern kept putting back the timetable for its emergence from Chapter 11. The examiner reported to the court that Texas Air indeed had paid too little for prepetition transfers of assets from Eastern, further eroding the creditors' confidence in Lorenzo.

Eastern's Chapter 11 gave a new meaning to the economic law of diminishing returns when, in April, Eastern provided its fifth projection to its creditors and, like each prior amended plan, it was worse than its predecessor. When Lorenzo steadfastly refused to commit a significant infusion of cash from Texas Air to help out Eastern, the creditors asked that the judge appoint a trustee. Much to everyone's surprise Judge Lifland did so, appointing as Chapter 11 trustee Martin R. Shugrue, who had been fired by Lorenzo as the president of Continental.

Had Judge Lifland turned antibusiness? Was this the end of megacorporate hegemony in bankruptcy court? Would Chapter 11 be unfriendly to megacorporations from now on? No. No. No. The Eastern case stands for the proposition that there is a limit to the level of incompetence that a bankruptcy court will tolerate, even if that limit is extreme.

There is a bankruptcy protocol for management, even if it is not expressed. There is no problem with kicking around employees. It is acceptable to string out a case until the creditors cry "uncle." It is acceptable to be aloof—even contemptuous—of the bankruptcy process and the judge, because that only confirms the power and the prestige of the megacorporate management. It is O.K. to lose money, lots of money . . . for a while. However, it is not acceptable to continue to hemorrhage money *with no feasible plan to stop it.* Missing projection after projection indicates to the judge either that management is scamming the court or that it has no idea what it is doing. The tipping point is when, after management has been given every benefit of the doubt over a long period of time, a judge becomes convinced that a trustee cannot possibly run the company as poorly as management has been doing.

The management of chairman Frank Lorenzo and president Phil Bakes had burned all of its credibility with Judge Lifland. Lorenzo had ceased to come across as a megacorporate baron and had begun to look like a dilettante. In referring to Eastern's losses since the bankruptcy was filed, Judge Lifland commented that Lorenzo and his management were "not competent to reorganize this estate. . . . Mr. Lorenzo has used $1.3 billion to fuel the reorganization." While the usual attorney-trustee often spells the death knell of an ongoing business, Lorenzo's bad luck was to have created his own successor by firing an apparently competent executive whom the judge could tap for the position. Finally, megacorporate Chapter 11s generally have megacorporate creditors. It was not Eastern's long-suffering employees who moved the judge to appoint the trustee, it was the scorn of big companies such as Marriott and Boeing for Lorenzo's dwindling offers that spurred the judge to make the change.

The amazing thing was that Judge Lifland still was firmly committed to saving Eastern, even in its horrible condition. The judge was so concerned that no gap in management occur that he appointed Shugrue based upon his qualifications on paper, turning down the creditors' request that more time be taken to choose who would be trustee. Judge Lifland also denied the creditors' request that the airline be liquidated, insisting that Shugrue operate it. To the judge, still intent on reorganizing Eastern whether internally or through its sale, "it would be *inappropriate* not to allow another management to address" Eastern's problems.

Frank Lorenzo virtually had walked away from Eastern. It would be up to Judge Lifland to effect a reorganization for him. After all Lifland had at least as much experience as Lorenzo in ramrodding mega-corporations through Chapter 11! As of mid-1990, Martin Shugrue still was insisting that he will turn around the company, not liquidate it.

Two other high profile bankruptcies illustrate the wide application of Chapter 11, from retailing to the world of public utilities.

Although no public utility had declared bankruptcy since the Depression, by the early Eighties a number were in deep trouble, drained of cash by costly nuclear power projects. As of mid-1984, three of them—Public Service Company of New Hampshire (Seabrook nuclear power plant), Long Island Lighting Company (Shoreham), and Public Service Company of Indiana (Marble Hill)—looked like they had reached the end of their respective lines of credit. However, the utilities held on for years, scraping up credit while fighting rearguard actions to open nuclear plants. (When the history of the twentieth century is written, the metamorphosis of members of the sleepy electric utility industry into giant nuclear power plant builders and operators—spenders of billions of dollars in the largest public works projects ever known to man in order to produce "cheap" power—will be recognized as one of the biggest boondoggles ever. Only the excesses of another formerly sleepy industry, the savings-and-loan business, will be found to have wasted more money for so little purpose.)

After three years of teetering on the brink while attempting to get approval to commence operations at Seabrook, PS New Hampshire ran out of time. Although it listed $2.95 billion in assets and "only" $1.7 billion in debt, 70 percent of those assets were tied up in Seabrook and the carrying costs on its loans had absorbed nearly all of its cash. On January 28, 1988, it filed a Chapter 11 case, earning it Top Ten status in the Bankruptcy Hall of Fame. The immediate cause of its filing was a ruling by the New Hampshire Supreme Court to the effect that the utility could not gain a rate increase for a facility (Seabrook) that was not producing power.

The safe harbor of Chapter 11 was an uncharted water for a public utility. The filing by PS New Hampshire raised a myriad of questions that had never been presented before. Would the bankruptcy supersede state regulations? Could a bankruptcy judge order a rate increase? How would consumers' interests be protected in what essentially was a commercial proceeding? And so on. Nevertheless, the management of PS

New Hampshire immediately breathed easier. The court and the creditors would not dare affect electrical service to consumers, and the bankruptcy canceled $100 million per year in interest.

Although PS New Hampshire set about trying to persuade its creditors and shareholders to accept a plan of recapitalization, its biggest problem was not with its creditors. Its cash-starved position had been caused by the state refusing to allow the utility rate increases. Like every utility, PS New Hampshire wanted to load its cost overruns on its captive customers rather than to pass its losses onto its shareholders who could invest elsewhere. In order for it to stick its customers, it would need relief from the state's regulations.

Having played the Chapter 11 card, PS New Hampshire followed up by asking the bankruptcy judge to rule that the company could bypass state regulation. Specifically, the utility asked the court to permit it to become a federally regulated utility, which would allow it to institute the rate increases that the state had denied. Judge James E. Yacos had no problem eliminating the state of New Hampshire as an impediment to the utility's path to reorganization, finding that Congress clearly had intended the bankruptcy law to supersede the "effective veto" over reorganizations that state regulatory agencies might otherwise have. Complaining that dealing with a state agency is hard when it "trundles a cannon up to the negotiating field" to enforce its narrow view that rates must be kept down, the judge ruled that it could be bypassed.

The ruling freed the utility to impose its losses on its hapless customers, who already suffered from rates that were among the highest in the country. It also attracted the interest of several other utilities that would be able to help the company recapitalize. In February 1990, the court approved a Plan of Reorganization, which included the sale of the company to Northeast Utilities, New England's largest utility. The plan included a whopping rate increase of 38.5 percent, spread over seven years. Thanks to Chapter 11, the company was able to direct the fallout of its mismanagement to its customers without the inconvenience of following state law.

The other end of the spectrum from electric utilities is the world of high fashion. PS New Hampshire hardly is a household name, but the American public was shocked in August 1989 at the news of the Chapter 11 filings of Bonwit Teller and B. Altman and Co.

It turned out that the problems of Bonwit Teller and B. Altman stemmed only partly from sluggish sales but more seriously from the financing and real estate problems of their distant owner, Hooker Corporation of Australia. Hooker Corporation was the plaything of corporate empire-builder George Herscu. After Herscu became enamored with American retailing, Hooker overextended itself in buying half-a-dozen American retail companies and opening three regional shopping centers in the space of two years. High interest rates and a poor real estate market in Australia then doomed Hooker to liquidation under Australian law.

B. Altman and Bonwit Teller suffered under Herscu's absentee management. B. Altman, with a 124-year history of quality and gentility, began to look seedy. The companies lacked funds to pay their vendors adequately and began to have difficulty acquiring inventory. Whether from lack of attention or lack of retailing exprience, Herscu had taken two venerable names in American retailing and had damaged them—more victims of the megalomania that fuels the conglomeratization of business. When the retailers filed bankruptcy, it was the first time that a megacorporation based offshore had used Chapter 11 to attempt to save ailing divisions. (The immediate parent of Bonwit Teller and B. Altman in the Hooker hierarchy, the U.S. unit L. J. Hooker Corporation, as well as thirteen other units, also filed Chapter 11 cases.)

With much fanfare, the retailers called in Sanford Sigoloff. Mr. Sigoloff had been available since he gave up his position as the head of Wickes when it was bought by an investment banking firm eight months before. No doubt his involvement with Hooker had a lot to do with the units filing Chapter 11. In an interview Sigoloff modestly allowed that his presence on the scene would result in the two retail chains getting the credit they needed to operate.

Sigoloff's magic could not save B. Altman. It was too far gone. Vendors had stopped shipping to it on credit long before Sigoloff had come on board. Losses of $4 million a month could have been tolerated at a larger chain, but with only seven stores with which to work, no substantial restructuring of operations was possible. Before the end of the year, shoppers on Fifth Avenue were jamming B. Altman's flagship store once more, but this time because the signs outside said GOING OUT OF BUSINESS and CLOSING OUR DOORS FOREVER. It was another end-of-an-era happening in a decade that seemed to specialize in them. Soon the public would be shocked by the bankruptcy filings of other famous retailing names that also were done in by corporate manipulation. Bonwit Teller limps along as a two-store chain after most of its stores were closed and a few were sold to Donald Trump's Pyramid Companies.

Ames Department Stores also expanded too quickly by taking on three hundred ailing Zayre stores in 1988. In Chapter 11 since April 1990, it is cutting about 30 percent of its fifty thousand employees and closing hundreds of stores. Since it has much more to work with than the Hooker retailers, it most likely will survive.

The late Eighties saw a full complement of megacorporate Chapter 11s in addition to the high-profile cases. Two Chapter 11s that saw little publicity nevertheless were among the biggest bankruptcies ever filed.

In January 1986, Global Marine, an offshore oil driller, filed for protection of its creditors. With about $1.8 billion in book assets as well as liabilities, it was perhaps the largest corporate victim of the American oil bust and one of the Top Ten bankruptcies ever. Its largest creditor was the federal Maritime Administration, which had guaranteed $200 million of Global's debts. (That government largess had funded the company's overexpansion.) When Global reorganized in 1988, its plan was very simple: its creditors were given 97.5 percent of the company. Although the industry is still very sick, Global remains as one of its larger members; and, thanks to its reorganization, it will be well situated when times get better.

Strong foreign competition in the shipping industry forced McLean Industries, operator of U.S. Lines, to seek Chapter 11 protection in November 1986. With about the same value of assets as Global, McLean also made the Top Ten to date. McLean sold off its fleet while in Chapter 11, including several brand-new jumbo container ships, and reorganized as . . . a real estate company.

Allegheny International has not attracted the attention of the general public, but it has attracted a number of buy-out artists who have been led on a merry chase by Allegheny's management.

The manufacturer of Sunbeam and Oster surprised the business community when it filed a Chapter 11 proceeding in February 1988. However successful its products were, it had been suffering for several years from the $543 million in debt incurred to purchase Sunbeam. A cash crunch and a standoff with its lenders brought on the filing. In a sign of the times, the company announced that the Chapter 11 would allow it to operate more aggressively, and financial analysts were pleased that the company had solved its immediate cash flow problem.

Several groups and individuals have taken a run at the company. Allegheny attempted to block a group of shareholders, led by a brokerage house, from staging a coup by refusing to hold a shareholders' meeting. By the time it was ordered to do so by a federal court, management had solidified its position and retained control of the company's board. Victor Kiam, head of Remington Products (the electric shaver people), kicked the tires. Management had on-again-off-again deals with investment banking house Donaldson, Lufkin and Jenrette Securities, eventually snubbing its overtures. In early 1990, management rebuffed another suitor and successfully engineered a reorganization fueled by stock.

The revolving door of bankruptcy court turned without much fanfare for other large corporations. Although Wheeling and LTV received the most press, McLouth Steel Corporation, the eleventh largest steel producer, filed Chapter 11 on December 8, 1988, to achieve debt and wage concessions. In September 1989, Braniff filed its second Chapter 11 of the decade and cut its work force in half. The carrier, which previously had been sold off by the Hyatt Hotels-Pritzker interests, restructured as a charter carrier. United Press International filed for Chapter 11 and achieved a reorganization (45 percent payment to creditors) through sale to a partnership headed by Mexican publisher Mario Vazquez-Rana. When Rusty Jones, the concern that provides auto undercoating, filed a Chapter 11 proceeding, it became possible for it to break all of its outstanding guarantees to users of its product.

Just as Chrysler's declaration of insolvency presaged the 1980s, two Chapter 11s of the late Eighties are a glimpse of the Nineties.

Southmark Corporation, a giant real estate company with interests also in the weak industries of health care, oil and gas, and insurance, filed for protection from its creditors in mid-1989. Shortly before its filing, Southmark managed to lose a staggering $1.04 billion *in one quarter* due to write-downs in the value of its real estate holdings, wiping out its owners' equity completely. The news was so bad, it was good. What with competition from the Great Federal Government S&L Real Estate Sell-Off (not to be confused with the Great S&L Rip-Off that preceded it), the real estate market is so bad that no one wants to force a liquidation auction of Southmark. Instead the company will sell its assets over a period of time. Creditors are likely to take a bath, and the company's shareholders no doubt will fare worse. Southmark's Chapter 11 is the first large bankruptcy directly related to the deflation in real estate values that started in 1986 with changes in the tax laws and will accelerate in the Nineties due to the S&L debacle and other downward pressures on real estate—but it will not be the last, by far.

The Chapter 11 of Revco D.S. is also a portent of the future. The company had been taken private in a $1.25 billion leveraged buyout in December 1986, and almost immediately ran into problems. Once the premier discount drug chain, with one thousand nine hundred stores in twenty-seven states, its cash flow problems caused by the leveraged buyout resulted in inventory problems and damage to its image with customers. When it filed its Chapter 11 petition at the federal courthouse in Akron, Ohio, in July 1988, it listed $1.2 billion in assets and $1.5 billion in debt—another Top Ten loser!

The filing came when Revco missed a $46 million semiannual interest payment on $703.5 millon in "junk" bonds, and holders refused to take stock in the company for their claims, several large holders instead demanding accelerated payments. That was bad-news-good-news for Revco's management, who most likely would have lost control in the recapitalization. Revco's chairman, Boake A. Sells, insists that he did everything possible to keep Revco out of Chapter 11, but that his hand was forced. Chalk up another Br'er Rabbit thrown into the briar patch.

Once in bankruptcy, Revco's leveraged buyout came back to bite it. As part of the transaction, Revco's lenders, recognizing how thinly capitalized the company would become, demanded a first lien position for the amount of their loans. As a result, unlike most large corporations, Revco was liened to the hilt when it filed Chapter 11, and the interest clock on the bank debt continued to run. (Interest ceased to run on the unsecured bonds.)

So far Revco has withstood some overtures by outsiders to take over the company. The "exclusive period," as extended by the presiding bankruptcy judge, has helped management fend off those proposals. The latest plan of action for the company is to sell off about a quarter of its locations in order to raise cash to fund a reorganization.

Although many of the megabankruptcies of the late Eighties received scant publicity, the level of filings of business bankruptcies in general and megabankruptcies in particular did not slack off. It looks like

Chapter 11 as a corporate tool is here to stay. The bankruptcies of the Eighties, as well as certain financial and debt trends, can give us clues as to the shape that the animal will take in the nineties.

Chapter 15

The Restructuring of American Industry—Again

"What's past
is prologue."
—William Shakespeare,
The Tempest

Which American megacorporations will find themselves in the sequel
to this book at the turn of the century?

What will the 1990s bring for American business? Will the economy
stay on an even keel or will it tip? Will the Beast of Inflation rear its
ugly head again? What opportunities will exist for businesses, and what
will be the pitfalls? What will be the megablunders of the megacorporations? It appears that competitive pressures in the world economy will be high, and there is little evidence that American business is
up to the challenge. One thing is for sure: unless Congress makes
changes in the Bankruptcy Code, Chapter 11 will be there to act as the
shield to protect them from their follies and as the sword to help them
get what they want.

Business swims in the economic stream. There always will be some
business people who are successful swimming against the current and
some who make a mess of things under even the most advantageous
conditions, but in general the odds of a business doing well are

improved if it is working consistent with the flow.

While it always is dangerous to predict general economic trends—so many smart, well-connected people miss them until after the fact— certain elements of economic life that became established in the Eighties as major determinants of the financial picture may be projected to have an effect into the Nineties. As sure as macro-economics has micro effects, those major components of the world's financial structure have an impact that affects not only the common man and woman on the street and in their homes but also the world's most powerful companies. Some of those pressures will lead a number of the largest corporations in the world to file bankruptcies.

Oil is the "500 pound gorilla" of the world's commodities. It is a $400 billion a year business that directly affects the cost of many products, from gasoline and electrical power to fertilizer and plastic bags. When the countries that formed OPEC gained control over their destinies in the early Seventies, the world's economy teetered on the brink. After Saudi politics led to the dismissal as oil minister of Sheik Ahmed Zaki Yamani, the master player in the oil game, OPEC disunity came to the forefront and prevented outright dictation of the world's oil prices during the late Eighties.

During 1989 and 1990, the price of oil moved fitfully in the $17– $20 per barrel range, pulled in different directions at different times by different causes. OPEC's lack of unity prevented it from exerting an upward force on oil prices for any substantial length of time. The major oil companies maintained sufficient market power to move the price of gasoline quickly in response to short-term changes, in order to protect their profit margins and, at times, significantly pad them.

The prior two years had been good ones for oil company profits. With the price of crude soft, the majors nevertheless had been able to maintain retail gasoline prices at a level that included a fat profit. Just when profit margins began to feel a squeeze along came the March 24, 1989, oil spill of the *Exxon Valdez*. Citing the disaster as the cause of a "shortage," the majors jacked up prices accordingly. The price of gasoline in California shot up forty-nine cents a gallon within days after the spill, and nationally the increase in gasoline prices during April set a record. (No doubt that run-up in prices added greatly to Exxon's kitty for cleaning up the ecological disaster and paying any fines.) In May, the average price of all grades of gasoline nationally was $1.254 on news of a disruption in North Sea production.

However, after the public balked at the usual "summer driving season" price gouging, prices moderated for the remainder of the year. As summer 1990 approached, gasoline prices began approaching a five-year high.

(Hurricane Chantal, which disrupted Gulf of Mexico operations in July 1989, also was associated with a brief run-up in gasoline prices. Can it really be true that the world's supply of oil and gasoline is so fragile that a brief disruption of one element of its distribution system can cause such extreme results? Are there no substantial reserves of oil not in the ground? Are there no reserves of gasoline to call upon to smooth out a short-term crisis? Or, is the price of gasoline the result of monopoly power acting upon pretexts? Exxon simplified the issue for the public. When called before Congress to explain the high cost of gasoline after the *Exxon Valdez* spill, Exxon blamed it on OPEC.)

The American public's reliance on gasoline will continue during the Nineties unless a sharp turn is made in U.S. policies. The driving public is renewing its interest in gas guzzlers, and most freight moves on the highways. The fact is that successive administrations of the United States Government, starting with President Eisenhower developing the federal interstate system "for defense," has encouraged and facilitated Americans' yearning for the open road and desire for a personal auto as a status symbol. The studious ignoring of public transportation as a means to move Americans by the Reagan administration no doubt will be continued by President Bush, who after all has spent his entire working career in the oil industry. As suburbs push farther out into the cornfields with no effective regional transportation systems other than one-car-for-one-person, the United States will continue to be hooked on foreign oil and gasoline refined by the majors. Everybody knows that junkies must feed their habit, and it is expensive.

While the major American oil companies have a great deal to say about the price of gasoline, diesel fuel, and heating oil, among other oil products, the price of OPEC oil still is of great concern to American business. Although energy usage in this country is more efficient than during the energy crises of the Seventies, for manufacturing it still is only half as efficient as in West Germany and Japan. The policies of Presidents Reagan and Bush, as well as those of the Seven Sisters, have insured that the United States is still hugely dependent on foreign oil. Domestic drilling continues only at minimal levels, the oil companies telling us that the price of oil is not high enough to induce them to undertake substantial drilling in the United States. Output from the North Slope of Alaska peaked in 1988 and is sliding slowly. As a result, U.S. oil production, flat at a little under nine million barrels of crude a day for almost the entire Eighties, is now on a downward trend below eight million. In 1989, the United States imported 46.1 percent of the oil which it consumed, a percentage exceeded only by the record of 47.7 percent set in 1977. In January 1990, a 44 percent surge in oil imports led to a $1.57 billion widening in the U.S. trade deficit, in the face of improving exports. If current trends continue, the country soon will be passing the 50 percent mark for imported oil on an annual average.

Sheik Yamani recently commented on the effect of American oil policies. "I am concerned about the impact of a decline in the U.S. oil industry. Considerable damage has already been done. It must stop. Otherwise America will be forced to rely on the Persian Gulf, which is a part of the world, I assure you, that you do not wish to allow yourselves to rely upon. Some day, maybe as soon as the 1990s, Americans will look back and curse the officials who allowed this to happen."

The net result of the oil situation is that American industry will continue to be hurt by energy costs that are set by a few countries and a few companies. The price of energy appears to be slowly but steadily rising, the U.S. price of a barrel of oil already having risen more than 35 percent since the beginning of last year. If OPEC can get its act together, and it is trying to do so every day, the world could be in for a price shock. Surely the American megacorporations that control the distribution of the world's oil (and gas and uranium, and to a large extent, coal) will be pleased to pass along every penny of the insult and toss in a few more for good measure. If that happens, the lines will be forming quickly at the filing desks of the clerks of the nation's bankruptcy courts.

As this book goes to print, Saddam Hussein of Iraq has just shaken the world's complacency by his takeover of Kuwait. The oil barons have jacked up the price of oil and gasoline because a shortage *might* result. The ripple effect *will* be played out in bankruptcy court.

Another major determinant of the health of American companies is Japan Inc. During the Nineties, Japan and Germany will dominate the world's markets, providing stiff competition for American exports; and Japan will dominate the American market for goods, finances, and real estate.

Gone are the days when Japanese companies merely were clever and good copycats of American technology. In spite of comforting theories on how and why the Japanese economic miracle would run out of steam by now, Japan continues to grow steadily in industrial might as past successes form the basis for future conquests. Unlike American megacorporations that expend their energies on short-term schemes to keep shareholders happy, such as asset shuffling among companies and stock and bond manipulation, Japanese companies are putting their money into capital spending for expansion, cost cutting, improvement of existing products, development of new products, and research and development. Nonresidential investment as a percentage of Gross National Product in Japan has increased during the Eighties from more than 14 percent to almost 20 percent. (In the United States, it has drifted downward during the 1980s from 12 percent to 10 percent.) Starting in 1988, capital outlays for Japanese companies began to exceed those of American business, even though the total Japanese output of goods and services is less than two-thirds that of America's. By the end of this decade, Japan's economy is likely to be the same size as this country's.

Much ado is made about the opening of Japanese markets to American products. It is a red herring. While certain American commodities, such as tobacco (cigarettes), timber, citrus, and a few custom items such as supercomputers and satellites, have natural markets in Japan and should be freed to compete there, most American products are not desirable enough to the Japanese to make a serious dent. Japanese protectionism in its many forms *is* unfair and should be attacked, but the immediate results for American business will be small.

We have lost valuable time. The timidity toward Japan shown by the United States government in the last twenty years has allowed Japan to have the best of both worlds—a substantially open U.S. market for goods but a protected local economy. In 1981, the U.S. merchandise trade deficit with Japan was under $20 billion annually; it is now $60 billion. Now that Japan has become a trading colossus, American bargaining power to achieve real changes in how Japan does business has weakened. With the exception of intermittent grandstanding by Congress, the realities of the Nineties will require that the U.S. negotiating posture toward Japan become even *more* timid than it has been. The Bush administration understands this. It has been persuading U.S. companies to drop "unfair trade" complaints against Japanese companies in favor of delicate government-to-government negotiations that will get nowhere. There is absolutely no chance that the Bush administration will get tough on Japan even when it is branded for its unfair trade policies. As stated by Takahashi Korekiyo, then Japanese minister of finance, in 1936, "It is much harder to nullify the results of an economic conquest than those of a military conquest."

The Japanese people increasingly see Americans as inefficient at best and lazy at worst, crime and drug ridden, and pompous. Are they wrong? Some figures from 1987 are illustrative. Average production worker's week: Japan—43.2 hours; U.S.—38.5 hours. Time lost to labor disputes: Japan—256,000 worker-days; U.S.—4,481,000 worker-days. Unemployment rate: Japan—2.8 percent; U.S.—6.2 percent. Household savings rate: Japan—18.3 percent; U.S.—6.3 percent. Japanese businesses invest an amount equal to 26 percent of the nation's output, compared to only 14 percent in the U.S. The U.S. crime and drug rates are too depressing even to make a comparison. Urban high schools in the United States have graduation rates of 50 percent.

Japanese financial institutions also are invading the U.S. markets. Japanese financial companies and banks have an inherent advantage in that interest rates are quite a bit lower in Japan. Not only are interest rates cheaper, but the Japanese banks make loans to industries, such as steel, that American financial institutions have abandoned—in favor of "good" loans like those to South American countries! Japanese-owned banks now control 25 percent of the banking market in California and 10 percent of the banking assets nationwide. In 1990, Orix Corporation became the first Japanese company to go into the aircraft leasing business—essentially a financing device—when it picked up troubled Braniff's option to buy seventy-four planes. Chances are that major American companies increasingly will find themselves debtors to Japanese-owned banks. While those financial institutions can be expected to tread lightly initially, it has to be disturbing to Americans that the fate of their industries will rest in the hands of foreign bankers.

Japanese companies are beginning to flex their financial muscles in a new way: by "rescuing" failing American industries, no doubt for their own future benefit.

The steel industry is an example. Looking toward the termination of import quotas on March 31, 1992 (in July 1989, President Bush extended them until then), every American steelmaker except Bethlehem Steel Corporation has allied itself with a Japanese steel manufacturer in at least one joint venture. The Japanese companies are supplying the American companies with their superior technology and with much-needed financing. (Bethlehem spent millions buying Japanese technology outright, much like Japanese companies did with American technology in earlier days.) The Japanese partners will be well positioned to take over the partnerships as the price for supplying future capital or technology. Are the American steel companies worried? They need the Japanese so badly that they are in no position to even think about the negative possibilities.

Another struggling industry reaching out to the Japanese is the American semiconductor manufacturers. The following alliances between American computer chip manufacturers and Japanese companies were forged in 1990: Texas Instruments and Kobe Steel; American Telephone and Telegraph and NEC, AT&T and Mitsubishi; Advanced Micro Devices and Sony Corporation; and Intel Corporation and NMB Semiconductor Company. Texas Instruments and Hitachi Corporation got together in 1988; and Motorola and Toshiba in 1986. The companies that have allied themselves with Japanese partners may avoid bankruptcy in the Nineties.

Another tactic that will have a large effect in this decade is Japan's old standby: acquiring technology in targeted industries and then gearing up to produce cheaper, improved versions. Toshiba Corporation has formed an alliance with American's Sun Microsystems that will allow the Japanese company to make inroads into the "workstation" market. NEC Corporation of Japan is allowing American Telephone and Telegraph Company to sell NEC's advanced logic chips in return for receiving some of AT&T's computer-aided design technology. AT&T also has entered into a similar relationship with Mitsubishi Electric Company. Toyota Motor Corporation's joint venture with General Motors in an auto production plant, commenced in 1985, in California provided the Japanese with an excellent introduction to U.S. employees and supply and distribution systems. (GM managers involved in the experiment complain that GM failed to make use of Japanese methods learned by them.) And the list goes on. American industries that Japan has targeted can be expected to see a substantial number of bankruptcies in the Nineties.

The evidence of Japan's next big industrial coup is staring us in our collective face.

With a strong helping hand from the United States government—initiated by the Reagan administration and finalized by President Bush—Japan is now gaining extensive knowledge in aviation technology. The immediate mode of transfer is the U.S. to Japan joint development of the FSX jet fighter plane, based on the American F16. The participation of the United States in the $6.5 billion project effectively was authorized when the Senate failed to pass a resolution of disapproval in May 1989. (Under a special provision, the deal could have been killed had both houses of Congress voted disapproval. Since the Senate failed to disapprove, a House vote was not necessary.) The Senate did require that certain elements of engine technology be kept secret and that American firms receive at least 40 percent of the subcontracting work, provisions that the Bush administration no doubt will be as disinclined to enforce as other rules of trade that Japan regularly violates. Hoping to have a piece of the pie, General Dynamics, Boeing, and McDonnell Douglas testified in favor of the joint project. Mitsubishi Heavy Industries, Japan's largest defense contractor, will be the project's contractor.

Senator Alan J. Dixon of Illinois was one of the main opponents of the deal. He argued the view that the U.S. should not provide a plum of a deal to an unfair trading partner and that the technology transfer to the Japanese would come back to haunt us. In a public letter he stated: "The Japanese will use this technology—which we are virtually giving away—to compete with our own commercial aviation industry, and we will get little or nothing in return. . . . When are we going to learn? We virtually gave away our technology in the VCR and semiconductor industries." Senator Dixon urged that we send a message to Japan by scrapping the FSX project. Instead, with the approval of the project, the United States government has sent a very different message.

The FSX project will be but one stepping-stone for a Japanese assault on the U.S. aerospace industry. Japanese companies already are almost on a parity with their U.S. counterparts in airborne electronics. The Pentagon already buys Japanese carbon-composites for airplane wings. In 1990, Daimler-Benz AG and Mitsubishi Heavy Industries, both of whom produced their country's fighter planes in World War II, agreed to team up on aeronautical and aerospace projects. During the Nineties, the United States government is likely to insist that Japan bear more of its own defense costs, allowing the industries of that country to make further inroads into aeronautics, aerospace, radar technology, and electronics.

Many feel that the lead of the United States over Japan is so great that the U.S. will not lose its preeminence soon. When have we heard that before? The American aerospace companies are inefficient due to decades of federal government largess and will be weakened by defense cutbacks. Thousands of small and mid-sized subcontractors to the industry will be easy pickings. It is a good bet that the next generation of American jet fighters will bear the stamp "Made in Japan."

The Japanese may be kind and help us out. In a recent interview Sony chairman Akio Morita offered, "We have acquired a great deal of technology from American industry—many licenses.... American industry may be behind today, but I'm not saying they have no chance to catch up. If it's necessary, we can help you by making our technology available." It probably is not wise to count on that promise. It is far more likely that a large percentage of victims of Japanese economic competition in the aerospace industry, including a number of mega-corporations, will attempt to respond to Japanese inroads by filing Chapter 11s.

An industry that has been under Japanese siege for more than a decade has been that of the U.S. automakers. Predictions that the Japanese automakers would suffer from a rebirth of the Big Three, from Korean manufacturers, from its own successes, from higher wages, from a stronger yen, from the cheaper dollar mandated in 1985, or from other problems that wishful thinking of Americans could conjure, have proven to be dead wrong.

Although American manufacturers had a good year in 1988, the Japanese automakers scored solid gains in 1989 almost without trying. Top executives at General Motors and Ford recently have admitted that Japanese autos still are superior. Although Lee Iacocca has refused to admit the same, the buying public also has been casting its votes increasingly for the Japanese automakers, both in customer-satisfaction surveys and in their purchases. By mid-1989, Japanese auto manufacturers controlled a record 24 percent of the American market, and it looks like they will equal or surpass that percentage for 1990. The percentage decrease in profits of the American auto industry from the first quarter of 1989 to the same period of 1990 was (minus) 64 percent, the worst industry average for all of American manufacturing.

What about the future? The U.S. production facilities of American auto manufacturers are being closed roughly at the rate that Japanese corporations are opening theirs. Japanese-operated auto plants in the United States consistently outperform those of the American-owned companies. For the period 1990 to 1993, the Japanese automakers are planning to introduce the same number of new products in the U.S. as the American manufacturers. It is predicted that by the end of the century—not too far away—the Big Three will be Toyota, Nissan, and Honda.

Is there a Chapter 11 or two or three in the future for U.S. automakers? Why not? Chrysler is closing its third assembly plant (out of nine). When sales fell for the U.S. manufacturers recently, it was Chrysler that was hit the hardest. The company has a $1.2 billion unfunded pension plan. In June 1990, Moody's Investor Service downgraded $22.2 billion of Chrysler's debt to the lowest level above "junk" bonds, which will make it more difficult and more costly for Chrysler to raise cash. Now that this country's megacorporations have had a decade's experience with the Bankruptcy Code, perhaps Lee Iacocca has changed his mind about Chapter 11. Besides, it is doubtful that he can go back to Congress's well again. Ford has not made any profits on its North American operations for some time. The market share of General Motors has steadily slipped along with its consumer-satisfaction ratings. Maybe the giant automakers will decide that the Nineties is the time to break their unions through a bankruptcy "crisis."

The recent decades of success have provided Japan with a new format for the conquest of American industries—buying them. Japanese companies are loaded with cash. Eight of the world's ten largest banks are Japanese, eager to finance acquisitions. Publicly reported acquisitions of American companies by Japanese climbed 8 percent in 1989 to a record $13.7 billion. In 1990, the Ito-Yokado Company offered to rescue ailing Southland Corporation, the operators of 7-Eleven stores, by purchasing 75 percent of Southland. The strong yen that supposedly was going to hurt Japanese exports (but has not) has made the prices of U.S. businesses look cheap. Japanese banks, along with a few European banks, have pushed all of the American banks out of the Top Ten worldwide and have stepped up their investment in, and purchase of, American financial institutions. Dai-Ichi Kangyo Bank has bought into Manufacturers Hanover and has purchased a controlling interest in that bank's finance company subsidiary. Recently, Japanese investments in

American farmland, ranches, and food-processing companies have been burgeoning. It is likely that Japan will surpass England this year as the source of the most foreign investment in the United States annually.

The heavy Japanese presence in American business, finance, and real estate will be changing the rules of the game for American-owned companies. When American megacorporations get in trouble, they may hear the siren song of Japanese investors. They may avoid bankruptcy by persuading creditors to compromise their debts in return for the injection of capital by Japanese investors. Southland did just that. At least the American companies captured that way will be less likely to need Chapter 11—until the Japanese learn about its great benefits for their American investments! Another scenario envisions Japanese investors becoming wise to the bankruptcy system and waiting until after Chapter 11s are filed, when a company can be had for much less money, to take a run at it.

Other factors besides predatory actions by foreigners will affect business in the Nineties. A major problem is that there will not be enough cash and credit to go around.

It will be very difficult for companies to find financing or refinancing, except possibly from the Japanese. The federal government will be in the credit market in a big way, to pay for the S&L debacle as well as the stubborn federal deficit, and it will soak up investment funds. Credit will be tight as the nation's bankers recoil from their excesses of the Eighties that brought us the S&L scandal. Pulling the economies of Eastern Europe and Russia out of the toilet will divert *substantial* amounts of investment capital away from domestic development, starving it for financing and raising interest rates. The bills for massive deferred maintenance in public works (the "infrastructure") will be coming due. (During the last decade, Japan has invested about 5 percent of its total output annually in public works. The United States has managed only .3 percent.) At the same time, U.S. industry will be called upon to finance technological advances and a whopping bill for environmental improvements. It is estimated that the Clean Air Act of 1990 alone will cost U.S. industry $21.5 billion a year when fully implemented. Although there are differences of opinion on the subject, the lack of enough capital to go aound very likely will result in interest rates rising at least several percentage points.

Rising interest rates will affect American business greatly.

Corporations large and small, as well as consumers, have been on a debt binge for the last several years. Borrowing to make acquisitions—leveraged buyout takeovers—had added another huge layer of debt for megacorporations. In 1980, American corporations on the average paid 5 percent of their pretax profits in interest payments; in 1990, debt service absorbs about 60 percent. Most borrowing, including many junk bond instruments, provides for a floating interest rate. Consequently, any material increase in interest rates will spark numerous defaults and bankruptcies. Interest rates (and inflation) will be moderated somewhat by the facts that defense spending probably will be reined in and that the S&L disaster and tax laws will hurt the prices of real estate significantly. Nevertheless, scarce capital will mean an abundance of bankruptcies, even for megacorporations.

A "benefit" of higher interest rates will be the continued interest of foreign investors in supporting the United States government, a legacy of the Reagan years. During the Reagan administration, the United States was turned from the world's largest creditor, with net foreign assets of $95 billion, to the world's largest debtor, with net liabilities of more than $400 billion—a $500 billion swing! The government's insatiable need for cash has been answered by foreign investors, the Japanese alone becoming major purchasers of Treasury bills with the power to affect their interest rates. The United States government thus has ceded its control over its own finances, and any substantial redeployment of capital by foreign investors could imperil the American economy and even the government of the United States. In 1990, some of that investment capital has been withdrawn to fuel the reawakened European economy, a portent of things to come.

The natural result of the scarcity of capital and the increase in interest rates will be that American companies will scrimp on capital spending, further eroding their competitive position. As of early 1990, that pattern is beginning to assert itself.

Of course, business can always count on the good ol' consumer to fuel the economy—or can it? Apparently it is consumer spending that has prevented the American economy from slipping into recession over the last two years; but the consumer has become overburdened. Adjusting for the official rate of inflation, the average American household's income increased only 3 percent between 1980 and 1990. Allowing for forms of inflation that are likely to strike the middle class harder than average figures indicate, such as tax increases in all areas other than federal income tax, adjustable rate mortgages, medical costs, and college expenses, it is quite possible that the American standard of living has slipped during the last decade. The economic trends already mentioned point to a continuation of that. A harbinger is the Consumer Price Index for the first quarter of 1990, which showed annualized price increases of 8.5 percent—the highest rate in eight years. Certainly, the trend in personal bankruptcies, likely to hit an all-time high of 600,000 in 1990, supports that conclusion. The result of the trends will be a fickle consumer, strapped for cash, who will send large and small retailers that are not at their absolute best into Chapter 11.

American business is not doing very well even at this time. For the first quarter of 1990, worker productivity in the U.S. declined at an annual rate of 2.7 percent, the poorest showing since the 1981–1982 depression, yet wages increased at an annualized 7 percent. The ranks of middle management in the megacorporations, the men and women leading the soldiers on the corporate battle lines, have been decimated and demoralized by the mania for cost cutting that has been brought about by mergers and acquisitions and other inefficiencies of megacorporate organization. During the Eighties, most mergers made sense only because one plus one only equaled one-and-a-half. Machiavelli would have loved it.

It is pretty well decided that neither American business nor the federal government can waste precious capital in a futile attempt to chase the Japanese in the development of the next generation of high-powered computer chips or high-definition television. Companies that have had "no layoff" policies in the past, such as International Business Machines, Digital Equipment, Hewlett-Packard, Polaroid, and Federal Express, have changed their policies, whether expressly or under euphemisms such as "voluntary severance." The slippage that has already occurred can be summarized in one "bottom line" figure: corporate profits of U.S. companies as a percentage of the country's Gross National Product have dropped steadily from about 12 percent in 1966 to less than 5 percent in 1989.

As might be expected, the general business climate at the turn of the decade already is producing its share of bankruptcies. Business bankruptcies jumped 34 percent in the fourth quarter of 1989 and are expected to continue upward during 1990. Megacorporations are contributing their fair share of the total. If there is any pattern to megacorporate bankruptcies of 1990 so far, it is the continuation of that of the 1980s: wide diversification of troubled companies as to industry and cause. The major change is the addition of the first wave of bankruptcies induced by failed leveraged buyouts and junk bonds.

Several large retailers who are overextended or otherwise not at the top of their game have fallen into Chapter 11. Ames Department Stores apparently made a mistake in attempting to absorb three hundred stores from the ailing Zayre chain in 1988. In Chapter 11, it has canceled leases and closed hundreds of stores and terminated about 30 percent of its fifty thousand employees. Since it has much more to work with than the Hooker retailers, no doubt it will survive. Circle K Corporation, the second-largest convenience store chain in the country, will be correcting its overexpansion and marketing errors—for which its creditors will pay dearly—in Chapter 11.

In addition to retailing, 1990 has already brought us a nice collection of bankruptcies of megacorporations suffering from general business conditions or their own management goofs, or both. Greyhound Lines, beset by a strike, filed Chapter 11 to prevent lessors of a substantial portion of its fleet from repossessing its buses. At the filing, management spoke quite bitterly about the Amalgamated Transit Union, and, while busting the union was not discussed, it was obvious that the company feels that it has nothing left to lose by playing hardball in bankruptcy. Doskocil Companies, a little-known name that became a megacorporation by taking over Wilson Foods (yes, the Chapter 11 union buster) in 1988, found itself caught in commodity and financing squeezes at the same time and repaired to bankruptcy court to lick its wounds and reorganize its debt. General Development Corporation, a large Florida developer, filed its Chapter 11 in Miami. The company may try to chisel a $100 million restitution settlement it had made based upon charges that it had defrauded home buyers. Colorado-Ute Electric Association, an electric power producer, filed a Chapter 11 due to rate problems. Perhaps the biggest splash in the bankruptcy pool was caused by Drexel Burnham Lambert, which appeared to the public as liquidating, but actually is attempting some type of reorganization. More about that later.

Of course, bankruptcy has wider uses than merely as a safety net for the incompetent and for those caught in the wrong financial place at the wrong time. There is an amazing flexibility and utility of Chapter 11 as a tool for top management to make someone else pay for its follies.

Perhaps the hottest area of business bankruptcy during the 1990s will involve unraveling one of the great excesses of the 1980s: the mania for the related activities of leveraged buyouts, leveraged take-overs, and "junk" bond financing. (Technically, a buyout occurs when one or more executives at a company buy substantially all of its stock, whether from a few holders or from the public through a tender offer. A takeover occurs when the stock is purchased by investors who have had no prior material connection with the target company. The financ-ing, or leveraging, principles of the two types are the same. For the sake of convenience, either type will be referred to by the term that has taken on generic meaning, "leveraged buyout," or "LBO.") Chapter 11 will play a central part in determining who will have won and who will have lost in the financial restructuring of American busi-ness that was the result of the new forms of financing developed in those years.

Actually, the whole thing started on July 18, 1974. On that date, International Nickel of Canada, advised by investment banking house Morgan Stanley, made a tender offer for all of the shares of ESB, a Philadelphia battery maker, without the permission of ESB's manage-ment. When ESB publicly described the tactic as a "hostile" takeover that term entered into the business lexicon. The fact that Morgan Stan-ley, an old-line conservative investment house, was involved helped to make the process legitimate for large corporations to engage in.

The next important watershed did not involve an unwanted takeover. On April 7, 1977, three former members of a large investment house together bought A. J. Industries, a small truck suspension maker, for $25.6 million. The partnership, Kohlberg Kravis Roberts and Com-pany, put up only $1.7 million of its own capital, borrowing the rest. Using borrowed money to buy a business was nothing new—leveraging one's capital by supplementing it with borrowed money was a basic money-making tactic in business and real estate—but the percentage of borrowed funds was. The secret was that KKR had persuaded its lender that the company was worth substantially more than its purchase price, thus giving it security for its loan beyond what showed on the company's books. KKR was right. It sold the company in 1985 for $75 million.

KKR's partners realized that there were many more potential targets waiting to be scooped up. They felt that the stock market was going through a period when the quoted value of the stock of many companies was less than the actual fair market value of the assets of those companies. Therefore, if such a company were to be purchased through an LBO, the risk could be substantially lessened quickly by selling off a division or subsidiary or two or three at a premium price, thus creating equity. (In its extreme form, the technique has been referred to as a "bust up" acquisition.) By continuing to pick underpriced companies wisely, KKR showed the business community that the (highly) leveraged buyout could bring great returns from relatively small investments with only moderately more risk than usual financing entailed.

Because the technique depended upon a shrewd assessment of the target company, the investment world beat a path to KKR's door to finance whatever KKR's latest venture might be. While people like Carl Icahn and T. Boone Pickens made most of the news in the late Seventies with their corporate "greenmail"—buying a few percent of a company's stock, threatening to toss out management, and then accepting a premium to sell the stock—KKR was showing others how to have the whole apple with one bite.

The next step was the development of a formal mechanism to expand the pool of capital that could become available for hostile or friendly LBOs. The problem was that the technique was so free form and the loans such a large part of the purchase prices that LBOs violated every rule of prudent finance. How could big money managers like pension funds and insurance companies and rich sources of capital such as banks and S&Ls (which had been freed to invest in things other than real estate) be persuaded to put large amounts of money on the line to finance highly leveraged acquisitions? It would take a supersalesman to persuade those conservative lenders to swing with the "kinky" LBO deals.

Michael Milken, working out of the Los Angeles office of Drexel Burnham Lambert in the early Eighties, was that man. With good credentials and a presence that was part financial messiah and part snake-oil salesman, Mike Milken began crisscrossing the country to raise financing for leveraged buyouts. The message he touted was simple: high returns awaited lenders who would back takeover attempts with short-term loans until bonds could be issued, and those who then invested in the high risk bonds would provide the permanent LBO financing. Milken would line up a takeover deal by allying himself with someone like KKR and then selling the hell out of the financing aspect. He made Drexel, an also-ran in the stock brokerage business, the most powerful broker in the country for a few years.

Milken's timing was so perfect that if he did not exist, someone else would have stumbled into his spot. At the time, banks and savings institutions were beginning to emerge from the cocoon of regulation. They were free to attract deposits by offering higher interest rates, but accordingly they were under considerable pressure to earn more from their investments and loans. The new breed of financier wanted to get *rich*, not run a sleepy operation that made a few points on the spread above the Fed's interbank rate. They were *very* interested to learn how they could earn higher interest rates. Of course, the more conservatively operated institutions turned away from "bridge" loans for take-overs and junk bonds, but the new breed of go-go financial executives were *ready*.

Once a few successful deals were done, it all looked like easy money. Banks charged outrageous transaction fees, and the banking officers who plunged into the business became heroes. Soon the bankers' and money managers' herd instincts—or is it lemming instincts?—took over. No one wanted to be left out at the money trough, and so the professional lenders and investors began throwing money at deals. Rules of prudent lending were trampled in the stampede.

An example illustrates the extent to which all caution was thrown to the winds. When leveraged buyouts were beginning to gain in popularity, banks required that there be *some* equity capital put into the deals, so that company assets would exceed liabilities by some small margin. As LBO fever caught on, the cushion of collateral to support the loans began to narrow down to nothing. At that point, even bankers in a feeding frenzy realized that they could not sell the loans to their boards unless some color of collateral were added to deals. Thus was born the "highly confident letter."

When a lender is asked to do bridge financing until permanent investment capital can be raised through a stock or bond offering, he or she wants to feel secure that the bridge loan will be "taken out" in a timely fashion and that the risk will be terminated. Put another way, no lender wants to make a bridge loan to a borrower who cannot complete the contemplated offering. A common practice that has been developed is for the prospective lender to require the company to get a statement from its investment banker to the effect that the investment banker believes that it can sell out the stock or bond offering to investors at no less than a target price. The statement, called a "highly confident letter" because of its form and usual wording ("Dear Mr. Smith: We are highly confident that we can place..."), historically has had no legal significance. It does not reach the standard of a legal guaranty, and its adds no collateral. It does not provide security for the loan, but it is the banker's security blanket.

When the pressure to do LBO deals got intense, lenders began to rethink their lending practices. They decided that a "highly confident letter" provided additional security for a loan since the investment bankers were selling the junk bond permanent financing like hot cakes. If the investment houses were that reliable, who cared whether there were any free assets after financing the company to the hilt? (It was not until 1989 that an investment banker reneged on a letter. When Morgan Stanley withdrew its "highly confident letter" to John B. Coleman and Company, its reputation was hurt, and the world of finance was thrown into a tizzy at the unprecedented action. Coleman, which claims to have passed up other financing opportunities in reliance on Morgan Stanley's letter, has sued.)

The next step was for the institutions to buy the junk bonds themselves. The risk was for a longer duration, but the interest rate "carrot" dangled in front of them was irresistible. Bank purchases of the bonds made good sense to the bankers because they helped to grease the LBOs from which they were sucking up huge fees. Once the banks were in, money managers caring for billions of dollars in insurance, pension, and mutual funds jumped in. Of course stockbrokers were touting the new product madly. Between 1985 and 1989, total investment in junk bonds increased each year.

As long as the deals were good—the companies bought at good prices and then operated very profitably or, more likely, chopped up to get at the asset value premium—there was good money to be had. When the deals later turned out to be not so good and the value of the junk bonds deteriorated significantly, the financial stability of numerous institutions, including some very large banks and many S&Ls, were threatened. (Also, many people found their retirement funds severely depleted by pension fund losses.) During the fourth quarter of 1989 and the first quarter of 1990, financial institutions wrote off 20 percent to 50 percent of the value of their junk bond holdings. It has been estimated that junk bond holdings constituted about 17 percent of the $7.5 billion in losses suffered by the thrift industry during the fourth quarter of 1989. Columbia Savings and Loan Association, of Beverly Hills, California, has invested more than $4 *billion* in junk bonds. When their prices plummeted, Columbia reported a first-quarter 1990 loss of $293.3 million and promptly declared itself insolvent. First Executive Corporation, a giant insurance holding company, has been in deep trouble because it holds $8 billion in junk bonds. In an example of poetic justice, it was the diminution of the value of junk bonds held by Drexel Burnham Lambert for its own account that drove it into Chapter 11.

The write-downs have wreaked havoc on the already poor financial position of many S&Ls. The decrease in value of junk bond portfolios has caused many S&Ls to fall below minimum capital requirements. The nation's largest investor in junk bonds by the end of 1990 most likely will be you and me—that is, our federal government. Because of the horrendous volume of failed thrifts and the large percentage of their assets that were invested in junk bonds, *it is estimated that as of the second quarter of 1990, the federal government is steward to 32 percent of the total of all outstanding junk bonds.* Thus the federal deposit insurance programs have accomplished a rare piece of governmental efficiency, providing corporate welfare not only to those who have run this nation's financial institutions into the ground, but also to the issuers of junk bonds who will cause those assets to decline even further in value while the government holds them.

In the mature phase of junk bond LBOs, in the late Eighties, deals made sense only by positing the most rosy scenarios for the future of the companies and the economy. Interest rates on the bonds typically floated, but it was assumed in the transactions that the prime rate would never rise during the terms of the bonds. It was assumed that divisions and subsidiaries marked for sale could be sold quickly and at premium prices. No thought of a downturn in any bond issuer's industry or in the economy could be had.

How could the cold, calculating bankers who grill a car-loan applicant mercilessly not see the folly? The reason is that any realistic view would have sunk the deals and stopped the flow of exorbitant fees to investment bankers and banks. How else can you explain the fact that in 1980 the average junk bond issuer had twice as much annual earnings before taxes as interest expense, but by 1988 the average company was earning only 71 percent of what it needed to pay its interest expense. In 1980 the average issuer's debt amounted to 60 percent of its assets; in 1988 that figure was 203 percent! With the pigs at the trough in a feeding frenzy, there were no cool assessments by the professionals to dampen the LBO fever of the corporate barons. That is why Robert Campeau, a generally savvy megacorporate businessman, could be led into paying $500 million too much for Federated Stores on the advice of his investment banker, Bruce Wasserstein. That is why Fruehauf Corporation foolishly paid a 34 percent premium above market price for the company's stock. That is why the $1.3 billion LBO of Revco, of which $1.1 billion was financed, was in trouble before the ink dried. Could the bankers and investment bankers be liable for fraud on junk bonds bought by the public? Maybe.

There were a few voices crying out in the wilderness. In 1984, John Shad, the chairman of the Securities and Exchange Commission, decried the "leveraging-up of American enterprise," which deflects cash flow from investment in plants and equipment, and warned, "The more leveraged takeovers and buyouts today, the more bankruptcies tomorrow." (Mr. Shad apparently decided that he would rather switch than fight. He later became the chairman and CEO of Drexel Burnham Lambert.) Felix Rohatyn called for legislation to sharply restrict the use of debt financing in acquisitions. While the debate raged, American corporations were on a borrowing binge. From 1984 to 1987 alone, corporate equity fell by $313.3 billion and corporate loans increased by $613.3 billion. Junk bond financing became the functional equivalent of the real estate financing technique that brought down the S&L industry: the overvaluation of property in order to borrow more on it than it is worth.

By and large, the potential for tremendous negative impact that junk bonds carried was studiously ignored or rationalized. A number of influential business people and commentators praised the ability to raise capital that junk bonds permitted. Junk bonds in general and Michael Milken in particular really did help some struggling businesses, including those owned by minorities, that could not secure customary forms of financing. Sanford Sigoloff has said of Michael Milken, "Mike brought the less-favored people the opportunity to participate in America, as opposed to standing in line for rationing of bank debt. . . . When the historians look back to the last quarter of the twentieth century . . . they will talk about the legacy of one of the greatest capitalists of that time—a capitalist of such Faustian proportions that his genius changed the world of financial competition." Congress temporized itself out of the issue entirely by failing to pass any legislation on the subject.

Meanwhile, the players in the game were too busy living their most amazing fantasies to care. The lenders and investment bankers were making obscene transaction fees, and the corporate barons were acquiring whole empires to treat as their own private fiefdoms. In effect, vast amounts of corporate wealth were transferred into the hands of the corporate transaction facilitators. Michael Milken, the leading facilitator, who could raise billions at a whim, ruled America's corporate world. The system of checks and balances previously provided by administrative regulations had been stripped away, and nothing could stop them until the scam had played itself out. (The scam was not what got Milken into criminal trouble, because it was too big to be censured. It consisted of a giant conspiracy of financial and corporate experts who willfully or negligently oversold the concept of highly leveraged corporate financing for their short-term gain, irrespective of the likely consequences to businesses and their employees, financial institutions and their employees, and the economy and competitiveness of this country. In the Eighties that was not criminal—it was considered good business. What brought Milken down was his feeling of omnipotence that allowed him to ignore basic insider-trading laws as mere inconveniences. He did not need to break the laws—he already was filthy rich. His power over the junk bond market was so awesome that he could not resist the temptation to play God with the stock prices of takeover targets. Because he copped a plea to the violation of federal securities laws, the full extent of his illegal activities may never be known.)

Which issuers of junk bonds are in trouble? Record numbers of debt issues are being downgraded, forcing higher interest rates and lower trading prices, and causing companies to violate financial covenants. There are so many companies in trouble over their junk bond financing, including those stewarded by the biggest names in investment banking, that it would be impossible to name all of them and unfair to name examples. It would be a far shorter list to name the major American companies that are not highly leveraged!

Beyond being "in trouble," a number of corporations have defaulted on their junk bond obligations. As of mid-1990 that list includes William Farley's West Point-Pepperell, which got caught in the collapse of the junk market still in its bridge-financing stage and before it could finalize its LBO transaction; Simplicity Pattern Company; Seaman Furniture, a Kohlberg Kravis Roberts project; and Mr. Success himself, Donald Trump. Quoth Mr. Trump, in what could be a junk bond motto: "The 1990s sure aren't anything like the 1980s." Whatever were the benefits of junk bond financing, an epidemic of defaults was an obvious and entirely predictable result of the excesses. There was no way that many companies could meet the promised interest rates in the upper teens—yes, some junk bonds carry interest rates of more than 19 percent! Default rates were estimated at 34 percent during the first quarter of 1989. No doubt they are much higher now. The final numbers for the junk bond crash are going to be astronomical, since LBOs probably accounted for at least 25 percent of all deals in the last several years.

Corporations are using a variety of tactics to stay afloat. Some companies, such as Fruehauf Corporation, Circle K Corporation, and Cineplex Odeon Corporation, have put themselves up for sale in order to recapitalize; however, many are finding no takers due to their debt loads. When possible, conglomerates are selling divisions—Rupert Murdock's News Corporation and Harcourt Brace Jovanovich's sale of its Sea World theme parks are examples—but there is a glut of large companies for sale, and it is hard to achieve the level of premium price that will meaningfully reduce debt. Of course deep cuts in corporate work forces, such as Prime Computer's slashing of 20 percent of its employees and the halving of the work force at Western Union Corporation, are the order of the day. The natural result of the division shuffling and cost cutting necessitated by LBOs is employee resentment and operational inefficiencies.

The latest technique is to squeeze the junk-bond holders. Junk bonds now are selling at only fractions of their face value on the open market, many drawing buyers only in the range of 20 to 50 percent. That has allowed some issuing companies that have access to capital to offer buybacks at rates slightly over the market but nevertheless at steep discounts. Hallmark Cards has offered to buy back $270 million of its junk debt for 40 percent of face value; and Ingersoll Publications has made a 55 percent offer. Interco, a furniture and shoe company that had borrowed $2 billion to fight off a raider, is offering cash and stock for its issues, one of which is trading at five cents on the dollar. Western Union is attempting to convert its junk bonds into stock.

Wiliam Farley is offering to make his bridge lenders majority owners of his West Point-Pepperell. Greyhound Lines offered 45 percent but could not raise enough money to fund it.

Buybacks of junk bonds hit a record $2.5 billion during the first quarter of 1990. The revaluing of the paper at deep discounts merely brings corporate financing into line with reality, now that the party is over. As usual, the investing public wakes up too late, like the drunk that has been fleeced.

There always is Chapter 11, a fact that has put a chill on buybacks. A decision in the bankruptcy case of LTV has called into question the value of the claims of junk-bond holders in bankruptcy. In that case Bankruptcy Judge Burton Lifland ruled in January 1990 that bondholders who have agreed to swaps of their debt for debt securities of a lesser value have a claim in bankruptcy only in the lesser amount, not the face value of the original bond. The judge ruled that the swap value and not the face value of the bond is the "fair market value." The natural result of the ruling is that bondholders who help out a troubled company by agreeing to a ratcheting down of the company's debt may find that their dividend under a Chapter 11 reorganization plan is slashed by the fact that their claim is discounted *before* the plan's percentage payment is applied.

Because of the prevalence of junk bond financing in American corporate life, junk bonds are involved in most—if not all—of the large Chapter 11s filed in the late 1980s, whether as a direct cause or simply one of the problems. (To some wags, LBO has come to stand for "large bankruptcy opportunity.") Because there is no specific collateral backing junk bonds, holders of those debt securities are nothing more than a class of unsecured creditors, only one step above shareholders on the bankruptcy totem pole. (In most cases banks hold senior debt, secured by collateral, for their bridge loans, although they often also are buyers of junk bonds. Some classes of bonds may be subordinate to other debts by the express terms of the issues.)

In most bankruptcy reorganizations, junk-bond holders will get the short end of the stick. Because their rights are subordinate to those of other creditors, it is unlikely that they will be offered anything more than stock and a small percentage of cash under a Plan of Reorganization. Of course, because the troubled company is so highly leveraged, the stock is actually worthless at the time it is issued. Further, under an arcane provision of the Bankruptcy Code, a small group of the company's existing shareholders such as its top executives can keep control of the corporation by infusing a relatively modest amount of fresh capital. Thus junk-bond holders can be reduced to minority shareholders in a reorganized corporation—as low as one can get in the business world! At this time, management-led shareholders are attempting that coup in the Revco and Wheeling-Pittsburgh Steel cases.

Does the story of junk bond financing inevitably lead to bankruptcy court? Why not? Chapter 11 is a perfect device for ratcheting down the excessive debt of a company at the expense of those who so foolishly provided it. By degrading the positions of the large amounts of junk bond (and other bond) financing in Chapter 11, megacorporations will keep themselves from drowning in their debt by climbing on the backs of their suckers—er, investors.

Companies burdened by junk bond debt receive the same generous benefits of Chapter 11 available to other types of bankruptcy debtors. Junk-bond holders and other creditors immediately are prevented from declaring or acting on defaults, and their momentum is blunted while they are shunted into such activities as forming committees, reviewing bankruptcy papers, and so on. The interest clock immediately ceases to run on all bonds and other unsecured debts. Since the junk bond claims obviously will be paid a pittance at best, bank lenders are happy to provide financing during the bankruptcy on more conventional, *secured* terms. In fact, if the Chapter 11 company can show dire need, the presiding judge may authorize a lender providing financing during the Chapter 11 case to have a secured position ahead of prepetition secured creditors.

Moving on to a Plan of Reorganization is quite simple in an LBO-induced Chapter 11 (although the company may want to clean up other pesky problems as long as it has the opportunity). It is a simple matter to show that the junk bonds have little or no actual value since the company is so far under water. It follows that the holders should receive little or nothing under a Plan. Q.E.D.

What are the dangers of a Chapter 11 to management? None, really. Any legal exposure on the part of the masterminds of the LBO or its bankers for fraud or mismanagement—and there are some legal theories being tested in the courts now—exist irrespective of the bankruptcy of the company. Management may lose control or see its majority stock ownership diluted, but the company presumably is in such bad shape that bankruptcy is unlikely to make those matters worse either. Consequently, while the public sees danger and risk for management in Chapter 11, the corporate barons see only another opportunity to score big.

In actuality, bankruptcy simply is another arena in the continuing gamesmanship of trying to steal a company at the lowest possible price. Management knows that megacorporations in Chapter 11 *will* be reorganized and that it will be the junk-bond holders who will suffer. The only real issue is who will end up in control of the company when it has been restructured, and Chapter 11 is very helpful to management in that regard. In Chapter 11, all the momentum for solving the company's problems belongs to management. The judge can maintain that exclusive period in which creditors are barred from proposing a Plan of Reorganization for quite a long time.

The icing on the cake for the businessman who rode an LBO into the executive suite is that Chapter 11 gives him a chance to steal the company again. Under bankruptcy rules, he has the opportunity mentioned previously respecting Revco, the chance to maintain a majority shareholder's position by supplying some relatively modest additional capital to the corporation. The judge need only rule that the proffered additional capital and the promise to provide managerial talent and effort in the future to the reorganized company are sufficient "new value" to the company, and effective control of the company going forward can be achieved. The LBO mastermind will continue in control of a company cleansed of much of its legitimate debt and will have paid a pittance.

Seen in this light, the main peril to the LBO manipulators in Chapter 11 will be not from the bondholders or other creditors, but from the other sharks in the water—the investment bankers and other corporate raiders—who may offer to add greater "new value" to the Chapter 11 corporation. As long as management can control the "exclusive period," it has the upper hand. Will the judges be more inclined than in the past to lift the prohibition and allow others to bid for companies? Will bankruptcy court turn into an arena for companies "in play"? Stay glued to your seats for the further adventures of LBO Barons in Bankruptcy, playing at a bankruptcy court near you.

Not surprisingly, the LBO Chapter 11s have begun to manifest themselves. As with the megabankruptcies of the early Eighties, as they progress they will encourage yet more filings. The bankruptcy courts will be the infirmaries for the later stages of LBO mania. The lawyers will get rich, the megacorporate manipulators will stay rich, and the investors in junk bonds will find themselves with little but pretty pieces of paper for their troubles.

The highest profile LBO debacle thus far has been that involving Robert Campeau and his two primary retailing operations, Federated Department Stores and Allied Stores Corporation. Although *Fortune* magazine termed Campeau's LBO purchase of Federated "The Biggest Looniest Deal Ever," it was neither. Although the numbers were impressive, the course of Campeau's LBO mania was common. It was just another LBO deal that never had much of a chance from its inception.

Campeau, a Canadian who had made a fortune in real estate, caught the fever one day and decided to become one of the biggest retailers in the United States. First he bought Allied, which included such names as Ann Taylor, Bonwit Teller (later to meet its fate at the hands of George Herscu and his Hooker companies), Bon Marché, Brooks Brothers, Jordan Marsh, and sixteen other retailers. Then he scooped up Federated, which included retailers Abraham and Straus, Bloomingdale's, Bullock's, Burdines, Filene's, Foley's, Gold Circle, I. Magnin, Lazarus, and MainStreet. The plan was typical of that demented period: Campeau simply would sell twenty-five divisions (keeping eleven) to reduce $13 billion in debt to $8 billion.

Although the biggest names in finance and investment banking took part in the package, no one seemed to notice that the numbers worked only under the most perfect of scenarios. The remaining eleven divisions would have to carry at least *$200 million a year in interest more than they had ever earned in their best years*. The shortfall would have to be matched by operating cuts on a level that had never been tried before on those well-known retailers. Then they all would have to have their best years ever, for the foreseeable future. No one involved seemed to care that Mr. Campeau was inexperienced in retailing and that he was so fixated on building an empire that he appeared to be paying about $500 million too much for Federated.

Although Campeau had been reasonably successful in real estate, he did not have anywhere near the cash necessary for his Campeau Corporation to take a run at his first target, Allied, at the end of 1986. When Bruce Wasserstein of First Boston investment banking firm found lenders for $3 billion, Campeau had to borrow the $300 million in "equity" that was his contribution. With all that financing available Campeau simply bought all of Allied's stock on the market, acquiring a majority quickly. (Shortly after that the SEC barred that method of takeover.) Through what amounted to 100 percent financing, he had acquired a conglomerate ten times larger than his Campeau Corporation.

The aftermath did not go badly. The bridge loans were repaid from a $1.1 billion junk bond offering in March 1987. During the course of 1987, Campeau built a good record of paying down his debt, so bankers began falling over themselves to offer him money just as he began planning to take over Federated.

On January 25, 1988, Campeau made an offer of $47 per share for Federated. When he encountered competition from several other chains for the prize, he eventually drove them out of the market with the exceedingly generous offer of $73.50 per share and the promise to spin off I. Magnin and Bullock's to one of them (Macy's). Lenders were eager to provide bridge financing of $2 billion. The advisors and bankers took home $350 million in fees. No one at the party was seen to complain about the host, even when he joked about paying $500 million too much for Federated.

Of course, Allied and Federated did not have their best years ever. Campeau had trouble attracting and then keeping top executives from the small pool of those with experience in running megacorporate retailers. Ann Taylor, a chain that Campeau had vowed to keep, was sold to raise cash. Investors were wary about Federated in its disorganized state, and so $1.1 billion in junk bonds offering 14 percent interest in fall 1988 did not sell, the company ultimately getting only $723 million and having to give 17.75 percent. By the holiday season of 1989, Federated was so short of cash and its stores so disheveled that its big-name retailers were offering large discounts to snag the customers off the streets—which killed profits for Federated and other large retailers that are Federated's competition. Suppliers began backing off from long-standing credit arrangements. For the fiscal year ending January 31, 1990, Federal and Allied reported losses of an amazing $2.4 billion. The jobs of 100,000 of Campeau's retailer employees were on the line.

By early 1990, the conglomerate was in a state of collapse. The board of Campeau Corporation actually fired Robert Campeau and brought in more professional management. (Campeau still is heavily involved with the companies.) A deal was patched together—with borrowed funds, of course—to offer Federated and Allied junk-bond holders a swap for stock (such a deal!), but the wounded nature of the retailers was so apparent that it could not be done. The board put Federated, Allied, and sixty-five related entities into Chapter 11 in Cincinnati, Ohio, on January 15, 1990. One more business megalomaniac has had his fun with other people's money.

The companies were in bad shape, but that did not mean that they would be shut down in bankruptcy. Banking syndicates offered $2.4 billion in financing. The companies also won the approval of the presiding bankruptcy judge, J. Vincent Aug, to offer a package of financial incentives to employees, to boost morale and avoid defections. Listing $11.5 billion in book assets, $8.7 billion in long-term debt, and a minus $138 million in shareholders' equity, the retailers began the rebuilding process under Chapter 11. It is highly doubtful that the companies will be liquidated on the auction block. Chapter 11 to the rescue!

Numerous other megacorporations are in bankruptcy as a direct result of junk bond financing. They include, in alphabetical order:

Drexel Burnham Lambert—forced in by the declining value of its own junk bond portfolio—now has five hundred employees instead of five thousand four hundred

Greyhound Lines—two weeks after offering to buy back its bonds at half price, due to a lack of the necessary financing

Hillsborough Holdings Corporation

Integrated Resources (financial services)

Resorts International—Merv Griffin had the misfortune of winning a bidding war for the casino, which defaulted nine months into the deal—quickly offered eighteen cents on the dollar plus stock to bondholders

Revco D.S.—ahead of its time

Southland Corporation

Southmark Corporation (real estate)

The rash of major bankruptcies caused by junk bonds will not soon end. The bondholders who provided the wherewithal to one of the great robber-baron eras in this country's history will be squashed through Chapter 11. The next generation of megacorporate manipulators, plus some recycled from the first decade of junk bond history, will whisk some very good megacorporations out of the bankruptcy courts of this country at very attractice prices, all of them ready to take on more debt in further exploits. So, what else is new?

Chapter 11 of the Bankruptcy Code: The All-Purpose Tool

Clearly, Chapter 11 of the federal Bankruptcy Code will be used in the Nineties to correct a variety of financial ills of American businesses, including the very largest. However, the bankruptcy lessons of the Eighties go far beyond that. Whether it was Frank Lorenzo blowing off Continental's unions or John McKinney or Claiborne Robins disdainfully treating injured and dying people as mere ciphers subordinate to the lives of their glorious corporations, the rule in bankruptcy was: Where There Is a Megacorporate Debtor There Is a Way. Several general principles established in the Eighties that favor megacorporate debtors remain firmly entrenched in the legal framework of Chapter 11s.

For one thing, a megacorporation may seek bankruptcy court protection even though it may have only one sticky problem. That problem can be one lawsuit, a particular cause of liability, unwise leases, or a union contract. As long as it is a *big* problem, it may be compromised through a Chapter 11—and judges are not particularly interested in closely inspecting the Chapter 11 company's assertion that the problem is big enough to warrant the protections of Chapter 11.

There has been no rollback whatsoever of the concept that an ongoing business may seek Chapter 11 as a preemptive strike against possible insolvency, without having to prove its existence on the date of filing by any particular test. In fact, the decisions on the insolvency issue really go beyond that. They generally affirm that, *at least for megacorporations*, the doors of the bankruptcy court stand open anytime they need sanctuary—whatever the reason.

Because of the solid establishment of the aforementioned bankruptcy principles in the Eighties on behalf of megacorporations, the thought that a bankruptcy judge will bounce a megacorporation out of bankruptcy because of notions of technical "bad faith" is now discredited. If a 500-pound gorilla of the corporate world wishes to take up residence in a bankruptcy courtroom, who is to stop it? Certainly not a bankruptcy judge.

There are various likely uses of Chapter 11 in the Nineties as a tool to attack and defeat a whole host of special business problems while loading the majority of the real losses onto hapless outsiders to the executive suites. Some of those uses of Chapter 11 have already been tested in the Eighties, and no doubt clever corporate managers and attorneys will find ways to reinforce and extend them. Others will constitute the new frontiers of bankruptcy.

It is firmly established that collective-bargaining agreements are ongoing contracts that may be canceled in Chapter 11 and that the national interests in promoting and enforcing collective action by employees are not paramount to the perceived national interests in reorganizing companies. It is true that subsequent to the Supreme Court's Bildisco decision, Congress passed legislation that limited the scope of the ruling. However, its purpose was to eliminate the more extreme ramifications of the ruling, not reverse it.

Essentially, Congress legislated that a company had to show that it really was in economic trouble before it could force the employees to contribute to its rehabilitation and that the company must bargain with the employees first in an effort to win voluntary concessions. The first requirement merely prevents a financially solid company from doing an end run around the labor laws out of pique and should not be difficult for a company suffering real competitive problems to meet (even if they may be attributed only partly to the union contract). The second requirement merely forces the parties to talk to each other for a period of time, which increases the odds that a voluntary agreement may be reached that will prevent litigation. If the company still believes that the union contract must go in order for it to be competitive, it can then exercise its rights under bankruptcy to act unilaterally on the union contract.

The most important feature of labor relations in bankruptcy court is that the provisions of the law generally will be interpreted by judges committed to the reorganization of the megacorporation. If there is a question on the application of a legal provision, a contract term, or the facts of the parties' bargaining, the megacorporation is going to receive the benefit of the doubt every time—and usually by a very wide margin. Megacorporations will learn that if they just make sure to touch all the bases, they can hit a home run against unions in the friendly confines of bankruptcy court.

Chapter 11 still is a great place to unload pension obligations, which are nothing more than unsecured claims in bankruptcy. As this book was being finalized, the United States Supreme Court ruled on the pension fund litigation between LTV and the federal Pension Benefit Guaranty Corporation. What the newspapers are trumpeting as a great victory for employees at closer reading looks like a megacorporate coup—but then again it was a no-lose situation for LTV no matter what.

First it should be noted what the Supreme Court did *not* do. It did not make a general ruling on the status of pension claims in bankruptcy. It did not say that a Chapter 11 company must contribute to its pension plans. It did not say that the PBGC gets reimbursed in full for canceled pension plans. In fact, the LTV case was unique, and the consequences of the Supreme Court's ruling will easily be sidestepped by companies in the future.

LTV had abandoned any pretense of fulfilling its obligations to its pension plans covering sixty thousand retirees and forty thousand active workers, and, as is the customary policy of the PBGC, that agency canceled LTV's pension plans in order to avoid the further accrual of additional unfunded liabilities. By law the $2 *billion* in unfunded liabilities became the responsibility of the PBGC, to be paid on a percentage basis—corporate welfare. Shortly after the PBGC acted, LTV entered into a new collective-bargaining agreement with the steelworkers' union in which it chiseled the employees' wages but agreed to install new pension plans with similar terms as the cancelled plans (called "follow-on" plans).

The institution of the follow-on plans raised the ire of the PBGC, normally not an aggressive agency. It claimed that the new plans really were an extension of the old, and so LTV's liabilities for the old attached to the new. (It has taken the same position with respect to follow-on plans of other companies that also have dumped unfunded liabilities onto the PBGC, which has a $5 billion deficit not counting LTV's plans.) It fought LTV all the way to the Supreme Court, and in an 8 to 1 decision that court agreed with the PBGC.

The Supreme Court did not discuss all of the possible ramifications of its ruling, and as usual its decision raised as many new questions as it answered. It does not appear that LTV's only choice is to accept the full liabilities of the former plans, and it is highly unlikely that the company will do so without umpteen more years of litigation (in which the creditors will be on its side). It is highly unlikely that Bankruptcy Judge Lifland will allow pension liabilities to stand in the way of LTV's reorganization. It is far more likely that LTV simply will tell the union that if the Supreme Court is requiring it to have serial plans or none, then it will have none, sorry about that. Another distinct possibility is that the PBGC, having established the legal principle it sought, will be content negotiating some modest contribution from LTV towards meeting the obligations of the canceled plans rather than face endless litigation with LTV over the nuances of the Supreme Court's ruling. (No matter what happens, certainly one thing that LTV got from the litigation that cannot be taken away from it was four years under the protection of Chapter 11 while the issue was litigated. It is possible that LTV will spend a good part of the Nineties under bankruptcy protection while the pension snafu is litigated further.)

The ramifications for other companies are easier to see. They still can force the PBGC to cancel their pension plans and to accept the unfunded liabilities in return for an unsecured prepetition claim. However, when the union comes calling to rebuild benefits for their employees, they can say "Gee, we would love to give them pension benefits, but the Supreme Court will not let us"—or something like that. Perhaps the corporate executives will shed a few crocodile tears. After all, what good is corporate welfare if you cannot tap into it!

Nothing in the Manville or Robins cases indicates that the bankruptcy courts will be inhospitable places for toxic tortfeasors. To the contrary, there hardly seems to be any reason for a company with its back to the wall in tort cases not to use Chapter 11. It works like a charm.

Although the toxic-torts bankruptcy case seems contentious and chaotic, those features really aid the Chapter 11 company in softening up the plaintiffs. As the case drags on, it becomes clear that the corporation will live forever, but the plaintiffs will not. The Chapter 11 company seems to gain legitimacy because the bankruptcy court is not the least bit interested in looking into the nefarious acts of which it stands accused (and convicted, in state courts). Meanwhile the "automatic stay" prevents plaintiffs and other creditors from seeking redress in other courts, and, typically, the continuation of the "exclusive period" maintains control of the case firmly in the hands of the management that caused the damage. The plaintiffs and their attorneys, many of whom have already spent much money and years of their lives chasing the corporation through state courts, get tired.

Manville has shown that Chapter 11 can make a winner out of a loser. Although there has been some irritation on the part of trial judges at Manville's immunity to asbestos injury suit installed by its Plan of Reorganization in light of the fact that its trust is almost broke, it will require many years of hard litigation if anyone has a hope of blasting that barrier from around the company. By that time nearly all of Manville's victims will be dead and therefore presumably easier to deal with. The Manville pattern—corporate immunity in return for funding a trust—will be a handy template for future asbestos bankruptcies.

There will not be a shortage of toxic tort problems during the Nineties.

Asbestos litigation continues to be a major, major chunk of injury litigation in the federal and state courts of this country, almost totally clogging the dockets in some districts. Several companies followed Manville into Chapter 11, but there are quite a few that have not yet taken the plunge. When their insurance coverage runs out, no doubt they will run for the cover of bankruptcy.

A product with the potential to cause injury litigation on the scale of asbestos litigation involves that killer weed, tobacco. It may be that the damage caused by cigarettes—perhaps the only consumer product that is dangerous when used as intended—is so immense that the courts will refrain forever from imposing liability on the tobacco companies. It also may be that the tremendous financial resources that the tobacco companies bring to bear in every lawsuit will squash litigation for the foreseeable future. (Even the asbestos producers fear the tobacco companies' economic power and have backed away from attempting to draw the cigarette producers into injury suits in spite of clear evidence that cigarette smoking multiplies the health risks of asbestos exposure.) Indeed, thus far the tobacco companies have maintained a *perfect* record in the defense of their product, juries blaming smokers for the diseases instigated by smoking and refusing to find that cigarette advertising has been false or misleading. Ironically, the warnings on packages of cigarettes mandated by federal law have provided the manufacturers with defenses. The rare cases in which juries have found against cigarette producers have *all* been overturned on appeal.

However, there is evidence that the tide may be turning, much like it did with asbestos litigation. Plaintiffs' lawyers and antismoking activists have begun to organize into groups such as the Tobacco Products Liability Project and to share information and tactics. In two separate cases at the turn of the decade, courts ruled that juries may decide that cigarettes are "inherently dangerous" products in that their dangers outweigh their benefits. If cigarettes are found to be inherently dangerous products, then defenses such as assumption of risk (that is, the user voluntarily exposed himself or herself to the dangers) and contributory negligence (the user was careless of his or her own safety), big elements of cigarette company defenses, will not apply. That change in legal theory, away from negligence, may result in victories for plaintiffs exactly the way the tide turned for asbestos litigation with the *Borel* decision in 1964. Ward Stephenson must be smiling in heaven.

Actually, the tobacco industry has been preparing carefully for some time for the tide to turn. The tobacco producers have been transferring their immense profits over the last ten years into acquisitions of megacorporations in other industries whose assets could not be touched by cigarette liability if imposed. If and when the dam breaks and liability insurance (if the producers have any) is depleted, it will be time to run the cigarette companies through bankruptcy. Can it happen in the Nineties? It gets more likely every day.

The drug industry also is susceptible to creating mass liabilities from products. The Copper-7 IUD put out by G. D. Searle and Company (which is now owned by Monsanto) does not have the horrendous reputation that Robins's Dalkon Shield developed, but it has had its share of dissatisfied—and injured—customers. Suits against Searle's IUD so far have numbered only in the hundreds. However, embarrassing internal documents unearthed in a Minneapolis suit that resulted in an $8.7 million verdict against Searle in September 1986 may result in further suits, judgments and, therefore, larger settlements. Other products that have produced "mass" lawsuits have been: the DES pregnancy drug marketed by a number of companies between 1947 and 1971, which can produce vaginal cancer not only in the users but in their daughters; Bendectin, marketed from 1957 to 1983 by Dow Chemical as an antinausea drug during pregnancy; inoculations for various diseases, including swine flu; and Rely tampons, made by Procter and Gamble, which caused what has been termed "toxic shock syndrome."

Although so far this country has been spared a significant mass tort epidemic in industries other than asbestos, the potential is always there. The chemical industry, manufacturing such things as pesticides and herbicides, is highly susceptible to being found to deal in inherently dangerous products. In a landmark decision with immense implications, in March 1990, the Texas Supreme Court ruled that foreigners may sue American chemical companies in the United States for injuries from pesticides used in foreign countries. Providing a domestic forum for such suits will give foreign nationals access to higher damage awards from American juries. Wide distribution of food products is a big accident waiting to happen, and some localized epidemics of salmonella poisoning have occurred. Perhaps suits will begin to appear concerning carcinogens in food products, such as the aflatoxin contamination that crept into this nation's corn and peanut crop in the drought of 1988.

Nuclear power plants, which enjoy limited liability for accidents courtesy of federal legislation, may not enjoy that partial immunity for diseases caused by slow leakage or improper disposal of irradiated material. Blood banks have been sued by those contracting AIDS from transfusion. Alcohol distillers are in the early stages of defending suits arising from birth defects and other health problems and diseases alleged to have been caused by alcohol consumption. Lawsuits against weight-loss programs for damage to health are growing. Anybody operating a factory may suffer liability from a leak or explosion. The $470 million that Union Carbide agreed to pay 3,300 victims of a gas leak at its Bhopal, India, facility would pale next to the amount of liability that would arise from a similar incident in the United States.

Liability arising from allegations other than mass tort claims may be enough to cause a company to seek the protection of the bankruptcy court. Inflation and every day's news about megacorporations has taught jurors to think in big numbers. Texaco showed us that no company is safe from the wrath of even one jury. In 1989, Santa Fe Southern Pacific Company suffered a $1 billion antitrust judgment at the hands of a pipeline company that apparently it drove out of business. Early in 1990 W. R. Grace was hit with a $75 million judgment for fraudulently obtaining a loan on a dry oil field. Pettibone Corporation, a manufacturer of heavy duty vehicles, was forced into bankruptcy after suffering personal injury judgments involving its forklift truck when its insurance carrier was declared insolvent.

As demonstrated by the *Exxon Valdez* incident, an oil spill at sea can generate a large liabiity for the damage to the environment and private property as well as clean-up costs. About 150 lawsuits have been filed against Exxon entities by, among other, the state of Alaska, Indian tribes, fish hatcheries, and environmental groups. Exxon's assets and insurance policies (and ability to control gasoline prices) give comfort that it will be able to cover liabilities that easily may exceed $1 billion, but what if a smaller company owned the *Valdez*? It was lucky for the people of Alaska that Exxon was shipping in its own "bottom," because it is one of the *very few* companies in the world that can handle such a staggering liability from one big tanker accident. (The oil companies now are shifting to tankers owned by smaller companies to ship into U.S. waters.)

Of course, incidents, accidents, and allegations do not a bankruptcy make. Megacorporations have mega-insurance coverage and mega-assets and mega-income from which to pay for liability not covered by insurance. However, juries' notions of proper compensation have been rocketing upward, and it does not take too many large judgments against a company to start insurance companies backpedaling on coverage and lenders asking for more collateral, putting the company at risk of defaults. In our mass society, there are many liabilities just waiting to happen.

Three issues being litigated throughout our legal system also will effect enormously the likelihood of bankruptcy arising from mass claims.

The first involves the extent to which mass tort defendants should be held liable for punitive damages. Defendants have argued in court and in Congress that a little punishment is enough, and once a company has been chastised by one or a few juries up to some modest amount, punishment should cease. They also have made the point that, unlike other kinds of damages, there are no rules of proof or guidelines on how much should be assessed. Juries who are asked by plaintiffs' atorneys to "send a message" to corporate defendants obviously feel that only one delivered in very large numbers will be heard—and felt. The plaintiffs' bar argues that punitive damages are the only effective means of making liability for injuries something more than a mere cost of doing business, so that megacorporations will be more careful about the products they produce. Corporations argue that plaintiffs' lawyers just want to keep open the chance for a big score. Those representing injured people say that all corporations care about is not having to pay judgments out of their own pockets. (Insurance does not cover punitive damages.) One suggestion by corporations is to throw punitive damages in mass tort situations—but not the underlying cases for compensatory damages—into one class action, with no opportunity for plaintiffs to "opt out" as is allowed in most other types of class actions. Presumably the result will be one punitive damage award that will be less than serial punishments by a number of juries.

The punitive damage issue has brought out industry's big guns, which are firing in every direction. Lobbyists continue to press Congress for legislation limiting the scope and amount of punitive damages. The American College of Trial Lawyers, an organization of attorneys who generally defend companies in injury cases, issued a "report" in 1989 recommending sharply limited punitive damages grouped in class actions. (Leon Silverman was the group's president in 1982.) A committee of the American Bar Association has made similar recommendations. Business lobbyists have achieved the enactment of statutory limitations on punitive damages by the legislatures of several states. Vice-president J. Danforth Quayle recently proposed a massive overhaul of product liability laws that would greatly favor industry, including limiting punitive damages.

Throughout the debate, the United States Supreme Court has not been totally silent. In June 1989, it rejected an argument that punitive damages violate the prohibition in the United States Constitution against "excessive fines," observing that the section historically has been applied only to fines established by government agencies. However, the court seemed to invite a challenge on "due process" grounds. In April 1990, the court agreed to hear a case involving a punitive damage award. While the ruling may establish ground rules for determining the amount of individual awards, the case does not involve a mass tort situation.

A second issue involves finding the right party to sue. Aside from the basic issues of proving liability in cases where much time has elapsed between exposure and disease—which by no means is easy, notwithstanding the cries for protective legislation by corporate defendants—in many situations it is not possible to determine the specific company that sold the offending product. Prescriptions may have been filled generically or by the same drug under a different brand name. Memories and records may be gone. The alternative is to allow manufacturers of a dangerous product a form of immunity from liability.

In response to the problem, plaintiffs' lawyers have developed theories of liability that lump all manufacturers together as defendants in any given case. Juries then are asked to find all manufacturers of the product liable, either equally or in the percentage of their market shares. (One nice feature for plaintiffs is that the concept puts companies in the unseemly position of pointing the finger at each other in a case rather than at the plaintiff. Plaintiffs' lawyers know that such a situation is a sure winner.) Needless to say, industries facing mass tort claims have been fighting the theory to the limit. Communal liability for the sins of one is a concept at odds with historical legal models.

At this time, the proverbial jury is still out on the issue. The supreme courts of states having considered the issue have split on establishing the theory of liability. (The courts of New York and California typically are harbingers of the legal future. The high court of New York recently adopted market-share liability, but California's Supreme Court recently reversed a 1980 decision and refused to permit market-share liability in a DES case. The United States Supreme Court thus far has refused to hear the issue.) The natural effect of a trend towards shared liability would be to encourage lawsuits by people who otherwise could not meet the burden of proving exactly which brand of drug or chemical was used.

The third major personal litigation issue involves the proper amount of time within which an injured person must bring suit—the "statute of limitations." In most accidents, the statute of limitations is not important, because injured people suffer the consequences within a short period of time and the various statutes of states only provide for a limited number of years within which to sue. (There is quite a bit of variation among the states, a fact that vexes the plaintiffs' bar.) However, in mass tort situations with delayed-reaction diseases, a too-conservative reading of a state's statute of limitations may result in a person losing the right to sue before having fair chance to discover the injury. There are also some sub-issues concerning the time to sue. Rulings on the issue can have a huge effect on the number of people allowed to sue a company.

As may be seen, some rather large issues in American liability law are not as well settled as one may have expected. Other important issues in flux that also affect the size and frequency of judgments include: when required arbitration or other forms of trial without access to juries at the first level of litigation may be foisted on plaintiffs; the level of scientific proof necessary to establish the cause of a delayed injury; the responsibility of companies that are successors to the ones that did the damage; insurance coverage issues; and other forms of proposed limits on plaintiffs generally lumped under the euphemism of "tort reform." Court rulings during the Nineties respecting the leading edge of the law will have a huge impact on the financial stability of many American companies and their need to pick up the Chapter 11 tool to clean house of annoying tort liabilities.

The Brave New World of bankruptcy law for the Nineties will involve Chapter 11s filed to deal with pollution liabilities. The size of those liabilities in the Nineties will be immense, and the antipollution laws on the books and likely to be enacted in this decade will place a huge burden on private industry, straining finances to the limit.

Businesses operating in the Nineties will face not only ordinary capital costs and expenses to stay current with rapid changes in technology, but also big bucks required to meet ever-increasing standards for air and water emissions and waste disposal. It is estimated that the "clean-air" federal legislation of 1990 alone will cost American industry and utilities an extra $21.5 billion *a year*. Utilities, especially those in the Midwest that burn Midwestern coal, will face heavy costs in eliminating the causes of acid rain and reducing other forms of pollution. Businesses are just beginning to feel the effects of a federal statute that requires them to clean up solid-waste storage facilities and landfills and provide for their upkeep for at least the next thirty years. Underground storage tanks, favored by regulators over the last thirty years because of an increasing concern for environmental aesthetics, are now *verboten* because leaks cannot easily be detected. They will have to be moved aboveground all across the country.

Of course, it will be the consumer who will pay for the capital improvements mandated by the fight against pollution. This alone is cause for concern, since the burden when filtered down will reduce the available cash in consumers' pocketbooks. However, as with other examples of rapid increases in costs such as the oil "crisis" of the Seventies and commercial real estate taxes of the late Eighties, business will not be able to fully pass along its environmental expenditures. The amount of the future costs is so uncertain that they cannot fully be built into prices—companies consistently will be learning their true costs after the fact and therefore will be playing catch-up. Also, there is a limit as to how much in cost leaps can be passed along to the consumer without a revolt.

Besides improving future practices, we must clean up the mess we have already made. There are about twenty-seven thousand waste sites in the United States. The estimated cost to America's businesses for cleaning up the nine hundred dumps already discovered to be leaking dangerous chemicals into the groundwater and about three hundred other likely sites is $300 billion, more than three times the profits of the entire "Fortune 500" in 1987. There are a number of laws already on the books that mandate the course of cleaning up the United States in the Nineties.

By far the most important environmental law is the 1980 act, supplemented in 1986, entitled the Comprehensive Environmental Response, Compensation, and Liability Act, sometimes called CERCLA but more popularly known as "Superfund." (Many states have "little Superfund" laws.) Superfund describes the procedures by which the United States Environmental Protection Agency identifies sites that are hazardous to health and either cleans them up or gets those responsible to do it under its supervision. If the EPA must bear costs to clean up a site, including costs of supervision, it may sue those responsible for the site. If cleaned up privately by responsible parties, they may then sue other responsible parties for reimbursement. The real rub in the law is the definition of "responsible parties."

Without getting too technical, "responsible parties" are not just the owners of the property but also include anyone who ever put waste onto the site. That includes all those who ever operated the site, all those who dumped things into the site, all those who gave the things to those who put things in the site, all the trucking companies who transported things to the site, and, in some circumstances, those who loaned money to those who owned the site. "Responsible parties" include individuals, companies, and those at the companies who made the decision to put the things directly or indirectly into the site, whether they own the company or are merely functionaries in an organization. Under the law, Joe Schmoe, the general manager of Widget Corporation, and his boss Moe Jough, the president of the company, can each be assessed the cost of cleaning up a dump site that the company used!

Here is another rub for American business: to be liable, it is not necessary to have done anything wrong. The main purpose of Superfund is not to punish wrongdoers; it is to make companies clean up their trash even if they had been entirely within the law when they disposed of it. It is a bill for cleaning services rendered long after the fact. Fraud, negligence, intent—they have nothing to do with liability. If the company cannot prove the percentage of waste that it generated at a Superfund site, it may be assessed the *entire* cost of cleaning up the site (as may individuals associated with the company). The EPA is asserting in court cases that it has the right to ignore basic law to the effect that corporations are each separate entities and may assess the "parents" of responsible corporations which have done nothing except to hold the stock of the subsidiary. The EPA knocks on the door of a company and says, "You have to throw out your trash from the last ten (or twenty, or thirty) years again, in a new and better way, and you have to pay for digging it up and disposing it under our supervision. The bill is $10 million, or $50 million, or so. Pay up right now." (Note that most people's conception of Superfund, that it is a government fund that pays for cleaning up sites, is not accurate. The federal government pays for cleaning up sites only until it can force the responsible parties to reimburse it.)

Many decent and honorable companies that have adhered to the law faithfully in their disposal techniques now find that they owe a huge amount of money to the government that they cannot possibly pay. (The midnight dumpers and secret sewer pourers cannot be found.) If the EPA deems the company to be uncooperative or a foot-dragger, it may assess the company up to three times its actual costs. The SEC is now taking the position that "public" corporations should recognize likely future costs of Superfund cleanups in their balance sheets once the EPA has come calling, in order to properly inform investors of their true financial condition. Needless to say, megacorporate executives are not in agreement with that view and are not rushing to make balance sheet *mea culpas*. If and when companies are forced to bare their future environmental problems in their present-day balance sheets, they will find it much harder to raise capital.

Insurance will not help much. Most companies are covered by customary liability insurance, which protects companies from "occurrences," normally thought of as "accidents." As the scope of the nation's corporate liability for pollution cleanup has become more apparent, insurance companies' resistance to paying for it has grown apace. In response to most claims arising now, insurance companies are denying coverage. The position of the insurance industry is not without merit. The carriers say that there was no intention to insure the type of liability that Superfund and other environmental laws confer, which after all arises slowly over a long period of time through regular business practices, not by an incident or accident. Had there been that intention, there would have been higher premiums charged.

The problem with the insurance dispute is that both sides are dealing with something that neither considered at the time policies were written. If a company is being assessed for its waste disposal for the 1970s, a not uncommon situation, generally it is the insurer(s) of the company for that period that are being asked to pay the liabiliy based on policies in force at that time. Neither side was able to assess its risks and determine its true costs because they were altered by Superfund retroactively. Insurance companies and their customers are in the same small boat, and it is sinking fast. (Insurance that expressly provides pollution cleanup coverage is now very expensive, when it can be had at all. Insurers now know the problem, but still cannot determine the cost of the solution because of additional likely environmental liabilities that will be added in the future retroactively. It still is not possible to assess the risks sufficiently to responsibly set a premium.)

As in the asbestos industry, insurer and insured are at odds, and the outcome of the fight will cost one side or the other billions of dollars. At this time the court decisions are split, but a majority favor the insurance industry. There will be many companies who will have to face demands for Superfund payment while, at best, embroiled in litigation with their insurance carriers that will take years to come to a head, or, at worst, knowing that they will be "going naked" in facing pollution liability.

Given the coverage of Superfund, it is hard to see how very many American industrial companies can avoid liability. There are virtually no defenses. The pressure to clean up hazardous waste is strong. The EPA has the legal tools, and at least half the money (!) to do the job. There is, however, one way to gain immunity from Superfund—be an oil company. Section 9601(4) of Superfund states that petroleum (oil) is excepted from the definition of "hazardous substance." It seems that some animals are more equal than others on this animal farm, too.

The assessment of overwhelming liability for Superfund or other pollution statutes has already begun. In December 1988, a jury found Shell Oil Company—and not its insurer—liable for the cleanup costs at its Rocky Mountain Arsenal near Denver. The cost may run to $2 billion. Nicolet, an asbestos manufacturer, managed to keep out of bankruptcy while defending against thousands of suits by injured people, but was forced into Chapter 11 by EPA action to clean up one of its former factory sites. Superior Toy and Manufacturing of Rockford, Illinois, developed financial problems from environmental problems at its plant and is now in Chapter 11. Chicago Modern Metal Plating Company is in bankruptcy after it failed to get financing to install required water purification equipment. Banks did not want to take a mortgage because they feared that metallic waste may lie under the company's plant. The list is growing every day.

What can a megacompany do when its capital costs have outreached its resources? What can be done when lenders are demanding more collateral and big paydowns? What will a CEO do when informed that his company just has received a bill for $200 million to clean up waste sites? The answer: call cost-busters (the bankruptcy lawyers)!

Many people think that the environmental laws are so important that they have a special status in bankruptcy court, but that is not true. There is not a word in CERCLA or any other pollution statute addressing the rights of governmental agencies or others who claim reimbursement for the costs of a pollution cleanup against a company or individual in bankruptcy. Absent any special legislation, a claim for the cost of cleaning up someone else's mess is just another unsecured claim if that someone files a bankruptcy.

The case decisions are starting to come in. In March 1990, a federal district court judge ruled that environmental problems created before LTV filed bankruptcy but not discovered until afterward would not be treated as costs arising during the Chapter 11 case, which must be paid in full under any Plan of Reorganization, but rather as a simple prepetition unsecured claim which can be compromised under a plan. If upheld on appeal and followed by other courts, it will mean that a company may rid itself of environmental liabilities it has created before filing bankruptcy *irrespective of when they are discovered.* Pollution liability discovered after the conclusion of a Chapter 11 bankruptcy case probably can be treated under existing sections of the Bankruptcy Code by reopening the case and modifying the plan. The LTV ruling should be a great help to corporate reorganizations. A similarly helpful ruling in the Wheeling-Pittsburgh Steel case allowed the company to reject a contract under which it was a partner in a polluted coal mine, pushing a claim for cleanup costs arising under the contract into prepetition unsecured status. However, some earlier cases involving shuttered companies have given cleanup costs a priority over other creditors.

In 1986, Congress amended CERCLA to provide that the EPA may file a lien against a responsible party for its claim, and at least six states—the list is still growing—have passed similar statutes. Companies nevertheless may avoid being subject to any such lien by being nimble enough to file Chapter 11 after the pollution has been caused and preferably after someone else has cleaned up the property and established a definitive claim, but no later than ninety days after a lien is filed. (Bankruptcy law allows a lien to be voided as "preference" if perfected within ninety days prior to the filing of bankruptcy.) Under the LTV ruling, a bankruptcy would be effective if filed any time after the pollution was caused, even before it is cleaned up or a claim for a definite amount made.

It remains to be seen whether environmental liens will stand up in bankruptcy court. There are good arguments to the effect that they should not be enforced in bankruptcy because they are not commercial liens, and they are at variance with the purposes of bankruptcy. It should not be assumed that the general policy of funding environmental cleanups will take money out of the pockets of innocent creditors, who after all did not knowingly take the risk of horrendous pollution liability when extending credit.

In attempting to predict the outcome of future court decisions relating to the environmental liability of companies in Chapter 11, two important considerations should not be forgotten. First, each dispute will be heard initially in a bankruptcy court by a judge who most likely is committed to reorganizing the subject company. Second, when a megacorporation is involved, the court will go to great lengths and jump through many practical, legal, logical, and philosophical hoops to see to it that *nothing* stands in the way of a mega-reorganization. Do not count out the corporations with immense pollution liability too quickly. Remember, where there is a Chapter 11 there is a way, especially for a megacorporation!

Chapter 17

What If?

Now that we have had ten years experience with Chapter 11 of the Bankruptcy Code, it is time to review how it has operated in practice and seriously examine, perhaps for the first time, the validity of its philosophical underpinnings.

Like Dr. Frankenstein, Congress did not fully understand its creation. Although during the consideration of the bankruptcy bills, great debate was had on the effects that the new law would have upon consumer bankruptices—whether the poor souls who were buried under consumer debt could keep a few more of their life's possessions—little serious thought was given to the effect of the changes in the business reorganization sections. In adopting an expansive "modern" code, Congress clearly intended to expand the safety net for families and small business people whipsawed by inflation and high interest rates, but it is not so clear that Congress anticipated how user-friendly bankruptcy reorganization would become for large conglomerates.

Congress created a monster when it fashioned Chapter 11. Whether knowingly or not, the final bankruptcy bill approved by Congress essentially was a welfare program for large corporations, available for the asking. Although camouflaged with the trappings of an adversarial litigation process, Chapter 11 became merely the delivery system for billions of dollars in benefits to megacorporations.

The federal judiciary, picking up Congress's cues, consistently has permitted megacorporate debtors to totally control their Chapter 11 cases. Judges, whether those presiding over the bankruptcy courts or the full federal judges superior to them, have repeatedly read the

Bankruptcy Code expansively, *especially* when a megacorporate debtor can be aided. Under that thinking, all the ingenuity that those judges can muster is brought to bear to facilitate the reorganization of mega-corporations, no matter what the consequences to others might be and no matter how many rules of law must be bent. The lack of interest of the appellate courts in truly reviewing the rulings of the lower court judges has given them *carte blanche* to bend the rules further yet in aid of megacorporate debtors. With the "can do" attitude of the bankrupt-cy court harnessed on behalf of megacorporate debtors, all legal, prac-tical, and human obstacles to reorganization are swept out of the way.

Because the primary job of the judiciary in a megacorporate Chapter 11 is to supervise what is essentially an administrative program of benefits, it is not surprising that the judges do not act judicial. Megacorporate debtors are allowed—encouraged, even—to flex every bit of their muscle to get what they want from the bankruptcy. Judges take unseemly advantage of their position to aid maneuvers on behalf of megacorporate debtors or even initiate them themselves. Attorneys for creditors who take positions contrary to those favored by the debtor routinely are threatened and punished in subtle and not-so-subtle ways by the court, most notably when it comes time for the judge to review their fee applications; and they soon come to realize how financially costly, psychologically painful, and eminently useless it is to oppose the program. As a result, for all of the drama and apparent uncertainty surrounding megacorporate Chapter 11s, they turn out to be cookie-cutter cases.

Because the welfare program is disguised as a court proceeding, the rule of law suffers. It is not too much to say that in most mega-corporate Chapter 11 cases, the judicial function is perverted to a greater or lesser extent by those in black robes who have taken as their mission the successful reorganization of the Chapter 11 company. When the judge has placed himself or herself at the disposal of one of the litigants, there can be no justice. Every stage-managed ruling in favor of a giant corporation, every "successful" reorganization, becomes a mockery of Americans' belief in their judicial system. What must a company do to have "the fix" put in? It need only be big. It matters not what reprehensible things it may have done on its way to the bankruptcy court.

What about the federal agencies whose job it is to protect the public? They understand that their job is to stay out of the way. An example is the Securities and Exchange Commission, the watchdog agency for shareholders and debentureholders. The SEC has been active in large bankruptcies ever since that agency's chairman in 1938, William O. Douglas, instituted its oversight program.

As part of the Reagan administration's deregulation philosophy, the SEC scaled back its presence in the megacorporate bankruptcies of the early 1980s to almost nothing, taking the attitude that the checks and balances built into the bankruptcy system were sufficient protection for shareholders. In December 1983, the SEC made its *de facto* program official. By a vote of the commission, the oversight activities of the SEC in bankruptcies were withdrawn. Two commissioners, James Treadway and Bevis Longstreth, expressed the sentiment that the fledgling United States Trustee system could pick up the slack. Any bankruptcy lawyer could have told them, if they really cared, that there was no comparison. The end result was that, at first unofficially and later officially, during the Reagan era, megacorporations could do what they wanted to do in Chapter 11 without having to worry about the SEC—the watchdog that they feared the most. To this day, the presence of any federal regulatory agencies in megabankruptcies is almost nonexistent, although the junk bond bankruptcies are beginning to draw some attention.

What if large corporations were prohibited from invoking Chapter 11?

It might be argued that establishing and maintaining a court reorganization process is a legitimate and absolutely necessary program to save large corporations and the jobs they provide. Many feel that Big Business, like individuals and small companies, should have a safety net, too. However, that view rests on two misconceptions.

It is an intuitive but nevertheless unproven assumption that it is more beneficial to our society that troubled entities be "saved" rather than "liquidated." Most people, including the judges who preside over court reorganizations, do not seriously analyze that emotion. They ignore perfectly sound economic theory to the effect that the bankruptcy system diverts scarce assets such as capital to inefficient producers, thereby allowing them to remain in existence at an added expense to society. By giving debtors an out, it reallocates bargaining power as against creditors. For small companies with little bargaining power, Chapter 11 may be justified as providing a needed measure of protection for the owners, who almost always bear personal liability to the company's lenders. However, in regulating the financial matters of large corporations, mercy should not be a guiding governmental principle.

In fact, megabankruptcies save few, if any, jobs. In bankruptcy, megacorporations shed their employees, divisions, and businesses at will and with no compunctions. They liquidate portions of themselves anyway, by selling profitable units and closing others. Often the surviving portion of the reorganized company looks so little like its prebankruptcy self that one must wonder just what has happened. The answer is simple: the jobs, salaries, and perks of those in the executive suite, the fat fees of the professionals who man (and woman) the system, and the tax benefits that can be used for future adventures have been "saved." The divisions that were strong and that survived the bankruptcy would have survived a liquidation of the parent company—they would have been sold intact. In the meantime, the Chapter 11 companies have tied up assets and withheld payment from many creditors large and small for years, many of whom were in dire need of those funds.

The second unproven assumption is that in order to save sick megacompanies, it is necessary to have a statutory scheme of court reorganization as a safety net. To the contrary, any large corporation has a great deal of resources and is entirely capable of taking care of itself across the negotiation table from its lenders and other creditors. Bankers are not too quick to foreclose on assets that will shutter a giant company, for many obvious reasons. Suppliers are even slower to act against an important customer. The existence of Chapter 11 does nothing more than distort the parties' bargaining. Even worse, through the magic of Chapter 11, megacorporations can transform vendors and lenders into unwilling investors. There is no reason why the federal government should throw a megacorporate debtor an extra shield and a quiver of arrows in the midst of the battle, except for an unspoken—and unwise—policy of welfare for Big Business. (Putting the shoe on the other foot, if creditors were to be denied the right to throw a megacorporation into an "involuntary" bankruptcy and were limited to individual suits to collect their debts, they would not suffer hardship.)

Even *if* there are benefits to providing federal aid in the form of bankruptcy reorganization to sick megacorporations, it is legitimate to question whether the system has swung too far in the debtor's favor.

Because Chapter 11 has become an impenetrable Star Wars shield behind which they can do virtually what they want, and because Chapter 11 has proven to have little effect on sales, it is an extremely attractive option. Even *if* Chapter 11 is necessary medicine for sick megacompanies, the problem is that it has become such a cure-all drug that it has become difficult to persuade only mildly ill companies not to partake.

That gentle persuasion is particularly hard to get across to large corporations because of the nature of today's top executives. For the last several decades, American management consistently has taken the routes of least resistance to short-term profits. Personal fortunes were made by CEOs shuffling corporate entities and selling overinflated junk bonds to the public, and, in spite of lip service to the contrary, little time or energy has been spent securing the long-term health of the companies that they stewarded. In reacting to the rewriting of the bankruptcy law, the corporate barons did what they do best, spotting the loopholes in the statute and then charging through them. Their perception that Chapter 11 was a safe harbor from which large companies could wage financial warfare rather than a fearsome, threatening presence proved to be entirely correct. As a result, many of America's largest corporations found it easier to file a bankruptcy reorganization and to pick the pockets of others than to become truly competitive. Chapter 11 crisis management became a "profit center," at almost no risk.

Believe it or not, some troubled megacorporations made it through the early 1980s without the help of Chapter 11.

The foremost example was International Harvester Company. International Harvester has had a long, proud history, but the economy of the early Eighties devastated its core businesses. IH was mentioned in virtually every article about the bankruptcy epidemic of the early 1980s as the "next" big bankruptcy. One reason why Chapter 11 for IH was a foregone conclusion was that it was well known that its chairman, Archie McCardell, was dead set against asking the federal government for a bailout.

International Harvester was an immense company. In 1979, IH was the twenty-seventh largest U.S. manufacturing corporation. It was the leading U.S. manufacturer of heavy- and medium-duty trucks, the number two manufacturer of farm equipment in the world, and a leading producer of gas turbines and construction equipment. Its 98,000 employees in forty-one plants around the world generated annual sales of $8.4 billion and profits of $370 million. Then Chairman Volcker prescribed his strong medicine for the economy, and IH was sent reeling, on its way to losing $800 million during the first two years of the decade. IH would go through not one, not two, but three restructurings in close order.

In 1981, International Harvester management and its 205 lenders worked closely under crisis conditions to put together a structure "workout"—an out-of-court reorganization—for about $5 billion in debt. The tentative agreement was a two-way street. The lenders were willing to maintain the level of IH's financing and restructure the debt to relieve cash shortages, but in return they wanted a whole panoply of concessions from the company, including asset sales to pay down the bank debt, restraints on IH's financing of its sick dealers, cutbacks in inventory, and other limitations on the company's freedom of action. Most importantly, they wanted to improve the security for their loans by taking additional collateral. The package was presented to the IH board of directors for approval.

The board of directors was divided on the issue. The thing that the board feared the most was a double-whammy—agreeing to concessions to IH's lenders and *then* having to file a Chapter 11 proceeding. The thing that the board feared next most was a Chapter 11 proceeding at *any* time. They were uncertain of the effect of what would be by far the largest bankruptcy ever filed. What if their decision to file a bankruptcy case resulted in the liquidation of the proud company? Would they be sued personally if they made the wrong decision? Archie McCardell later noted, "There had never been a company our size that had filed a Chapter 11 . . . and nobody knew what would happen."

At a pivotal meeting of the board in December 1981, Vern Countryman, a Harvard Law School professor and one of the country's acknowledged experts on bankruptcy, was called in to give a discourse on the relatively new Bankruptcy Code. Although he outlined the favorable aspects of the new law for debtors, some directors saw only the abyss. A split board of directors authorized the out-of-court restructuring that had been negotiated by McCardell rather than a Chapter 11.

Almost before the ink was dry, IH was in trouble again. Its sales were sinking faster than the company could respond. It had to find hundreds of millions of dollars in cost savings. The company adopted

Chrysler's "equality of sacrifice." Asking all the constituencies from its employees to its trade creditors to make concessions, it acquired $200 million in union concessions and $85 million from suppliers. By April, the company was near technical default of formulas built into the loan agreement, and Archie McCardell was forced out of the driver's seat for not foreseeing the company's (and the economy's) immense problems. In 1982, IH went through its second restructuring, its banks converting $350 million in debt to stock.

Over the next two years, the company remained in the doldrums. In 1983, IH went through its third restructuring of debt in as many years, its banks canceling another $500 million in debt in return for stock. With "only" $900 million in debt remaining, the company was able to stabilize its situation. In 1984, it gave up on farm equipment, selling that business at a big loss to Tenneco. IH continued on as a manufacturer of trucks and engines.

The restructuring of International Harvester obviously was painful to the company and required giving up substantial control over business decisions to its creditors. However, working cooperatively, a massive reordering of the company's debt and operations was accomplished. Of its thousands of creditors, none acted precipitately to torpedo the company.

Viewed in the light of history, the directors of IH were very foolish and old fashioned to undertake the program. There is no question that IH could have done better for itself in Chapter 11. Crisis could have been changed to stasis, in that the creditors would have had virtually no choice but to wait for IH to decide what to do. Although all constituencies gave up concessions in the out-of-court reorganization, shifting additional bargaining power to IH in a Chapter 11 would have shifted the results accordingly. IH could have tapped into the federal welfare system. Nevertheless, the reorganization of IH also stands as a shining example of how a sick megacorporation can cure itself without the crutch of Chapter 11.

So, the answer to the question "What if...?" is "Nothing terrible would happen." Judges would stop being cheerleaders, and the judicial system would regain some integrity. Giant corporations would hold their own in dealing with their creditors and would retain sufficient tools to work through crises. Megacorporations would be more likely to pay their suppliers in a timely fashion, a circumstance that will help the economy just as much as, if not more than, allowing the megadebtors to hide in bankruptcy. It is even possible that CEOs otherwise intent on betting the store on an unwise move might develop a modicum of restraint! The federal government would take one small step back from favoring the barons of industry, those wonderful folks who brought us rampant asbestosis and other nationwide toxic torts, junky bonds and other megamanipulations of the investing public, and part and parcel, the decline of American industry.

Is that solution too extreme? Some bankruptcy attorneys have suggested that misuse of the bankruptcy system could be prevented if an insolvency test were adopted for businesses invoking Chapter 11. Unfortunately, that would do nothing to alleviate the problem. Any definition of insolvency would be subject to interpretation by the same judges who bend over backwards to help big companies. Changing one section of the bankruptcy statute would do nothing to change the operation of the system for the benefit of megacorporations.

Some would argue that the bankruptcy system has provided a way of dealing with mass torts not available in the general court system. I say that bankruptcy has failed miserably, because the system is so oriented toward aiding the megacorporate debtor. While there is a lot to be said for a procedure that deals with the present and future liability of a company that has done widespread damage to people or property rather than permit endless individual suits, the primary focus in bankruptcy court has been nothing more than to reestablish corporations' good financial health. Other interests, particularly those of injured individuals, have been virtually ignored, although the camouflage of bankruptcy has hidden that fact. The end result has been a boon for megatortfeasors in bankruptcy.

Since the job of the bankruptcy judges is to reorganize megacorporate debtors, other goals of the court system have not been served. Bankruptcy judges' almost total lack of interest in investigating the causes of the mass injuries in the cases before them has removed simple justice from the system. When the human need of victims to see punishment of wrongdoers is openly belittled by those judges as illegitimate emotions in a bankruptcy proceeding, and yet that proceeding effectively blocks other avenues of gaining satisfaction, great damage has been done to the court system. When a judicial proceeding that is supposed to be a fair forum for a clash of interests turns out to be a secret delivery system of benefits to one of the parties, the rule of law has suffered a grave injury. When litigants are favored solely because they are large corporations, most Americans get the short end of the stick.

The system could be made more fair for mass tort claimants. At some point, the weight of individual cases against a company or companies in an industry could trigger a consolidation procedure, either under present federal procedures for class actions or multidistrict litigation or under a new, mass tort procedure. It is assumed that the procedure will not be invoked until a number of individual cases have firmly established the nature and general extent of the liability of the defendant(s). Accordingly, the proceeding will be able to adopt a new primary goal: delivering the maximum amount of compensation to the company's creditors. A radical new idea would be to set the extent of the company's future liability to the claimants' group according to the extent of the wrongdoing. The law could direct a judge presiding over such a mass case to appoint an independent investigator to determine the culpability of the company. The more guilty that management has been, the more the company should be operated in the future as a public trust for those whom it has damaged. The less culpable the company's officers have been, the more it will be able to retain future profits for its own unrestricted corporate purposes.

Fairness to tort claimants will not mean that other types of creditors must be ignored. There has been some debate over whether mass tort claimants have a higher moral claim to the moneys of a Chapter 11 debtor to the extent that they should be paid in full before commercial creditors can receive anything on their claims. That seems to punish the wrong people. Some balance will have to be reached concerning the legitimate claims of suppliers and lenders, but the point is that the megacorporate debtors' self-centered interests will be subordinate to whatever balance is reached between the different types of creditors. The main purpose of the proceeding would be for claimants to receive all that they can get from the perpetrator, consistent with the assessment of the degree of the company's wrongdoing. That will hurt the shareholders, but presumably they benefited financially from the illegal operation of the company that they allowed to occur.

Injured claimants should also be given psychological satisfaction. An important purpose of the consolidated proceeding should be to pursue claims for personal liability against those in top management who were responsible for the widespread injury, both in civil and criminal proceedings. While the cost of the investigation and prosecution may decrease the pot available to creditors—in Leon Silverman's words, "It will not put one penny in their pockets"—most mass injury victims would be more than happy to, in effect, contribute a portion of their compensation to that end.

Capital markets may or may not be favorable for a company paying its debt to society, but in any event that consideration will be subordinate to the needs of those it has injured.

In other words, justice could be done.

Could the bankruptcy system be made fair for mass tort claimants? In my opinion that is highly doubtful. The bankruptcy courts, with their narrow scope of purpose, are not well versed in considering larger issues of justice. Bankruptcy judges are incapable of truly standing up to megacorporations. Further, as long as bankruptcy policy favors megacorporate debtors above all other interests, the system is too structurally flawed to accomplish wider goals. Resolution of thorny mass tort issues is best left to the federal judges of general jurisdiction at the district court level.

In summary, there would be no loss to the justice system if larger companies—say, individual or related corporations that have assets of $100 million or more—were barred from becoming Chapter 11 debtors. Changing the Bankruptcy Code to establish such a standard would be easy. However, persuading Congress to make such a change would be hard.

Perhaps, as with the many arcane provisions aiding megacorporations that have crept into the Internal Revenue Code, the extreme slant of the Bankruptcy Code was not accidental. Perhaps the members of Congress who spearheaded the change in the bankruptcy law knew the full extent of the megacorporate welfare system that they were creating. However, because there is no public evidence that Congress intended to aid large conglomerates to the tune of billions of dollars through changes in the bankruptcy law, let us give our senators and representatives the benefit of the doubt and assume that they knew not what they did.

Whether or not Congress intended to provide a welfare system for megacorporations in the Bankruptcy Code, the plain fact is that it created an expansive bankruptcy code which easily was co-opted by large companies and it has done nothing (except giving organized labor one leg to stand on concerning cancellation of collective-bargaining agreements) to alter the balance of power. It has been studiously indifferent to the use—some would call it abuse—of the system by megacorporations. It has shown no inclination to change the bankruptcy law. Consequently, one must assume that it is content with the bankruptcy process as it now stands. It is happy to be the handmaiden to megacorporations. Changing the bankruptcy law will require a change of heart of the national legislature.

On a practical note, Congress may genuinely fear opening hearings into the bankruptcy law. The last major change—the creation of the Bankruptcy Code—took almost a decade of development and a large amount of Congress's time and energies in eleventh-hour wrangling. The need for Congress to amend the law due to the Supreme Court's *Marathon* decision brought out many special interest groups and produced an excruciating situation for Congress. There will be many in Washington who will wince at the thought of picking up that tar baby again.

So, as we enter the 1990s, the bankruptcy courts stand ready for megacorporations, much as the welfare office opens for business each morning. During the last decade of the twentieth century, strains in the economy caused by oil price increases and other factors will threaten balance sheets, and junk bonds will become inconvenient obligations for corporations. For many megacorporations, a stop at the welfare office/bankruptcy court will be a slightly embarrassing but highly rewarding experience. Only Congress can toss the bums in the silk suits out of the line.

Notes

Chapter 2

Oil as a utility. Auspitz, Joseph Lee. "Oil: The Strategic Utility." *The New Republic*, April 26, 1975, pp. 13–17.

Business Week, on price increases. Business Week, June 23, 1973, p. 16.

Influential article. Akins, James E. "The Oil Crisis: This Time the Wolf is Here." *Foreign Affairs* 51 (April 1973): pp. 462–85.

Perfectly serious articles. Auspitz. Op. cit. Ignotus, Miles. "Seizing Arab Oil." *Harper's Magazine*, March 1975, pp. 45–60.

Future generations. Pollack, Gerald A. "The Economic Consequences of the Energy Crisis." *Foreign Affairs* 52 (April 1974): pp. 452–71.

President Ford, control. Carroll, Peter N. *It Seemed Like Nothing Happened.* New York: Holt, Rinehart & Winston, 1982: p. 173.

Akobo. Newsweek, October 6, 1975, p. 63.

Time survey. Time, March 17, 1975, p. 16.

Business Week, on inflation. Business Week, May 22, 1978, p. 106.

Reagan. Carroll. Op cit., p. 216.

Chapter 3

Amendments. Lee, "Legislative History of the New Bankruptcy Law," 28 *DePaul Law Review* 942, 955 n. 127 (Summer 1979).

See, for example, the rather compelling and logical arguments made in the case of *In re Wildman*, printed in *West's Bankruptcy Reporter*, vol. 30, p. 133, by Chicago Bankruptcy Judge Richard L. Merrick, who later resigned in protest of the rule and the demotion of bankruptcy judges.

Chapter 4

Townsend. Moritz, Michael, and Barrett Seaman. *Going for Broke: The Chrysler Story.* Garden City, New York: Doubleday & Co., Inc., 1981: p. 117.

Riccardo. Reich, Robert B., and John D. Donahue. *New Deals: The Chrysler Revival and the American System.* New York: Times Books, 1985: p. 28.

Iacocca, on RV sales. Newsweek, August 13, 1979, p. 55.

Newsweek. Ibid., pp. 52–61.

Iacocca book. Iacocca, Lee. *Iacocca.* Toronto: Bantam Books, 1986.

Davidson. Reich. Op. cit., p. 134.

Proxmire. Reich. Op. cit., p. 132.

Iacocca, bar of the press. Fortune, March 23, 1981, p. 146.

Iacocca, flimflam and penalty. Wall Street Journal, January 24, 1989, p. 1.

Wall Street Journal, equality of sacrifice. Wall Street Journal, July 15, 1983, p. 1.

Wall Street Journal, biggest reorganization. Ibid.

Chapter 6

Wall Street Journal. Wall Street Journal, January 31, 1980, p. 1.

Rohatyn. Business Week, March 24, 1980, p. 105.

Critique of Volcker. Washington Monthly, June 1982, pp. 12–21. (Quote at 20.)

Walter Heller. Time, June 16, 1980, p. 67.

Volcker interview. New York Times Magazine, September 19, 1982, p. 73.

Jake Garn. U.S. News & World Report, February 22, 1982, p. 42.

Howard Baker. Time, February 8, 1982, p. 52.

White's announcement. Wall Street Journal, September 5, 1980, p. 3.

Dealer's reaction. Business Week, September 22, 1980, p. 35.

Maloon. Wall Street Journal, January 20, 1981, p. 4.

Insufficient documentation. Ibid.

Vote of confidence. Wall Street Journal, June 8, 1981, p. 29.

Sad, sad day. Petzinger, Jr., Thomas. "AM International Gets a Vital Second Chance by Using Chapter 11." *Wall Street Journal*, April 23, 1981, p. 1.

A business fact of life. Ibid.

Legal boilerplate. Ibid.

Uncertainty removed. Op. cit., p. 25.

Forbes article. Stern, Richard L., and Paul Bornstein. "Now You See 'Em, Now You Don't." *Forbes*, July 19, 1982, pp. 34–36.

Presto accounting. Op. cit., p. 34.

DeLorean assets. Wall Street Journal, October 27, 1982, p. 16.

Solomon. Business Week, May 9, 1983, p. 71.

Reign of terror. Business Week, April 23, 1984, p. 54.

GHR as Chrysler. Ibid.

Wall Street Journal. McCoy, Charles F., and Matt Moffett. "Energy Firm Expands Even in Chapter 11, Wears Out Creditors." *Wall Street Journal*, July 30, 1987, p. 1.

McCardell. Marsh, Barbara. *A Corporate Tragedy: The Agony of International Harvester Company.* Doubleday & Company, Inc. Garden City, New York: 1985, p. 262.

Chapter 7

Fortune. Fortune, April 30, 1984, p. 266.

"I'm the kind. . . ." Wall Street Journal, March 30, 1982, p. 52.

Sigoloff management philosophy. Better, Nancy Marx, and Peter M. Stevenson. "Salvaging the Eighties." *Manhattan, Inc.*, December 1989, p. 72.

Suntan. Ibid.

Executions. Op. cit., p. 74.

Sigoloff pose. Op cit., p. 68.

18-hour days. Wall Street Journal, March 31, 1982, p. 31.

Truly impossible requests. Wall Street Journal, August 2, 1985, p. 5.

Banker's comments. Op cit., p. 1.

"Maybe I Know Something. . . ." Business Week, April 12, 1982, p. 120.

Swamp. Wall Street Journal, August 2, 1985, p. 5.

100 cents. Ibid.

Good or lucky. Wall Street Journal, July 10, 1985, p. 13.

Sigoloff, on G&W. Wall Street Journal, June 18, 1985, p. 14.

Chapter 8

Wall Street Journal. Carley, William M., and Brenton R. Schlender. "Conditions That Did in Braniff Could Ground Other Weak Lines." *Wall Street Journal*, May 14, 1982, p. 1.

Banker. Op. cit., p. 3.

Countryman. Ibid.

King. Work, Clemmens P. "Bankruptcy: An Escape Hatch for Ailing Firms." *U.S. News & World Report*, August 22, 1983, p. 66.

Kennedy. Sorenson, Laurel. "Chapter 11 Filing by Wilson Foods Roils Workers' Lives, Tests Law." *Wall Street Journal*, May 23, 1983, p. 37.

Business Week. *Business Week*, May 9, 1983, p. 33.

Business Week Editorial. *Business Week*, October 10, 1983, p. 132.

Skewing of forces. Smith, Mark Wesley, and Mark S. Pulliam. "Congress Wrote Continental's Ticket." *Wall Street Journal*, October 11, 1983, p. 23.

Sole problem is labor. Ruthart, Dean, and Bryan Burrough. "As Continental Airlines Takes Bankruptcy Step, Rivals Plan to Move In." *Wall Street Journal*, September 26, 1983, p. 1.

Countryman on Continental. Ibid.

Lorenzo and deregulation. *Business Week*, November 7, 1983, p. 111.

Report of Continental hearing. *Wall Street Journal*, October 14, 1983, p. 3.

Chapter 9

Jury verdicts. Borel v. Fiberboard Paper Products Corporation, *West's Federal Reporter*, 2nd ed., vol. 496, p. 1076 (Fifth Circuit Court of Appeals, 1973).

Borel decision. Ibid.

Chapter 10

McKinney on emerging from chapter 11. *Wall Street Journal*, September 3, 1982, p. 17.

Reactions to Manville's bankruptcy filing. *Wall Street Journal*, August 27, 1982, p. 1; *Newsweek*, September 6, 1982, 54; *Business Week*, September 19, 1982, p. 34; Greer, Edward. "The Manville Maneuver: Going Bankrupt to Fleece the Public." *The Nation*, October 16, 1982, p. 360.

Robert Dole. *Wall Street Journal*, August 30, 1982, p. 3.

ERI report. Epidemiology Resources, Inc. Final Report, reprinted in *Asbestos Litigation Reporter* (Andrew Publishing Company, Edgemont, Pennsylvania), September 24, 1982, pp. 5585–5597.

John Jerome. Op. cit., September 23, 1983, p. 7120.

Lifland, "generals." *Wall Street Journal*, October 28, 1983, p. 60.

Lifland's opinion on motions to dismiss. In re Johns-Manville Corporation, *West's Bankruptcy Reporter*, vol. 36, pp. 727–743; appeal denied, vol. 39, p. 234; reargument denied, vol. 39, p. 998; mandamus denied, *West's Federal Reporter*, 2nd ed., vol. 749, p. 3.

Lifland's opinion on "legal representative." In re Johns-Manville Corporation, *West's Bankruptcy Reporter*, vol. 36, pp. 743–758.

Hart, UNR. Asbestos Litigation Reporter, April 8, 1983, p. 6468.

Chapter 11

Paean to Lifland. Silverman, Leon. "Application for Final Allowance by the Legal Representative for Future Claimants and His Counsel." *In re Johns-Manville Corporation, et al.*, United States Bankruptcy Court for the Southern District of New York cases 82 B 11656 through 11662 and 82 B 11665 through 11676: October 17, 1988, pp. 4–5.

Job description. Op. cit., p. 5.

Clear right to shareholder meeting. Saxon Industries v. NKFW Partners. Delaware Supreme Court. Reported in *West's Atlantic Reporter*, 2nd Ed., vol. 488: 1985, p. 1298.

Parker testimony. In re Johns-Manville Corporation, et al. United States Bankruptcy Court for the Southern District of New York. Reported in *West's Bankruptcy Reporter*, Vol. 66: 1986, p. 538.

In terrorem. Op. cit., p. 535.

Silverman's description of his role. Silverman, Leon. "Application . . . ," Op cit., p. 44.

Chapter 12

Davis and the Pill. Susan Perry and Jim Dawson. *Nightmare: Women and the Dalkon Shield.* New York: Macmillan Publishing Company, 1985: p. 44.

Ross reaction. Ibid., p. 192.

Fench memo. Ibid., p. 85.

Robins brochures. Ibid., pp. 96, 101.

Lillian Yin. Ibid., p. 185.

Nickless memo. Mintz, Morton. *At Any Cost: Corporate Greed, Women, and the Dalkon Shield.* New York: Pantheon Books, 1985: p. 125.

Moore memo. Ibid., p. 134.

Robins deposition. Engelmayer, Sheldon, and Robert Wagman. *Lord's Justice.* Garden City, New York: Anchor Press/Doubleday, 1985: pp. 148–149.

Populist; Miles Lord interview. Siegel, Barry. "Miles Lord: Champion or Zealot?" *Los Angeles Times,* June 28, 1984.

Miles Lord speech. To Minneapolis Council of Churches, November 12, 1981, reproduced in Mintz, *Op. cit.,* pp. 256–263.

Reprimand to Robins officers. "A Plea for Corporate Conscience." Reproduced in *Harper's,* June 1984, pp. 13–14.

Insulted attorney. Engelmayer, *Op. cit.,* p. 222.

Lord's request to Robins officers. Ibid., p. 254.

Robins annual meeting. Perry and Dawson, *(Nightmare),* Op. cit., p. 209.

Eighth Circuit statement. Engelmayer, Op. cit., p. 287.

Judge Theis observation. Perry and Dawson *(Nightmare),* Op. cit., pp. 202–203.

Chapter 13

Dalkon Shield group leader. "The Bankruptcy Refuge: How to Reward the Criminals." *The Nation,* February 13, 1989, p. 193.

Shelter of choice. Ibid., 192.

All-consuming trials. A. H. Robins Company v. Piccinin, *West's Federal Reporter,* 2nd ed., vol. 788, p. 1013 (Fourth Circuit Court of Appeals, 1986).

Chapter 14

Clear message. Wall Street Journal, April 15, 1988, p. 14.

Wall Street Journal article on LTV. Hill, G. Christian. "Concerns Deep in Debt and Those That Aren't Fare Very Differently," *Wall Street Journal,* April 30, 1982, p. 1.

Bunker Hunt. Time, December 29, 1980, p. 51.

Damn straight. Wall Street Journal, April 14, 1987, p. 12.

Ten-Gallon Outrage. Wall Street Journal, April 14, 1987, p. 32.

Banging heads. Wall Street Journal, March 21, 1989, p. A3.

Flagpole. Wall Street Journal, May 23, 1989, p. A23.

Cows come home. Wall Street Journal, May 26, 1989, p. A4.

Inappropriate. Wall Street Journal, April 19, 1990, p. A3 (emphasis added).

Not competent. Newsweek, April 30, 1990, p. 49.

$1.3 billion fuel. Chicago Tribune, April 19, 1990, section 3, p. 1.

Chapter 15

Yamani. Robinson, Jeffrey. *Yamani.* New York: The Atlantic Monthly Press, 1989, p. 286.

Korekiyo. Schlosstein, Steven. *Trade War.* New York: Congdon & Weed: 1984, p. 28.

Shad. Wall Street Journal, June 8, 1984, p. 8.

Sigoloff. Better, Nancy Marx, and Peter M. Stevenson. "Salvaging the Eighties." *Manhattan, Inc.,* December 1989, p. 77.

Looney. Loomis, Carol J. "The Biggest Looniest Deal Ever." *Fortune,* June 18, 1990, pp. 48–72.

Trump. Newsweek, June 18, 1990, p. 38.

Index